# PEACE AND CONFLICT STUDIES

## THIRD EDITION

### DAVID P. BARASH
*University of Washington, Seattle*

### CHARLES P. WEBEL
*University of New York in Prague*

**SAGE**

Los Angeles | London | New Delhi
Singapore | Washington DC

Los Angeles | London | New Delhi
Singapore | Washington DC

FOR INFORMATION:

SAGE Publications, Inc.
2455 Teller Road
Thousand Oaks, California 91320
E-mail: order@sagepub.com

SAGE Publications Ltd.
1 Oliver's Yard
55 City Road
London EC1Y 1SP
United Kingdom

SAGE Publications India Pvt. Ltd.
B 1/I 1 Mohan Cooperative Industrial Area
Mathura Road, New Delhi 110 044
India

SAGE Publications Asia-Pacific Pte. Ltd.
3 Church Street
#10-04 Samsung Hub
Singapore 049483

Acquisitions Editor:   Reid Hester
Editorial Assistant:   Sarita Sarak
Production Editor:   Eric Garner
Copy Editor:   Michelle Ponce
Typesetter:   C&M Digitals (P) Ltd.
Proofreader:   Joyce Li
Indexer:   Jean Casalegno
Cover Designer:   Gail Buschman
Marketing Manager:   Lisa Sheldon Brown
Permissions Editor:   Karen Ehrmann

Printed in the United States of America

*A catalog record of this book is available from the Library of Congress.*

978-1-4522-0295-2

This book is printed on acid-free paper.

Certified Chain of Custody
Promoting Sustainable Forestry
www.sfiprogram.org
SFI-01268

SFI label applies to text stock

14 15 16 17 10 9 8 7 6 5 4 3 2

# Brief Contents

# Detailed Contents

# Preface to the Third Edition

Welcome to the 3rd edition of *Peace and Conflict Studies*. Not surprisingly, a lot has happened since we wrote the 2nd edition, about four years ago. Although it isn't clear whether the pace of events is quicker now than in the past, it often feels that way.

In any event, it is striking to consider how rapidly the world of politics changes compared to that of any academic discipline: That's why it's called "current events"! Since the 2nd edition of this book, the United States of America elected its first mixed-race president; much of the developed world was gripped by a Great Recession; both the Arab World and the United States have been convulsed by a remarkable series of prodemocracy movements, and numerous assumptions about the stability of global relationships were shattered. The rate of change sometimes seems so dizzying that it has been hard to keep up, and periodically we wish that we were specialists in such "stable" fields as ancient languages or Baroque harpsichord music.

But fortunately—at least for those who write textbooks and teach about these events and their significance—some things remain unchanged, namely the historical and philosophical background of world affairs as well as the implications of what has happened and is happening for what is likely to take place in the future. Perhaps more than any other discipline, peace and conflict studies (the subject) as well as *Peace and Conflict Studies* (the book) are deeply enmeshed in and concerned about that world. Thus, you are about to enter an academic discipline but also much more than that.

As we emphasize throughout this text, peace and conflict studies differs from other branches of scholarship, not so much in the richness of its intellectual material but in its commitment to help create a better world and in its overt hope that you, the reader, will undertake your own personal commitment to do just this. Toward that end, we have sought to combine our own sociopolitical orientation with informed scholarship, to incorporate recent events while not getting mired in short-term issues of the moment, and, where appropriate, to engage in advocacy without sacrificing academic rigor. As is often the case with co-authored books, we are not in complete accord about everything in this book, notably the degree to which academic style and referencing are suitable for a project of this kind. But we are in agreement about virtually every substantive issue covered in this long book, which is remarkable considering the number and range of topics covered! And we also concur that you, the reader, should reflect on and debate the issues of greatest interest to you, and, more generally, to humanity in general.

We welcome feedback in this regard—and, indeed, in anything related to either the style or substance of this book—from students as well as faculty, just as we welcome all of you to this important subject, something as challenging, frustrating, rewarding, and important as anything we can imagine.

David P. Barash
Redmond, Washington

Charles P. Webel
Emeryville, California

# Acknowledgments

We would like to acknowledge the sterling contributions of Laurie Calhoun and Dina Soliman, who assisted with the sections "Gender, War, and Peace," and "Cutting-Edge Military Technologies," respectively.

SAGE Publications gratefully acknowledges the contributions of the following reviewers:

Carol Shaw Austad, Central Connecticut State University

Walton Brown-Foster, Central Connecticut State University

Mark Davidheiser, Nova Southeastern University

David Drews, Juniata College

**PART I**

# The Promise of Peace, the Problems of War

*"Only the dead have seen the end of war."*

—Plato as cited by General Douglas MacArthur

At the beginning of the 21st century, human beings are faced with many problems. Our planet is becoming increasingly polluted and otherwise threatened. The Earth is composed of finite resources whose limits may soon be reached. Moreover, the Earth's global warming may result in unprecedented catastrophes. Human societies contain gross maldistributions of wealth and power, which prevent the overwhelming majority of human beings from realizing their potential and ensure that vast numbers die prematurely. Our cultural systems perpetuate regrettable patterns of economic, social, and political injustice in which racism, sexism, homophobia, militarism, and other forms of unfairness abound and in which representative government is relatively rare and torture and other forms of oppression are distressingly common. The natural balance upon which all life depends (including our own) has been increasingly disrupted. And this is only a partial list.

Yet, despite all of these difficulties, the remarkable fact is that enormous sums of money and vast resources of material, time, and energy are expended, not in solving what we might call the "problems of peace" but rather in threatening and actually making war on one another. Although it seems unlikely that human beings will ever achieve anything approaching heaven on Earth, or what the philosopher Kant called "Perpetual Peace," it does seem reasonable to hope—and perhaps even to demand—that we will someday behave far more responsibly and establish a global community based on the needs of the entire planet and the beings who inhabit it, a planetary society that is just and sustainable and not characterized by repeated major outbreaks of violence.

In this book, we explore some of the aspirations, needs, prospects, and obstacles involved in achieving such a world. After opening chapters on the meanings and measurement of peace, we proceed to an examination of war—its causes and prevention. This is one of humanity's most serious challenges, because behind the threat of war—especially global nuclear and/or biochemical war—lies the prospect that human beings may end their civilization and perhaps all life on Earth.

Part I looks specifically at the promise of peace and the problems of war. Although war and peace are not polar opposites, there is nonetheless a fundamental tension between them, two differing ways in which people interact. Part II considers war and its apparent causes, and Part III looks at possible routes toward preventing and abolishing it. Part IV turns to deeper aspects of peace, examining our dilemmas and considering some solutions, including the creation of positive structures of peace—steps that go beyond the mere prevention of war. Throughout the entire book, we hope to challenge you, the reader, not only intellectually but also in many other dimensions of your life.

# CHAPTER 1

## THE MEANINGS OF PEACE

A man releasing a dove, which is widely considered a symbol of world peace.

*Source:* © Nathan Lau/Design Pics/Corbis.

*We need an essentially new way of thinking if mankind is to survive. Men must radically change their attitudes toward each other and their views of the future. Force must no longer be an instrument of politics. . . . Today, we do not have much time left; it is up to our generation to succeed in thinking differently. If we fail, the days of civilized humanity are numbered.*

—Albert Einstein

This text is based on a number of assumptions. War is one of humanity's most pressing problems; peace is almost always preferable to war and, moreover, can and must include not only the absence of war but also the establishment of positive, life-enhancing values and social structures. We also assume, with regret, that there are no simple solutions to the problems of war. Most aspects of the war-peace dilemma are complex, interconnected, and, even when well understood, difficult to move from theory to practice. On the other hand, much can be gained by exploring the various dimensions of war and peace, including the possibility of achieving a more just and sustainable world—a way of living that can nurture life itself and of which all people can be proud.

Throughout this book, we maintain that there is good reason for such hope, not simply as an article of faith but based on the realistic premise that human beings are capable of understanding the global situation and of recognizing their own species-wide best interests. Humans can behave rationally, creatively, and with compassion. Positive steps can be taken that will diminish our species' reliance on violence in attempting to settle disputes and that will facilitate the development of a more just, sustainable, and truly peaceful world.

Most people think they know what *peace* means, but in fact different people often have very different understandings of this seemingly simple word. And although most would agree that some form of peace—whatever it means—is desirable, there are often vigorous, even violent, disagreements over how to obtain it.

# The Meanings of Peace

Peace, like many theoretical terms, is difficult to define. Like happiness, harmony, justice, and freedom, peace is something we often recognize by its absence. Consequently, Johan Galtung, a founder of peace studies and peace research, has proposed the important distinction between "positive" and "negative" peace. "Positive" peace denotes the simultaneous presence of many desirable states of mind and society, such as harmony, justice, equity, and so on. "Negative" peace has historically denoted the "absence of war" and other forms of large-scale violent human conflict.

Many philosophical, religious, and cultural traditions have referred to peace in its positive sense. In Chinese, for example, the word *heping* denotes world peace, or peace among nations, while the words *an* and *mingsi* denote an "inner peace," a tranquil and harmonious state of mind and being, akin to a meditative mental state. Other languages also frame peace in its "inner" and "outer" dimensions.

The English lexicon is quite rich in its supply of terms that refer to peace. In *Webster's Third New International Dictionary*, for example, peace is initially defined as "freedom from civil clamor and confusion" and positively as "a state of public quiet."[1] This denotes negative and positive peace in their political or "outer" sense. *Webster's* proceeds further to define (political or outer) peace positively as "a state of security or order within a community provided for by law, custom, or public opinion."

The second definition of peace, according to *Webster's*, is a "mental or spiritual condition marked by freedom from disquieting or oppressive thoughts or emotions." This is peace in its personal or "inner" sense, "peace of mind," as well as "calmness of mind and heart: serenity of spirit" (*inner peace*). Third, peace is defined as "a tranquil state of freedom from outside disturbances and harassment." Peace also implies "harmony in human or personal relations: mutual concord and esteem." This is what we might call *interpersonal* or *intersubjective peace*.

Peace is then defined by *Webster's* as "a state of mutual concord between governments: absence of hostilities or war." This is the conventional meaning of peace, as "negative" peace, caused by "the period of such freedom from war." The sixth definition of peace is the "absence of activity and noise: deep stillness: quietness," or what may be called *positive inner peace*. And in its seventh and final lexicographical meaning, peace is personified as "one that makes, gives, or maintains tranquility." This is what might be called *divine or perpetual peace*, with God as the ultimate cause of peace on Earth.

In some cases, the word *peace* even has an undesirable connotation. The Roman poet Tacitus spoke of making a desert and calling it "peace," an unwanted place of sterility and emptiness. Similarly, although nearly everyone seeks "peace of mind" or "inner peace," the undesired "peace" of a coma or even of death may not seem so desirable. To be *pacified* (derived from the Latin word for peace, *pax*) often means to be lulled into a false and misleading quietude. Indeed, *appeasement*—buying off a would-be aggressor—has a very bad name indeed. In the most notorious example, British prime minister Neville Chamberlain appeased Hitler in September 1938, famously declaring as he signed the Munich Agreement, which essentially gave in to all of Hitler's demands: "I believe it is peace for our time." (Less than a year later, Hitler invaded Poland, effectively starting World War II on the European continent.) By contrast, even the most peace-loving among us recognize the merits of certain martial and aggressive attitudes, acts, and metaphors, especially when they refer to something other than direct military engagements: President Lyndon Johnson's "war on poverty," for example, or the medical "war on cancer" and "battle against AIDS."

## Some Eastern Concepts of Peace

The foregoing is not simply a matter of playing with words. Fighting, striving, and engaging in various forms of conflict and combat (especially when they are successful) are widely associated with vigor, energy, courage, and other positive virtues. Nonetheless, it is no exaggeration to claim that peace may be (with happiness) the most longed-for human condition.

Chinese philosopher Lao Tzu (6th century BCE), founder of Taoism and author of the *Tao Te Ching*, emphasized that military force is not the *Tao*, or "Way," for human beings to follow. He frequently referred to peaceful images of water or wind—both of them soft and yielding yet ultimately triumphant over such hard substances as rock or iron. The teachings of K'ung fu-tzu (or Confucius, approximately 551–479 BCE) are often thought by most Westerners to revolve exclusively around respect for tradition, including elders and ancestors. But Confucius did not hold to these ideas because he valued obedience and order as virtues in themselves; rather, he maintained that the attainment of peace was the ultimate human goal and that peace came from social harmony and equilibrium. His best-known collection of writings, the *Analects,* also emphasizes the doctrine of *jen* (empathy), founded on a kind of hierarchical Golden Rule: Treat your subordinates as you would like to be treated by your superiors.

The writings of another renowned ancient Chinese philosopher and religious leader, Mo Tzu (468–391 BCE), took a more radical perspective. He argued against war and in favor of all-embracing love as a universal human virtue and the highest earthly goal, yet one that is within the grasp of each of us. Mo Tzu said, "Those who love others will also be loved in return. Do good to others and others will do good to you. Hate people and be hated by them. Hurt them and they will hurt you. What is hard about that?"[2] In what is now India, Buddhist monarch Ashoka (3rd century BCE) was renowned for abandoning his successful military campaigns in the middle of his career and devoting himself to the religious conversion of his adversaries by nonviolent means.

The great Indian text, the Hindu epic *Maha-bha-rata* (written about 200 BCE), contains as perhaps its most important segment the *Bhagavad Gita*. This is a mythic account of a vicious civil war in ancient India, in which one of the principal warriors, Arjuna, is reluctant to fight because many of his friends and relatives are on the opposing side. Arjuna is ultimately persuaded to engage in combat by the god Krishna, who convinces Arjuna that he must fight, not out of hatred or hope for personal gain but out of selfless duty. Although the *Gita* can be and has been interpreted as supporting caste loyalty and the obligation to kill when bidden by a superior party to do so, it also inspired the great 20th-century Indian leader Mohandas Gandhi as an allegory for the de-emphasis of individual self in the pursuit of higher goals. The *Gita* was also cited by the "father of the atomic bomb," J. Robert Oppenheimer, when he described the first atomic explosion as a contemporary incarnation of Krishna: "I am become Death, the Destroyer of Worlds."

## Some Judeo-Christian Concepts of Peace

Peace per se is not prominent in the Old Testament. The God (Yahweh) of Abraham, Moses, and David is frequently portrayed as rather bellicose, even bloodthirsty, and the ancient Israelites were often merciless warriors. Exceptions to this norm exist, however, such as the prophet Isaiah, who praised the reign of peace and described war not as a reward or a route to success but rather as a punishment to be inflicted on those who have failed God.

Under the influence of Isaiah and later Hebrew prophets—and despite the ostensibly defensive violence of the Maccabees and Zealots (who opposed Roman rule in Palestine and have sometimes been called history's first recorded terrorists)—Jewish tradition has tended to strongly endorse peacefulness. On the other hand, it can also be argued that with the emergence of Israel as a militarily threatened—and threatening—state, this tradition has been substantially changed. In fact, Jewish, Christian, and Islamic traditions all have bellicose components and elements in their history. A key question is whether these militaristic activities—often quite persistent and widespread—are part of a pattern of faithfulness to, or a deviation from, their underlying religious worldview.

A deep irony underlies the concept of peace in these three great Western religious systems. Christianity, for example, gave rise to one of the great warrior traditions in the world, yet it is unique among Western religions in the degree to which it was founded upon a message of peace, love, and nonviolence. "My peace I give unto you," declares Jesus, according to the New Testament, along with "the peace of God, which passeth all understanding." Although definitions of peace often vary and hypocrisy is not infrequent, most human beings share a positive presumption in favor of peace, in accord with the stated aspirations of these great religions.

# Positive and Negative Peace

Let us recall the important distinction between positive and negative peace. Negative peace usually denotes the absence of war. It is a condition in which no active, organized military violence is taking place. When the noted 20th-century French intellectual Raymond Aron defined peace as a condition of "more or less lasting suspension of rivalry between political units," he was thinking of negative peace.[3] Aron's is the most common understanding of peace in the context of conventional political science and international relations, and it epitomizes the so-called *realist* view that peace is found whenever war or other direct forms of organized state violence are absent. From this perspective, the peace proclamations of Pharaonic Egypt, the *Philanthropa*, were actually statements of negative peace, expressions of benevolence from a stronger party toward those who were weaker. Similarly, the well-known *pax* of Roman times really indicated little more than the absence of overt organized violence, typically a condition of nonresistance or even acquiescence enforced by local arrangements and the military might of the Roman legions. The negative peace of the *Pax Romana* was created and maintained through social and political repression of those who lived under Roman law.

An alternative view to this realist (or *Realpolitik*) perspective is one that emphasizes the importance of positive peace and that has been particularly advanced by Norwegian peace researcher Galtung and others. Positive peace refers to a social condition in which exploitation is minimized or eliminated and in which there is neither overt violence nor the more subtle phenomenon of underlying *structural violence*. It denotes the continuing presence of an equitable and just social order as well as ecological harmony.

## Structural and Cultural Violence

One commonly understood meaning of violence is that it is physical and readily apparent through observable bodily injury and/or the infliction of pain. But it is important to recognize the existence of other forms of violence, ones that are more indirect and insidious. This structural and cultural violence is typically built into the very nature of social, cultural, and economic institutions. (For example, both ancient Egypt and imperial Rome practiced slavery and were highly despotic, although they were technically in states of negative peace for long periods of time.)

Structural violence usually has the effect of denying people important rights, such as economic well-being; social, political, and sexual equality; a sense of personal fulfillment and self-worth; and so on. When people starve to death or even go hungry, a kind of violence is taking place. Similarly, when people suffer from preventable diseases or when they are denied a decent education, affordable housing, freedom of expression and peaceful assembly, or opportunities to work, play, or raise a family, a kind of violence is occurring, even if no bullets are shot or no clubs are wielded. A society commits violence against its members when it forcibly stunts their development and undermines their well-being, whether because of religion, ethnicity, gender, age, sexual preference, or some other social reason. Structural violence is a serious form of social oppression, which can also be identified with respect to treatment of the natural environment. However defined, structural violence is widespread yet often unacknowledged.

Under conditions of structural violence, many people who behave as good citizens and who think of themselves as peace-loving people may, according to Galtung, participate in "settings within which individuals may do enormous amounts of harm to other human beings without ever intending to do so, just performing their regular duties as a job defined in the structure."[4] Reviewing the role of "normal" people, such as Adolf Eichmann, who helped organize the Holocaust during World War II, noted philosopher Hannah Arendt referred to the "banality of evil," emphasizing that routine, workaday behavior by otherwise normal and decent people can contribute to mass murder, social oppression, and structural violence.

Structural violence, including hunger, political repression, and psychological alienation, often is unnoticed and works slowly to erode humanistic values and impoverish human lives. By contrast, direct violence generally works much faster and is more visible and dramatic. In cases of overt violence, even those people not specifically involved in the conflict may be inclined to take sides. News coverage of these events is often intense (as in the O. J. Simpson and Rodney King episodes, not to mention the Persian Gulf War, the war in Kosovo, and the wars in Afghanistan and Iraq). And because the outcome is often quite visible and undeniable (e.g., the forcible extraction of Iraq's forces from Kuwait and of Serbia's troops from Kosovo or the violent removal of Chinese citizens from Tiananmen Square by Chinese Army troops), the viewer is more likely to pay attention to this tangible violence than to the underlying structural factors that may have led to the conflict.

The concept of *cultural violence* can be seen as a follow-up to Galtung's previously introduced idea of structural violence.[5] Cultural violence is any aspect (often symbolic) of a culture that can be used to legitimize violence in its direct or structural forms. Symbolic violence built into a culture does not kill or maim like direct violence or the violence built into the social structure. However, it is used to legitimize either or both, as for instance in the theory of a *Herrenvolk,* or a superior race. Cultural violence provides legitimizing frameworks for structural and direct violence, occurring at the levels of religion, ideology, art, language, and (pseudo-)science.

Structural and cultural violence are, however, contested concepts. Clearly, structural and/or cultural violence take place wherever there is slavery or gross political, cultural, and/or economic oppression; it remains debatable, on the other hand, whether social inequality constitutes structural violence and whether differing cultural norms and practices constitute violence. And what about skewed access to education, jobs, or medical care? Does simple social hierarchy (as, for example, in a family or classroom) constitute structural violence, and do culturally relative forms of life amount to cultural violence?

## Achieving Positive Peace

Many cultural and spiritual traditions have identified political and social goals that are closer to positive peace than to negative peace. The ancient Greek concept of *eireinei* (see the related English word *irenic*) denotes harmony and justice as well as peace. Similarly, the Arabic *salaam* and the Hebrew *shalom* connote not only the absence of violence but also the presence of well-being, wholeness, and harmony within oneself, a community, and among all nations and peoples. The Sanskrit word *shanti* refers not only to peace but also to spiritual tranquility, an integration of outward and inward modes of being, just as the Chinese noun *ping* denotes harmony and the achievement of unity from diversity. In Russian, the word *mir* means peace, a village community, and the entire world.

Attention to negative peace, or the simple absence of war, usually results in a diplomatic emphasis on peacekeeping or peace restoring (if a war has already broken out). By contrast, positive peace focuses on peace building, the establishment of nonexploitative social structures, and a determination to work toward that goal even when a war is not ongoing or imminent. Negative peace is thus a more conservative goal, as it seeks to keep things the way they are (if a war is not actually taking place), whereas positive peace is more active and bolder, implying the creation of something that does not currently exist.

Moreover, just as there is disagreement about how best to avoid a war—that is, about how to achieve a negative peace—even among decision makers who may be well intentioned, there is at least as much disagreement about the best routes toward positive peace. Peace in its positive form is more difficult to articulate, and possibly more difficult to achieve, than its negative version. And although there is relatively little debate now about the desired end point in the pursuit of negative peace, most people agree that war in general is a bad thing. People may disagree, however, about the justification for any particular war. And when it comes to positive peace, there is substantial disagreement about specific goals and the means to achieve them. Some theorists have argued, for example, that peace should exist only as a negative symbol (the avoidance of war), because once defined as a specific ideal system to be achieved, peace becomes something to strive for, even perhaps to the point of going to war!

As Quincy Wright, one of the 20th century's preeminent researchers into the causes of war, put it:

> Wars have been fought for the sanctity of treaties, for the preservation of law, for the achievement of justice, for the promotion of religion, even to end war and to secure peace. When peace assumes a positive form, therefore, it ceases to be peace. Peace requires that no end should justify violence as a means to its attainment.[6]

Other notable figures, on the other hand, have maintained that a free society may justify—or even require—occasional violence. Thomas Jefferson, for example, wrote in 1787 that "the tree of liberty must be refreshed from time to time with the blood of patriots and tyrants." This apparent paradox—violence as a precondition for attaining its alternative—is a recurring theme in the study of and quest for peace.

There are other ways, however, in which peace can assume a positive form. And these are more than mere clichés: for example, cooperation, harmony, equity, justice, and love. Supporters of positive peace uniformly agree that a repressive society, even if it is not at war, should be considered at peace only in a very narrow sense. In addition, a nation at peace that tolerates outbreaks of domestic violence on a widespread level, despite an absence of violent conflicts with other nations, is not really at peace with itself.

## Social Justice

Having recognized the importance and underdeveloped nature of positive peace, we now pay further attention to a related notion: social justice. Although almost everyone today agrees that a just society is desirable, widespread disagreement continues as to what, exactly, a just society looks like. For example, whereas capitalists and individualists tend to privilege economic freedom (from state intervention) and individual liberty—often at the cost of mass poverty, malnutrition, and homelessness—socialists and collectivists tend to value economic and social security, sometimes at the price of individual political freedoms. Also, many Western individualists assert that nations with capitalist economies and democratic political systems seldom if ever go to war with one another, whereas many non-Western and dissident Western critics of capitalism claim that capitalism by its very expansionistic nature is inherently predatory and militaristic, frequently impelling ostensibly democratic nations to invade and occupy undemocratic but economically and/or strategically important countries.

## The Peace-War Continuum

"War is not sharply distinguished from peace," according to Quincy Wright. Moreover:

> Progress of war and peace between a pair of states may be represented by a curve: the curve descends toward war as tensions, military preparations, and limited hostilities culminate in total conflict; and it rises toward peace as tensions relax, arms budgets decline, disputes are settled, trade increases, and cooperative activities develop.[7]

Many people, if pressed, would agree that with respect to overt and direct violence, war and peace are two ends of a continuum, with only a vague and uncertain transition between the two. But the fact that two things may lack precise boundaries does not mean that they are indistinguishable.

For example, at dawn, night grades almost imperceptibly into day and vice versa at dusk. Yet when two things are very distinct, we say that "they are as different as night and day." The transition from war to peace may often be similarly imprecise (although the move from peace to war may be all too clear and dramatic, as was evident at the beginning of World War II, both in Europe and in the Pacific), but the characteristics of either state of affairs are often quite apparent.

Consider, for example, that the U.S. involvement in Vietnam and the rest of Southeast Asia began in the early 1950s with economic and military aid to French forces seeking to retain their colonial possessions in that part of the world. It progressed to include the deployment of relatively small numbers of "technical advisers" in the early 1960s to what was then called South Vietnam. Larger numbers of American "advisers" were then added, accompanied by combat troops in small numbers, followed by limited and eventually massive bombing of all of Vietnam (and its neighbors Laos and Cambodia). Finally, even though more than 500,000 American troops were committed to propping up a corrupt and autocratic South Vietnamese government engaged in a civil war with its own people and with what was then called North Vietnam, and even though more than 50,000 Americans died as did perhaps as many as 2 million Vietnamese, the United States never formally declared war! Yet there was no doubt that a state of war existed.

There is an increasing tendency—especially since the Vietnam War and notably during America's "War on Terror(ism)"—for nations to fight wars without formal declarations announcing their beginnings and, similarly, without solemn peace ceremonies or treaties signaling their end. The Korean War, for example, which began in 1950, was never officially declared and has never really ended (although there has been a prolonged cease-fire between North and South Korea lasting more than a half-century). One of the most destructive wars of the second half of the 20th century, the conflict between Iran and Iraq in the 1980s, which produced casualties that may well have numbered in the millions (and during which Iraq was believed to have used chemical weapons and to have been developing biological weapons), was never declared. In fact, most of the world's armed conflicts involve revolutionary, counterrevolutionary, genocidal, and/or terrorist violence with no declarations of war whatsoever, as in East Timor, Kashmir, Sudan, Congo (Zaire), Rwanda, and much of the rest of central Africa; in the former Yugoslavia and several independent nations spawned from the former Soviet Union; and in El Salvador, Nicaragua, Guatemala, Afghanistan, Angola, and Cambodia. By the same token, the U.S.-led invasions of Afghanistan and Iraq were not preceded by formal declarations of war and seem unlikely to conclude with official announcements of peace.

The reluctance of most governments to declare war, as opposed to their willingness to fight or promote wars, may also result from the fact that although wars continue to be fought and to break out, most citizens and politicians are not proud of that fact. And despite the potential for theoretical arguments over the precise transition points between different stages of conflicts, most people know at a gut level what is meant by war. There is also little doubt that, given the choice, most would prefer peace.

# Measuring Peace

## Defining and Redefining Peace

The concept of peace remains notoriously difficult to define, the foregoing passages notwithstanding. The difficulties in defining the concept of peace may partly explain why there have been so few attempts to measure states of peace across nations. Although scholars have made numerous attempts to measure and operationalize "war," it is only recently that similar efforts have been made to measure peace.

Is it possible to identify the social structures and political institutions that create and maintain peace, however defined? The Global Peace Index (GPI) is a step in this direction: a measurement of peace as the "absence of violence" that seeks to determine what cultural attributes and institutions are associated with states of peace. [8]

# The Global Peace Index

Unlike such things as Gross National Product or unemployment rate, the peacefulness of a country does not readily lend itself to direct measurement. However, the GPI, produced by the Institute for Economics and Peace in Sydney, Australia, and updated annually, has succeeded in generating a credible assessment. The GPI offers the promise of enabling researchers not only to rank countries with regard to their peacefulness, but—more importantly—to begin assessing what factors correlate with peaceful versus nonpeaceful societies. Toward this end, the 2012 GPI, for example, examined 158 countries, using 23 qualitative and quantitative indicators that reflect three broad themes, namely, each country's 1) level of internal safety and security, 2) involvement in domestic or international conflict, and 3) degree of militarization.

## GPI Results

The GPI for 2012 shows the relative peacefulness of advanced industrial societies, primarily in Europe, compared with war-torn and impoverished nations, predominantly African and Asian. It also suggests that for the first time since 2009, the world improved in peacefulness overall. All regions, excluding the Middle East and North Africa, saw an improvement. This follows two consecutive years of overall decline in peacefulness, when many countries experienced heightened disharmony linked to rapid rises in food, fuel, and commodity prices and the global economic downturn.

Iceland is ranked as the country most at peace, followed by Denmark and New Zealand. Small, stable, and democratic countries are consistently ranked highest; most of the top 20 are western or central European nations. The Asia-Pacific region experienced the largest average rise in peacefulness, with the most significant gains in Sri Lanka, Bhutan, Philippines, and Nepal. Syria's descent into civil war caused its score to deteriorate by the largest margin. Africa became slightly more peaceful, with notable improvements in Zimbabwe, Madagascar, and Gabon and, for the first time since the GPI was launched in 2007, it is not the least peaceful region—that dubious honor falls to the Middle East and North Africa.

Qatar is the highest placed Middle Eastern country (and nondemocracy), in 12th position. Bhutan moved into the top 20 for the first time, mainly as a result of easing tensions surrounding ethnic Nepali refugees. Norway dropped out of the top 10 to 18th position, the result of a murderous rampage by a deranged white supremacist in July 2011. Sri Lanka experienced the greatest improvement in its overall peacefulness, following the apparent ending of decades of civil war. War-ravaged Somalia remained the country least at peace in 2012, with ongoing conflict in several regions (with the notable exception of Somaliland, a self-styled independent state). Afghanistan dropped to the second-lowest position. The United States ranks 88th, one notch ahead of China and below such countries as Jordan, Mongolia, Sierra Leone, and Vietnam. And Russia is number 153, just behind North Korea and three positions ahead of Israel.

**Figure 1.1** GPI 2012 Rank Ordering of Nations

**Rank Country Score**

| | | |
|---|---|---|
| 1. Iceland 1.113 | 37. Laos 1.662 | 71. Ukraine 1.953 |
| 2. Denmark 1.239 | 38. Italy 1.690 | 72. Tunisia 1.955 |
| 3. New Zealand 1.239 | 39. Bulgaria 1.699 | 73. Cyprus 1.957 |
| 4. Canada 1.317 | 40. France 1.710 | 74. Gambia 1.961 |
| 5. Japan 1.326 | 41. Estonia 1.715 | 75. Gabon 1.972 |
| 6. Austria 1.328 | 42. South Korea 1.734 | 76. Paraguay 1.973 |
| 7. Ireland 1.328 | 43. Lithuania 1.741 | 77. Greece 1.976 |
| 8. Slovenia 1.330 | 44. Argentina 1.763 | 78. Senegal 1.994 |
| 9. Finland 1.348 | 45. Latvia 1.774 | 79. Peru 1.995 |
| 10. Switzerland 1.349 | 46. United Arab Emirates 1.785 | 80. Nepal 2.001 |
| 11. Belgium 1.376 | 47. Kuwait 1.792 | 81. Montenegro 2.006 |
| 12. Qatar 1.395 | 48. Mozambique 1.796 | 81. Nicaragua 2.006 |
| 13. Czech Republic 1.396 | 49. Namibia 1.804 | 83. Brazil 2.017 |
| 14. Sweden 1.419 | 50. Ghana 1.807 | 84. Bolivia 2.021 |
| 15. Germany 1.424 | 51. Zambia 1.830 | 85. Ecuador 2.028 |
| 16. Portugal 1.470 | 52. Sierra Leone 1.855 | 86. Swaziland 2.028 |
| 17. Hungary 1.476 | 53. Lesotho 1.864 | 87. Equatorial Guinea 2.039 |
| 18. Norway 1.480 | 54. Morocco 1.867 | 88. United States of America 2.058 |
| 19. Bhutan 1.481 | 55. Tanzania 1.873 | 89. China 2.061 |
| 20. Malaysia 1.485 | 56. Burkina Faso 1.881 | 90. Dominican Republic 2.068 |
| 21. Mauritius 1.487 | 56. Djibouti 1.881 | 91. Bangladesh 2.071 |
| 22. Australia 1.494 | 58. Mongolia 1.884 | 92. Guinea 2.073 |
| 23. Singapore 1.521 | 59. Oman 1.887 | 93. Papua New Guinea 2.076 |
| 24. Poland 1.524 | 60. Malawi 1.894 | 94. Trinidad and Tobago 2.082 |
| 25. Spain 1.548 | 61. Panama 1.899 | 95. Angola 2.105 |
| 26. Slovakia 1.590 | 62. Jordan 1.905 | 95. Guinea-Bissau 2.105 |
| 27. Taiwan 1.602 | 63. Indonesia 1.913 | 97. Cameroon 2.113 |
| 28. Netherlands 1.606 | 64. Serbia 1.920 | 98. Uganda 2.121 |
| 29. United Kingdom 1.609 | 65. Bosnia and Herzegovina 1.923 | 99. Madagascar 2.124 |
| 30. Chile 1.616 | 66. Albania 1.927 | 99. Tajikistan 2.124 |
| 31. Botswana 1.621 | 66. Moldova 1.927 | 101. Liberia 2.131 |
| 32. Romania 1.627 | 68. Macedonia (FYR) 1.935 | 102. Mali 2.132 |
| 33. Uruguay 1.628 | 69. Guyana 1.937 | |
| 34. Vietnam 1.641 | 70. Cuba 1.951 | |
| 35. Croatia 1.648 | | |
| 36. Costa Rica 1.659 | | |

| | | |
|---|---|---|
| 103. Sri Lanka 2.145 | 122. Eritrea 2.264 | 142. India 2.549 |
| 104. Republic of Congo 2.148 | 123. Venezuela 2.278 | 143. Yemen 2.601 |
| 105. Kazakhstan 2.151 | 124. Guatemala 2.287 | 144. Colombia 2.625 |
| 106. Saudi Arabia 2.178 | 125. Mauritania 2.301 | 145. Chad 2.671 |
| 107. Haiti 2.179 | 126. Thailand 2.303 | 146. Nigeria 2.801 |
| 108. Cambodia 2.207 | 127. South Africa 2.321 | 147. Libya 2.830 |
| 109. Belarus 2.208 | 128. Iran 2.324 | 147. Syria 2.830 |
| 110. Uzbekistan 2.219 | 129. Honduras 2.339 | 149. Pakistan 2.833 |
| 111. Egypt 2.220 | 130. Turkey 2.344 | 150. Israel 2.842 |
| 111. El Salvador 2.220 | 131. Kyrgyz Republic 2.359 | 151. Central African Republic 2.872 |
| 113. Jamaica 2.222 | 132. Azerbaijan 2.360 | 152. North Korea 2.932 |
| 114. Benin 2.231 | 133. Philippines 2.415 | 153. Russia 2.938 |
| 115. Armenia 2.238 | 134. Ivory Coast 2.419 | 154. Democratic Republic of the Congo 3.073 |
| 116. Niger 2.241 | 135. Mexico 2.445 | 155. Iraq 3.192 |
| 117. Turkmenistan 2.242 | 136. Lebanon 2.459 | 156. Sudan 3.193 |
| 118. Bahrain 2.247 | 137. Ethiopia 2.504 | 157. Afghanistan 3.252 |
| 119. Rwanda 2.250 | 138. Burundi 2.524 | 158. Somalia 3.392 |
| 120. Kenya 2.252 | 139. Myanmar 2.525 | |
| 121. Algeria 2.255 | 140. Zimbabwe 2.538 | |
| | 141. Georgia 2.541 | |

*Source:* Institute for Economics & Peace and Global Peace Index.

The GPI researchers explored possible correlations between the GPI and other economic and societal indicators—including measures of democracy and transparency, education, and material wellbeing. Among the GPI indicators, "Level of perceived criminality in society" showed a substantial overall deterioration. The five factors that diminished most substantially were all measures of the security situation, reflecting the turmoil that has roiled the Arab world and beyond. The Political Terror Scale showed the greatest improvement, although there were also gains in several indicators of militarization. (Since annual GPI findings are largely based on data accumulated during the prior 12-month period, they can be expected to fluctuate in response to current events.)

There is a statistically significant correlation, although not a dramatic one, between Gross Domestic Product (GDP) per capita and the peacefulness of a country.

## The United States

The United States was selected for the first national peace index, principally due to the high quality of state-level data dating back to the early 1980s and the existence of a large literature of related studies, which estimate the various costs of violence as well as the costs associated with containing violence. Compared to other nations in the Global Peace Index, the United States is

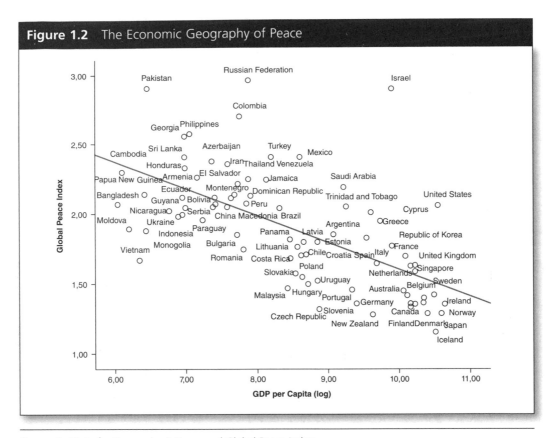

**Figure 1.2** The Economic Geography of Peace

*Source:* Institute for Economics & Peace and Global Peace Index.

midranking. The peacefulness of the United States can be further analyzed by comparing the internal U.S. peace score from the Global Peace Index with the average GPI score for each of the categories measured. The United States performs relatively well on the majority of these internal indicators when compared to the rest of the world and particularly well on measures of internal cohesion: low levels of organized internal conflict and a high level of political stability. The United States also performs well on citizen perception of crime within the country and on the likelihood of violent demonstrations.

However, as noted—and is worth repeating—the overall score of the United States ranks it a less-than-impressive 88th worldwide out of the 158-ranked nations, mainly due to its wars and defense expenditures. The United States is commonly characterized as having a higher rate of violence than many other developed economies, yet trends in crime over the past 20 years have fluctuated substantially, for reasons that have been much debated. At the beginning of the 1980s, the U.S. crime rate was comparable to that of other developed nations; violence then steadily increased to a peak in the mid-1990s and has since been falling. However, this reduction has been accompanied by a steadily *increasing* incarceration rate, which has significant economic consequences.

It is striking that the United States, with the largest economy in the world and one of the highest per capita GDP, nonetheless has a relatively low level of peacefulness compared with other developed economies. This suggests that the potential economic gains of domestic peacefulness may well be considerable. In the context of the lingering effects of the Global Financial Crisis, this is especially pertinent, because the additional economic activity that would be created through improvements in peace can provide a powerful stimulus to aid economic recovery.

The opportunity to move expenditures from violence-containment industries to more economically productive industries is significant. This can be exemplified by the opportunity to build a highway instead of a jail or the expansion of employment in teachers rather than prison guards. Although such efforts would not necessarily generate additional economic activity in themselves, they would create the foundation for a more productive economy. The realization of such additional economic activity is defined as the "dynamic peace dividend," which can result in a substantial lift in GDP and employment.

Compared to most other countries, additional data are available for the United States, permitting a more fine-grained analysis. The results indicate that states in the northern part of the United States are consistently more peaceful than those in the south, and also that the United States performs well on the majority of internal indicators compared with the rest of the world. These indicators are:

- Number of homicides per 100,000 people
- Number of violent crimes per 100,000 people
- Number of jailed population per 100,000 people
- Number of police officers per 100,000 people
- Availability of small arms

*Source:* Institute for Economics & Peace and Global Peace Index.

# Key Findings of the U.S. Peace Index

1. **From 1995 to 2009, the United States became more peaceful**

   Peace improved by 8% from 1995 to 2009, driven by a substantial decrease in the rates of homicide and violent crime. However, these improvements were largely offset by increases in the incarceration rate, which, as of year-end 2010, stood at 0.7% of resident adults, the highest in the world.

2. **The five most peaceful states are Maine, New Hampshire, Vermont, Minnesota, and North Dakota**

   The Northeast is the most peaceful region in the United States., with all of its states ranking in the top half of the U.S. Peace Index. This includes the heavily populated states of New York, Pennsylvania, and New Jersey. The least peaceful states are Louisiana, Tennessee, Nevada, Florida, and Alabama.

3. **Peace is linked to opportunity, health, education, and the economy**

   Statistically significant correlations were found between a state's peacefulness and 15 different social and economic factors. These related to health, education, demographics and economic opportunity but not to political affiliation.

Many of these factors can be seen as measures of opportunity. States that ranked higher on these social and economic factors tended to have higher scores in peace, which suggests that access to basic services including education, health care, and ultimately the opportunity to succeed are key prerequisites to a more peaceful society.

4.  **Peace is not linked to political affiliation**

    Neither predominantly Republican nor Democratic states had a discernible advantage in peace. Although the top five states are largely Democratic and the bottom five states are largely Republican, once the mid-ranking states were included in the analysis, no overall political effect was found.

5.  **The potential economic gains from improvements in peace are significant**

    Improvements in peace would result in the realization of substantial savings for both governments and society. If the United States reduced its violence to the same levels as Canada, for example, local governments would collectively save about $89 billion, while the same reductions in the level of violence would provide an economic stimulus of approximately $272 billion. The release of "trapped productivity" via a reduction of violence would create a stimulus that could generate an additional 2.7 million new jobs, effectively lowering the U.S. unemployment rate by 20%.

6.  **On a per capita basis, the top five states with the most to gain from reductions in violence are Louisiana, Florida, Nevada, Alaska, and New Mexico**

    The total economic effect of violence tends to be greatest in the most violent states; however, several states have a structurally higher cost of violence because of the nature of that violence. For instance, lost productivity from assault and lost productivity from incarceration are the largest shares of the total cost of violence, so states with high levels of incarceration and assault tend to have a higher per capita cost. The large populous states with high levels of incarceration have the most to gain, such as California, Florida, and Texas.

7.  **Growing incarceration is a drag on the economy and in recent years has not had a significant effect on violent crime**

    While homicide and violent crime rates have fallen, the economic benefits to flow from these decreases have been largely offset by the costs associated with the increase in the incarceration rate. In recent years, there has been no statistically meaningful relationship between increases in incarceration rates and decreases in violent crime.

8.  **There is a strong correlation between people's satisfaction with their access to basic services and the peacefulness within each state.**

    The Gallup Basic Access sub-index is based on a survey in which 13 questions assess availability of basic needs for a healthy life, specifically, access to clean water, medicine, a safe place to exercise, and affordable fruits and vegetables; enough money for food, shelter, and health care; having health insurance, access to a doctor and a dentist; as well as satisfaction with one's community, which includes a sense that it is improving as a place to live, and that the respondents feel safe walking alone at night.

9. **Six of the 10 most populous states were also among the top 10 states whose peacefulness improved**

These were New York, California, Texas, Georgia, Illinois, and Michigan.

10. **North Dakota, South Dakota, and Montana had the three most significant declines in peacefulness**

This result stands out, since these three states all declined in peacefulness by over 40%; nonetheless, they are still relatively peaceful and in the top half of the states generally.

# Culture of Peace

In 1999, the United Nations (UN) General Assembly launched a program of action to build a "culture of peace" for the world's children, which envisaged working toward a positive peace of justice, tolerance, and plenty. The UN defined a culture of peace as involving values, attitudes, and behaviors that

- reject violence,
- endeavor to prevent conflicts by addressing root causes, and
- aim at solving problems through dialogue and negotiation.

The UN proposed that such a culture of peace would be furthered by actions promoting education for peace and sustainable development, which it suggested was based on human rights, gender equality, democratic participation, tolerant solidarity, open communication, and international security. However, these links between the concept of peace and its all alleged causes were presumed rather than systematically measured. For example, while advocates of liberal peace theory have held that democratic states rarely attack each other, the ongoing wars in Iraq, Afghanistan, and elsewhere demonstrate how some democratic countries can be militant or belligerent—the justification for war often being that peace is ultimately secured through violence or the threat of violence.

## A FINAL NOTE ON THE MEANINGS OF PEACE

Neither the study nor the pursuit of peace ignores the importance of conflict. Peace and conflict studies do not aim to abolish conflict any more than peace practitioners expect to eliminate rivalry or competition in a world of finite resources and imperfect human conduct. (Analogously, the field of medicine does not realistically seek to eliminate all bacteria or viruses from the world, although it is committed to struggling against them for human betterment.)

Where possible, peace and conflict studies seek to develop new avenues for cooperation, as well as to reduce violence, especially organized, state-sanctioned violence and the terrorizing violence perpetrated by and against nonstate actors. It is this violence, by any definition the polar opposite of peace, that has so blemished human history and that—with the advent of nuclear weapons, biochemical weapons, and other weapons of global destruction—now threatens the future of all life on this planet. And it is the horror of such violence, as well as the glorious and perhaps even realistic hope of peace (both negative and positive), that make peace and conflict studies especially frustrating, fascinating, and essential.

## NOTES

1. *Webster's Third New International Dictionary.* 1993. Springfield, MA: Merriam-Webster, Inc., 1660.

2. Mo Tzu. 1967. *Basic Writings of Mo Tzu.* New York: Columbia University Press.

3. Raymond Aron. 1966. *Peace and War.* New York: Doubleday.

4. Johan Galtung. 1985. "Twenty-Five Years of Peace Research: Ten Challenges and Responses." Journal of Peace Research 22: 141–158.

5. Johan Galtung. 1990. "Cultural Violence." *Journal of Peace Research, August 1990, vol. 27 no. 3, 291-305.*

6. Quincy Wright. 1964. *A Study of War.* Chicago: University of Chicago Press.

7. Ibid.

8. For the Global Peace Index and related documents, see: http://www.visionofhumanity.org/gpi-data/#/2011/scor. Tables reproduced with permission by Vision of Humanity.

## QUESTIONS FOR FURTHER REFLECTION

1. Is peace an absolute, or are there degrees of peace, both outer and inner?

2. To what extent are peace and war, and nonviolence and violence, mutually exclusive?

3. Under which circumstances, if any, is conflict inescapable and perhaps even desirable?

4. Under which circumstances, if any, is violence inescapable and perhaps even desirable?

5. Assess the strengths and weaknesses of such empirical tools as the GPI for measuring peace and its absence.

## SUGGESTIONS FOR FURTHER READING

Antony Adolf. 2009. *Peace A World History.* Cambridge, UK: Polity Press.

David Barash, ed. 2010. *Approaches to Peace: A Reader in Peace Studies.* Second Edition. New York and Oxford: Oxford University Press.

Elise Boulding. 2000. *Cultures of Peace: The Hidden Side of History.* Syracuse, NY: Syracuse University Press.

David Cortright. 2009. *Peace: A History of Movements and Ideas.* Cambridge and New York: Cambridge University Press.

Johan Galtung, Carl G. Jacobsen, and Kai Fritjof Brand-Jacobsen. 2002. *Searching for Peace: The Road to TRANSCEND.* London: Pluto Press.

Charles Webel and Jorgen Johansen. 2012. *Peace and Conflict Studies: A Reader.* London and New York: Routledge.

Charles Webel and Johan Galtung, eds. 2009. *The Handbook of Peace and Conflict Studies.* London and New York: Routledge.

Nigel J. Young, editor in chief. 2010. *The Oxford International Encyclopedia of Peace*, Four Volumes. Oxford and New York: Oxford University Press.

# CHAPTER 2

# PEACE AND CONFLICT STUDIES, EDUCATION, AND RESEARCH

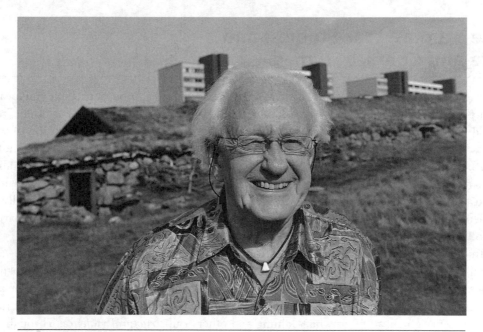

Johan Galtung, a founder of peace studies and peace research.

*Source:* Used with permission.

*Peace does not appear so distant as it did. I hope it will come soon, and come to stay; and so come to be worth the keeping in all future time.*[1]

—President Abraham Lincoln

*Conflict is a theme that has occupied the thinking of men more than any other, save God and love.*[2]

—Anatol Rapoport

Peace studies is a child of its time, which in this case is the nuclear and Cold War era. As a transdisciplinary inquiry into the nature of peace and the reasons for wars and other forms of human conflict, peace studies has grown exponentially since its birth during the mid-20th century.

Precursors of peace studies, peace education, and peace research go back to ancient times. But the systematic practice of peace education began in the early 20th century, partly in reaction to World War I. It took off after World War II, as did the earliest higher education-based peace studies programs.[3]

Similarly, although the origins of peace research date back to religious and ethical debates on peace and war scattered across various world cultures and traditions, and the forerunners of scientific approaches to investigating war and peace emerged in conjunction with World War I, peace and conflict research as a distinct scholarly discipline took off soon after World War II. It continues to be alive and vibrant today.

## Peace Studies, War Studies, and Peace and Conflict Studies

How does one study peace? Whereas there have been different approaches to studying peace, contemporary Western peace studies (or *irenology,* from the Greek "eirene" or "Irene," the goddess of peace) focuses on the analysis and prevention, de-escalation and solution of conflicts by peaceful, or nonviolent means, thereby seeking victory for all parties involved in the conflict. This is in contrast to war studies (or what Johan Galtung, a founder of peace studies, calls *polemology,* from the Greek "polemos," or "the spirit of war") and security studies, which tend to focus on the factors leading to victory or defeat in conflicts waged principally by violent means and to the increased or decreased "security" of one or more, but not all, parties involved.

Importantly, since peace studies investigates the reasons for and outcomes of large- and small-scale conflicts, as well as the preconditions for peace, the discipline is also known as *peace and conflict studies* (PCS or PACS). PCS allows one to examine the reasons for and prevention of wars, as well as the nature of violence, including social oppression, discrimination, and marginalization, or what Galtung and others call *structural violence.* Through the rigorous analysis of peace and conflict, one can also learn peace-making strategies. Peace and conflict studies is accordingly an academic field that identifies and analyzes individual and collective violent and nonviolent behaviors as well as the structural mechanisms underlying social conflicts in order to understand and transform those processes that might lead to a more peaceful planet.

Peace and conflict studies also addresses the effects of political and social violence, the causes of this violence, and what can be done to resolve conflicts peacefully. The rapid growth in these programs in colleges and universities in North America, Western Europe, and elsewhere reflects growing popular alarm about war violence, and other global perils (including the nuclear threat, low intensity conflict, the costs of arms races, environmental destruction, domestic violence, ethnic and regional conflicts, terrorism, etc.). People concerned about violence are turning to education as a means to heighten awareness about the causes of violence and to promote nonviolent alternatives to violent means of conflict resolution.

# Peace Education

Peace education is the theory and practice of education about peace and nonviolence and a commitment to building a more cooperative society by utilizing the concepts and practices of peace studies, conflict resolution, and nonviolence. The first initiatives to develop peace education mainly focused on the horrors of war and statistics about weapon systems. Today, peace education comprises a wide variety of courses and programs aimed at giving students at all levels and of all ages the tools to reduce violence and oppression. These include strategies for avoiding bullying and increasing citizen empowerment.

According to Betty Reardon, a noted American peace educator,

> the general purpose of peace education . . . is the development of an authentic planetary consciousness that will enable us to function as global citizens and to transform the present human condition by changing the social structures and patterns of thought that have created it.[4]

Like other progressive peace educators, Reardon takes "a transformational approach," one, that, like peace studies, is based on peace research. The goal of peace education at all levels, from this point of view, is the development and transmission of pedagogy and practices that shift current conventional values, thinking, behaviors, and institutions away from violence and toward nonviolent solutions to interpersonal, social, and political disputes.

Toward this end, The Peace Education Foundation writes and publishes materials for conflict-resolution curricula currently in use in more than 20,000 schools around the world. Like others in the field, this nongovernmental organization (NGO) views its mission as the education of children and adults in the dynamics of conflict and the promotion of the skills of peacemaking in homes, schools, communities, nation-states, and the world.

There are also numerous United Nations (UN) declarations on the importance of peace education. Koichiro Matsuura, past director-general of the United Nations Educational, Scientific, and Cultural Organization (UNESCO), has written that peace education is of "fundamental importance to the mission of UNESCO and the United Nations." There has also been some recent integration of peace education with education for democracy, human rights, and nonviolent conflict resolution.

The Israeli peace educator Gavriel Salomon has presented some major challenges facing peace educators around the world today, especially those working in zones of ongoing and seemingly intractable conflict (such as Israel and Palestine).[5] In addition to political opposition to their programs and severe socioeconomic inequalities in the regions where they operate, peace education practitioners also face such challenges as conflicting collective narratives, historical memories, and contradictory beliefs. According to Salomon, additional challenges

> that appear to concern the heart of peace education [are] the need to create a societal "ripple effect" whereby the impact of peace education programs spreads to wider social circles . . . increasing the endurance of desired program effects . . . the need for diverse programs . . . [and] the need to find ways to bridge the gap that divides the cultivation of desired general dispositions, principles, and values and their application in specific situations.

To maximize the enduring social impact of peace education, effective programs of peace education should take ethnic and social differences into account and combine general dispositions to peace with specific context-sensitive applications of peace pedagogy and practice. Peace and conflict studies may be viewed, in part, as the dimension of peace education that is increasingly focused on institutions of higher learning.

# The Dimensions of Peace and Conflict Studies

As a scholarly enterprise, PCS is multi- or transdisciplinary, incorporating important theories and research findings from anthropology, sociology, political science, international relations, psychology, evolutionary biology, ethics, theology, and history. PCS is also multilevel, since it examines intrapersonal (or inner) peace and conflict, as well as peaceful and conflictual *irenic and polemic* relations between individuals, neighbors, ethnic groups, organizations, states, and civilizations (or outer peace and conflict).

Central to peace studies, peace education, and peace research is a concern not just with understanding the world but with changing it. This is a bone of contention for academics who espouse "value neutrality and scientific impartiality," especially by such more conventional disciplines as political science, international relations, and strategic or security studies.

PCS is both normative (or prescriptive) and analytic (or descriptive). As a normative discipline, peace and conflict studies often makes value judgments, such as peace and nonviolence are *better* than war and violence. But it makes these judgments both on the basis of ethical postulates (i.e., humans *should* resolve conflicts as nonviolently as possible) and of analytic descriptions (i.e., most violent efforts to resolve conflicts *in fact* result in less social stability than nonviolent means of conflict resolution).

The Canadian peace scholar Conrad Brunk argues that the explicit value commitment of peace studies to peace requires another "value central to the very definition of Peace Studies— that violence is undesirable, and that where the same human goods can be achieved by them, nonviolent means are preferable to violent ones."[6] Therefore, the normative components of PCS are no different from many other scholarly endeavor. Accordingly, what distinguishes PCS from most academic fields are principally its subject matter—peace, violence, conflict, and power—its inter- (or multi-) disciplinary methodology, and its aim of identifying, testing, and implementing many different strategies for dealing with conflict situations.

Peace and conflict studies is both theoretical and applied. Johan Galtung is a Norwegian sociologist and pioneer of the field who founded Transcend Peace University, a website that offers certificate-level courses and a master's degree in peace and conflict transformation. "Peace studies," writes Galtung,

> is about relationship repair on all levels, so it's crucial that these programs include both theory and practice. The field is moving beyond conflict resolution toward the teaching and practice of conflict transformation and reconciliation, which includes healing past wounds and creating long-term, sustainable peace between antagonistic parties.

At the theoretical level, PCS aims to uncover the roots of conflict and cooperation by examining and proposing theoretical models to explain violent and nonviolent individual and collective behaviors, both historically and cross-culturally. By revealing the underlying structures that give rise to human conflict and that support conflict resolution, PCS also hopes to transform the underlying causes, develop preventive strategies, and teach conflict transformation skills.

Fieldwork is often an important part of peace studies, with students taking extended internships in conflict zones where they can learn and apply dialogue, negotiation, and mediation skills. The fruits of peace studies may sometimes be difficult to see and take long to come to fruition, but that does not discourage Mary King, a professor at the University for Peace (in Costa Rica), who has stated, "When you are dealing with millennia during which war has been the ultimate arbiter of conflicts, you can't expect change in a decade or two."

Peace and conflict studies also aspires to be multicultural and cosmopolitan, in part citing the lives and works of Gandhi and Martin Luther King, Jr. as its paragons. However, true multiculturalism and cosmopolitanism remain more an aspiration than a reality for the field, since most peace studies programs and centers are located in the West (although their influence is increasing elsewhere, particularly in Australasia).

Peace and conflict studies is both a pedagogical activity, in which teachers and learners come together to understand the roots of peace and conflict, and a research enterprise, in which researchers propose rigorous theories and methods for formulating and testing hypotheses about the sources of conflict and the institutionalization of lasting cultures of peace.

PCS teachers, students, and researchers are a key component of the more generic field of peace education, which ranges from primary school to postdoctoral pedagogical activities. And they may also interact with peace and antiwar activists and political movements engaged in "peace work." This reflects the dual nature of PCS as a scholarly enterprise and as a force for the pacification of the Earth. Peace education and peace research, as complements to peace studies, strive not just to study but also to achieve peace.

## PCS as Pedagogical Activity

Everyday citizens, teachers, and students have long been motivated by an interest in peace. American student interest in what is today considered peace studies first appeared in the form of campus clubs at U.S. colleges in the years immediately following the Civil War. Similar movements appeared in Sweden at the end of the 19th century and elsewhere in Europe soon after. These were usually student-originated discussion groups, not formal courses included in college curricula.

Because of its destructiveness, World War I, or "The War to End All Wars," was a turning point in many Western attitudes to war. When the leaders of France, Britain, and the United States (led by Georges Clemenceau, David Lloyd George, and Woodrow Wilson) met to sign the Treaty of Paris in 1919, and to decide the postwar future of Europe, President Wilson proposed his famous Fourteen Points for peacemaking. These included breaking up European empires into nation-states and the establishment of a League of Nations. These proposals were the background to a number of developments in the emergence of PCS as an academic discipline, such as the founding in 1919 of the first chair in International Relations (at Aberystwyth University in Wales).

As the noted peace scholar Elise Boulding has pointed out, peace studies was initiated by scholars who were consciously separating themselves from the older, more established discipline of international relations. Other peace studies educators have argued that the field of international relations itself was initially developed with a peace studies focus to avoid war. Peace studies started out on most American college campuses within departments emphasizing international relations, which to many scholars and activists had reneged on the study and promotion of war avoidance. To address this pedagogical gap, peace studies began to develop a broader base on colleges and universities throughout North America.

Just after World War II, many university courses on peace and war were established. The first undergraduate academic program in peace studies in the United States was created in 1948 at Manchester College in Indiana. It was not until the late 1960s in the United States that student and professorial objections to the Vietnam War stimulated more universities to offer courses about peace, whether in an undergraduate major or postgraduate degree program or as a course within such traditional majors as political science and sociology. For example, Manhattan College, a Catholic college in New York City, began its peace studies program in 1968, while Colgate University started one in 1969.

In England, the first school of peace studies was founded at Bradford University in 1973. Like many others, Bradford's program defines peace not just as an absence of large-scale conflict and violence—known as negative peace—but also as structural cooperation that fosters justice and freedom, also known as positive peace, based on human rights, equal access to education, and just social and political structures.

In the 1970s, many North American universities offered courses about the war in Vietnam. Many faculty who created these programs were responding to student demands to create courses that "had relevance to their lives."

Growth in peace studies programs accelerated during the 1980s as students and the general public became increasingly concerned about the prospects of nuclear war. Their concern about the fate of the planet spurred the creation a host of new courses and programs aimed at promoting global survival. Key components of peace studies during this period included courses on violence and war, the nuclear arms race and the threat of nuclear destruction, international conflict, alleged aggressive tendencies in human nature, disarmament, discrimination against minorities, group conflicts, nonviolent action, defense policy, group dynamics, environmental damage, cultural integration, the unequal distribution of wealth, women's roles, Central America, and structural violence.

With the dissolution of the Soviet Union and the end of the Cold War in 1991, the emphasis of peace studies courses at many North American colleges shifted somewhat from international politics to the domestic scene, emphasizing structural, domestic, and civil violence. In 1991, the United States Institute of Peace[7] published *Approaches to Peace: An Intellectual Map,* which listed the following headings for the study of peace: traditional approaches (collective security and deterrence); international law approaches (international law, interstate organizations, third-party dispute settlement); new approaches (transnationalism, behavioral approaches, conflict resolution); and political systems approaches (internal systems and systemic theories/world systems). Many international organizations, agencies, and NGOs, from the United Nations, Organization for Security and Cooperation in Europe (OSCE), European Union (EU), and the World Bank to the International Crisis Group, International Alert, and others, began to draw on PCS research. By the mid-1990s, peace studies curricula in the United States had somewhat shifted from research and teaching about negative peace to positive peace.

Since the beginning of the new millennium, course offerings in peace studies have expanded to include topics such as: north-south relations; development, debt, and global poverty; the environment, population growth and resource scarcity; feminist perspectives on peace, militarism, and political violence; and nonviolent alternatives to terrorism. There is also an increasing emphasis on conflict resolution and transformation.

# PCS Today

Peace and conflict studies today is widely researched and taught in a large and growing number of institutions. The number of universities offering peace and conflict studies courses is hard to estimate, mostly because courses may be taught in different departments and have different names. The International Peace Research Association website (http://www.iprafoundation.org) provides one of the most authoritative listings available.

A 2008 article in the *International Herald Tribune* mentions over 400 programs of teaching and research in peace and conflict studies, noting in particular those at the United World Colleges, The Peace Research Institute Oslo (PRIO), the American University (Washington, D.C.), Notre Dame University, George Mason University (Virginia), Syracuse University, the University of Bradford (which is said to have the largest and most comprehensive university-based peace studies program), the UN-mandated Peace University (UPEACE in Ciudad Colón, Costa Rica), Lund and Uppsala Universities (Sweden), the Universities of Queensland and Sydney (Australia), Innsbruck and Klagenfurt Universities (Austria), Universitat Jaume I in Castellón de la Plana (Spain), and the Universities of Oslo and Tromsø (Norway). Other notable programs can be found at the University of Waterloo (Canada), University of Hiroshima (Japan), King's College (Department of War Studies, University of London), London Metropolitan University, Sabanci University (Istanbul, Turkey), Marburg University (Germany), Sciences Po (Paris), University of Amsterdam (The Netherlands), the University of Otago (New Zealand), St Andrews University (Scotland), and the Universities of Coventry and York (England). The Rotary Foundation, the Joan B. Kroc Foundation, and the UN University (Tokyo) support several international academic teaching and research programs.

Of the several hundred North American colleges and universities with peace studies programs, about 1/2 are in church-related schools, about a third are in large public universities (such as the University of California at Berkeley and the University of Washington), approximately one-fifth are in non-church-related private colleges, and a smaller number are in community colleges. About half of the church-related schools that have peace studies programs are Roman Catholic. Other religious denominations with more than one college or university with a peace studies program are the Mennonites, Quakers, United Church of Christ, and Church of the Brethren. About 80% of these programs are at the undergraduate level and the rest at the graduate level. Only about 10% of these North American colleges and universities have both undergraduate and graduate programs.

The Joan Kroc Institute for International Peace Studies at the University of Notre Dame recently added a new doctoral program. Other institutions of higher education responding to the burgeoning interest in the field include the University for Peace—established by the United Nations in demilitarized Costa Rica in 1980. Peace studies programs are noticeable by their absence at elite private universities, where departments of Political Science and Government hold sway along with programs in Security and International Studies.

PCS programs and international security and diplomacy research agendas have also become common in institutions located in conflict, postconflict, and developing countries and regions, for example, the National Peace Council (Sri Lanka), Centre for Human Rights (University of

Sarajevo, Bosnia), Chulalongkorn University (Thailand), National University of Timor (Timor-Leste), University of Kabul (Afghanistan), Makerere University (Uganda), Tel Aviv University (Israel), and so on.

At the present time, PCS is somewhat shifting its focus from interstate rivalry to intrastate conflict, as well as to problems caused by interpersonal violence. Whereas peace studies faculty used to come mostly from international relations and political science, they now are drawn from many different fields, including social welfare and education, such conventional disciplines as psychology, philosophy, and sociology, and recently minted graduate-degree programs in PCS itself. While the original emphasis of PCS in the United State was on the cessation of war (most specifically the war in Vietnam), today, the field is addressing such hot-button issues as intrapsychic and interpersonal conflicts as well as wars, terrorism, trafficking, refugees, treaties, and international efforts to curtail war and to promote an ecologically sustainable future. Additionally, many scholars on university campuses are trying to apply the insights of principled and strategic nonviolence (to be discussed in Chapter 23) to diverse settings.

## PCS as Research

Although individual thinkers such as Plato and Kant long recognized the centrality of peace for inner and outer harmony, it was not until the 1950s and 1960s that peace studies began to emerge as an academic discipline with its own research tools, a specialized set of concepts, and such forums for discussion as conferences and journals. Peace research institutes were established in Europe in the 1960s, although many of these do not offer formal peace studies courses. Some of the oldest and most prominent peace research centers include PRIO in Oslo, founded in 1959; the Department of Peace and Conflict Research at Uppsala University in Sweden; and the Stockholm International Peace Research Institute (SIPRI). The work of such peace researchers as Johan Galtung and John Burton, and the establishment as of such scholarly journals as *The Journal of Conflict Resolution* and *The Journal of Peace Research* in the 1950s and 1960s, reflected the growing interest in and academic stature of the field.

In 1963, the Peace Research Society was founded in Sweden. The group of initial members included Walter Isard, Kenneth Boulding, and Anatol Rapoport. In 1973, this group became the Peace Science Society. Peace science was viewed by these academics as an interdisciplinary and international effort to develop a set of theories, techniques, and data to better understand and mitigate conflict. Peace science attempts to use quantitative techniques developed in economics and political science, especially game theory and econometrics, otherwise seldom used by researchers in peace studies. The Peace Science Society website makes available the *Correlates of War*, one of the best-known collections of data on international conflict. The society also publishes two scholarly journals: *The Journal of Conflict Resolution* and *Conflict Management and Peace Science*.

In 1964, the International Peace Research Association (IPRA) was formed at a conference organized by Quakers in Switzerland. The IPRA holds a biennial conference. IPRA research typically focuses on qualitative, comparative, institutional, and historical research.

In 2001, the Peace and Justice Studies Association (PJSA) was created after the merger of two precursor organizations. The PJSA is the North American affiliate of IPRA.It publishes a newsletter (*The Peace Chronicle*) and holds annual conferences on themes related to the organization's mission "to create a just and peaceful world" through research, scholarship, pedagogy, and activism.

# Some Contributions of PCS

Scholars and others working in peace and conflict studies have made significant contributions to the policies of many nongovernmental organizations, development agencies, international financial institutions, and the UN system as well as to human knowledge more generally. Specific scholarly contributions have been made to conflict resolution and citizen diplomacy; economic, social, and political development and reform; peacekeeping, mediation, early warning, prevention, statebuilding and peacebuilding; and the causes of war and the reasons for peace, among others.

More recently, social scientists and other peace researchers, while still in part focusing on assessing historical trends in warfare and violence, have also increasingly analyzed the comparative efficacy or failure of violent and nonviolent strategies and tactics of revolutionary and other movements of social and political change. This represents a shift in interest from conflict management approaches, or a negative peace orientation to conflict resolution, to peacebuilding approaches aimed at a positive peace. This shift started at the end of the Cold War and was encapsulated in the report of then-UN secretary-general Boutros Boutros-Ghali, *An Agenda for Peace*. What has been called *liberal peacebuilding* or *statebuilding*, is based largely on the work that has been carried out in this area.[8] A notable case of bringing theory to practice has involved applying specific techniques for nonviolent revolution to the Arab Spring and other prodemocracy movements. These techniques, initially developed by peace researcher Gene Sharp, have been so widely (and successfully) adopted that Sharp has been called the godfather of these stunning events.

Peace researchers also investigate, catalog, and analyze arms production, trade, disarmament, and their political and economic impact comparing them with those of peace.

After the limited successes of liberal peacebuilding or statebuilding in places as diverse as Cambodia, the Balkans, Timor Leste, Sierra Leone, Liberia, Nepal, Tunisia, Egypt, and Burma/Myanmar, some PCS scholars have advocated an emancipatory form of peacebuilding, based upon an international "Responsibility to Protect" (R2P), human security, local ownership, and popular participation in democracy-building processes.

## Conflicts within PCS

Not surprisingly, there are disagreements within PCS. Although many PCS observers and critics smile when they hear about conflicts among those studying conflicts, the reality is that just as doctors sometimes get diseases, PCS scholars and practitioners now and then have disputes. (Thus far, however, they have all been resolved nonviolently!)

For example, as we have noted, peace studies is now often referred to as peace and conflict studies, reflecting the integration of studying peace and understanding the nature of conflict. But some leaders in the field believe that by doing so, peace studies risks becoming more like war studies, because so much attention in peace research is devoted to war research and conflict resolution rather than to building peace and transforming conflicts by peaceful and not bellicose means.[9]

The inclusion of the analysis of (violent) conflict within peace studies has sparked a debate not only with mainstream international relations and its dominant Realpolitik orientation but also in the field of peace studies itself. Most research on large-scale conflicts is focused on armed ones.

Wars have been studied from many different perspectives since the first works in this field were published. This tradition, from pioneers such as Lewis Richardson and Quincy Wright, has dominated most conflict research ever since. The exceptions are few but very important.

The history of peace discourse and movements is intertwined with opposition to war and the advocacy of conflict *reduction* and war cessation, dating back to the ancient Romans and Chinese. Accordingly, for PCS, analysis of the reasons for war and other forms of violent conflict is linked to its aspiration for violence prevention, reduction, and possible elimination.

Also, some PCS researchers and activists claim that if we could simply persuade people to be more tolerant and open-minded, conflicts would no longer be harmful or may even disappear altogether. Others focus on how people behave, maintaining that the problem is humanity's use of violent and aggressive means of trying to resolve conflict. And some conflict transformers argue that what matters is that existing social and economic contradictions be resolved or transcended. All three perspectives have some fundamentalists, but a growing majority of PCS researchers and conflict specialists see the need to include them all.

An old controversy within PCS concerns the relation between inner and outer peace. Should one first strive to achieve peace within one's self or initially try to create greater peace in society at large? Which comes first, healing one's self to gain inner peace, or changing a violent world to gain outer peace? Despite different views, many peace researchers and activists view this as a false dilemma and see the need for both inner and outer peace.

Some peace scholars and educators are absolute pacifists (opposing the use of military force in all circumstances), but many are not, and there is no litmus test to decide the matter. Scholars and peacebuilders are united not by ideology but by a commitment to finding *nonviolent solutions rooted in justice.* Many see themselves as contributing to a body of knowledge and practice that historically has been neglected in favor of the study and practice of war. But peace studies is not antimilitary. Many peace scholars are in conversations with the military, and many in the military are supportive of peace studies.

As in other social and human sciences, there is considerable debate about methodology within PCS. Should the emphasis be on quantitative or qualitative studies in order to get the best understanding of a conflict or a peace movement? At present, the majority of those who are close to the political science and international relations side use more quantitative methodologies, while the social movement and nonviolent side conducts more qualitative studies. Both approaches contribute importantly to the field.

When initiatives are taken to have new PCS programs at universities, there have often been spirited discussions regarding whether the best way to create a PCS degree is to include PCS in already existing fields (like international relations) and institutions (like Divisions of Social Science) or to set up separate PCS centers. Around the world there is now an expansion of both types.

Many academic fields have a theoretical component —PCS included. Good theories are essential for anyone who wants to understand the world. The complexity of conflicts makes it a challenge to have a complete understanding of such a multifaceted political reality. As with most human sciences, PCS finds it difficult to do experiments and tests that can be repeated. This is not to say that empirical observation and facts are without significance for PCS. The more and better case studies available to the researchers, the more accurate should be the theories based on these observations.

Comparing PCS with meteorology and the early history of public health may help clarify some of the challenges faced by the field. The complexity of weather forecasting is probably similar to the complexity of many conflicts. Meteorologists today are pretty good at predicting a five-day weather forecast. By identifying, measuring, and analyzing the many variables that influence the weather, they are able to forecast the probability of how weather will develop in the near future. However, it is almost impossible to accurately predict the more distant future. Early warning systems for predicting the development of human conflicts face similar or even more difficult challenges. Human beings significantly alter the Earth's climate, especially global warming, but have little influence on day-to-day weather. Natural forces create weather and human behavior creates conflicts.

To understand human behavior is essential, but not sufficient, for students of PCS, because PCS is an ethical and applied social science as well as an analytical one. Like public health professionals who were trying about a century ago simultaneously to forge a disciplinary identity separate from the medical establishment as well as scientifically to analyze and treat epidemics, contemporary peace scholars, researchers, and students attempt not merely to understand the world but to improve it. But before acting, one must have sufficient knowledge and skills. For a medical student doing surgery or for a public health worker combating a mass infection, this is obvious. Many soldiers are normally given at least a year of training prior to being sent to a conflict zone. Similarly, peace and conflict workers should be equipped with a comparable toolbox of conflict resolution skills and nonviolent techniques before they intervene in a conflict.

All tools, theories, and kinds of knowledge can be misused. Medical science is a gift to humanity but was misused by some doctors in Nazi Germany. Many of those who employ torture are using legally, psychologically, and medically trained personnel to help them be more efficient. Many PCS scholars and activists feel a need to include a humanitarian ethic in the teaching of PCS. Johan Galtung has suggested a version of the Hippocratic Oath, which may as useful for students of PCS as the original oath has been for medical students.[10]

## Criticisms of PCS and Responses

Critics of the field have sometimes claimed that PCS research is diffuse, wooly, and insufficiently rigorous. Such views have been strongly opposed by scholars who have done interdisciplinary, theoretical, methodological, and empirical research into the causes of violence and dynamics of peace.

Some academics and nonacademic critics have asserted that peace studies approaches are not objective, are derived from mainly leftist and/or inexpert sources, are not practical, support certain forms of violence and terrorism rather than reject them, or have not led to useful policy developments.

PCS defenders respond that other social and human sciences are also normatively oriented and involve subjective choices; sociology, political science, psychology, and even economics, for example, are not neutral, value-free sciences. They typically value, for example, social stability (in the case of sociology), democracy and freedom (political science), sanity (psychology), and capitalism (economics). The sources on which PCS educators and researchers rely are often the same books, journals, and databases as other academic fields and reflect the full range of ideological and political orientations. PCS action proposals are almost entirely nonviolent and anti-terrorist in orientation. And while these proposals may or may not be operationalized, they are neither more nor less practical than action plans drawn up outside PCS.

Furthermore, the development of UN and major donor policies (including the European Union, United States, United Kingdom, Japan, Canada, Norway, etc.) in conflict and postconflict countries have been heavily influenced by PCS. Since roughly the year 2000, a range of key policy documents has been developed by these governments, as have such UN (or related) documents as "Agenda for Peace," "Agenda for Development," "Agenda for Democratization," the "Millennium Development Goals," and the "Responsibility to Protect." PCS research has also been influential in the work of, among others, the United Nations, the United Nations Development Program (UNDP), the UN Peacebuilding Commission, the UN High Commission on Refugees (UNHCR), the World Bank, the European Union, and the Organization for Security and Cooperation in Europe (OSCE).

PCS also influences such international NGOs as International Alert, International Crisis Group, Amnesty International, Human Rights Watch, and many local NGOs. And major databases have been generated by the work of PCS scholars, such as "The Correlates of War" by the Peace Science Society, and, for example, also by PRIO, SIPRI, and the International Center for Nonviolent Conflict.

Finally, peace and conflict studies debates have generally confirmed, not undermined, a broad consensus (Western and beyond) on the importance of human security, human rights, equitable and sustainable economic development, democracy, and the rule of law (though there is a vibrant debate ongoing about the contextual variations and applications of these frameworks).

A necessary but insufficient condition for peace is the absence of war. The main task for peace researchers should be to help in building peace with peaceful means. It seems natural for avowed peace researchers to study the most peaceful cases of conflict resolution and transformation in order to learn how to handle all forms of conflict.

# The Future of PCS

The growth of peace studies programs in Canada, the United States, Australia, New Zealand, India, Western Europe, and elsewhere indicates a concern for the future of life on this planet. Faculty members are using their professional skills to educate students about the causes of war while pointing out concrete alternatives to violent behavior. PCS programs vary considerably as to their scope, content, and structure. More conventional programs emphasizing the study of treaty arrangements, alliance systems, deterrence theories, and the study of war between sovereign nation-states have been complemented by newer programs focusing on subnational groups and movements that cut across the boundaries of nation-states.

PCS programs, especially at the graduate level, increasingly require a core curriculum comprising the history of PCS theories and movements; qualitative and quantitative research methodologies; ethics, philosophical, and religious contributions to the field; and case studies and other applications of conflict resolution methods to current conflicts, including peacebuilding and fieldwork.

Many PCS faculty members work with peace and social justice organizations in their communities. Such efforts at peacebuilding may help build a support base for academic peace studies programs. Institutional and increased financial support is needed to give PCS programs both an ongoing identity and a continuing vitality on college and university campuses. Without institutional support, these programs tend to rely too much on the good will of a few committed faculty members, who can easily become burned out as they try to juggle peace studies with their existing academic and personal commitments.

As we move further into the 21st century, there is a danger that many peace studies courses and programs will disappear as faculty and administrators who were attracted to peace studies as a result of the war in Vietnam or the nuclear threat retire. Many graduate programs produce young scholars, committed to peace paradigms, but quite a few of these recent PhDs have trouble finding work in universities that are downsizing and whose faculty and administrators are committed to traditional subject matter. Younger scholars, originally attracted to the idealistic visions of peace education, may become frustrated and disappointed at the academy's inability to incorporate them. Many budding and even established multidisciplinary scholars feel they are peripheral to traditional academic disciplines.

Scholarly debate about the value of multidisciplinary programs also provides a challenge for PCS. Most scholars are accustomed to looking at the world through the lenses of the disciplines in which they were trained. Peace studies, rather than relying on a unidisciplinary perspective, can provide a potentially unifying center for political scientists, educators, sociologists, theologians, psychologists, biological scientists, lawyers, anthropologists, and philosophers seeking to use their academic skills to shed light on how peace and conflict affect humanity and the Earth. Nonetheless, although colleges and universities typically pay lip service to interdisciplinary studies, the reality is that such programs are difficult to establish and to maintain; in this regard, PCS, sadly, is no exception.

Studies of the causes of and remedies for violence are so multifaceted that they should not be limited to one discipline. PCS students are frequently educated in multidimensional and rigorous ways not often rewarded in traditional academic settings. Many peace studies programs are student centered, based upon dialogue (and not lecture) and group and experiential learning, value laden in their commitment to justice, and passionate in their aversion to violence. Such pedagogy has brought forth critics who accuse PCS of being soft or lacking in rigor, as well as champions, especially among the graduates of PCS programs, who frequently laud their educational experiences.

The recent re-emergence of peace, social justice, antiwar, and democracy movements, most notably the Arab Spring and Occupy movements, has created new opportunities for PCS programs. With energized peace and nonviolent democracy movements demanding that attention be paid to problems of violence and injustice, PCS may gain wider acceptance by the West and the rest of the world, as citizens looking for solutions to violent conflict, ecological destruction, and socioeconomic inequity turn to peace researchers and activists for education and support.

Nonetheless, in spite of the tremendous carnage of the 20th century, and the worldwide renaissance of nonviolent movements for social and political change, PCS is still in danger of academic and political marginalization. The mass media's and mainstream politicians' emphasis on responding to violence with greater violence make it hard to build a foundation of support for peace studies among citizenries and decision-makers who see the pursuit of peace by peaceful means as idealistic, unglamorous, impractical, and/or unprofitable.

The pursuit of peace is often labeled idealistic because it is assumed that human beings will always be violent due to human nature, and any talk about building a peaceful global community is seen as dangerous and naive. It is also considered unglamorous in the sense that bloody and dramatic events make headlines; an old saying in journalism is that "If it bleeds, it leads." Peaceful living usually not covered by mainstream mass media seeking to titillate an audience that has been raised on glamorous and unrealistic images of violence promoted on television, in novels, movies, video games, and popular music. News reports obsessively cover the protagonists and antagonists in violent conflicts but generally ignore the peacemakers who may be present and trying to resolve conflicts nonviolently. And the business of war and preparations for war (aka the Military-Industrial Complex) is a multitrillion dollar global enterprise whose economic and political clout currently dwarfs that of PCS. Accordingly, PCS needs to find ways to dramatize the work of peace heroes and heroines and to signal the successes of nonviolent movements for social, political, and economic equity. It is crucial that the struggle to build a peaceful world be a dynamic part of the public debate, so that the 21st century that will not be as dominated by violence and war as was the 20th century.

PCS faces problems of definition, influence, continuity, legitimacy, status, and funding, but it does so with hundreds of programs, thousands of graduates, and an immense global need for peaceful conflict resolution.

What are some possible futures for PCS? The field may collapse entirely (which at the present time is unlikely), may plateau (which is possible), or may continue to expand. Theories of conflicts based on the knowledge of what most conflicts have in common—from individual conflicts to group and national conflicts to international and global disputes—are increasingly being developed, tested, and refined. With new generations of students graduating from PCS and many moving on to graduate-level programs, recognition of the field as a legitimate, evidence-based discipline should grow. For judicious and effective action to take place, theories need to be combined with in-depth knowledge of actual cases. Informed critical evaluations of past conflicts will help peace activists to act more appropriately to address future ones.

## A FINAL NOTE ON PEACE AND CONFLICT STUDIES, EDUCATION, AND RESEARCH

When Gandhi said that the theory and practice of nonviolence was at the same level as electricity in Edison's day, he was probably right. "Peace by peaceful means" has taken the first step on the long road from being a slogan to becoming a reality. With serious research, creative action, and compassion, PCS educators, activists, and students can better address future global challenges. We hope this textbook will be a useful tool for those taking that path.

Like peace itself, peace studies and peace education are very much works in progress. We invite you to discuss and debate the values and methods used by these fields to propagate their vision and mission of creating more peace on earth via education, research, and lifestyle change.

## NOTES

1. Letter of Abraham Lincoln, *Collected Works of Abraham Lincoln*, vol. 6. 1991. Rutgers, 410.

2. Anatol Rapoport, paraphrasing R. Duncan Luce and Howard Raiffa. 1991. *The Origins of Violence*. New Brunswick, NJ: Transaction Publishers, xxi.

3. "Peace Studies is an interdisciplinary field encompassing systematic research and teaching on the causes of war and the conditions of peace. It focuses on the causes of . . . violence. While there is disagreement of the exact content of the field, and even on the definition of peace, most would agree that peace studies began to be identified as a separate field of inquiry during the first few decades after World War II . . . the field is multidisciplinary . . . international . . . policy oriented . . . and . . . value explicit." Carolyn M. Stephenson. 1999. "Peace Studies, Overview," in L. Kurtz & J. Turpin, eds., *The Encyclopaedia of Violence, Peace and Conflict*. San Diego: Academic Press, Vol. 2, 809–10.

4. Betty Reardon. 1988. *Comprehensive Peace Education Educating for Global Responsibility.* New York and London: Teachers College Press, Columbia University, ix–x.

5. Gavriel Salomon. 2012. "Four Major Challenges Facing Peace Education in Regions of Intractable Conflict," in Charles P. Webel and Jorgen Johansen, eds., *Peace and Conflict Studies: A Reader.* London & New York: Routledge, 25–35.

6. Conrad G. Brunk. 2012. "Shaping a Vision: The Nature of Peace Studies," in Charles P. Webel and Jorgen Johansen, eds., *Peace and Conflict Studies: A Reader.* London & New York: Routledge, 10–24.

7. The United States Institute of Peace (USIP) was established in 1984 by Congress as a publicly funded national institution chartered to "serve the American people and the federal government through the widest possible range of education and training, basic and applied research opportunities, and peace information services on the means to promote international peace and the resolution of conflicts among the nations and peoples of the world without recourse to violence."

8. See Oliver Richmond's books: *A Post-Liberal Peace.* London: Routledge, 2011; *Liberal Peace Transitions: Between Peacebuilding and Statebuilding,* with Jason Franks. Edinburgh, UK: Edinburgh University Press, 2009; *Peace in International Relations.* London: Routledge, 2008; and *The Transformation of Peace.* New York: Palgrave Macmillan, 2007.

9. See Jorgen Johansen, "Peace Research Needs to Re-Orient," in Hunter, A. ed., *Peace Studies in the Chinese Century.* Aldershot, UK: Ashgate Publishing Ltd., 2006, 31–38; and Peter Wallensteen, *Peace Research: Theory and Practice.* New York: Routledge, 2011.

10. Johan Galtung's proposed "oath" can be found at http://www.pbs.org/wgbh/nova/body/hippocratic-oath-today.html.

## QUESTIONS FOR REFLECTION AND DISCUSSION

1. From what you've now read about Peace and Conflict Studies, what would you consider to be the strengths and weaknesses of this field?

2. If you were to design a peace education program for your community/nation, what would you include?

3. Do you think global peace is achievable in your lifetime? Why/why not?

4. What are the most and least fruitful areas of PCS research?

5. How do you envision the future of PCS?

## SUGGESTIONS FOR FURTHER READING

Ian M. Harris and Amy L. Schuster, 2006. *Global Directory of Peace Studies and Conflict Resolution Programs.* San Francisco: Peace and Justice Studies Association (PJSA) and the International Peace Research Association Foundation (IPRAF).

Timothy A. McElwee, B. Welling Hall, Joseph Liechty, and Julie Garber, eds. 2009. *Peace, Justice, and Security Studies: A Curriculum Guide.* Boulder and London: Lynne Rienner.

James S. Page. 2008. *Peace Education: Exploring Ethical and Philosophical Foundations.* Charlotte, NC: Information Age Publishing.

Gavriel Saloman and B. Nevo, eds. 2002. *Peace Education: The Concepts, Principles, and Practices around the World.* Mahwah, NJ: Lawrence Erlbaum Associates.

Peter Wallensteen. 2011. *Peace Research: Theory and Practice.* New York: Routledge.

## JOURNALS

*Journal of Peace Research (JPR):* http://jpr.sagepub.com/

*Journal of Conflict Resolution:* http://jcr.sagepub.com/

*Peace and Change:* http://www.wiley.com/bw/journal.asp?ref=0149–0508

*Peace and Conflict: Journal of Peace Psychology*

*Peace Review:* http://www.tandf.co.uk/journals/titles/10402659.asp

*The International Journal of Peace Studies:* http://www.gmu.edu/programs/icar/ijps/

## WEBSITES

International Peace Research Association (IPRA): http://www.iprafoundation.org/

Peace and Justice Studies Association (PJSA): http://www.peacejusticestudies.org/

Peace Science Society: http://pss.la.psu.edu/

Peace Research Association Oslo (PRIO): http://www.prio.no/

PUGWASH: http://www.pugwash.org/

Stockholm International Peace Research Institute (SIPRI): http://www.sipri.org/

Transcend International: http://www.transcend.org/

# CHAPTER 3

# THE MEANINGS OF WARS

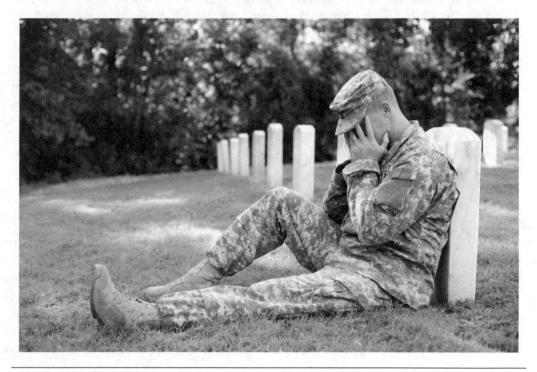

An American war veteran at the graves of his deceased fellow soldiers.

*Source:* Istock/ Jonathan Brizendine.

> *Man's body is so small, yet his capacity for suffering is so immense.*
>
> —Rabindranath Tagore

> *War is a series of catastrophes that results in a victor.*
>
> —Georges Clemenceau

Most human activities—buying and selling, sowing and reaping, loving, learning, eating, sleeping, worshipping—take place with a minimum of overt conflict and certainly without anything even remotely like war. Warfare nonetheless has a special importance for human beings, particularly since the invention of nuclear weapons in 1945, which raised the very real possibility that war could extinguish human civilization and, possibly, life on Earth. Peace researcher Quincy Wright began his *A Study of War* by noting that

> to different people war may have very different meanings. To some it is a plague which ought to be eliminated; to some, a mistake which should be avoided; to others, a crime which ought to be punished; to still others, it is an anachronism which no longer serves any purpose. On the other hand, there are some who take a more receptive attitude toward war and regard it as an adventure which may be interesting, an instrument which may be useful, a procedure which may be legitimate and appropriate, or a condition of existence for which one must be prepared.[1]

If wars are to be understood and, ultimately, overcome, we must first agree as to what they are. In this text, we will mainly consider "hot" wars—that is, overt violent conflicts between governments or rival subnational groups hoping to establish governments. In recent times, an official declaration of war has been relatively rare; nonetheless, in many cases, "wars" can still easily be recognized, not only between different nation-states but also as civil wars and so-called wars of liberation. We shall largely exclude feuds, disputes, or cases of banditry, as well as trade wars, propaganda wars, or "cold" wars, except insofar as these have a bearing on hot wars.

## Defining Wars

According to *Webster's Third New International Dictionary,* the term *war* ultimately derives from the Old High English noun *werra,* meaning "confusion." This term is perhaps derived from an ancient Greek verb meaning "to go to ruin." The modern English noun *war,* according to *Webster's,* denotes two such "confusing" and/or "ruinous" conditions. The first is a state of hostile and armed conflict between such political units as states, countries, and nations, while the second is a more general state of conflict, opposition, and antagonism between "mental, physical, social, or other forces."[2]

Many people have tried to compile data on wars throughout history, both to help identify the issue and to test various empirical hypotheses about the causes of war. However, researchers have not always agreed which armed struggles deserve to be included in such a compilation. There is little doubt, for example, that World Wars I and II are major examples, but what about the War of the Bavarian Succession (1778–1779)? In this "war," fully armed Prussian and Austrian troops marched while drums rolled, but not a shot was fired. War was declared, but no one died. By contrast, consider the Korean War, in which more than 2 million people (military and civilian) were killed: The United States was a major protagonist, and yet war was never declared. (In fact, neither was peace. This conflict is still officially unresolved, with an ongoing armed truce.) Instead, it was officially known as a United Nations (UN) "police action." Or consider the Vietnam War, in which, once again, no official state of war was ever acknowledged.

Quincy Wright considered a war to have taken place either when it was formally declared or when a certain number of troops were involved; he suggested 50,000 as a baseline. Lewis Richardson, another pioneering peace researcher, sought to define war by the number of deaths incurred. J. D. Singer and M. Small have focused on a minimum of 1,000 combat-related fatalities. Whatever the technicalities involved, most people might agree that war can be described in much the same way as a jurist's observation about pornography: "I may not be able to define it, but I know it when I see it."

Similarly, there can be debate over exactly when a given war began. The United States entered World War II in December 1941, after the Japanese attack on Pearl Harbor, just as the Soviet Union had entered the war 6 months earlier, after it had been attacked by Germany in June. Most historians (and virtually all Europeans), however, consider that World War II began with Hitler's invasion of Poland in 1939, after which France and Great Britain declared war on Germany. On the other hand, some argue that World War II began with Italy's invasion of Ethiopia (1935) or even earlier, with Japan's initial incursion into China (1931). And some historians have even maintained that in fact World War II began when World War I ended, with the Treaty of Versailles (1919), which created great resentment among the German people, leading ultimately to a resumption of armed hostilities 20 years later. The long Cold War (1945–1991) between the United States and the Soviet Union was never declared, but when the Soviet Union collapsed, it was widely considered to have been "won" by the United States.

Psychologically, the essence of war is found in the intensely hostile attitudes among two or more contending groups. Economically, war often involves the forced diversion of major resources from civilian to military pursuits. Sociologically, it frequently results in a rigid structuring of society, with prominence given to military functions. Perhaps the most famous definition of war, however, speaks to its political significance. Karl von Clausewitz (1780–1831), a Prussian army officer best known for the treatise *On War,* defined it as "an act of violence intended to compel our opponents to fulfill our will." He further emphasized that war was "the continuation of politics by other means," by which he meant war should not simply reflect senseless fury; rather, it should be an orchestrated action, with a particular political goal in mind. Very often, that political goal is the preservation of the power of those statesmen and other elites who orchestrate and hope to benefit from a particular war. It is the victors among warring elites who, in its aftermath, will normally declare the war to have been "good" and/or "just." The losers and victims of wars generally have a different view.

# The Frequency and Intensity of Wars

By some measures, wars have been relatively infrequent. Based on the number of nation-states existing since 1815, there have been between 16,000 and 20,000 nation-years, and during this time, war has occupied about 4% of the possible total. The 20th century was a very warlike one, with, by one count, about 87 million war deaths (60/40 civilian to military fatalities). But more than 85% of these occurred during the two World Wars, and since 1945, according to the scholar Joshua Goldstein, "war has decreased . . . and stands at perhaps at an all-time low" (due, according to Goldstein, principally to the "UN system in general and peacekeeping in particular").[3] And modern warfare, even with its enormous devastation, was directly responsible for fewer than about 2% of all deaths occurring during the past century. Note, however, that there have also been many indirect casualties of war, since wars and the preparations for wars divert resources that might be directed against other causes of death, such as disease and starvation.

In Iraq, for example, between 1991, when the first Gulf War began, and 2012, the number of civilian casualties occurring as a result of these factors—initiated during the devastating Gulf War, aggravated by sanctions imposed on Iraq by the United Nations under prodding by the United States, and compounded since the second coalition invasion in 2003—has far exceeded the number of military and civilian deaths that occurred during the wars themselves. And in Sudan, particularly in Darfur, millions of displaced and prematurely deceased civilians have been casualties of a multisided civil war. The extraordinary horror and the impact of wars derive from their extraordinary violence and the scale and intensity of needless human suffering that results.

Scholars estimate that between 1500 and 1942 there was an average of nearly one formally declared war per year. This does not count armed revolutions, of which between 1900 and 1965 there were approximately 350, an average of 5 or more per year. According to Lewis Richardson, there were at least 59 million deaths from human violence between 1820 and 1946, of which fewer than 10 million were attributable to individual and small-group violence; the remainder occurred as a result of wars.

Unfortunately, wars between nations in the contemporary world are ongoing in many places and imminent in many others. Since 1955, the number of armed conflicts has ranged from about 20 (in the late 1950s) to nearly 60 (in the late 1980s). During the 1990s and until 2002, the overall number of wars declined somewhat but remained between 30 and 40 per year. In 2010, according to the Uppsala Conflict Data Program (UCDP), the global total of major and minor inter- and intra-state armed conflicts was 30, which is a substantial reduction from the 36 active conflicts recorded in 2009 and the lowest number of active conflicts since 2003. Between 1946 and 2010 a total of 246 armed conflicts have been active according to UCDP criteria. Out of the current 30 or so armed conflicts, four have reached the intensity level of "war," meaning that, by the UCDP's criterion, more than 1,000 battle-related deaths were recorded in the conflict throughout the year. These armed conflicts were the ones in Afghanistan, Iraq, Pakistan, and Somalia.[4]

## Indirect Killing

In addition to the direct casualties, war kills indirectly, particularly by disease among armed forces personnel as well as by starvation as a result of disrupted food production and distribution services. For example, more than 8 million soldiers and 1 million civilians died during World War I, with approximately 18 million additional people dying during the influenza epidemic of 1918. Historically, in fact, more soldiers have died of diseases and of exposure than from enemy fire: More than eight times as many French soldiers died from cholera during the Crimean War (1853–1856) than from battle. Similarly, of Napoleon's forces that invaded Russia in 1812, many more died from the cold and pneumonia than from Russian military resistance. During the Thirty Years' War (1618–1648), the armies of Gustavus Adolphus and Albrecht von Wallenstein, facing each other outside Nuremberg, lost 18,000 men to typhus and scurvy and then separated without a shot having been fired.

In modern times, deaths due to disease have become less prominent during times of war, as a result of improved medical technology. At the same time, advances in military technology have made wars themselves more deadly, especially for nearby civilians: Military deaths were roughly the same in World Wars I and II (about 17 million in each war), but civilian deaths in World War II (approximately 35 million) were about seven times greater than in World War I. In the past, civilians often suffered horribly during wars, notably during the Thirty Years' War, when an estimated third of the German population was killed, and during the sacking of fallen cities, such as Carthage at the end of its long Punic Wars with Rome. But through most of human history, war casualties were overwhelmingly concentrated among military forces. With advances in military technology, not only have casualties generally increased but the ratio of civilian to military deaths also rose to unprecedented levels during the 20th century; this trend appears to be continuing in the 21st century. In the event of nuclear or biochemical war, whether deliberate or accidental, the casualties could well include essentially all the civilian population on both sides—and possibly billions of bystanders in other countries as well.

## The Waste of War

The sheer wastefulness of war has been appalling, even with conventional (non-nuclear) weapons. During the Battle of the Somme (1916) in World War I, for example, the British sought to pierce the German lines, gaining a mere 120 square miles at a cost of 420,000 men while the Germans lost 445,000. At the Battle of Ypres (1917), the British advanced 45 square miles, in the process losing 370,000 men. During World War I alone, Europe lost virtually an entire generation of young men. Here is F. Scott Fitzgerald's description of the Somme battlefield:

> See that little stream—we could walk to it in two minutes. It took the British a month to walk to it—a whole empire walking very slowly, dying in front and pushing forward behind. And another empire walked very slowly backward, a few inches a day, leaving the dead like a million bloody rugs.[5]

Numbers can be numbing. For example, of the 2,900,000 men and women who served in the U.S. armed forces during the Vietnam War (average age 19), 300,000 were wounded and 55,000 were killed. Yet these figures convey very little of the war's significance or of its horror, both for those who served and for the country at large—especially among the people of Vietnam. They also ignore the war's devastating socioeconomic consequences for Vietnam, Laos, and Cambodia, as well as for the United States, where it had profound social effects, including widespread alienation of millions of young people and massive antiwar demonstrations around the country. There were also political consequences, not all of them negative, including a hesitancy to engage U.S. servicemen and servicewomen in foreign conflicts (the "Vietnam syndrome"). In Vietnam itself, the economy and natural environment were devastated, and several million Vietnamese were killed. Decades after it has ended, the Iraq and Afghanistan wars may similarly have devastating consequences not only for the millions of Iraqis and Afghans displaced, killed, or maimed by the conflict but also for coalition soldiers and civilians who return home only to be afflicted by post-traumatic stress disorder and other indicators of an "Iraq/Afghan syndrome."

It is deceptively easy to present a sanitized summary, often in statistical form, of incalculable carnage and misery, thereby synopsizing ineffable horrors in a few well-chosen words. In this book, we plead guilty to this form of euphemism and linguistic sanitation, offering only the excuse that the demands of space (and cost) do not permit the reproduction of photos that could reveal the atrocity of warfare infinitely better than a written text.

# Historical Trends in War

The following list of (admittedly bloodless) facts and figures should give some idea of how war has evolved over the past half-millennium. Consider, for example, these trends:

1. *An increase in the human, environmental, and economic costs of war; a decrease in the casualty rate among combatants; and an increase in the number of civilian casualties.* In the Middle Ages, for example, the defeated side, typically the one that broke and ran, would be cut down by the victors, often losing as many as 50% of its fighting men. By modern standards, however, the actual numbers in question were small: thousands or, at most, tens of thousands involved in combat, as opposed to modern armies numbering in the hundreds of thousands. Up to the 16th century, about 25% of combatants died; by the 17th century, this proportion was about 20%, dwindling to 15% in the 18th century, 10% in the 19th century, and 6% in the 20th century (perhaps fewer in the first decade of the 21st century). This is partly because with modern technology, a larger proportion of "combatants" are engaged in support and supply rather than actual fighting. In addition, the proportion of combat injuries leading to death had decreased because of better medical care for the wounded. And disease, once a major scourge during wartime, now causes fewer combat fatalities (although the indirect effects of combat may kill many civilians, as in Iraq since 1991). On the other hand, the proportion of the civilian population in the armed services has increased, and since the number and duration of battles has increased as well, the percentage of the national population dying in war has also gone up. In France, for example, approximately 11 out of every 1,000 deaths during the 17th century were due to military service; in the 18th century, this number had increased to 27; by the 19th century, 30; and in the 20th century, 63. The 20th century also witnessed the initiation of large-scale attacks on civilian shipping, especially with the use of submarines. Attacks on noncombatants became particularly pronounced with the use of air bombardment—of Ethiopians by Italy; of Spanish Loyalists by German and Italian "volunteers" during the Spanish Civil War; of Chinese by Japan; of Poles, Dutch, and English by Germany; of Finns by the USSR; of Japanese and Germans by the United States and Britain during World War II; and of Iraq, Afghanistan, Serbia, and Libya by the United States and its allies during the 1990s and first years of the 21st century. The ratio of civilian to military casualties at Hamburg, Dresden, Hiroshima, and Nagasaki was on the order of thousands to one.

2. *An increase in the speed at which wars spread to additional belligerents, in the number of belligerents involved in a given war, and in the area covered.* In ancient times, battles typically took place in, and were named for, cities or mountain passes: the Battles of Thermopylae, Waterloo, Gettysburg. During the 15th and 16th centuries, each war had, on average, just slightly more than two collective participants. By the 20th century, the number of states involved had jumped to five. In World War II, many battles had expanded yet more, to whole countries, even continents or oceans: the Battle of Britain, the Battle of the Atlantic; on land, the tides of battle swept across all of Europe, as well as across much of northern Africa, East Asia, and the Pacific Ocean. Following this tradition, World War III, like the current "War on Terror(ism)," would almost certainly be global.

3. *Since World War II, an increase in the frequency of so-called low-intensity conflicts (LICs), in which the United States and the former Soviet Union, especially, became indirectly involved in*

*Third World conflicts, revolutions, and counterrevolutions.* Both the United States and to a lesser degree the former Soviet Union tended to consider that their "national interests" included the outcome of struggles taking place virtually anywhere on the globe. Often, they interpreted strictly indigenous conflicts, especially those reflecting revolutionary nationalism, as evidence of meddling by the other side and regarded the nations involved, therefore, as pawns in the East-West conflict. As war has become potentially more destructive and more likely to engulf nuclear powers, military strategy has focused increasingly on fighting comparatively limited wars—for example, U.S. support for the contras in Nicaragua or the mujahideen in Afghanistan—that are perceived as less threatening to the major powers but that nonetheless allowed them to carry on their rivalry on someone else's soil. The U.S. experience in the Vietnam War (and quite possibly, the Russian experiences in Afghanistan and Chechnya) also sensitized government leaders to the difficulties of conducting wars that are expensive, in terms of money as well as lives, and that do not enjoy strong public support. As a result, one might expect increased interest in the 21st century by the great powers in orchestrating LICs that are comparatively low profile and hence less controversial and domestically disruptive.

At the same time, the phrase low-intensity conflict is a euphemism, dangerously misleading as to the death and misery it may produce. Similar euphemisms would include the "police action" in Korea (1950–1953) and Vietnam (1962–1974), "peacekeeping" in the Dominican Republic (1965), and the "rescue operation" in Grenada (1983). To many defense strategists in the United States, who by the late 1980s were especially committed to the concept, an LIC is really a war, typically in the Third World, in which the number of U.S. combatants and casualties is kept low; for those directly affected, by contrast, the damage can be staggering. For example, consider the death toll in Nicaragua during the U.S.-sponsored contra war of the 1980s: more than 29,000. To gain a better perspective on this, imagine that Nicaragua's population (3.5 million) were that of the United States (about 285 million, at the time). A comparable cost to the United States would have been more than 2 million lives. Proportionately, the Nicaraguan death toll in this "low-intensity war" exceeded all U.S. losses in all the wars of its history, from the Revolutionary War to Iraq and Afghanistan.

Even "small" conventional wars can be devastating: For example, the Six-Day War between Israel and its Arab opponents in 1967 resulted in 21,000 battle-related deaths, far greater than the rate of killing per day that occurred during the Korean War. And between 1980 and 1988, the war between Iran and Iraq, generally considered a minor conflagration, may have claimed more than a million lives. Between 1991 and 2000, wars and "ethnic cleansing" in Rwanda, Burundi, Iraq, East Timor, and some parts of the former Soviet Union and Yugoslavia claimed vast numbers of civilian casualties. Millions of Iraqis and Afghans have been displaced, wounded, or killed since 1991. The civil war in Sudan, between an Islamic government in the northern part of that country and Christian and animist secessionists in the south, has claimed perhaps 2 million lives, both from direct fighting and from subsequent disease and mass starvation.

4. *The continuing increase in "asymmetrical" conflicts between nations or empires on the one hand and guerrillas, "freedom fighters," and/or "terrorists" on the other hand.* During the late 18th and early 19th centuries, the Napoleonic era of revolutionary wars initiated the phenomenon of "anti-imperialist," guerrilla warfare. Resistance and "terrorist" fighters had existed since antiquity; best known, perhaps, were the Zealots, dagger-wielding Jewish opponents of Roman rule in ancient Palestine. But the concept of guerrilla warfare as an organized if rather informal uprising on a national scale originated with the Spanish resistance to Napoleon. In fact, during the 5 years

of French occupation, Spanish guerrillas (aided by English forces in Portugal) accounted for as many French casualties as Napoleon's forces suffered during their ill-fated Russian campaign.

5. *An increase in religiously inspired armed conflicts since the Israeli occupation of Arab lands in 1967.* The phenomenon of resistance to imperial dominion by dedicated fighters in small groups has taken on an increasingly religious cast since the Euro-American and former Soviet occupation of much of the Middle East. The Soviet occupation of Afghanistan during the 1980s and the American-led occupations of Afghanistan and Iraq (and emplacement of military bases throughout the Middle East and Islamic world more generally) have been met by fierce resistance on the part of "freedom fighters" and "God's warriors" who believe that "Christian-Jewish crusaders," and their "infidel" Muslim backers, have desecrated the Islamic "holy land." *Jihadis* claim that they are defending their faith from an American-led attack against Islam itself. On the other hand, some conservative Western commentators have called militant Islam "Islamo-Fascism." While militant Islamists believe their "holy war" (*jihad*) to be a just struggle against "imperialists and infidels," many Westerners consider the global "War on Terror(ism)" to be a "just war" against "barbarism." "God's warriors" come in all denominations, and the escalation of violence by all of "God's warriors" has had infernal consequences for countless victims caught in the "divinely inspired" crossfire.

6. Finally, although the future—by definition—cannot be predicted with certainty, many experts anticipate extension of certain recent trends, such as the following: use of child soldiers, especially in impoverished regions (especially sub-Saharan Africa) that are better endowed with people than with financial resources; and increased reliance on robotically controlled munitions and private, mercenary armed forces, especially by wealthier countries.

# Modern Weaponry

We can identify four major eras of weaponry: (1) the earliest period (encompassing the entire preindustrial period), based primarily on muscle power; (2) an intermediate period (from approximately the Renaissance until the first half of the 20th century in the West and still the case in most of the rest of the world), powered by chemicals, especially gunpowder, as well as steam and internal combustion engines; (3) the second half of the 20th century, dominated by the threat of nuclear weapons and other weapons of potential mass destruction (especially biochemical weapons), and (4) the early 21st century, which, while preserving the dubious legacy of the late 20th century, may also be increasingly characterized by military adaptations of such cutting-edge technologies as robotics, drones (devices of unmanned "precision" killing at a distance), nanotechnology, space-based weaponry, and cyberwarfare. This "advance" from stone ax to hydrogen bomb and satellite gives particular urgency to peace and impels us to understand the instruments of war so as to appreciate the need for developing alternative, nonweapon "instruments" of peace.

Before 1939, it was assumed by many strategic thinkers that World War II would largely be a replay of the static trench warfare of World War I. Instead, the German Army used quick-moving armored forces closely coordinated with air strikes, in a new style of rapidly penetrating battle known as the *Blitzkrieg*, or "lightning war," which benefited the offense. In contrast with trench warfare, there were relatively few casualties in the Nazi conquest of Poland, the Low Countries (Holland, Belgium, and Luxembourg), and even France. The major loss of life in the European theater during World War II occurred during prolonged fighting on the eastern front, where the Soviet Union suffered more than 20 million casualties and Germany sustained nearly 90% of its wartime losses.

Toxic gas was used extensively by both sides during World War I. Japan employed chemical weapons against unprepared Chinese forces during the 1930s; Italy did the same in Ethiopia. Subsequently, advances in chemical and biological warfare (CBW) have raised new fears about the potentially devastating consequences of future wars, along with their possible use by terrorists (as in the 1995 attack on the Tokyo subway system by *Aum Shinrikyo*, a religious cult). Iraqi forces apparently used chemical weapons (mustard gases) in their war with Iran during the 1980s, as well as against Kurdish rebels inside Iraq itself, in both cases violating international law. And there may well be biochemical attacks on civilians in the United States and elsewhere during the ongoing "War on Terror(ism)" being conducted around the world.

There have been many innovations in war-fighting technology within the past hundred years: breech-loading artillery, landmines, grenades, torpedoes, machine guns, tanks, chemical warfare, powered ships (first steam, later diesel), iron-hulled ships, submarines, and aircraft, including fighters and bombers. Also, advances in rocketry have permitted swift, stealthy, and relatively accurate attacks on distant targets. The Battle of Leyte Gulf, during World War II, for example, was the greatest naval engagement of all time: In 5 days, Japan lost 4 aircraft carriers, 3 battleships, 6 heavy cruisers, and 11 destroyers (and, of course, many thousands of sailors), all destroyed by torpedoes launched by submarines or by bombs dropped by airplanes; there were no direct encounters between the surface vessels of the two sides.

Other developments in conventional weaponry involve improved armor plating for tanks and ships, as well as highly accurate *precision-guided munitions*—relatively inexpensive, highly accurate rocket-propelled devices that can be fired by small groups of soldiers and that endanger costly targets, such as tanks or aircraft. Many military analysts believe that the future will see further development of highly lethal munitions and robots, used on an increasingly automated, even electronic, battlefield, possibly conducted in space as well. These trends have culminated in what is probably the most important technological development in war making, the invention and high-speed delivery of nuclear weapons.

# Cutting-Edge Military Technologies

In their never-ending search for the "winning weapons," military strategists and planners have been busy developing new weapons systems and the means to deliver them. They have increasingly appropriated scientific, technological, and engineering innovations that have dual-use applications, that is, those for civilian and for military purposes. During the early 21st century, cutting-edge and futuristic military technologies include nanotechnological devices; drones, robots and other "terminator-like" weapons; chemical and biological warfare agents; cyberwarfare technologies; and satellites and other space-based weapons systems.

## Nanotechnological Devices

Nanotechnology (sometimes shortened to "nanotech," or NT) is the manipulation of matter, or the engineering of functional systems, on an atomic and molecular scale. Generally, NT deals with developing materials, devices, or other structures with at least one dimension sized from 1 to 100 nanometers (one nanometer, or nm, is one billionth, or $10^{-9}$, of a meter). NT has a wide range of applications. Molecular manufacturing, also known as molecular nanotechnology, is a field of NT that involves the manufacturing of products that are built one atom or molecule at a time.

NT has military uses as well, especially for technologically advanced machinery and for soldiers. NT can be used to build materials and parts for machines and weapons; for soldiers, it can be used to build materials to enhance clothing, and there is the possibility, according to the Defense Advanced Research Projects Agency (DARPA), of creating sensor microchips that can be implanted in soldiers to monitor their health and vital signs during combat. According to DARPA, this technology could revolutionize war, as the chips would allow the U.S. military and its medical personnel to receive instant updates about any potential medical problems in soldiers, thus expediting medical evacuations. DARPA may also develop chips allowing for treatment of medical conditions from within the body. Whether these chips prove successful in relaying health information and possibly treating medical conditions remains to be seen; however, it is important to consider the future implications of such devices. Since these chips are meant for military uses, they could be developed to do harm to the body from the inside, potentially as a means of torture. There is also the possibility that NT could be developed for surveillance purposes (via nanoscale microphones or cameras) to be used for such covert military operations as spying.

Despite the possible benefits of molecular nanotechnology, such as the potential to improve medical procedures and treatments and to develop alternative energy sources, there are risks associated with its military applications. These risks include potential dangers to soldiers' health; the threat of technologically "improved nuclear" warfare; social and economic disruption, and the threat of criminal or terrorist use of NT.

Nanoparticles used on weapons and machinery (i.e., drones, tanks, planes, etc.) to make surfaces harder, smoother, and more stealthy for covert military operations could erode and enter the body through the respiratory system, possibly leading to lung infections or cancers that could spread to the rest of the body and cause a multitude of health problems. NT that is used to improve human performance can also pose human health risks, especially if injected into the bloodstream. For example, artificial blood cells called respirocytes can greatly enhance a soldier's performance on the battlefield, but such tampering of delicately balanced biological systems within the body could cause overheating of the body, dehydration, and even breakdown of tissues and organs if the immune system perceives the respirocytes as a threat. Another example of NT that can be used to improve human performance is the introduction of nanoscale receptor enhancers that are designed to increase alertness and reduce reaction times. With repeated use, however, these enhancers could cause addiction and, with chronic use, could lead to Chronic Fatigue Syndrome, which in turn often leads to weakness, neural damage, and even to death. (The drug Provigil is already used by military pilots on long-range missions and has been employed by civilians seeking to keep themselves productive despite sleep deprivation.)

Perhaps the most terrifying risk of militarized NT lies in the possible increased likelihood of nuclear war due to the advent of sophisticated molecular nanotechnology. Nuclear war has the potential to be facilitated by nanotechnology devices (i.e., atomic firing, molecular-based lasers, etc.), and nanotechnology weapons can be developed to destroy specific targets with considerable ease and speed once NT itself has progressed to develop inexpensively manufactured military products. Because molecular nanotechnology focuses on the nanoscale, and because the advent of nuclear weapons has added to our knowledge of the atomic scale, the sophistication of nuclear warfare that incorporates elements of NT weapons has the potential to be not only devastating on the battlefield but also to become the driving force of a new and unstable arms race. Nanotechnology weapons could themselves become part of this arms race, because NT is easier to use, easier to transport, easier to manufacture, and easier to develop into weaponry than most conventional and nuclear technologies. Unless restrictions are put on the applications of NT to nuclear weapons, the number of nations whose military forces are based on nanotechnology weapons could be much greater than the number of nations that have nuclear arsenals, thus increasing the likelihood that a regional conflict could arise as a result of an arms race. As nations are increasingly encouraged to get involved in nanotechnology research due to its implications for military weaponry, superpowers could well lose their current ability to "police" the international arena, thus encouraging the breakup of existing relationships and alliances between nations and contributing to additional global instability.[6]

## Drones, Robots, and "Terminator"-Like Weapons

A drone, otherwise known as an unmanned aerial vehicle (UAV), is an aircraft without a human pilot onboard. Its flight is either controlled autonomously by computers in the vehicle or under the remote control of a navigator on the ground or in another vehicle. Although they are also used in a small but growing number of civil applications, such as firefighting or non-military security work (i.e., the surveillance of pipelines), drones are most noted for their military applications and are often preferred for missions that are too dull, dirty, or dangerous for manned aircraft.

Between September 11, 2001 and early 2012, the Pentagon increased the drone inventory from a handful to 7,500, comprising approximately one-third of all U.S. military aircraft. As advances in Artificial Intelligence (AI) continue to be made, drones and other robotic systems designed for military use (e.g., ground-based robots assigned with a wide variety of tasks, such as evacuating wounded soldiers) may be able to make combat decisions without human input.[7] In essence, the usefulness of these robots lies in the fact that they can carry out specific kinds of jobs that human forces would not be able to perform: dull jobs that go beyond the limitations of human endurance or involve extended patrolling; dirty jobs that involve work with hazardous materials or environments (e.g., underwater or even in space); and dangerous jobs that involve direct interaction with enemies or other hostiles. However, another kind of job could feasibly be assigned to these robots, namely the ability to act with dispassion; in other words, robots do not have the emotional capacity to prevent them from committing war crimes, nor be negatively affected by adrenaline, hunger, sleep deprivation, or anything else that has the potential to cloud human judgment. This could have the potential to remove human forces completely from the battlefield and therefore minimize causalities—something that is considered to be the top priority in combat situations. It could also generate serious problems.

This technology still has a long way to go. Taking its usefulness for granted could prove a horrible mistake, impacting relations with other countries. For example, in May 2012, a U.S. military aerial drone attacked a convoy of alleged al-Qaeda militants in Yemen, killing 247 of the alleged militants, 55 military personnel, 18 local militiamen, and 18 civilians. In other cases, drone attacks on supposed Taliban operatives in Afghanistan as well as in Pakistan have instead targeted wedding parties and other purely civilian events, resulting in the deaths of dozens of innocent people and generating immense anger in the host countries. In such cases, official U.S. government policy is to pay reparations to surviving family members, which is consistent with local Islamic tradition in such regions. However, it is appropriate to ask whether the perceived benefit of remotely terminating alleged terrorists exceeds the cost of civilian lives, in addition to the added cost of antagonizing people whose hearts and minds are supposedly being courted.

This is one of many ethical dilemmas arising from the military uses of such technologies. Another dilemma arises when considering accountability: who is accountable for, say, the killing of civilians in a strike? The commander who can override its orders? The politician(s) who authorized its use? The manufacturer of the robot if its equipment is proven to be faulty? (As of late 2012, authorization of drone attacks in Yemen and Afghanistan in particular has been handled by the Central Intelligence Agency, not the U.S. military command.) In addition: 1) allowing machines to make life-and-death decisions during combat requires extensive legal and ethical constraints; 2) such constraints and policies must be put in place in order to guide future technological developments; and, 3) using unmanned military technology removes major psychological barriers to wars (e.g., the cost of human lives, distances, etc.), making them easier to start.

## Space Technologies

No longer a part of science fiction, space technologies are becoming more useful for military purposes, including tiny disposable satellites, material breakthroughs to maximize the efficiency of solar cells for satellites, and even small nuclear reactors for satellite systems and other spacecraft. An additional technology is the unmanned OTV (Orbital Test Vehicle), the U.S. Air Force's mysterious robotic X-37B space plane, a secret reusable spacecraft that looks like a miniature version of a space shuttle.

DARPA's "SeeMe" program includes the use of tiny satellites that could swarm battlefields, allowing soldiers to have much wider and constant surveillance coverage from space and therefore be instantly updated during combat situations. It could also be very cost effective, much less expensive than the flying robots that comprise the U.S. military's drone fleet. According to DARPA, two dozen of these tiny satellites could be launched from missiles fired via aircraft into space, where they would maintain their orbit for a minimum of 45 days, sending updated images of the battlefield taken from space to soldiers on the ground via handheld devices within an hour and a half of receiving image requests. Although this technology is still in the works, its implications are far reaching. From an ethical standpoint, if successful, it would introduce to other nations the necessity of developing technology to shoot down the satellites in order to delay information relay to the battlefield. This could cause political conflict; also, any remaining debris in space could prove detrimental to other spacecraft as well as to soldiers on the ground if it falls through the Earth's atmosphere. In addition, if the technology gets in the wrong hands (i.e., that of terrorists or militant groups), it could be used for spying and theft of information.

Furthermore, the U.S. Air Force has plans to increase the amount of energy available for use by its satellite systems for military-based missions. As Mark Maybury, chief scientist for the U.S. Air Force notes, "Space is the 'ultimate high ground,' providing access to every part of the globe.... Space also has the unique characteristic that once space assets reach space, they require comparatively small amounts of energy to perform their mission, much of which is renewable."[8] Additional technologies that can be utilized to provide energy for even ground-based facilities include small modular nuclear reactors and space tethers, which—when developed—could harvest energy from the Earth's geomagnetic field. Although space tethers are in the far distant future, small modular nuclear reactors are not. In fact, nuclear energy has already been demonstrated for several satellite systems and has been shown to provide a consistent source of power at a much higher level than current technologies. As the size of these nuclear reactors decreases, their utility onboard satellite systems and other spacecraft increases. However, such a technology can easily have catastrophic consequences if not properly maintained or if it ends up in the wrong hands. For instance, it is possible that such technology could be used to build small nuclear weapons or more powerful conventional weapons. Attached to missiles, rockets, or even hand grenades, if small enough, such technology could prove extremely dangerous both physically and politically.

## Biological and Chemical Weapons

Biological and chemical agents have been used during warfare throughout history. Today, such weapons are sometimes known as "the poor man's nuclear weapon" because of the ease of developing them compared with nuclear weapons.

Biological agents include pathogens or other microscopic organisms capable of causing disease, such as bacteria (e.g., anthrax), viruses (e.g., smallpox), fungi, and toxins. Biological agents differ from chemical agents in that their release and their effects are not immediately noticeable, simply because infection of the human body requires a certain amount of time to become an illness.[9]

Chemical agents include: 1. nerve agents (e.g., GB, or sarin), 2) blister agents (e.g., HD, or sulfur mustard), and 3) choking agents (e.g., CG, or phosgene). Nerve agents are particularly toxic, as with VX, or methylphosphonothioic acid, which causes death after 15 minutes of absorption, and GB, which can cause death in 1 to 2 minutes if enough is absorbed. Nerve agents are particularly toxic because of their ability to inhibit the enzyme acetylcholineresterase, which is responsible for the hydrolyzation of acetylcholine wherever it is released. Nerve agents irreversibly inhibit acetylcholinesterase, which in turn causes the neurotransmitter acetylcholine to accumulate in the body; victims of nerve agents ultimately die of suffocation because they are unable to control their breathing. Blister agents do not immediately kill like nerve agents; they are meant to limit fighting ability rather than to cause casualties, although exposure to such agents can be fatal. HD (sulfur mustard) is particularly toxic, due to its stability; it attacks not only the skin but also the eyes and the respiratory tract. Choking agents utilize chemical agents that attack lung tissue. Phosgene is the most dangerous of these agents, as it causes massive pulmonary edema and can result in death within 24 to 48 hours of exposure.

Clearly, the use of these weapons against human beings is a significant ethical issue, although it is worth considering why such things should be considered less tolerable than traditional explosive or penetrating weaponry based on gunpowder. Concerning biological agents: 1) they can spread very easily and rapidly if not contained, resulting in secondary infections far from the initial site of release, and 2) advances in biotechnology have made it easier to develop possibly dangerous agents with fewer resources, increasing worries about bioterrorism. The Convention on the Prohibition of the Development, Production and Stockpiling of Bacteriological (Biological) and Toxin Weapons and on their Destruction (usually referred to as the Biological Weapons Convention, or the BWC, or Biological and Toxin Weapons Convention, or BTWC) was the first multilateral disarmament treaty banning the production of an entire category of weapons. It was the result of prolonged efforts by the international community to establish a new instrument that would supplement the 1925 Geneva Protocol, which prohibited use but not possession or development of chemical and biological weapons. The BWC became effective in 1975. It currently commits the 165 states (but not Israel, Kazakhstan, and about 20 other nations) that are party to it to prohibit the development, production, and stockpiling of biological and toxin weapons. As of early 2012, an additional 12 states signed the BWC but have yet to ratify it. However, the absence of any formal verification regime to monitor compliance has limited the effectiveness of the Convention.

The Chemical Weapons Convention (CWC) is a similar arms control agreement outlawing the production, stockpiling, and use of chemical weapons. As of August 2010, 188 states are party to the CWC. By the end of 2011, about 71% of the world's (declared) stockpile of chemical weapons had been destroyed. The convention also has provisions for systematic evaluation of chemical and military production facilities, as well as for investigating allegations of use and production of chemical weapons.

Chemical agents, like NT and drones, pose their own array of grave ethical, legal, and political concerns. Would their use be the most efficient way to eradicate such alleged enemies as groups of terrorists? What about civilians caught in the crossfire? Is it ethically acceptable to wipe out villages with toxic nerve agents, for instance, in order to kill terrorist groups that have the potential to kill many more people? Also, what about countries that possess chemical weapons but are not under any legal imperatives to surrender them or to allow for their inspection and control? Syria, for example, is one of eight countries (including Israel and North Korea) that have not signed the CWC; Syria also supposedly has the world's largest remaining stockpile of undeclared chemical weapons, namely mustard gas and the VX nerve agent.

## Cyberwarfare

Cyberwarfare refers to politically and/or criminally motivated computer hacking. It is a form of information warfare sometimes seen as analogous to conventional warfare. Richard A. Clarke, former National Coordinator for Security and Counterterrorism and Special Adviser to the President for Cyber Security, defines "cyberwarfare" as "actions by a nation-state to penetrate another nation's computers or networks for the purposes of causing damage or disruption."[10] *The Economist* describes cyberspace as "the fifth domain of warfare, "and William J. Lynn, U.S. Deputy Secretary of Defense states that "as a doctrinal matter, the Pentagon has formally recognized cyberspace as a new domain in warfare ... which has become just as critical to military operations as land, sea, air, and space."[11]

In 2009, President Barack Obama declared America's digital infrastructure to be a "strategic national asset," and in May 2010, the Pentagon set up its new U.S. Cyber Command (USCYBERCOM) to defend American military networks and attack other countries' systems. The European Union has set up European Network and Information Security Agency (ENISA). The United Kingdom has also set up a cyber security and "operations centre." The USCYBERCOM is intended to protect only military assets, whereas civilian government and corporate infrastructures are primarily the responsibility of the Department of Homeland Security and private companies, respectively.

Numerous key sectors of national economies are currently at risk, including cyberthreats to public and private facilities, banking and finance, transportation, manufacturing, medicine, education, and government, all of which are dependent on computers for daily operations. In 2009, President Obama stated that "cyber intruders have probed our electrical grids." *The Economist* wrote that China has plans for "winning informationised wars by the mid-21st century." It claims that other countries are likewise organizing for cyberwar, among them Russia, Israel, and North Korea. Iran may have the world's second-largest cyberarmy; Iran has also been the subject of more cyberattacks than has any other country, reflecting efforts by Israel and the United States to interrupt Iranian nuclear programs.

Cyberwarfare is often depicted in movies as intense yet easy; with just one click of the mouse and a few keystrokes, the "good guys" (or the "bad guys") successfully hack into a multimillion dollar security system or insert a computer virus undetected. In reality, however, cyberattacks are much more complicated, time-consuming, and expensive. Also, cyberweapons are quite flexible and can be used for a variety of purposes, including propaganda, espionage, and even impersonation, in addition to destroying physical infrastructures (e.g., factories, powerplants, or nuclear enrichment centrifuges, in the case of Iran).

There is also the prospect of cyberterrorism. Many important infrastructures and services rely on the Internet to function, and so can in theory be controlled or manipulated from the Internet. Potentially, the most serious form of cyberwarfare is a targeted attack, designed to breach defenses and disable computerized functions of an individual, company, or organization. Highly sophisticated attacks, such as one against Google in 2009, succeed, despite top security efforts and procedures. As long as people—whether an individual, a small business, or even a large pharmaceutical company or corporation—have something of interest to attackers (e.g., source code, intellectual property, etc.), they are at risk of being victimized by a cyberattack.

Defensive measures against such attacks include not only such standard techniques as security software, firewalls, and encryption but also procedures for what to do after an attack has been successful. Preventive measures include backing up information to a secure outside source, developing advanced analytic software, and setting up network intelligence systems to create awareness of possible attacks and develop means of defense against them. Identification of a highly sophisticated targeted attack involves three steps: 1) detection, or recognizing the attack; 2) situational awareness, or determining the context of the situation (i.e., what information is being stolen); and 3) intelligence, or finding the solution to the problem. Most successful targeted attacks are designed to take advantage of vulnerabilities in software or programs.

Although sophisticated cyberattacks against Iran's nuclear facilities began under the Bush administration in 2006, President Obama accelerated the program under the code name "Olympic Games."[12] Most conspicuously, an American and Israeli cybereffort (later called "Stuxnet" by computer security experts) attacked Iran's Natanz nuclear plant. Additional attacks in the weeks following the initial assault temporarily disabled approximately 1,000 of the 5,000 uranium-enrichment centrifuges in that facility.

The implications of Stuxnet's success in disabling a significant part of Nantanz's operations are considerable, including the fact that the United States, whose economy relies greatly on computer networks, would appear to have the most to lose if and when cyberattack capability becomes widespread. With such cybertechnology, plans and programs in other countries can also be disrupted or sabotaged; however, it is not an easy matter, for there are significant disadvantages associated with using any cyberweapon.

First, cyberweapons are very time consuming in their development as well as in their transfer to the physical site of the target. The team that developed Stuxnet had to physically transfer it via thumb drives into the Nantanz facility, an operation that was both risky and time-consuming. Because many Middle Eastern infrastructure systems aren't accessible via the Internet, other measures have to be taken in order to infect them; this is why using a cyberweapon to attack Syrian armed forces, for instance, might be futile. The Pentagon is accelerating the development of equipment that utilizes radio signals to insert computer code into system hardware that is offline and therefore inaccessible from the Internet.

Second, cyberweapons have shown the capability to jump from one computer system to another and should therefore be extremely limited in their use as well as intended targets. The implications of this can be seen with Stuxnet's "escape" into the Internet; if Stuxnet were capable of targeting anything else but nuclear centrifuges, the possible damage that could occur might be catastrophic. Third, although unreliable, cyberweapons can be used as leverage to exert dominion over other nations. For instance, the ostensible reason for the cyberattacks against Iran was to prevent war between Israel and Iran.

Although the very nature of computer networks limits the kinds of cyber attacks that can be carried out, cyberwarfare is nonetheless coming to the forefront of weapons strategies. Similarly, cybersecurity measures and defenses are also becoming increasingly important, as DARPA and the USCYBERCOM are given billions of dollars for building and managing new cyberweapons as well as state of the art cybersecurity.

Like other new cutting-edge military technologies, for good and ill, future developments of cyberwarfare are unpredictable, risky, and ethically contentious. To paraphrase the noted ethicist Peter Singer, the growth of technology is exponential whereas that of human institutions and societies grows at a much slower—even glacial—pace. Cyberweapons are currently being developed outside of any regulatory framework. The "Stuxnet" computer worm was essentially the starting gun of what will likely become a unique kind of international competition. Unlike nuclear weapons, for example, in which countries enter into arms races while ostensibly hoping that those weapons will not be used, cyberwarfare is already upon us: Countries are not only developing various computer worms, viruses, and so on and then storing them for possible use in the future, they are actually using these weapons right now, without any overt state of war.

## Has Technology Made War Obsolete?

In the age of nuclear and biochemical weapons, some people claim that the destructiveness of these devices has made war obsolete. It is interesting to note, however, that this suggestion is not unique to contemporary weapons of mass destruction: Throughout history, people have regularly claimed that the latest advances in weaponry, by their very deadliness, will somehow prevent war. And then comes the next one. (This brings to mind Mark Twain's comment: "It is easy to stop smoking; I've done it many times.")

Following the invention of the bayonet, for example, an English editor wrote in 1715 that "perhaps Heaven hath in Judgment inflicted the Cruelty of this invention on purpose to fright Men into Amity and Peace, and into an Abhorrence of the Tumult and Inhumanity of War." Similarly, Alfred Nobel hoped that his new invention, dynamite, would make war impossible. In 1910, an Englishman, Norman Angell, wrote a best-selling book, *The Great Illusion,* in which he argued that because of the economic interconnectedness of nations, as well as the increased destructiveness of modern military forces, war had finally become impossible. The "great illusion" was that no one could rationally conceive of or wage war in the 20th century; ironically, World War I began just 3 years after the publication of Angell's book. And in that conflict, the invention of the machine gun made neither people nor war obsolete. Rather, it led to the deaths of hundreds of thousands, often in just a single military engagement, such as the Battle of the Somme.

Since the dawn of the nuclear age in 1945, some observers of the global military scene have once again suggested that since war has become unacceptably destructive—to a would-be aggressor and even to a supposed "victor"—the likelihood of war has actually decreased. Although this line of reasoning may appear somewhat comforting, it is also seriously flawed. Let us grant that nuclear war, because of its potential for global annihilation, is in a sense its own deterrent. States possessing nuclear weapons (especially the major superpowers) may well be especially cautious in any conflict with other nuclear weapons states. But at the same time, theories of mutual nuclear deterrence seem to have produced the expectation that because of the seriousness of nuclear war, each side can count on the other to refrain from anything resembling a nuclear provocation, which in turn makes the world yet more "safe for conventional war."

In addition, there is the great danger that in a nuclear confrontation, each side will presume that the other will be deterred by the prospect of annihilation and, therefore, expect the other to back down, while remaining determined to stand firm itself. Moreover, nuclear weapons carry with them an inherent ambiguity: Since the consequences of using them are so extreme, the threat to do so lacks credibility. As a result, although technological "progress" in war making has undeniably made war—especially nuclear war—horrifically destructive, it remains uncertain whether such developments have actually made war any less likely. In fact, it may well be true that a nuclear conflict, detonation, or accident is more, not less, likely in this century than in the previous one. This is because of the increased likelihood of "accidental" local (or *theater*) nuclear wars, as well as the likely proliferation of small nuclear devices (possibly deliverable in suitcases) and of "rogue states" and "terrorists" seeking to acquire them.

Perhaps most disturbing of all, the fact remains that human beings, including decision makers, are influenced by many things beyond a cool, rational calculation of their perceived best interests. Wars have been initiated for many reasons, often including mistaken judgment or faulty information. And when war takes place, the combatants make use of whatever weapons they have. Never in the history of human warfare to date has an effective weapon been invented and then allowed to rust without at some time being used.

Historically, the impact of "war is obsolete" reasoning has also been ironic: It has not so much discouraged governments from waging war as diminished whatever hesitation scientists, engineers, and industrialists might otherwise have had about lending their talents to the production of ever-more-destructive weapons. Even the liberal view of the perfectibility of human nature helped justify science's contribution to the manufacture of cannons, no less than steam engines or new techniques of manufacturing metal alloys. And from the late 1980s until the present, many scientists similarly justify their participation in "Star Wars" (Strategic Defense Initiative–Ballistic Missile Defense–related) research.

## Total War

One of the most important changes in modern war has been the combination of (1) increased destructiveness of the weapons and (2) decreased selectivity as to their targets. The weapons, in short, have become more deadly while at the same time been increasingly directed toward civilians, even as their actual targeting has become more accurate. Traditionally, noncombatants have been granted immunity during war—in theory, if not always in practice. In his book *A Sentimental Journey through France and Italy,* English author Laurence Sterne recounted how, in the 18th century, he went to France, entirely omitting the fact that at the time England and France were fighting the Seven Years' War! There was a time when states engaged in war without the lives of all their citizens poisoned, corrupted, or otherwise focused by the conflict. In 1808, for example, with the Napoleonic Wars raging, the French Institute conferred its gold medal on Sir Humphry Davy, an Englishman, who blithely crossed the English Channel to accept his award to the enthusiastic cheers of the great scientists of France. However, this separation between civilian and military, between the lives of the people and the behavior of their states, has changed dramatically with the "hardening" of political boundaries as well as the advent of what has come to be called *total war.*

Although to some extent military forces have long been raised by taxing the population at large, armies in the field had largely supported themselves by foraging, purchasing, or pillaging. With the advent of immense national forces that employed advanced technology and were unable to provide for themselves, it became necessary to mobilize the "home front" in order to provide needed food, clothing, and munitions. As entire populations were enlisted in the war effort, it became increasingly difficult to distinguish between combatants and noncombatants: After all, it was argued, how can the enemy be limited to the person who pulls a trigger, ignoring those who build the bombs, guns, ships, and other articles of war? Furthermore, why shouldn't war also be waged against those who make the clothing used in military uniforms or even those who grow the food, without which no military force can be maintained?

During the Russian retreat before Napoleon's invading French army, partisans destroyed crops and other civilian articles that might be useful to the invader. And toward the end of the War Between the States, also known as the Civil War in the United States, the Union's General Sherman marched destructively through Georgia, punishing the civilians in that part of the Confederacy no less than the rebel military. Total war was therefore not unknown by the 20th century; civilians, moreover, have in many cases suffered greatly after their side was militarily defeated, especially if their city was sacked. New in 20th-century total war, however, was the organized use of military force directly and explicitly against an opponent's homeland in order to win the war.

Total war became institutionalized during World War I, with the first use of the term *home front* and the direct and deliberate targeting of civilians maintaining that front. Italy had actually initiated military bombing of noncombatants during its 1911 campaign in Libya, but Germany's use of zeppelins to bomb London was the first major attack on a home front. To appreciate some of the ambivalence that this tactic raised among the perpetrators, consider the following letter from Captain Peter Strasser, chief of Germany's naval airship division, to his mother:

> We who strike the enemy where his heart beats have been slandered as "baby-killers" and "murderers of women." . . . What we do is repugnant to us too, but necessary. Very necessary. Nowadays there is no such animal as a non-combatant; modern warfare is total warfare. A soldier cannot function at the front without the factory worker, the farmer and all the other providers behind him. You and I, mother, have discussed this subject, and I know you understand what I say. My men are brave and honorable. Their cause is holy, so how can they sin while doing their duty? If what we do is frightful, then may frightfulness be Germany's salvation.[13]

## Loosening of Restraints

The tendency toward total war at that time was widespread and certainly not limited to Germany. For example, the British naval blockade of Germany during World War I caused great suffering and widespread malnutrition, leading to an estimated 800,000 additional civilian deaths. As the historian John Nef put it, "One consequence of industrialization was to loosen the restraints upon war. With the growing material power to make war, what was needed was more politeness, more art, more wit in the conduct of international relations. What came was more grossness."[14]

What also came, as a result of national commitment to total war, was an inability on the part of the belligerents to call a halt to the carnage. Thus, for example, the disputes leading up to World War I were in their own way no more serious than those of the 18th century, which were resolved with much less bloodshed. What happened, in part, was that, according to the military historian Gwynne Dyer:

> the techniques of war had completely overpowered the ability of governments to limit their commitment to it. The axiom that force can only be overcome by greater force drove them to make war total, and the scale of the sacrifices they then had to demand of their citizens required that the purposes of the war must also be great. . . . When the people's willingness to go on making sacrifices has been sustained in every country by hate propaganda that depicts the war as a moral crusade against fathomless evil—then governments cannot just stop the fighting, sort out the petty and obscure Balkan quarrel that triggered it, swap around a few colonies and trade routes, and thank the surviving soldiers and send them home. Total war requires the goal of total victory, and so the propaganda has become the truth: the future of the nation (or at least the survival of the regime) really does depend on victory, no matter what the war's origins were.[15]

## Strategic Bombing

The invention of airplanes, and with it the possibility of long-range, strategic bombing, opened up yet another phase in the march of total war. Following the horrors of trench warfare in World War I, some military analysts initially welcomed the possibility of attacking an enemy's homeland as a means of guaranteeing that future wars would be short and, on balance, less destructive than in the recent past. Foremost among these theorists was Italian Air Force General Guido Douhet (1869–1930), who emphasized that air power, applied directly to an enemy's industry and to the workforce that sustained its war effort, would destroy that side's "will to resist" and break its morale, resulting in a relatively quick and painless victory:

> A complete breakdown of the social structure cannot but take place in a country being subjected to . . . merciless pounding from the air. The time would soon come when, to put an end to horror and suffering, the people themselves, driven by the instinct of self-preservation, would rise up and demand an end to the war.[16]

In pursuit of total war, during the 1930s and continuing through World War II, numerous civilian targets were attacked. German bombers targeted Rotterdam (Holland) as well as

Coventry and London (Britain), while British and American strategic bombers eventually retaliated and then exceeded the initial German bombings, conducting large-scale raids against many German urban areas, including notably the firebombings of Hamburg and Dresden. In the Far East, U.S. bombers attacked Japanese civilian targets, culminating in the firebombing of Tokyo and the use of atomic bombs against the cities of Hiroshima and Nagasaki.

With the exception of these latter two cases, there is no evidence that the national will to resist was ever seriously shaken by total war; on the contrary, national will was typically hardened by such attacks (as in Iraq since the coalition's invasion and occupation of that country in 2003 and Serbia during the 1990s), even as the civilian casualty toll mounted. It is estimated, for example, that German bombs killed 60,000 British civilians during World War II and that Allied bombs killed more than 500,000 Germans and 500,000 Japanese. Perhaps most troubling of all, today many decision makers and others take civilian casualties for granted, as "collateral damage," even as they ostensibly attempt to minimize them. Admittedly, however, we have not yet reached Shakespeare's prediction in *Julius Caesar*:

> Blood and destruction shall be so in use
>
> And dreadful objects so familiar,
>
> That mothers shall but smile when they behold
>
> Their infants quartered with the hands of war. (III, i)

# Wars, Empires, Colonialism, and National Liberation

To some extent, the history of war *is* the history of civilization or, more accurately, a history of failures in our struggle to be civilized. The earliest peace treaties known are clay tablets dating from about 3000 BCE and that resulted from wars among the city-states of the Tigris and Euphrates valley. The rise and fall of empires and states have been marked—if not specifically caused—by a pattern of military successes followed eventually by defeats. Empires that rose by the sword generally died by the sword.

## Some Ancient Empires

In the ancient Near East, for example, the Sumerian empire was established around 2500 BCE and replaced by that of Sargon of Akkad, which in turn ended around 2000 BCE Hammurabi then forged a Babylonian empire, which lasted about 200 years, until it was conquered by the Mitanni and the Assyrians around 1400 BCE Egypt began uniting in approximately 3000 BCE, whereupon it spread via conquest and contacted the Mitanni, signing a nonaggression pact with them and with the Hittites around 1400 BCE But the Assyrians eventually conquered Egypt as they did the Babylonians. In turn, the Assyrian capital of Nineveh was destroyed by the revivified Egyptians and Medes in 612 BCE.

Next to rise to prominence were the Persians, who conquered Babylon in 538 BCE. The Persian Empire under Darius I in the 5th century BCE extended from what is now southern Russia to southern Egypt and from the Danube to the Indus rivers. But the Greeks held off the Persians, and following their rather unexpected victory, Athenian Greece entered into its

Golden Age, 500–400 BCE. However, this period of prosperity and cultural creativity was shattered by the devastating Peloponnesian War between Sparta and Athens, and the Greeks never regained their civic and military glory.

Ultimately, the Greeks were defeated by the Macedonians under Philip. Philip's son, Alexander the Great, unified the Greek city-states and enabled the Greeks to conquer Egypt and virtually everything previously held by the Persians. Meanwhile, Rome developed as a major force, conquering Macedonia and Greece and defeating its rival Carthage in the Punic Wars by the 3rd century BCE. The ensuing *Pax Romana* lasted about 500 years, but the western Roman Empire ceased to exist after CE 476, because of successful attacks by such "barbarians" as the Huns, Visigoths, and Vandals. The eastern (Byzantine) part of the Roman Empire later came under attack by Muslim Saracens and ultimately fell to the Turks in 1453. Before this, Islamic forces had conquered Egypt, northern Africa, Palestine, and Spain and were engaged in periodic wars with the Christian Crusaders.

## Medieval to Modern Empires

Muslim armies, however, were stopped in their advance into Europe at Tours, in modern-day France, by forces under the leadership of Charles Martel. Charlemagne, Martel's grandson, was subsequently crowned Holy Roman Emperor by the pope, in the forlorn hope of rekindling the power of ancient Rome. Several centuries later, in the 12th century, Genghis Khan, leader of nomadic Mongol herdsmen from central Asia, established the largest land empire ever known, while massacring perhaps tens of millions of people. Although Genghis Khan's army was never conclusively defeated, the Mongol empire eventually gave way as well, largely because the various subjugated peoples retained their cultural identity even as they assimilated certain Mongol traditions.

As the Mongol and Islamic empires receded, others gained prominence, each relying heavily on military power and each relatively short-lived. Thus, the Italian city-states, as well as Spain, Portugal, and the Netherlands, have all had their periods as major world powers, especially through their trading activities, secured by naval power. England and France contested the spoils of the New and Old Worlds for centuries, essentially to a draw. Napoleon, and, in more recent times, Hitler, attempted to conquer large parts of the known world, and although they succeeded briefly (at least in continental Europe), their imperial ambitions were defeated by countervailing military force.

From the 18th to the early 20th centuries, Britain was the dominant world power, but the British Empire has also declined, in large measure hastened by the bloodletting and economic costs of World Wars I and II. Neither the "thousand-year Reich" (Hitler's imperial design for Germany) nor the "greater east Asia co-prosperity sphere" (Japan's euphemism for its imperial sway over Asia) lasted for more than a few years. World War I brought about the end of most European monarchism and of four empires. World War II left the United States and the Soviet Union as the two preeminent global powers; soon thereafter, the Cold War was initiated between them. The end of European colonialism in the 20th century was hastened by numerous wars of national liberation. In the 21st century, what some regard as American Imperialism may be challenged by China's rise to global hegemony.

## Wars and Social Change

Although wars have been crucial to many of the major political changes on the world scene, paradoxically, they have often also served to prevent significant social and economic changes.

In this sense, the threat of war has helped maintain the status quo. The *Pax Romana,* during the period of Roman hegemony, was due largely to the ability of Rome to act essentially as (Western) world police. The same was true, but to a lesser extent, during the so-called *Pax Britannica,* from the late 18th century to the early 20th century. Following World War II, the United States attempted to forge a kind of *Pax Americana;* some would claim it succeeded. But it may well be that the only kind of peace likely to be truly lasting and socially significant will have to be something as yet unknown in modern times, a *Pax Mundi*—that is, a global peace associated not with an individual nation but with the entire world.

Owing largely to their advantages in science, socio economic and educational development, and military technology, the major European powers—and, to a lesser extent, the United States and the former Soviet Union—were able to conquer, or at least to dominate militarily and politically, large areas of the globe. In the early stages of European colonial expansion, such indigenous peoples as Native Americans, Africans, and Chinese had numerical superiority, but they lacked modern firearms and often the necessary social and political organization to resist effectively. Cortés, for example, conquered 8 million Aztecs with 400 men with muskets, 16 horses, and 3 cannons. Pizarro was similarly successful in Peru, as was Clive in India. Commodore Perry "opened" Japan with a handful of naval vessels. An Englishman, Hilaire Belloc, offered this sardonic commentary on the crucial role of technology in 19th-century British imperial conquest:

Whatever happens we have got

The Maxim gun, and they have not.

But just as Native Americans eventually obtained rifles (especially during the late 19th century), anti-*junta* rebels in El Salvador during the 1980s captured large amounts of military hardware, provided initially by the United States to the repressive, neocolonial Salvadoran government. And much of Saddam Hussein's Iraqi arsenal, as well as the arms controlled by the anti-Soviet *mujahideen* in Afghanistan, came by way of their eventual U.S. enemies.

Revolutionary nationalism, especially in the form of guerrilla warfare, has been very successful, particularly since World War II, in evicting the weakened European powers from such regions as eastern Africa, Algeria, Vietnam, and Indonesia. By contrast, revolutionary forces have only rarely triumphed over locally based, nationalist governments, except when those governments were corrupt and generally out of touch with their citizenry, as happened in Russia in 1917, China in 1949, Cuba in 1959, and Nicaragua and Iran in 1979.

## The Desirability of Peace Versus Justifications for Wars

Given the positive response that most people have to the word *peace,* it is fair to question why for almost all human cultures and for most of our history we have never attained it; at least, not for long. In fact, for many centuries, war has been considered acceptable, even honorable, by large numbers of people and most governments. How can one explain the conundrum that the same human beings who say they want peace will nonetheless kill other human beings, sometimes ruthlessly and indiscriminately, to obtain it and to protect their own "vital interests" and "national security"? What justifications are provided for violent conflicts, and what are the motivations that underlie decisions made by leaders who make war?

## Biological Justifications for Wars

War has long been the ultimate arbiter of human disputes and a way of achieving glory, both for individuals and for entire peoples and nations. Ares, the Greek god of war (Mars was his Roman equivalent), was a major deity, whereas Irene, the Greek goddess of peace, was a minor figure at best. According to Heraklitos, the pre-Socratic philosopher, war (or strife) "is the father of all things." And an influential 19th- and 20th-century intellectual movement, Social Darwinism, maintained that war was not only rewarding, virtuous, and manly but also biologically appropriate.

Social Darwinism attempted to apply (or misapply) the evolutionary concept of natural selection to human political and social activities by providing a biological rationale for national conquests, imperialism, military dictatorships, and the subjugation of "weaker" by "stronger" peoples. But in fact, Social Darwinism is not scientifically valid, since natural selection and thus the process of organic evolution favor living things that are most successful reproductively, not necessarily those that are the most aggressive. Moreover, there is no objective basis for assuming that just because something is the case in the biological world, it is therefore socially desirable, ethically defensible, or even characteristic of the human world. AIDS and typhoid fever, for example, are both "natural" and "organic," yet virtually all people agree that neither is desirable.

## Social and Political Justifications for Wars

Some influential Western philosophers, including Hobbes and Hegel, have at times expressed views that deem war not merely natural but beneficial to humanity because, in Hegel's words (intended as a critique of Immanuel Kant's pathbreaking essay *Perpetual Peace*), "war prevents a corruption of nations which a perpetual, let alone an eternal peace would produce."[17]

Although this view may be in disrepute today, throughout most of the "civilized" world the fact is that wars have frequently shaken up the existing (and often unjust) sociopolitical order and have resulted in many changes, not all of them for the worse. Through revolutionary wars and wars of national liberation, many peoples have won their independence from colonial powers, both by overthrowing despotic governments and by repulsing the efforts of other powers to force them back into subjugation. In some cases, however, revolutionary struggles have resulted in newer forms of autocracy, as in the Iranian revolution of 1979, in which the despotic pro-Western shah was overthrown, only to be replaced by the despotic Islamic fundamentalist Ayatollah Khomeini. Still, revolts against oppression should not automatically be condemned because they sometimes go astray after the insurrectionary groups have seized state power.

Thus, wars, especially those fought to throw off the shackles of despotic indigenous regimes or the sometimes less visible controls of imperial global powers, may at times serve the enticing ends of enhancing, at least for a short time, national self-determination and political liberty. Indigenous peoples, no less than those in advanced technological societies, also tend to "rally 'round the flag" in times of perceived military danger, and this sense of patriotic fervor and national unity is usually achieved at the cost of projecting a stereotyped, and often dehumanized, image of "the enemy." Indeed, domestic political elites often employ the unifying effect of war and the threat of war to distract their citizenry from domestic problems and scandals in order to increase electoral support for themselves.

# Social Justice and War

Social injustices, such as economic exploitation and political autocracy, are important not only as contributors to structural violence but also as major factors in the outbreak of wars. Perhaps ironically, although the United States of America originally arose following a war of independence from Great Britain in the late 18th century, during the final decades of the 20th century and continuing into the first decade of the 21st, the United States became widely perceived as both an antirevolutionary force and a "status quo power," the "policeman of the world." Not coincidentally, for most American citizens, as well as for privileged Europeans and other economic elites in less affluent societies, the military, cultural, and political hegemony of the United States at the beginning of this millennium is welcomed as the guarantor of their wealth, power, and status. For them, peace means the continuation of things as they now are, with the additional hope that overt violence will be minimized or prevented altogether. Others—perhaps a majority of the world's present population—yearn for dramatic social and economic change from the status quo. And for some of the most militant people, peace is something to kill and die for if it can bring about greater social justice and economic equity. As a Central American peasant is reported to have said, "I am for peace, but not peace with hunger." ·

The great 18th-century French philosopher Denis Diderot was convinced that a world of justice and plenty would mean a world free from tyranny and war. Hence, in his treatise, the *Encyclopédie,* Diderot hoped to establish peace by disseminating globally all of humanity's accumulated scientific and technical knowledge, from beekeeping and leather tanning to iron forging. Similar efforts continue today, although few advocates of economic and social development and equity claim that the problem of war can be solved simply by spreading knowledge or even by keeping everyone's belly full. It is indeed disquieting that in a time of historically unprecedented affluence in many nations (despite the global economic downturn since 2008) and of the increasing global dissemination of Western (particularly American) economic and cultural ideals, the inhabitants of this planet continue to dissipate their resources and lives fighting among themselves, or preparing to do so, for an increased share of Earth's abundance. Although there is nothing new in the human experience about recourse to war and political violence, what is new, as we shall see, is the global risk involved in these potentially cataclysmic squabbles.

# Political Ideologies and Militarism

The noted British historian Michael Howard introduced the term *bellicist* to refer to cultures "almost universal in the past, far from extinct in our own day, in which the settling of contentious issues by armed conflict is regarded as natural, inevitable and right." For example, Howard continues, bellicism during World War I "accounts not only for the demonstrations of passionate joy that greeted the outbreak of war but sustained the peoples of Europe uncomplainingly through years of hardship and suffering."[18]

While this account may overstate the "peoples of Europe's" toleration of horrific loss of life, it does point to the fact that many people are inclined (or manipulated) to identify perceived adversaries as bellicist, while claiming that they (and their governments) are peace loving, if not pacifist. The latter is a term of opprobrium hurled by many political leaders against opponents they wish to caricature as weak. Not coincidentally, certain political ideologies, notably Fascism and Nazism, have openly glorified war, not only as a means to alleged national political goals but also as a desirable end in itself.

## Some Conservative Viewpoints

In contrast with more liberal and progressive political worldviews, conservatism has long tended to look upon war more favorably. Nonetheless, even most conservative ideologies have espoused a preference for peace and war prevention. The mainstream Anglo-American conservative tradition, for example, traces its roots to a rather pessimistic, even bellicose, view of human nature. One of the philosophical founders of this tradition, the great 17th-century English philosopher Thomas Hobbes, warned that because of humanity's ostensibly inherent, competitive, and sinful nature, life for humans in what Hobbes termed "the state of nature" consisted of *bellum omnium contra omnes* (the war of everyone against everyone). For Hobbes, this "natural state" of war required people who wished to avoid violent death to impose on themselves an autocratic governmental authority (which he called the "Leviathan").

More than 2,000 years earlier, Socrates had also argued against democracy and popular sovereignty, though for very different reasons. Socrates claimed that the great majority of Athenian citizens were inclined to be misled and duped by political and religious demagogues and hence could not be trusted to make rational decisions (an assembly of Socrates' peers in fact condemned him to death for "impiety" and "misleading the young"). So, in Plato's *Republic,* Socrates is depicted as arguing that only philosopher-kings should rule, rather than the people as a whole. Plato also concluded from the Peloponnesian War that city-states must be hierarchically and stringently organized if they are to survive in a violent, unruly world in which war seems an unavoidable fact of life.

The mainstream Western conservative tradition also suggests that strong moral and governmental controls over individual conduct are necessary if social order and peace are to be secured. To many conservatives, wars usually occur because we are, at bottom, predatory and aggressive animals by nature and also because social order and political stability constantly threaten to break down. Since social organizations are regarded by most conservatives as basically unstable and often irrational, peace, security, and stability can be safeguarded only by strong laws and the efficacious use of force, thereby achieving a desirable combination of deterrence (to prevent breaches of the peace) and punishment (in case deterrence fails).

For Hobbes, and for many in the mainstream Western conservative tradition, virtually nothing justifies the overthrow of a monarch or duly elected political authority. From this perspective, the "state of nature" is so dangerous and abhorrent that the people make a *social contract* with political authority, whereby they cede to the Leviathan their allegiance (and forgo their right to rebel) in return for protection against real and alleged enemies, foreign and domestic. This is a contract whose purpose is to minimize the risk of *anarchy* (lack of order) within a nation-state. But Hobbes also noted that states interacted with other nations in what was essentially an anarchic situation. "The state of Commonwealths considered in themselves is natural, that is to say, hostile," he declared in *The Citizen,* and so "neither if they cease from fighting, is it therefore to be called peace; but rather a breathing time."[19]

According to mainstream Western conservative political ideology, if power is properly and securely held and wielded, there should be little reason for war or insurrection, except perhaps for occasional brief wars to adjust the "international state system"—that is, for what has come to be called "reasons of state." War may be acceptable, even laudable, if it serves to prevent civic and moral breakdown. For example, the Roman historian Livy (59 BCE to CE 17) reported approvingly in *The Early History of Rome* that the Roman Senate had "ordered an immediate raising of troops and a general mobilization on the largest possible scale" in the hope that the revolutionary proposals that some Roman tribunes were bringing forth might be forgotten in the bustle and excitement of three imminent military campaigns against Rome's perceived enemies. The Roman general Vegetius is first credited with having coined the phrase *si vis pacem, para bellum* ("if you wish peace, prepare for war"). And in more recent times, the doctrines of "balance of power," "peace through strength," "national security," and "*Realpolitik*" have continued this line of conservative political thought.

Probably the most articulate spokesperson for conservative political theory in the English-speaking world was the 18th-century orator and statesman Edmund Burke. Reacting to the violent extremes of the French Revolution, Burke articulated mainstream Anglo-American conservative political doctrine by stressing the primacy of "community" and "tradition," the importance of preserving existing institutional order, and skepticism about the perfectibility of human societies and individual persons. According to Burke, society is a partnership "not only between those who are living, but between those who are living, those who are dead, and those who are to be born."[20] This philosophy has long been motivated by a lack of trust in the rational potential of autonomous individual citizens and by a deep suspicion of democracy.

Not surprisingly, most conservatives have long been especially concerned about the alleged threats of disorder and subversion being imported from abroad. Writing about the French Revolution, Burke observed, "It is a war between the partisans of the ancient, civil, moral, and political order of Europe the monarchy against a set of fanatical and ambitious atheists which means to change them all." For most conservatives, the traditions inherited from past generations must be respected. Social cohesion and political stability are seen to come from reverence for, and deference to, established authority (which is one reason why K'ung fu-tzu, or Confucius, is also considered a conservative social thinker). Authority per se, and usually patriarchy and authoritarianism as well, are typically valued over equality, spontaneity, and change.

Social hierarchies have also been generally admired by most mainstream conservative political theorists. Hierarchical social and political relations are claimed by conservatives to provide a citizenry with necessary reference points and stability. In the 19th and 20th centuries, however, with the overthrow of hereditary monarchy in most of Europe, mainstream Western conservatism shifted its focus away from a prior veneration of established political authorities and began instead to concentrate more on the advocacy of "rugged individualism" and "free enterprise and free markets," unimpeded by "state interference." This is an ironic inversion of the classical Greco-Roman privileging of community and society over individualism. Many contemporary Anglo-American conservative thinkers in particular have also become ambivalent about the state, generally opposing big government (except in the realm of military expenditures and in support of what has been called "the prison-industrial complex"), yet also revering patriotism and loyalty to the state.

During the late 1990s and through the first decade of the 21st century, a new trend gained momentum within conservative circles, especially in the United States. So-called neo-cons (for "new conservatives") advocated a pro-interventionist foreign policy aimed at toppling regimes deemed unfriendly to the United States and installing governments that are sympathetic to both democracy and free enterprise. This approach differs from the older, "paleoconservative" perspective, which, although generally more bellicist than its liberal counterpart, takes a more pessimistic view of human nature and thus of the prospects of changing political and socioeconomic systems in other countries. Neo-cons were especially influential during the presidency of George W. Bush; however, their impact waned somewhat as the failures of the Iraq War became increasingly apparent even to traditional war-supporting conservatives.

## Some Liberal Viewpoints

Most Anglo-American political liberals have valued highly the autonomous individual, free from political and ecclesiastical authority. Major liberal theorists in the Anglo-American tradition include John Locke, Thomas Jefferson, Jeremy Bentham, John Stuart Mill, John Maynard Keynes, John Kenneth Galbraith, and John Rawls. According to the mainstream liberal tradition in the English-speaking world, political and legal equality are more desirable than social hierarchy. The classical liberalism of the early 18th century (represented most keenly by Jefferson, Bentham, and J. S. Mill) was opposed to monarchism and in favor of free-market entrepreneurship. This early defense of capitalism by classical liberals may come as a surprise to many contemporary conservatives, who have associated liberalism with advocacy of the welfare state. But the two leading theorists and early defenders of capitalist economics, Adam Smith and David Ricardo, were considered the leading liberals of their day. The liberal theorist Norman Angell even claimed in 1910 that capitalists were necessarily opposed to war because "the capitalist has no country, and he knows . . . that arms and conquests and juggling with frontiers serve no ends of his and may very well defeat them, through the great destruction that such wars will generate."[21]

Another major strand in Western liberal political thought addresses the issue of peace from an economic perspective. In *The Spirit of Laws*, the 18th-century French political philosopher Montesquieu proposed that international trade and commerce would naturally tend to promote peace: "Two nations which trade with each other become reciprocally dependent; if it is to the advantage of one to buy, it is to the advantage of the other to sell; and all unions are founded on mutual needs." (This foreshadows the widespread view, sometimes known as "liberal peace theory," that democracies do not go to war against each other in large measure because their economic interests would be severely undermined by international conflicts.) Montesquieu also argued that trade leads to an improvement in manners and basic civility: "It is almost a general rule that wherever there are tender manners, there is commerce, and wherever there is commerce, there are tender manners."[22] In a similar vein, J. S. Mill claimed that "it is commerce which is rapidly rendering war obsolete, by strengthening and multiplying the personal interests which act in natural opposition to it."[23]

Mill's and Montesquieu's views soon became part of the liberal antiwar credo: By expanding commerce and spreading free-market capitalism around the world, as well as by promoting democracy and harnessing public opinion, war could be made obsolete. The leaders of the so-called Manchester School of British economic theory, Richard Cobden and John Bright, for example, in the mid- to late 19th century opposed foreign interventionism by the British crown and maintained that maximum free trade between peoples would serve to make war not only unnecessary but also impossible. As the process of economic globalization gathered steam at the beginning of the 21st century, its supporters have argued similarly that increased trade and economic interdependence would contribute not only to enhanced wealth for most nations but also to peace. The opponents of contemporary globalization disagree vehemently with these claims.

In a reversal of theoretical roles, however, 20th-century liberals, especially in the United States, placed greater emphasis on social responsibility and community than have the conservative champions of free enterprise and possessive individualism, except possibly in the area of civil liberties, where liberals defend individual rights and freedom and most conservatives prioritize traditional social units, such as the family, church, and state.

With regard to the establishment of peace and the reasons for wars, Anglo-American liberals have decried the excessive power of nation-states and their often imperious leaders. However, most liberals were also caught off guard by the rise of Fascist, racist, and xenophobic movements in 20th-century central Europe, especially in Austria, Germany, and Italy, and in 21st-century Eastern Europe (where Roma, aka gypsies, have been particularly targeted by racists and xenophobics). Perhaps ironically, these countries were also the birthplace of many liberal and progressive ideas, social movements, and political parties. Nonetheless, a combination of right-wing populism, virulent nationalism, and xenophobic ethnocentrism led directly to political authoritarianism and militarist campaigns against perceived threats to the established political orders. With their optimistic view of human nature, most liberals have had great difficulty understanding how this could take place within advanced industrial societies with long-standing democratic traditions and humanistic cultural values.

After World War II, conservatives generally saw the rise of Communism in the former Soviet Union and in "Red China" as the chief peril to "the free world," and they were prepared to use any military and propaganda means necessary to defeat it. By contrast, most Western liberals were less rhetorically aggressive in promoting the "war against Communism," while nonetheless continuing to allocate massive expenditures to military and espionage activities aimed at defeating left-wing governments, many of which were more nationalist than "communist inspired." Both liberals and conservatives applauded in triumphalist ways the apparent end of Soviet Marxism and the breakup of the former Soviet Union in 1991. Still, compared with conservatives, Anglo-American liberals tend to be more favorably disposed to arms control agreements with the Russians and other perceived threats to national security, and they place more hope in the peacemaking and peacekeeping roles of international organizations, such as the United Nations, than do most conservatives, who tend to be quite skeptical of any supranational institutions.

Liberals have on occasion supported specific wars. The Spanish Civil War (1936–1939), for example, was initially seen by virtually all Western progressives as an unambiguously just war, the defense of a popularly elected (socialist) government against an attack by reactionary forces aided by Fascist dictatorships in Germany and Italy. America's entry into World War II occurred under the administration of perhaps the most liberal American president of the 20th century, Franklin Delano Roosevelt. Many liberals associated with the Kennedy and Johnson administrations initially supported America's war in Southeast Asia. And virtually all prominent liberal congressional figures in the United States also were in favor of American involvement in the Persian Gulf War, the war in Kosovo, the invasion of Afghanistan in late 2001, and The North Atlantic Treaty Organization's (NATO) intervention in Libya in 2011. At the same time, the rationale for American involvement in wars of the 1990s shifted from its previous anticommunist rhetoric to a defense of human rights in the face of potentially genocidal *ethnic cleansing* (a term initially employed to depict the actions by ethnic Serbs in Bosnia against Bosnian Muslims and Croats) or in defense of the republic against terrorists "and the states that support or harbor them."

Liberals have typically been more ambivalent about war than most conservatives and typically require a "better rationale" for military action. Nonetheless, by the beginning of the 21st century, traditional liberal and conservative perspectives on war and peace had become even more fractionated. Some conservatives, for example, embraced an isolationist approach to international relations, while others, especially in the United States, favored selective military interventions in order to maintain and enhance the global military and economic preeminence of the United States. Some liberals favor military intervention for humanitarian purposes or to vanquish terrorism, while others oppose any military incursion into another country. Once again, the Iraq War created strange political bedfellows within the United States. Just as some old-line conservatives opposed that war (while neo-cons orchestrated it), an important contingent of "liberal internationalists" or "Wilsonian liberals" (named for their parallel to President Woodrow Wilson's enthusiasm for World War I as a means of reworking global politics) also supported the U.S. overthrow of Saddam Hussein.

## Some Progressive or Leftist Viewpoints

Political movements of the far right (and even some moderate right-wing or conservative parties) have rarely if ever professed peace as an important national political goal. By contrast, most left-wing (progressive and/or radical) thinkers and parties have traditionally claimed a strong association with world peace (although, as we have just seen, many of the less radical members of progressive political movements and parties have frequently approved of war under certain conditions). The most explicit and best-known example of a radical left-wing (communist) leader supporting war is Mao Tse-tung, who wrote,

> Political power grows out of the barrel of a gun. . . . All things grow out of the barrel of a gun. . . . Some people ridicule us as advocates of the "omnipotence of war." Yes, we are advocates of the omnipotence of revolutionary war; that is good, not bad. . . . We are advocates of the abolition of war, we do not want war; but war can only be abolished through war, and in order to get rid of the gun it is necessary to take up the gun.[24]

Mao's apparently paradoxical rationale for war (as the best means to abolish war) is the quintessential *Realpolitik* perspective, one that justifies war as the best means to end class violence and social oppression. Ironically, whereas the purported goals of left-wing revolutionary wars differ from the espoused aims of right-wing military campaigns, people from all political perspectives have justified the use of organized state violence as a defensible (if sometimes regrettable) means of attaining allegedly higher political, social, and economic goals, such as freedom and national security.

Within left-wing political traditions, stemming from Karl Marx and continuing through Lenin, Mao, and Che Guevara to the present, there is a further justification for the selective use of revolutionary violence (and even of terror) against established "reactionary" regimes or in defense of "progressive" ones. This is found in the ostensibly humanistic social goals of the use of "selective" violence: the emancipation of workers and other oppressed peoples from capitalist domination and exploitation and the construction of socialism (leading eventually perhaps to a classless, or "communist," society) both domestically and globally.

This radical political tradition is often in opposition to another viewpoint—namely, an antimilitarist, socialist-pacifist tradition, represented in the 20th-century European progressive movements by Rosa Luxemburg, Karl Liebknecht, and Bertrand Russell and in the United States by Eugene V. Debs, Norman Thomas, Emma Goldman, and A. J. Muste. For Muste in particular, religious considerations loomed large, such as the necessity of personal, faith-based "witness" against war. Muste is particularly well known for his insistence that "there is no way to peace; peace is the way" and that "wars will end when men refuse to fight."

Prior to World War I, European pacifists and socialists had hoped that *worker solidarity* would prevent the outbreak of war. But the war that erupted between 1914 and 1918 was an enormous blow to the optimism of many socialist-pacifists, especially since overwhelming majorities in the European Socialist and Social Democratic parties elected to support their governments' war efforts (with such notable exceptions as Rosa Luxemburg and Karl Liebknecht), rather than to organize antiwar protests and demonstrations. Eighty-five years later, in 1999, many members of the European Left—especially those with important political offices in England and Germany— enthusiastically supported NATO's bombing campaigns in Serbia and Kosovo, despite the protests of many more pacifistically inclined members of their own political parties (such as the Labour, Social Democratic, and Green parties). And in response to the attacks on the United States in 2001, and on Madrid in 2004 and London in 2005, many hitherto "pacifists" on the red/ green left sanctioned the use of violence against terrorists in the Middle East and elsewhere.

Similarly troublesome issues arise when there is a significant disparity in wealth and power between two contending parties, with the militarily stronger one satisfied with the status quo and the weaker one, dissatisfied. This is largely the case, for example, in Israel and Palestine: Most Israelis want peace, as do most Palestinians. However, most Israelis are also content with the current situation, whereas most Palestinians are not. Peace, for most Israelis, therefore involves keeping things as they are, whereas for most Palestinians, peace requires change. As a result, insofar as nonviolent means fail to induce such change, many Palestinians—as well as their sympathizers— have become increasingly convinced that only violence will get the other side's attention, never mind actually achieving their desired results.

From a mainstream Israeli perspective, as a senior adviser to the government has pointed out, Israel "cannot make peace while there is violence and when there is no violence it sees little reason to make peace." The situation that emerges is like the paradox of when to repair a leaky roof: You don't want to do it while it is raining (i.e., while violence is occurring, since this can appear to be appeasement), and when it isn't raining, there seems little reason to do anything! This perpetuates a status quo that at least one major party in the conflict, the Palestinians, finds unacceptable and increases the risk of an escalation of violence by all parties.

In summary, radical leftists and other political progressives have long advocated opposition to war in general, although many have believed that the abolition of war, the prevention of genocide, and the struggle against terrorism—and in some cases, even social justice itself—can be accomplished only via war. With the fall of the Soviet Union and the end of the 20th-century Cold War, many progressives have become more involved in local, often environmentally related movements, rather than in the mass antiwar and antinuclear movements with which they had been closely identified between 1950 and 1990, their opposition to the invasion and occupation of Iraq notwithstanding. Whether this continues in the first part of this millennium remains to be seen.

# Is War Inevitable?

Many 19th-century liberals viewed war as a deplorable interruption in the linear progression of our species to a better, more peaceful world. Even today, many liberal views of the reasons for wars emphasize the role of misperceptions and cognitive errors (rather than human iniquity on the part of political leaders who initiate wars). War is, in this view, a blunder, the consequence of human fallibility: If decision makers would only operate more carefully and thoughtfully, most wars could be prevented.

In contrast, there is another, sterner tradition associated with conservative viewpoints. The emphasis here is on innate human weakness, sin, and/or the allegedly unalterable fact of "evil" in human nature. According to one of the most important conservative politicians of the 20th century, Winston Churchill, "The story of the human race is war." From this perspective, wars do not in general occur because one side, presumably the more peace-loving one, misunderstands the other. Rather, wars are usually forced on otherwise rational and peace-loving national leaders because their "vital interests" have been assaulted or because they realistically perceive an impending threat to their "national security" and hence must defend themselves and others against those who would do them harm. According to this view, epitomized by the administration of George W. Bush but not in principle disputed by the Obama administration, the defense of freedom requires a political willingness by national statesmen to go to war if need be.

Regardless of one's thinking about the ultimate, underlying causes of wars, the belief that war is inevitable carries a great danger. Consider, for instance, the idea of a *self-fulfilling prophecy,* in which something that is not necessarily true may become true if enough people believe it will occur. Thus, if one believes that another person or country is an enemy and acts on this assumption, the belief may create a new reality. Similarly, if war is deemed inevitable and societies therefore prepare to fight against each other—by drafting an army, procuring and deploying weapons systems that threaten their neighbors, and/or engaging in bellicose foreign policy—war may well result. Such a war may then be cited as "proof" that it was inevitable from the start. Moreover, it may be used to justify similar bellicose behavior in the future (as was often the case during the Cold War of the late 20th century).

Importantly, many social practices once common and widely viewed by many as inevitable—such as slavery and dueling—are virtually unknown today. If opponents of slavery and dueling had simply conceded the inevitability (if undesirability) of this ancient social practice, they would not have struggled to end it. Nonetheless, it must be acknowledged that ending slavery and dueling may well have been easy compared with ending war, since these social changes were often feasible without regard to what other nation-states, especially the most heavily armed, were doing. A state that renounces war as a means of settling international conflicts may, by contrast, find itself vulnerable to demands and threats made by other, better-armed nations, particularly by nuclear states. In short, unlike the case of slavery in the United States, an end to war cannot be simply declared by a Lincoln-like "emancipation proclamation," which is then unilaterally implemented. An end to war in this millennium seems to require a global will to do so, although this does *not* mean that individual countries are powerless in this respect until everyone agrees.

# Can Nations Change?

There are some reasons for guarded optimism. For example, history provides many examples of societies changing dramatically from warlike to peaceful. During the early Middle Ages, the Swiss were among Europe's most bellicose people, fighting successfully against the French in northern Italy and fighting for their own independence against the Holy Roman Empire. But Switzerland hasn't fought a war since 1515, when it was defeated by France and adopted a policy of permanent neutrality. Today, Switzerland's vaunted "neutrality" (most keenly compromised during World War II due to the support by many Swiss for Nazi Germany) is undergirded by a large, well-equipped, defensively oriented modern army and by a civilian network of underground shelters.

Japan has also changed notably over the centuries. It gave birth to one of the world's great warrior traditions, the code of *Bushidō* and the very aggressive samurai. Within several decades after European firearms reached Japan via Portuguese traders (in 1542), Japanese musketry was among the most advanced in the world. But a century later, guns were virtually absent from all of Japan. And when Commodore Matthew Perry "opened" Japan (for Western trade) in 1853, Japanese warfare was technologically medieval.

The process of Japan's transformation had been remarkable. The 16th-century shogun Tokugawa, upon being victorious over his rivals, centralized all firearms manufacture and arranged for all gunpowder weapons gradually to be destroyed, without replacement. His decision was not based on a wholehearted devotion to peace; rather, it reflected the samurais' great distaste for muskets and cannons, which threatened to ruin the cult of the warrior/nobleman. Despite the reasons for this "conversion," the Japanese example is still inspiring, since it demonstrates that militarism can be curtailed and whole societies reorganized along more peaceful lines, once the authorities (and in democracies, the citizenry) consider such changes to be in their best interest.

However, demilitarization can be reversed, as was the case in Japan during the latter half of the 19th century. After being humiliated by Perry, Japan modernized very rapidly and initiated successful wars against China (1894) and Russia (1904–1905). But Japan's increasingly aggressive and warlike ventures, including its attacks on China and much of the rest of Asia in the late 1930s and on the United States in 1941 at Pearl Harbor, culminated in its defeat and the atomic devastation of Hiroshima and Nagasaki in 1945. Since the end of World War II, Japan has kept its military force considerably smaller than that of comparably affluent nations (in part because it has been "protected by America's nuclear umbrella") and has instead devoted its energies to economic growth (although there is currently much internal debate about Japan increasing its military role).

Germany has been similarly variable in its war/peace behavior. After the devastating Thirty Years' War, the principalities and kingdoms in the German-speaking world went on to become the philosophical, musical, and scientific centers of central Europe, although militarism continued to flourish in Prussia, the most influential of the German states. Beginning around 1860, with the wars of German unification, the newly constituted state of Germany became increasingly militarized, a process culminating in Germany's military aggression during World War I and World War II and in its total defeat by the Allies in 1945. Since then, Germany (like Japan) has been comparatively demilitarized, although it participated directly in NATO's military strikes against Serbia in 1999 and has played a "support" role in Afghanistan, much to the consternation of Germany's considerable antiwar movement.

Peaceful traditions can be ruptured by war, just as peaceful societies can become militarized. For example, despite long-standing Jewish advocacy of peace and nonviolence, modern-day Israel expends about 30% of its Gross National Product on its military, and Israel has been involved in five wars (1948, 1956, 1967, 1974, and 2006), as well as many military incursions into Lebanon, during its brief existence. On the other hand, nations that had previously been rent by war and domestic violence can renounce those behaviors, as did Costa Rica in 1948, when the government abolished its standing army.

War can become a national habit, and militarism a way of life. But so can peace. Long-standing traditions of war and conflict may, with sufficient popular support, give way to nonbellicose traditions. Great Britain and France, for example, which were bitter opponents for hundreds of years and had fought many devastating wars against each other, were close allies for much of the 20th century, as were other longtime enemies, such as the United States and Great Britain. Kenneth Boulding, one of the founders of peace studies, has pointed out that a zone of "stable peace" has spread to include most of Western Europe (though notably not in the Balkans or in Northern Ireland and the Basque region of Spain), North America, and Oceania (Australia and New Zealand). Within this zone, war seems very unlikely to break out between democratically governed nation-states.

The case of Northern Ireland provides another, more recent example of a transition from war to peace. In 2005, the (Catholic) Irish Republican Army disarmed and pledged never to resume its unsuccessful, violent campaign to drive Britain out of Northern Ireland, while the (Protestant) Ulster Volunteer Force made a parallel commitment, with both sides agreeing to political power sharing. There has been violent conflict between Irish Catholics and Protestant English essentially since the Norman conquest in 1066, and more actively since Henry VIII sought to impose Protestantism and English land ownership on an overwhelmingly Catholic indigenous Irish population. It is certainly possible that the current agreement will break down at some point, but the fact that these belligerents have finally agreed to peace after literally centuries of violent animosity must be seen as a hopeful step and a powerful statement of the capacity of people to change.

## Are We "Winning the War Against War" and the "Fight Against Violence?"

According to the noted psychologist Steven Pinker and the military historian Joshua Goldstein, the answer, perhaps surprisingly, is a qualified yes, because long-term historical trends indicate [25]

1. Wars today are measurably fewer and smaller than 30 years ago.

2. The number of people killed directly by war violence has decreased by 75% in that period.

3. Interstate wars have become very infrequent and relatively small.

4. Wars between "great powers" have not occurred for more than 50 years.

5. The number of civil wars is also shrinking, though less dramatically, as old ones end faster than new ones begin.

Based on these recent trends, Goldstein concludes that "For now peace is increasing. Year by year, we are winning the war on war." Why? Because, according to Goldstein, of the "efforts of international peacekeepers, diplomats, peace movements, and other international organizations" (such as the UN, EU, NATO, African Union, as well as other nongovernmental actors and individuals) "in war-torn and postwar countries . . . ." Bottom line: "World peace is not preordained and inevitable, but neither is a return to large-scale war."

And Pinker argues that "believe it or not . . . today we may be living in the most peaceable era in our species existence . . . ." This "makes the present less sinister and the past less innocent." Pinker's evidence for this possibly striking and counterintuitive claim includes the facts that:

1. Homicide rates in Europe have declined 30-fold since the Middle Ages.

2. Human sacrifice, slavery, punitive torture, and mutilation have been abolished around the world.

3. Wars between developed countries have vanished, and even in the developing world (civil) wars kill a fraction of the numbers they did decades ago.

4. Rape, battering, hate crimes, deadly riots, child abuse, cruelty to animals—"every category of violence from deaths in war to the spanking of children to the number of motion pictures in which animals were harmed . . . declined."

5. "Forms of institutionalized violence that can be eliminated by the stroke of a pen—such as capital punishment, the criminalization of homosexuality . . . and the corporal punishment of children in schools—will continue to decline."

However one judges the merits of these claims, the desirability of peace or the legitimacy of (at least some) wars, and the defensibility of at least some forms of violence, such as "self-defense," it should be clear that peace and war exist on a continuum of violent/nonviolent national behaviors and that they constantly fluctuate. Neither should be taken for granted, and neither is humanity's "natural state." The human condition—whether to wage war or to strive to build an enduring peace—is for us to decide.

# The Nature and Functions of Conflict

We end this chapter with a brief discussion of various ways of conceptualizing conflict. The word *rivalry,* for example, originated with the Latin *rivus* (river or stream). Rivals were literally "those who use a stream in common." Competitors, by contrast, are those who seek to obtain something that is present in limited supply, such as water, food, mates, or status. But the word *enemy* derives from the Latin *in* (not) plus *amicus* (friendly), and it implies a state of active hostility. Rivals necessarily compete, if there is a scarcity of a sought-after resource—this much is unavoidable— but they do not have to be enemies. The word *conflict,* on the other hand, derives from the Latin *confligere,* which means literally "to strike together." It is impossible for two physical objects, such as two billiard balls, to occupy the same space. They conflict, and if either is in motion, the conflict will be resolved by a new position for both of them.

Within the human realm, conflict occurs when different social groups are rivals or otherwise in competition. Such conflicts can have many different outcomes: one side changed, one side eliminated, both sides changed, neither side changed, or (rarely) both sides eliminated. Conflicts can be resolved in many ways: by violence, by the issues changing over time, by the deaths (natural or otherwise) of one or more of the conflicting parties, or by mutual agreement. Most people would agree that the latter is best.

## A FINAL NOTE ON WAR

Today's armed conflicts, as previously noted, rarely involve a formal declaration of war, probably because, in general, diplomatic formalities are less prominent, and war is increasingly considered an illegitimate way to settle grievances. However, wars—often under various euphemisms—are still taking place, causing immense destruction and misery. Moreover, the threat of war remains great, with its likely consequences more severe and potentially far-reaching than ever.

The history of war in the 20th and early 21st centuries shows that human life certainly is *not* considered priceless. It also shows that some lives are valued more than others, especially those of white, Western male soldiers and decision makers when they choose to perform military "operations" on other people. Moreover, a great danger lurks in a very special kind of calamity—nuclear or chemical-biological war—that could be catastrophic not only for all humans but also, perhaps, for all life on Earth.

## NOTES

1.  Quincy Wright. 1964. *A Study of War.* Chicago: University of Chicago Press.

2.  *Webster's Third New International Dictionary of the English Language Unabridged.* 1993. Springfield, MA: Merriam-Webster, Inc., 2575.

3.  Joshua Goldstein. 2011. *Winning the War on War: The Decline of Armed Conflict Worldwide.* New York: Dutton, esp. 12-44.

4.  The Worldwatch Institute. 2005. *State of the World. Redefining Global Security.* New York: W.W. Norton & Company, 12–13. See the Uppsala report at: http://www.pcr.uu.se/research/ucdp/faq/#How_many_conflicts_were_there_in_the_world_in_2009.

5.  F. Scott Fitzgerald. 1934. *Tender Is the Night.* New York: Scribner.

6.  "Nanotechnology: Future Military Environmental Health Considerations." 2005. *Global Futures Studies & Research.* The Millenium Project. http://www.millenniumproject.org/millennium/nanotechnology-military.pdf.

7.  Bernd Debusmann. "More Drones, More Robots, More Wars." *Thomson Reuters.* Thomson Reuters, 31 Jan 2012. <http://blogs.reuters.com/bernddebusmann/2012/01/31/more-drones-more-robots-more-wars/>.

8.  Mark Maybury. United States Air Force. *Energy S&T Vision 2011-2026.* 2011. <http://www.af.mil/shared/media/document/AFD-120209-060.pdf>.

9.  "Chemical and Biological Warfare (CBW)." *Science Tracer Bullets Online.* The Library of Congress, 8 Feb 2011. <http://www.loc.gov/rr/scitech/tracer-bullets/chemicalbiotb.html>.

10.  Clarke, Richard and Robert C. Knake. 2010. *Cyber War: The Next Threat to National Security and What to Do About It.* New York: Harper-Collins/Ecco Publishing.

11.  William J. Lynn, III. "Defending a New Domain: The Pentagon's Cyberstrategy." *Foreign Affairs,* Sept/Oct. 2010, 97–108.

12.  David Sanger. "Obama Order Sped Up Wave of Cyberattacks Against Iran." *The New York Times.* June 1, 2012. <http://www.nytimes.com/2012/06/01/world/middleeast/obama-ordered-wave-of-cyberattacks-against-iran.htm?_r=1&pagewanted=all>.

13.  From A. Normal. 1969. *The Great War.* New York: Macmillan.

14.  John U. Nef. 1950. *War and Human Progress.* Cambridge, MA: Harvard University Press.

15.  Gwynne Dyer. 1985. *War.* New York: Crown.

16.  Guido Douhet. 1942. *The Command of the Air.* New York: Coward-McCann.

17.  G. W. F. Hegel. 1942. *Philosophy of Right.* T. M. Knox, trans. Oxford: Clarendon.

18.   Michael Howard. 1986. *The Causes of Wars.* Cambridge, MA: Harvard University Press.

19.   Thomas Hobbes. 1949. *The Citizen.* New York: Appleton-Century-Crofts.

20.   Edmund Burke. 1961. *Reflections on the Revolution in France.* New York: Doubleday.

21.   Norman Angell. 1913. *The Great Illusion.* London: Heinemann.

22.   C. L. Montesquieu. 1977. *The Spirit of Laws.* David Carrithers, trans. Berkeley: University of California Press.

23.   John Stuart Mill. 1958. *Considerations on Representative Government.* New York: Liberal Arts Press.

24.   Mao Zedong. 1966. *Basic Tactics.* Stuart R. Schram, trans. New York: Praeger.

25.   Steven Pinker. 2011. *The Better Angels of Our Nature.* New York: Viking. Also see Andrew Lawler, "The Battle Over Violence." *Science*, Vol. 336, 18 May 2012, 829–830; and Joshua Goldstein and Steven Pinker, "War Really Is Going Out of Style." *New York Times*, 17 December, 2011.

## QUESTIONS FOR FURTHER REFLECTION

1.   Are there any persuasive justifications for war? If so, which ones? If not, why not?

2.   Is it possible to end war? Why or why not?

3.   Are some wars more "just" or "unjust"? Why?

4.   Can and should there be ways of resolving bitter conflicts without going to war?

5.   Do you think we, as a species, are becoming more or less belligerent and violent? Why or why not?

## SUGGESTIONS FOR FURTHER READING

Anatol Rapoport. 1997. *The Origins of Violence: Approaches to the Study of Conflict.* New Brunswick, NJ: Transaction Publishers.

Joshua Goldstein. 2011. *Winning the War on War: The Decline of Armed Conflict Worldwide.* New York: Dutton.

Arnold J. Toynbee. 1950. *War and Civilization.* New York: Oxford University Press.

Michael Howard. 1986. *The Causes of Wars.* Cambridge, MA: Harvard University Press.

Quincy Wright. 1964. *A Study of War.* Chicago: University of Chicago Press.

Raymond Aron. 1966. *Peace and War.* New York: Doubleday.

Stephen Pinker. 2011. *The Better Angels of Our Nature Why Violence Has Declines.* New York: Viking.

# CHAPTER 4

# TERRORISM VERSUS COUNTERTERRORISM

## *A War Without End?*

The second hijacked commercial plane about to hit the second tower of the World Trade Center in New York City on September 11, 2001.

*Source:* © 2008 Corbis Corporation.

> *This is a battle, not a war. There is a way to fight this battle without violence: reconciliation between the terrorists and their enemies.*
>
> —Survivor of September 11, 2001,
> attacks on the World Trade Center in New York

On September 11, 2001, the cities of New York and Washington, D.C., were attacked by Islamic terrorists. The loss of life in a single day due to these attacks (about 3,000 civilians) was exceeded in American history only by battles during the Civil War. However, many bombing attacks on urban centers during World War II resulted in far greater casualties to noncombatants in other countries. Raids on Hamburg, Dresden, and Tokyo caused tens of thousands of deaths, not to mention the atomic bombings of Hiroshima and Nagasaki, each of which resulted in at least 100,000 dead and wounded noncombatants.

What may be unprecedented is that the attacks of 9/11 were perpetrated by foreign Islamic terrorists on American soil, that U.S. civilian airplanes were transformed into weapons of mass destruction, that the United States was not in a declared state of war at the time, and that although the leadership of certain countries (notably Afghanistan) was perceived in many Western circles to be sympathetic to the attacks, the actual perpetrators were nonstate actors, mostly citizens of Saudi Arabia.

The instigators of the 9/11 attacks—and the perpetrators of bombings in Madrid in 2004, in London in 2005, and in other cities around the world since 9/11—have been almost universally depicted as terrorists in most of the non-Islamic world and in large parts of the Islamic world as well. On the other hand, they have been praised as God-fearing martyrs by some Muslims. Although terrorism and terrorists predated the attacks on New York and Washington, D.C., since 9/11 they have emerged as headline issues for the mass media—even if there is little global consensus as to the meaning of terrorism, the identity of terrorists, and what to do about the problem.

## What Is Terrorism? Who Are "Terrorists"?

*Terrorism* is a vexing term. Any actual or threatened attack against civilian noncombatants may be considered an act of "terrorism." "Terrorists" are people who typically feel unable to confront their perceived enemies directly and who accordingly use violence, or the threat of violence, against noncombatants to achieve their political aims.

"Terrorism" is also a contemporary variant of what has been described as guerrilla and insurrectionary warfare, dating back at least to the anticolonialist and anti-imperialist struggles for national liberation conducted in North America and Western Europe during the late 18th and early 19th centuries and continuing after World War II in Africa and South Asia against such European empires as the British, French, Dutch, and Portuguese.

Placing "terrorist" in quotation marks may be jarring for some readers, who consider the designation self-evident. We do so, however, not to minimize the horror of such acts but to emphasize the value of qualifying righteous indignation by recognizing that often one person's "terrorist" is another's "freedom fighter." Thus, who is or is not a terrorist and what may or may not be acts of terrorism depend largely on the perspective of the person or group using these terms. Here are some contemporary, and contending, definitions of terrorism:

> The term "terrorism" means premeditated, politically motivated violence perpetrated against noncombatant targets by sub-national groups or clandestine agents, usually intended to influence an audience.[1]

This is perhaps the most commonly understood contemporary definition of terrorism in the West, and it was penned by the U.S. Central Intelligence Agency (CIA).

A second, widely held definition of terrorism is articulated by an influential American terrorism expert, Bruce Hoffman (formerly of the RAND Corporation):

Terrorism is fundamentally a form of psychological warfare. Terrorism is designed, as it has always been, to have profound psychological repercussions on a target audience. Fear and intimidation are precisely the terrorists' timeless stock-in-trade. . . . It is used to create unbridled fear, dark insecurity, and reverberating panic. Terrorists seek to elicit an irrational, emotional response.[2]

In contrast, a philosopher has argued that terrorism is

non-sharply demarcated from other types/forms of individual or collective violence. The major types of terrorism are: predatory, retaliatory, political, and political-moralistic/religious. The terrorism may be domestic or international, "from above"—i.e., state or state-sponsored terrorism, or "from below."[3]

Finally, a political theorist states that

terrorism is meant to cause terror (extreme fear) and, when successful, does so. Terrorism is intimidation with a purpose: the terror is meant to cause others to do things they would otherwise not do. Terrorism is coercive intimidation.[4]

Although it is possibly the most contested concept in the contemporary political lexicon, "terrorism" has been used most often to denote politically motivated attacks by subnational agents (this part is virtually uncontested among Western scholars) and/or states (this is widely debated but increasingly accepted outside the United States) on noncombatants (and, some would argue, on police and other state representatives as well), usually in the context of war, revolution, and struggles for national liberation. In this sense, "terrorism" is as old as violent human conflict.

However, there is little consensus on who, precisely, is or is not a "terrorist" or on what is or is not an act of "terrorism." Thus, it is notable that even the United Nations (UN) has been unable to agree on defining terrorism, despite decades of debating the issue.

"Terrorism" is clearly a subcategory of violence in general and of political violence in particular. Almost all current definitions focus on the violent acts committed (or threatened) by "terrorists" and neglect the effects of those acts on their victims. Hence these are *agent-centered* conceptions of terrorism, probably the majority position for the current terrorism industry. But there are also *victim-centered* understandings of terrorism—a minority position in most of the West but not uncommon in the rest of the world. Victim-centered views of terrorism focus on the terrifying effects of certain violent acts on the victims of those acts, rather than on continuing the never-ending debate as to who is or is not a "terrorist."

Despite disagreements regarding the nature and perpetrators of "terrorism," for functional purposes, we propose the following definition:

Terrorism is a premeditated, usually politically motivated, use, or threatened use, of violence, in order to induce a state of terror in its immediate victims, usually for the purpose of influencing another, less reachable audience, such as a government. Such victims may include civilian noncombatants but are not necessarily limited to them.

Note that under this definition, both nation-states—which commit "terrorism from above" (TFA)—and subnational entities (individuals and groups alike)—which engage in "terrorism from below" (TFB)—may commit acts of terrorism. This conceptualization distinguishes our understanding of terrorism from the "official" one of the U.S. government and from that of many, but not all, writers on this topic.[5] It also distinguishes political terrorism from other forms of terrorism, especially criminal terrorism.

In considering who "is" and who may "become" a "terrorist," it is also important to dispel some popular misconceptions. Recent work conducted by the political scientist Robert Pape and also at the National Consortium for the Study of Terrorism and Responses to Terrorism (START) at the University of Maryland challenges some long-accepted notions—for example, that terrorists are pathological, driven by religious fanaticism, and/or spurred by poverty. According to a study published in *Science*, "It's now well established that many terrorists are well-educated and seemingly rational. Economists in particular have explored a disturbing notion, probing terrorism as a form of 'altruism' and comparing it to exclusive groups."[6] In this light, it should come as little surprise that some of yesterday's "altruistic" terrorists have become heads of state and even Nobel Peace Prize winners.

## The Politics of Terrorism: Yesterday's Terrorist, Tomorrow's Nobel Peace Prize Winner?

"Terrorism" is at bottom a political construct: a historically variable and ideologically useful way of branding those who may violently oppose a particular policy or government as beyond the moral pale and hence "not worthy" of diplomacy and negotiations. Moreover, yesterday's "terrorist" may become today's or tomorrow's chief of state—if successful in seizing or otherwise gaining state power.

Historical examples abound, from the "barbarian" Teutonic insurgents who overthrew the Roman Empire to the Jacobins during the early days of the French Revolution. Moreover, prior to the U.S. Civil War, militant abolitionists such as John Brown were considered terrorists and are now widely seen as abolitionist freedom fighters. During the 1940s, Menachem Begin—who subsequently became prime minister of Israel and a close ally of the United States—headed a militant Zionist group known as the *Irgun*; this organization conducted numerous acts of violence, primarily against British-occupied Palestine, including the notorious bombing of the King David Hotel, a civilian target.

The late Yasser Arafat, longtime head of the Palestine Liberation Organization, has similarly been denounced (in the West and in Israel) as a terrorist; among Palestinians, he is widely regarded as a heroic leader. The government of Pakistan, which criticized "terror attacks" on the United States as "un-Islamic," has long sponsored violent agitators in Kashmir, who are considered terrorists by the government of India. The Irish Republican Army (IRA) has been widely regarded in Great Britain as a terrorist organization, yet many Irish Catholics consider this group laudably patriotic, and much of its funding has come from donations raised in the United States. Nelson Mandela and other leaders of the antiapartheid resistance movement in South Africa used violence to promote their political ends. When asked if he and his African National Congress (ANC) were terrorists, Mandela replied, "Of course. . . . " Mandela later won the Nobel Peace Prize, as did Yasser Arafat. (On the other hand, so did Henry Kissinger, an architect of the Vietnam War and of the "Christmas bombing" campaign that killed many Vietnamese civilians just before the American withdrawal from Vietnam.) After accession to state power, the victors often (re)write the history books to (re)label themselves as "freedom fighters," "patriots," and/or proponents of "national liberation" and denote their vanquished adversaries as "terrorists," "autocrats," "imperialists," "dictators," and so on.

Terrorism therefore may acquire its political content retrospectively, based on the success or failure of those who employ political violence in achieving specific political goals, such as anti-imperialism, revolutionary insurrection, nation-building, and/or radical Islamic *jihad*, and so on. Many politically powerful contemporary opponents of "terrorism" claim for themselves a kind of moral superiority, an "ethical high ground" that permits and justifies virtually any means (designated "counterterrorism" and/or "preemptive war")—including bombings that result in many civilian casualties ("collateral damage")—to win "the war against terror/ism." But this often precipitates an escalating series of attacks and counterattacks, a "cycle of violence" that has global, and potentially homicidal, implications.

# A Brief History of Terrorism

The lexicography and history of terrorism are important. The term *terrorism* derives originally from the French Revolution, when it was initially used approvingly in 1793–1794 by newly installed defenders of the revolutionary regime to denote the "reign of terror" that they believed was needed to safeguard the new state against its enemies, alleged "counter-revolutionaries" both domestic and foreign. At the turn of the 19th century, therefore, terrorism was political violence deployed by agents of a government against its real and alleged internal and external foes—"enemy combatants"—and the people who supported them.

Two centuries later, the term *terrorism* has been inverted. Today, in most of the Western world at least, terrorism usually denotes political violence, intimidation, and psychological warfare deployed by subnational groups mainly against civilian noncombatants. In other words, what some analysts have called TFA: Terrorism From Above, or state-conducted and/or supported political violence, intimidation, and psychological warfare—has largely been excluded from most official and even popular conceptions of terrorism. Instead, most people in the West have learned to identify "terrorism" exclusively with TFB: Terrorism From Below, or political violence, intimidation, and psychological warfare conducted by nonstate actors.

This is a shift of profound importance, for it permits states and the mass media to legitimize the violence, intimidation, and coercion of state-sanctioned "counterterrorist" operations, ostensibly conducted in defense of freedom and national security. And it also delegitimizes and morally condemns domestic and foreign opponents of state authority. The current "Global War on Terrorism" is the quintessential example of this transformation. To a considerable degree, it is the logical extension of trends in warfare dating back to the end of World War I and to World War II, when "total war" included the massive bombing of civilian noncombatants.

## Warfare as Terrorism From Above

Terror bombings of civilians during wartime have resulted in many *more* casualties (numbered in the millions) than all acts of "terrorism from below" combined (perhaps tens of thousands). In fact, more than 99% of the victims of political violence between 1968 and 1988 were killed by agents of *state* terror. [7]

Furthermore, aerial bombings of civilians have rarely resulted in achieving their declared political objectives: The firebombings of German and Japanese cities did *not* by themselves significantly induce the German and Japanese governments to surrender; rather, they tended to harden the resolve of the indigenous populations to fight harder (as did the German *Blitz* of

England during 1940). Some historians have also made the case that even the nuclear bombings of Hiroshima and Nagasaki did not significantly accelerate the outcome of the War in the Pacific, because the Japanese government had already signaled its willingness to capitulate before the bombings. On the other hand, the terror firebombing of Rotterdam in 1940 (which may not have been intended by the *Luftwaffe*) was followed almost immediately by the surrender of the Dutch to the Germans. Similarly, Serbia withdrew from Kosovo soon after Belgrade and other Yugoslavian cities were bombed by NATO in 1999. And NATO's bombing of Colonel Qaddafi's forces in Libya in 2011 eventually resulted in his being driven from power and executed. But in these two cases, the bombing was brief and civilian casualties were probably in the hundreds, not in the hundreds of thousands as they were in Germany and Japan during World War II.

Accordingly, the terror bombings committed by Great Britain and the United States, as well as by Nazi Germany and by Japan (principally in China), are classic examples of TFA or "state terrorism," and they resulted in millions of civilian casualties, without accomplishing their most important political objectives—namely, the profound demoralization of the civilian populations and prompt surrender of their antagonists. But what these state terrorists did accomplish, like their TFB counterparts, was to terrorize huge numbers of people, to use persons as a means toward political ends, and to dehumanize their victims.

Consequently, this Age of Global Terrorism, dating from the early 20th century, when "total war" and "strategic bombing" became acceptable components of military and diplomatic strategy, has culminated in the progressive obliteration of important, previously held moral and military distinctions. Most notably, there has been a gradual collapse of the distinction between "illegitimate" (i.e., civilian noncombatants) and "legitimate" (i.e., military) "targets," as well as of the distinction between "terrorists" and "the states" that allegedly support them.

Finally, this century-long process is leading to erosion of the boundary between "terrorism" and "war." Thus, since at least the early days of World War II, for the civilian populations of the affected states, war has become indistinguishable from terrorism. Terrorism, or psychological warfare, has become a predictable tool to be employed by war planners and policymakers, whether from "above" or "below." Terrorism has also become a tool in the arsenal of enemies of the state and government policymakers, both locally and globally.

## Homegrown American Terrorists From Below

The United States has its own tradition of homegrown insurrectionary groups and terrorist actions. From the standpoint of the British government, during the American War of Independence, or Revolutionary War (1776–1783), such American "founding fathers" as Paul Revere, George Washington, John Adams, and Thomas Jefferson were probably deemed the equivalent of "terrorists" because of their opposition to colonial rule and espousal of revolutionary, insurrectionary, and belligerent strategies and tactics to gain independence from England. Terrifying raids and murders were also perpetrated by John Brown and other violent abolitionists in the 19th century. Just prior to the American Civil War, for example, pro- and antislavery groups had frequent battles, particularly in Kansas, their principal battleground. More than 200 people were killed there, which is why during the late 1850s it came to be known as "Bleeding Kansas."

Following the Civil War, Confederate veterans, some organized in the Ku Klux Klan (KKK), terrorized the newly freed blacks of the American South as well as their white Republican allies. They named it after the Greek word *kuklos*, which means circle. The name Ku Klux Klan means "Circle of Brothers." The Klan worked to curb the education, economic advancement, voting rights, and right to keep and bear arms of blacks. In the late 1860s, the Klan spread into nearly every southern state, launching a "reign of terror" against Republican leaders both black and white. Those political leaders assassinated during the campaign included Arkansas Congressman James M. Hinds and three members of the South Carolina legislature. The KKK continued to lynch blacks and to murder white liberals well into the 20th century, especially during the early days of the Civil Rights Movement.

During the 1990s, the number of violent right-wing groups and hate crimes went up dramatically. White Protestant militia groups, such as The Order, and similar Christian Patriot organizations promoted fiercely anti-Semitic, anti-Islamic, antigovernment, and xenophobic views. And neo-Nazi groups, such as the *Volksfront and White Revolution,* have hoped for an "Aryan Revolution," with many believing that a "racial holy war" is inevitable.

On April 19, 1995, Timothy McVeigh, an adherent of white supremacist ideology, bombed a federal building in Oklahoma City and killed innocent civilians. McVeigh was a United States Army veteran and security guard, who detonated a truck bomb in front of the Alfred P. Murrah Federal Building. Commonly referred to as the Oklahoma City Bombing, this attack killed 168 people and injured more than 800; it was the deadliest act of terrorism within the United States prior to the September 11, 2001 attacks. McVeigh hoped to inspire a revolt against what he considered to be a tyrannical federal government. He was convicted of 11 federal offenses and executed in 2001; two others were also convicted and sentenced to life imprisonment as co-conspirators in the plot.

Although such home-grown "militia movements" have become less public in the ensuing decade, some right-wing Christian militants, possibly inspired by a shadowy organization called the Army of God (AOG), have intimidated, assaulted, and even murdered workers at abortion clinics. The earliest documented incidence of the AOG being involved with anti-abortion activity occurred in 1982. The "East Coast division" of the AOG planted bombs at seven abortion clinics in 1985. The AOG claimed responsibility for Eric Robert Rudolph's 1997 nail bombing of abortion clinics in Atlanta and Birmingham, as well as an attack on an Atlanta lesbian bar. Clayton Waagner, claiming to act on the part of the "Virginia Dare Chapter" of the AOG, mailed over 500 letters containing white powder to 280 abortion providers in 2001. The letters claimed that the powder was anthrax; though it was not identified as such, the tactic took advantage of the U.S. public's fear of biological warfare after the recent real anthrax attacks. The AOG is also associated with a number of assassinations of abortion providers. Some of these assassins claimed association with the AOG; in other cases, while the assassin expressed no affiliation with the group, the AOG has lionized their acts and taken up their cause.

Like their terrorist fellow travelers at other times and in other cultures, many members of these American groups believe they are conducting a "righteous," even "God-ordained" struggle against "evil," particularly against federal and state authorities they sometimes regard as an infernal enemy.

## The Historical Tension Between State Terrorism From Above and Nonstate Terrorism From Below

To designate a beginning point (or an end) of terrorism is arbitrary. Nonetheless, since the Middle East today is widely but inaccurately considered to be the font of all terrorism and the birthplace of most terrorists, it is useful to consider it as an illustration of the tension between state and antistate violence, also known as terrorisms from above and from below.

## Roman Terrorism From Above and Jewish Terrorism From Below

From biblical times until the zenith of the Roman Empire (roughly from just before the time of Christ to the early 5th century CE), the Middle East comprised a hodgepodge of nomadic ethnic groups and city-states within what we now call the nation-states of Egypt, Israel (and Palestine), Tunisia, Libya, Greece, Jordan, Syria, Lebanon, Saudi Arabia, Iraq, the Gulf States, and Turkey. By the 1st century BCE, almost all these territories lay within the Roman Empire. It is here that the bloodcurdling dialectic between state terrorism (TFA) and nonstate terrorism (TFB) may have begun, and—after some long intervals of relative peace, mainly under Islam— was revived during and shortly after World War I.

Conventional histories of terrorism depict the Roman Empire as having deployed its considerable resources to quash popular revolts against its rule in the Roman province of Judea (contemporary Israel and Palestine). In so doing, according to St. Augustine, the Romans created a desert and called it peace: "Peace and war had a contest in cruelty, and peace won the prize." [9] The political theorist Michael Walzer has stated, "Terrorizing ordinary men and women is first of all the work of domestic tyranny," and, as Aristotle wrote, "The first aim and end of tyrants is to break the spirit of their subjects." [10] This is what the Romans attempted to do, especially in their eastern provinces.

"Terrorism" (more accurately, TFB) itself is identified with the political revolts and religious uprisings of Rome's Jewish opponents, especially the dagger-wielding Zealots of the 1st century CE. These accounts depict the links between religion (or "holy terror"), anti-imperial insurrections, and terrorism. Less often, they identify TFA with the widespread acts of political violence committed by the Romans in their efforts to create, expand, and defend their empire. About two centuries after the fall of the Roman Empire, Islam replaced Christianity and Rome as the dominant religious and political force in the Middle East.

## Islam: Religion of Peace, Religion of *Jihad*

Former president George W. Bush, supported by some American Muslim clerics, once announced that Islam was "a religion of peace" that had been "hijacked" by such violent groups as al-Qaeda. But this apparently reassuring statement was immediately disputed by those who claimed that Islam is much more accurately seen as "the religion of war." Those who take the latter view of Islam cite the Muslim belief that the world is divided by a continuous struggle between the *dar al-Islam* (the unified house of Islam) and the *dar al-Harb* (the house of war); allegedly, the Muslim believer is therefore duty-bound to participate in a "holy war" *(jihad)*. In Arabic, "*Islam*" literally means "submission" (to the will of God, or Allah), from the root of *aslama*, "he resigned, he surrendered, he submitted," and related to *salam*, "peace." This implies that peace is one prerequisite of Islam.

But belief in *jihad* is also central to Islam, as attested by many sacred texts. For example, as one *hadith* (saying of the Prophet Muhammad) proclaims: "There is no monasticism in Islam; the monasticism of this community is the holy war." It is also historically true that Islam began in battle. Exiled for his subversive beliefs, the Prophet Muhammad gained warrior allies in the Saudi hinterlands, defeated his numerically superior opponents, and returned as a conqueror to his natal city of Mecca.

Muhammad was a great war leader as well as a spiritual redeemer, promising his followers not only admission to heaven in the next world but also concrete spoils of victory in this one. Those early Muslims who did not participate in *jihad* were considered lacking in religious merit. Those who fell in battle were guaranteed immediate entrance into paradise. (A similar claim was widespread among militant Christians, especially during the Crusades.)

Nor did Islam become exclusively a religion of peace after Muhammad's death (632 CE). Instead, Muslim warriors battled on against the powerful Persian and Byzantine empires. Their eventual victory validated their message for their millions of followers and also established the foundation for the great Islamic dynasties—Umayyad, Marwanid, Abbasid, Buyid, Fatimid, Seljuk, Ottoman, and Safavid—which were eventually to rule from Morocco to India.

Yet a portrait of Islam as a warlike religion is as simplistic as the alternative image of Islam as a religion of peace. (Consider, as a parallel, how misleading it is to describe Christianity as simply a "religion of peace" or a "religion of war," given that Christ's redeeming message is widely seen as intimately bound up with peace and that Christianity also became one of the world's great warrior religions!) Although many Muslims divide the world into warring camps of believers and unbelievers, in real life it is not so easy to decide who is who, since "only God knows" the true content of the human heart.

In this context, many Muslims have interpreted the injunction for *jihad* as a command to purify the self by ridding one's own heart of hypocrisy (sometimes called the "greater jihad"). With self-doubt, spiritual introspection, and resigned acceptance of the inevitable plurality of beliefs as major religious themes in Islam, war against the external heathen (the "lesser jihad") has usually been secondary to war against the internal Pharisee.

Nor has conversion to Islam by former nonbelievers usually been at the point of a sword; instead it has most often been a voluntary response to Muslim egalitarianism and the Prophet's expansive message of salvation. In this environment, Islamic pogroms against Jews, Christians, and other minorities were considerably less common in the premodern Middle East than in premodern Christian Europe. For much of the Islamic world, all the descendants of Abraham (including Jews and Christians) were honored as fellow "people of the book" and recognized as having a fundamental kinship with their Muslim brothers and sisters.

## Jihad and Terrorism: Are They Synonymous?

In many Western and even in some Muslim-jihadist circles, jihad and terrorism appear related, even synonymous. But according to the contemporary Muslim writer Yasmeen Ali:

> Terrorism is no Jihad. Western media is more often than not, awash with the details of 'jihadists' who commit atrocious acts in the name of religion. More and more, Islam is projected as a religion of violence, hatred and vengeance. However, Islam comes from the root word Salaam, which means peace. It also means submitting one's will to Allah. The word Salaam is also an attribute of God. In this context, it means 'The Giver of Peace'. Terrorism, is a different concept altogether. According to Jason Burke, it may be defined as 'the use or threat of serious violence to advance some kind of cause'.[11]

But does Islam condone terrorism? Are terrorism and jihad ever one and the same? Not according to Ali, for whom:

> Military conflict is to be directed only against fighting troops and not against civilians. As a matter of fact, all religions of 'The Book,' promote peace and tolerance, not violence. Attacking innocent civilians, women, children, sick in hospitals, people going about their daily chores who are not at war with you is terrorism. If there is a threat to human life, property and honor, fighting for defending life, property and honor is deemed as Jihad.

For some violent jihadists then and now, though, the West and its Middle Eastern surrogates do present such a "threat" to their lives, property, honor, and sacred polity.

## Reestablishing the Sacred Polity

Similar to recent times, when many Muslims have felt assaulted by "heathens" inside and outside their community, more than a millennium ago many Muslims who had participated in Muhammad's "umma" could not accept the disintegration of their unified and charismatic collective so easily. They nostalgically and imaginatively remembered the promises of the Prophet and what they perceived as the divinely consecrated commune of all Muslims—memories (or longings) that continue today to activate religious resistance to secular government. Muslims have thus constantly sought more sanctified candidates to fill the post of ruler over an Islamic collective. This quest, in its most extreme manifestations, has animated the unique brand of religious-political terrorism practiced in the name of Islam since the death of the Prophet Muhammad.

### The Kharijites

For many Muslims, there have been two main approaches to reestablishing the sacred polity. The first was taken by those referred to as the *Kharijites,* "those who go out." These originally were early tribal followers of Muhammad who later favored Ali (the prophet's son-in-law and nephew) against the alliance of military elites and Meccan aristocrats. But when Ali vainly sought negotiation with his enemies, the Kharijites rejected him as a poseur and assassinated him. They then established radically egalitarian religious republics, wherein only the most pious and able would rule, regardless of family, ancestral spirituality, priority of conversion, or any other claim. In some Kharijite groups, even women were given the same rights as men (something unknown or rejected by much of the rest of the Islamic world, even today). Pitiless opponents of all who objected to their egalitarianism, the Kharijites saw themselves as "the people of heaven" battling against "the people of hell."

Despite an absence of political success, the Kharijite impulse to a transcendent morality and political egalitarianism has had an affinity ever since with devout Muslim rebels who refuse to accept secular rule or elite domination. Even today, modern Islamist radicals—from the Muslim Brotherhood and Islamic Jihad in Egypt and the Saudi peninsula to Jamaat-e-Islami in Pakistan, and including the Taliban and al-Qaeda in Afghanistan, Yemen, and Iraq—are execrated by more orthodox clerics as "Kharijites" because of their radical egalitarianism, moral self-righteousness, willingness to use violence against those with whom they disagree, and relentless opposition to central authority.[12] In turn, the Islamist radicals denounce their moderate opponents as apostates for accepting the "un-Islamic" commands of the corrupt and despotic rulers of secular Islamic states—whose political leaders are widely perceived to be manipulated and paid off by the West in general and by the United States in particular.

### The Shiites: Partisans of Ali and Opponents of Sunni Traditionalists

Although the rebellious and anarchistically inclined Kharijites long were a thorn in the side of Middle Eastern authoritarian and repressive regimes, and though their message still has a powerful appeal, a more effective source of sustained sacred opposition to the status quo came from a very different ideological direction. Instead of arguing for a radically egalitarian community of believers who freely elect as a leader the person best among them—as the Kharijites had done— these rebels subordinated themselves to a sacred authority whose word was absolute law. For them, Muhammad's charisma was reincarnated in his descendants, notably in Ali, who served as the fourth caliph after the prophet's death. These are the Shiites, or "partisans," of Ali, who have argued that, since Muhammad had no sons, Ali had inherited Muhammad's spiritual power and must be recognized as Imam, the sacred ruler of all of Islam.[13]

For those following Ali or other lineal descendants of the Prophet, the problem of authority was solved by recognizing that one particular member of the Prophet's kin group had spiritual ascendance above all others and therefore had the intrinsic right to rule. The first crisis of faith occurred when Ali was assassinated by a poisoned sword wielded by a Kharijite fanatic—an indi- cation that assassination as a form of political terrorism began very early in the history of Islam, about 1,250 years ago.

Shiite resentment over Sunni rule and the perceived injustices of this world continues to fan subversive acts of opposition, which have sometimes included terrorism. Shiite Islam rejects the first three caliphs who followed the Prophet Muhammad as "usurpers." Its adher- ents remain "partisans of Ali," the fourth caliph, whom it recognizes as the legitimate heir of the Prophet.

In contrast, Sunni (from the Arabic word *sunna*, meaning "tradition") Islam recognizes the legitimacy of the order of succession of the first four caliphs who succeeded the Prophet Muhammad. Sunni Islam, unlike Shiite Islam, has no centralized clerical institution, comprises four schools of Islamic law (*sharia*), and ranges ideologically from the expressive Sufis to the puritanical Wahhabis (who are discussed later in this chapter).

But despite numerous disputes *between* Shiite and Sunni Muslims and *by* Shiite and Sunni rebels against despised state representatives, rarely has insurrectionary violence directed against political elites kindled a general spark of rebellion among the disenfranchised masses. Very pos- sibly most Muslims in the past, like most Muslims now, have been satisfied to have a stable, if tyrannical, regime in power, following the local precept that "60 years of an unjust Imam are better than one night without a Sultan." A despotic "enemy we know" is often preferred to the risk of the chaos that might be unleashed by the overthrow of central authority.

### The Nizari

Perhaps the most relevant historical precedent for the present is to be found in the extraor- dinary trajectory of the Nizari Shiites. The prototypical assassins, they found refuge in several remote mountain enclaves at the margins of the Seljuk Empire (in Turkey) at the end of the 11th century. Because of their fervor, their willingness to die for their beliefs, and their practice of assassination (always with daggers) as a political tool, the Nizari gave rise to legends of hashish- intoxicated madmen and mystical voluptuaries, dying at the whim of their mysterious master.

These legends disguised something even more remarkable: tightly disciplined communities of absolute believers, all imbued with a spirit that placed their ultimate mission above any personal desire—even above the desire for life. Although the Nizari assassins did not intend to kill anyone but their political targets, they were the precursors of, and prototypes for, the self- sacrificing, suicidal bombers and terrorists who have spread from the Middle East throughout the entire world.

The Nizari epitomize the general historical tendency of religiously motivated violent groups to use terrorist tactics (such as assassinations) to achieve political goals and to rationalize murder by appealing to a "sacred" justification for their killing. Their history also exemplifies the "cycle of violence"—of murder "from above or below" and murderous retaliation by the victim's survivors against the perpetrators and anyone else unfortunate enough to be nearby when "payback" takes place. The Nizari were a weak and relatively isolated group who could not confront the might of the Seljuk Empire and its allies directly, but in assassination they found an effective tool for disrupting the empire. Moreover, they are precursors of U.S. government–designated "terrorist" groups today.

Despite their limited successes, the Nizari eventually abandoned assassination as a tactic and accommodated themselves to the local imperial regime. The fact is that most Muslims then, as now, found assassinations in particular, and political terrorism more generally, reprehensible, and they would not follow Nizari leadership.

The trajectory of this archetypal band of religious terrorists is both unexpected and instructive. Most of the Nizari emigrated to India in the 13th century in order to escape the invading Mongol hordes. Now known as Khojas, they soon became wealthy entrepreneurs. Al-Qaeda and other "successful" global terrorist organizations—and their Western adversaries—have long since discovered that even with "God on one's side," to conduct a "holy war" successfully, it helps to have working modems and numbered Swiss bank accounts.[14]

## The Iranian Revolution and Shiite Militancy

The great oppositional Islamic upheaval of modern times is the Iranian revolution of 1979, led by Ayatollah Khomeini. Throughout the Middle East as a whole, the Shiite clergy has had much greater independence than Sunni clerics, and Shiites, unlike most Sunnis, believe that certain scholars, known as Ayatollahs, are sacred authorities in themselves. (The word *Ayatollah* is an honorific term designating a wise leader who is blessed with the *ayat*, or "sign," of God, "Allah.") Because Iranian Ayatollahs have had such great spiritual authority and wealth, they have, until very recently, been able to resist secularizing trends in government, even prior to the advent of the deposed former despot of Iran, Reza Shah. The shah was convincingly portrayed by the Ayatollah Khomeini and his mainly student followers as the modern *Yazid,* a puppet of the (Western) "capitalist devils" and "The Great Satan" (a.k.a. the United States).

The old Shiite eschatology was reawakened, transformed, and reinvigorated by Khomeini and his acolytes; followers could now redeem the ancient stain of betrayal by actively purging this world of evil, starting in Iran and expanding to combat actively such alleged enemies of righteousness as "The Great Satan," "the evil one." This message inspired acts of self-sacrifice and ended in the overthrow of the shah but also led to terrorist attacks against Americans and others.[15] (Iranians are painfully aware that the shah was placed on his throne in 1953 as a result of a coup orchestrated by U.S. and British intelligence services, which overthrew Mohammed Mossadegh, the democratically elected Iranian president.) Subsequent violent assaults against both perceived political adversaries and civilian emissaries of despised foreign powers were justified on the grounds that in the battle against Satan, any methods were acceptable. This is an age-old rationale for murder and terrorism. Acts of extreme violence are "justified" by those who would wage "holy war" against the West as well as by what much of the Islamic world regards as latter-day "crusaders" now conducting a war against Muslims disguised as a "war against terror."

## Sunni Islam and the Salafi/Wahhabist Movement

Although there are significant doctrinal differences between Shiite and Sunni clerics, dating back to the struggle over the succession to the Prophet Muhammad, it is the political cleft between the majority Sunnis (constituting more than 80% of the billion-plus Muslims today) and the minority Shiites (based largely in and near Iran) that has widened and engulfed the Middle East in factional violence.

Wahhabism denotes a "Salafist" reform movement (*Salafi* means, in Arabic, "the righteous ancestors," Sunni Muslims who wish to emulate the first generations of the original, 7th-century Islamic community). It dates back to the late 18th century, when it was founded by Muhammad al-Wahab, who preached the controversial message that all modifications to Islam after the late 10th century must be purged. Al-Wahab converted the Saudi tribe to this ascetic branch of Sunni Islam, and Salafist-Wahhabis have been extremely influential in Saudi Arabia, the birthplace of Osama bin Laden and many of his most militant followers. But Egypt has been the home of perhaps the most significant Sunni Islamist movement of the 20th century, the Muslim Brotherhood.

## The Muslim Brotherhood and Sayyid Qutb

For more than a millennium, Cairo has been the prime center of Sunni scholasticism, and modern Sunni Islamic militancy arose there following the end of World War I. Perhaps the most important source of ideological and political inspiration for contemporary *jihadis* ("holy warriors," as well as the *mujahideen*, or "strugglers for jihad") has been the Muslim Brotherhood, a religious and social reform movement founded in 1928 in Egypt by Hassan al-Banna, widely considered the father of what is today known as modern political Islamism (whose ideological followers are "Islamists"). Following the "Arab Spring" and the removal of Hosni Mubarak from power in 2011, the Muslim Brotherhood has enjoyed considerable popular and electoral success in Egypt, a "mainstreaming" of this once "fringe" Islamic "fundamentalist" movement.

Like the Kharijites before them, militant Islamists today hope to "reform" Islamic society by reviving the original Islamic community. From an Islamist point of view, this entails relentless opposition, by any means necessary, to all existing Muslim "infidels," especially corrupt and ruthless local Muslim rulers and their "Christian-Zionist" supporters. (It is noteworthy that in addition to shared religious ideology, a major unifying force among militant Islamists is a shared antipathy toward the state of Israel, which is widely considered to be politically illegitimate since its founding involved expropriation of what had been Palestinian land.)

For many Sunni Islamists, including the two men most closely associated with al-Qaeda "central"—Ahman al-Zawahiri and Osama bin Laden—the person most worthy of adulation and imitation was the Egyptian political rebel and writer Sayyid Qutb. For 3 years, Qutb lived in the United States, which he found empty, decadent, sexually depraved, materialistic, ignorant, and godless. (This, incidentally, should be a cautionary note for those who automatically assume that Islamic exposure to the West will automatically result in the acceptance of Western ideals and lifestyles, or vice versa!) Qutb then returned to Cairo and, in 1953, joined the Muslim Brotherhood. He was subsequently imprisoned, tortured, and hanged (in 1966) by the Egyptian government.

While in prison, Qutb wrote a book called *Milestones*, whose religious-revolutionary message— that "mankind today is on the brink of a precipice" and to be saved needs a "system of high ideals and values previously unknown in the West," or a purified Islam—has become a battle cry for militant Sunni Islamists, locally and globally.[16] What is widely referred to as "al-Qaeda" has heard, and acted on, Qutb's appeal.

## Al-Qaeda

It is difficult to write authoritatively about an organization as contemporary and elusive as al-Qaeda. This section should thereby be considered as not unlike its subject matter—a work in progress.

In Arabic, *al-Qaeda* can refer to a base or foundation of a house (or of a political movement), as well as to a principle, rule, formula, or model. Al-Qaeda, whose perceived leaders Osama bin Laden and Ahman al-Zawarhiri were reared in Sunni antiestablishment circles, gained their political experience in the 1980s as Arab volunteers for the predominantly Shiite *mujahideen* Islamic resistance to the Soviet occupation of Afghanistan. Ironically, funding to the Afghan *mujahideen* groups was provided by the United States and channeled through the Pakistani government, as well as by the Saudi government and Persian Gulf–based mosque charities. Twenty years later, the U.S., Pakistan, Saudi, and Gulf governments—early backers of anti-Soviet Islamic *jihadis* and *mujahideen*—became targets of al-Qaeda.

For the decade or two that Western intelligence and counterterrorist agencies have focused on it, al-Qaeda appears to have operated less like a formal organization and more like a network with an ideology that inspires a worldwide political movement. In 1996, Osama bin Laden, until his death in 2011 widely considered the chief ideologist of al-Qaeda, (with Ahman al-Zawahiri, who apparently succeeded bin Laden, viewed as its principal strategist) issued a key statement titled "A Declaration of War Against the Americans Occupying the Land of the Two Holy Places."

Most of bin Laden's declaration focuses on the alleged failures of the House of Saud, rulers of Saudi Arabia and custodians of the cities of Mecca and Medina, which are for Muslims intimately associated with the life of the prophet Muhammad and with the holy book of Islam, the Quran. The Saudi government, according to bin Laden, committed an unpardonable sacrilege when, in the early 1990s, it accepted the American offer of military assistance to defend it against the Iraqi army of Saddam Hussein, which had invaded and occupied Kuwait and seemed poised to do the same in Saudi Arabia. (Bin Laden's offer of military assistance was rejected by the Saudis, and he left the country.) The subsequent stationing of U.S. military forces in their "holy land," and more generally throughout the Islamic world, shocked millions of Muslims.

Bin Laden's declaration is designed not just to evoke Muslim fury about the U.S.-led occupation of Islamic lands but also to arouse Arab resentment regarding a century of Western exploitation and a millennium of what he calls "aggression, iniquity and injustice imposed by the Zionist-Crusader alliance and their collaborators. . . ." Bin Laden points to cases of Muslim blood being "spilled in Palestine and Iraq. . . . Massacres in Tajikistan, Burma, Kashmir, Assam, the Philippines . . . Ogaden, Somalia, Eritrea, Chechnya and Bosnia-Herzegovina." For him, the U.S. occupation of the holy sites in Saudi Arabia and the Israeli occupation of Palestinian territory (especially the al-Aqsa mosque in Jerusalem) are against the will of Allah. Consequently, bin Laden calls for a *jihad* "to expel the occupying enemy out of the country of the two holy places, to re-establish the greatness of the umma and to liberate its occupied sanctuaries."[17]

To accomplish this mission, al-Qaeda views itself—like numerous TFB groups throughout history—as the vanguard of a local and global *jihad* against occupying forces in the Middle East.

Also targeted are the states that sponsor them and the civilians—Christian, Jewish, and Muslim—who wittingly or unwittingly perpetuate occupation and other alleged anti-Islamic policies.

Like Sayyid Qutb and the Muslim Brotherhood, Osama bin Laden and al-Qaeda apparently have believed themselves to be in a "cosmic struggle" against the enemies of Islam. This *jihad* is global and has no defined end point. To win it, *jihadis* must "hit the enemy with an iron fist." On September 11, 2001, supporters of al-Qaeda-inspired *jihad* hit the World Trade Center in New York and the Pentagon near Washington, D.C.— tangible symbols of American economic power and military might—with "fists" garbed as civilian airplanes.

Since 9/11 and the U.S.-led invasions and occupations of Iraq and Afghanistan—where al-Qaeda had operated training camps dating back to 1996—bin Laden, al-Zawahiri, their closest supporters, and some of the Afghan Taliban leaders who had provided them a haven apparently fled to the parlous sanctuary of tribal lands straddling Afghanistan's mountainous border with Pakistan and then to northwestern Pakistan itself (where bin Laden was killed). Al-Qaeda itself may have metamorphosed from a relatively small group of Sunni-led Islamic terrorists to the ideological fringe of a broad Islamist movement, whose historical roots may be found in the mission and methods of such *jihadis* as the Kharijites and Nizaris. But unlike their forefathers, today's *jihadis* wage their war on a global as well as a local scale. In the most extreme cases, this can mean terroristic martyrdom, usually but not always in the form of suicide bombings.

Although the future of this struggle is unclear, notwithstanding the well-publicized killings of bin Laden, the American citizen Anwar Al-Awlaki (who, with his 16-year-old son, were killed in an American drone attack in Yemen in fall, 2011), and al-Qaeda's deputy leader, Abu Yahya al-Libi (killed in a drone strike in northern Pakistan in June, 2012), what has become evident since 9/11 is that suicide terrorism is a prime weapon in al-Qaeda's and the Islamic *jihadis*' arsenal—a weapon of the weak in striking their adversaries' most vulnerable bases, their homelands. Al-Qaeda "central" as a self-sufficient entity may or may not survive. But its mission will likely endure, unless the social and political conditions that give rise to al-Qaeda and its emulators are transformed.

## Suicide Terrorism

Islamist terrorist groups have grabbed the headlines of the mass media since 9/11. But it is important to note that this is a relatively recent development and that until the formation of the state of Israel just after the end of World War II and the U.S.-led occupation of Middle Eastern lands several decades later, terrorism from below in that part of the world was committed mainly by Arab subnational groups against other Arabs, principally against secular political authorities.

Furthermore, there is a popular conception in the West that most suicidal terrorists are Muslim and that virtually all of them have predominantly *religious* motivations—martyrdom allegedly for the sake of Islam. The facts are that suicide terrorism was historically launched by Jewish Zealots against the Romans centuries before Islam even existed and that until very recently the most frequent users of suicide attacks have been *Hindus*—the Tamil Tigers in Sri Lanka.[18] Other notably destructive terrorist groups include the Hindu-extremist RSS, the Lord's Resistance Army of Uganda, and Colombia's FARC. In recent memory, the United States has supported antigovernment, right-wing terrorist groups, such as UNITA in Angola and the *contras* in Nicaragua. In addition, during the 19th and 20th centuries, Christian, Sikh, Buddhist, and Shinto terrorists also carried out suicide attacks—sometimes with, and sometimes without explicitly religious motivations. Moreover, Islamist suicide bombers display a range of secular and/or religious motivations for their deadly attacks, primarily revenge against Israeli raids and "targeted assassinations" and/or to end the Israeli occupation of Palestinian territory.

Contrary to popular belief that a single terrorist suffices to carry out a suicide terrorist attack, there are several people involved in the process of preparing the human bomb for explosion. Usually, they make up a team for the serial production of living bombs. First of all, a recruiter must find and select suitable candidates for journey to "paradise." In the 1990s, when "religious terrorist organizations" such as Hamas and the Islamic Jihad were the primary sources for suicide bombers, the main pool of future suicide-bombers was a mosque, and the recruiter was someone connected to that mosque. Now, when the "secular terrorist organizations" such as the People's Front for Liberation of Palestine employ suicide bombers, recruitment can take place anywhere, from hospitals or restaurants to primary schools—the youngest suicide bomber arrested by Israeli security services was just 13 years old, the youngest who blew up was 16.

Further on down the chain, there is an agent, who has to select the target of a terrorist act and to collect information about it. Terrorists' choice of their objective is far from random. In Israel/Palestine, the agent is usually a Palestinian Arab with a work permit in Israel, or less often an Israeli Arab. The agent often works or had worked in the target location, such as a restaurant, a hotel, or a banquet hall. The engineer prepares the bomb and its separate components. The "mule," who brings the terrorist closer to her or his target is sometimes an Israeli Arab, more often a Palestinian with a work permit. Usually she or he is not a member of a terrorist organization, but an experienced car-thief, familiar with Israeli society. The planner who commands the operation is the leader of the group, an active member of a "terrorist organization" (Hamas, Fatah, etc.) who is the "field captain" of the terrorists. In addition to the planner, there is often another person who deals with the operation's finances.

This is not a hard and fast structure. Often a single person performs several tasks, for example, recruitment and command, or several terrorists work on the same task. The bomb is usually constructed by two or three people—the head "engineer" and his or her assistants.

Contemporary suicide bombings fit into an ancient tradition as a tactic employed by political groups too weak to confront their enemies directly, so instead they kill (or, from a *jihadi* point of view, "martyr") themselves and as many "enemy" soldiers or civilians as they can. Most often, this is done in order to pressure a vastly more powerful force—the state—to change its policies once it becomes luridly evident that the price of continuing them will be the lives of many of its citizens.

## State and State-Sponsored Terrorism

In explaining and preventing Terrorism From Below, it is important to understand that terrorist actions by Islamist and other cultic groups would have little popular resonance on "the Arab street" and elsewhere if it were not for one other aspect of terrorism—namely the terror perpetrated by the state on its own people.

In contrast to Islamist-cultic terrorist organizations, state-sponsored terrorism from above very rarely makes any claim to sacred justification. It is quite baldly the assertion of ruthless force for the purpose of breaking all resistance to internal tyranny. Such brutal violence is in part a confirmation of the widely perceived illegitimacy of the secular state itself, which, from the earliest times, in the eyes of most Muslims has always suffered in comparison with the history of sacred rule by the Prophet and his caliphs. (A caliph is the head of state in a caliphate and the title for the ruler of the Islamic *Ummah*, ruled by the Shari'ah, Islam's moral code and religious law.)

Lacking any sacred justification, popular compliance to the decrees of corrupt secular Muslim rulers has generally been a result of mass terror from above. Popular resentment is usually directed toward the ruling elites of oil-rich Arab states, in particular, which are perceived to be backed by the United States and other "Christian-Zionist" nations (especially including Israel). The "Arab Spring" movement is a quintessential expression of this long-held attitude.

As one Muslim writes, the state is popularly understood "as a source of evil and harm, and those who hold power tend to be unjust, to break the law, and to play with other people's lives. . . . Injustice is the rule, the abuse of power is the rule; the proper, adequate use of power is the exception."[19] Such structural violence of the state—its neglect of basic human rights and its promotion of repressive policies—although endemic in the Middle East and elsewhere, is rarely confronted directly by those who are its everyday victims . . . notwithstanding "The Arab Spring," which has been a notable exception.

In former times, the violence and terrorism of Middle Eastern rulers were restrained both by traditional standards of honor and by the relative weakness of the regimes themselves. As a consequence, most Sultans (the word itself simply means "power") were content to torture, maim, and kill mainly members of their own immediate entourage, leaving the populace relatively unscathed as long as taxes were paid and order was maintained. However, contemporary Middle Eastern rulers (irrespective of their religious or political leanings) have greater ambitions as well as greater means at their disposal for the infliction of violence and mass terror. As a result, state-sponsored terrorism in that region has substantially increased—evidenced, for example, by the mass violence orchestrated by Syria's ruling elites against popular resistance to the rule of dictator Bashar al Assad.

Iraq, under Saddam Hussein, may have been the most frightening and well-publicized instance of state terror, but the use of terrorism from above has been widely practiced throughout the region. A conservative estimate is that more than 100,000 citizens "disappeared" during the reign of Saddam Hussein, with the real number probably closer to 250,000. Compare this to the 30,000 who "disappeared" during the "dirty war" in Argentina. Other regimes, from Algeria to Sudan and from Libya to Taliban Afghanistan, have lesser, but equally horrifying, human rights records. One cannot understand the appearance of religiously based terrorist movements in the modern Middle East without also taking into account the ways such states maintain their power through coercion of and violence against their own people.

Terrorism from above and from below reinforce each other in the Middle East as elsewhere. The crucial difference between recent history and the past is that terrorism from below has gone global and not been confined to the region, as evidenced by the attacks on the World Trade Center in 1993 and 2001. But so has terrorism from above, sometimes clad in the garb of "counterterrorism."

Political violence and terrorism have a long history in Middle Eastern Muslim societies. Whether they are more prevalent in this part of the world than elsewhere is unclear.[20] But a deep sense of the illegitimacy of the secular state, coupled with a millennial tradition of charismatic leadership can undoubtedly favor the rise of Islamist groups willing to use terrorism to bring the promised land into being. The popular appeal of such groups varies greatly, fluctuating according to the degree of oppression and alienation felt by the Muslim masses, also known as "the Arab street."

## Terrorism in the Name of God

It is easy to paint Islam as either essentially pacifist or bellicose—just as it is easy to draw passages from the Bible or from the Torah to make either case about Christians and Jews. The truth about all great religions is that the written record is ambiguous: Islamic scripture, like that of the Christians and Jews (or Hindus or Buddhists for that matter), can be interpreted in various ways for various purposes.

In a real sense, it is the protean character of great religions that makes them so appealing—and so dangerous. Islam is no different in this respect: Its adherents can be pacifists or terrorists or somewhere in between. All faiths can equally call on holy writ to "justify" themselves and their murderous deeds. Neither terrorism nor pacifism reflects some essential aspect of Islam any more than the slavery and genocide that stain European and American history are a direct and inevitable consequence of the message of Jesus. The problem lies in neither the Quran nor the Bible but in the violent behavior of some Muslims, Christians, and Jews who believe not only that "God is on our side" but that their terrorizing acts are morally, divinely, and politically sanctioned. And the mass media and "terrorism industry" play an essential role in "framing" both Islam and "our side."

# The Terrorism Industry and the Mass Media

Since the Vietnam War, there has arisen a caste of political and military pundits who "advise" Western governments about the real and alleged threats posed by subnational groups to Western—particularly American—economic and geopolitical interests around the world. Since the Reagan administration in the 1980s, they also have actively worked for the mass media. Most have military intelligence, CIA, and/or U.S. State Department backgrounds. Since 9/11, these consultants and advisers have contributed to a revived and influential "terrorism industry" (which also includes mercenaries and the purveyors of military hardware and services).

The wars conducted by the United States in Central America, Africa, and South Asia from the 1980s to the present have routinely been cast by these foreign policy and security analysts, and hence by the mass media, as *defensive* in nature and as necessary to promote freedom and democracy in nations endangered by "terrorists" and by the governments that harbor them. Much of this dates from 1979, when both the Sandinistas in Nicaragua and the Islamic clerics in Iran swept to power in relatively nonviolent revolutions against U.S.-supported autocracies. To combat these "antidemocratic" "extremists," "fanatics," and "militants," governments that are allied with the West have frequently deployed death squads and other paramilitary forces (as in El Salvador, Guatemala, and Honduras) to quell populist insurrections.

These TFA forces frequently received training, logistical support, and munitions from the United States. Until 2000, the United States Army School of the Americas (USARSA)—alternatively known as the "School of the Assassins"—was the principal training site for U.S. and Latin American military and police personnel. Critics note that much of the training that occurred at USARSA, located at Fort Benning, Georgia, provided expertise in antidemocratic terrorism whereby right-wing military dictatorships, supported by the U.S. government, practiced TFA against their own people.

Millions of civilian noncombatants worldwide have been casualties of what have been called "counterinsurgency operations," ranging from Indonesia and Vietnam in the 1960s and 1970s, to Central America and central Africa in the 1980s, and to Iraq and Afghanistan from 1991 to the present.

These "casualties of war" have rarely been portrayed by the mass media as the innocent victims of state and state-supported terrorism. And yet, counterinsurgency and counterterrorist operations, especially in Asia, Africa, and Latin America, have frequently inflamed rather than quelled popular resistance to local authorities and to Western intervention. Such "blowback" is in part due to the widespread perception in many impoverished countries that these activities serve principally to prop up corrupt and despotic regimes and to channel indigenous natural resources—such as oil—to affluent consumers in industrialized countries while benefiting the local elites rather than the native population. In addition, the civilian and noncombatant casualties caused by "precision bombing" and other "counterterrorist" measures further enrage those people who are to be "liberated" from "terrorists" and/or "rogue regimes." In particular, this often serves to radicalize disaffected youth and abets the efforts of violent insurgents who would recruit them as suicide bombers.

The mass media tend to follow the agenda framed by powerful political and economic elites, and only later, if at all, do they question the vision, strategy, tactics, and motives of decision makers and their lobbyists. The war in Iraq, as part of the global "War on Terrorism," is a prime example.

# The Global "War on Terrorism"

After the attacks on the World Trade Center in New York City and the Pentagon near Washington, D.C., many Americans agreed with pronouncements by many senior politicians that the United States was "at war" with "terrorism." Yet, to many disempowered people in other regions, "Americans are the worst terrorists in the world" (according to Osama bin Laden in an American TV interview). Following the attacks, former president George W. Bush announced that the United States "would make no distinction between terrorists and the countries that harbor them." For large numbers of frustrated, impoverished, infuriated people—who view the United States as a terrorist country—attacks on American civilians were justified in precisely this way: making no distinction between a "terrorist state" and the citizens who aid and abet that state.

Moreover, promilitarists within the United States and elsewhere have found the existence of "worldwide terrorism" to be especially convenient. This is particularly true since the end of the Cold War might have otherwise deprived them of a suitable enemy. The case can even be made that if al-Qaeda did not exist, the West would have been obliged to invent it. A more perfect foil to replace "the communist threat" could scarcely be imagined than a worldwide conspiracy of Islamic terrorists bent on our destruction and headed by "the evil one." Whatever its real structure and function, the *image* of al-Qaeda as the quintessential terrorist organization, like "The Red Menace" before it, is the ideal vehicle for motivating a "global war against terrorism" and "in defense of freedom." In addition, because terrorists are not manifested in the government of a particular country, against which a declaration of war could be declared, or which could ever be clearly defeated, such a "war" can never be definitively won. It therefore threatens (or, for its supporters, promises) to go on indefinitely.

## Countering Terrorism From Below

What seems particularly novel and terrorizing about the political state of affairs in the early 21st century are the global scope of terrorist and counterterrorist operations and the suddenness and lethality of such actions. In addition, whereas people often demand swift and decisive responses from their government in the face of violent events of this sort, the perpetrators are typically elusive and often difficult to identify, much less to apprehend or punish. The dominant strategy of Anglo-American terrorism-fighters is "counter-terrorism."

Counterterrorism comprises the practices, tactics, techniques, and strategies that governments, militaries, police departments, and corporations adopt to attack real and perceived terrorist threats and/or acts. Counterterrorism includes both the detection of potential acts and the response to "terrorist" events. If the terrorism is part of a broader insurgency, counterterrorism may also form part of a counterinsurgency doctrine, but political, economic, and other measures may focus more on the insurgency than the specific acts of terror.

According to the Department of Homeland Security (DHS), created after 9/11:

> Protecting the American people from terrorist threats is the founding purpose of the Department and our highest priority. The Department's efforts to battle terrorism, include detecting explosives in public spaces and transportation networks, helping protect critical infrastructure and cybernetworks from attack, detecting agents of biological warfare, and building information-sharing partnerships with state and local law enforcement that can enable law enforcement to mitigate threats. [21]

Any "battle" or "war" to "counter" terrorism is part of an increasingly recognized 21st-century pattern: so-called asymmetric warfare. In this circumstance, large, wealthy, heavily armed, and technologically sophisticated countries and their military forces find themselves aligned against small, poor, lightly armed, low-tech opponents, who are often willing to die for their cause. Although the latter can typically be defeated in straightforward "set-piece battles," the former—in part because of the openness of their civil societies as well as the fact that they offer a "target-rich" environment—are likely to remain vulnerable.

In this regard, another major concern is the "law of unintended consequences," whereby actions (especially violent ones) often bring about results that are unpredictable as well as undesirable. This can apply to those responding to terrorism no less than to the perpetrators. Thus, violent retribution by the leaders of a victimized country runs the risk not only of killing additional innocent civilians but also of generating yet more attacks, in a potentially endless cycle of violence. (This problem is exacerbated when terrorist perpetrators are difficult to identify and target.)

In the specific case of the events unleashed following the attacks of 9/11, what some Muslims regard as a U.S.-led "crusade" against terrorism has been seen as a war against Islam, which has in turn threatened to destabilize certain "moderate" Islamic regimes, resulting in governments that are yet more extremist and violence prone. Given that the United States has a long history of supporting military dictatorships—for example, in Pakistan, now a nuclear weapons state—such concerns seem especially cogent.

There is even has a term for this sort of thing: *blowback*, which, according to Chalmers Johnson, does not just mean

> retaliation for things our government has done to, and in, foreign countries. It refers specifically to retaliation for illegal operations carried out abroad *that were kept totally secret from the American public*. These operations have included the clandestine overthrow of governments various administrations did not like, the training of foreign militaries in the techniques of state terrorism, the rigging of elections in foreign countries, interference with

the economic viability of countries that seemed to threaten the interests of influential American corporations, as well as the torture or assassination of selected foreigners. The fact that these actions were, at least originally, secret meant that when retaliation does come—as it did so spectacularly on September 11, 2001—the American public is incapable of putting the events in context. Not surprisingly, then, Americans tend to support speedy acts of revenge intended to punish the actual, or alleged, perpetrators. These moments of lashing out, of course, only prepare the ground for yet another cycle of blowback.[22]

Historically, terrorists have sought not only to cause death, injury, and terror itself but often to induce their victims to strike back; the more bloody and indiscriminating the retaliation, the more perceived benefit derived by the terrorists themselves. Thus, a violent response tends not only to ethically delegitimize the retaliators; it also plays into the hands of the original perpetrators by recruiting others, newly victimized, to their cause. When there is an asymmetry between perpetrators and responders, such that the perpetrators are indigenous—as with the Taliban in Afghanistan and Pakistan—and the responders are foreigners, as with the United States and NATO forces who respond violently, for instance, to Taliban attacks, there is a notable tendency for the local population to blame the responders while exonerating the perpetrators.

Then there are the internal costs, both economic and human, of conducting a "war" against terrorism. Torture; "extraordinary rendition" (abduction of others in foreign countries without due process and their deportation to countries where they are likely to be tortured); the use of detention camps and jails in which human rights are typically denied, such as Guantánamo Bay and Abu Ghraib; violations of civil liberties; unlawful surveillance; the "targeted assassinations" of real and suspected "terrorists," both foreign and American; and much else have been conducted by the United States. and its partners in the name of protecting the homeland and apprehending terrorists. There is also the expenditure of over $2 trillion, funds that could have been devoted to such other "wars" as the "wars" against cancer, poverty, and so on. And while no one can say with certainty how many civilians have died in these wars, researchers at Brown University's Watson Institute for International Studies found that between 12,000 and 14,000 noncombatants perished in Afghanistan and at least 120,000 have died in Iraq.

Globally, officially designated terrorist attacks have dramatically increased since the commencement of the "Global War on Terror" (GWOT) more than a decade ago, despite the killings of numerous suspected terrorist leaders and the apparent absence of successful terrorist attacks on the American homeland since 9/11. According to the 2010 Report by the National Counterterrorism Center (NCTC), official U.S. government data indicate that

- the worldwide number of U.S.-designated terrorist attacks (excluding Iraq) increased from 7,763 in 2006 to 8,916 in 2010;
- the number of global deaths (excluding Iraq) attributed to these attacks increased from 7,191 in 2006 to 9,822 in 2010; but that
- the number of U.S. civilian deaths attributed to these attacks was only 15 out of 13,186 total deaths associated with terrorist attacks, including Iraq. These trends are consistent with data from 2002 through 2006.

Over 11,500 U.S. government-designated terrorist attacks occurred in 72 countries in 2010, resulting in approximately 50,000 victims, including almost 13,200 deaths. Although the number of attacks rose by almost 5 over the previous year, the number of deaths declined for a third consecutive year, dropping 12% from 2009. This decline reflects a combination of two factors: a decrease in the number of attacks causing more than five deaths along with an increase in attacks causing no deaths. The largest number of reported attacks occurred in South Asia, which also had the largest number of victims for the third consecutive year. More than 75% of the world's terrorist attacks and deaths took place in South Asia and the Near East. The Near East and South Asia in 2010 suffered a combined total of 8,960 attacks, causing 9,960 deaths. Attacks in Afghanistan and Iraq rose in 2010. Almost a quarter of worldwide attacks occurred in Iraq, a slight increase from 2009, although deaths fell for the fourth consecutive year. The number of attacks and deaths in Europe and Eurasia declined slightly in 2010, with the vast majority again occurring in Russia. The fewest incidents in 2010 were reported in the Western Hemisphere, where both attacks and deaths declined by roughly 25%. Western Hemisphere attacks fell from 444 in 2009 to 340 in 2010, and deaths fell from 377 in 2009 to 279 in 2010.

Sunni extremists committed almost 60% of all worldwide terrorist attacks. These attacks caused approximately 70% of terrorism-related deaths, a significant increase from the almost 62% in 2009. Of the remaining attacks, secular, political, or anarchist groups accounted for almost 16% of the total, roughly the same proportion as in 2009. Christian extremist attacks fell sharply from 1,052 in 2009 to 321 in 2010. The fact that almost 99.9% of the victims of global terrorist attacks are *not Americans* may be a significant reason why, in the United States at least, there is a widespread (mis)perception that terrorism is decreasing.[23]

When counting costs, one should also include the possibly permanent damage done to Islamic culture and traditions, not to mention the affront to the collective self-esteem of Muslims. After all:

> For many centuries the world of Islam was in the forefront of human civilization and achievement. In the Muslims' own perception, Islam was indeed coterminous with civilization, and beyond its borders there were only barbarians and infidels.[24]

In sum, the conventional counterterrorist strategy of negative peacemaking, put into effect in September 2001—more than a decade ago—has

- not defeated radical Islamism,
- resulted in hundreds of thousands of casualties,
- led to a global clash between extreme elements of Western and Islamist civilizations, and
- threatened to escalate to a war of the world in which nonstate terrorists and state counterterrorists may both employ weapons of mass destruction.

A peace-oriented perspective condemns not only terrorist attacks but also any violent response to them. It is tempting to conclude that, under such circumstances, violence is always counterproductive. Nonetheless, an alternative view also deserves respect. Consider a country that refuses to respond forcefully after large numbers of its citizens are attacked: It must be acknowledged that well-meaning, well-informed people honestly disagree as to whether such a policy might actually encourage more attacks, resulting in reduced overall security. Although vengeance is not highly regarded by most civilized persons, justice is. Accordingly, the best response to such terrible events is often maddeningly unclear and should not be made precipitously, in the heat of the moment. How does one "counter" terrorism without resorting to terror? Any policy for countering terrorism would seem to profit by an understanding and analysis of when, where, how, and why officially designated "terrorist" groups (from below) have ended.

## How Do Terrorist Groups End?

In 2008, the RAND Corporation presented to the United States House Armed Services Committees the results of a comprehensive study for "Defeating Terrorist Groups."[25] The study concluded: "By far the most effective strategy against religious groups has been the use of local police and intelligence services, which were responsible for the end of 73% of terrorist groups since 1968." The RAND report recommended

- "the U.S. military should generally resist being drawn into combat operations in Muslim countries where its presence is likely to increase terrorist recruitment;" and
- "ending the notion of a 'war' on terrorism" and "moving away from military references would indicate that there was no battlefield solution to countering terrorism."

These data as seen in Figure 4.1 clearly indicate that politicization and policing are much more often a winning strategy than is military force alone for governments seeking to "defeat" insurgent and/or perceived terrorist groups, since the combination of politicization (43%) and policing (40%) results in the end of such groups (Total N= 268) much more often than any other. According to this figure, governments are seldom able to end terrorist groups by the use of military force (7% of the time), and are also very unlikely to achieve a "victory" over them (10% of the time).

Similarly, according to both Figure 4.1 and Table 4.1, insurgent groups are more likely to achieve their aims via "politicization" (43%), i.e., political negotiations with the government(s) they oppose leading to incorporation in the available political processes than by force of arms alone. And government-designated insurgent and other ("terrorist") groups are much more likely to end by "splintering" (N=136 according to Table 4.1), i.e., through internal disintegration, or by effective government intelligence gathering and police work (N=107), than by violent state counterterrorism efforts (i.e., the combination of "military force/victory:" N=47). For both parties, military force unaccompanied by dialogue is usually a losing strategy.

**Figure 4.1**  RAND Findings: How Terrorist Groups End

*Source:* RAND Corporation.

| Table 4.1    RAND Finding: How Insurgent Groups End | | |
|---|---|---|
| *End of Group* | *Insurgents* | *Others* |
| Splintering | 4 | 132 |
| Policing | 2 | 105 |
| Victory | 10 | 17 |
| Military force | 8 | 12 |
| Politics | 18 | 96 |

*Source:* RAND Corporation.

Accordingly, the RAND authors stress that "there is no battlefield solution to terrorism," and that, citing journalist Peter Bergen, "Creating a world of enemies is never a winning strategy," and that "terrorist groups typically end due to a combination of strategies." Perhaps inconsistently they also claim that "a political solution" between the United States/West and al-Qaeda and "a negotiated settlement" between al-Qaeda and Middle Eastern governments, [are]"not possible." But if the incorporation of official terrorist groups in the political process combined with the efforts of police and intelligence services to prevent terrorist attacks results in a success rate (ending terrorist actions) far greater than other strategies, why shouldn't this strategy replace the Global War on Terrorism, also known as "Overseas Contingency Operations," with its associated counterterrorist strategy?

## Countering Terrorism via Antiterrorism

Antiterrorism includes those measures taken to protect society from terrorist acts. Antiterrorism focuses on nonmilitary preventive actions. It is part of the "human security paradigm," which outlines a nonmilitary approach that aims to address the enduring underlying inequalities and injustices (both real and perceived) that fuel terrorist activity. Causal factors need to be delineated and measures implemented that allow equal access to resources and sustainability for all people. Such activities empower citizens providing "freedom from fear" and "freedom from want." According to the philosopher Haig Khatchadourian, antiterrorism refers to:

> The administrative, police, psychological resources, tactics, equipments, security, judicial, and political measures employed by governments . . . designed to prevent terrorist attacks. . . . Antiterrorist measures include the use of judicial and penal systems as a whole to bring terrorists to justice. Thus antiterrorism has both a deterrent and a punitive aspect: to deter and so to prevent terrorism, to apprehend and bring to justice suspected terrorists, and to punish convicted terrorists. . . . Therefore, antiterrorist measures and strategies are, ideally speaking, nonviolent and in accord . . . with extant international law.[25]

Antiterrorism is a multilateral strategy congruent with human security that advocates ethical, legally sanctioned methods for establishing effective communication and just relations between adversaries, resolving conflicts peacefully, and bringing terrorists to justice. Antiterrorism is a less violent, or even a nonviolent, alternative to counterterrorism (TFA). One possibility is to replace *counter*terrorist violence with *anti*terrorist prevention and interception measures. This may include negotiations with members or representatives of antistate terrorist groups.

Additionally, consistent with a human-security, antiterrorist approach, one course of nonviolent action might be for international organizations such as the United Nations and the International Court of Justice to be empowered to bring to justice the perpetrators of such crimes against humanity as acts of terrorism involving the mass murder of civilians. Implied in such an approach is that "terrorism" should evoke a response involving international police activity and that "terrorists" should be brought to justice in the same way as other alleged lawbreakers.

Another move would be for the West to recognize that occupation, historically and currently, is probably the principal political reason for terrorist attacks against the occupying powers and their citizens locally and globally. Therefore, the United States and Great Britain might seriously consider dramatically altering their Middle East strategic policy. This would probably necessitate the withdrawal of all Western combat forces from the countries in the region and the redeployment of some of those forces offshore—until a comprehensive Middle East peace plan could be negotiated by all the affected parties, whereupon those forces would be permanently withdrawn.

Moreover, Western nations could make more sustained efforts to more fully integrate Islamic and other immigrants, particularly disaffected young men, and also to wean themselves gradually from dependence on Middle East oil. If successful, the West would be more insulated from its current perceived need to intervene in Arab and other Muslim states.

Unfortunately, at the present time it is unlikely that there will be direct negotiations between the major adversaries: the United States, Great Britain, and their allies on the one hand and a shifting congeries of radical Islamist cells ostensibly directed and/or inspired by al-Qaeda on the other. But that was also the case for much of the 20th century in Northern Ireland and Great Britain. Then came the Good Friday accords, a complex of agreements signed in 1998 that officially disarmed the "terrorist" IRA organization and brought a fragile but continuing peace to Ireland after "the troubles" which had persisted for centuries. Similarly, the French negotiated their withdrawal from Algeria with "terrorists" from the Front de Libération Nationale, or National Liberation Front (FLN). And few thought that apartheid in South Africa would end peacefully, but the ANC—another onetime "terrorist" organization—and the racist Afrikaner-led government in Pretoria negotiated a relatively nonviolent transition to black rule and ultimately, to national reconciliation as well. The Palestinian Liberation Organization (PLO), a longtime "terrorist group" in the eyes of many Israelis and Americans, and the Israeli government have been negotiating for decades. And it is likely that no "peace process" will succeed until all parties—including Hamas—are included. So there are numerous examples of governments doing business and concluding peace treaties with what they long deemed "terrorist groups" and of "liberation fronts" laying down their arms in return for political and economic concessions.

Just as there is now substantial mutual demonization between successive U.S. administrations and militant, violent Islamists, a similar dynamic characterized the IRA and pro-British "loyalists" in Northern Ireland. But eventually, due in part to the skillful intervention of third parties, they came more peacefully to coexist and even to share power.

But it is difficult to negotiate directly with an adversary that is geographically distant, decentralized, culturally very different, and without a nation-state to call home. But on more than one occasion, al-Qaeda has publicly indicated its willingness to suspend hostilities and to declare a kind of truce with its Western and Islamic adversaries. Western governments have officially refused to take up this invitation. But this was also the case for years with the IRA and with the ANC. And there are ongoing efforts to negotiate nonviolent resolutions to the conflicts between the West and North Korea and Iran, respectively, over their nuclear programs.

Good-faith negotiations between the Western powers and militant Islamists—possibly through back channels conducted by third parties, such as the Arab League, the Organization of the Islamic Conference, and the UN—may or may not result in a reduction of terrorist attacks and counterterrorist operations. But the alternative—an open-ended global conflict with the potential to escalate to the use of nuclear and other weapons of mass destruction—would likely be so destructive as to warrant that any and all nonviolent efforts should be made to end the "War on Terror," rechristened "Global Contingency Operations" by the Obama administration. Certainly, any policy—military, diplomatic, and/or economic—must be chosen with the greatest care and with the utmost respect for human life. To end terrorism means, among other things, to change the political reality and the mentality that give rise to it.

## A FINAL NOTE ON TERRORISM

Terrorism is simultaneously one of the oldest and one of the most recent incarnations of political violence. Whether employed from above or from below, it has existed for millennia. Accordingly, it is wishful thinking to believe that terrorism can be ended overnight or even, perhaps, within the lifetimes of the writers and readers of this book.

It is not, however, wishful thinking to believe that we must begin now to struggle forcefully, but if possible nonviolently, against all forms of political violence, no matter the origin, position, or creed of its perpetrators. Ending terrorism would entail, among other things, changing the political reality and mentality that engender it. Although we may not see the end of terrorism in the foreseeable future, perhaps by confronting political mass murder with reason and under-standing—rather than with violence in kind—while we still live we may see the beginning of the end of terrorism.

## NOTES

1. DCI Counterterrorist Center, Central Intelligence Agency. Undated October, 3.

2. Bruce Hoffman. October, 2002. "Lessons of 9/11." RAND, CT-201, http://www.rand.org/pubs/testimonies/CT201/.

3. Haig Khatchadourian. 1998. *The Morality of Terrorism*. New York: Peter Lang, 11.

4. Igor Primoratz. 1990. "What Is Terrorism?" *Journal of Applied Philosophy* 7(2): 129–130.

5. According to Noam Chomsky, "Terrorism is the use of coercive means aimed at civilian populations to achieve political, religious, or other aims. That's what the World Trade Center attack was, a particularly horrifying terrorist crime. Terrorism, according to the official definitions, is simply part of state action, official doctrine, and not just of the U.S., of course." Noam Chomsky. 2001. *9/11*. New York: Seven Stories Press, 57, 90.

6. Eliot Marshall, "Parsing Terrorism." *Science*, 18 May 2012, Vol. 336, 820-23.

7. See Edward S. Herman and Gerry O. Sullivan. 1991. "'Terrorism' as Ideology and Culture Industry." In *Western State Terrorism,* ed. Alexander George. Oxford: Polity Press, 41–42.

8. See James M. Lutz and Brenda J. Lutz. 2005. *Terrorism Origins and Evolution.* New York: Palgrave Macmillan, 49–51, 133–134.

9. Quoted in Jean Bethke Elshtain. 2003. *Just War Against Terror.* New York: Basic Books, 50.

10. Aristotle. *Politics* (13142). Cited in Michael Walzer. 1977. *Just and Unjust Wars.* New York: Basic Books, 198.

11. Yasmeen Ali. 2010 May. Available at: http://www.opinion-maker.org/2010/05/jihad-and-terrorism-are-both-synonymous/.

12. See Gilles Kepel. 2002. *Jihad: The Trail of Political Islam.* 2002. Cambridge, MA: Harvard University Press, 24–30, for the Muslim Brotherhood; John L. Esposito. 2002. *Unholy War: Terror in the Name of Islam.* Oxford: Oxford University Press, 84–87, for Islamic Jihad and Jamaat-e-Islami; and Ahmed Rashid. 2000. *Taliban.* New Haven, CT: Yale University Press. Also see Jessica Stern. 2003. *Terror in the Name of God: Why Religious Militants Kill.* New York: Ecco, for interviews with many contemporary Islamic "terrorists."

13. For a synopsis of the differences between Sunni and Shiite Muslims, see Bernard Lewis. 1997. *The Middle East.* New York: Simon & Schuster Touchstone Books, 67, 139.

14. For al-Qaeda and its selective appropriation of Western technology and modernity, see John Gray. 2003. *Al Qaeda and What It Means to Be Modern.* New York: The New Press.

15. Charles Webel interviewed one of the Americans who was kidnapped in 1979 from the U.S. Embassy in Teheran by followers of Khomeini. This captive's experience, along with the stories of many other contemporary victims of TFB and TFA, are related in Webel's 2007 book *Terror, Terrorism, and the Human Condition.* New York: Palgrave Macmillan.

16. See Jason Burke. 2004. *Al-Qaeda: The True Story of Radical Islam.* New York: Penguin Books, 52–55.

17. Osama bin Laden as cited in Burke, *Al-Qaeda,* op. cit., 163.

18. See Robert A. Pape. 2005. *Dying to Win the Strategic Logic of Suicide Terrorism.* New York: Random House.

19. Muhammad Guessous, quoted in Kevin Dwyer. 1991. *Arab Voices: The Human Rights Debate in the Middle East.* Berkeley: University of California Press, 120.

20. Walter Laqueur, in *The Age of Terrorism,* p. 8, citing U.S. State Department statistics, claims that from 1980 to 1985 there were many times more acts of terrorism (which Laqueur restricts to acts of violence by *non*-state actors) in Latin America (369) and Western Europe (458) than in the Middle East (84).

21. Department of Homeland Security website: http://www.dhs.gov/files/counterterrorism.shtm

22. Chalmers Johnson. 2004. *The Sorrows of Empire: Militarism, Secrecy, and the End of the Republic.* New York: Holt.

23. *2010 NCTC Report on Terrorism.* 8 April 2011. Available at: http://www.nctc.gov/site/index.html.

24. Bernard Lewis. 2002. *What Went Wrong? The Clash Between Islam and Modernity in the Middle East.* New York: HarperCollins, 3.

25. See Seth Jones and Martin C. Libicki. 2008. *How Terrorist Groups End: Lessons for Countering al Qaida.* Santa Monica, CA: Rand; and Audrey Kurth Cronin. 2009. *How Terrorism Ends: Understanding the Decline and Demise of Terrorist Campaigns.* Princeton, NJ: Princeton University Press.

26. Haig Khatchadourian. 2011. *The Morality of Terrorism.* New York: Peter Lang, 113–14, ff.

## QUESTIONS FOR FURTHER REFLECTION

1. Consider the contending definitions of terrorism. Which seem most appropriate, and why?

2. In thinking about TFA by states and TFB by subnational agents, are they comparable, or is one worse than the other? Why?

3. To what degree do you consider the current wars and terrorism in the Middle East to be a continuity, or a rupture, with Middle Eastern political history since the rise of Islam in the 7th century?

4. Is the "War on Terrorism" a war? Are antiterrorist measures more likely than counterterrorist measures to diminish or to increase terrorism around the world?

5. Why do people become "terrorists"? How might this be prevented?

## SUGGESTIONS FOR FURTHER READING

Alexander George, ed. 1991. *Western State Terrorism*. Oxford: Polity Press.

Bruce Hoffmann. 1998. *Inside Terrorism*. New York: Columbia University Press.

Haig Khatchadourian. 2011. *The Morality of Terrorism*. New York: Peter Lang.

Gus Martin. 2013. *Understanding Terrorism*. 4th Edition. Los Angeles: SAGE.

Charles Webel. 2007. *Terror, Terrorism, and the Human Condition*. New York: Palgrave Macmillan.

Charles Webel and John Arnaldi, eds. 2011. *The Ethics and Efficacy of the Global War on Terrorism Fighting Terror With Terror*. New York: Palgrave Macmillan.

James M. Lutz and Brenda J. Lutz. 2005. *Terrorism: Origins and Evolution*. New York: Palgrave Macmillan.

Robert A. Pape. 2005. *Dying to Win: The Strategic Logic of Suicide Terrorism*. New York: Random House.

# CHAPTER 5

# THE SPECIAL SIGNIFICANCE OF NUCLEAR WEAPONS

Thermonuclear device detonated over the Bikini Atoll in the Pacific in March 1954; at 11 megatons, it was the third largest nuclear test ever conducted by the United States.

*Source:* © 2008 Corbis Corporation.

> *The splitting of the atom has changed everything but our way of thinking, and hence we drift toward unparalleled catastrophe.*
>
> —Albert Einstein

> *We are here to make a choice between the quick and the dead. . . . If we fail, then we have damned every man to be the slave of fear.*
>
> —Bernard Baruch

*Today I can declare my hope and declare it from the bottom of my heart that we will eventually see the time come when that number of nuclear weapons is down to zero and the world is a much better place.*

- Colin Powell

**A**lbert Einstein once noted that, as a child, he had been taught that modern times began with the fall of the Roman Empire. But everything changed with the atomic bombings of Hiroshima and Nagasaki: Now, Einstein observed, we must say that modern times began in 1945.

There is indeed something special about nuclear weapons. They represent a dramatic discontinuity in human history, and they offer the possibility of an even more dramatic break: a canceling of the past, an end to the present, and a negating of the future. As destructive and dangerous as conventional warfare has been—and continues to be—it clearly takes a backseat to the sheer terror and horrific consequences of nuclear war. One of the ironies of the early 21st century is that with the end of the Cold War, other concerns (including, but not limited to global warming, economic inequality, abuse of human rights, and terrorism) have eclipsed anxiety about nuclear weapons as such. And yet, even as the risk of all-out global thermonuclear war—"World War III"—seems to have abated, the risk that nuclear weapons will be used in anger has not lessened; it may have even increased.

Moreover, as President Barack Obama has noted, "as the only nuclear power to have used a nuclear weapon, the United States has a particular moral responsibility to act." And according to Takashi Hiraoka, mayor of Hiroshima, in the "Hiroshima Peace Declaration," on the 50th anniversary of that city's nuclear destruction (6 August 1995): "So long as such weapons exist, it is inevitable that the horror of Hiroshima and Nagasaki will be repeated—somewhere, sometime—in an unforgivable affront to humanity itself." And so, we turn to a consideration of these uniquely terrible weapons.

At least four factors must be understood if one is to grasp the nature of nuclear war and the urgency as well as the prospects of preventing it: (1) the weapons—bombs and warheads—and their effects; (2) "delivery systems," the means by which nuclear weapons are to be directed to their targets; (3) "strategic doctrine," concerned with the plans and strategies for the use of nuclear weapons; and (4) the problems of nuclear proliferation and nuclear terrorism.

# The Nature of Nuclear Weapons

Nuclear weapons derive their explosive power from the conversion of matter into energy. This conversion takes place according to the well-known equation, $E = mc^2$, in which $E$ is the amount of energy released, $m$ is the mass to be converted into energy, and $c$ is the speed of light. Since the speed of light is itself a very large number (186,000 miles or 300,000 kilometers per second) which is squared in the equation, the resulting energy release is truly enormous. Nuclear fusion drives the sun and the stars; prior to 1945, the explosive power of nuclear energy had never been released by humans.

The power of nuclear weapons exceeds that of most conventional explosives by approximately a factor of 1 million. Herein rests the underlying significance of nuclear weapons and nuclear war: Something radically new and qualitatively different from previous human experience has been introduced into the world of war and into strategic thinking about conflicts. However, in some cases strategic thinking hasn't changed significantly, and herein lies a further problem!

Atomic bombs result from *nuclear fission,* the splitting of large, unstable atoms, most commonly uranium-235 (a radioactive isotope of the element uranium) or plutonium-239 (another radioactive element, one that is essentially man-made). When enough fissionable material is gathered together in one place and exposed to a barrage of neutrons, some of the unstable nuclei are split, releasing energy as well as additional neutrons. These neutrons, in turn, split the nuclei of other atoms, releasing yet more energy and neutrons, which continue to split additional nuclei in a chain reaction that accelerates geometrically and, thus, at extraordinary speed. The material has reached *critical mass* when each nucleus, after being split (or "fissioned"), releases enough neutrons to split approximately two nearby nuclei. As a result, an immense amount of energy can be released in a very short time. For example, in 0.00000058 second, $2^{57}$ nuclei (approximately 2 followed by 24 zeros) will have been split, releasing the energy equivalent to 100,000 tons of TNT.

Atomic, or fission, explosions are typically measured in *kilotons* (KT)—that is, the equivalent energy that would be released by the detonation of thousands of tons of TNT. Thus, a 12-KT atomic explosion—the size that destroyed the Japanese city of Hiroshima—releases the same amount of energy as would be released if 12,000 tons of TNT were to detonate.

The first nuclear weapons were based on fission. Most nuclear weapons today, however, are *fusion,* or *thermonuclear,* devices. They derive much of their energy from the squeezing together of very small atoms, notably deuterium and tritium, two isotopes of hydrogen. In the process, the element helium is produced, and through the conversion of mass into energy, vast amounts of energy are released. When plutonium, for example, is split, the total mass of the fission products that are formed—such as iron, cobalt, and manganese—is slightly less than that of the parent nucleus with which the process started. Similarly, the total mass of the helium nuclei produced by fusion is slightly less than the mass of the hydrogen isotopes with which a fusion reaction begins. This mass has not been "lost." Rather, it has been converted into energy.

Fusion is more efficient than fission in that more energy per starting mass is released. But fusion is also more difficult to initiate than fission, since great heat and pressure are required literally to squeeze the hydrogen nuclei together. Therefore, fusion explosions—or "hydrogen bombs," as they are often known—start with a relatively small "atomic" explosion, which serves as a trigger to initiate the much more powerful fusion reaction. This requirement of great heat and pressure is why fusion reactions are also known as *thermo*nuclear explosions. Fusion explosions are also typically boosted with an additional fission component, as the energy released by the fusion is captured by a lower-grade form of uranium, usually U-238, which is induced to split as well. So the typical thermonuclear (H-bomb or hydrogen bomb) explosion is fission-fusion-fission, all occurring in a minuscule fraction of a second. The energy released in such detonations can extend into the range of *megatons* (Mt), equivalent to millions of tons of TNT. Although nuclear explosives are often referred to as *bombs,* if deployed by nation-states, they are in fact more likely to be carried by a missile, in which case they are known as *warheads.* If deployed by some subnational actors, small nuclear devices and "dirty" bombs may be carried in a variety of ways, possibly including backpacks and suitcases. In addition, nuclear weapons are often designated as either *tactical* or *strategic.* The former usually refers to weapons intended for use on a battlefield; the latter are normally intended for use against an adversary's (usually distant) homeland. As a result, tactical nuclear weapons are typically smaller than their strategic counterparts.

# The Effects of Nuclear Weapons

Given that nuclear weapons have only twice been exploded in wartime (both in 1945, at Hiroshima and Nagasaki), it may seem strange that they should command so much attention. The reason is simple and related primarily to their effects: Nuclear explosions are extraordinarily powerful and devastating. Consider this account of the first atomic bomb test, at Alamogordo, New Mexico, in July 1945:

> No man-made phenomenon of such tremendous power had ever occurred before. The lighting effects beggared description. The whole country was lighted by a searing light with the intensity many times that of the midday sun. It was golden, purple, violet, gray and blue. It lighted every peak, crevasse and mountain range with a clarity and beauty that cannot be described but must be seen to be imagined. It was the beauty the great poets dream about but describe most poorly and inadequately. Thirty seconds after the explosion came . . . to be followed almost immediately by the strong, sustained, awesome roar which warned of doomsday and made us feel that we puny things were blasphemous to dare tamper with the forces heretofore reserved to the Almighty. Words are inadequate tools for the job of acquainting those not present with the physical, mental and psychological effects. It had to be witnessed to be realized.[1]

For insight into the effects of a nuclear explosion on the world as we live in it, however, it is more useful to consider eyewitness accounts of the actual use of atomic weapons, such as this one describing the impact on Nagasaki:

> For some 1,000 yards, or three-fifths of a mile, in all directions from the epicenter . . . it was as if a malevolent god had suddenly focused a gigantic blowtorch on a small section of our planet. Within that perimeter, nearly all unprotected living organisms . . . perished instantly. Flowers, trees, grass, plants, all shriveled and died. Wood burst into flames. Metal beams . . . began to bubble, and the soft gooey masses twisted into grotesque shapes. Stones were pulverized, and for a second every last bit of air was burned away. The people exposed within that doomed section neither knew nor felt anything, and their blackened, unrecognizable forms dropped silently where they stood.[2]

During the height of the Cold War, pronuclear strategists on both sides argued for "civil defense" as a way of minimizing damage in a nuclear war, although antinuclear opponents maintained that such efforts were neither "civil" nor "defense," since they would provide no real safety and if anything, increased the risk that such weapons might be used insofar as they were perceived to be survivable. Former Soviet communist party chairman, Nikita Khrushchev, once observed that following a nuclear war, the survivors would envy the dead.

Nagasaki and Hiroshima were both hit with atomic bombs, carrying the explosive power of about 20 KT and 12 KT, respectively. These are very small compared with the bombs and warheads now available: Hydrogen bombs have been produced and deployed in the multimegaton range. Since 1 Mt is equivalent in energy to 1 million tons of TNT, it follows that a 9-Mt bomb is slightly less than 1,000 times more powerful than the one that destroyed Hiroshima. Most bombs and warheads in the strategic arsenal of the United States and Russia are about 100 to 500 KT, or approximately 8 to 40 times more powerful than the Hiroshima explosion. In 2010, the total U.S. strategic arsenal was about 1,700 Mt; by comparison, the entire explosive force detonated (by both sides) during World War II was approximately 3 Mt.

Despite some cuts in the nuclear arsenals of the two nuclear superpowers (the United States and Russia) since the end of the Cold War, in 2010 there were still an estimated 19,000 nuclear weapons in the world. Of these, some 4,800 warheads are considered operational, of which nearly 2,000 U.S. and Russian warheads are on high alert, ready for use on short notice. The exact number of nuclear weapons in each country's possession is a closely held national secret. The other "declared nuclear states"—the United Kingdom, France, China, India, and Pakistan—each possess roughly 100 to 300 nuclear warheads and/or bombs, as does another undeclared but undoubted nuclear state: Israel. North Korea possesses a nuclear arsenal of uncertain number (perhaps as many as a dozen or so) and questionable reliability. Iran is widely suspected of attempting to develop nuclear weapons. It is also widely believed that subnational and terrorist groups, as well as possibly a few nonnuclear states, have been seeking to develop, or acquire, nuclear devices.

## Immediate Effects of Nuclear Weapons

Most estimates of nuclear war fatalities are lower than they should be, because the relevant effects are generally considered separately. In reality, however, all would occur simultaneously: People would be trapped in collapsing buildings (blast), which would then likely burn (heat), while the survivors would also have to contend with radiation. Infections are a serious complication of burns, and radiation reduces the body's ability to ward off infection. Many victims would likely be burned and irradiated and might also suffer from crushing or piercing injuries. In addition, most hospitals and medical personnel are located in major cities, which would almost certainly be targeted and destroyed, and pharmaceuticals would be almost entirely unavailable; ditto for emergency services of all sorts. Firefighting would also be virtually impossible, because streets would be impassably blocked with the debris of collapsed buildings, water pressure would be nonexistent because of the rupture of pipes, and potential firefighters would likely be dead or contending with their own personal tragedies.

Of the approximately 200,000 fatalities resulting from the bombing at Hiroshima, about 50% were due to burns, while about 30% were due to lethal doses of radiation. Another 75,000 people eventually perished due to the atomic bombing of Nagasaki. Although technical knowledge of this sort is important, such sanitized data are grossly inadequate for conveying the full horror of nuclear war. Numbers are numbing. Another kind of knowledge, more personal and visceral, may be more meaningful.

There are harrowing accounts of people with empty eye sockets whose eyeballs were literally melted, of infants attempting to nurse at the corpses of dead mothers, of burn victims with their skin hanging in loose strips, and of family members trying to rescue relatives who had been trapped under collapsed and burning buildings. One survivor gives this account:

> The sight of the soldiers was more dreadful than the dead people . . . I came upon . . . many, burned from the hips up . . . where the skin had peeled, their flesh was wet and mushy . . . And they had no faces! Their eyes, noses, and mouths had been burned away, and it looked like their ears had melted off. It was hard to tell front from back.[3]

Even for those not physically injured, the psychological effects of such an immense and sudden disaster were overwhelming for most survivors. A Hiroshima physician describes some survivors leaving the city:

> Those who were able walked silently toward the suburbs in the distant hills, their spirits broken, their initiative gone. . . . They were so broken and confused that they moved and behaved like automatons . . . a people who walked in the realm of dreams. . . . A spiritless people had forsaken a destroyed city.[4]

The Hiroshima and Nagasaki bombs were very small by today's standards. Moreover, at that time there was an "outside world" from which aid eventually reached the survivors. In the event of full-fledged nuclear war today, the experience would be many times worse, with virtually no prospect of recovery.

## The Effects of Nuclear Weapons on Social, Economic, and Political Organization

In addition to the radioactive fallout that would follow nuclear explosions, a major mid-range effect of nuclear war would be its impact on social, economic, and political organizations. Food storage regions would likely be destroyed or inaccessible; cities would be devastated, with rescue, firefighting, and medical services largely unavailable; transportation might well cease altogether. Electricity-generating plants would almost certainly be destroyed, along with oil refineries. Most sources of power—for communication, transportation, manufacturing, and agriculture—would be eliminated, perhaps permanently. A simple barter system would probably replace traditional money-based economies for any possible survivors. As economist John Kenneth Galbraith has emphasized, communism and capitalism (as well as Christianity, Islam, Judaism, Hinduism, Buddhism, and so forth) might well be indistinguishable in the ashes. Diseases such as cholera would spread rapidly, with sanitation and public hygiene virtually eliminated, and billions of insects and trillions of bacteria would multiply in the rotting, unburied corpses.

Shortly before he was assassinated in 1979, Lord Mountbatten gave a speech in which he asked:

> And when it is all over, what will the world be like? Our . . . great buildings, our homes will exist no more. The thousands of years it took to develop our civilization will have been in vain. Our works of art will be lost. Radio, television, newspapers will disappear. There will be no means of transport. There will be no hospitals. No help can be expected for the few mutilated survivors . . . there will be no neighboring towns left, no neighbors . . . there will be no hope.[5]

By contrast, many nuclear strategists calculated that nuclear war might be survivable, at least for some people and with appropriate precautions, such as (in the early 1960s) blast and/or fallout shelters and (in the 1980s) crisis relocation plans, which were intended to organize the evacuation of the citizenry from high-risk areas to other regions, thought to be untargeted. Such thinking was especially prominent among those nuclear strategists who fretted that "excessive" anxiety about the effects of nuclear war might erode U.S. willingness to stand up to its possible adversaries.

They worried also about the possibility that antinuclear anxiety would diminish the credibility of the stated U.S. intention to resort to nuclear weapons under certain circumstances, such as an invasion of Western Europe or in retaliation for a nuclear attack on the United States. In addition, some conservative politicians were long concerned that nuclear fears might undermine a continuing commitment by the United States to ever-more weaponry and undercut the "better dead than red" mentality, which had been prevalent among many Cold Warriors.

By the 1990s, however, such thinking became increasingly difficult to defend, largely as a result of the widespread publicity concerning the horrific prompt and intermediate effects of nuclear war, as well as revelations concerning their likely long-term effects. The peace movement, both in the United States and worldwide, can take substantial credit for awakening many government leaders to the unacceptable consequences of nuclear war, as epitomized in the belated observation by President Reagan (who took office with a seemingly cavalier attitude toward the effects of nuclear war) that a "nuclear war can never be won and must never be fought."

## Long-Term Consequences of Nuclear Weapons

Long-term effects of nuclear weapons would include dramatically increased levels of background radiation (due to radioactive fallout) as well as significant depletion of stratospheric ozone (O3), which otherwise protects the Earth's inhabitants from dangerous cancer- and blindness-inducing levels of natural ultraviolet radiation from the sun. Undoubtedly, however, the most serious long-term consequence would be the phenomenon of *nuclear winter*. This refers to the cooling and darkening of the planetary environment that most atmospheric scientists believe would result from an all-out nuclear war. The basic concept of nuclear winter is as follows: A nuclear war would produce not only immense amounts of dust but—far more important—enormous fires, which in turn would generate huge quantities of smoke and soot. Rising into the upper atmosphere, this material would absorb incoming heat and light from the sun, thereby making the Earth cold and dark.

Some estimates show that nuclear winter could be triggered by the detonation of as "little" as 100 Mt, a tiny fraction of the world's arsenals. The effects would be worldwide and catastrophic: Temperatures could plummet as much as 50° F, which would result in extreme freezing over widespread areas and total disruption of agriculture and natural ecosystems, as well as perhaps making fresh water unavailable for people, plants, and/or animals for prolonged periods of time. Certainly, such an event would greatly complicate the problems of survival in what is sometimes, in a sanitized way, referred to as the "postattack environment."

The nuclear winter scenario generated considerable controversy, as specialists questioned some of its assumptions, such as precisely how much smoke would be produced, how it would be distributed globally, and how intense and how persistent the climatic darkening and freezing would therefore be. There is also debate over the possible modulating effect of the oceans and the effect of increased cloud cover, as well as questions as to what proportion of the targeted cities would actually burn. Thus far, however, most of the conclusions reached by scientists studying the issue have proven to be quite robust, although the prospect of nuclear winter is, fortunately, still only theoretical.

At present, and despite a growing consensus that nuclear war is an unacceptable option, some aspects of nuclear strategy depend on the willingness of governments to employ nuclear weapons or, at least, on the belief by an adversary that such willingness exists. Hence, one comes across such statements as the observation by Henry Kissinger (now a self-professed nuclear abolitionist) that nuclear diplomacy "requires strong nerves" and that, accordingly, the United States should "leave no doubt about our readiness and our ability to face a final showdown."[7]

During the early years of the Reagan administration, for example, official pronouncements appeared to minimize the likely consequences of nuclear war. In 1982, Deputy Undersecretary of Defense T. K. Jones claimed that

> everybody's going to make it if there are enough shovels to go around. . . . Dig a hole, cover it with a couple of doors and then throw three feet of dirt on top. It's the dirt that does it.[8]

Other pronouncements of this sort, combined with a massive and unprecedented military buildup of both conventional and nuclear weapons, stimulated renewed interest in—and anxiety about—the effects of nuclear war.

By the late 1990s, antinuclear peace movement activities had succeeded in making it unacceptable for politicians and strategic planners to speak lightly of precipitating a nuclear holocaust. Toward the latter years of the Reagan and during both Bush administrations, official pronouncements on this topic became much more circumspect, testimony to the impact of a populace and a peace movement that had become increasingly antinuclear because of these administrations' policies. President Obama then became the first U.S. president to make nuclear abolitionism a centerpiece of foreign policy; in a much-touted speech in Prague, in 2009, he laid out a possible road map toward a nuclear-free world. In addition, the Obama administration canceled financing for a new nuclear warhead sought by both Bush administrations, thereby terminating plans to develop and deploy this low-yield, deeply burrowing "bunker buster" nuclear warhead that the Pentagon had sought to strike buried targets, like the nuclear facilities in North Korea and Iran.

# Nuclear Delivery Systems

The technology—and the peace/war implications—of delivering nuclear weapons to their targets are almost as important as that of the weapons themselves. The strategic nuclear forces of both the United States and Russia are based on a *triad* of three distinct components: long-range bombers, land-based intercontinental missiles, and missile-carrying submarines, as well as cruise missiles. The other nuclear powers—China, France, Great Britain, India, Pakistan, Israel, and possibly North Korea—each employ one or, at most, two "legs" of such a triad.

## Bombers

Bombers were originally intended to attack targets by dropping gravity bombs. That role has to some extent been superseded by the use of bombers as "launch platforms" for a variety of air-to-land and cruise missiles. More recently, however, interest has been revived in using bombers as "penetrating aircraft," as in *stealth bombers,* this time having them fly very low, thereby ducking under radar detection. The wars conducted by the North Atlantic Treaty Organization (NATO) over Serbia, Kosovo, and Libya, and by the United States and its allies over Iraq and Afghanistan, made heavy use of both high-altitude conventional bombing as well as missile-launched conventional warheads, which resulted in very few (in some cases, zero) casualties for the fliers and significant casualties for civilians and soldiers who happened to be in the path of "precision-guided" and/or "errant" munitions.

## Intercontinental Ballistic Missiles

Ballistic missiles are rockets. They travel very rapidly, reaching speeds of greater than 10,000 miles per hour, and during intercontinental flight they actually leave the Earth's atmosphere, to reenter before striking their targets. Intercontinental ballistic missiles, or ICBMs, are located underground, in steel- and concrete-reinforced silos. The United States maintains up to 1,000 ICBMs (as with all such weapons for all countries, the exact numbers keep changing, when older models are phased out and new ones are brought into service). Russia and, increasingly, China have also invested heavily in ICBMs.

ICBMs have typically been *MIRV*ed, that is, equipped with Multiple, Independently-targeted Reentry Vehicles. A single MIRVed missile can carry 10 or more warheads, each of which can be aimed at a different target. Fifty MIRVED missiles can thus destroy 500 distinct targets, each with a warhead of between 350 KT (nearly 30 times the power of the Hiroshima bomb) and 2 Megatons. Russian missiles have historically tended to be larger than their U.S. counterparts, a fact that has caused great consternation to some in the United States and that was long used to buttress claims that the United States was "behind" in ICBMs, thereby helping generate support for additional missile programs. But in fact, the smaller size of U.S. ICBMs was an indication of the *superiority,* not inferiority, of U.S. missile technology.

According to the physics of nuclear explosions, the accuracy of a warhead is far more important than its explosive size: A small increase in accuracy is equivalent—in the probability of destroying a given "hardened" target—to a very large increase in total explosive force. The U.S. arsenal achieved very high degrees of accuracy (thanks in part to the same technology now widely employed in global positioning system devices); as a result, it has been possible to decrease the megatonnage and also to employ ICBMs that are significantly smaller than the first, relatively bulky missiles. It would take approximately 30 minutes for ICBMs fired by one nuclear superpower to devastate the other and much less time for regional nuclear powers to obliterate one another.

## Submarine-Launched Ballistic Missiles

Nuclear submarines can be nuclear in two senses: They are typically propelled by nuclear power plants, and they also carry nuclear missiles, known as SLBMs, for submarine-launched ballistic missiles. These missiles are designed to be fired while the submarine remains submerged. The particular advantage of strategic submarines is that, unlike bombers or ICBMs, they cannot be targeted by an adversary once they are on deep-ocean patrol. In terms of strategic doctrine, they have therefore long been considered an ideal deterrent weapon, since they offer the prospect of a secure "second strike" force—that is, one that could absorb a "first strike" and still be able to deliver retaliation that would be unacceptable to a would-be nuclear aggressor. However, SLBMs have certain disadvantages, notably the fact that it is often quite difficult to communicate with deeply submerged submarines.

Strategic submarines carry many SLBMs; U.S. *Trident* submarines, for example, carry 24 missiles. Like ICBMs, SLBMs tend to be MIRVed, although the United States has progressed further than

Russia in this regard. When it comes to strategic submarines, the United States also enjoys an immense geographic advantage over Russia because of its extensive, ice-free ocean coastlines. The United States is also acknowledged to have a substantial lead over any competitors in submarine technology, including antisubmarine warfare.

## Cruise Missiles

Since the early 1990s, cruise missiles have become increasingly prominent and are now in a sense the fourth leg of America's "triad." Cruise missiles are pilotless jet aircraft that travel comparatively slowly (about the speed of sound) but close to the ground and are therefore difficult for radar to detect. They are also relatively inexpensive to produce, roughly $1 million each. Equipped with modern navigational and homing devices, they are also becoming extremely accurate. In addition, cruise missiles are quite small, perhaps 20 feet long. Thus, once they have been deployed in large numbers, verification of their elimination at any time in the future, even if countries possessing them muster the political will to do so, becomes extremely difficult if not impossible. Cruise missiles can be armed with conventional or nuclear warheads, and at present there is no way to distinguish the two kinds from a distance. Cruise missiles with conventional warheads were used by the United States against Iraq during its two wars against that country, as well as by NATO in Libya and Afghanistan.

# Strategic Doctrine: Deterrence

*Strategic doctrine* refers to the plans that purportedly underlie the accumulation of nuclear weapons, the justifications for their existence, and the expectations as to their use. The major component of U.S. strategic doctrine is alleged to be *deterrence,* the idea that nuclear war will be prevented by the threat that any attacker would suffer unacceptable retaliation. Realizing this, the would-be attacker would therefore be deterred.

Deterrence as such is not unique to nuclear weapons. What is unique to nuclear deterrence, however, is the consequence of failure and the fact that, heretofore, military forces that ostensibly provided deterrence also did double duty in providing defense, should deterrence fail. For centuries, for example, the Roman legions defended Rome and its colonies by deterring would-be attackers, but when attacks nonetheless occurred, the legions were also available to defend Rome. In the nuclear age, despite efforts at achieving strategic missile defense, the fact remains that the offense is all-powerful, despite hopes by some that a National Missile Defense (NMD) program might lessen the dominance of offense; if nuclear deterrence between nuclear superpowers should fail, there is currently no effective defense. Moreover, most independent experts agree that any conceivable missile defense system would readily be overwhelmed by a concerted ballistic missile attack, as well as easily confused by such countermeasures as decoys. Shortly after World War II, American strategic analyst Bernard Brodie recognized the qualitative change in deterrence ushered in by nuclear weapons:

> The first and most vital step in any American security program for the age of atomic bombs is to take measures to guarantee . . . in case of attack the possibility of retaliation in kind. The writer . . . is not . . . concerned about who will *win* the next war in which atomic

bombs have been used. Thus far the chief purpose of our military establishment has been to win wars. From now on its chief purpose must be to avert them. It can have almost no other useful purpose.[9]

Nonetheless, advocates of missile defense maintain that even though it could not function effectively against a concerted attack by a well-armed opponent (e.g., Russia), it might be useful against a very limited first strike by a nuclear "mini-power" such as North Korea or, possibly, Iran. At present, the United States is the only country that actively seeks to develop strategic missile defense, which has emerged as a favorite of conservative "hawks." Efforts to deploy such a "Star Wars" system against a hypothetical attack emanating from Iran or North Korea, however, have met strong resistance from Russia, whose leaders claim that it is actually directed against their missile system, thereby threatening the alleged stability of deterrence . . . ultimately based on continuing vulnerability on the part of each participant.

Strategic deterrence theory has been modified and adjusted many times, varying with the state of U.S.-Russian relations and weaponry. However, the basic premise of deterrence has remained that no country would use nuclear weapons against the other so long as the victim retains the ability to cause unacceptable damage to the attacker. In such thinking, the initial attack is referred to as a *first strike,* and a *first-strike capability* is generally taken to mean the ability to conduct an initial assault that will render the victim unable to retaliate.

According to conventional deterrence theory as it applies to nation-states, therefore, it behooves each country to maintain a *second-strike capability,* the capacity to absorb a first strike and still retaliate. If one side has a second-strike capability, the other, by definition, lacks a first-strike capability. The result is considered *strategic stability,* a situation in which neither side can profit by striking first; thus, war should not occur. This, of course, is not peace at all but rather a kind of suspended animation in which overt warfare is merely postponed (in theory).

## Skeletons in the Closet of Deterrence

Deterrence theory is not as cut and dried, or even as reliable, as its proponents might wish. A number of factors—or "skeletons in the closet"—have consistently undermined the presumed goal of strategic nuclear stability based on mutual deterrence.

*Skeleton 1: How much is enough?* No simple rule of thumb or straightforward quantitative measure can assure national leaders that they have accumulated enough retaliatory force to deter an adversary. Indeed, if one side is willing to be annihilated in a counterattack, it cannot be deterred. And if one side is convinced of the other's implacable hostility, no amount of weaponry can ever be "enough." So long as money is made by accumulating weapons, and so long as prestige and careers are served by designing, producing, and deploying new "generations" of nuclear forces, there will be continuing insistence on yet more weapons. Finally, insofar as nuclear weapons also in part serve symbolic, psychological needs, such as conveying legitimacy to otherwise insecure leaders and countries—thereby ostensibly demonstrating the scientific and technological accomplishments of a nation—then once again, there is no rational way to put a cap on the optimum size of one's arsenal. Strategic planners have further declared that to be "prudent," each leg of the strategic triad should be able to deliver 400 Mt. However, because of the many factors that drive the nuclear arms race—and, to some extent, arms races in general—the arsenals of both the United States and Russia have expanded to many times this amount. Given that a single nuclear bomb or warhead delivered on any major city would cause staggering loss of lives and property, it is difficult to understand the deterrent rationale for maintaining literally thousands of times that destructive capacity.

*Skeleton 2: Credibility.* A second major difficulty of deterrence theory is the problem inherent in basing security on the threat to do something that is grossly self-destructive and therefore lacking in credibility. Thus, granted that one side would be irrational to attack a nuclear-armed opponent that had a second-strike capability, the victim would be equally irrational to reply with nuclear weapons. Not only would retaliation be useless, but it would almost certainly be counterproductive, adding to worldwide destruction (through fallout, ozone depletion, nuclear winter, etc.) while also raising the possibility of yet another attack from the aggressor's remaining nuclear forces. In addition, given the ethical issues raised by a willingness to commit mass murder on the largest scale in human history, there might be additional reason to doubt a nuclear state's willingness to do so.

"One cannot fashion a credible deterrent out of an incredible action," wrote former defense secretary Robert McNamara. "Thus, security for the United States and its allies can only arise from the possession of a range of graduated deterrents, each of them fully credible in its own context."[10] Such thinking led, in turn, to the notion of "flexible response," according to which NATO should possess a range of military options, including a diversity of nuclear responses short of all-out nuclear war.

There are, however, serious problems with doctrines of limited war fighting. First, to be credible, such doctrines must be based on weapons and tactics that are in fact usable: generally, missiles, bombs, and warheads that are smaller and highly accurate and that produce relatively less *collateral damage* (the killing of civilians and the destruction of their property). So in order to be effective, which in the case of nuclear weapons means in order *not to be used,* these weapons must be made *more usable.* But this poses a major paradox, one that may someday be catastrophic: The more usable, hence credible, they are, the more likely they are actually to be used. And numerous studies have shown that in the event of nuclear war between nuclear powers, no matter how small and controlled the opening shots, the confrontation is very likely to escalate to an all-out strategic exchange, with catastrophic consequences for all involved. Moreover, even without such escalation, a limited nuclear war, in Europe or between regional nuclear powers (such as between India and Pakistan, between Israel and her adversaries, or by the United States and a "rogue state" or "terrorists"), for example, would appear quite unlimited to the Europeans, South Asians, or people in the Middle East, for whose benefit the war was ostensibly being fought. As a result of all this, even limited nuclear war—hence, nuclear deterrence—may be seen as lacking in credibility after all.

*Skeleton 3: Vulnerability.* As already mentioned, deterrence requires that the nuclear weapons of each side remain invulnerable to attack or, at least, that the probability of them being destroyed in a first strike be very low. Over time, however, as nuclear missiles have become increasingly accurate, concerns have been raised about the growing vulnerability of these weapons (note: not vulnerability *of the population,* which is fundamental to deterrence). The alleged vulnerability of nuclear weapons themselves has been enhanced by the development of so-called *counterforce* doctrines, policies and capabilities that focus on targeting an adversary's weapons rather than population centers. Although counterforce appears less unethical than its alternative, *countervalue* targeting (or the deliberate targeting of civilian populations in cities), it also raises concerns that the other side may be planning a first strike since, in theory at least, a successful counterforce attack would preclude retaliation. The perception of vulnerability can lead to strategic instability. On the one hand, the side possessing a first-strike capability may be tempted to make such an attack, especially under conditions of crisis, when war seems likely and perhaps inevitable. On the other hand, the vulnerable side might well calculate that since its opponent has the ability to strike a devastating first blow, it ought to preempt such an attack by striking first. This is also more likely during an international crisis. (There is virtually no limit to this chain of reasoning: Side A, fearing that side B is about to preempt in this way, may be tempted to pre-preempt, leading side B, which anticipates such a pre-preemption, to consider pre-pre-preempting, and so forth.) The result—so-called crisis instability—is very dangerous in that it threatens to undermine deterrence.

One of the most important contributions toward reducing crisis instability was the ABM Treaty according to which signatories agreed to forgo the deployment of antimissile defenses. Although the evidence is overwhelming that such "Star Wars" antiballistic missile systems could not successfully defend major population centers, it is at least theoretically possible that they might succeed in protecting some of a country's nuclear arsenal after it had launched a nuclear attack against its opponent's weapons. If a would-be attacker had confidence that its ballistic missile defenses could be somewhat successful against a "ragged retaliation," it might be tempted to launch such an attack in the first place, thereby seriously undermining deterrence. The George W. Bush administration withdrew the United States from the ABM Treaty in 2001 and announced plans to install a limited ABM system, ostensibly to defend against a possible attack from Iran. The Russian government, in turn, objected vigorously, claiming that such a system—even if technologically flawed and susceptible to countermeasures—would dangerously erode nuclear stability. The Bush administration nonetheless announced plans to deploy ABM components in Poland and the Czech Republic, a plan that was vigorously opposed by many Czechs and Poles and the Russian government, which views the emplacement of such a system as destabilizing and a potential "first-strike" move by the United States. Subsequently, the Obama administration backed away from this proposed land-based ABM system in favor of a more limited one, to be based primarily on warships in the open ocean.

*Skeleton 4: Human psychology.* Deterrence theory assumes optimal "rationality" in decision makers or, at least, that those with their fingers on the nuclear triggers will remain calm and cognitively unimpaired under extremely stressful conditions. It also assumes that leaders will always retain control over their nuclear forces and that, moreover, they will always retain control over their emotions as well, making decisions based solely on the basis of a cool calculation of the costs and benefits associated with each course of action. Deterrence theory thus maintains that each side will scare the other with the prospect of the most hideous, unimaginable consequences and that the persons thus terrified will then behave with the utmost in cool, precise instrumental rationality. Ironically, virtually everything we know about human psychology suggests precisely the opposite.

Deterrence theory also ignores the fact that, even without intense fear, many people often behave in ways that are irrational, vengeful, and even spiteful and self-destructive (i.e., hurtful to themselves as well as others). Moreover, they may be the victims of insufficient or faulty information or of various other perceptual distortions that cause them to make incorrect judgments as to the intentions of others, the probabilities of various alternative courses of action, and so on. It requires no arcane strategic wisdom to know that people often act out of anger, despair, insanity, stubbornness, revenge, and/or dogmatic conviction. And finally, in certain situations—such as when either side is convinced that war is inevitable or when the pressures to avoid losing face are especially intense—an irrational act, even a lethal one, may appear quite "rational" or otherwise appropriate, even unavoidable.

*Skeleton 5: Deterring terrorists.* How can people who do not fear violent death and who do not have a fixed location be deterred? Clearly, deterrence theory is therefore of dubious relevance for committed terrorists, most of whom do not have a return address, are immersed within the very societies they are inclined to attack or are in very remote locations, and/or will not be "deterred" because they do not fear—and may even welcome—"martyrdom." How can people who believe their violence is "sacred" and will be rewarded, either by God or by the community, be deterred, or even found and targeted, especially if they are within urban, civilian communities?

Even more problematic is that the cycle of terrorist/counterterrorist violence may spiral out of control. Tit for tat, an eye for an eye, a city for a city, a nation for a nation: There is no lasting security in a world in which terror matches terror and neither the terrorists nor the counterterrorists are deterred by the prospect of greater violence. This extends from the local detonation of car bombs and "precision-guided" weaponry to the deployment, locally and globally, of weapons of mass destruction.

## Has Deterrence Worked?

Many strategic analysts would say, "Of course." They would claim that we can attribute the fact that there has been no nuclear or conventional war between nuclear states to the existence of nuclear deterrence. Some would also claim that the fall of the Soviet Union and the "defeat of Communism" were also brought about by the West's "robust" nuclear deterrent, which allegedly prevented the former Soviet Union from invading Western Europe.

Others, however, argue that the absence of a war between the United States and its NATO allies, on the one hand, and the former Soviet Union and its Warsaw Pact allies, on the other hand, was not primarily due to nuclear deterrence but to other factors, such as the absence of any wars between America and Russia prior to the advent of the nuclear age and to internal domestic considerations within each country. In any event, should "deterrence fail," there will likely be no strategists or historians left to debate the reasons for its failure.

# How a Nuclear War Could Start

There are many possible scenarios (imagined sequences of interactions) according to which nuclear war could occur. Here are some examples; although these scenarios were originally developed with an eye to the Cold War between the United States and the Soviet Union, most of them could apply to other confrontations, notably between India and Pakistan; between Israel and a nuclear-armed Iran, and so forth:

*Bolt out of the blue.* Although most laypeople imagine a surprise, middle-of-the-night attack, most experts agree that a so-called bolt out of the blue, or BOOB attack is the least likely scenario of all. Neither side would come out ahead, and unless other factors are operating, deterrence should prevent any such calculated madness. On the other hand, strategic analysts worry constantly that one side may be tempted to attack preemptively if it becomes convinced that its perceived adversary's weapons could be destroyed in a surprise first strike. More-realistic scenarios for BOOB attacks generally depend on some combination of the various other scenarios discussed below.

*A game of "chicken."* A popular but risky game played by teenagers and captured memorably in the 1950s James Dean movie *Rebel Without a Cause* was to play "chicken" in automobiles. Two drivers would drive toward a cliff at high speed. The first one to bail out lost; the one who persevered was the winner. In a game of chicken, therefore, the goal is to induce the opponent to back away and not to do so oneself.

Philosopher and antinuclear campaigner Bertrand Russell made an even more dramatic analogy between strategic games of chicken and two drivers heading toward each other, straddling the white line, each seeking to induce the other to turn aside. The most dramatic example of nuclear chicken occurred during the Cuban Missile Crisis in 1962, when the Soviet Union attempted to install medium-range nuclear missiles in Cuba, hoping to deter the United States from invading Cuba and to "balance" the American deployment of nuclear-tipped missiles in Turkey (bordering the former Soviet Union) and Great Britain.

The United States demanded that the missiles be withdrawn; the Soviets refused. After considering and rejecting various options—including a conventional attack on the missile sites, an invasion of Cuba, and a preemptive nuclear strike against the Soviet Union—President John F. Kennedy decided on a naval blockade (designated at the time as a "quarantine"). The situation was exceedingly tense, and President Kennedy subsequently stated that he thought the chance of nuclear war had been between one in two and one in three. Premier Khrushchev ordered Soviet naval vessels to turn back, and an accommodation was reached in which the Soviet missile site was dismantled and the United States promised not to invade Cuba. (An unofficial part of the deal was that the United States would quietly decommission its medium-range missiles in Turkey, something it had already planned to do before the Cuban Missile Crisis.)

As then–secretary of state Dean Rusk put it, "We were eyeball to eyeball, and the other guy blinked." In other words, the Soviets turned aside in that game of nuclear chicken. They may have been induced to do so, at least in part, by the fact that the Soviet Union was militarily inferior to the United States at the time, both in conventional forces in the Caribbean and in nuclear arms as well. However, the United States and Russia now appear equally capable of destroying each other, as well as the rest of the world, completely, and neither side is likely to accept the ignominy of being the one to swerve. In contests of nuclear chicken, when each side insists that the other one turn aside, the result is likely to be "fried chicken."

*Escalated conventional war.* Military forces of the United States and Russia have not engaged in direct hostilities since the United States—along with the other Western powers—tried unsuccessfully to undo the Bolshevik Revolution. It is quite possible (some would say, likely) that such restraint has been due to the shared possession of nuclear weapons. Nonetheless, each side has been engaged in conventional fighting—the Soviets, for example, in Hungary (1956), Czechoslovakia (1968), and Afghanistan (1979–1988); the Russians in Chechnya (1996–present); and the United States in Korea (1950–1953), Vietnam (1962–1974), Beirut (1982), Grenada (1983), Panama (1989), the Persian Gulf (1990–1991), the former Yugoslavia (1999), Afghanistan (2001–present), and Iraq (2003–present), to mention just a few cases.

The United States has seriously considered the use of nuclear weapons many times, from 1946, when President Truman threatened to employ nuclear weapons unless Stalin withdrew his forces from Iran (which he did), to 1968, when American generals considered the poible use of nuclear weapons to help lift the siege of Khe Sanh in Vietnam. The United States under former president George H. W. Bush may also have contemplated using nuclear weapons against Iraq during the Gulf War. And the administration of George W. Bush refused to rule out the first use of nuclear weapons, although President Obama also revised U.S. policy on the use of nuclear weapons in a Nuclear Policy Review required of all presidents, declaring for the first time that the United States would not use nuclear weapons against nonnuclear states that were compliant with the Nuclear Non-Proliferation Treaty. This policy shift also renounced development of any new nuclear weapons.

Thus far, existing international threats and confrontations have been resolved short of nuclear war, but there is no assurance that this can continue indefinitely. There is also an ongoing threat that, during conventional warfare, nuclear weapons will be used in a last-ditch effort to win the war or simply to prevent one's homeland from being overrun. Many experts believe that the greatest current threat of nuclear use is posed by India and Pakistan, two nuclear-armed countries with shared borders, continuing conflict over a disputed geographic region (Kashmir), and a long history of wars during the past few decades. It is all too possible that should a conventional war break out between them, the losing side might resort to nuclear weapons. Ironically, it is even possible that the winning side would also be tempted, out of fear that the other might do so in desperation and, thus, in the hope of beating it to the punch!

Nearly 20 years after leaving the Defense Department, Robert McNamara warned that

> we face a future in which . . . we must contemplate continuing confrontation between East and West. Any one of these confrontations can escalate . . . into military conflict. And that conflict will be between blocs that possess fifty thousand nuclear warheads—warheads that are deployed on the battlefields and integrated into the war plans. . . . In the tense atmosphere of a crisis, each side will feel pressure to delegate authority to fire nuclear war weapons to battlefield commanders. As the likelihood of attack increases, these commanders will face a desperate dilemma: use them or lose them.[11]

*Nuclear accidents.* An accidental nuclear detonation has never officially taken place, although both Russia and the United States have come close. In several cases, the conventional explosive that is part of a nuclear weapon has detonated, scattering large amounts of radioactive material. Furthermore, nuclear-armed bombers and submarines have crashed, exploded, and/or sunk. Given the chaos that doubtlessly would follow an accidental nuclear explosion, it is always possible that such an event would lead to retaliation. A full-fledged nuclear detonation would dwarf such accidents as those that occurred at the Three Mile Island (United States), Chernobyl (Ukraine, at the time part of the Soviet Union), and Fukushima (Japan) nuclear power plants. Nor is the United States immune from possible nuclear blunders: In 2007, a B-52 bomber flew from North Dakota to Louisiana carrying five armed nuclear warheads, apparently unbeknownst to the crew or any other authorities. The plane and its lethal cargo remained unguarded on a runway for 11 hours before the situation was discovered. Moreover, if a nuclear explosion occurred during a time of international tension, the consequences may well be extremely grave for all parties.

*Unauthorized use, "loose nukes," and nuclear terrorism.* Both the United States and Russia until the late 1990s kept relatively tight, centralized control over their nuclear weapons, in an effort to make certain that they will be employed only if appropriate orders are given by the highest level of political leadership. Numerous fail-safe devices are incorporated into U.S. weapons design, and until the 1990s it was widely assumed that comparable controls existed on the Russians' part as well. However, there is no guarantee that something could not go wrong, and as a result, someone relatively low in military/political rank could wind up starting a nuclear war.

Since the collapse of the Soviet Union in 1991, the danger of "loose nukes" not subject to stringent command and control procedures has emerged as a major worry, in response to which the United States has invested hundreds of millions of dollars in its "Fissile Material Disposition" and "Global Threat Reduction" programs, designed to improve security around nuclear facilities in the former Soviet Union, as well as transporting high level nuclear materials for disposal. It remains debatable, however, whether these measures have been adequate to the task.

Adding to the uncertainty is the continuing possibility that fissionable materials could be stolen and then fabricated into nuclear weapons or even that small nuclear bombs or warheads could be sold to interested buyers. It is often rumored that nuclear weapons formerly under Soviet hands are for sale to the highest bidder. It has also been suggested that, given the economic and social decline of post-Soviet Russia, formerly well-paid weapons designers have become willing to sell their expertise to the highest bidder. It is also conceivable that governments or terrorist groups could steal ready-made bombs, warheads, or bomb-ready fissile material while they are in transit or in storage depots. It is widely acknowledged, for example, that Israel's nuclear weapons program benefited when that country commandeered a shipload of enriched uranium in the late 1960s. In addition, governments could purchase ready-made nuclear weapons: At one time, Libya, for example, attempted unsuccessfully to buy nuclear bombs from China.

Finally, since September 11, 2001, there have been numerous successful terrorist attacks on major Western (including the United States, the United Kingdom, and Spain) and Western-allied (Indonesia, Turkey, India, and Morocco) "soft," or civilian, targets. There have also been an unknown number of aborted, alleged terrorist attacks in the making (in Germany, the United Kingdom, the United States, etc.). Still, many Western terrorism "experts" believe it is only a matter of time before subnational terrorist groups succeed in acquiring and/or detonating nuclear devices, dirty bombs (that would spew radioactive materials, although without a nuclear explosion), and/or other weapons of mass destruction.

Enormous resources are being devoted by law enforcement, military, information technology, intelligence-gathering, counterterrorist, and customs agencies to prevent nuclear and weapons of mass destruction (WMD) attacks by official and as-yet-unknown terrorist groups. But if these prevention and interdiction measures should fail—even once—there will be tremendous pressure on the government of the attacked nation to retaliate quickly and with overwhelming force (as there was on the United States immediately after the terrorist attack of 9/11). The deployment of nuclear weapons against the alleged perpetrators of a nuclear terrorist attack might be done by decision makers who are understandably angry, but it might not be the most prudent or rational course of action. And it might result in such potentially catastrophic unintended (but foreseeable) consequences as massive civilian casualties and global thermonuclear war.

*Irrational use.* It can readily be argued that *any* use of nuclear weapons constitutes irrational use. Beyond this, however, the possibility also exists that those persons exercising the highest political authority may themselves go insane or behave irrationally. Many famous leaders throughout history were severely emotionally disturbed and/or experienced psychotic episodes: Caligula, Nero, and probably Adolf Hitler and Joseph Stalin as well. Woodrow Wilson and

Dwight Eisenhower suffered serious strokes while in office, which compromised their ability to perform their duties and to think clearly. During the final days before resigning his presidency in 1974, Richard Nixon is said to have acted irrationally, possibly due in large measure to the stress of the Watergate investigations. No precedent and no set of guidelines currently exists for countermanding the orders of a sitting president, no matter how dangerous or unwise such orders might be, and the use of nuclear weapons could legally be ordered without a formal declaration of war by Congress and even without any prior consultation. In other nuclear states, including Russia, China, India, Pakistan, and Israel, the possibility of unnerved political decision makers, or "rogue officers," authorizing the use of nuclear and/or other weapons of mass destruction is at least as high as in the United States.

*False alarms.* One of the most chilling—because the most likely—scenario for nuclear war involves failure in the command, control, communications, and intelligence (C3I) systems of a nuclear state. Before the nuclear age, countries worried about being the victims of a surprise attack, as happened to the United States at Pearl Harbor and to the Soviet Union when Germany suddenly invaded it in June 1941. In the era of nuclear weapons, a danger even greater than surprise attack, paradoxically, is that one side—thinking it is under attack—may "retaliate" when in fact it had not actually been attacked at all or, in the case of a nuclear and/or WMD attack by unidentified terrorists, may retaliate massively against a nation or people unconnected with the initial attack.

The leadership of all nuclear states is essentially hostage to the correct functioning of their warning systems. And during times of international stress or crisis, this connection may be especially perilous. Thus, there have been many false alarms: According to the Senate Armed Services Committee, there were 151 "serious" nuclear false alarms and 3,703 lesser alerts during a (presumably representative) period between January 1979 and July 1980. In the past, radar signals bouncing off the newly risen moon have been taken for enemy missiles, migrating geese have been similarly misinterpreted, and a fire in a Siberian natural gas pipeline set off a satellite sensor, which identified it as the exhausts of a Soviet missile launch. In 1980, a practice war-games tape was erroneously read by military computers as an actual attack, and faulty microchips have several times generated unnecessary alerts.

Because the extreme destructive power of nuclear weapons is combined with exceedingly high speed and short warning times—literally, a matter of minutes—there would be great pressure on decision makers to know quickly whether such an attack is under way and, if so, to respond immediately. In addition, as nuclear delivery systems became increasingly accurate, counterforce weapons have made it more and more feasible (at least in theory) for the attacking side to demolish the victim's nuclear forces. And as that feasibility increases, reports of such an attack become more believable. The result is to put great pressure on a prospective victim to "use it or lose it," with a resulting increased risk of severe miscalculation and premature launch. The hot line between the White House and the Kremlin—installed after the Cuban Missile Crisis—and the crisis control centers are supposed to reduce the danger that similar false alarms will lead to nuclear war by miscalculation. But it remains unclear what sort of communication would reassure a side that believes it is being attacked and feels that it must respond immediately.

*Launch on warning.* Nuclear deterrence depends, essentially, on the other side believing that, if attacked, the victim will retaliate. But as we have also seen, nuclear deterrence must deal with the problem of *credibility:* Having suffered immense destruction in an initial attack, an attacked nation has literally nothing to be gained by retaliating and, moreover, a great deal to lose, if the attacker responds to the victim's retaliation by firing yet more missiles. In addition, the great speed and increasing accuracy of strategic missiles have led some strategic analysts to conclude that, at least in theory, an opponent could target a large proportion of the victim's land-based missiles. So it has been argued that to shore up the credibility of nuclear deterrence, it will always be necessary to employ a system known as *launch on warning,* in which the decision to launch is made upon warning of an attack, rather than waiting until the attacker's warheads have literally begun exploding on the target country's soil. Moreover, to bolster the credibility that the victim will actually make such a retaliation, launch on warning is also often taken to mean that the "decision" to launch will be removed from human beings and placed in the hands of computers, pre-programmed to launch when advised of an impending attack. There have been numerous reports of near launches based on computer, satellite sensor, and/or human mistakes. And with the increased reliance on computer systems (which are never perfect) and the decreased control by Moscow of the nuclear weapons in the former Soviet Union, the danger of nuclear retaliation to "avenge" a real or perceived attack on either side has not decreased since the end of the Cold War and especially since September 11, 2001.

Launch on warning, the supremely "logical" consequence of nuclear deterrence theory itself, thus carries immense dangers. First, it drastically reduces the time span in which a decision must be made—perhaps the most fateful decision in the history of the world. Second, it places the fate of the Earth in the hands of potentially fallible sensor and warning systems. And third, it makes us all dependent on the correct functioning of computers. It is widely acknowledged that Russian, Chinese, Indian, and Pakistani computer systems are less efficient than those computers used by the Pentagon, the United Kingdom, or France, which are themselves hardly fail-safe. Moreover, it seems likely that if other countries (e.g., Iran or North Korea) with less robustly developed technological infrastructure develop their own nuclear arsenals, their "fail-safe" command and control systems will likely be even more vulnerable to accidents and false alarms, especially when and if their governments are engaged in a tense diplomatic, political, and/or military standoff with a nuclear-armed opponent.

# Nuclear Proliferation

We have focused on the two nuclear superpowers because the United States and Russia still account for over 90% of the world's nuclear weapons. In addition, the United States and Russia are primarily responsible for the qualitative as well as the quantitative dimensions of the nuclear arms production. We have accordingly focused on what has been called *vertical proliferation,* the accumulation of weapons and delivery systems by the nuclear superpowers. However, there is substantial reason to be concerned as well about *horizontal proliferation,* the acquisition of nuclear weapons by other, previously nonnuclear countries, especially those with long-standing traditions of hostility between them (such as between India and Pakistan and between Israel and its Middle Eastern neighbors, especially Iran).

There are numerous potential routes to nuclear proliferation, including the following:

1. Buying, stealing, or otherwise obtaining already-made nuclear weapons that are currently deployed or stockpiled by countries now possessing these weapons: This has apparently not happened yet.

2. Somehow obtaining sufficient quantities of plutonium or highly enriched uranium to be able to construct one's own nuclear weapons: It is widely believed that Israel's initial development of nuclear weapons was facilitated by that country's successful diversion of a merchant vessel carrying uranium in the early 1960s.

3. Making illegal or clandestine use of the products of nuclear power plants or research reactors, especially plutonium: Plutonium is unavoidably created in all currently operating reactors, and although it is difficult to safely separate it from other, nonfissile byproducts, it is technically feasible. Importantly, there aren't two distinct kinds of radioactive plutonium: the "good" kind produced in power and research reactors and the "bad" kind, used in nuclear weapons. Rather, there is only one kind of plutonium atom. North Korea's weaponization program was achieved by use of reactor-generated plutonium.

4. Using various chemical and mechanical processes to increase the concentration of uranium-235: Although present in only minute concentrations (less than 1%) in natural uranium ore, once concentrated to 3-5%, U-235 can power nuclear reactors. Increased to 90% or more, it can constitute an atomic bomb. Since all uranium atoms are chemically identical, it is quite difficult to separate U-235 from relatively inert U-238, which makes up the overwhelming bulk of raw uranium ore; however, this can be done using ultra-high-speed centrifuges, which take advantage of the slightly lesser weight of the U-235 isotope. Iran's apparent pursuit of nuclear weapons has largely emphasized this avenue of proliferation.

Regardless of the means of proliferation, there is widespread agreement that especially with the end of the Cold War, horizontal proliferation has equaled if not surpassed vertical proliferation as a source of legitimate anxiety.

But there is also another view. It has been argued that since nuclear weapons, in the hands of the Great Powers, have ostensibly helped "keep the peace," these same weapons, widely proliferated, might conceivably be a stabilizing influence on world affairs. (After all, if the U.S. and Russian publics are supposed to believe that nuclear weapons are good for them, why wouldn't nuclear weapons be equally good for, say, Iran, Nigeria, Iraq, North Korea, Syria, Brazil, South Africa, or Argentina?) This is the so-called porcupine theory, that a world composed of many nuclear-armed states would be a safe one because each state would carefully avoid antagonizing its neighbors, just as porcupines walk in relative safety through the forest. More often, however, the argument is reversed, with the assumption that horizontal proliferation is in fact profoundly dangerous: Insofar as some people argue in favor of certain countries (notably the United States) maintaining its nuclear weapons, how can one legitimately argue against other countries deriving similar benefit from retaining theirs, or, for that matter, what is the basis for opposing nuclear weapons in the hands of any country that might want them?

From the perspective of a would-be proliferator, perhaps even more significant than *how* to "go nuclear" is the question of *whether* to do so. Thus, numerous countries that could readily go nuclear have not done so—Sweden, Canada, Germany, Japan, Australia, the Netherlands, and Switzerland—while others (Ukraine, Kazakhstan, South Africa) have voluntarily given up their nuclear weapons. As the same time, Pakistan and India, with much less-developed economic and technological bases, have joined the nuclear "club," leaving other nations as possible future entrants. On the other hand, Libya, which was widely believed to be capable of developing weapons of mass destruction (WMDs), abandoned its nuclear ambitions—due to the incentives of enhanced market opportunities and security guarantees.

Among the acknowledged nuclear powers, the proliferation path has been much like a chain of dominoes: The United States initiated a nuclear weapons program out of fear of being beaten to the punch by Germany during World War II and to intimidate the Soviet Union; the Soviet Union followed suit, in response to the U.S. nuclear monopoly; China went nuclear largely because of the Soviet Union; India developed nuclear weapons primarily because of China; and Pakistan developed its nuclear arsenal in response to India. For its part, Israel furtively became a nuclear power ostensibly to deter conventional and chemical attacks from its Arab neighbors. If Iran or some other Islamic country were to develop nuclear weapons and the systems to deliver them, the likely rationale would be to "deter" a possible attack by Israel and/or the United States.

As of 2012, Iran has continued to produce and stockpile low enriched uranium in defiance of UN Security Council resolutions that have repeatedly called for a suspension of its sensitive nuclear fuel cycle activities while a diplomatic solution is pursued. Even as international sanctions were heightened, the Iranian government expanded its nuclear infrastructure, especially the use of high-speed centrifuges to produce increasingly concentrated Uranium-235, the prime ingredient in atomic bombs and warheads. This action was counter to demands from the International Atomic Energy Agency (IAEA) that Iran abide by its treaty obligations with regard to nuclear safeguards. It has also led to the complaint that Iran (like North Korea) has been partaking of a classic "run-out-the-clock" strategy, engaging in time-consuming negotiations while simultaneously defying the international community by moving toward a nuclear "break out." Tehran has also announced an intention to accelerate uranium enrichment of uranium to the 20% level, which exceeds the 5% level justified for nuclear power generation and can plausibly be explained only by the fact that stockpiling 20%-enriched uranium would shorten the time needed to convert such material to weapons grade, should that country decide to make a quick dash to nuclear weapons capability. In turn, this heightens the risk that Israel and/or the United States might attempt a military strike in addition to cyberattacks, to preempt such a development.

It remains to be seen whether Iran intends to become a nuclear-armed state, or whether its government plans to use the threat of doing so as a lever by which to negotiate certain benefits from the international community, action criticized by some as blackmail but considered by others to be *Realpolitik*. Either way, it is a dangerous "game," since threatened proliferation by a country (e.g., Iran) that also expresses belligerent antagonism toward another country (Israel) runs the risk of evoking a pre-emptive attack, with unforeseeable consequences for the region and the world.

The possibility also exists that if Iran develops nuclear weapons, other Middle East countries will follow suit. This is because there are substantial ethnic and religious differences and competition between Iran and most other Middle East states (Iran is largely Shi'ite, whereas most Arab countries are largely Sunni, and Iranians are ethnically Persian, not Arab). Saudi Arabia and Egypt, in particular, have threatened to respond with their own nuclear programs if Iran develops and deploys its own nuclear arsenal. Similarly, even though North Korea's nuclear arsenal is small and of uncertain reliability—plus it lacks suitable delivery vehicles—its nuclearization has already begun pressuring South Korean militarists to do the same. Japan, also, feels threatened by further nuclear "advances" on the part of North Korea, although thus far, that country has effectively resisted calls for nuclearization from the far right, in large part because its history of experiencing the nuclear destruction of Hiroshima and Nagasaki in the last days of World War II has to date immunized that country against developing its own indigenous nuclear force. A disastrous near-meltdown, with substantial release of nuclear radioactivity at Japan's Fukushima power plant following a massive tsunami in 2011 has also reduced the likelihood that Japan will "go nuclear" . . . at least for the immediate future.

In some cases of proliferation, states went nuclear after they discovered that the nuclear superpowers could not be counted on to provide a "nuclear guarantee"—that is, to risk nuclear war on their behalf. Nuclear states cannot really be blamed for hesitating to run such a grave risk as nuclear war, even on behalf of an ally. The problem is closely intertwined with that of state sovereignty: States insist on their absolute sovereignty and freedom of action in a world that is increasingly interdependent and in which *globalization* is the latest buzzword.

There is also another, more general motivation behind would-be proliferators: pride and political status. Britain and France, for example, had little strategic motivation for developing their own nuclear arsenals, but both countries in the 1950s and 1960s were contending with the dismantling of their overseas empires and with the psychological stress of having to forgo their previous position as "Great Powers." If it possesses nuclear weapons, a state is virtually guaranteed a place in world councils, and it should not be surprising that many leaders in less economically advanced nations believe that their country, their people, and their culture deserve the same recognition that more affluent societies have arrogated to themselves.

In addition, international events in the early 21st century appear to have exerted additional pressure in favor of nuclear proliferation. Thus, it was not lost on the political leaders of North Korea and Iran that the U.S. invasion of Iraq and Afghanistan would probably not have occurred had those countries possessed their own nuclear arsenals. Combined with a willingness on the part of the United States to support "regime change," it is not unlikely that the governments in North Korea and Iran have concluded that acquiring nuclear weapons may be in their national interest.

Many legitimate reasons for opposing nuclear proliferation exist, including the following:

1. As more people, small groups, and political-religious organizations have their "finger on the button," it becomes more likely that someone, somewhere, will for some reason press it.

2. In many less economically developed countries, political power is held by military dictators and political autocrats who are not accountable to their citizenry, who have obtained power without democratic checks and balances, and who may be psychologically unstable.

3. Countries with a limited technological base may be hesitant to invest heavily in various "fail-safe" protective devices, thereby increasing the danger of accidental detonations, unauthorized use, or war by false alarm. Subnational groups are virtually certain not to do so.

4. According to standard deterrence theory, states with a very small nuclear arsenal may actually be more at risk of preemptive attack than those having an ability to absorb such an attack and then retaliate. In this sense, it is paradoxically true that a comparatively large nuclear arsenal may actually lead to greater "crisis stability" than a small arsenal of the sort North Korea currently possesses and Iran would have, as well, if it continues down that path. Moreover, for their part, terrorist organizations probably are unconcerned with retaliation.

5. Many would-be proliferators are currently engaged in active or smoldering hostilities directly on their borders. This is especially the case along the India-Pakistan border, the Israel-Palestinian conflict, and in the republics in and near the former Soviet Union. Terrorist groups might well make use of nuclear weapons if they obtain them or engage in nuclear blackmail.

The existing nuclear powers have a shared interest in restricting nuclear proliferation, and they have established an international framework toward that end, the Non-Proliferation Treaty (NPT), which, regrettably, has not been signed by India, Pakistan, or Israel, and from which North Korea has withdrawn. Signatories agree to forgo nuclear ambitions (if they are nuclear "have-not" states) and to permit inspection of their declared nuclear facilities, whereas states possessing nuclear weapons agree to cooperate in sharing nuclear power technology with the latter. This itself is problematic, since there is no clear dividing line between the technology necessary for nuclear power and that which enables the development of nuclear weapons. In addition, nuclear states are bound by the NPT to make good-faith efforts to reduce and eventually eliminate their nuclear arsenals. Thus, today's nuclear powers are ill situated to criticize other countries for seeking to obtain nuclear weapons so long as they continue to add to and modernize their own vast arsenals: "Do as I say," they appear to be pronouncing, "not as I do."

In addition to continuing anxiety about possible nuclear proliferation itself, there is, ironically, a growing risk that efforts to *prevent* proliferation might themselves precipitate conventional war—or that claims of would-be proliferation will serve as a trumped-up excuse for such war. In 1981, Israeli warplanes destroyed an Iraqi nuclear reactor, evidently in an effort to prevent Iraq from developing nuclear weapons. A similar attack occurred again in 2007, with Israeli warplanes this time attacking a facility in Syria believed to be associated with nuclear weapons. The United States government claimed Iraqi possession of "weapons of mass destruction" as the major justification for its invasion of Iraq in 2003 and has since threatened war with North Korea and Iran over their nuclear weapons programs.

A detailed report prepared by the Institute for Science and International Security concluded that

Despite the current political dialogue in Israel and the United States about a growing urgency to strike Iran, short of full-scale war or occupation, most military options are oversold as to their ability to end or even significantly delay Iran's nuclear program. Limited bombing campaigns are unlikely to destroy Iran's main capability to produce weapon-grade uranium. . . . More importantly, Iran has mastered the construction of centrifuges and has likely even secretly stockpiled an unknown number. . . . An ineffective bombing campaign that does not eliminate these capabilities would leave Iran able to quickly rebuild its program and would motivate it to launch its own Manhattan Project, resulting in a Middle East region that is far more dangerous and unstable.[12]

To the foregoing must be added the likely costs of precipitating conventional war in the Middle East, with all its unpredictable consequences. In the meanwhile, nonproliferation efforts short of military strikes directed at Iran (and likely to be encountered by other would-be proliferators in the future) have included strenuous economic and political sanctions and inspection of ships and planes bound for Iran, as well as other, illegal but widely acknowledged measures such as cyberattacks (e.g., the "Stuxnet" computer worm, believed to have been engineered by Israel and the United States, which partially disabled Iranian uranium enrichment facilities) and even the assassination of Iranian military officials and leading nuclear scientists.

Less prominent than nuclear proliferation as such, but nearly as important, is proliferation of "delivery systems" (most commonly ballistic missiles) capable of conveying nuclear warheads to a potential target. First generation nuclear weapons—of the sort developed by North Korea, for example—are too large and heavy to be placed atop a missile; with increasing sophistication, however, the warheads are miniaturized and thus rendered more "deliverable." In this regard, much international attention focused on North Korea's test launch of a long-range missile in 2012. Although ostensibly intended for placing a weather satellite in Earth's orbit, the reality is that any missile capable of doing this is also capable of delivering a nuclear warhead at intercontinental range. The North Korean launch was a failure; however, it may herald more such efforts in the future. [13]

There have also been clear signs of an emerging "missile race" in south Asia. In 2012, India successfully launched a ballistic missile capable of reaching Shanghai and Beijing, thereby joining the small group of nations (all nuclear-capable) that also possess long-range missiles: China, the United Kingdom, France, Russia, Israel, and the United States. This, in turn, threatens to provoke an arms race between the two Asian giants, India and China. Further emphasizing the growing militarization of this region is the fact that India has become the world's most active weapons importer, while pressure mounts in Japan and South Korea (both of whose industrial infrastructures are capable of expanding into missile design and production) to join their Asian neighbors/competitors.

The horror of nuclear war is so great that fear of nuclear weapons (with or without suitable delivery systems) falling "into the wrong hands" seems likely to induce instability in the future, along with the possible need for even well-intentioned governments to decide whether to risk "preemptive" war as a preventive measure. This raises the question of whether nuclear weapons can ever be "in the right hands."

## Other Proliferation Problems

In addition to the problem of nuclear proliferation, there are other, related issues, notably the proliferation of chemical or biological warfare capabilities, of conventional weapons with near-nuclear effects, and of ballistic missile and land- and/or space-based antimissile and antisatellite technology. Chemical weapons have been called the "poor man's atomic bomb," and in fact, the manufacture of highly toxic chemical munitions is relatively easy and inexpensive. Iraq used such weapons against Iran and its own Kurdish rebels and may have attempted to use them during the Gulf War; Libya—assisted by a German chemical firm—constructed a chemical warfare facility, which has subsequently been dismantled. France, Russia, and the United States have maintained large chemical weapons stockpiles until very recently. Of these, the U.S. arsenal has been the most sophisticated, consisting of "binary" chemicals, two subcomponents that are not lethal in themselves but become highly toxic when combined immediately prior to use.

The major holders of these weapons have indicated their intention of destroying their chemical arsenals, but not all have done so, while others—notably Syria and Iran—have developed their own. In the final years of the Clinton administration and continuing through the two terms of George W. Bush's administration, official U.S. doctrine came to include the implied threat that the United States might employ nuclear weapons in response to nonnuclear—chemical and/or biological—attacks against its interests. Although this policy was rescinded under President

Barack Obama, it was matched by the declaration of the Russian government under Vladimir Putin that Russia might use nuclear weapons to defend itself against a nonnuclear attack, a significant change in policy from its avowed "no first use" doctrine of the latter half of the 20th century. Just as chemical and biological weapons have been called the "poor man's nuclear weapons," nuclear weapons themselves have become—for some would-be proliferators in particular—a "poor man's conventional weapons," since expensive and dangerous as they are, they may actually be cheaper (more "bang for the buck") than conventional armaments.

## What Might Be Done

While it is beyond the scope of this book to detail all the possible ways of reducing the risk of nuclear war, a few basic possibilities can be described. Naturally, these vary in their desirability and feasibility.

1. Rely even more heavily on nuclear weapons, in the hope of increasing whatever benefits they are presumed to have provided thus far. This might include encouraging the spread of nuclear weapons to other, currently nonnuclear countries, consistent with the idea that a nuclear armed world would be one in which countries avoided antagonizing each other

2. Continue with the status quo, hoping that catastrophe will somehow be averted—as, according to traditional deterrence theory, it has been in the past.

3. Engage in a vigorous effort at nuclear arms control via international treaties, including restrictions on bomb and warhead testing and development as well as reductions in the allowable numbers of delivery vehicles.

4. Move away from the current focus on peace via traditional nuclear deterrence, especially as this doctrine was established during the Cold War vis-à-vis the Soviet Union. Shakespeare's play, *The Winter's Tale*, includes this famous stage direction, which generations of theater professionals have struggled to represent on stage: "Exit, pursued by a bear." Rethinking current nuclear strategy would require going beyond decades of assumptions about the need to structure such weaponry and doctrine in response to the West being pursued by the Russian Bear. Although the Cold War is over, it persists in determining (and, possibly deforming) the thinking of many of today's strategic analysts and weapons procurers.

5. Engage in a vigorous policy of de-alerting, thereby interjecting more time before nuclear weapons can be employed. This could involve physically storing bombs and warheads separately from their delivery vehicles, imposing greater code restrictions on their arming and actual use, removing guidance systems from missiles, pinning open the switches that fire missile motors. Such actions would not only diminish the likelihood of nuclear war by accident or false alarm, they would also enhance the confidence of all sides that others are unlikely to attempt a surprise attack, or to "retaliate" in advance of having been attacked.

6. Encourage the further spread of nuclear-free zones, regions within which—by treaty—(as in Latin America and New Zealand) no nuclear weapons are permitted. This would require willingness to engage in the latest in verification technology (a robust international monitoring system is already in place, capable of identifying very small nuclear tests as well as test missile launches), including submission to onsite inspection.

7. Engage in unilateral reductions in nuclear weaponry, including delivery systems. Given the excessive numbers of both—especially within the arsenals of the United States and Russia—either side could afford to initiate substantial reductions without compromising its security. The likelihood, in fact, is that such actions would stimulate other countries to do the same. By contrast, so long as the nuclear powers jealously guard their arsenals, other countries can scarcely be blamed for doing the same, or planning to increase their holdings.

8. Encourage an international environment that helps delegitimize any reliance upon nuclear weapons. Although such an approach would not be sufficient in itself, and may appear to rely on wishful thinking, it is worth noting, for example, that it is virtually inconceivable that France and the United Kingdom would now go to war, even though they have a long history of violent competition. Various "soft power" connections (economic, social, cultural, and political ties) between the two countries have made war unimaginable. Similarly, the likelihood is quite low that poison gas or biological weapons will be used in the future, largely because social and cultural norms have rendered their employment "beyond the pale." By the same token, it is altogether possible that vigorous worldwide public efforts to label nuclear weapons "uncivilized" and "unacceptable" could have the practical effect of literally making their use inconceivable by any civilized society, thereby making their development, deployment, and—most important—their use extremely unlikely. Perhaps we should take President Obama's calls for a nuclear-free world literally—and demand follow-up actions to make this "dream" come true.

In 2012, U. S. Congressman Edward Markey introduced model legislation called the Smarter Approach to Nuclear Expenditures (SANE) Act. It would have cut $100 billion from the U.S. nuclear weapons budget over the next decade by delaying a proposed new bomber program, ending the nuclear mission of strategic bombers, delaying the purchase of new nuclear armed Trident submarines, and reducing the current U.S. strategic SLBM holdings. "America's nuclear weapons budget is locked in a Cold War time machine," the congressman noted at the time. "It doesn't reflect our twenty-first-century security needs. It makes no sense. It's insane."

He went on to explain: "It's insane to spend $10 billion building new plants to make uranium and plutonium for new nuclear bombs when we're cutting our nuclear arsenal and the plants we have now work just fine." Furthermore: "It's insane that we're going to spend $84 billion for up to fourteen new nuclear submarines when just one sub, with 96 nuclear bombs on board, can blow up every major city in Iran, China and North Korea." Finally, "it is insane to spend hundreds of billions on new nuclear bombs and delivery systems . . . while seeking to cut Medicare, Medicaid and social programs that millions of Americans depend on."

## A FINAL NOTE ON NUCLEAR WEAPONS

There is an ancient Chinese proverb: "Unless we change direction, we shall end up where we are headed." The proliferation of nuclear weapons and of other weapons of mass destruction—both vertically and horizontally—poses the most serious imaginable threat to human beings and to the planet. As we have emphasized, a world that is truly at peace must be more than one not actively at war. It is our planet, our lives, and we have the right, even the duty, to aim high. Yet, when it comes to nuclear weapons, the narrow goal of simply preventing war is so essential that it seems satisfactory as an end in itself. Given the extraordinary dangers of nuclear war, however, mere prevention—from day to day, year to year—is not sufficient; we must aim for a higher degree of confidence. Undoubtedly, any satisfactory solution to the nuclear dilemma must be political and ethical, not just technological. But at the same time, peace in the nuclear age utterly demands the elimination of the nuclear threat itself. In the long run, nothing less will do.

"We are not condemned to repeat the lessons of 40 years at the nuclear brink," said General Lee Butler, former commander of the U.S. Strategic Air Command, in a speech at the State of the World Forum, in San Francisco, in 1996. "We can do better than condone a world in which nuclear weapons are enshrined as the ultimate arbiter of conflict. The price already paid is too dear, the risks run too great. The nuclear beast must be chained, its soul expunged, its lair laid waste. The task is daunting but we cannot shrink from it. The opportunity may not come again."

## NOTES

1.  Quoted in L. Groves. 1962. *Now It Can Be Told.* New York: Harper & Row.

2.  Frank Chinnock. 1969. *Nagasaki: The Forgotten Bomb.* New York: World.

3.  From John Hersey. 1946. *Hiroshima.* New York: Modern Library.

4.  From M. Hachiya. 1955. *Hiroshima Diary.* Chapel Hill: University of North Carolina Press.

5.  From a speech delivered by Lord Mountbatten in Strasbourg, France, 1979.

6.  Quoted in Robert Scheer. 1982. *With Enough Shovels.* New York: Random House.

7.  Henry Kissinger. 1957. *Nuclear Weapons and Foreign Policy.* New York: Norton.

8.  Quoted in Scheer. *With Enough Shovels.*

9.  Bernard Brodie. 1946. *The Absolute Weapon.* New York: Harcourt Brace Jovanovich.

10. Robert McNamara. 1968. *The Essence of Security.* New York: Harper & Row.

11. Robert McNamara. 1986. *Blundering Into Disaster: Surviving the First Century of the Nuclear Age.* New York: Pantheon.

12. D. Albright, P. Brannan, A. Stricker C. Walrond, and H. Wood. 2012. "Preventing Iran From Getting Nuclear Weapons." Institute for Science and International Security: Washington, DC.

13. Worth noting: For this failed launch, North Korea had constructed a new site near the Chinese border, at a cost of about $400 million; the rocket itself likely cost another $450 million, and one consequence of the test was the loss of previously agreed-upon food aid from the United States, worth another $200 million. Thus, altogether the effective cost of this event exceeded $1 billion . . . for a country unable even to feed its own people.

## QUESTIONS FOR FURTHER REFLECTION

1.  What are the justifications for the development, possession, and deployment of nuclear and other weapons of mass destruction? How do you evaluate them?

2.  What are the rationales for the reduction and elimination of nuclear and WMD arsenals? How do you assess them?

3   Is nuclear proliferation inevitable? Is it desirable?

4. Would the world be safer with a few, many, or no nuclear weapons?

5. Were the atomic bombings of Hiroshima and Nagasaki justified? Is there a circumstance today that would justify the use of nuclear weapons?

## SUGGESTIONS FOR FURTHER READING

Jeremy Bernstein. 2010. *Nuclear Weapons: What You Need to Know*. Cambridge MA: Cambridge University Press.

Michael E. Brown, Owen R. Coté, Jr., Sean M. Lynn-Jones, and Steven E. Miller, eds. 2010. *Going Nuclear: Nuclear Proliferation and International Security in the 21st Century*. Cambridge, MA: The MIT Press.

Jonathan Schell. 2000. *The Fate of the Earth and the Abolition*. Stanford, CA: Stanford University Press.

Karl Jaspers. 1961. *The Future of Mankind*. Trans. E. B. Ashton. Chicago: University of Chicago Press.

Michio Kaku and David Axelrod. 1987. *To Win a Nuclear War: The Pentagon's Secret War Plans*. Boston: South End Press.

Robert Jay Lifton and Richard Falk. 1982. *Indefensible Weapons: The Political and Psychological Case Against Nuclearism*. New York: Basic Books.

Ron Rosenbaum. 2012. *How the End Begins: The Road to a Nuclear World War III*. New York: Simon & Schuster.

The Weapons of Mass Destruction Commission. 2006. *Weapons of Terror: Freeing the World of Nuclear, Biological and Chemical Arms*. Stockholm, Sweden: WMDC.

# PART II

# The Reasons for Wars

*The central reality of our time is that the advent of globalization and the revolution in information technology have magnified both the creative and destructive potential of every individual, tribe, and nation on our planet.*

—President Bill Clinton

In Part I, we presented an overview of peace and war. The absence of war is a necessary but not a sufficient condition for the realization of peace. It is insufficient because a life without war can nonetheless also be lacking in peace. But at the same time, the prevention of war is necessary if any meaningful peace is ever to be achieved. Enduring peace simply cannot coexist with war. And so our hopes for peace, and our work toward it, must take account of war; in particular, we must turn to the reasons for wars, if our suggestions, means, and goals are to enjoy any realistic prospect of success.

For too long, students of peace—in their legitimate eagerness to embrace a new and more peaceful world—have abandoned the understanding of war and other forms of violent human conflict to their "hardheaded," "realistic" colleagues in the more traditional academic disciplines of political science, security studies, and international relations. As a result of this division of responsibility, while centers for strategic studies and the like engage in the planning and legitimation of war and other acts of government-initiated violence, many people in peace and conflict studies and in peace movements spend much time trying to conceptualize peace while avoiding the very real problems of war and violence. In doing so, they have run the risk of becoming increasingly marginalized, not only in academic circles but also with respect to their potential influence in the real world. This is not to propose that peace and conflict studies students and teachers should become handmaidens of the academic war establishment, whether cold or hot; rather, they should get to know their "enemy." And that enemy, more than anything else, is violence and war.

"War" does not exist; there are, rather, individual wars. And just as the species *Homo sapiens* does not, per se, exist, there are, rather, individual people. Furthermore, it is far easier to understand individual people than to encompass the complexity and diversity of the more than 7 billion souls who constitute the human species. Just as we can make useful generalizations about the human species, we can do the same about the "species" of violent human conflict known as war.

In doing so, it is helpful to distinguish between the *real* or *underlying reasons* (or what in much of the relevant literature has been referred to as the *causes*) of a particular war and the *ostensible reasons* (or pretexts) for such wars. The former refer to the underlying factors that actually give rise to the war; the latter refer to the propagandistic excuses frequently enunciated by governments to justify their actions. We are primarily concerned in this part of the book with the reasons for wars, insofar as they can be identified. Then in Part III of this book, we assess various suggestions for preventing war. The task is daunting. Indeed, trying to specify the reasons for war generally—that is, the motives that led decision makers to make war or even just the causes of any one war—is a bit like the story of the blind men and the elephant by the 19th-century American John Saxe:

It was six men from Industan, to learning much inclined,

Who went to see the elephant (though all of them were blind)

That each by observation might satisfy his mind. . . .

Not surprisingly, each one felt a different part so that the one touching the legs thought they were tree trunks, the one touching the tail thought it was a snake, etc.

And so, at the end, they disputed loud and long,

Each in his opinion stiff and strong,

Though each was partly in the right, and all of them were wrong.[1]

In reviewing the various proposed reasons for wars, we shall proceed from the most reductionistic interpretations to the most inclusive. Thus, we begin with an examination of the reasons for wars at the personal level, moving through a consideration of wars among small groups of preindustrial and nontechnological peoples to the functioning of large, advanced social units and nation-states. Then we examine decision making by national leaders, assess the role of social and economic factors, and finally summarize the reasons for wars. Although we shall necessarily consider these explanations one at a time, let us try to avoid the blind men's blunder by recognizing at the outset that war, like an elephant, is a complex and integrated phenomenon, which to be understood must be taken in its entirety and with a hefty dose of humility.

Consider, for example, that someone has just died. We might ask, "What was the cause of death?" And perhaps we are told, "He died of disease." "What kind of disease?" "Heart disease." "What was the nature of the heart disease?" "Hardening of the arteries leading to a massive stroke—that is, a coronary thrombosis." And if we then inquire, "What was the cause of that?" we are likely to get any number of answers: poor dietary habits, a genetic predisposition to high cholesterol levels, a lack of regular medical care, too much stress, a history of heavy smoking and not enough exercise, and so forth. One of these might be the precipitating factor, but it is most likely that several of them, taken in combination, were ultimately responsible. The social, psychological, and historical reasons for wars can be at least as complex as the physical causes of one person's death.

We should also keep in mind the logical distinction between *necessary* and *sufficient* conditions. Thus, for war to occur, it may be necessary for human beings to exist in societies, but it certainly is not sufficient—there are human societies that have apparently never known war.

Similarly, it may be necessary for individuals to be motivated so as to participate in the preparations and conduct of war, but once again, this is not sufficient—people often get angry, but this does not necessarily mean that their country goes to war as a result. Moreover, wars often occur without very much personal anger being involved.

Every scholar of peace and war, it appears, has a different framework for understanding the reasons for organized human violence. Peace and conflict historian Quincy Wright, for example, identified four major factors—idealistic, psychological, political, and legalistic—arguing that

> individuals and masses have been moved to war (1) because of enthusiasm for ideals expressed in the impersonal symbols of a religion, a nation, an empire, a civilization, or humanity, the blessings of which it is thought may be secured or spread by coercion of the recalcitrant [idealistic]; or (2) because of the hope to escape from conditions which they find unsatisfactory, inconvenient, perplexing, unprofitable, intolerable, dangerous, or merely boring [psychological]. Conditions of this kind have produced unrest and have facilitated the acceptance of ideals and violent methods for achieving them. Governments and organized factions have initiated war (3) because in a particular situation war appeared to them a necessary or convenient means to carry out a foreign policy, to establish, maintain, or expand the power of a government, party, or class within the state; to maintain or expand the power of the state in relation to other states; or to reorganize the community of nations [political]; or (4) because incidents have occurred or circumstances have arisen which they thought violated law and impaired rights and for which war was the normal or expected remedy according to the jural standards of the time [legalistic].[2]

Although there is disagreement over the most useful way to categorize the reasons for wars, there is consensus that every war—just like every human being—must have progenitors. Efforts at identifying warmongering culprits, as individuals rather than impersonal forces, have been especially frequent in the aftermath of every major war. One scholar described the chronology of such culprit hunting as follows:

> In the eighteenth century many philosophers thought that the ambitions of absolute monarchs were the main cause of war: pull down the mighty, and wars would become rare. Another theory contended that many wars came from the Anglo-French rivalry for colonies and commerce: restrain that quest, and peace would be more easily preserved. The wars following the French Revolution fostered an idea that popular revolutions were becoming the main cause of international war. In the nineteenth century, monarchs who sought to unite their troubled country by a glorious foreign war were widely seen as culprits. At the end of that century the capitalists' chase for markets or investment outlets became a popular villain. The First World War convinced many writers that armaments races and arms salesmen had become the villains, and both world wars fostered the idea that militarist regimes were the main disturbers of the peace.[3]

Similarly, the Vietnam War—to take just one example—was said to have been caused by

> the desire of American capitalists for markets and investment outlets, by the pressures for markets and investment outlets, by the pressures of American military suppliers, by the American hostility to communism, by the crusading ambitions of Moscow and Peking, the aggressive nationalism or communism of Hanoi, the corruption or aggression of Saigon, or the headlong clash of other aims.[4]

Clearly, for the Vietnam War—or just about any other—a host of different causes can be identified, many of which might be operating simultaneously, some of which may involve individuals, and others of which may pose more frustrating and faceless considerations. In their yearning for truth, however, many people are dissatisfied with complex, multifactorial explanations. For example, it is tempting to say that the country that initiates a war is the one that "started" it and, therefore, the one that "caused" it—that is, the culprit. But the real world is rarely this simple.

When the United States "started" the War of 1812 with Britain, it was at least partly in response to the impressment of American sailors by British naval forces. (It was also in part because of U.S. imperialistic designs on British Canada.) And although nearly everyone considers that Nazi Germany initiated the European part of World War II, the fact remains that Britain and France first declared war on Germany, not the other way around—but only after Germany invaded Poland in 1939.

Wars, in short, often occur as a result of preexisting antagonisms that lead to provocations so that the underlying reasons for a war may lie further back in time. And of course, those provocations are themselves the result of yet earlier factors. The German invasion of Poland, for example, was itself "caused" in part by Britain and France's earlier appeasement of Hitler, which convinced the German leader that aggression against Poland would go unpunished. Meanwhile, Hitler's aggressive and expansionist policies were also "caused," at least in part, not only by his own personal idiosyncrasies but also by German anger over the terms of the Treaty of Versailles, which ended World War I. And so it has gone.

The dominant Western conception of causality requires that for every effect (including war), there must be a preexisting cause. It also suggests that this cause should be clear-cut, direct, and linear. Even if we grant the legitimacy of cause and effect, however, there is no reason why reasons—especially for something so complicated as war—should not be diffuse, indirect, curvilinear, and multifaceted. In short, war is, to borrow the psychoanalytic term, *overdetermined*; it has multiple reasons for its existence, both in general and in specific violent conflicts.

But this is not to claim that efforts to answer the question "Why war?" are a waste of time, even though the results can sometimes be misleading. Out of that search can come a deeper appreciation of the devastating conundrum that is war. Moreover, our judgment as to the reasons for war will have great influence on our preferred methods for preventing specific wars and our hopes for eliminating war altogether.

## NOTES

1. John Saxe. 1892. "The Blind Men and the Elephant." *The Poetical Works of John Godfrey Saxe*. Boston: Houghton.

2. Quincy Wright. 1966. "Analysis of the Causes of War." In R. Falk and S. Mendlovitz, eds., *Toward a Theory of War Prevention*. New York: World Law Fund.

3. Geoffrey Blainey. 1973. *The Causes of War*. New York: Free Press.

4. Ibid.

# CHAPTER 6

# THE INDIVIDUAL LEVEL

Small arms are the principal weapon of choice in acts of individual aggression.

*Source:* Istock/Vinicius Ramalho Tupinamba.

> *A weapon is an enemy even to its owner.*
>
> —Turkish proverb

Wars require the organized activity of large numbers of people. But even the facts of complex organization and massive numbers do not eliminate the personal involvement and responsibility of individuals. To some degree, individual people acquiesce to war, prepare for it, and often participate in it, either passively (by permitting it to occur) or actively (by providing material assistance or actually doing the fighting). If individuals didn't allow, encourage, or engage in them, wars wouldn't happen. Hence, without denying the importance of other dimensions—which we shall explore in subsequent chapters—our search for the reasons for wars will commence by looking to the inclinations and behavior of individual people.

The preamble to the constitution of the United Nations Educational, Scientific, and Cultural Organization (UNESCO) states that "wars begin in the minds of men" (and, we must add, women, although possibly to a somewhat lesser extent). It takes no great stretch of imagination to charge the human psyche with prime responsibility for the initiation of war.

Former senator J. William Fulbright emphasized the personal dimension of war making (and, thus, war preventing) when he wrote:

> The first, indispensable step toward the realization of a new concept of community in the world is the acquisition of a new dimension of self-understanding. We have got to understand . . . why it is, psychologically and biologically, that men and nations fight; why it is . . . that they always find *something* to fight about.[1]

When we concern ourselves with peace and war, we normally talk about the actions of large social units, often entire countries. But, at least in part, when we say that a social unit "acts" in a particular way, what we really mean is that many individuals within those units act in such a manner. Thus, we say that the state acts, often meaning that the people within it—especially decision makers in and outside the government—act.

First, we focus on the level of the individual person: instinct theory, sociobiology (and evolutionary psychology), Freudian and post-Freudian psychoanalysis, and the postulation of innate human depravity. These perspectives, while differing in significant ways, share an emphasis on the role of inborn, biological factors. Then, after considering some criticisms of these "human nature" approaches, we consider a variety of other factors believed to operate at the individual level, all of which involve greater attention to social experiences.

# Aggression, Drives, and Instincts

Many thinkers have assumed human beings to be instinctively aggressive. A particularly influential version of instinctivist theory has developed around presumed biological traits of the human species. Thus, Hans Morgenthau's extremely influential textbook on international relations begins as follows: "The drives to live, to propagate, and to dominate are common to all men."[2]

According to such notions, human warfare can be traced to our biological heritage, attributable directly to genetic, hormonal, neurobiological, and/or evolutionary mechanisms, including a tendency to form dominance hierarchies, to defend territories, and to behave aggressively toward others. Much emphasis is placed on the existence of comparable behavior patterns among certain animals and the presumption that the behavior of animals reflects underlying principles that hold for the human species as well.

## The Lorenzian Approach

Perhaps the most influential exponent of this deterministic perspective was the Nobel Prize–winning Austrian ethologist (the study of the biology of animal behavior) Konrad Lorenz. Lorenz helped conceptualize a view of instinctive behavior according to which animals are endowed with certain behaviors, called "fixed action patterns," whose physical performance is genetically fixed and unvarying from one individual to another. In his book *On Aggression,* Lorenz argued that certain "species preserving" aspects of aggression applied to human beings as well. They include the following:

1. Providing an opportunity for competition within a species, after which the most fit will emerge to produce the next generation

2. Achieving spacing and population control, to minimize the disadvantages of overpopulation

3. Establishing a means whereby the pair bond can be strengthened, as by shared aggression of a mated pair against competitors

Lorenz was not concerned with extolling human aggression but with understanding it. He noted that, in moderate amounts, aggression may well be functional and healthy, but, at the same time, he deplored its occurrence in excess, especially when combined with what he called "militant enthusiasm," the tendency of people to lose their normal inhibitions against violence when united with others similarly motivated.

Lorenz also emphasized that animals, such as wolves or hawks, that have lethal natural weapons also tend to possess innate inhibitions against employing such weapons against members of the same species. By contrast, animals such as rabbits, doves, or human beings—not naturally equipped with lethal weapons—lack such inhibitions. According to this line of thought, the human condition is especially perilous because while we have developed the ability, by technological means, to kill our fellow humans, quickly, easily, and in great numbers, our biological evolution remains far behind our technological progress. We continue to lack genetically based mechanisms to keep our newfound lethality in check.

The Lorenzian approach, which tends to "extrapolate war from human instinct," is in some ways a caricature of biological (ethological) views. According to what might be called the *classical ethological approach,* aggression is genetically controlled behavior, such that the actual behavior patterns are rigidly stereotyped, invariant, and independent of learning. In this perspective, aggression can also emerge spontaneously; that is, individuals have a *need* to discharge this drive by behaving aggressively.

Lorenz suggests that one way to deal with our instinctive penchant for aggression and militant enthusiasm is by rechanneling this biological energy in socially useful (or, at least, nondestructive) forms of competition, such as athletics, the exploration of space, or medical research. Nonetheless, Lorenz is led to a pessimistic assessment of the human future:

> An unprejudiced observer from another planet, looking down on man as he is today, in his hand the atom bomb, the product of his intelligence, in his heart the aggressive drive inherited from his anthropoid ancestors, which this same intelligence cannot control, would not prophesy long life for the species.[3]

## Is War in Our Genes?

Although biology may well provide valuable insights into the current state of the world, simplistic extrapolations from animal to human can be dangerously misleading. For example, it is no more valid to argue that human beings are naturally murderous because baboons sometimes kill other baboons than it is to conclude that human beings are naturally vegetarians because gorillas exclusively eat plants or that humans can fly because birds have wings.

There is a danger that by accepting war as part of "human nature," one thereby justifies war itself, in part by diminishing the human responsibility to behave more peacefully. If war is "in our genes," presumably we cannot act otherwise, so we should not be blamed for what we do; maybe, then, we shouldn't even bother trying to do anything about our warlike inclinations. At minimum— and perhaps, at its most pernicious—such biological fatalism supports a pessimistic perspective on the human condition, one that provides an excuse for the maintenance of large military forces and leads to profound and possibly lethal distrust of others. There is, indeed, evidence that people who are generally promilitary tend to be disproportionate believers in the doctrine that war is somehow etched in our DNA.

To address (and scientifically to refute) biological determinism, a group of prominent behavioral scientists from 12 nations met in 1986 in Seville, Spain, and agreed on the "Seville Statement." The document provides scientific information contradicting the myth that the human capacity for aggression makes war and violence inevitable and identifies in sociocultural factors the main causes of violence. Most importantly, it also highlights the role of education in preventing, diminishing, and eliminating violence. The document was also endorsed by a number of well-known significant scientific organizations, including the American Psychological Association, the American Anthropological Association, the American Sociological Association, and other scholarly organizations. Some excerpts from this statement are as follows:

- It is scientifically incorrect to say that we have inherited a tendency to make war from our animal ancestors. Warfare is a peculiarly human phenomenon and does not occur in other animals.
- It is scientifically incorrect to say that war or any other violent behavior is genetically programmed into our human nature.
- It is scientifically incorrect to say that in the course of human evolution there has been a selection for aggressive behavior more than for other kinds of behavior.
- It is scientifically incorrect to say that humans have a "violent brain." While we do have a neural apparatus to act violently, there is nothing in our neurophysiology that compels us to.
- It is scientifically incorrect to say that war is caused by "instinct" or any single motivation. The technology of modern war has exaggerated traits associated with violence both in the training of actual combatants and in the preparation of support for war in the general population.
- We conclude that biology does not condemn humanity to war, and that humanity can be freed from the bondage of biological pessimism. . . . The same species . . . [that] invented war is capable of inventing peace.

Approximately a quarter century after the original "Seville Statement," in September 2011, an international conference on violence was held in Rome. The conference, entitled "The Seville Statement on Violence: Twenty-Five Years Later," was held to more effectively analyze the complex relationships among brain, aggression, and society. Participants discussed the opportunity of re-examining and improving the "Seville Statement." They concluded that the fundamental thesis enunciated in the original Seville Statement is still valid; namely, that human violence is not inevitable, since it is not biologically determined but is basically related to sociocultural factors. At the same time, this reevaluation of the Seville Statement concluded by recommending that this thesis be further developed in the light of the new research findings that have been obtained in the last 25 years.

# Sociobiology and Evolutionary Psychology

A more sophisticated version of instinctivism is associated with the discipline of sociobiology, whose best-known practitioner is Edward O. Wilson. The mainstream sociobiological approach, which in the 1990s was somewhat superseded by an even more recent discipline known as evolutionary psychology, differs from instinctivism in that it places new emphasis on evolution as a process rather than a historical event. That is, sociobiologists and evolutionary psychologists are particularly concerned with the *adaptive significance* of behavior, or the way in which particular behavior patterns are maintained and promoted in a population because they contribute to the reproductive success of individuals (not species) that possess these traits.

A sociobiological or evolutionary psychological view of human war examines such phenomena as ecological competition (for food, nesting sites, etc.), male-male competition (for dominance in the pecking order and for mates), and the role of kinship patterns in directing aggressive behavior in particular ways. Among many species, for example, males tend to be larger, showier, and more aggressive than females. In addition, biological differences between males and females mean, among other things, that one male can successfully fertilize many females. Sexual differences of this sort, in turn, convey a reproductive payoff (enhanced evolutionary fitness) to individuals—especially males—who succeed in defeating their rivals, whether in symbolic display or outright combat.

Consistent with this theory is the finding that men tend to be more aggressive than women (especially outside the family) and also that men are more likely to be involved in violence of all sorts, including war. Another important tenet of sociobiological theory is the role of genetic relatedness: Individuals who share genes probably will behave benevolently (altruistically) toward each other, because such behavior tends to contribute to the success of genes predisposing toward such behavior; conversely, a low probability of genetic relatedness is likely to be associated with aggressiveness. Therefore, appeals to patriotism often involve what anthropologists call *fictive kinship,* calling on citizens to stand up for the motherland, fatherland, Uncle Sam, "brothers and sisters," and so forth.

Competition has been defined by Wilson as "the active demand by two or more individuals . . . for a common resource or requirement that is actually or potentially limiting."[4] Many studies have pointed to the role of primitive war in gaining access to mates, animal protein, and social prestige, such that warfare among preindustrial or nontechnological peoples, which in the past appeared to be irrational and nonadaptive, is now increasingly seen to possess an internal logic of its own—although not necessarily a logic that is consciously understood by the participants.

## Both Nature and Nurture

It is misleading to ask whether a given behavior is either instinctive or learned, since all behavior results from the interaction of genetic potential with experience, both nature and nurture. "In order to be adaptive," writes Wilson,

> it is enough that aggressive patterns be evoked only under certain conditions of stress such as those that might arise during food shortages and periodic high population densities. It also does not matter whether the aggression is wholly innate or is acquired in part or wholly by learning. We are now sophisticated enough to know that the capacity to learn certain behaviors is itself a genetically controlled and therefore evolved trait.[5]

Finally, another important evolutionary perspective considers war to have had a prominent role in the early evolution of the human species. Conceivably, proto-human warrior bands were a major selective force in our own early evolution, with successful groups killing off those that were less successful. Large brains could well have contributed to success in violent intergroup conflict by promoting relatively sophisticated communication, formation of social alliances, and effective use of weapons. Those experiencing such outcomes would presumably have left more descendants, who in turn were likely to possess these favored traits and capacities.

# Freudian and Post-Freudian Psychoanalytic Theory

Sigmund Freud was the creator of psychoanalysis and in many ways the founder of modern psychiatry. He is particularly noteworthy for his emphasis on the role of the unconscious in human behavior. Freud himself was a pacifist, and he especially deplored what he saw as a vicious, lethal streak among human beings.

To Freud, human history is in large part the history of human violence, with the human race having exchanged "numerous, and indeed unending, minor wars for wars on a grand scale that are rare but all the more destructive." In his later work, Freud attributed much of humanity's more "inhumane" behavior to the operation of *Thanatos,* or the death instinct, which he saw as opposed to *Eros,* the life (or erotic) instinct, which may "encourage the growth of emotional ties between men [and] must operate against war."

In a famous letter to Albert Einstein, Freud noted, "We are led to conclude that this [death] instinct functions in every living being, striving to work its ruin and to reduce life to its primal state of inert matter."[6] When Thanatos is thwarted by Eros, its energy is displaced outward onto subjects other than oneself, resulting in aggression between individuals or among groups.

The notion of a death instinct remains associated with Freud's thought, but he also argued that, regardless of whether Thanatos exists within the human psyche or if we are "simply" aggressive by nature, civilization demands that people repress their primitive tendencies toward destructive and aggressive behavior if they are to live together with a minimum of violent conflict. Parents must provide discipline for their children, society must restrict its citizens, and, ultimately, some form of supranational authority will be necessary to enforce a system of world government over individual states that would otherwise function anarchically. Hence, civilization demands the repression of both Eros and Thanatos, which in turn necessarily produces discontent (and neurosis) among its populace. Like Einstein, Freud argued that "Wars will only be prevented . . . if mankind unites in setting up a central authority to which the right of giving judgment upon all conflicts of interest shall be handed over. There are clearly two separate requirements . . . "the creation of a supreme authority and its endowment with the necessary power. One without the other would be useless."

Another important Freudian concept especially relevant to war is that of *narcissistic injury.* Narcissism involves infatuation with one's self, and in moderation it is considered a normal stage in personality development. But when the individual associates himself or herself with a larger group, especially with the nation-state, slights or injuries to the group are easy to perceive as injuries to one's self. The resulting "narcissistic rage" may involve an unrelenting compulsion to undo the hurt; in the pursuit of this vengeful "justice," great violence may be self-righteously employed. Many of the most destructive wars in the 20th century were perpetrated by people seeking to retake territory that had been wrested from them by others (e.g., the French yearning to recapture the provinces of Alsace and Lorraine from Germany, which was a major reason for World War I, or the Viet Cong and North Vietnamese, who sought during the Vietnam War to reunite their country). Other wars have been instigated by ethnic groups seeking to secede from a central governmental authority, only to precipitate intervention by armed forces from the nation-state from which they hoped to disconnect (as in Nigeria, Ethiopia, Indonesia, the former Yugoslavia, Sudan, and Russia).

Like the Lorenzian and (to a lesser extent) the sociobiological and evolutionary psychological approaches, the orthodox Freudian perspective tends to be pessimistic about the prospects for ameliorating, much less eliminating, "this ineradicable defect in human nature." Thus, Freud maintained, for example, that we really shouldn't be disillusioned about atrocities during wartime, because the notion that humankind is fundamentally civilized is itself illusory.

Furthermore, according to Melanie Klein (a prominent follower of Freud), human aggression is ultimately rooted in the earliest "primitive" states of human existence, before there is an ego or a language to modulate, rechannel, or defuse it. Human destructiveness manifests itself, among other things, in the "paranoid-schizoid" anxieties and defenses (such as splitting and projection) initially used by infants to ward off feelings of abandonment—by the mother or other caregivers—and fears of annihilation and disintegration.

According to Kleinian theory, human aggression is implicit even in the womb. It emerges full-blown during the first years of life (when the infant quite literally bites the mother's hand and breast that feed it) and persists throughout the entire life span, either as unconscious sadomasochistic fantasies or overtly in self- and other destructive behaviors. The goal of psychoanalytic therapy from a Kleinian perspective is accordingly to induce the "malignant" (destructive and disowned) parts of the self to become "reintegrated" within a "whole-object" psyche, not to seek in vain to eradicate aggression from either the individual or the human species.

Some students of human behavior have concluded that much human misery, including even the penchant for war itself, derives in part from the consequences of being mistreated as children. It is further argued that many acts of violence toward children—whether overt, such as beating or sexual abuse, or more subtle, such as severe criticism and belittling by significant others in a child's early environment—have in turn been buttressed by the view that human beings are inherently sinful and depraved. From a more secular perspective, the neo-Kleinian psychoanalytic theorist and pediatrician D. W. Winnicott claimed that with "good enough mothering," the infant's proclivities toward aggression could be mollified. Conversely, without a nurturing environment, babies and young children who are deprived of maternal love and positive reinforcement are at risk of developing pathological character structures and engaging in destructive behaviors.

Other prominent psychoanalysts have not been as pessimistic as most Kleinians and have in fact rejected the notion of a death drive (as do virtually all biologists). Wilhelm Reich, for example, argued that the unprecedented violence and destructiveness unleashed on Europe during the first part of the 20th century were not simply the latest manifestation of the eternal battle between Eros and Thanatos but could instead be better explained in terms of the historical development of character pathologies ("armor") and socially induced aggression under modern capitalism. And more contemporary schools of psychoanalytic theory and therapy—notably the ego, self, relational, and critical psychologists—have also stressed the roles of environment, culture, social interaction, and socialization in eliciting and reinforcing aggressive and destructive behaviors.

# "Innate Depravity" and "Human Nature"

Some thoughtful people have long maintained that human beings are innately depraved, nasty, and evil, basing this claim on a loosely argued blend of biology, moral outrage, and, on occasion, theology. Looking over the bloodletting of the English Civil War (1642–1649), Thomas Hobbes concluded that there was "a general inclination of all mankind, a perpetual and restless desire for power after power that ceaseth only in death."[7] To some extent, Hobbes's pessimism can be traced to a biblical—especially a conservative Christian—tradition that sees human nature as inherently flawed. Suffused with original sin, humans are deemed to be inherently incapable of becoming good. Consider these sentiments from the 16th-century theologian John Calvin, perhaps the most influential advocate of this perspective:

> Even infants themselves, as they bring their condemnation into the world with them, are rendered subject to punishment of their own sinfulness. . . . For though they have not yet produced the fruits of their iniquity, yet they have had the seed of it in them. Their whole nature is, as it were, a seed of sin and therefore cannot but be . . . abominable to God.[8]

In Calvinist theology, because of our allegedly innate human sinfulness, we were cast out of the Garden of Eden, doomed to death. We therefore deserve—indeed, we require—to be treated sternly and punished vigorously. In any event, according to this pessimistic Christian view, a true state of personal peace can be achieved only by grace, just as a state of political peace requires the Second Coming of Christ. And until then, war is inevitable.

This attitude is not limited to conservative Christians, however. Another approach, rarely articulated, emphasizes that human beings have not only a capacity for violence but also a deep-seated love of bloodletting, hatred, and destruction.[9] In the 17th century, John Milton wrote that

> even if our species were rendered somehow impervious to injury from all outside forces, yet the perverseness of our folly is so bent, that we should never cease hammering out of our own hearts, as it were out of a flint, the seeds and sparkles of new misery to ourselves, till all were in a blaze again.[10]

From this perspective, war is an evil unique to humanity. The influential 20th-century theologian Reinhold Niebuhr argued that it was the "sinful character of man" that necessitated "the balancing of power with power."[11] The philosophers Spinoza and Kant located the evils of human violence in the fact that our rational faculties are regularly overwhelmed by our irrational and untamed emotions.

This is only a very limited sampling of a widespread notion. Although it is virtually impossible to verify, the idea of innate human weakness and depravity remains popular, especially among the lay public. It has also been particularly influential among those who are sympathetic to military force, if not to war itself. Thus, if human nature is inherently nasty and warlike, we can never have any confidence in morality, law, or anything else to deliver us from war, since these are only frail, artificial institutions constructed by fundamentally flawed human beings. Accordingly, from this perspective, because human nature presumably cannot be changed, the best way to safeguard personal or national security is by recourse to arms.

## Criticisms of Human Nature Theories

The various human nature theories about the reasons for human violence all contain flaws. For example, human beings undoubtedly have the biological capacity to kill one another—proven by the fact that they have often done so! The danger is that such a broad generalization may be useless in analyzing the past or predicting the future. Other, more specific problems in these theories exist as well. For example, consider the following:

1. Although war is a widespread human trait, it is not a universal one; certain cultures, such as the South African Bushmen (or San), the Semai (in Southeast Asia), and the Inuit (in northern North America), apparently never engaged in war, although interpersonal violence is not unknown. Explanations based on human nature should apply to these peoples no less than to others. Although some societies are clearly more war prone than others, there is also no evidence that such differences reflect inherent differences in human nature.

2. Even among war-prone cultures, there have been many years of peace. If human nature caused World War II or the Vietnam War, what about the peace that preceded and followed these wars? If human nature causes war, it must also cause peace—the neutrality of Sweden, the demilitarized U.S.-Canadian border, Gandhi's nonviolence, and so on. Any explanation that is so broad becomes useless. To paraphrase a military metaphor of Karl von Clausewitz, he who seeks to explain everything explains nothing.

3. Even within war-prone cultures, there have been war resisters, peace advocates, and longtime nonviolent traditions such as the Mennonites and the Quakers; are they less "human," or less "natural," than their more violent fellow citizens?

4. The fact that animals behave in certain ways does not necessarily mean that human beings do so; we have the capacity for complex, abstract, and symbolic thought, which gives us the opportunity to reason, to analyze, and to rise above our unpleasant or dangerous inclinations.

5. If war is a result of a fixed human nature, it seems predestined and unavoidable, since we cannot—by definition—behave counter to our own nature. There is a special danger in the belief that war is inevitable, because it is likely to discourage people from seeking to end war and to promote peace. Moreover, it can also serve to *justify* war by making it appear somehow "good" because it is natural.

The above criticisms oversimplify the more sophisticated human nature arguments. Most biologically inclined theorists recognize that genetic factors do not irrevocably commit a person, or a society, to a given course of action. Rather, they create *predispositions* for behaving aggressively or violently when circumstances are appropriate; similarly, nothing in sociobiological or evolutionary psychological theory suggests that such predispositions could not be overridden by religious beliefs, historical circumstances, collective social action, and so on. There is nothing inconsistent with the proponents of such theories suggesting that human beings can say No, even if it seems difficult or feels "unnatural," to their genes, neurons, and/or hormones.

### Human Nature and Genetic Determinism

There is a great difference between a possible genetic *influence* on war-proneness and the doctrine of genetic *determinism*. The former implies the existence of tendencies, likely to be subtle and capable of being overridden, whereas the latter implies rigid, ironclad automatic responses. There may well be genetic and neurobiological influences that human beings, if they are to be peaceful, must overcome or sublimate. But this is not to say that our genes, neurons, and/or hormones predetermine our behavior, condemning us to violence.

As to morality, advocates—and critics—of biologically based arguments should be wary of what the philosopher David Hume first identified—and what was later labeled by the 20th-century British philosopher G. E. Moore—as the *naturalistic fallacy,* the mistaken belief that "*is* implies *ought*." In other words, whatever insights evolutionary theory and neuroscience might provide regarding how the natural world and the human brain work are distinct from ethical guidance as to what is good. Typhoid is natural; this does not mean that it is good. War may or may not be natural; whether it is good, however, is an entirely different question. In any event, if typhoid, or war, is to be prevented or cured, we must understand its causation, whether or not we are pleased by what we find.

# Social Learning Theories

Thinkers since Aristotle have debated the primary causes of human behavior, often dividing them into "nature" versus "nurture." We have just reviewed some of the main theories involving "human nature." Next, we turn to the major alternative: a variety of hypotheses involving the role of experience and the environment, in short, "nurture," which typically focus on social learning as well as cultural traditions and expectations.

### Frustration-Aggression

Among explanations for war that do not depend on explicit assumptions about human nature, one of the most influential has been the frustration-aggression hypothesis, which was developed to explain individual aggressiveness as well. According to this theory, first proposed in 1939 by John Dollard and Neal Miller, aggressiveness is produced by frustration, which in turn is defined as "an interference with the occurrence of an instigated goal-response at its proper time in the behavior sequence."[12] Thus, if a hungry rat is presented with food, after which a glass wall is interposed between the animal and its desire, the rat is likely to become aggressive. A similar thing happens with people who have been seeking something unsuccessfully—food, political freedoms, access to a disputed territory, union with others who practice the same customs— or who have obtained partial success only to be prevented from achieving their ultimate goals. When circumstances disallow people from achieving their goals, individuals are likely to engage in aggressive behavior. This theory attempts to explain why people create scapegoats and claims that when the source of the frustration cannot be challenged, the aggression gets displaced onto an innocent target.

In its initial formulation, frustration theory was presented rather dogmatically. "The occurrence of aggressive behavior always presupposes the existence of frustration, and contrariwise, the existence of frustration always leads to some form of aggression."[13] This rigidity led to problems comparable to those encountered with some human nature theories: The argument can become circular if all cases of aggression are defined as revealing preexisting frustration, and vice versa, if any behavior that follows frustration is defined as aggression. Additionally, aggression is not always the response to frustration. Furthermore, there is little empirical support for frustration theory as such, even though researchers have studied it for more than 70 years. Another issue is that this theory suggests that frustrated, prejudiced individuals should act more aggressively toward outgroups they are prejudiced against, whereas studies have shown that they are more aggressive toward *everyone*. The theory also has another limitation: for example, it cannot say why some outgroups are chosen to be scapegoats while others are not.

Frustration theory has subsequently been modified to recognize that frustration creates a predisposition or readiness for aggression, by producing an intervening emotional state: anger. In addition, environmental stimuli are necessary for aggression to be produced. Finally, an individual's learning experiences and society's expectations exert a powerful influence on the connection between frustration and aggression. Of course, other responses to frustration are also possible—namely, submission, resignation, alienation, withdrawal, avoidance, or even acceptance—but this does not in itself argue against a possible frustration-aggression link.

Frustration can also result in resentment, which (like the above responses) may or may not subsequently produce aggressive behavior. Frustration may be especially high when there is a discrepancy between expectations and realities: Bad social conditions, such as poverty or political repression, are made to seem even worse by high expectations that conflict with unpleasant realities. Accordingly, the "revolution of rising expectations," particularly in the less advanced economies, has been associated with frustration and violence. In his influential book, *Why Men Fight*, political scientist Ted Gurr developed the concept of "relative deprivation"— people's sense of their socioeconomic standing relative to others—showing that higher relative deprivation correlated with a greater propensity for revolutionary violence.

Political and military authorities often respond to collective efforts to promote social change with increased repression, but the forceful repression of strongly felt needs (such as the yearning for Palestinian self-determination and, before that, of Zionists for a Jewish state) can in itself be highly frustrating and thereby ultimately increase hostility and aggression. In some cases, frustration finds its outlet in aggressive behavior against others who are not actually the perceived frustrating agent.

There is another possible twist to the connection between frustration and war: namely, boredom. It has been suggested that war is especially appealing to those whose lives are lacking in excitement and interest. "The absence of delight in daily living," wrote the historian John Nef, "has helped to leave many lives empty and sterile and so, fair game for any excitement, including the most terrific of worldly excitements, that of war."[14] Furthermore, once a society has elevated military values, has trained men and boys (and, increasingly, women and girls) to be warriors, and has institutionalized and mythologized the war experience, people may be especially prone to be frustrated and bored with peace. Of course, warfare itself actually involves prolonged periods of boredom and monotony. The endless repetition, drill, and "hurry up and wait" behavior that characterize military routine are hardly antidotes for civilian ennui. Military boredom may lead, however, to frustration, which in turn may lead to greater willingness to go to war, if only to "see action" and thereby finally break the suspense.

Beginning with experiments conducted at Yale in 1961 and culminating in the publication of his book *Obedience to Authority* (1974), the social psychologist Stanley Milgram showed the importance of situational factors in explaining aggressive and brutal behavior under conditions in which individuals feel pressured by authority figures.

## Social Learning

Clearly, human beings are strongly influenced by their experiences—those that occur early in development and that also characterize later socialization—as well as society's norms and expectations. Many psychologists and most sociologists maintain that human violence arises in response to experiences, rather than bubbling up out of our genetic constitution.

Social learning theory explains human behavior in terms of continuous reciprocal interaction among cognitive, behavioral, and environmental influences. According to the influential social psychologist Albert Bandura, people learn through observing others' behavior, attitudes, and outcomes of those behaviors: "Most human behavior is learned observationally through modeling: from observing others, one forms an idea of how new behaviors are performed, and on later occasions this coded information serves as a guide for action." Bandura, who was analyzing adolescent aggression, believed in "reciprocal determinism," that is, the world and a person's behavior cause each other.

"The important fact," wrote psychologist John Paul Scott, "is that the chain of causation in every case eventually traces back to the outside. There is no physiological evidence of any spontaneous stimulation for fighting arising within the body."[15] Scott emphasized that individuals are particularly likely to fight if they have fought successfully in the past and that aggression often results from a breakdown in social structures. (It is also noteworthy, on the other hand, that some of the most aggressive societies have been highly structured: Nazi Germany as well as Fascist Italy and pre–World War II Japan, for example.)

## Conditioning

One of the most important developments in 20th-century psychology revolved around the phenomenon known as *instrumental* or *operant conditioning,* especially associated with the work of B. F. Skinner. The basic idea is that behavior will be influenced by its consequences for the individual: Certain behaviors tend to be *reinforcing*—that is, they make it more likely that the individual will repeat the previous actions. Some authorities employ the phrase *instrumental aggression* to refer to aggressive behavior that is oriented primarily toward attaining some goal, such as winning a war or recovering territory, rather than causing injury as such.

Conditioning theory applied to human aggressiveness suggests that people will behave aggressively when such behavior leads to reinforcing (i.e., positive) results and, conversely, that the likelihood of aggression will be reduced if it leads to negative results. By extrapolation, members of whole societies can presumably be influenced similarly, making war more probable if their behavior has been positively reinforced (rewarded) or negatively reinforced (punished). For example, the international aggressiveness of Nazi Germany was positively reinforced during most of the 1930s by the appeasement policies of the West; by contrast, it can be argued that international adventuring on the part of the United States was negatively reinforced by its divisive and ultimately unsuccessful involvement in Southeast Asia (resulting in a subsequent reluctance to commit American ground troops to foreign combat, the so-called Vietnam syndrome). If so, the effects are disputable, since the "Vietnam syndrome" did not inhibit two subsequent U.S.-led invasions of Iraq; moreover, one of the expressed motivations for these military adventures was to "get rid of the Vietnam syndrome, once and for all."

## Socialization to Aggressiveness

Some societies actively encourage aggressiveness from early childhood. For example, consider the Fulani people of northern Nigeria, among whom most males seek to embody the ideals of "aggressive dominance." As boys, young Fulani males are taught to beat their cattle to prevent them from wandering off and to fight back unhesitatingly whenever they have been attacked. If they refrain from retaliating, they are mocked as cowards. They show virtually no emotion when struck with sticks during increasingly serious fights, and by the time they are young men, the Fulani are proud of their battle scars. Not surprisingly, they are also prone to personal fighting as well as warfare.

Mark May, an influential social psychologist, summed up the dominant American view of the 1940s when he wrote that "men not only learn when it is best to fight or not to fight, whom to fight and whom to appease, how to fight and how not to; but they also learn whom, when, and how to hate." May went on to discuss the phenomenon of social learning for group aggressiveness:

> Learning to fight and to hate involves much more than learning to box, to duel, or to participate in other forms of group violence. Systematic education for aggressive warfare in ancient Sparta or in modern Germany includes, besides physical education in games and contests, universal compulsory military training; the inculcation of certain attitudes, prejudices, beliefs; and devotion to leaders and ideals. The whole purpose and direction of such education is toward group aggression.[16]

Also important in this context is the phenomenon of "imitative learning," whereby individuals are prone to do something if they witness others doing the same thing. Thus, aggressiveness and hostility—or, alternatively, an inclination to settle disputes peacefully—can become part of the ethos of a society.

# Gender, War, and Peace

The recorded history of warfare is made up of wars waged and fought almost entirely by men. Only recently have women been admitted to the military, and until 2013, women were excluded from combat in the US military. Pacifists and others would prefer both men and women to be excluded; if they were, there would be no combat!

In centuries past, women filled primarily supportive roles in society, beginning most obviously with motherhood. The question naturally arises whether women, regarded throughout history as the weaker but also the gentler sex, might help to temper the bellicose tendencies of men, if only they were to occupy more high positions in government, from which the military takes it orders. There have been female leaders who never waged or promoted any wars, but the same can be said of male leaders, too. In cases involving less powerful nations, where war is not really an option for anyone, no matter who the leader of the land may be, the fact that a female leader did not draw her country into war cannot serve as evidence for the claim that women are more pacific than men.

A few salient examples—including Britain's former prime minister Margaret Thatcher, former U.S. secretary of state Madeleine Albright, India's former prime minister Indira Gandhi, Israel's former prime minister Golda Meir, and former U.S. secretary of state Condoleezza Rice—appear on their face to challenge the idea that women might be intrinsically more pacific than men. In 1982, Thatcher famously sent British troops to assume control of the Falkland Islands, a disputed Argentinian territory, and earned the epithet "The Iron Lady," in part for her tough positions and willingness to wield the weapons of war. Madeleine Albright was a staunch proponent of the 1999 NATO bombing of Kosovo. Earlier, while serving as the U.S. ambassador to the United Nations, Albright infamously asked then-head of the Joint Chiefs of Staff Colin Powell, "What's the point of having this superb military that you're always talking about if we can't use it?" And Condoleezza Rice was one of the most outspoken advocates of the 2003 invasion of Iraq, even in the face of vehement opposition by millions of people the world over, and she joined her fellow male war architects in a brazen show of disdain for the Charter of the United Nations, according to which war must be waged only as a last resort and with the blessing of the UN Security Council.

How are we to understand such cases? One way is simply to take these examples on their face as refutations of the thesis that women are inherently more pacific than men. In reality, however, it is important to understand how the corridors of power come to be filled in such militarily powerful lands as Britain and the United States. Such nations, with long histories filled with wars, have been shaped politically along the way so as to effectively preclude the ascent to power of nearly anyone who opposes, on principle, the use of deadly force as a means resolving international conflict. In other words, although men in the same or similar positions as these women may well have supported the use of military force—and these women's colleagues of course did—this does not show anything more than that the people who gain access to the corridors of power regard the use of military force in such circumstances as perfectly valid.

The reasons for this promilitary bias in the selection of leaders are manifold. The rhetoric of defense is used in persuading voters to support candidates, and those who spurn the use of military force are lambasted by media pundits as weak, naive, and unfit for leadership. The populace tends unreflectively to accept the status quo view that the military is a necessary institution that must be funded and supported. At the same time, powerful economic forces are poised to support promilitary candidates and, above all, those who can be counted on to pass legislation likely to be lucrative to military industry and its many subcontractors. The implements of war are very expensive and profitable to produce. The implements of peace, negotiation, and dialogue are not generally viewed as sufficiently profitable to powerful corporations and their associated interests. As a result, promilitary candidates are at a great advantage, enjoying political approval from the populace in general and the financial support of military industry and its subcontractors as well.

This complex situation makes it extremely difficult to tease out the necessary variables to determine whether women are intrinsically more pacific than men. Not only are elected officials likely to be more hawkish, but the people whom they appoint, such as secretaries of state, share their views and values. To complicate matters, the few women who have achieved such positions may feel the need to flex their military muscle, so to speak, in order to refute the prevailing cultural dogma according to which women are weak. They may adopt and espouse exceptionally hawkish positions during times of conflict, as did Thatcher, Albright, Rice, and others.

Institutions are by nature conservative, concerned first and foremost with their own preservation and perpetuation in their current state, and military institutions are no exception to the rule. What the cases of female leaders such as Thatcher, Albright, and Rice reveal, in the end, is only that access to the corridors of power in military states presupposes a promilitary stance, given the structures already in place, which were usually erected by men. We do not know what contemporary social and political institutions might have looked like had they been created by women, because they were not.

But we do know that many cherished myths about the relation between gender and war/peace roles have gone down in flames due to lack of scientific support, including claims about alleged "matriarchies," of a separate genetic code for men, about the alleged causal link between testosterone levels and aggression on the one hand and between female hormones and peacefulness on the other hand, and the allegation that most women oppose wars and hence choose not to participate in combat.[17] Like most social phenomena, gender matters when it comes to belligerent and peaceful behavior. But we are still investigating how much, or how little, it matters.

## Self-Fulfilling Behaviors

An important sociological concept has been called the *self-fulfilling prophecy* (formulated by the sociologist Robert Merton[18]), according to which a belief becomes true if enough people believe that it is true. In the realm of aggressive behavior, hostility often begets hostility on the part of others, which in turn not only reinforces the initial hostility but also intensifies it. People may create their own interpersonal environments simply by behaving with a certain expectation: If someone is suspicious, secretive, and blameful, he or she is likely to elicit comparable behavior. This pattern has the makings of a vicious circle, in which hostility becomes self-reinforcing in a kind of positive feedback.

A similar pattern can apply to international relations as well. For example, if country A, convinced of the hostility of country B, increases its armaments, B may well respond in kind. This in turn reinforces the "enemy image" already present, leading to further militarily oriented actions, each of which may truly be intended to be "defensive" but that, taken as a whole, diminish the security of all participants. Such a process characterizes much of the history of arms races.

## Redirected Aggression

Other patterns in behavioral development also take place, often without the explicit intent of producing aggressiveness. For example, in *displaced* or *redirected* aggression, a victim will attack an innocent third party who may have had nothing to do with the initial victimization. The Bible describes how the ancient Israelites designated an animal as a *scapegoat*, which would be abused and driven from the herd, ostensibly taking with it the sins and anger of those who remained behind—uninjured and purified.

Frequently, the victims of redirected aggression are smaller, weaker, or already the subjects of social abuse: a religious or racial minority, advocates of unpopular political doctrines, and so on. Blacks, communists, and dark-skinned immigrants in the United States; Arab immigrants in France; and religious and ethnic minorities (especially those with dark skin, such as the Roma, or Gypsies) in countries spawned by the collapse of the former Soviet Union and Yugoslavia all have borne the brunt of redirected aggression by people who are themselves deprived or disadvantaged. Although local minorities provide convenient "targets of opportunity," foreign nationals are particularly targeted as objects of redirected group anger.

Immediately prior to the U.S.-led invasion of Iraq in 2003, the following ditty made its way around the Internet (to the tune of the children's song, "If You're Happy and You Know It, Clap Your Hands"):

> "If you cannot find Osama, bomb Iraq.
>
> If the market's hurt your momma, bomb Iraq.
>
> If they've repossessed your Audi, and the terrorists are Saudi,
>
> And you're feeling kind of rowdy . . . bomb Iraq."

There are many possible reasons why the Bush administration chose to bomb Iraq and then either "liberate" or "invade" it (depending on one's perspective). What is clear, however, is that Saddam Hussein was not responsible for the terrorist attacks of 9/11. But for most Americans, the agony of that attack demanded that something be done—something violent—and that someone be held accountable and made to suffer, preferably someone already known to be nasty and who could readily be defeated. The initial object of American wrath was Afghanistan, whose appropriateness for U.S.-led invasion and occupation will long be debated. But the Iraq invasion seemed a total nonsequitur as a response to 9/11. So why did it happen?

Here is Thomas Friedman writing in *the New York Times*, in June of 2003:

> The 'real reason' for this war, which was never stated, was that after 9/11 America needed to stick it to someone in the Arab-Muslim world. . . . Smashing Saudi Arabia or Syria would have been fine. But we attacked Saddam for one simple reason: because we could, and because he deserved it, and because he was right in the heart of that world.

According to former chief UN weapons inspector Hans Blix, in his book, *Disarming Iraq*, "It is clear that the U.S. determination to take on Iraq was not triggered by anything Iraq did, but by the wounds inflicted by Al-Qaeda." U.S. counterterrorism expert Richard Clarke noted that "Having been attacked by Al Qaeda, for us to go bombing Iraq in response was like our invading Mexico after the Japanese attacked us at Pearl Harbor." As illogical as such actions may appear, they fit rather well into the definition of redirected aggression.

## Authoritarian and Machiavellian Personalities

Following World War II and the Holocaust in which 6 million of Europe's Jews (as well as millions of pacifists, gays, Roma, war resisters, mentally disabled people, political dissidents, and civilian noncombatants) were murdered, researchers led by the German philosopher Theodor Adorno, a leading member of the "Frankfurt School" of critical theory, and the American social psychologist Nevitt Sanford sought to identify those personal traits and experiences that predispose people toward anti-Semitism and related authoritarian and antidemocratic ideologies and practices. The results were published in one of the most influential and controversial works of social psychology, *The Authoritarian Personality* (1950). Their work resulted in the F Scale (for Fascist), a personality test, which supposedly provides a rough measure of an individual's tendency toward authoritarianism.

The F-scale purportedly measures an "antidemocratic personality structure" according to subjects' responses to questions tapping several different components of authoritarianism. The scale specifically examines the following personality dimensions: conventionalism: one's conformity to the traditional societal norms and values of the middle class; authoritarian submission: a passive notion toward adhering to conventional norms and values; and authoritarian aggression: punishing and condemning individuals who don't adhere to conventional values. Other dimensions include: superstition and stereotype, power and "toughness," destructiveness, and cynicism.

The *authoritarian personality* is positively correlated with a rigidly hierarchical family structure: the husband dominant over the wife; and parents (especially fathers) demanding unquestioned obedience and respect from their children. This moralistic and disciplinarian style of child rearing was often combined with a strongly nationalistic outlook, ready submission to powerful external authority, and fear of weakness and of moral "contamination" by "aliens and other outsiders." "The authoritarian personality" is negatively associated with peace-supportiveness, while "the liberal-democratic personality" is allegedly positively associated with peace-supportiveness and nonviolence.

The F Scale has been heavily criticized by many psychologists because it may be a better indicator of conservatism, an old-fashioned outlook, and a tendency to say "yes" to anything, rather than a measure of authoritarianism. In short, it may not predict authoritarian behavior. However, it does express sentiments tending toward the political right and sentiments characteristic of less-educated and unsophisticated people. The F Scale may also reflect cultural norms rather than underlying authoritarian personality dimensions.

Like the "authoritarian personality," "the Machiavellian personality," as described by Richard Christie and Florence Geis in their *Studies in Machiavellianism* (1970), is likely to support unjust and violent behavior, if profitable for the person involved. In opposition to the Machiavellian personality stands the altruistic personality—emphatic, moral, and highly peace-supportive (but also, perhaps, more likely to be taken advantage of).

The notion of an authoritarian personality has largely gone out of fashion among mainstream psychologists. Closely connected to it, however, is the concept of *identification with the aggressor.* Here, the victim tends reflexively to adopt the attributes of a powerful punishing agent (parent, government) in order to alleviate anxiety; in the process, the victim is transformed into an aggressor, either directly or indirectly by supporting aggression on the part of others. It may be significant that comparatively permissive societies seem to be less warlike than those with high levels of physical punishment of children and of sexual repression.

## Alienation and Totalism

Psychoanalysts Erich Fromm and Erik Erikson have emphasized, more than their drive-oriented colleagues, the influences of culture, society, and the environment on people's propensity for engaging in violent and other antisocial conduct. They have also focused on the role of painful, or traumatic, experiences operating through nonrational psychic processes.

Fromm distinguished between *defensive aggression* and *malignant aggression,* with the latter involving a passionate drive to hurt others (sadism) or oneself (masochism). But unlike the human nature theorists, he attributed malignant aggression to social conditions rather than to innate human traits. In particular, Fromm blamed *alienation,* an acute loneliness and disconnectedness from others, for the inclination by some people to avenge their pain by acts of extreme destruction. According to Fromm, those who are extremely alienated are also ripe candidates for inclusion in violent organizations, where they can find satisfaction in a group that is united by its hatred of others. This might include the Ku Klux Klan and other neo-Nazis in the United States, skinheads in Great Britain, and other "terrorist" and hate groups worldwide. It must also be noted, however, that feelings of social and political alienation might also motivate psychologically healthy personalities to participate in social movements to *oppose* injustices and wars.

In a similar vein, Erikson pointed out that, especially when it is changing rapidly, a society may generate ambiguities and unresolved stresses that combine with the individual's developmental problems to produce *totalism,* a susceptibility to all-or-nothing simplifications: us versus them, good versus evil, God versus the devil. War demands substantial sacrifices, not only economic and political but also a willingness to sacrifice one's life and to go against the standard societal prohibition against taking another's life. Accordingly, it is not surprising that totalistic thinking goes hand-in-hand with war.

## Prejudice, Images of the Enemy, and Human Needs

During the 1950s, the psychologist Gordon Allport argued that individual prejudice is founded on ignorance of others; therefore, less ignorance would mean less prejudice. Allport claimed that conflicts escalate due to ignorance of one's adversaries. According to Allport's "contact hypothesis," an increase in social interaction between members of in- and out-groups could reduce intergroup prejudice. Intergroup contact would lead to reduced intergroup prejudice if the contact situation embodies four conditions: 1) equal status between the groups in the situation; 2) common goals; 3) no competition between the groups; and 4) authority sanction for the contact. Subsequent research has shown that, in fact, increased intergroup contact correlates with reduced intergroup prejudice. About a decade after Allport's work, the psychiatrist Jerome Frank and the political psychologist Ralph White emphasized the dangers of developing diabolical enemy images people tend to create especially when they feel threatened.

Many violent conflicts result from the suppression of human needs, in large part because, according to the noted peace researcher John Burton, basic needs, such as security, and such core values as freedom are not negotiable, unlike interests, which are negotiable and depend on circumstances. And Johan Galtung also emphasizes the primacy of human needs, which, if frustrated, may engender intrastate and destructive identity conflicts. He argues that sustainable peace requires the satisfaction of our needs for security, identity, well-being, and self-determination.

## Attributions and Just-World Theories of Behavior

Attributions refer to the causal explanations that people devise in order rationalize both physical events and human behavior, especially acts perceived as successes or failures and that benefit or harm oneself and others. Attribution theory is especially relevant for understanding behavior that is based on cognitive errors and biases and that may often lead to interpersonal and group conflict.

These attributions are governed by such attribution biases as the "illusion of control." This is an idea put forward by contemporary "just-world theory," according to which there is a strong tendency for people to believe that the world is a just place, one in which people get what they deserve: "good things happen to good people and bad things happen to bad people." Therefore, we tend to blame the victim for his or her misfortune, and not the society, culture, economy, or environment. If our thinking is "self-serving" and "other-blaming," then it's easy to valorize one's "own" group and demean or demonize others and to rationalize "our" good fortune and the misfortune of others.

Biased attributions may also be present at the level of larger-scale societal, class, religious, cultural, and even civilizational attributions. For example, many Westerners, especially affluent ones, tend to make more dispositional attributions ("individuals make their own destinies"), based on shared cultural assumptions of Western individualism, whereas people in non-Western cultures may attribute beneficial or harmful events and actions to fate, nature, the collectivity, or the "will of God." This provides an ideological and motivational basis for a "clash of civilizations" and a "war between cultures," with all participants in the conflict believing they are "good," their adversaries are "evil," and "God is on our side."

The social-psychological process of categorizing individuals into in-groups and out-groups may lead to depersonalization: individuals are perceived as without distinctive features and as anonymous members of a "mass." And "they" may no longer viewed as (fully) human, especially when language of dehumanization is at play. The discourse of dehumanization motivates and activates stereotypical and ethnocentric thinking and behavior; once viewed as "sub-human," other individuals and groups are easily stripped of their dignity, and their humanity is denied. Discriminatory, belligerent, and even genocidal behavior against "nonpersons" may therefore be "justifiable."

Crimes against humanity share a common language of dehumanization. Labeling people as more or less human facilitates or makes possible denying them their basic and essential dignity as full-fledged human beings. To psychologist Marilyn Brewer, an important part of the solution to human oppression is therefore to change from dehumanizing, "toxic" rhetoric to life-affirming alternatives. Brewer speaks of an "expansive definition of humanity," one that embraces all human beings regardless of their physical characteristics or stage of life.[19]

## Altruism, Aggression, and Reconciliation

In sharp contrast to the paradigm that human behavior is primarily individualistic and egoistic, altruism denotes activities that are costly to individuals themselves but benefit others. According to the "empathy-altruism hypothesis," empathic concern (an emotional reaction brought about by the act of perspective-taking and characterized by such feelings as compassion, tenderness, soft-heartedness, and sympathy for another) leads to truly selfless motivation to help another person. In his 1759 book, *The Theory of the Moral Sentiments*, Adam Smith—better known as an early theorist of capitalism—wrote of the universality of such perceptions:

> How selfish soever man may be supposed, there are evidently some principles in his nature, which interest him in the fortunes of others, and render their happiness necessary to him, though he derives nothing from it, except the pleasure of seeing it. Of this kind is pity or compassion, the emotion we feel for the misery of others, when we either see it, or are made to conceive it in a very lively manner. That we often derive sorrow from the sorrows of others, is a matter of fact too obvious to require any instances to prove it; for this sentiment, like all the other original passions of human nature, is by no means confined to the virtuous or the humane, though they perhaps may feel it with the most exquisite sensibility. The greatest ruffian, the most hardened violator of the laws of society, is not altogether without it.

The distinguished Dutch ethologist Franz De Waal argues against the allegedly antisocial character of aggression and instead proposes a "reconciliation hypothesis," according to which aggression is a well-integrated part of social life. By examining the dynamics of social interactions among nonhuman primates, de Waal argues that confrontation should not be viewed as a barrier to sociality but rather as an unavoidable element upon which social relationships can be built and strengthened through reconciliation. Social animals, including but not limited to human beings, seek contact with former opponents and engage in postconflict reunion practices like kissing, embracing, sexual intercourse, grooming, and so on. Reconciliation serves to decrease aggression and socially destabilizing anxiety. It occurs especially after a conflict between parties whose possible partnership may have a high socially reproductive value.

De Waal's demonstration of reconciliation in both monkeys and apes supports the idea that forgiveness and peacemaking are widespread among nonhuman primates. The evolutionary advantages of reconciliation are obvious for animals that survive through mutual aid, that is., the continuation of cooperation among parties with partially conflicting interests. De Waal's findings regarding nonhuman primates (especially among the young) may also have significant potential applications for understanding human conflict resolution: with reconciliation seen as a shared heritage of the primate order.

# The Attractions of War

In *Notes From Underground,* Dostoyevsky wrote, "In former days we saw justice in bloodshed and with our conscience at peace exterminated those we thought proper to kill. Now we do think bloodshed abominable and yet we engage in this abomination, and with more energy than ever."[20] This energy derives at least in part from the fact that some people find war a positive experience. Many combatants have extolled the sheer intensity of confronting the basic phenomena of life and death and, in the process, exploring the boundaries of one's capacities. For some soldiers, especially young men, there is something exhilarating about meeting death face-to-face, perhaps even heroically and for a noble cause, rather than being overtaken alone in the night. Pierre Teilhard de Chardin (who served in World War I) wrote:

> The front cannot but attract us, because it is . . . the extreme boundary between what you are already aware of, and what is still in the process of formation. Not only do you see there things that you experience nowhere else, but you also see emerge from within yourself an underlying stream of clarity, energy, and freedom that is to be found hardly anywhere else in ordinary life. . . . This exaltation is accompanied by a certain pain. Nonetheless it is indeed an exaltation. And that is why one likes the front in spite of everything, and misses it.[21]

For others, there may be a compelling sexual component, as revealed in this passage from the American novelist Norman Mailer:

> All the deep, dark urges of man, the sacrifices on the hilltops, the churning lusts of night and sleep, weren't all of them contained in the shattering, screaming burst of a shell? The phallus-like shell that rides through a shining vagina of steel. The curve of sexual excitement and discharge, which is, after all, the physical core of life.[22]

Most significant of all, perhaps, is the satisfaction of "belonging" and companionship, particularly a kind of male bonding, which most men do not experience during civilian life. Shakespeare's Henry V rhapsodizes about the pleasure the forthcoming battle holds for

> We few, we happy few, we band of brothers;
>
> For he to-day that sheds his blood with me
>
> Shall be my brother. (*Henry V,* IV, iii)

The American philosopher and psychologist William James (1842–1910) believed that the raw emotional appeal of war constituted one of the greatest difficulties in overcoming it. In a renowned essay, James presented the case for war's attractiveness:

> The war against war is going to be no holiday excursion or camping party. The military feelings are too deeply grounded to abdicate their place among our ideals until better substitutes are offered. . . . Showing war's irrationality and horror is of no effect upon him. The horrors make the fascination. War is the *strong* life; it is life in *extremis*. . . . Its "horrors" are a cheap price to pay for rescue from the only alternative supposed, of a world of clerks and teachers, of . . . consumer's leagues and associated charities, of industrialism unlimited. . . . Militarism is the great preserver of our ideals of hardihood, and human life with no use for hardihood would be contemptible. Without risks or prizes for the darer, history would be insipid indeed.[23]

James then suggested that these attractions could be overcome only by substituting other crusades, involving risk, daring, and hard work, which he called "the moral equivalent of war."

These selections involve not so much enthusiasm for war as a grudging recognition that *even* war has not only its horrors but also its attractions. Other approaches have been more admiring of war itself. Thus, a famous *Bushidō* tract from ancient Japan advises that "when all things in life are false, there is only one thing true, death."[24] Although even the most war-prone ideologies generally claim that their long-term goals are to eliminate war, there is a notable modern exception: fascism. Fascism glorifies war, and (judging by its success in the 20th century) it struck a favorable chord in many people. "War alone," wrote Italian dictator Benito Mussolini,

> brings up to their highest tension all human energies and puts a stamp of nobility upon the people who have the courage to meet it. All other trials are substitutes, which never really put a man in front of himself in the alternative of life and death. A doctrine, therefore, which begins with a prejudice in favor of peace is foreign to Fascism.[25]

A final contributing reason for war, working at the individual level, may well be a kind of sanitized romanticizing of battle, found in many children's cartoons and toys, movies, music, art, and literature. For example, consider the following verse by English poet A. E. Housman:

> I did not lose my heart in summer's eve,
>
> When roses to the moonrise burst apart:
>
> When plumes were under heel and lead was flying,
>
> In blood and smoke and flame I lost my heart.
>
> I lost it to a soldier and a foeman,
>
> A chap that did not kill me, but he tried;

That took the sabre straight and took it striking

And laughed and kissed his hand to me and died.[26]

To be sure, there also exists a rich catalog of antiwar songs, stories, movies, and poems, ranging from the delicate and plaintive (as in the songs "Where Have All the Flowers Gone?" and "The Drums of War") to the unrelentingly realistic and grotesque (as in *All Quiet on the Western Front, Johnny Got His Gun, Catch-22, Saving Private Ryan,* and *The Hurt Locker*). Opponents of war, however, are obliged to recognize those aspects of war that have long exercised a positive appeal for many humans.

# Inhibitions Against War

The history of warfare shows that people are capable of the most heinous acts of brutality. From American history alone, consider the massacre of Sioux Indians at Wounded Knee in South Dakota in the late 19th century or the massacre at My Lai in Vietnam about 100 years later: In both cases, hundreds of men, women, and children were slaughtered wantonly. Indeed, the preceding sections may leave the impression that war exerts a virtually irresistible attraction to human beings at the individual level, whether through our innate characteristics, through our experiences, or via the lure of excitement, camaraderie, and ideology. But in fact, even beyond ethical and religious strictures, there are many inhibitions that serve to check the personal propensity for war.

One of these inhibiting factors is fear for one's own life. In Euripides' *The Suppliants,* the Theban herald points out that "if death had been before their own eyes when they were giving their votes, Hellas [Greece] would never have rushed to her doom in mad desire for battle." There are, in fact, very few authentic heroes during a war; most soldiers seek to do the minimum necessary to save themselves and their close colleagues.

As to alleged bloodlust and war fever, consider that during World War II, rarely did more than 25% of American soldiers fire their guns in battle; even during intense battles, about 15% opened fire. And this applied to highly trained combat infantrymen. A study sponsored by the U.S. Army concluded that "it is therefore reasonable to believe that the average and healthy individual—the man who can endure the mental and physical stresses of combat—still has such an inner and usually unrealized resistance toward killing a fellow man that he will not of his own volition take life if it is possible to turn away from that responsibility."[27] It can even be argued that, in many wars before 1950, fear of killing, rather than fear of being killed, was the largest cause of battle failure.

By the Korean and Vietnam wars, however, the percentage of soldiers willing to fire their weapons appears to have gone up significantly, largely because of modified training and greater emphasis on establishing within-group solidarity among individual combat units. A major part of military training (especially in boot camp) seeks to countermand the basic moral teaching—not limited, incidentally, to Western tradition—"Thou shalt not kill." The goal of basic training, in the armed forces of most countries, has not so much been the teaching of new techniques and skills as the inculcation of new attitudes: unquestioning obedience to military superiors and a willingness to kill. Despite some resistance, most people can in fact learn these things, usually in just a few weeks. This should not be surprising, since a profound asymmetry of power exists between the recruits and the officers who train them: "Recruits usually have no more than twenty years' experience of the world, most of it as children, while the armies have had all of history to practice and perfect their techniques."[28]

Actual killing during combat is widely considered the role of enlisted men or, at most, junior officers. By 1914, for example, lieutenants and captains in the British Army led men into battle carrying only a swagger stick or, at most, a pistol. "Officers do not kill" was the common understanding at that time, and there is reason to believe that, if they had the choice, most enlisted men would not have done so either. George Orwell, for example, who fought as an anti-Fascist volunteer on the Loyalist side during the Spanish Civil War, recounted that he was unable to shoot an enemy soldier whom he observed

> half-dressed and . . . holding up his trousers with both hands. . . . I did not shoot partly because of that detail about his trousers. . . . A man who is holding up his trousers isn't a "Fascist," he is visibly a fellow-creature, similar to yourself, and you don't feel like shooting him.[29]

## Some Issues in Nuclear Psychology

When it comes to nuclear war, feelings of attraction and revulsion are particularly intense. Some people evince a strange love for weapons of such all-encompassing power (hence the title of the famous satirical movie *Dr. Strangelove or: How I Learned to Stop Worrying and Love the Bomb*). Others, by contrast, are especially repelled by the grisly prospect of ending life on so massive a scale. And yet, because a full-fledged nuclear conflict has not occurred and because, in addition, the effects of nuclear explosions are so powerful as literally to stagger the human imagination, most people have difficulty focusing their minds and energies on such a topic, which is at once horrifying and yet strangely unreal.

When confronted with deeply unpleasant information, for example, people often respond with *denial.* This process is particularly well known with respect to personal death: Virtually every cognitively unimpaired adult recognizes that eventually he or she will die; however, most of us go about our lives as though our own death holds little reality. When confronted with facts, we generally concur; if not, we often practice denial. Something similar can be identified with respect to the nuclear danger: Most of us go about our daily lives as though the prospect of instantaneous nuclear holocaust does not hang over us, simply because such an overwhelming threat is too painful and emotionally disruptive to admit into our moment-by-moment consciousness.

This behavior, although presumably adaptive for the individual, also has unintended and potentially dangerous consequences. By refusing to confront unpleasant realities, people who might otherwise become mobilized in opposition to nuclear weapons are likely to place their attention and energy elsewhere. Moreover, they abandon the field to those who have insulated themselves from the negative consequences of their activities and who, by virtue of career advancement or ideology, have committed themselves to a more pronuclear, and possibly prowar, orientation.

Denial is encouraged by the fact that nuclear weapons tend to lack psychological reality: They are kept in secret, restricted installations, and in the United States the Department of Defense refuses, as a matter of policy, either to "confirm or deny" their presence. This policy has ostensibly been adopted so as to keep information from would-be nuclear terrorists. Regardless, one important effect of official secrecy clearly is to keep the American public uninformed and, to some extent, to facilitate denial. Hence, for most people, nuclear weapons cannot be seen, touched, smelled, or heard, so it requires a conscious effort to consider that they exist at all.

Closely related to denial is another personal, psychological phenomenon of the nuclear age, often called *psychic numbing.* This phrase was originally applied by psychiatrist Robert J. Lifton to the *hibakusha,* the victims of the atomic bombing of Hiroshima and Nagasaki. Psychic numbing refers to a loss of emotional sensitivity and awareness that appeared to result from the survivors' immersion in the mass death that characterized those events. It can be argued that, to some extent, we are all victims of Hiroshima and Nagasaki, in that all of us suffer from some degree of psychic numbing, as the nuclear menace pervades our unconscious.

## A FINAL NOTE ON INDIVIDUAL-LEVEL EXPLANATIONS OF WARS

Approximately 1% to 2% of human deaths during the 20th century were inflicted by other human beings. In other words, 98% to 99% of recent human deaths were *not* caused directly by intentional, individually inflicted violence. Moreover, of those deaths caused by other people, the majority are due to collective violence rather than to individual aggression.

Many social scientists have insisted that war is a human invention, not a biological necessity. They cite the high level of social organization and structuring involved in any military enterprise and the fact that different societies make war, if they do so at all, in very different ways, depending on the social structures and technological options. Different societies also make war for different reasons, including pride, prestige, revenge, and the quest for resources. It can also be argued that decisions regarding war, especially in large, modern societies, are not made at the individual level, or at least not at the level of the average citizen. Certainly, such decisions do not involve the simple summation of all individual inclinations within the population; nor do they follow the results of plebiscites or referenda submitted to the citizenry to vote for or against a particular war. Rather, war is decided by political (and often military, economic, and strategic) elites, after which the populace generally goes along, sometimes eagerly but usually only after considerable manipulation or even outright coercion. And sometimes, war isn't really deliberatively "decided" at all; it just seems to "happen," often by mistake or misjudgment.

In addition, although war typically *arouses* great passions, it is not always true that war is the *result* of such passions. In some cases, wars appear to have been chosen by intelligent, instrumentally rational individuals, after carefully calculating the costs and benefits of alternative courses of action. According to military historian Michael Howard:

> In general, men have fought during the past two hundred years neither because they are aggressive nor because they are acquisitive animals, but because they are reasoning ones: because they discern, or believe they can discern, dangers before they become immediate, the possibility of threats before they are made.[30]

Humans also fight when they can perceive—whether accurately or not—that they will gain substantially by doing so.

One influential view, then, is that, rather than being a result of instinctive human nature, war can be the consequence of our coolest, most cerebral faculties. Individuals may fight with passion when placed in warlike situations, but throughout history, authorities have often had to force their supposedly vicious, hotheaded, and war-loving citizens to fight at all. Traditionally, many soldiers have been forced into battle with guns at their backs, hating and fearing their officers and military discipline more than the "enemy."

In any event, any serious effort to prevent war—and to establish a just and lasting peace—must take into account the inclinations and behavior of individual people, especially people with wealth and power. However, the "war against war" should not limit itself to the level of individual psychology, since, as we shall soon see, the behavior of organized groups may differ significantly from that predicted by a study of personal motivation or biology.

## NOTES

1. J. William Fulbright. Preface to Jerome D. Frank. 1967. *Sanity and Survival.* New York: Random House.

2. Hans Morgenthau. 1967. *Politics Among Nations.* New York: Knopf.

3. Konrad Lorenz. 1966. *On Aggression.* New York: Harcourt, Brace & World.

4. Edward O. Wilson. 1971. In J. Eisenberg and W. Dillon, eds., *Man and Beast: Comparative Social Behavior.* Washington, DC: Smithsonian Institution Press.

5. Edward O. Wilson. 1975. *Sociobiology: The New Synthesis.* Cambridge, MA: Harvard University Press.

6. Sigmund Freud. 1964. Reprinted in J. Strachey, ed. and trans., *The Standard Edition of the Complete Psychological Works of Sigmund Freud.* London: Hogarth.

7. Thomas Hobbes. 1930. *Selections.* F. J. E. Woodbridge, ed. New York: Scribner.

8. John Calvin. 1956. *On God and Man.* F. W. Strothmann, ed. New York: Frederick Ungar.

9. Freud. *The Standard Edition.*

10. John Milton. 1953–1982. "The Doctrine and Discipline of Divorce." In *Complete Prose Works.* New Haven, CT: Yale University Press.

11. Reinhold Niebuhr. 1940. *Christianity and Power Politics.* New York: Scribner.

12. John Dollard et al. 1939. *Frustration and Aggression.* New Haven, CT: Yale University Press.

13. Ibid.

14. John Nef. 1950. *War and Human Progress.* Cambridge, MA: Harvard University Press.

15. John Paul Scott. 1975. *Aggression.* Chicago: University of Chicago Press.

16. Mark May. 1943. *A Social Psychology of War and Peace.* New Haven, CT: Yale University Press.

17. See Joshua Goldstein. 2010. *War and Gender.* Cambridge and New York: Cambridge University Press: 403-07.

18. According to Merton, "The self-fulfilling prophecy is, in the beginning, a *false* definition of the situation evoking a new behavior which makes the original false conception come 'true'. This specious validity of the self-fulfilling prophecy perpetuates a reign of error. For the prophet will cite the actual course of events as proof that he was right from the very beginning." Robert K. Merton. 1968. *Social Theory and Social Structure.* New York: Free Press, 477.

19. M. B. Brewer. 1991. "The Social Self—On Being the Same and Different at the Same Time." *Personality and Social Psychology Bulletin*, 17(5): 475–482; M. B. Brewer. 2000. "Superordinate Goals Versus Superordinate Identity as Bases for Intergroup Cooperation," in D. Capozza and R. Brown, eds., *Social Identity Processes* (pp. 117–132). London: Sage; and M. B. Brewer. 2007. "The Importance of Being We: Human Nature and Intergroup Relations." *American Psychologist*, 62: 728–738.

20. Fyodor Dostoyevsky. 1960. *Notes From Underground.* New York: E. P. Dutton.

21. Pierre Teilhard de Chardin. 1965. *The Making of a Mind: Letters From a Soldier-Priest, 1914–1919.* New York: Harper & Row.

22. Norman Mailer. 1968. *The Armies of the Night.* New York: New American Library.

23. William James. 1911. "The Moral Equivalent of War." In *Memories and Studies.* New York: Longmans, Green.

24. Z. Tamotsu. 1937. *Cultural Nippon.* Iwado, ed. and trans. Tokyo: Nippon Cultural Foundation.

25. Quoted in Seyom Brown. 1987. *The Causes and Prevention of War.* New York: St. Martin's.

26. From A. E. Housman. 1936. *More Poems.* New York: Knopf.

27. S. L. A. Marshall. 1947. *Men Against Fire.* New York: William Morrow.

28. Gwynn Dyer. 1987. *War.* New York: Crown.

29. George Orwell. 1968. *Homage to Catalonia.* New York: Harcourt Brace Jovanovich.

30. Michael Howard. 1984. *The Causes of War.* Cambridge, MA: Harvard University Press.

## QUESTIONS FOR FURTHER REFLECTION

1. To what degree is aggression "in our genes"? Is it learned, innate, or something in between?

2. How do you evaluate the Freudian claim that human beings have a "death drive"? What are the arguments for and against this view?

3. Do the attractions of war outweigh our inhibitions against it? Why or why not?

4. To what extent is war a biological necessity or a human invention, a learned behavior that could be unlearned?

5. What are the strengths and weaknesses of individual-level explanations of wars?

## SUGGESTIONS FOR FURTHER READING

Albert Camus. 1972. *Neither Victims Nor Executioners.* Chicago: World Without War Publications.

John Dippel. 2010. *War and Sex: A Brief History of Men's Urge for Battle.* Amherst, NY: Prometheus Books.

Chris Hedges. 2004. *War Is a Force That Gives Us Meaning.* New York: Public Affairs.

Edward O. Wilson. 1979. *On Human Nature.* Cambridge, MA: Harvard University Press.

Ervin Staub. 2003. *The Psychology of Good and Evil.* Cambridge, UK: Cambridge University Press.

Sigmund Freud. 1963. *Character and Culture.* New York: Colliers Books.

D. J. Christie., R.V. Wagner., and D.D. Winter. 2001. *Peace, Conflict, and Violence: Peace Psychology for the 21st Century.* Upper Saddle River, NJ: Prentice-Hall.

Franz de Waal. 1990. *Peacemaking Among Primates.* Cambridge, MA: Harvard University Press.

# CHAPTER 7

# THE GROUP LEVEL

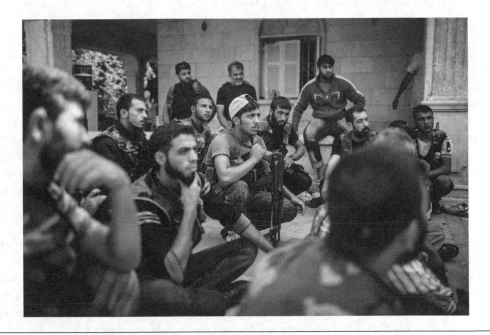

Fighters from the "Free Syrian Army" listening to their commander before going to battle during the Syrian Civil War, in 2012.

*Source:* © 2008 Corbis Corporation.

*Man is a social animal who dislikes his fellow man.*

—Eugène Delacroix

*It is not easy to see how the more extreme forms of nationalism can long survive when men have seen the Earth in its true perspective as a single small globe against the stars.*

—Arthur C. Clarke

Regardless of individual participants, war remains fundamentally a group activity. A single person may be able to incite or catalyze international or domestic conflict, as did the assassin who killed Archduke Franz Ferdinand in 1914, thereby "causing" World War I, or Adolf Hitler, who "caused" World War II in Europe. Similarly, individuals can *go to* war, by enlisting or being conscripted. But an individual cannot *make* war, since it is by definition a group endeavor. And strange things happen when collective concerns become more important than individual differences among the group members.

Let us take a brief look at the early history of warfare and then quickly review its occurrence among premodern and nontechnological peoples, not because war was necessarily responsible for shaping part of our behavior as a species but because it has characterized much of human prehistory and history, and because the "group-loving" as well as "group-opposing" aspects of humanity provide powerful indicators of our likely future.

# War: Its Prehistory and Early History

## War and Human Evolution

Very little is known about the earliest human warfare. It seems likely, however, that social grouping among primitive human beings was highly adaptive—that is, it probably contributed to cultural and biological survival. By associating with other individuals living near them, our ancestors were able to share information and resources, to gain assistance in caring for their young, and to defend themselves against predators. Presumably, social grouping also enabled prehistoric human beings to bring down larger prey than would have been possible for a solitary hunter.

Some anthropologists have suggested that the early stages of human social evolution were promoted by selection for effective hunting, which favored the ability to fashion and use tools, to walk upright (thereby freeing the hands), and to communicate effectively with one's fellow hunters. This "hunting hypothesis" has been disputed, however, by others who emphasize the importance of gathering and digging roots. While the hunting hypothesis focuses on the dominant role of men, the foraging hypothesis places more emphasis on the role of women.

The role of war in early human evolution has also been disputed. One extreme view holds that war—even prehistoric or preindustrial war—is such a recent development that it exerted essentially no influence on the human species. The other view, and one that may be equally extreme, claims that warfare was an essential component of human evolution, perhaps *the* major selective force operating in our early history. From this perspective, groups and their constituent individuals that were more successful in hostilities with other groups were more likely to leave offspring who themselves possessed traits leading to such success.

The widespread dispersion of early human groups probably made contact—and thus potential hostility—with other group members rare. Nonetheless, significant interactions likely still took place in regions of common interest: at waterholes, in areas of local food abundance, and so on. We may never know whether early war was important in shaping human evolution; even if it was, however, it seems unlikely that this would somehow doom the human species to unending war in the future. After all, war often entails such socially desirable elements as courage, initiative, coordination, self-restraint, and self-sacrifice. A winning group would presumably be one that cooperated well . . . at least internally. Making airborne missiles, for example, whether spears or intercontinental ballistic missiles (ICBMs), is not a frenzied act of passion but rather a labor of considered intelligence. (Launching these missiles, especially in retaliation, however, may in part involve more-primitive mental processes.)

No clear evidence of warfare—as opposed to fighting and skirmishing between mobile bands—can be found during Paleolithic (early Stone Age) or even Mesolithic times, from 10,000 to 8000 BCE. At this point, hunting and gathering societies were slowly replaced by economies based on the domestication of plants and animals. War is first discernible during the early Neolithic period, which began around 8000 BCE The remains of the ancient city of Jericho (dating from 7500 BCE) show clear signs of fortified towers and walls, suggesting that they were military defenses, probably necessitated by the accumulation of wealth via agriculture, artisan-ship, and trade, which in turn made such places targets for aggressive raiding or war.

## Why Study Premodern and Nontechnological Warfare?

Anthropologists studying modern peoples have found examples of warfare that may in some ways predate the maintenance of fixed and fortified cities for the defending of accumulated wealth. The actions of certain nontechnological societies, even if "primitive" by Western stan-dards, are not the same as those that occurred in earlier stages of human history. Nonetheless, by examining nontechnological "war" among contemporary people (e.g., in the Amazon basin or the outback of Australia), we may learn something about our ancestors' behavior in pre-Neolithic days. And this in turn might yield some insight into underlying tendencies among human beings as a species.

A study of the diversity of human war making might lead to some useful generalizations beyond the following claims, most clearly articulated by the historian Arnold Toynbee: Extremes of climate (both very hot and very cold) are less conducive to the development of large-scale war making than are temperate climates; prairie and seacoast dwellers tend to be more war prone than mountain or forest inhabitants; pastoralists (nomads) are similarly more war prone than are settled agriculturalists. We can also go beyond the simplistic (and misleading) generalizations that human beings have always fought wars, that they have hardly ever fought wars, that they always fight wars for practical reasons, or that they never do so.

# Functions of Nontechnological Wars

Most analysts of war, whether of technological or nontechnological conflict, agree that warfare is, in most cases, ethically a "bad thing." But there is disagreement among sociologists studying Western war and among anthropologists studying its nontechnological counterparts as to whether war is adaptive or maladaptive. Advocates of the latter, *dysfunctional* perspective empha-size the disruptive and retrogressive aspects of war: how it prevents growth, development, and material and social progress, as well as the obviously negative effects of destruction, suffering, and death. Proponents of the former viewpoint claim that preindustrial and nontechnological war can be *eufunctional*—that is, it can serve an overall positive role for its participants by provid-ing social solidarity within each competing unit, by yielding access to resources (notably food, territory, and/or mates) or by enhancing the prestige of the victors.

Walter Bagehot, a noted economist, expressed the eufunctional perspective when he wrote that "civilization begins because the beginning of civilization is a military advantage." Herbert Spencer, a distinguished 19th-century proto-sociologist, also emphasized the prosocial aspects of war: "From the very beginning, the conquest of one people over another has been, in the main, the conquest of the social man over the anti-social man." This is a challenging suggestion, especially for people who think of war as the extreme in antisocial behavior.

War is not a simple or unitary phenomenon among modern nation-states; nor is it readily explained among nontechnological peoples. The following functions of premodern war have been suggested:

1. Provide outlets for aggressiveness of young men and thus reduce within-society tensions.

2. Provide opportunities for social advancement via enhancement of prestige.

3. Gain access to food resources, notably animal protein.

4. Obtain women from neighboring groups.

5. Obtain land from neighboring groups.

6. Correct imbalance in the sex ratio—in certain societies, female infanticide creates an excess of males, which can be corrected by mortality during war.

7. Achieve revenge, which often carries both symbolic and social payoffs.

8. Provide the opportunity for enlargement of tribal domain and (rarely) for certain individuals to establish large kingdoms or empires.

At its simplest level, nontechnological war appears to be largely concerned with interpersonal competition and struggles to obtain individual prestige, rather than with large-scale conflicts between social groups or even with the accumulation of land, women, or other resources. Thus, in premodern war, involvement and motivation tend to be at the personal level, as compared with its modern counterpart, which is mainly directed toward conquest or the advancement of state interests. In modern technological warfare, personal involvement and motivation tend to be relatively less intense because the benefits to be derived are more diffuse, often ideological rather than practical and immediate. It should be noted, however, that anthropologists are divided over the degree to which ecological forces are responsible for human war and, if so, which forces might predominate.

# Characteristics of Premodern and Nontechnological Wars

The renowned anthropologist Bronislaw Malinowski identified six categories of armed aggressive behavior among nontechnological peoples:

1. "Fighting, private and angry," which serves as the prototype of criminal behavior

2. "Fighting, collective and organized," among groups within the same cultural unit

3. "Armed raids, as a type of man-hunting sport, for purposes of headhunting, cannibalism, human sacrifices, and the collection of other trophies"

4. "Warfare as the political expression of early nationalism, that is, the tendency to make the tribe-nation and tribe-state coincide"

5. "Military expeditions of organized pillage, slave-raiding and collective robbery"

6. "Wars between two culturally differentiated groups as an instrument of national policy"[1]

Premodern war can be understood by considering its apparent functions. "Among almost all American Indians," according to one authority, ". . . war existed to bring glory to the individual, and since war was relatively safe, everyone was happy even though few tactical, strategic and economic advantages for a whole people were obtained."[2] Even the causing of death or injury to one's opponents was not always a goal for premodern warriors, and mortality appears generally to have been low; premodern and nontechnological "wars" often end after a single death or even a serious injury. The Dani people of New Guinea, for instance, traditionally do not use feathers on their war arrows, thereby reducing accuracy and keeping casualties down. And the Ibo of Nigeria used to count up their dead after a war, after which the side losing fewer warriors would compensate the "losers" with money, to avoid any grudges.

Premodern war has typically been bounded by numerous rules, specific to each tribe. For example, the Nuer of Sudan were forbidden from using spears against anyone living within a given proximity; beyond that distance, such lethal weapons were allowed. Among the Dani, truces automatically occurred at nightfall, although a battle was considered unfinished until at least one person was killed on either side.

Premodern wars have usually been fought for limited goals and in a limited way. Warfare among nontechnological peoples is typically of this sort—over revenge, women, animal protein, prestige, or, occasionally, access to physical space for hunting, farming, or living. Only rarely does lethal group conflict erupt due to contesting ideologies. In fact, neighboring groups, usually the opponents in nontechnological wars, typically share the same culture, language, and worldview. And the goal of such conflict only rarely includes complete destruction of the other side or anything approaching "unconditional surrender."

Among the most widespread customs associated with premodern warfare are those involving the extensive use of rituals to signal the initiation of warfare, as well as the change of one's status from civilian to warrior. Magic amulets were common, as were special ways of shaving and adorning the body, typically with paint and/or feathers. Such techniques ostensibly help ward off evil and bad luck, but their more practical function appears to be the promotion of group solidarity. This includes modern-day uniforms and "totemic" symbols such as insignias, regimental banners, and national flags. Ritual abstinence, notably from food or sex, apparently helped relieve the guilt of killing while also signifying that one was special, different, and thus permitted to do certain things that were forbidden during peacetime. Repetitive dancing and singing, often with the use of drugs, has been characteristic of warfare among people in Asia, Africa, Polynesia, and certain Native American tribes; this apparently reduces fear and helps cement commitment among members of a war party. Rehearsals of battle serve to diminish anxiety and also provide practice for warriors going into combat.

Typically, elaborate rituals are also performed after a battle, especially if the warrior has actually killed somebody. The great majority of societies consider that anyone who kills—even in war—is somehow "unclean" and must be ritually purified before being readmitted into civilian life: Fasting or abstinence is common, often with varying periods of isolation from the home group. In modern societies, returning soldiers are often accorded medals, parades, membership in special veterans' organizations, and their own cemeteries.

# Alternatives to Nontechnological Warfare

There are a variety of seemingly peaceful societies, defined variously as (1) not having wars fought on their soil, (2) not fighting wars with other groups, or (3) not experiencing any civil wars or internal collective violence. (Interestingly, the frequency of external war has very little correlation with that of internal war.) Some examples of the most peaceable societies include the Semai of Malaysia, the Siriono of Bolivia, the Mbuti pygmies of central Africa, the !Kung Bushmen of the African Kalahari Desert, and the Copper Eskimos of northern Canada.

It is increasingly recognized that certain nontechnological people are notable not so much for their lack of aggression as for their effective and nonviolent way of coping with it. For example, the Eskimos of central Greenland slap each other's faces; in western and eastern Greenland, they engage in prolonged singing duels, with individuals competing to be more imaginative and to engage their audience more effectively. Many inhabitants of Alaska, Siberia, and Baffin Island have traditionally settled their disputes by wrestling. The Kwakiutl Indians of the northwest coast of North America have competed via potlatch feasts, in which chiefs sought to outdo each other by demonstrating how much wealth they could sacrifice. And the African Bushmen (!Kung) and pygmies use laughter and ridicule.

In other stateless human societies, war is either absent or quite rare. Among those factors that help prevent the outbreak of organized civil violence, the following appear to be especially important (although not all are present at the same time): (1) socialization toward the peaceful settling of conflicts and disapproval of violence or force, (2) the presence of a group or tribal decision-making system that applies effective sanctions against violent transgressors, (3) the opportunity for dissidents to emigrate to other groups, and (4) the existence of economic interdependence within the group.

As to the maintenance of peace between groups, several factors can be identified, although the enormous diversity of human cultures makes any generalizations hazardous. The perception of shared ancestry between different groups tends to inhibit violence between them, just as an emphasis on relatedness within a group (terms such as motherland, fatherland, "brothers and sisters," etc.) tends to foster greater internal group solidarity combined with an increased willingness to close ranks against other groups perceived as unrelated, foreign, and thus enemies. Similarly, peaceful relations among groups are often enhanced by establishing kinship ties through marriage.

According to the structuralist school of anthropology (whose most noted representative was the French anthropologist Claude Lévi-Strauss), a primary reason for the incest taboo is that by inducing people to marry outside the family, group members establish cooperative relationships with other groups, thereby minimizing the likelihood of destructive warfare between them. The phenomenon of establishing politically useful alliances via marriage has a long history in the West as well, at least at the level of ruling houses among the European monarchies.

Encouragement as well as insight can also be gained by looking into what have been called "peace systems," arrangements among neighboring societies that are specifically designed to achieve peace among the members. A recent review examined three such peace systems—the Upper Xingu River basin tribes of Brazil, the Iroquois Confederacy of upper New York State, and the European Union—and highlighted six features considered important in the creation and maintenance of intersocietal peace. There are: (1) a shared social identity among the participants; (2) interconnections among the subgroups, achieved by intermarriage, enhanced communication, and so forth; (3) interdependence, such that the well-being of the various subgroups is dependent upon peaceful coordination—as achieved, for example, via trade or other exchanges whereby all participants benefit; (4) "nonwarring values," which means the overt acknowledgment that peace is far better than war, which includes valorizing peacemakers more than war makers; (5) symbolism and public ceremonies that reinforce peace as both an ideal and a practical goal; and (6) superordinate institutions that manage conflicts when they arise. The existence of peace systems is consistent with what famed peace researcher Kenneth Boulding once proclaimed as his "First Law": If something exists, then it is possible![3]

# Underlying Group Processes

Human beings are highly social creatures. One of the most powerful human tendencies is to aggregate and somehow to distinguish the members of each group from other, comparable ones. This is typically achieved by shared language, customs, patterns of adornment, mythological and religious beliefs and practices, and so forth. Others who speak different languages (or even the same language but with a different accent), who worship different gods, or who follow a different political or economic system are readily identified as different and are often perceived as threatening. Sigmund Freud once wrote of the "narcissism of minor differences," whereby many people tend to focus on, and exaggerate, relatively inconsequential cultural traits that distinguish them from their neighbors.

## Benefits

Clearly, group life has important and empowering components, including the ability to pool resources, to cooperate, to achieve a division of labor, to learn and to teach, and simply to receive stimulation from the presence of one's fellows. As William James once wrote, "All the qualities of a man acquire dignity when he knows that the service of the collectivity that owns him need them. If proud of the collectivity, his own pride rises in proportion."[4] There is a powerful allure to being needed and appreciated and a strong tendency to associate oneself with a larger whole, thereby enhancing one's self-esteem and self-worth. There may also be genetic benefits, conveyed by enhanced reproductive success among returning warriors (balanced, to be sure, by costs incurred by those who don't return), as well as the possibility that even if individually unsuccessful, war-fighting genetic inclinations may experience higher evolutionary fitness if reflected in greater success among a warrior's relatives. There is currently a heated debate among biologists as to whether evolution proceeds via comparative success among individuals and their genes, or by the differential benefit accorded to groups. Either way, it is clear that as a general rule, larger groups have been able to defeat smaller ones, which itself may be responsible for the widespread preference for establishing group affiliations in the first place.

## Costs

But there are also disadvantages. Of these, one of the most significant is the loss of inhibitions that can result from immersion in a crowd, as a result of which a *mob psychology* can take over, through which individuals can engage in acts that would rarely if ever be done if they were acting alone. It can be debated whether war-making groups literally produce a new kind of entity, a social one having its own tendencies and characteristics, or whether groups simply give social sanction to individual tendencies—notably, aggressiveness, intolerance, and rage. Freud once commented that he could shame a single Nazi storm trooper, sent to search his apartment in Vienna, but when two were sent together, they became "good Nazis." And of course, once associated in a group, individuals become vulnerable to the "decisions" made by the collectivity, whether or not such actions are in their personal best interest.

## De-individuating

The process of *de-individuating* is an important part of group violence; it appears to involve four major components:

1. *The effect of validation by one's peers.* Members of homogeneous groups are more likely to respond to conflictual situations with hostility than are groups whose membership is more heterogeneous. Individual aggressiveness, when validated by the expressed aggressiveness of others, is more likely to be released.

2. *Diminished individual profile.* Biologists have identified something known as the "selfish herd" phenomenon, whereby animals as diverse as fish or starlings appear to flock together because, by doing so, each individual increases the chances that its neighbor—rather than itself—will fall victim to an approaching predator. Similarly, a human crowd seems to provide not only a feeling (as well as the reality) of strength in numbers but also a shield of protective anonymity.

3. *Leadership.* Groups are usually associated with highly visible and persuasive leaders, who may provide the impetus for group hostility by actively fomenting as well as directing violence that might not otherwise occur if individuals were left to their personal inclinations. And finally, the simple presence of leaders also tends to suggest to the group members that the leaders, rather than the followers, are likely to be at risk for retaliation, which in turn diminishes reluctance of the followers to participate.

4. *Contagious or imitative behavior.* A frustrated or angry person is much more likely to behave aggressively if he or she perceives others doing so. This may involve not only "getting the idea" of violence but also gaining a kind of social "permission" to behave in this way. Thus, it is well known that violence (or, to put a more favorable cast upon it, resistance to oppression) tends to spread when others witness or hear about the events. Examples include the violence of the French Revolution of 1789, the Luddite uprising in early-19th-century Britain, and the U.S. African American ghetto uprisings of the late 1960s. Less violent cases include the active resistance of Chinese students and workers in 1989, of Buddhist monks and civilians in Myanmar in 2007, and the recent Arab Spring.

## Dehumanization

Another prominent characteristic of group functioning is the tendency to *dehumanize* members of other groups—that is, to give the impression (to compatriots and, at least on a subconscious level, to oneself) that the other group members are not really (or fully) human at all. It is especially easy to dehumanize those who are recognizably different because of language, appearance, cultural practices, religion, political ideology, and so on.

Among various nontechnological peoples, even the word *human* is the same as the name for the tribe; members of different tribes are thus denied their humanity, as a result of which they can be killed with little or no remorse. Among modern technological peoples, language patterns during times of hostility reflect this tendency, especially with the use of animal terms to describe the opponent: vermin, insects, rats, pigs, dogs, and so forth. Even nonanimal slang terms have a similar effect: wogs, slants, kikes, niggers, krauts, honkies, reds, and so on.

A terrorism expert at the RAND Corporation (a think tank heavily supported by the U.S. Department of Defense), testified as follows to a U.S. House of Representatives subcommittee in June 2007: "Unless we can impede radicalization and recruitment, then we are condemned to a strategy of stepping on cockroaches one at a time." Unless we can impede such dehumanizing thought processes, we may all be condemned to an unacceptably violent future.

Group associations may also contribute to war by engaging people in a cumulative process by which the hostility of a few serves essentially to contaminate most, if not all, others. One writer poses the question as follows: "Imagine a group of tribes living within reach of one another. If all choose the way of peace, then all may live in peace. But what if all but one choose peace?"[5]

# A Conclusion on Premodern and Nontechnological Warfare

We may never fully know the earliest history of human warfare; nor whether premodern warfare among contemporary nontechnological, stateless societies casts much light on the evolution of human warfare generally. In addition to its intrinsic interest, however, premodern warfare undoubtedly illuminates at least some facets of modern, contemporary war that might otherwise be obscured by the complexity of modern social life and by our own involvement in current affairs. Moreover, certain fundamental underlying principles of individual motivation, group association, and intergroup aggression appear to be prefigured in an examination of nontechnological war. The fact remains, nonetheless, that the fundamental issues of peace and war in the modern world are played out in a different arena, that of larger groups often functioning at the level of nations.

# Nations, States, Ethnic Groups, and Nationalism

## Nations and States

In a sense, nations are ethnic groups writ large. Just as tribal or ethnic groups are composed of individuals sharing a strong sense of shared social identity, nations are similarly united, only the populations are much larger and, typically, more complex internally. *Ethnic* comes from the ancient Greek word *ethnos,* meaning a race, tribe, or group of people; the term *nation,* on the other hand, derives from the Latin *natio,* referring to birth (as in prenatal or native). Although the word *nation* is often used loosely to indicate a state—that is, a political and geographic entity—in fact it refers more precisely to a large group of people, ideally united by a common language, origin, history, religion, and culture. No formal process exists for identifying nations; rather, a nation exists when a group considers itself a nation and is recognized as such by already existing nations.

A *state*, by contrast, is a political unit, an area of land whose people are governed independent of other, comparable states. A nation-state exists if a nation and a state have the same geographic boundaries. For example, for a brief period after World War I, Lithuanians, Latvians, and Estonians each constituted separate nation-states, the Baltic states of Lithuania, Latvia, and Estonia. Then they were incorporated into a larger state, the former Soviet Union, from which they eventually gained independence and became nation-states once more as the Soviet Union broke up. Russia today, like the former Soviet Union, is a large state but not a single nation; rather, it is composed of many nationalities, including not only ethnic Russians but also Tatars, Chechens, and many other ethnic groups.

## Nationalism

The phenomenon of *nationalism* is one of the most powerful sociopolitical forces of modern times. It refers to the yearnings of a people to constitute themselves as part of a nation, typically to form a nation-state and often to adjust geographic boundaries so as to increase the size of their domain, to incorporate others who share the same sense of national identity, and frequently to establish their nation as significant, if not preeminent. According to one definition, nationalism is "a people's sense of collective destiny through a common past and the vision of a common future."[6]

This hints at an important component of nationalism—namely, the emotional appeal of belonging, of shared deeds, and of extending the boundaries of one's individual identity to comprise a larger and seemingly more glorious whole. In the words of 19th-century French philosopher and historian J. Ernest Renan, "What constitutes a nation is not speaking the same tongue or belonging to the same ethnic group, but having accomplished great things in common in the past and the wish to accomplish them in the future." In perhaps the most famous definition of this phenomenon, Renan also suggested that nationalism is

> a grand solidarity constituted by the sentiment of sacrifices which one has made and those that time is disposed to make again. It supposes a past, it renews itself especially in the present by a tangible deed: the approval, the desire, clearly expressed to continue the communal life. The existence of a nation is an everyday plebiscite.[7]

Increasingly, however, the sense of national identity has moved beyond the standard textbook definition, which emphasizes cultural unity. To a great extent, large nation-states are not so much natural social constructs as arbitrary groupings of people, cobbled together for political and economic purposes. The result has been a strong tendency to confer unity by establishing national symbols shared by many persons, regardless of their ethnic identity. National flags, heroes, myths, and anthems all have a remarkable hold over most people, and virtually all nations seek to inculcate recognition and respect for such symbols, typically requiring oaths, pledges, or other specific acts of allegiance.

During times of perceived stress—especially if the stress comes from an external threat—nationalist sentiments are likely to become particularly intense. Often the threat serves to enhance pronational emotions that may previously have been ebbing. The German invasion of the Soviet Union in 1941, for example, enabled Stalin to build on a "war nationalism" that overcame much disaffection with his purges and heavy-handed dictatorship. (At the same time, some nationalists—notably in the Baltic states and Ukraine—allied themselves with Nazi Germany during World War II, hoping to fulfill their own nationalist aspirations of separating from the Soviet Union.) The Japanese attack on China also evoked solidarity born of war nationalism, causing the government of Chiang Kai-shek and the revolutionary forces of Mao Tse-tung to make common cause, at least for a time, in the interest of Chinese national survival against the invaders. Even long after national struggles have ceased, the existence of martyrs and of regular days for remembrance also serve to whip up nationalist sentiment and keep it fresh. A notorious example of this was how Serbian dictator and demagogue, Slobodan Milošević, whipped up Serbian nationalism (and leading eventually to genocide against Bosnian Muslims) just prior to the Bosnian War of 1992 to 1995 by invoking the memory of a famous Serb military defeat by Muslim Turks 500 years earlier.

Nationalism can, in theory, be limited to love for one's nation; in practice, however, it is often combined with antagonism toward other nations. "By nationalism," wrote George Orwell,

> I mean first of all the habit of assuming that human beings can be classified like insects and that whole blocks of millions or tens of millions of people can be confidently labeled "good" or "bad." But secondly—and this is much more important—I mean the habit of identifying oneself with a single nation or other unit, placing it beyond good or evil and recognizing no other duty than that of advancing its own interests.[8]

This occurs, in part, because the nation provides a way of submerging the comparatively small, vulnerable individual self into a much larger, more powerful other. As the distinguished theologian H. Richard Niebuhr describes the ardent nationalist,

> The national life is for him the reality whence his own life derives its worth. He relies on the nation as a source of his own value. He trusts it; first, perhaps, in the sense of looking constantly to it as the enduring reality out of which he has issued, into whose ongoing cultural life his own actions and being will merge. His life has meaning because it is part of that context, like a word in a sentence. It has value because it fits into a valuable whole.[9]

Unfortunately, the tendency to identify one's group, tribe, or "own people" as a "valuable whole" carries along with it another tendency: to devalue other, similar groups or, worse yet, to see them as threatening to one's fundamental values. Therefore, these "others" become suitable targets for competition, conflict, and often violence.

# A Brief History of Nationalist Wars

## Early-Modern European Nationalism

The sense of nationhood, as opposed to ethnic group or tribal affiliation, is relatively recent. During the Middle Ages, for example, individuals typically felt that they belonged to a city or to a local reigning monarch. Thus, the loyalty of someone whom we now identify as "French" might have included local affiliation to family and village, and personal fealty to the duke of Lyon, the king of France, the Holy Roman Emperor, and the Pope, but not to "France" as such.

European nation-states began to develop during the late Middle Ages. After the Treaty of Westphalia (1648), which ended the Thirty Years' War, European peoples became increasingly aware of the existence of others who were similar to themselves, as well as of others, generally farther away, who were quite different. Moreover, centralized authorities—abetted by gunpowder— were able to demolish the castles of local rulers and enforce a broader allegiance: to kings, whose domains also tended to include greater numbers of similar people. At the same time, loyalty to local rulers and religious leaders tended to diminish. Spain, Portugal, France, and England were nation-states by the 16th century; later, the phenomenon of nationalism, particularly in central Europe, received an enormous boost, largely in reaction to revolutionary and Napoleonic France.

In the course of its revolution in the late 18th century, France developed the first truly national anthem, "La Marseillaise," and substituted adherence to the nation for fealty to a monarch. In addition, Napoleonic conquests of other nations helped generate strong feelings of national pride on the part of those who had been invaded. Nationalistic sentiments were widespread by the early 19th century, largely coalescing around the doctrine of national self-determination, the belief that each national group had the right to form its own state. Under this impetus, Greece won its independence from Turkey in 1829, and Belgium was declared independent from the Netherlands in 1830. The Dutch republic had achieved its own national self-determination several centuries earlier, from the Spanish empire, after a protracted and bloody conflict; the Dutch revolt was the first modern successful war of national liberation.

## Nationalism in the United States

Within the United States, the Revolutionary War was largely a war of independence rather than of nationalism or of class-based social upheaval (the latter characterized the French Revolution). Nonetheless, U.S. nationalism later expressed itself through the doctrine of *manifest destiny,* which claimed that it was "manifestly" the "destiny" of the American people to expand across all of North America. Moreover, dreams of a major worldwide role for the United States led to other military adventures, including the little-remembered War of 1812. Senator Henry Clay of Kentucky, leader of an ultranationalist group known as the War Hawks, expressed both local pride and nationalist fervor when he proclaimed,

> It is said that no object is attainable by war with Great Britain. . . . I say that the conquest of Canada is in your power. I trust that I shall not be deemed presumptuous when I state that I verily believe that the militia of Kentucky are alone competent to place Montreal and all of Upper Canada at your feet.[10]

The resulting war was one of the least successful in U.S. history—1,877 Americans killed, 9,700 taken prisoner, and a cost of $200 million, including the burning of Washington, D.C., by the British. And no territory was gained. (Interestingly, this same war—which receives very little attention in U.S. history books—is widely celebrated as a success in Canada, since the expansionist designs of the "colossus of the north" was defeated.) Nonetheless, U.S. nationalist sentiment contributed to such expansionist adventures as the Mexican-American War and the Spanish-American War, as well as to a growing series of armed interventions, notably in Latin America and the Far East.

## European Nationalism in the 19th and 20th Centuries

By the late 19th century, Western European nationalism had become especially pronounced in Germany and Italy, each of which had been divided into numerous mini-states and principalities.

Italian unification was finally achieved in 1870, after a militant struggle primarily against the Austrian empire (itself composed of many nations). Meanwhile, formal unification of such German mini-states as Saxony, Hanover, and Silesia was completed in 1871, with Prussia the undisputed leader of the new German nation-state. German unification was achieved by the Prussian leader Otto von Bismarck, who successfully engineered a series of wars, first against Denmark and then against Austria, culminating in the Franco-Prussian War.

Whereas Western European nationalism primarily involved the amalgamation of previously disunited regions and states, nationalism in Eastern Europe took a somewhat different form, ultimately resulting in the carving out of nation-states from the large, heterogeneous Ottoman (Turkish), Austro-Hungarian, and Russian empires. Nationalistic demands, especially on the part of the newly created Balkan states—and the tensions they provoked, especially within the Austro-Hungarian empire—played a major role in initiating World War I.

The Austrian leadership of that empire, for example, was desperately worried that it would not be able to hold together its unstable, heterogeneous assemblage of restive nations, consisting of Hungarians, Serbs, Croats, Montenegrins, Slovenians, and so on. Following the assassination in 1914 of the Austrian Archduke Franz Ferdinand by a Serbian extremist, the Austrians feared that Serbian nationalism was about to unleash additional nationalist demands that would ultimately result in the disintegration of the already rickety Austrian empire. And so it was decided to "punish" the Serbs. Russia stood by tiny Serbia, in a show of national solidarity, as it did during the North Atlantic Treaty Organization's (NATO) bombing of Serbia in 1999: Serbs, like Russians, are ethnically Slavic. Germany, in turn, stood by Austria, which was its ally. France was already allied to Russia and was independently hungering to regain the provinces of Alsace and Lorraine, lost to Germany 40 years before, in the Franco-Prussian War—and a continuing insult to French national pride. Furthermore, the war plans of Germany demanded an invasion of neutral Belgium, which in turn brought Great Britain into the war. National passions, fears, demands, and misunderstandings resulted in the first catastrophic 20th-century war.

Following World War I (or, as it was called at the time, "the Great War"), numerous nations were not granted self-determination. The state of Yugoslavia, for example, was created as a patchwork quilt of seven "national republics"—consisting of Serbs, Croats, Bosnians, Macedonians, Slovenians, Montenegrins, and Albanians—all of whom consider themselves distinct nations. These groups were held together, at least in part, by a powerful leader, Josip Tito, a renowned Croatian anti-Nazi partisan during World War II. Following Tito's death, nationalist unrest commenced in Yugoslavia during 1988 to 1989, culminating in the relatively nonviolent secession of Slovenia and Macedonia, the moderately violent withdrawal of Croatia, and extremely violent wars in Bosnia and Kosovo (Kosovo itself is a predominantly Albanian-oriented nationalist enclave currently within Serbia but pressing for independence). As a general principle, the national aspirations of defeated people are often trampled on by the victors.

Nonetheless, nationalist sentiments can be extraordinarily resilient. For example, Poles retained their national identity for decades when "Poland" didn't exist (it was gobbled up in the late 18th century by Germany, Russia, and Austria). Citizens of Venice considered themselves Italians even while part of Austria, French-speaking residents of Quebec have resisted Anglicization of their culture by the rest of English-speaking Canada and periodically agitate for complete political independence, most Basques consider themselves Basques rather than Spaniards, and so forth. Kurds constitute the largest nation that is not associated with its own state; their population is spread across Turkey, Iraq, Iran, and Syria. Despite continual yearnings—and frequent violence—it seems unlikely that Kurdish nationalist aspirations will be gratified, at least in the near future. This is largely because the existing states resist any such separation, which would threaten their current boundaries.

Intrastate nationalist movements have generally resisted the efforts—even the violent efforts— of states to deprive them of their identity. Nonetheless, there have been some examples of *assimilation,* in which isolated national groups lose their identity in favor of a larger group in which they are embedded. Most American Indians and Hawaiians, for example, despite awareness of their particular ethnic heritage, think of themselves as Americans. Ditto for Alaskan "Eskimos" (Inuit).

## National Liberation and Revolutionary Nationalism

By the 19th century, the colonizing activities of the European powers had created a situation in which large segments of the globe were under military domination by people who had little similarity to, or cultural affinity for, the much larger number of "natives" being subjugated. Wars of national liberation were notably successful in Latin America during the 1800s, as the Spanish empire crumbled in the south, and the brief French ascendancy in Mexico was also ended. Revolutionary nationalism during the 19th century was less successful, however, in Africa and Asia: The Zulus were eventually crushed by the British in South Africa, for example, and despite bloody uprisings (of which the so-called Sepoy Mutiny, 1857 to 1859, is best known), Britain maintained control over India as well as Egypt and, indeed, over a large part of the inhabited planet.

Although China was not directly occupied by imperialist powers, except for Hong Kong and Macao (both of which were returned to China by the end of the 20th century), the weak and decentralized Chinese government was regularly humiliated and forced to submit to economic ravishment, including the forced "opening" of the country to opium trading. The resulting Opium Wars caused yet more local resentment, adding to the growing urgency of Chinese nationalism, as did the Boxer Rebellion and, from 1850 to 1864, the ill-fated Taiping Rebellion. (This latter struggle, little known in the West, resulted in an estimated *20 million* fatalities.)

In the aftermath of the two world wars of the 20th century, revolutionary nationalism and counterrevolutionary and antimodern ethnocentrism have essentially triumphed throughout much of the "postmodern" world. In some cases this has occurred through protracted conventional war, in others by guerrilla operations, and in yet others by peaceful transitions, whereby the occupying colonial power granted independence, albeit grudgingly. Colonial holdings were not typically bounded in ways that were naturally (i.e., nationally) meaningful. As a result, many of the newly independent former colonies, especially those established since the end of World War II, have had to cope with substantial national and ethnic divisions of their own, many of which have led to war. The boundaries of the modern-day states of Iraq and the Democratic Republic of Congo (formerly Zaire), for example, do not correspond to natural, ethnic, or tribal-based geographical entities; the former results from British colonialism and the latter, Belgian. Not surprisingly, these and other such arbitrary political units have been caught up in considerable postcolonial violence.

Take, for example, Sudan. Previously one of the geographically largest countries in Africa, "Sudan" was a creation of joint British and Egyptian colonialism until it became independent in 1956. But even then, Sudan was a heterogeneous assemblage, consisting particularly of light-skinned Muslims in the north, dark-skinned Muslims and animists in the west (Darfur), and dark-skinned Christians and animists in the south. After considerable oppression and genocide promulgated by the dominant north against residents of Darfur, as well as a prolonged civil war instituted by forces in the south, an independent state of South Sudan was created and internationally recognized in 2011. However, even though some nationalist aspirations have finally to some extent been met, the situation between Sudan and South Sudan remains highly unsettled and militarily contentious.

# Types of Nationalist Wars

## National Independence

National independence need not always be preceded by war. Burma, Malaysia, the Slovak Republic, Ukraine, the Baltic states, and Slovenia, for example, achieved statehood and self-determination with relatively little bloodshed. Canada and Norway became independent from Britain and Sweden, respectively, with no violence whatsoever. On the other hand, warfare is a frequent prelude to national independence, as witnessed by the birth of the United States. Indonesia fought for four years to gain independence from Holland, and East Timor fought Indonesia for its autonomy. Algeria became separate from France only after 8 years of fighting, which cost 250,000 Algerian and French lives.

## National Prestige

Many of the classic interstate wars of modern history have been stimulated by issues of national prestige. Enthusiasm within the United States for the Spanish-American War (1898) was largely generated by American desires to enter the arena of worldwide colonial acquisitions. The government of Spain, for its part, appears to have fought back largely because it would have been embarrassing to give up without doing so. Similarly, the aggressive appetite of both Germany and Japan in the 20th century was whetted by a pervasive sense that these great nations had not achieved world status commensurate with their economic or technological accomplishments or their self-proclaimed racial superiority. There are fears that China, Russia, and Brazil (as well as possibly India, Japan, and Germany) may act in a similar way during the 21st century.

India has long taken the lead in condemning worldwide militarism in general and the nuclear arms race in particular. But when Prime Minister Rajiv Gandhi announced in February 1988 that his country had successfully developed and tested a surface-to-surface liquid-fueled missile—entirely with Indian technology—he received a standing ovation in the Indian Parliament. And a decade later, India publicly exploded nuclear devices, supposedly in response to the threat posed to it by Pakistan. Of course, Pakistan claimed it had tested and developed its nuclear arsenal in response to the alleged threat to its national identity posed by a nuclear-armed India.

Pride and prestige, sometimes on a personal level as well, can loom large. Thus, President Lyndon Johnson persevered in the Vietnam War in large part because of his private determination not to be "the first U.S. president to lose a war," and for President Nixon the worst outcome for the United States in that conflict was humiliation. "If, when the chips are down," he announced,

> the world's most powerful nation, the United States of America, acts like a pitiful, helpless giant, the forces of totalitarianism and anarchy will threaten free nations and free institutions throughout the world. It is not our power but our will and character that is being tested.[11]

Frustration among American ruling elites was particularly acute during the period from late 1979 to early 1981, when revolutionary Iranians held the staff of the U.S. embassy captive. The resulting sense of national humiliation contributed greatly to the election of Ronald Reagan and to the military buildup that followed. Similarly, the U.S. invasion of Grenada in 1983 served partly to assuage the emotional pain of a devastating car bomb attack on the temporary U.S. Marine barracks in Beirut, Lebanon, just a few days before. Also during the Reagan administration, U.S. bombers attacked Tripoli, Libya, in retaliation for acts of terrorism allegedly committed by Libyan nationals. And shortly afterward, the United States sank Iranian naval vessels in the Persian Gulf. These actions provided an outlet for frustration and an opportunity to redeem a sense of diminished national pride. At the same time, what redeems the pride of one nation typically diminishes that of another, leading in turn to a felt need for revenge, which creates yet more need to assuage the now-reinjured pride, and so on.

The maintenance of national prestige and the avoidance of humiliation loom large in the calculation of almost every state. For example, immediately after NATO's air war over Serbia and Kosovo—which Russia opposed—Russian military units used a ruse to secure the airport in Priština (Kosovo's capital), thereby attempting to assert Russian national pride in the face of NATO's overwhelming military might and Russia's "defeat" in the Cold War. Similarly, Arab pride was sorely wounded by Israel's string of military victories in 1948, 1956, and 1967. The October War of 1973, although technically yet another Arab defeat, came close enough to victory to demolish the myth of Israeli invincibility and sufficiently restored Egyptian self-respect and prestige that President Anwar Sadat felt empowered to make his stunning trip to Jerusalem in 1977, to conclude the Camp David Accords in 1978, and to sign an Egyptian-Israeli peace treaty (the first one between Israel and an Arab state) in 1979. Many Arabs, even those who normally oppose militant Islamists, were pleased by Hezbollah's military performance during Israel's incursion into Lebanon in 2006.

## Secessionism

Sentiments of national unity are often associated with yearnings of a group of people to secede from a larger collectivity of which they do not feel a part. In 1967, for example, about 50,000 Ibos, who had migrated to northern Nigeria, were slaughtered by the more numerous Hausas, who resented Ibo economic success. Another 1 million Ibos were driven out of the north, after which the Ibo "nation" sought to secede and form its own nation-state of Biafra. The result was a civil war in which hundreds of thousands died and many more suffered severe malnutrition and starvation. The war ended, unsuccessfully for the would-be secessionists, in 1970. Secessionism is a major factor in organized violence today, which has been particularly intense in the armed struggles by Kosovars and Chechens to secede from Yugoslavia and Russia, respectively, and for Hindu-affiliated Tamils seeking to separate from Buddhist-oriented Sinhalese in Sri Lanka. Separatist movements, of varying degrees of violence and with varying prospects of success—but always cohering around nationalist associations and ambitions—are found on every continent except Antarctica.

## International or Transnational Solidarity

The sense of "nationhood" and of "national solidarity" often extends across political boundaries (which have often been drawn without regard to "natural" national groupings), resulting in strong feelings of empathy and connectedness with fellow nationals living in another state. When these people are considered abused, war can be evoked by a felt need to extend protection to fellow nationals living elsewhere. Thus, India felt justified in entering the 1971 Pakistani civil war between mostly Bengalis in what was then East Pakistan and Pashtuns in West Pakistan, because India's Bengali population found it intolerable to stand idly by during Pakistan's slaughter of its own Bengali population.[12] Many Arab states send money in support of Palestinian nationalism, thereby expressing solidarity with fellow Arabs. The (mostly black) states of sub-Saharan Africa were especially opposed to South African apartheid because of the oppression of its black population. Turkey has come to the aid of the Turkish population on Cyprus, just as Greece has been seen as the protector of the Greek population there. Irish Americans have historically supported Irish independence from the United Kingdom (including, to some degree, financial aid to the violent Irish Republican Army), just as Jewish Americans tend to support Israel in its conflict with the Palestinians.

Of course, this is not the whole story, and extending international solidarity can also be a pretext for aggression. For a clear example, Hitler annexed Czechoslovakia and invaded Poland, using alleged mistreatment of Czech and Polish "Germans" as an excuse. The U.S. invasion of Grenada in 1983 was officially justified at the time by the U.S. government's claim that American medical students on that island were in danger of being taken hostage, just as the U.S. invasion of Panama in 1989 was ostensibly undertaken to protect American lives in that country. In short, national solidarity has often been used to provide legal and political justifications that rationalize a conflict or intervention whose roots may well lie elsewhere.

In many cases, states stop short of war but nonetheless provide "fraternal" aid to ethnic groups in other states. This is often done to promote their own interests, even if those interests are limited to satisfying otherwise restive, kindred national elements within their own borders. India, for example, was drawn into the fighting in Sri Lanka (formerly Ceylon) because both India and Sri Lanka have a large Tamil population, which is overwhelmingly Hindu.

Russia is also an amalgamation of many ethnic groups (although much less so than the former Soviet Union, many of whose republics gained autonomy in 1991). In addition, there are currently large ethnic Russian populations in many of the now-independent states of the former Soviet Union (in what Russia refers to as its "near abroad"). The danger therefore exists that a nationalist government in Russia might attempt to intervene in, say, Estonia, Latvia, Moldova, Georgia, Ukraine, or Kazakhstan, ostensibly on behalf of Russians in those countries. This danger is augmented by the fact that the Baltic states, much to Russia's chagrin, have entered NATO, and Ukraine appears bent on doing so as well. Moreover, Russian political and military leadership has been acutely concerned that Islamic fundamentalism might spread from the south to the heartland of Russia itself—a not-unjustified worry given the numerous Islamist terrorist attacks in Russia during the past two decades. This, in turn, has provided a justification for Soviet/Russian wars in Afghanistan, Chechnya, and elsewhere.

The future of nationalism is impossible to predict. On the one hand, "transnationalism"— communication and commerce across national borders, especially facilitated by the rise of cell phones and the Internet—was predicted to lead to enhanced nationalism, as members of various national *diasporas* (people who have migrated to other countries but nonetheless retain a sense of ethnic and national identity) connect with each other, thereby forming a more potent social and political force. At the same time, however, others anticipated a rapid decline in nation-states, with their parochial political and linguistic boundaries, in the face of globalization.

To date, neither prediction has clearly been confirmed. In addition, some nationalists object to what they see as globalization's dilution of their culture and traditions, while others eagerly anticipate that globalization will bring about prosperity and in the process strengthen nation-building and pronationalist sentiment. Just as the future of nationalism points in multiple directions, so does the effect of nationalist sentiment.

## Nationalist Threats to States

One might ask why many governments so strenuously resist the various secessionist and reintegrationist national movements. Aren't the West Pakistanis better off not being artificially united to 100 million resentful Bengalis? What would be the harm to Spaniards if the troublesome Basques seceded and formed their own tiny nation-state?

Part of the answer may itself reflect a kind of national pride, the hope for a larger and therefore greater state. In addition, the resisting peoples are typically those who profit economically and socially from the presence of the would-be seceders. British and American support for national self-determination for Kuwait (invaded by Iraq in 1990) and Brunei (long coveted by Indonesia) derives largely from interest in the oil resources of these small countries. Similarly, Belgium's support in 1960 for attempts by residents of Katanga to secede from the Congo was keyed to the copper wealth of that province. Had Biafra been carved out of Nigeria, much of that state's industrial capacity and natural resources would have gone, along with the Ibo people. When Hitler seized the Sudetenland, he not only "liberated" 3 million Sudeten Germans but also—not coincidentally—about three quarters of Czechoslovakia's industrial capacity, including an important armaments industry. South Sudan has oil, which North Sudan lacks.

When states are heterogeneous (composed of many ethnic groups and republics), political leaders often worry that demands for national self-determination may lead to additional popular demands and possibly to the breakup of the home country. This happened, for example, in the former Yugoslavia during the 1990s. Such fears drove the Austrian government's policies at the onset of World War I and the Russian government's actions from the late 1990s to the present. Furthermore, it is not clear that further *Balkanization* (the breakup of a larger region into small constituent states, as happened in the Balkans) of Africa, India, or anywhere else will necessarily further the cause of peace. Certainly, the Balkan Peninsula, known as the "tinderbox of Europe," has not been a good advertisement for the benefits of nationalist sentiment, as was abundantly clear during the last decade of the 20th century.

In addition, although nationalism is generally seen as a force for unity within a political entity, this is only true if such an entity is mostly homogeneous. When diverse nations are contained within a single state, even if civil war and secessionism are avoided, the resulting social divisions may get in the way of unity rather than promoting it. Political leadership in such cases may be hamstrung, unable to provide coherent policy because of the danger of alienating one national faction or another. Examples include Egypt, divided between majority Muslim and minority Coptic Christian, and Lebanon, a small country that nevertheless includes numerous religious-ethnic factions, such as Maronite Christian, Greek Orthodox, Palestinian refugees, Druze, Chaldean Catholic, and so forth.

# Racial and Cultural Intolerance

Whenever individuals associate, especially if they do so on the basis of shared characteristics that exclude others and make for a distinction between "Us" and "Them," and political leaders declare, "You're either with us or against us," there are the dangers of racism, ethnocentrism, xenophobia, and other forms of intolerance. All of these can contribute to war and other violent acts against racial and ethnic minorities, as well as against "foreigners."

Many of the world's hostilities involve different nationalities and ethnic groups in conflict. Of course, the mere fact of ethnic difference is not a sufficient cause for war; many pluralistic societies live peacefully, both *intra*nationally—the multiethnic population of Hawaii, for example, or multilingual Switzerland—and *inter*nationally. In addition, distinct racial or cultural differences are not necessary for war, either: Paraguay and its racially and culturally similar neighbors fought some extraordinarily bloody wars in the 19th century, as did Austrians and Prussians, North and South Koreans, and North and South Vietnamese, not to mention the long and tragic history of civil wars within such relatively ethnically homogeneous nations as Spain and China.

## Ethnic Antagonisms and Ethnic Cleansing

A high proportion of armed conflicts, however, do involve members of different ethnic/religious/cultural/linguistic groups, such as Iraq (Arab) versus Iran (Persian), Jews versus Arabs in the Middle East, Irish Catholics versus English-oriented Protestants in Northern Ireland, Tamils versus Sinhalese in Sri Lanka, Orthodox Christians against Muslims in the former Yugoslavia and Russia, Tutsis versus Hutus in Rwanda and Burundi, and so on. The horrific culmination of these conflicts has been the forced "ethnic cleansing" committed by militarily superior groups upon ethnic minorities, as in large areas of the former Yugoslavia and central Africa. The result has been the slaughter of hundreds of thousands, perhaps millions, of people and often forced dislocation from their ancestral homelands.

In a sense, there is nothing new about this. Hatred based on ethnic and religious differences was at the root of many wars throughout history, including the Crusades of the Middle Ages (European Christians versus Arab Muslims) and the Thirty Years' War (largely Catholics versus Protestants), which devastated central Europe in the 17th century. To a degree, no clear separation can be drawn between national antagonisms based on religion and those based on race and ethnicity. Many of the 20th-century intra-African wars (Ibo/Hausa, Hutu/Tutsi) have been more ethnic than religious; the India-Pakistan wars, on the other hand, have been primarily religious, although the differences between Hindus and Muslims are so fundamental to Indian and Pakistani society that they include ethnic distinctions as well. The Iran-Iraq and Arab-Israeli conflicts involve both religious and ethnic differences, although economic and political factors are involved as well.

Clearly, many other considerations apply to each of these conflicts: border disputes, a history of antagonism based at least partly on generations of real or perceived oppression, economic rivalries, and the like. And typically, these various "causes" provide the immediate stimulus for each outbreak of violence. But it also seems clear that national and often racial sentiments linger in the background as a crucial underlying cause and also as an explanation for the persistence and intensity of many conflicts. In addition, once war erupts—even if for other immediate reasons—the belligerents quickly seize on any discernible differences between themselves and their opponents, typically magnifying these differences, elevating their own traits, and devaluing those of the other side. Often it is sufficient just to point to the opponents as different—that is, as Hondurans rather than Salvadorans or as Koreans rather than Japanese—to evoke potent antagonisms. Dehumanizing language and racial/ethnic scapegoating are often introduced at this point as well.

A year after the beginning of World War I, Einstein lamented humanity's insistence on primitive hatred and its use of nationalism as the vehicle for that hatred:

> When posterity recounts the achievements of Europe, shall we let men say that three centuries of painstaking cultural effort carried us no further than from the fanaticism of religion to the insanity of nationalism? It would seem that men always seek some idiotic fiction in the name of which they can hate one another. Once it was religion; now it is the state.[13]

It is worth emphasizing that "state worship" and nationalism, of the sort that Einstein so decried, come together, especially in fascism and in other ultranationalist ideologies of statism.

# Nationalism and the Public Mood

Public opinion counts, especially when it comes to issues of peace or war. And this is even truer in a democracy. "Opinion," wrote Alexander Hamilton, "whether well or ill-founded is the governing principle of human affairs." And Abraham Lincoln noted that "he who molds public sentiment goes deeper than he who enacts statutes or pronounces decisions." Wars can be provoked for many reasons, including so-called reasons of state (*raisons d'état*), which, at the outset, evoke very little nationalist passion on the part of the participants; rather, they proceed in large part from the machinations of leadership. To prosecute wars, however, especially in the modern era, it has proven necessary for governments, through the mass media, to inflame the public, often by use of nationalist passions.

## Manipulating Public Opinion and Arousing Public Passions

In modern times, war requires the mobilization of national sentiment, so if real affronts to national dignity, honor, or well-being are not available, pretexts are typically arranged. Even Hitler, who clearly sought to invade Poland in 1939, found it necessary to stage a phony "incident" to justify his actions and help arouse German national indignation: He staged an attack, allegedly by Polish forces (but actually by Germans wearing Polish uniforms), against a German radio station. The so-called Gulf of Tonkin Incident, in which U.S. destroyers were supposed to have been attacked by North Vietnamese forces in 1964, is now acknowledged to have been exaggerated and manipulated by the U.S. government, so as to induce Congressional authorization and public support for the unrestricted involvement of U.S. combat units in Vietnam.

Effective orators and publicists have long been able to sway public mood, often generating enthusiasm for war and often disregarding "inconvenient" facts. The ancient Greek historian Thucydides recounted that the Athenian general Alcibiades stirred up irresistible public enthusiasm for glory, booty, and adventure. "With this enthusiasm of the majority," noted Thucydides, "the few that liked it not feared to appear unpatriotic by holding up their hands against it, and so they kept quiet." The result was an expedition against Syracuse (in modern-day Sicily) that ultimately proved disastrous.

In the 2nd century BCE, when Carthage had long ceased to be a threat to Rome, the elderly and eloquent Cato would repeat, after each of his speeches, *Carthago delenda est* ("Carthage must be destroyed"). And in the ensuing Punic War, it was. The U.S. entry into the Spanish-American War was promoted by lurid and often inaccurate accounts of alleged Spanish atrocities in Cuba: The so-called yellow journalism of the Hearst newspaper chain, which favored war. The U.S. battleship *Maine* was blown up while in Havana harbor, allegedly by Spanish agents; this acutely inflamed American passions, and "Remember the *Maine*" became a slogan of that war. Some historians now maintain that the *Maine* was actually sunk by a prowar group to provide a pretext for the hostilities that followed.

A consequence of manipulating public opinion so as to arouse popular passion is that many of today's nationalist and ethnic wars remain unresolved, partly because relatively few recent wars have been successful in ending the underlying conflict that generated the war itself. Korea, for example, remains divided and heavily armed, approximately 60 years after the Korean War; India and Pakistan are in a state of ongoing antagonism, especially over control of Kashmir; the Middle East remains a tinderbox; and Cyprus, the Balkans, and much of central Asia and Africa are still divided among warring ethnic factions. Nationalist passions keep age-old rivalries simmering, interfering with the prospect of reconciling old disputes or healing ancient injuries.

In some cases, however, closure on a nationalist war has been achieved, generally when the most intensely pronationalist side wins: This happened in Vietnam, as in most anticolonial wars of national liberation. In other cases, a decisive move by a national leader—as with former Egyptian president Sadat's overtures to Israel—can overcome the prowar drift of nationalist passion.

# Nationalism and Political Ideology

Even so potent a force as political ideology can appear pallid compared with the energies unleashed by nationalism, which is in a sense a primitive and pervasive ideology of its own. The Soviets and the Chinese Communists were both officially Marxist, but, for the most part, they remained Russians and Chinese first, as witnessed by their history of armed border clashes and persistent antagonism in recent decades. Similarly, the Vietnamese and Chinese, despite a shared Marxist-Leninist ideology, fought a short but vicious war in 1979 and remain mutually distrustful today.

## World War I

Perhaps the most dramatic case, however, of the triumph of nationalism over ideology occurred in the early days of World War I. (More accurately, nationalist and imperialist ideology clashed with internationalist and socialist ideology—and the former won.) In the years prior to World War I, the European Socialist and Social Democratic parties were powerful, seemingly united, and for the most part committed to opposing the institution of war, which was seen by most socialists as part of capitalist exploitation of the proletariat. Through various resolutions associated with the Second International, as well as within each major European country, the large Socialist and Social Democratic parties (most influentially, those of Germany and France) asserted that if war ever appeared imminent, their memberships would smother it by general strikes and, if necessary, insurrections. Solidarity among the working class would make war impossible: "They" might declare a war, but no one would come.

Before war was in fact declared, however, French socialists began worrying that German socialists would be unable to restrain German militarism, which would leave France fettered while Germany triumphed. German socialists, in turn, anguished that antimilitary and antinationalist success on their part would leave Germany at the mercy of reactionary czarist Russia. In the end, an overwhelming majority within the socialist parties of each nation announced support for the coming war, because for *their* country, such a war would be defensive. The following declaration, by the Social Democratic Party of Germany in 1914, shows the tenor of thinking at the time:

> We are menaced by the terror of foreign invasion. The problem before us now is not the relative advisability of war or peace, but a consideration of just what steps must be taken for the protection of our country. . . . It devolves upon us, therefore, to avert this danger, to shelter the civilization and independence of our native land.[14]

## Ideology and Nationalism

On the other hand, sometimes political ideology and nationalism go hand-in-hand, producing a combination that is especially potent. War-prone imperialist France during the 18th and 19th centuries, for example, was committed to its *mission civilisatrice,* the notion that France had a special mission to civilize the non-French world. Similarly, German national militarism in the 20th century was buttressed by Nazi yearnings for a "thousand-year *Reich*" peopled by a triumphant "Aryan race." The former Soviet Union's support for Third World national revolutions derived in part from its devotion to Marxist-Leninist ideology, just as the American ideology of free-market capitalism and the vision of the United States as the "new Jerusalem," a shining "city on the hill," uniquely pleasing to God and man, undergirded U.S. territorial expansionism during the 19th century and overcame its penchant for isolationism in substantial periods of the 20th and early 21st centuries.

In most cases, peace movements fare poorly during wartime, overwhelmed by militant national enthusiasm. There are exceptions, however: Notably, a kind of "war weariness" can set in, especially when the war itself is controversial or appears to be stalemated. The Vietnam War was such an example, controversial from the start and terminated in large part because the enthusiasm of the American citizenry was insufficient and turned increasingly to public outrage. World War I turned out to be much bloodier than expected and, after several years, seemed nowhere near resolution. Although citizen support remained generally high (except in Russia), mutinies became frequent: Fifty-four divisions (about half of the total) of the French Army mutinied in April 1917; 25,000 men were eventually court-martialed. Such behavior was contagious: The following month, 400,000 Italian troops deserted the field at Caporetto, and around the same time, German and Russian troops were fraternizing openly.

President Obama inherited two wars from the administration of George W. Bush. The war in Iraq was essentially terminated as far as the United States is officially concerned (as indicated, at least, by the withdrawal of U.S. ground troops) by the end of 2011. The war between Iraqis continues. The other and longer war, in Afghanistan, is scheduled to be officially concluded by American combat troops in 2014. Although both wars became increasingly unpopular with the American people as they dragged on, bringing hundreds of thousands of casualties (mostly Afghan and Iraqi) and few demonstrable payoffs, neither war generated the kind of large-scale popular resistance that characterized, for example, public disaffection with the Vietnam War 40 years earlier.[15]

# The Tension Between Peace and Freedom

For all the legitimate criticism of war and nationalism's frequent role in stimulating violent group-oriented passions, there has also been a positive side to nationalist sentiment in relation to war. Thus, some of humanity's most stirring visions and most memorable sacrifices have been made ostensibly on behalf of freedom—typically efforts of national groups to achieve self-determination. Consider, for example, the blood-tingling sentiments of these lines from Robert Burns's poem (later set to music) "Scots Wha Hae," originally written in support of renewed Scottish national independence (Scotland was once an independent state, before being incorporated into Great Britain):

> By oppression's woes and pain! By your sons in servile chains!
>
> We will drain our dearest veins, but they shall be free!
>
> Lay the proud usurpers low! Tyrants fall in every foe!
>
> Liberty's in every blow! Let us do or die.

Many people think of nationalism and ethnocentrism as major reasons for wars, and they are at least partly correct. Certainly, nationalist sentiments, such as those expressed by Burns, are not likely to lead to the peaceful resolution of conflicts. It may be somewhat surprising, therefore, to learn that through much of the 19th and 20th centuries, nationalism was widely viewed as a potentially strong contributor to *peace*. After all, ethnically unified nations would seem less prone to civil war. However, the civil wars of Spain and China during the mid-20th century and, more recently, in Iraq, Afghanistan, Libya and in much of central Africa give the lie to this somewhat wishful thinking.

On the other hand, by producing a crosscutting loyalty—one that transcends connections of economic class, local leadership, and even religion—feelings of national identity and ethnic solidarity do appear to have sometimes contributed to peace and social stability. Nationalism has helped end many instances of endemic subnational conflict. Following the establishment of nation-states in Western Europe, for example, the low-level feuding and banditry as well as the religious and class violence that had long characterized that region was virtually ended—at least until the resurgence of genocidal ethnic cleansing and xenophobia during the 1990s in the Balkans. Although the future of Iraq and Afghanistan remains unclear at this time, it is at least possible that the prospect of peace in those devastated countries depends on whether their citizens act upon a supranational identity as united "Iraqis," rather than as ethnically based national groups—notably, Sunni Arabs, Shiite Arabs, and Kurds, and as "Afghans" rather than Pashtun, Tajik, Hazara, Uzbek, and so on.

The U.S. Civil War took place in part because feelings of regional identity (especially in the South) were stronger than national identity. Perhaps greater nationalism might have kept the peace, at least in this instance. The idea of nationalism as a route to peace is nonetheless ironic in that the first nation-state to have achieved what is generally regarded as a modern level of national self-consciousness—Napoleonic France—proceeded almost immediately to embark upon the most expansive, domestically motivated series of wars that Europe had experienced up to that time.

By the turn of the 20th century, the mainstream liberal European attitude toward nationalism had become ambivalent: Support for oppressed minorities—"captive nations" within oppressive empires—tempered with anxiety about a world divided into numerous feisty, competing, and independent units. And by the beginning of the 21st century, despite widespread sympathy in the United States for the national aspirations of various ethnic groups (Chechens, Tatars, etc.) within

Russia, the American government has maintained a policy in favor of maintaining Russia's geographic integrity. Similarly, U.S. foreign policy has consistently undercut the prospects of Kurdish nationalism, opting instead for the status quo, largely so as not to upset NATO ally Turkey. By the same token, the United States and Western countries generally tend to tread very carefully when it comes to questioning China's oppression of native Tibetans or of its indigenous Uighur people, who are Muslim and also ethnically different from the Han Chinese majority.

## The Post–World War II International Scene

In the sense of avoiding major armed conflict, Europe was largely peaceful from World War II until the Balkan Wars in the former Yugoslavia and NATO's unprecedented military intervention in 1999. But Europe has also achieved a fair degree of national self-determination: Just about all French live in France, virtually all Germans in Germany (or Austria or the German-speaking part of Switzerland), nearly all Poles in Poland, and so forth. There are, however, Austrians in northern Italy (the Tyrol) and Hungarians in Romania, and, until 1999, there were Albanians in Serbia (i.e., in Kosovo); there are also Gypsies (Roma) in much of Eastern Europe and many "guest workers" from northern Africa, Southern Europe, and Turkey in Northern and Western Europe, as well as increasing numbers of Arabs from northern Africa and the Middle East. The presence of minority groups in many European countries has led to a backlash against foreigners, who are (usually incorrectly) perceived as taking jobs away from the ethnic majorities. Right-wing politicians have in some cases (notably Austria, France, Italy, Holland, and Switzerland) capitalized on widespread feelings of resentment and ethnic chauvinism. This has also led to substantial unease and occasional violence (especially in France, which has the largest such minority population).

In addition, there are simmering separatist movements among the Spanish Basques and Catalans, Catholics in Northern Ireland, and, occasionally, Swiss in the Jura region, as well as tension between Flemings (speaking a Dutch/German dialect) and French-speaking Walloons in Belgium. These difficulties have been most acute in the former Yugoslavia, which came apart violently in the 1990s. The resurgence of jingoism, ethnocentrism, and xenophobia in many parts of Western and Central Europe shows few signs of abating during the first decade of the 21st century and threatens to reverse the relatively halcyon conditions that prevailed in most of Europe during the second half of the 20th century.

Other regions of the planet did not experience the Cold War "peace" that prevailed in most of Europe between 1945 and 1990. Palestinians continue to strive for national self-determination, which may yet be attainable but only if Israel makes what it perceives to be concessions to the Palestinians and Arab nations surrounding it. India is a patchwork of dozens, perhaps hundreds, of potential nations speaking more than a thousand languages; China contains more than 50 million non-Chinese, of which the Tibetans and Uighurs (ethnically Turkic and overwhelmingly Muslim citizens of western China) are the most notably oppressed and resentful; and Russia, like its predecessor, the former Soviet Union, is a vast heterogeneous assemblage of territories and regions dominated by different ethnic groups. Finally, the boundaries of many of the postcolonial African states are nothing less than a disaster, since they were drawn (by Europeans) with virtually no regard to the nationality of their people.

## The Effects of Political Ideology

There remains the prickly question of fundamental values: Peace, admittedly, is a great value, but is it of greater value than anything else? Is it so worthy an end that it should be maintained at all costs? Similarly, what of the connection between peace and freedom or between peace and justice? What if justice—including national self-determination—cannot be obtained short of war? Since 1945, many Western advocates of peace have tended to see nationalism as an evil if practiced by the Western powers, not only because it has led in the past to imperialism but also because it may contribute to a growing danger of nuclear war. At the same time, there is a tendency to look favorably on wars of national liberation, if directed by the oppressed against their oppressors—for example, the Algerian struggles against France during the 1950s and 1960s, the Mau Mau movement for independence of Kenya from Britain during that same time, the Vietnamese conflict with the United States, and even the struggles by Chechens and Kosovars to detach themselves from Russia and Serbia, respectively.

At the same time, right-wing anticommunists, while deploring revolutionary nationalist violence (which they have typically seen as communist inspired and therefore especially "illegitimate"), have applauded various equally violent counter-revolutionary wars, such as that of the contras in Nicaragua, UNITA in Angola, and the anti-Soviet *mujahedeen* in Afghanistan. Seemingly, extreme right- and left-wing ideologues are willing to value freedom over peace, so long as freedom is defined as either (in the first case) freedom from Marxist governments or (in the second case) freedom from colonial or right-wing military dictators.

During the second half of the 20th century, there was a tendency among American partisans of the political right (i.e., conservatives) to see antiestablishment revolutionary movements as necessarily aligned with worldwide communism. By contrast, centrists and leftists have been more likely to emphasize the nationalist, rather than the ideological, underpinnings of such activities. They point out, for example, that Tito, anti-Nazi partisan leader and later president of Yugoslavia, was a nationalist first and a communist second (he withdrew Yugoslavia from the Soviet-dominated Warsaw Pact, for example). Similarly, Ho Chi Minh's commitment was to Vietnamese nationalism more than to communism of either the Chinese or Soviet variety. The effort to achieve freedom via national struggle has produced many wars of liberation and, more recently, of counter-liberation. At the same time, there has been reluctance—at least among many U.S. citizens—to acknowledge the role of nationalist sentiment in Iraq and Afghanistan in generating hostility toward U.S. and NATO military forces.

# The Question of "National Character"

There is no evidence for any genetically influenced behavioral differences among people of differing nationalities. Nonetheless, there remains a persistent belief that a nation can in some cases be characterized by certain summed personality traits. In fact, there have been numerous errors of political judgment resulting from a misreading of the "national character" of a prospective opponent. Hitler, for example—and Napoleon before him—believed that Britain was a "nation of shopkeepers" and therefore neither willing nor able to resist aggression. During the 18th century, Germans were widely considered to be either philosophical metaphysicians or incurable romantics, not cut out for heavy industry or any other practical undertakings; the Italians, by contrast, were seen as highly rational and scientifically inclined. Today, these two stereotypes have to some extent been reversed.

Often such perceptions are self- (or, rather, nation-) serving, as well as incorrect. During World War II, for example, part of the Allied justification for bombing German cities was that unlike the dauntless British moral fiber, the German will to persevere would "crack" under bombardment, leading perhaps to revolt and thereby shortening the war. Official government documents claim that "the evidence at our disposal goes to show that the morale of the average German civilian will weaken quicker than that of a population such as our own as a consequence of direct attack."[16] There is debate about whether strategic bombing actually shortened World War II by creating shortages of critical materials, notably ball bearings and petroleum, in the final months. However, it is widely acknowledged that, if anything, bombing *increased* the German will to resist. Certainly, the German "national character" did not crack.

Later, the United States also underestimated the ability and willingness of the North Vietnamese to absorb bomb attacks and yet persevere in a war to which they, as a nation, were committed (whereas the United States, increasingly, was not). Despite what are perceived to be eventual defeats, Serbs during the war over Kosovo, Chechens during the bombardments perpetrated by Russia, all endured longer than most Western political "experts" expected. This may in part be explained by a "rally 'round the flag" effect that strengthens ties of national and ethnic solidarity when under attack by a "foreign" power, even if the domestic regime is also perceived as corrupt and autocratic. Much of the resistance by Iraqi "insurgents" and by Afghan Taliban followers to U.S.-led occupation—and which was unanticipated by the Bush and Obama administrations—was similarly due to a near-universal inclination toward national solidarity in the face of foreign occupation.

The persistence of the idea of national character is probably due to the fact that, while it is incorrect biologically, it has the appearance of psychological and sociological reality. Thus, a "national style," in speech, clothing, or even responses to stress or to potential enemies, can sometimes be exhibited. These styles can and do change over time, but they nonetheless often have limited consistency. For example, some Mediterranean peoples (Italians, Greeks) seem to be relatively more voluble and excitable than peoples from more northern climes (Scandinavians, Germans, British). Latin Americans and Arabs tend to maintain less interpersonal distance than do Americans or Europeans, which sometimes leads to misunderstandings at international gatherings. Japanese and Chinese seem (by mainstream American standards) unusually concerned with politeness and social formality. And Russians and Americans often misinterpret each other. For example, when Soviet premier Khrushchev arrived in the United States for a summit conference with President Eisenhower, he unwittingly antagonized many Americans by clasping both hands above his head, in a gesture used to signal "victory" by U.S. prizefighters; in the former Soviet Union, the same action had been used to communicate friendship and solidarity.

Patterns of family life and personal development can also influence behavior patterns characteristic of the nation as a whole. According to the psychoanalyst Erik Erikson, the political appeal of Nazism to Germans in the 1930s was based at least partly on the authoritarian style of the typical German family, in which the father was often both tyrannical and remote:

> When the father comes home from work, even the walls seem to pull themselves together. The children hold their breath, for the father does not approve of "nonsense"—that is, neither of the mother's feminine moods nor of the children's playfulness. . . . Later, when the boy comes to observe the father in company, when he notices his father's submission to superiors, and when he observes his excessive sentimentality when he drinks and sings with his equals, the boy acquires . . . a deep doubt of the dignity of man—or at any rate, of the "old man."[17]

Whatever the role of national character, and of shared national or ethnic experiences in molding such apparent traits, the power of national self-image, or ethnic identity, is undeniable. Nations and ethnic groups invariably see themselves as well-meaning and motivated only by the purest of goals; their opponents, on the other hand, typically see themselves differently. For example, Americans generally perceived their efforts on behalf of post–World War II reconstruction (the Truman Doctrine and the Marshall Plan), which included assistance to defeated Germany and Japan, as generous and laudable. To the Soviets, this appeared entirely self-serving: A form of economic imperialism, a device to relieve American postwar overproduction, and a political and military weapon directed against the Soviet Union.

More recently, many Americans see the post–Cold War status of their nation (having emerged—at least for a time—as the sole superpower) as a validation of its political and economic ideology of "democratic capitalism." At the same time, many other countries (especially Russia, much of the Islamic world, and increasingly China) regard this posture as U.S. arrogance and as a dangerously inflated self-righteousness combined with a failure to acknowledge its diminished international standing in the aftermath of the Great Recession that began in 2008, combined with the immense costs of the wars in Iraq and Afghanistan.

## A FINAL NOTE ON NATIONALISM AND ETHNOCENTRISM

On the one hand, nationalism and ethnic solidarity can sometimes evoke compassion, love, and community pride and can even serve as a positive force for human cooperation and ecological awareness. Love of the land, the people, the culture, and the ecosystem can contribute to dignity, caring, altruism, and some of the finer emotions of which human beings are capable. At the same time, however, nationalism and ethnocentrism can become malevolent when they foster ethnic chauvinism, when they create violent divisions between people, and when they threaten to destroy the humanistic values they supposedly venerate. Nationalism and ethnocentrism pump people up, and they may often generate conditions that bring them down as well.

In his essay "Christianity and Patriotism," Leo Tolstoy pitied "the good-natured foolish people, who, showing their healthy white teeth as they smile, gape like children, naively delighted at the dressed-up admirals and presidents, at the flags waving above them, and at the fireworks, and the playing bands." Tolstoy warned that this euphoria is typically short-lived, and the flags and cheerful bands are quickly replaced by "only the desolate wet plain, cold, hunger, misery—in front of them the slaughterous enemy, behind them the relentless government, blood, wounds, agonies, rotting corpses and a senseless, useless death."[18]

One of the great challenges to students and practitioners of peace and conflict resolution is accordingly to channel the benevolent aspects of nationalism and ethnic solidarity while guarding against their horrors.

## NOTES

1. Bronislaw Malinowski. 1941. "An Anthropological Analysis of War." *American Journal of Sociology,* 46: 521–550.

2. H. H. Turner-High. 1949. *Primitive War.* Columbia: University of South Carolina Press.

3. D. Fry. 2012. "Life Without War." *Science,* 336: 879–894.

4. William James. 1911. "The Moral Equivalent of War." In *Memories and Studies.* New York: Longman, Green.

5.  Andrew Schmookler. 1984. *The Parable of the Tribes.* Berkeley: University of California Press.

6.  John Stoessinger. 1962. *The Might of Nations.* New York: Random House.

7.  J. Ernest Renan. 1882. *Qu'est-ce qu'une nation?* Paris: Calmann-Levy.

8.  Gorge Orwell. 1953. *Such, Such Were the Joys.* New York: Harcourt, Brace.

9.  H. Richard Niebuhr. 1970. *Radical Monotheism and Western Culture.* New York: Harper & Row.

10. Quoted in G. G. Van Deusen. 1937. *The Life of Henry Clay.* Boston: Little, Brown.

11. Richard M. Nixon. Radio and TV address to the nation, April 10, 1970.

12. Bengalis and Pashtuns are both predominantly Muslims, but each constitute a different ethnic group (and thus, different "nations") in terms of language, customs, and to some extent, physical characteristics.

13. Albert Einstein. 1979. *Einstein: A Centenary Volume.* Cambridge, MA: Harvard University Press.

14. Quoted in Kenneth Waltz. 1959. *Man, the State, and War.* New York: Columbia University Press.

15. Not coincidentally, U.S. and NATO combat casualties in Iraq and Afghanistan were significantly lower than in the Vietnam War.

16. Quoted in C. Webster and N. Frankland. 1961. *The Strategic Air Offensive Against Germany.* London: HMSO.

17. Erik Erikson. 1950. *Childhood and Society.* New York: Norton.

18. Leo Tolstoy. 1987. *Writings on Civil Disobedience and Nonviolence.* Philadelphia: New Society Publishers.

## QUESTIONS FOR FURTHER REFLECTION

1.  What similarities and differences are there between premodern, nontechnological wars and contemporary hi-tech wars?

2.  How does "mob psychology" work in terms of peer-group pressure among students and political decision makers?

3.  In current international and domestic conflicts, what role does dehumanization play?

4.  What are some advantages and disadvantages of nationalism in 20th-century and early-21st-century political struggles?

5.  How has public opinion been determined and manipulated during the Iraq and Afghanistan wars?

## SUGGESTIONS FOR FURTHER READING

Douglas R. Fry. 2007. *Beyond War: The Human Potential for Peace.* New York: Oxford University Press.
Paul R. Ehrlich. 2000. *Human Natures: Genes, Cultures, and the Human Prospect.* New York: Penguin Books.
Ernest Gellner. 2009. *Nations and Nationalism,* 2nd ed. Ithaca, NY: Cornell University Press.
Stanley Milgram. 1975. *Obedience to Authority: An Experimental View.* New York: Harper & Row.
E. J. Hobsbawm. 2012. *Nations and Nationalism Since 1780.* Cambridge, UK: Cambridge University Press.

# CHAPTER 8

## THE STATE LEVEL

President Barack Obama announcing the end of formal U.S. military action in the Iraq War. Such decisions are typically made at the "state level."

*Source:* © Kristoffer Tripplaar/Pool/Corbis.

*Nothing appears more surprising to those who consider human affairs with a philosophical eye, than the easiness with which the many are governed by the few.*

—David Hume

We now come to the role of states in our analysis of the reasons for wars. For many people, and for perhaps most political scientists, states are the prime movers of wars. But while states are often necessary for international conflicts, it is unclear if they are sufficient, especially since in the 21st century, the boundaries between state and nonstate belligerents are becoming increasingly blurred.

# Defining the State

As we have seen, popular usage (especially in the United States) often refers to *nation* when the correct word is *state*: The former correctly refers to a collection of people and the latter to an entity that functions in the world political arena. More generally, however, a state can be defined as a sovereign political unit that may include many different communities and that operates via a centralized government, which has the authority and power to decree and enforce laws, collect taxes, and act as the legally recognized representative of its citizens in exchanges with other states, including the waging of war.

The relationship between nations and states is complex. Although there have long been efforts to make national and state borders coincide, thus creating nation-states, states also tend to suppress national movements within their borders. It has been estimated that there are about 200 states containing approximately 800 nationalist movements (more than 7,000 if ethnic identity alone is taken as the criterion for nationhood). At the same time, states promote their own forms of "nationalism," often calling it "patriotism," and glorify those who participate while denouncing those who don't. Thus, the leaders of states often seek to create a national or patriotic identity by unifying the diverse peoples living within state borders. The concept of statehood has often been imbued with an idealistic and almost metaphysical significance (so, for that matter, has the concept of nationhood). "What is the State essentially?" asked Randolph S. Bourne:

> The more closely we examine it, the more mystical and personal it becomes. On the Nation we can put our hand as a definite social group, with attitudes and qualities exact enough to mean something. On the Government we can put our hand as a certain organization of ruling functions, the machinery of law-making and law-enforcing. The Administration is a recognizable group of political functionaries, temporarily in charge of the government. But the State stands as an idea behind them all, eternal, sanctified, and from it Government and Administration conceive themselves to have the breath of life.[1]

This abstract description notwithstanding, the modern state performs numerous specific functions and has immense power, including the power to wage war. When discussion of the state is not enveloped in emotional rhetoric ("wrapping one's self in the flag"), states often justify their existence by appeals to political realism and to principles of efficiency and regularity. Yet scholars increasingly recognize that perhaps the most crucial characteristic of the state is its monopoly on the use of "legitimate" physical violence within its territory—that is, states reserve unto themselves the privilege of taking human life, without being answerable to any higher secular authority.

The two political ideologies that particularly value the state—elevating it above the individual—are the authoritarian left and the far right. Thus, in some Communist Party–governed countries, individuals may be held to be less important than the collectivity, typically represented by the state. Whereas Marxist theory calls for the eventual "withering away of the state," in practice, the governments of most Communist Party–ruled states are notably intrusive (as in China, Vietnam, and Cuba).

Speaking from the perspective of the far right, Benito Mussolini wrote,

> The fascist conception of life stresses the importance of the State and accepts the individual only in so far as his interests coincide with those of the State . . . the fascist conception of the State is all-embracing; outside of it no human or spiritual values can exist, much less have value.[2]

Increasingly, mainstream liberals and conservatives seem also to be placing greater emphasis on the state, with many liberals looking toward the promise of a benevolent "social welfare state" and conservatives lauding the role of patriotism and the "national security state." Peace activists and progressive scholars, however, frequently criticize what they regard as excessive emphasis on states. They claim that an inordinately state-centered view of world politics makes the continuation of states a foregone conclusion, thereby shutting out the possibility of other kinds of political organization. But however the state is imagined, whether we like it or not, and whatever our goals may be for states in general and our own state in particular, states are the primary actors on the world's political stage (just as multinational corporations are the major actors on the world's economic stage), so we had better understand what they are about.

# State Sovereignty

An important concept related to the theory and practice of states is sovereignty, defined by French political economist Jean Bodin (in 1576) as "the state's supreme authority over citizens and subjects." In other words, under the doctrine of sovereignty, states are the final arbiter of earthly disputes and issues. There is no higher recourse. This is supposed to be true during peacetime but is, if anything, exaggerated during war (at least with respect to a state's control over its own citizens). Writing during the time of reigning monarchs, Bodin conceived of sovereignty especially in the sense of one's "sovereign lord," emphasizing the relationship of a subject to his or her ruler.

The Dutch jurist Hugo Grotius, writing a century later, made major contributions to the development of international law by considering the relationship of sovereign rulers to each other. He contended that in the light of state sovereignty, no ruler could be subject to legal control by another state. This principle still applies today, so in theory the United States is legally on a par with, for example, Malta, an island state in the Mediterranean Sea, one-tenth the size of Rhode Island and containing about one-third as many people.

## The Price of State Sovereignty

A crucial consequence of state sovereignty is international "anarchy." In a world composed of separate states, each of which is sovereign and thus legally equal, by definition there cannot be any recourse to higher authority in the solving of disputes. Conflicting claims among cities can be adjudicated by the government of a province or whatever may be designated the next higher administrative unit (confusingly known in the United States as a "state," such as Illinois or California). Conflicts among provinces can be adjudicated by a federal government that in some sense sits "above" these provinces. But if different federal governments are truly sovereign unto themselves, there is no guarantee of orderly process—never mind harmony—when these entities quarrel. They may agree to submit their dispute to mediation, arbitration, or other forms of negotiation, or they may seek to employ diplomacy. But such efforts depend entirely on the voluntary goodwill of the states involved; that is, they involve temporary, and readily revoked, surrender of sovereignty. The Charter of the United Nations, for example, clearly says that it does not seek to restrict the sovereignty of the states making up this international organization. By the same token, international weapons treaties, for example, typically include a provision by which any participating state can withdraw if it determines that its "supreme interests" require doing so.

When states disagree seriously, given that they are legally coequals, they are in theory "free" to engage in a violent test of strength: that is, war. (Or, to put it differently, one might say that sovereign states engage in war when they agree: namely, that war is the most expedient way to resolve the issue between them.) In short, the doctrine of state sovereignty results in the lack of an over-riding central authority with the legitimacy and power to carry out its decrees. Note that this does not necessarily imply disorder. In fact, much of the diplomatic exchange between states is highly structured. Rather, it follows from the absence of any overarching authority, superior to that of states themselves. Bodin as well as Thomas Hobbes recognized that interstate violence, or war, is the price paid for the system of state sovereignty, which, they claimed, nonetheless, maintains a degree of peace within states.

Others have placed much of the blame for war at the doorstep of the state system, although this has not necessarily led to rejection (even in theory) of the system of nation-states. More often, the mood is one of resignation.

## Violations of State Sovereignty

The doctrine of state sovereignty is powerful. All states claim to support it, although in fact efforts at spying and subversion (which are frequent and sometimes continual between certain states) are common violations of that doctrine, along with outright invasion.

In 1979, for example, when the government of Tanzania, with the aid of Ugandan exiles, invaded Uganda and ousted the Ugandan despot Idi Amin, other governments generally applauded or remained silent, not so much out of disrespect for Ugandan sovereignty as because the Amin government was almost universally reviled. In 1956, the former Soviet Union trampled on Hungarian sovereignty, putting down efforts at liberalization; the same was done to Czechoslovakia in 1968, and Poland was implicitly threatened in 1981. These violations were tolerated by the international community largely because the Soviet Union was so powerful, and also because of a tacit recognition that its *de facto*[3] "sovereignty" included the "satellite states" of Eastern Europe. Later, under Mikhail Gorbachev, the former Soviet Union peacefully allowed Poland, Hungary, and other members of the Warsaw Pact to go their own way. Now, most of these Eastern European states are members of the North Atlantic Treaty Organization (NATO), to the consternation of many politicians in Russia. When a neo-Nazi political party became part of the governing coalition in Austria in 2000, many other governments expressed alarm, and the European Union nations sought to isolate Austria diplomatically. Others, including many people within Austria itself, expressed outrage at such actions and claimed these were efforts to interfere with that state's sovereignty.

The former Soviet Union may also be said to have violated the sovereignty of Afghanistan following its 1979 military move into that country; supporters of this action, however, claim that the Soviets were merely responding to requests for assistance by the recognized Afghan government. The U.S. government sought repeatedly to arrange for the assassination of Cuba's Fidel Castro in the 1960s, and attempted to kill Libya's leader, Muammar Gadhafi, by bombing his residence in 1986 (killing members of his household instead, including his 2-year-old daughter). The Central Intelligence Agency (CIA) engineered the forcible overthrow of democratically elected governments in Guatemala and Iran in the 1950s, and in 1973 it provided assistance to the right-wing forces that overthrew the democratically elected Socialist government of Salvador Allende in Chile. These are only some of the more widely acknowledged examples.

When Britain, France, and Israel invaded Egypt in 1956, capturing the Suez Canal, international outrage (especially from the United States) forced them to withdraw, arguing the need to respect Egyptian sovereignty. Yet in 1984, the government of the United States secretly and illegally planted mines in certain Nicaraguan harbors, despite the fact that Nicaraguan sovereignty—at least in theory—is no less worthy of respect than Egyptian (or American) sovereignty. In 1988, the U.S. government arranged for the extradition of an accused drug smuggler from Honduras, in clear violation of the Honduran constitution and Honduran sovereignty. Outraged Hondurans rioted in response. And in 1989, when the United States invaded Panama in clear violation of Panamanian sovereignty, worldwide condemnation of the action was widespread but ineffectual. There are questions, as well, regarding the legitimacy of military actions by the United States and its allies in Iraq (from the Persian Gulf War in 1990–1991 to the present), as well as in Afghanistan, Serbia, and Libya.

As part of its undeclared "war on terror," the U.S. government has made repeated use of missile attacks launched by unmanned drones on citizens of other sovereign states and within the territorial boundaries of these states, including Yemen, Afghanistan, and, notably Pakistan, whose government has publicly complained about such actions. In 2011, U.S. military units killed Osama bin Laden, in a raid occurring within the sovereign state of Pakistan. In short, although virtually all state governments pay lip service to the doctrine of state sovereignty, more powerful nations often invade and attack less powerful states as they see fit, violating state sovereignty in numerous ways.

At the same time, powerful states occasionally oppose international intervention into the domestic affairs of other states, claiming that such intrusions would violate state sovereignty. These arguments have been used by China, for example, in opposing UN intervention in Sudan and by Russia in opposing similar UN intervention in Serbia. In these and other cases, however, the real motivation appears to be concern that such actions might constitute precedents that could diminish their own sovereign powers in Chechnya (in the case of Russia) and Tibet (for China). And of course, it is beyond question that such governments oppose intervention in their own affairs!

## Limitations of State Sovereignty

States have traditionally been hesitant to allow the armed forces of another state to be stationed within their territory or even to pass through it. During World War II, for example, Spain's fascist government, led by the dictator Francisco Franco, although sympathetic to Nazi Germany, would not permit German troops to cross its territory. However, sovereignty can be surprisingly flexible. The government of South Korea hosts thousands of U.S. troops and many U.S. nuclear weapons. South Korean military forces are essentially under U.S. command, largely a consequence of the Korean War. In a remarkable—if limited—surrender of sovereignty, the government of Sri Lanka invited Indian troops to enter that country, so as to police an attempted truce with Tamil separatists; this led to Indian troops engaging in hostilities with Sri Lankans on Sri Lankan soil. During the period roughly 2004 through 2008, the United States claimed that the Iraqi government, established by American military force after the overthrow of dictator Saddam Hussein, was sovereign, even as it "hosted" tens of thousands of foreign troops, and Iraq's genuine sovereignty was very much in doubt.

In contrast, the states of Western Europe are also experiencing a kind of reduction in sovereignty, although this appears to be entirely voluntary. The European Parliament sets some economic and legal policy, in a sense over the heads of its constituent states, and the same can be said for the European Union. For example, by eliminating tariffs toward other members and setting rules for the conduct of trade among their member states, the rules of the European Union circumscribe the economic sovereignty of each participant, presumably for the good of all. In 1992, all trade barriers among member countries were lifted, and by the first decade of the 21st century, a common currency—the euro—had come into existence, replacing the currencies of many of the member states. Some suggest that this may be preliminary to the eventual establishment of a "United States of Europe." On the other hand, the European economic crisis that began in 2011—especially in some of those euro-zone countries with relatively weak economies such as Greece, Portugal, and Spain—may well have been exacerbated by the fact that countries suffering severe balance of payment deficits were unable to respond by devaluing their currency and thereby making their exports more affordable (which in turn would have improved their financial situation). Such monetary adjustments require sovereign control of each state's money supply, control which partially was given up when they agreed to the euro as a common currency.

Other economic unions—such as OPEC, the Organization of Petroleum Exporting Countries— have not always succeeded in getting their member states to subordinate their desires to those of the group as a whole, at least in part because these states have retained sovereign control over their own currencies as well as their foreign policies. When Saudi Arabia or Iran, for example, refuses to restrict or to raise its crude oil production, thereby foiling OPEC efforts to charge uniform oil prices, the members of OPEC defend their actions by relying on the principle of state sovereignty.

State sovereignty is to some extent enshrined in international law, part of which maintains that a procedure, if customary, has legal validity. But underlying any legal niceties, the fundamental legitimacy of sovereignty appears to rest on force: Just as states have a monopoly on sanctioned violence within their borders, there are no suprastate structures currently acknowledged legally capable of overriding a state's claim of sovereignty. In *The City of God,* St. Augustine tells the story of a pirate who had been captured by Alexander the Great. Alexander asked him what his justification was for infesting the sea, and the pirate answered, with uninhibited insolence, "The same as yours, in infesting the earth! But because I do it with a tiny craft, I'm called a pirate. Because you have a mighty navy, you're called an emperor."[4]

# The State System

## The Origins of States and the State System

Many theories have been proposed to explain the origin of the state. Aristotle maintained that it was "natural" and therefore needed no explanation. Rousseau viewed it as an historical curiosity. Some anthropologists have seen a relationship between the early production of agricultural surpluses (made possible by division of labor) and the presence of centralized organization to store, ship, and protect that surplus. Others have emphasized the early association of pretechnological civilization with arid environments (as in Babylonia and Egypt), as well as the possible advantage of economies of scale in providing for irrigation canals. On the other hand, in some cases (China, Mexico) states developed before irrigation. Orthodox Marxists maintain that states originated to police the dominance of one class over another. English philosopher Thomas

Hobbes was less concerned with the origin of states than with their function, arguing in his master work, *The Leviathan*, that the state was crucial to maintaining social stability, because it prevented people from acting on their more violent, selfish, belligerent, and antisocial inclinations.

Many social scientists and historians, however, ascribe special importance to interactions *among* states, leaning toward what may be called the "conquest" theory to explain the origins of the state. According to this view, larger, well-integrated sociopolitical groups succeeded in conquering smaller, less integrated rivals, eventually leading to the modern state system, which is widely thought to have originated in Europe with the Peace of Westphalia (1648), which ended the Thirty Years' War.

But even before this, states constituted a powerful force over their subjects. For example, in Sweden, during the Thirty Years' War, most of the taxes raised were appropriated for the war effort. From then on, European states began rationing food to the civilian population, as well as establishing armaments monopolies, appropriating private lands, and selling war bonds. In the pursuit of armed might, the state began to penetrate nearly every aspect of civilian life. Several centuries earlier, distinctions had already been blurred between the sacred and the secular, between religion and civil society. Similarly, in the conduct of modern war, boundaries were gradually erased between state and society. Just as medieval knights were closely connected with the Catholic Church, 17th-century armies (especially the Protestant forces) made virtually everyone into functionaries of the state.

## War and the State System

Whatever its origins, the organization of people into states constitutes a major fact of life in today's world, and the "state system" is crucial to issues of peace and war. Even though most people are organized in other ways as well—ethnically, vocationally, religiously, and so on—the state system has achieved a virtual monopoly not only over hard power (executions, wars) but also over political discourse and even the ability to imagine solutions to the problem of war. To a large extent, proposed courses of action within most peace-movement traditions are "state centered," and, within traditional governmental circles, policy options are focused almost entirely on the activities of states.

Increasingly, as states came to be accepted almost without question as sovereign over individuals within their boundaries, they were left free to act with other states so as to maintain and enhance their power and international position. According to military historian Michael Howard, as often as not states fight "not over any specific issue such as might otherwise have been resolved by peaceful means, but in order to acquire, to enhance, or to preserve their capacity to function as independent actors in the international system at all." And French political theorist Raymond Aron argued that "the stakes of war are the existence, the creation or the elimination of states." In short, the wars between states, which characterized so much of the state system, have typically been about states and the state system itself. On the other hand, since the end of World War II, the number of states in the world has tripled, largely because of decolonization, and yet the frequency of inter-state wars has not increased correspondingly, and has largely been replaced by intrastate ("civil") wars.

Historically, certain states have been disproportionately involved in wars. These tend overwhelmingly to be the "Great Powers," especially those of Europe. According to Quincy Wright, of the 2,600 most important battles involving European states between 1480 and 1940,

France participated in 47%, Austria-Hungary in 34%, Great Britain and Russia in 22%, Turkey in 15%, and Spain in 12%. Of 25 interstate wars since 1914, the Great Powers were involved in 19. Today, the United States alone spends about 60% of all military budgets worldwide—that is to say, more than all other countries combined—and the Great Powers (United States, Russia, Great Britain, France, Germany, Italy, China, and Japan) spend nearly 90%.[5] A War Participation Index, based on the total number of wars in which a state has participated, divided by the years of the state's political existence, ranks the United States first, Israel second, Turkey and the Ottoman Empire third, and Great Britain fourth.[6] Several centuries ago, Spain, Portugal, Turkey, Holland, and Sweden were involved in a high proportion of wars; with their decline as world powers, they have been substantially more peaceable as well.

These observations suggest that perhaps the problem of war is not so much a function of the *system* of states but rather of *certain* states and, particularly, of the relative importance of these states. Furthermore, it can be argued that there is not, in fact, a "system" of states but rather simply a number of separate entities, each pursuing its own interest (*Realpolitik*). Yet states often seem to act not only to preserve themselves but also to maintain the predominant international fabric of which they are part.

This leads to two rather different ways of thinking about the reasons for wars: (1) a kind of *systemic analysis,* in which the most significant factor is considered to be the preexisting organization—of states, of ideologies, or of individual or group inclinations—all of which interrogate the deep reasons for wars, versus (2) a *situational analysis,* which considers each crisis to be attributable largely to its own circumstances, a function of specific events, actors, and unique situations.

It should be emphasized that the system of states is not irretrievably wedded to war. After all, there have been numerous peaceful boundaries between states, such as the United States and Canada since 1812, the United States and Mexico since 1846, and Norway and Sweden since their peaceful separation in 1905. In addition, war between France and Germany, or Britain and France, is inconceivable today, although the animosity between these pairs of states goes back literally hundreds of years.

From a "structural" or "defensive realist" perspective, states' perceptions of the structure of international power strongly affect the risk of war. According to the political scientist Steven van Evera, states fight

- when they believe they'll win,
- when they think the strategic advantage will lie with the state the attacks first,
- when they fear their relative power may be declining,
- when they believe they can add to their resources, and
- if they think that conquest will be easy.[7]

Van Evera argues that together these factors and perceptions explain much about the reasons for modern wars, and in their absence, war rarely occurs. He also claims that while the actual structure of international power affects the risk of war, it is less important than the aforementioned factors and that in modern times the structure of power has been relative benign.

And the political scientist Charles Kupchan argues that "enemies become friends"; warring states set aside their grievances and construct a relationship precluding the prospect of armed conflict—if the strategic necessity for stable peace unfolds in four phases:

1. A state faced with insufficient resources to deal with existing threats resorts to unilateral accommodation to befriend an adversary;

2. reciprocal restraint then regularizes cooperation and dampens rivalry between the states;

3. societal integration builds institutional and personal linkages between the former adversaries; and

4. changes in political discourse replace former bellicose narratives with new ones of amity and the consolidation of shared identities.[8]

Nations need not be democratic or have any particular form of government to make friends, but they do need strong leaders willing to take the initiative. The United States and Great Britain during the late 19th and early 20th centuries are examples of former foes making friends (as are the North and South of the United States following the Civil War).

# Alliances Between States

States form alliances. They do so to increase their security, assuming that in unity there is strength. Surprisingly, perhaps, large states (such as the United States, Russia, Britain, and France) are more likely to enter into alliances than are small ones. Large states consider themselves to have large responsibilities and commitments, with their obligations often exceeding their resources; hence, they seek to ally with others. Alliances are also often formed among states that share common cultural or ideological features. They typically involve mutual pledges of assistance, often including the willingness to go to war in support of another alliance member.

## Alliances as a Cause of War . . .

It has been claimed that alliances can help deter war by confronting a would-be aggressor with stronger opposition. But it can also be argued that, overall, alliances have served more as a cause of war. Even the signing of an alliance can be a serious provocation, leading to efforts to test, undermine, or break rival alliances. The evidence is equivocal, although certainly alliances have a very strong influence on who goes to war and on which side, when and if war breaks out.

The events leading to World War I provide the most dramatic example of "entangling alliances" among states dragging them—sometimes unwillingly—to war. The United Kingdom. and France were allied (primarily against Germany) in an "entente cordiale," in response to which Germany and Austria-Hungary formed a competing pact, the so-called Triple Alliance (which included Italy, although in fact Italy ultimately ended up fighting against Austria). When the Austrian Archduke Ferdinand was assassinated by a Serbian nationalist at Sarajevo—now part of Bosnia—Austria-Hungary felt a need to assert its power as an effective and unified state (which it wasn't), while Russia felt compelled to back up tiny Serbia, with which Russia shared linguistic and religious ties. The German Kaiser promised full support to Austria-Hungary, Russia did the same for Serbia, and France pledged to fight along with Russia (because of its alliance commitment as well as a long-held grudge over the loss of Alsace and Lorraine to Germany during the Franco-Prussian War several decades earlier). Shortly afterward, when Germany followed its long-prepared war plan and invaded neutral Belgium to attack France, Britain felt compelled to enter the war as well. Many other factors were involved in precipitating World War I, which deserves to be called the War Nobody Wanted. There is no doubt, however, that the web of opposed alliances—some officially signed and equivalent to treaties, others based on strong feelings of connectedness—was crucial in dragging most of the states of Europe into war.

## . . . And the Absence of Alliances as a Cause of War

Ironically, just as World War I was caused in part by the state system of alliances, World War II was brought about in part by the *absence* of such alliances. Through much of the 1930s, Stalin sought to involve the Western powers in an alliance against Nazi Germany, but Britain and France, apparently disliking the Soviet Union even more than Hitler's Germany, resisted. Then, in 1938, French premier Édouard Daladier and British prime minister Neville Chamberlain agreed in Munich to allow Hitler to occupy the Sudetenland of Czechoslovakia. When Hitler also annexed Bohemia and Slovakia in the spring of 1939, Britain and France were finally ready to reinstitute the World War I Triple Entente against Germany. By this time, however, Stalin had given up on the West and had engineered his own pact with Hitler, calling for Germany and Russia to carve up Poland between them. When Germany invaded Poland in September 1939, France and Britain—having warned Hitler that they could not stand idly by—finally declared war on Germany. However, the ultimately successful alliance of Britain, France, the United States, and the Soviet Union did not come about until 1941, after Germany attacked its purported ally, the Soviet Union. Japan, allied to Germany, then attacked the United States at Pearl Harbor, after which Germany declared war on the United States. Just as the rigidities of the pre-1914 alliances in Europe helped precipitate World War I, the failure of the anti-Nazi and anti-fascist states to organize a united opposition seems to have encouraged German and Japanese expansionism.

In more recent times, supporters claim that NATO (and presumably the former Warsaw Pact as well) kept the East-West peace between 1945 and the fall of the Soviet Union in 1991. An alternative view is that these alliances in fact heightened tensions that might otherwise have subsided. In any event, it is noteworthy that the end of the Cold War has led to anxiety among many NATO officials that their alliance has become increasingly outdated, notwithstanding the leading role played by NATO in the militarily victorious campaign against Serbia in 1999, and in Libya in 2011, as well as NATO's less triumphal activities in Afghanistan since 2002.

In summary, alliances among states can be double-edged swords: Bringing about or preventing war, increasing or reducing tensions, or tying states together in ways that may not be anticipated by the leaders and can only with difficulty be understood, later, by historians.

## Alliances and the State System

Winston Churchill, for all his opposition to Hitler, detested Stalin and the Soviet Union at least as much—until Hitler's attack on the Soviet Union set the stage for Britain to ally itself with the Soviets against Nazi Germany. Again and again, alliances have been based primarily on matters of state convenience and power (*Realpolitik* considerations). Hence, they have shifted readily, depending on current perceptions of mutual advantage. As Great Britain's Lord Palmerston put it, "Great states have no permanent friends, only permanent interests."

Conventional political scientists have attempted to characterize the state system—both past and present—in terms of the pattern of major state actors and their alliances. Two primary dimensions are generally considered: polarity and connectedness. Thus, a bipolar system consists of primarily two states (such as the United States and the former Soviet Union) with their associated allies as minor accompaniments. By contrast, a multipolar system might consist of many states (e.g., the United States, Russia, Japan, China, India, Brazil, Nigeria, and the "superstate" of Europe). The dimension of connectedness refers to the closeness with which the various states are linked and thus the probability that a perturbation in one will cause some change in another. If this probability is high, the states are said to be "tightly" connected; if this probability is low, they are "loosely" connected. Thus, the state system at any given time could conceivably be "tight and bipolar," "tight and multipolar," "loose and bipolar," or "loose and multipolar."

Much effort has been expended trying not only to assess the nature of the world state system but to predict its future as well. Theories also abound as to which patterns are most war prone and which are most peace stable. For example, perhaps bipolar systems are more stable because each side can attend more accurately to the behavior of the other. Or perhaps multipolar systems are more stable for the same reason that biologically diverse ecosystems are more stable than monocultures: There are more players available to take up the slack and to prevent catastrophic breakdown. Many other interpretations are possible; the jury is still out on the war/peace significance of differing patterns of interstate alliances.

In any event, such issues are particularly the concern of political scientists and specialists in international relations, fields that are often closely allied with, and frequently apologists for, the state system. The field of peace and conflict studies, by contrast, tends to distance itself from analyses of this sort, considering instead that the state system is part of the problem and thus not likely to be part of the solution.

# *Realpolitik* and *Raisons d'État*

When a state behaves in a particular way, supposedly doing so for its own good, the French say that it is demonstrating *raisons d'état,* the state's own reasons for its actions. The phrase also implies the "right" of a state to act in its own best interests. Insofar as states are totally sovereign, *raisons d'état* are sufficient justifications unto themselves, legally if not morally.

Closely related is the concept of *Realpolitik,* derived from the German and referring to the conduct of international affairs under the assumption that a state's policy should be oriented toward and based on considerations of power and national security rather than on presumably "utopian" ethical ideals. *Realpolitik* is not necessarily any more "real" than other models of international relations, but its advocates fancy it to be.

In the early modern period, Niccolò Machiavelli was a major precursor of *Realpolitik;* during the 18th century Prussia's Frederick the Great and in the 19th century Austria's Metternich, Britain's Palmerston, and Germany's Bismarck practiced the tradition with particular success. In the second half of the 20th century, former U.S. secretary of state Henry Kissinger (a historian and devotee of Metternich) was a well-known practitioner, as was the political scientist Hans Morgenthau. These influential figures, and many others, claimed that *Realpolitik* requires statesmen to base policy decisions primarily on considerations of power and national self-interest—in other words, *raisons d'état.*

### *Realpolitik* and Power

Hans Morgenthau was especially concerned with outlining the *Realpolitik* basis for state conduct in world affairs. He maintained that the primary national interest was the quest for national security and that this was to be achieved fundamentally (although not exclusively) through national power. The goal of international politics, in Morgenthau's view, was therefore the maximization of national power, politics reducible to one of three basic goals: "to keep power, to increase power, or to demonstrate power." Power is to the national leader what wealth is to the economist or what morality is to the ethicist. States are assumed to be concerned—almost exclusively—with enhancing their power and not hesitant about going to war to do so.

Power, however, is not strictly limited to military strength. In 1941, the United States was far more powerful than Japan realized, not because of its military (which was relatively small at that time) but because of its population, its industrial potential, its geographic location, and its determination to prevail. Japan, similarly, is very powerful today, despite a relatively modest military force, because of the size of its economy and its ability to compete in international markets. (This in turn may be partly because Japan has invested in domestic productivity rather than weaponry.) There is also moral power, enjoyed by such neutral states as Sweden, Norway, and to some extent India because of its history of Gandhian nonviolence. The power of a state can be defined as the ability of that state to influence the behavior of other states. As such, power ("soft power," in the words of political scientist Joseph Nye) can derive from unity, ideology, effective leadership, geographic position, cultural influence, health and educational level of its citizens, and access to resources no less than raw military force and the willingness to use it (or "hard power," in Nye's formulation).

### *Realpolitik* and War

In the rough and tumble of *Realpolitik,* military power—however achieved, and whether direct or implied—is the "name of the game." Karl von Clausewitz, spokesperson for the military aspects of *Realpolitik,* made the renowned observation that war is "the continuation of politics by other means." He emphasized the subordination of military to political goals and wrote that although war is often brutal, it should not be senseless but rather "an act of violence to compel the enemy to fulfill our will." According to von Clausewitz, "Violence is therefore the means; imposing our will on the enemy, the end."

Part of the *Realpolitik* tradition in statecraft, accordingly, is the view that war is, ideally, not a consequence of error or irrational factors but rather a result of a coolheaded decision that more can be gained by going to war than by remaining at peace. By extension, wars begin when two parties disagree as to their relative strength, and wars end when they are in agreement—that is, when the victor is revealed to be stronger than the vanquished. (Of course, given that most wars have a loser, it can be argued that 50% of the time, states are wrong, or their initial decision process was less than ideal.)

It would be simplistic, however, to assume that practitioners of *Realpolitik* are necessarily warmongers. Rather, they advocate a constant and, as they see it, hardheaded sense of the ways of international relations, limiting war only to those cases in which it will contribute to the "national interest." Hans Morgenthau, for example, strongly opposed the Vietnam War but only because it was hurtful to the United States, not because it was wrong in any other respect. It could similarly be argued that insofar as Western (especially U.S.) policies toward the Islamic world were to be based on *Realpolitik*, it would help diminish existing Crusader-like inclinations to remake other countries in "our mold," which is to say: democratic, capitalist, and secular.

## *Realpolitik* and Morality

When the *realpolitik* of interstate behavior comes into conflict with more altruistic ethical principles, the latter almost always take a backseat. On the other hand, although states often use *Realpolitik* considerations in determining whether to go to war, they typically justify such a decision, publicly, in terms of morality or idealism. Consider the following argument from 19th-century British prime minister William Gladstone: "However deplorable wars may be, they are among the necessities of our condition; and there are times when justice, when faith, when the failure of mankind, require a man not to shrink from the responsibility of undertaking them." He argued that Britain had a moral obligation to aid the Bulgarians, at the time oppressed by the Turks, whose rule, according to Gladstone, involved "the basest and blackest outrage upon record within the present century, if not within the memory of man."[9] Yet, just 20 years earlier, Britain had gone to war in support of that same Ottoman Empire, against Russia (the Crimean War). The issue at that time, far from the abuses and outrages of Turkish policy, was in fact *Realpolitik,* in this case the competition between Britain and Russia for influence in the Black Sea region.

*Realpolitik* seems to transcend traditional liberal, radical, and conservative political ideologies. Thus, the British liberal statesman James Bright resigned from the cabinet in 1882 to protest Britain's bombardment of Alexandria and occupation of Egypt: "Be the Government Liberal or Tory much the same thing happens: war, with all its horrors and miseries and crimes and cost."[10] (However, Gladstone's attitude represented something of an ethical advance over previous principles of *Realpolitik* in that he emphasized the relation of war to the common interests of humankind, rather than simple considerations of state power.)

Ethical considerations loom large in more recent history as well. Yet, when ideals of nonviolence, fairness, and noninterference conflict with *Realpolitik,* the latter has generally triumphed. Immediately after World War II, for example, U.S. government officials harbored a number of former Nazi war criminals—especially those with expertise as rocket scientists or knowledge about left-wing movements in Europe—because it was believed these people could help the United States compete with and defeat the Soviet Union. The United States has repeatedly refrained from criticizing the ruthless tactics of China in forcing its rule upon Tibet, and in brutally suppressing the prodemocracy movement in Tiananmen Square during 1989, because trade with China is deemed economically important to America, and because for a while China served as a convenient ally in America's competition with the former Soviet Union. Similarly, the United States has long been willing to wink at Pakistan's violation of nuclear nonproliferation obligations because of that nation's role as a conduit for American military aid to the anti-Soviet *mujahideen* guerrillas in Afghanistan and as a counterbalance to India, often seen by the United States in the past as tilting toward the former Soviet Union. Recent years have seen a more positive U.S. stance toward India, perhaps in response to India's increasing technological and economic influence.

The United States has also continued a difficult courtship with Pakistan, as a result, the United States has funneled billions of dollars in military aid to the government of Pakistan, which it claims to value as a "partner in the war on terror" even though it is increasingly clear that the Pakistani government has long played a "double game" of fighting Islamic extremists within

Pakistan itself while covertly supporting components of the Taliban inside Afghanistan. In doing so, the Pakistani government is doubtless responding to its own *Realpolitik* calculations, which suggest that eventually the United States will depart Afghanistan, whereupon the Pakistani government will likely have to deal with an indigenous Islamist government in Kabul.

In the recent past, the United States readily collaborated with right-wing dictators and despots, often ignoring their abominable human rights records, because their anticommunist stance was judged useful in America's competition with the former Soviet bloc. President Franklin Roosevelt, for example, is said to have observed about the brutal Nicaraguan dictator Anastasio Somoza (who, after decades in power, was eventually overthrown by the Sandinistas in 1979) that "he may be an SOB but he's *our* SOB!" U.S. government policy toward Third World countries also resulted in large part from a *Realpolitik* desire to oppose and undermine left-wing governments, as in Nicaragua during the 1980s, in Venezuela during the presidency of Hugo Chávez, and in Cuba since 1961, and to oppose left-wing insurgencies against right-wing regimes friendly to the United States (as in El Salvador, Honduras, and Guatemala). During the Cold War, the Soviet Union was no less observant of *Realpolitik,* showing little hesitation about quashing prodemocracy movements in East Germany (1953), Hungary (1956), and Czechoslovakia (1968)—although it allowed these and its other Eastern European client states to leave the Soviet orbit between 1989 and 1991 (when the Soviet Union itself collapsed).

## Status Quo Versus Revisionist States

Considerations of *Realpolitik* also influence whether states are satisfied with current circumstances or advocate for change. The former are "status quo states," such as the United States; they generally seek to keep things as they are. Their wars are fought against those who try to change things, notably threatening aggressors such as Nazi Germany or, more recently, revolutionary nationalist and militant Islamist movements. The doctrine of deterrence—which is not limited to the nuclear age but which nonetheless looms especially large in the calculations of nuclear-armed superpowers, especially the United States—lends itself particularly well to states whose primary desire is to prevent change. Thus, deterrence represents a way of preventing another state from aggressing; by its nature, its greatest success is when nothing happens.

On the other hand, "revisionist states" are those that typically believe their international status is not commensurate with their economic power and geopolitical aspirations. Examples include Japan in 1905 (on the eve of the Russo-Japanese War) and again in the 1930s and early 1940s; Germany in the 1870s and again in the 1930s; and possibly China in our own time—although China, despite its increasing Great Power status and growing economic clout, has thus far been notably reticent when it comes to projecting military power beyond its borders—with the exception of Tibet. It is debated whether the Soviet Union in the late 20th century was a status quo or revisionist state. Under Mikhail Gorbachev, it became increasingly revisionist at home and abroad, culminating in its release of control over the states of Eastern Europe. By contrast, the United States seems to have become consistently a status quo power, both at home and abroad. On the other hand, the so-called Bush Doctrine, under which the United States pledged to support democratization in other countries, suggests possible revisionist inclinations. It remains to be seen, however, whether this claim is simply rhetorical, retrospectively used to justify the Iraq War, or whether it will be acted upon with respect to such long-standing but undemocratic allies as Saudi Arabia, or semifriendly, quasidemocratic states such as Russia under Vladimir Putin.

# Internal Cohesion

Considerations of *Realpolitik* and *raisons d'état* may lead politicians to engage in foreign wars so as to consolidate their domestic situation. We have seen that strong psychological and sociological pressures induce citizens to "rally 'round the flag," ignoring or postponing complaints with the current government so as to present a united front to the enemy. Jean Bodin, a major conceptualizer of state sovereignty, wrote that "the best way of preserving a state, and guaranteeing it against sedition, rebellion, and civil war, is to keep the subjects in amity with another, and to this end, to find an enemy against whom they can make common cause." Similarly, on the eve of the American Civil War, Secretary of State William Seward urged that President Lincoln declare war on France and Spain so as to unite Americans and preserve the union.

In Shakespeare's *Henry IV, part 2*, a dying King Henry advises his son how to respond when his subjects are unhappy with past abuses from their government: "Be it thy course, to *busy giddy minds With foreign quarrels*; that action, hence borne out, May waste the memory of the former days." And in George Orwell's *1984*, the world was divided into three megastates, which constantly made war against each other, not to win but rather to preserve their internal conditions:

> The war, therefore, if we judge it by the standards of previous wars, is merely an imposture. . . .
> The war is waged by each ruling group against its own subjects, and the object of the war is not to make or prevent conquests of territory, but to keep the structure of society intact.[11]

Wars can also serve states by providing an outlet for pent-up energy as well as surplus manpower. On the other hand, if wars have consistently been initiated so as to achieve internal cohesion, a correlation should exist between internal and external conflicts. Yet careful studies have not been able to demonstrate any significant statistical relationship between these variables; that is, states are not more likely to go to war when they are seriously threatened with heightened internal violence or dissension. Moreover, wars initiated in the hope of achieving national unity and minimizing domestic discontent don't always work out that way. If the war is prolonged and costly, citizen dissatisfaction can grow, despite the pressure for conformity that wars typically engender. Major reasons for resentment include the burden of added taxes to pay for the war, the mounting toll of casualties, unhappiness with the direction of the war, and, especially, anger if the war is lost.

It is relatively rare that ethical considerations loom large in generating popular dissatisfaction with a regime's warlike behavior, although the Vietnam War was an exception. Practical concerns are generally paramount. Thus, enormous Russian casualties during World War I were important in precipitating the Bolshevik Revolution of 1917, and popular resentment at the conduct and outcome of the Falklands War led to the downfall of General Galtieri's Argentine government in 1982. On the other hand, the government of the Ayatollah Khomeini in Iran was, if anything, strengthened by its bloody war with Iraq in the 1980s, as was Saddam Hussein's regime in the 1990s, despite costly military defeats at the hands of the United States and its allies. Of course, that regime was overthrown by the United States some years later. And part of the ostensible rationale for the U.S. invasion was its avowed abhorrence of weapons of mass destruction in the hands of "that evil dictator, Saddam Hussein." When no such weapons were found, the "moral" justification shifted to removing a tyrant from power, ostensibly to "spread democracy" throughout the Middle East.

Finally, since warfare requires a degree of national unity and effective central coordination, states that are internally disunited may be especially cautious and hesitant to engage in a war they could well end up losing.

# Arms Races

Short of war itself, an arms race is the most prominent and warlike form of competition between states. Arms races have been defined as "intense competitions between opposed powers or groups of powers, each trying to achieve an advantage in military power by increasing the quantity or improving the quality of its armaments or armed forces."[12]

Between 1945 and 1991, the nuclear arms race between the United States and the Soviet Union consumed considerable resources and attention. Despite the disintegration of the Soviet Union, the United States has continued to conduct an arms "race" against a range of hypothetical adversaries, including terrorists, "rogue states" (including Iran and North Korea), and possible rivals (most notably China). But arms races existed long before the invention of nuclear weapons. Moreover, arms races have long been a major arena for interstate competition, from the city-states of Greece to competing feudal overlords during the Middle Ages to modern times. As William James put it, "The intensely sharp competitive preparation for war by the nations is the real war, permanent, unceasing, and the battles are only a sort of public verification of the mastery gained during the 'peace' interval."[13] Writing of one of the first documented major wars in human history, the Pelopponesian War between Athens and Sparta, the historian Thucydides famously noted that "What made the war inevitable was the growth of Athenian power and the fear which this caused Sparta."

## Anxiety and the Fundamental Attribution Error

Reciprocal anxiety has often fueled arms races, with each side worried that the other was about to pull ahead or was already dangerously in the lead. Often, this involved incorrect estimates, which exaggerated the other side's forces. In 1914, for example, German intelligence estimated that the French Army had 121,000 more soldiers than the German army; at the same time, the French judged that the German Army exceeded the French by 134,000! From 1906 to 1914, when Great Britain and Germany were engaged in a vigorous naval arms race, each of the two states worried that the other was about to launch a preemptive attack. Such anxiety almost certainly played a part in the initiation of World War I. Edward Grey, British foreign secretary during the decade leading up to World War I, put it this way:

> Great armaments lead inevitably to war. The increase of armaments . . . produces a consciousness of the strength of other nations and a sense of fear. Fear begets suspicion and distrust and evil imaginings, till each Government feels it would be criminal and a betrayal of its country not to take every precaution, while every Government regards the precautions of every other Government as evidence of hostile intent.[14]

Governments and citizens often tend to make what psychologists call the *attribution error*. This involves attributing the behavior of one's opponent to ill will and aggressive designs, while interpreting one's own, comparable behavior to an understandable effort at self-protection.

## Failure to Act

We have already noted that in a parallel to the debate over whether alliances cause or prevent war, it can also be argued that just as the pre–World War I arms races helped precipitate that conflict, the *failure* of the Western powers—notably Britain and France—to engage Germany in an arms race may have helped bring about World War II. Hitler appears to have been emboldened by what he saw as the rise of pacifism in Western Europe. When Germany first began violating the provisions of the Versailles Treaty (which ended World War I and called essentially for the demilitarization of Germany), England and France were considerably stronger than Germany, yet they did not respond. Thus, when Germany rebuilt its military and reoccupied the Rhineland in 1936, in clear violation of its treaty obligations, England and France failed to act or even to engage in significant arming of their own. The German General Staff is now known to have been quite apprehensive about these early aggressive moves by Adolf Hitler: Had the Western allies responded more forcefully, it is possible that Germany would have backed down, and Hitler's aggressive momentum might have been ended before it gathered steam.

## Peaceful Resolution of Arms Races

In some cases, arms races have been resolved peacefully:

1. Great Britain versus France, navy, 1841–1865

2. Germany versus France, army, 1870s–1890s

3. Great Britain versus France and Russia, navy, 1884–1905

4. Chile versus Argentina, navy, 1890–1902

5. United States versus Great Britain, navy (cruisers), 1920–1930

6. United States versus the former Soviet Union, nuclear weapons, and other weapons of mass destruction (WMDs), 1945–1991, and to a lesser extent, versus Russia, 1991–present, and versus China, 2005-present

In case 1, one side gave up; in case 2, the competition simply petered out, at least temporarily; case 3 was resolved by an alliance among the racers; case 4 ended with a resolution of the existing boundary dispute; case 5 (and 4 as well) ended with an arms limitation treaty. The outcome of case 6 remains to be determined.

## Factors Driving Arms Races

Many factors drive arms races: The financial profits to be made, desire for advancement on the part of individuals whose careers depend on success in administering or commanding major new weapons programs, political leaders pandering to bellicose domestic sentiment, and interservice rivalry within a state. Another potential reason for these activities is genuine concern about the security needs of the state. Faced with an uncompromisingly hostile opponent, national leaders have often believed that military might was their only real protection. This leads to what has aptly been called the "security dilemma": When states perceive that they must increase their military power so as to achieve security, their rivals feel constrained to do the same. As a result, both sides enter into a dangerous competitive spiral by which all parties are made less secure. Each seeks to resolve its insecurity by acquiring more weapons, which only leads to even more insecurity, which leads in turn to even greater acquisitions of weapons, and so on.

British historian Herbert Butterfield suggested that perhaps "no state can ever achieve the security it desires without so tipping the balance that it becomes a menace to its neighbors." In the process, it becomes a menace to itself. But this has not prevented states from trying.

## Arms Races and War

Do arms races lead to war? One influential point of view claims that they do. Another maintains just the opposite: By being militarily strong, a state prevents war. Arguing in favor of greater military expenditures, President Ronald Reagan, for example, claimed that the United States never got into a war because it was too strong. (This ignores the Mexican-American and Spanish-American wars and perhaps the Vietnam and Iraq wars as well.) Proponents of military strength and arms races point to the "lessons of Munich," when World War II was made more likely by the failure of the West to answer Germany's strength with strength of its own. Opponents of arms races point to World War I, when arms races helped precipitate the European powers into an unwanted and unnecessary war.

It has proved virtually impossible to evaluate these propositions, although most attempts to examine the historical record have shown that arms races seem more likely to produce war than to prevent it. For example, one political scientist examined 99 serious international disputes between 1815 and 1965. Twenty-eight of these had been preceded by an arms race; 71 had not. Of the former, 23 (82%) resulted in a war, whereas of the 71 disputes not preceded by an arms race, only 3 (4%) resulted in war.[15] Although this study does not prove that arms races cause war, it does suggest that when a serious dispute occurs in conjunction with an ongoing arms race, war is far more likely than when the disputing nations have not also been competing militarily.

Nonetheless, many statesmen as well as citizens remain convinced that security often demands strength, and the pursuit of strength often generates an arms race. This theme is described in the famous Latin motto, formulated by the Roman general Vegetius: *Si vis pacem, para bellum* ("If you want peace, prepare for war"). "A wiser rule," according to sociologist William Graham Sumner, "would be to make up your mind soberly what you want, peace or war, and then to get ready for what you want; for what we prepare for is what we shall get."

## A FINAL NOTE ON WAR AND STATES

When it comes to war, states seem more often to be the problem than the solution, although most people would agree that if there is to be a solution, states will have to be a part of that as well. Increasingly, states appear to exist for their own sake, not for the benefit of their citizens. They enter into wars for their own *raisons d'état* and terminate them for the same reasons. If defense is the primary reason for people to associate into those large political entities known as states, what is to be done in the nuclear age, when that relationship has become potentially lethal, as well as one-sided? Nuclear weapons in particular may exist almost entirely because of the purported *Realpolitik* benefits they confer on states that possess them; however, it is increasingly difficult to argue that they confer security on the individual. Indeed, citizens of nonnuclear states, such as

New Zealand, Australia, Switzerland, Costa Rica, Finland and Sweden are in many ways more secure and prosperous than citizens of the nuclear powers.

The novelist E. L. Doctorow wrote,

> The time may be approaching when we will have to choose between two coincident reality systems: the historical human reality of feeling, of thought, of multitudinous expression, of life and love and natural death; or the supra-human statist reality of rigid, ahistorical, censorious and contending political myth structures, which may in our name and from the most barbaric impulses disenfranchise 99 percent of the world's population from even tragic participation in their fate.[16]

With the world in ecological and social crisis, states have largely compounded these problems through increasing violence and militarism. If one is to oppose war, is it also necessary, then, to oppose the state? Can positive peace be achieved within the current system of states? And if so, what about the various positive roles of the state, such as maintaining order, social welfare systems, and common purpose among its citizens? Many of the most important factors affecting people's lives occur on a global scale and may be to a large extent beyond the ability of individual states to manage.

In the first part of the 21st century, some states may increasingly turn their attention toward some of the global problems facing all human beings, such as poverty, global warming, ecological destruction, energy shortages and the urgent need for worldwide demilitarization, especially weapons of mass destruction. But except for nongovernmental organizations (NGOs) and international institutions such as the United Nations, it seems likely that *Realpolitik* and a narrowly defined sense of "the national interest" will continue to be the modus operandi for most states, particularly great powers such as the United States. As a result, students of peace and conflict studies can anticipate efforts by many organizations to go beyond existing state boundaries and to seek alternative or additional ways of resolving these planetary issues.

## NOTES

1. Randolph S. Bourne. 1964. *War and the Intellectuals, Collected Essays 1915–1919*. New York: Harper & Row.

2. Benito Mussolini. 1963. "The Doctrine of Fascism." In J. Somerville and R. Santoni, eds., *Social and Political Philosophy*. New York: Anchor.

3. De facto refers to a situation "in fact," whereas de jure refers to its legal or theoretical condition.

4. St. Augustine. 1950. *The City of God*. New York: Modern Library.

5. Quincy Wright. 1964. *A Study of War*. Chicago: University of Chicago Press.

6. See Johan Galtung, "From Early Warning to Early Action: Developing the EU's Response Crisis and Longer-Term Threats," lecture delivered to the EU Commission. Brussels: November 12, 2007.

7. Steven van Evera. 1999. *Causes of War: Power and the Roots of Conflict*. Ithaca, NY: Cornell University Press.

8. Charles A. Kupchan. 2010. *How Enemies Become Friends*. Princeton, NJ: Princeton University Press.

9. Quoted in J. Morley. 1903. *The Life of William Everett Gladstone*. New York: Macmillan.

10. Ibid.

11. George Orwell. 1949. *1984.* San Diego: Harcourt Brace Jovanovich.

12. Hedley Bull. 1965. *The Control of the Arms Race.* New York: Praeger.

13. William James. 1967. *The Writings of William James.* New York: Random House.

14. Quoted in John G. Stoessinger. 1985. *Why Nations Go to War.* New York: St. Martin's.

15. William D. Wallace. 1979. "Arms Races and Escalation." *Journal of Conflict Resolution* 23: 3–16.

16. E. L. Doctorow. 1983. "It's a Cold War Out There, Class of '83." *The Nation,* July 2.

## QUESTIONS FOR FURTHER REFLECTION

1. What are the advantages and disadvantages of unrestricted state sovereignty? Do the advantages outweigh the disadvantages?

2. If states are "the problem," the principal cause of war in the modern period, what is the solution?

3. To what degree is *Realpolitik* "realistic" in the contemporary world? To what degree is it moral or unethical?

4. To what degree do arms races today resemble or differ from those of the 20th century?

5. Are "national interest" and "national security" better served by war and the buildup to war or by peace? Why?

## SUGGESTIONS FOR FURTHER READING

Anne Clunan and Harold Trinkunas, eds. 2010. *Ungoverned Spaces: Alternatives to State Authority in an Era of Softened Sovereignty.* Stanford, CA: Stanford University Press.

E. Dougherty and R. L. Pfalzgraff. 2000. *Contending Theories of International Relations,* 5th ed. New York: Longman.

Hans Morgenthau. 1967. *Politics Among Nations.* New York: Alfred Knopf.

Joseph S. Nye, Jr. 2003. *Understanding International Conflicts,* 4th ed. New York: Pearson.

Robert J. Art and Robert Jervis. 2006. *International Politics: Enduring Concepts and Contemporary Issues,* 8th ed. New York: Longman.

William H. McNeill. 1982. *The Pursuit of Power.* Chicago: University of Chicago Press.

Kenneth N. Waltz. 2001. *Man, the State, and War: A theoretical analysis.* New York: Columbia University Press.

# CHAPTER 9

# THE DECISION-MAKING LEVEL

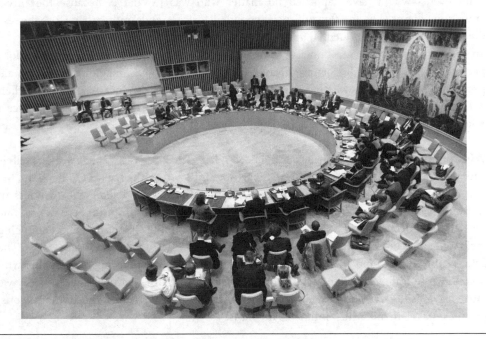

On March 26, 2003, at its headquarters in New York City, the Security Council of the United Nations holds it first public meeting since the beginning of the Iraq War.

*Source:* © 2008 Corbis Corporation.

*The offhand decision of some commonplace mind high in office at a critical moment influences the course of events for a hundred years.*

—Thomas Hardy

*No leader should put troops into the field merely to gratify his own spleen; no leader should fight a battle simply out of pique. But a kingdom that has once been destroyed can never come again into being; nor can the dead ever be brought back to life. Hence the enlightened leader is heedful, and the good leader full of caution.*

—Sun Tzu

Large groups of people are usually led by smaller groups, and, in many cases, the ultimate decisions of war and peace are made by very few people, sometimes just one person. It is therefore appropriate to consider decision making at the level of governmental and other influential leaders.

# The Role of Leaders

There has long been debate over the role of crucial individuals in the making of history. So-called great man theories maintain that the personality of certain select, major figures has had a determining effect on world events. By contrast, theories of "impersonal forces" claim that most significant events would have happened no matter who was in charge, because they are the culmination of large ebbs and flows of societies and historical trends, rather than from the results of the actions of a small, influential minority.

In various writings, but most notably in his novel, *War and Peace,* Leo Tolstoy argued for the impersonal forces theory. He portrayed Napoleon as a bit ridiculous, imagining himself making important decisions such as whether or not to go to war or how to conduct major battles, whereas major leaders are actually "history's slaves." In discussing the outbreak of war between France and Russia in 1812, Tolstoy raises the following questions:

> What produced this extraordinary occurrence? What were its causes? The historians tell us with naive assurance that its causes were the wrongs inflicted on the Duke of Oldenburg, the non-observance of the Continental System, the ambition of Napoleon, the firmness of Alexander, the mistakes of the diplomats, and so forth and so on. . . . And there was no one cause for that occurrence, but it had to occur because it had to! Millions of men, renouncing their human feelings and reason, had to go from West to East to slay their fellows. . . . The actions of Napoleon and Alexander were as little voluntary as the action of any soldier who was drawn into the campaign by lot or by conscription. . . . To elicit the laws of history we must leave aside kings, ministers and generals, and select for study the homogeneous, infinitesimal elements which influence the masses.[1]

Tolstoy's view that the common people are as responsible as their leaders derived from his conviction that individuals have the opportunity—indeed, the responsibility—to take things into their own hands and refuse to fight.

With regard to its causes, probably no war has been analyzed in greater detail than World War I, because the interweaving factors that culminated in that war were unusually complex, and because so many relevant government documents are available to historians. No single villain (and, certainly, no hero) emerges from all this scholarship, and some respected observers have even proposed that somehow war was "in the air," a view that does not ignore other concerns or causal factors but that emphasizes the irrational and impersonal:

> No single cause will explain the First World War. But the formal causes—the commercial and colonial rivalries, the cocked war establishments of Europe designed to mobilize, deploy, and conquer by the execution of a single and irreversible general-staff plan, the strident minorities and grandiose nationalisms, the disintegration of the Austro-Hungarian empire,

the colonial rivalries, the rot of Turkey, the instability of the balance of power—all these pale before the fact that Europe in 1914 wanted war and got it.[2]

While this debate may be irresolvable, it is still necessary to attend to the specific issue of leaders and their decision making, if only because leaders do exist and make decisions, and, moreover, there is good reason to think that these decisions are important—although perhaps not as important as most military and political leaders themselves would like to think.

## Strong Leaders

In the past, when rulers embodied the political and military power of their group, they clearly played a major role in deciding whether or not to go to war. In *The Education of a Christian Prince,* Erasmus (1456–1536) urged,

Although a prince ought nowhere to be precipitate in his plans, there is no place for him to be more deliberate and circumspect than in the matter of going to war. Some evils come from one source and others from another, but from war comes the shipwreck of all that is good and from it the sea of all calamities pours out.[3]

The role of individual leaders may well have been unduly glamorized, and decision makers often receive credit—and blame—that they do not entirely deserve. Yet certain individuals, by the force of their personalities and the decisions they made, have had enduring effects on history. Sometimes, they represent the culmination of currents within their societies, and they may also catalyze other events. Nonetheless, people such as Alexander the Great, Genghis Khan, Charlemagne, Joan of Arc, Napoleon, Bismarck, Hitler, Stalin, de Gaulle, Mao Tse-tung, Saddam Hussein, and George W. Bush have acted as lightning rods for popular discontent and, often, as precipitators of war. Less often have leaders of this ilk achieved renown as peacemakers.

On the other hand, when it becomes necessary for a state to accept defeat, a strong leader may be the only person capable of getting the populace to swallow the bitter pill. Marshal Pétain played this role in France in 1940, as did Carl Mannerheim in Finland in 1944 and Charles de Gaulle in France in 1961 when he acquiesced to independence for Algeria. Similarly, the warming of Sino-American relations during the Nixon administration was facilitated by the fact that Richard Nixon's reputation as a hard-line anticommunist insulated him against most accusations of "appeasement."

Many leaders may be moved by the desire to go down in history as peacemakers. Thus, the dramatic warming of relations between the United States and the former Soviet Union during the late 1980s and early 1990s must be attributed, at least partly, to a partial shift in perceptions and goals by President Reagan. This was even more the result of the commitment by Mikhail Gorbachev to *glasnost* ("political opening") and *perestroika* ("economic restructuring") inside the Soviet Union, which in turn helped lessen U.S.-Soviet tensions and facilitated advances in arms control, such as a partial reduction of conventional forces in Europe and a decrease in the number of strategic nuclear warheads. This almost certainly would not have taken place had any of Gorbachev's more Stalinist rivals assumed power in the Kremlin. On the other hand, Reagan's personal commitment to "Star Wars" (the Strategic Defense Initiative, or SDI) prevented even more dramatic cuts in U.S. and Soviet nuclear weapons. By the same token, U.S. withdrawal from the 1972 Anti-Ballistic Missile Treaty, ostensibly to build a Ballistic Missile Defense (BMD, also called a National Missile Defense or NMD) system, threatens to have a similar effect in the early 21st century.

The role of individual leaders was perhaps most clearly emphasized by events during the early days of World War II, when Britain stood virtually alone against Nazi Germany. Churchill not only personified British defiance and determination at that time, but he also helped generate it with such stirring rhetorical pronouncements as: "We shall fight on the beaches, we shall fight on the landing grounds, we shall fight in the fields and in the streets, we shall fight in the hills; we will never surrender." Nor does strong leadership only promote war: When President Sadat of Egypt went to Israel and negotiated a historic peace treaty with Israel's Begin, through the mediating efforts of President Carter, it was a triumph of the courage, vision, and hard work of a few individuals. (Sadat was later assassinated by violent Islamists.) Making peace typically requires as much if not more courage and determination than does making war.

In many cases, of course, wars are imposed on their people by the decisions of their leadership. The various "wars of succession" during the 18th century, for example, did not arise from the upwelling of public anger or concern; rather, they were decreed by leaders for *raisons d'état* and obediently entered into by most of the populace. At other times, charismatic leaders from Alexander the Great to Hitler have succeeded in generating wartime enthusiasm (although admittedly their messages could flourish only on fertile soil). In his war message to the American people in 1917, President Wilson expressed the oft-spoken distinction between people and their leadership, one that—true or not—has proven especially convenient during war:

> We have no quarrel with the German people. . . . It was not upon their impulse that their government acted. . . . It was a war determined as wars used to be determined upon in the old, unhappy days when people were nowhere consulted by their rulers and wars were provoked and waged in the interest of dynasties or of little groups of ambitious men who were accustomed to use their fellow men as pawns or tools.[4]

## Weak Leaders and the Role of "Villains"

It is not necessarily true that only strong leaders initiate wars. The weak political personalities of Germany's Kaiser Wilhelm and Russia's Czar Nicholas rendered them unable to hold their general staffs in check; stronger leadership on their part might have prevented World War I, just as stronger leadership in Britain and France during the 1930s might have averted World War II. In the former case, such strength would have been needed to restrain those, within the country, who felt bound to follow predesigned mobilization plans and who worried excessively about being preempted by the other side. In the latter case, strength would have been needed to restrain those outside the United Kingdom and France—notably Hitler and Mussolini.

The Cuban Missile Crisis—the closest humanity has apparently come to general nuclear war—was brought about in part because John F. Kennedy felt browbeaten by Soviet premier Khrushchev at their 1961 summit meeting in Vienna and was further humiliated by the debacle of the failed American-supported invasion of Cuba at the Bay of Pigs. The following year, Kennedy was determined that he would not be pushed around again by the Soviet leader; fortunately for the world, Khrushchev was willing (perhaps due largely to insufficient military strength) to back down.

Lyndon Johnson was personally determined not to be defeated by Ho Chi Minh and the North Vietnamese. The war between Iran and Iraq during the 1980s depended in large part on personal animosity between the two leaders, Saddam Hussein of Iraq and the Ayatollah Khomeini of Iran. The Persian Gulf War was fed by the hostility between Saddam Hussein and President George H. W. Bush, and the Iraq War was fed in turn by enmity between Hussein—who is widely believed to have tried to kill the first President Bush—and President George W. Bush. (It has also been suggested that George W. Bush hoped to outdo his father, who, during the Persian Gulf War had ordered coalition forces to refrain from overthrowing Saddam Hussein.)

Sometimes, wars result from the overwhelming personal ambition of leaders, something that is not restricted to modern tyrants or would-be conquerors. Consider this boast from Xerxes, King of Persia in 480 BCE (and recounted by Herodotus):

Once let us subdue this people [the Greeks] . . . and we shall extend the Persian territory beyond our borders; for I will pass through Europe from one end to the other, and make of all lands which it contains one country. . . . By this course then we shall bring all mankind under our yoke.[5]

Sometimes, the issue is one of face-saving, in which case leaders are especially likely to precipitate a crisis—or respond aggressively to one—if they are wary of opposition at home. Thus, President Truman, stung by criticism that he had "lost" China to communists, may have felt especially driven to intervene when North Korea subsequently invaded South Korea. John F. Kennedy seriously worried in 1962 that he might be impeached if he did not respond forcefully to the discovery of Soviet missile sites under construction in Cuba. Also that year, Indian prime minister Nehru stirred up anti-Chinese feeling in India, and when the Chinese resisted Indian territorial encroachments, he had to choose between fighting and losing face, even though the Chinese had overwhelming logistic advantages and 10 times as many troops.

We know very little about what produces personalities that are likely to achieve national leadership or what distinguishes a peacemaker from a warmonger. Alexander the Great grew up as one of many children in a royal, polygynous household. Contact with his father (Philip of Macedon) was rare, and young Alexander apparently had a very intense relationship with his mother, who was ambitious, energetic, demanding, punitive, and rather violent. Perhaps it is not surprising that Alexander's quest for approval included conquering much of the known world before he was 33. On the other hand, Prussia's Frederick—also known as the Great—had a submissive, ineffectual mother but a demanding, callous, and rather brutal father (who forced him to witness the beheading of his boyhood friend, with whom he may have had a homosexual relationship). In his book *The Anatomy of Human Destructiveness*, psychoanalyst Erich Fromm argued that the early experiences of Hitler and Stalin produced a kind of malignant sadism (Stalin) and necrophilia (Hitler).

Genghis Khan, Attila the Hun, Timur, Hitler: These leaders often appear as villains, and rightly so, insofar as they figured prominently in precipitating wars that resulted in the deaths of millions. But what of Cecil Rhodes, an architect of British imperialism; Alfred Krupp, German weapons manufacturer extraordinaire; and J. Robert Oppenheimer and the other American physicists who created the first atomic bombs, President Truman who ordered their use, the bomber crews who dropped them, Edward Teller, "father" of the hydrogen bomb, or the patriotic citizens who paid their taxes in support of the war effort as well as the nuclear arms race that followed? The point is that it may be relatively easy to assign villainy to a select number of prominent individuals, but by most measures there is more than enough blame to go around.

Political revolutions are often precipitated by the popular perception that leadership is particularly corrupt, incompetent, or villainous. Although the new leadership may enjoy wider popular support (at least for a time), it may become as bad as, or worse than, what it replaces: Robespierre, for example, became more dreaded than the French King Louis XVI, who was rather mild and fumbling by contrast. And Stalin was far worse than Czar Nicholas II. Ayatollah Khomeini, who replaced Mohammad Reza Pahlavi, Shah of Iran in 1979, was a very different leader in nearly every respect; it isn't at all clear, however, whether he was more or less dictatorial or war prone. Moreover, heroes in one nation are often perceived as evildoers in another, and vice versa, as was the case during the Persian Gulf War, with Saddam Hussein and President George H. W. Bush being demonized in each other's country. Similar behavior occurred between Venezuelan president Hugo Chávez and U.S. president George W. Bush. And although Osama bin Laden at the time of his death was substantially less popular in the Islamic world than had been the case shortly after 9/11, he was widely admired among many Muslims even as he was reviled in the West.

It is often difficult to assign villainy in matters of politics, and especially in war and peace, because supporting reasons often exist for even the most violent and inhumane acts. Nonetheless, in certain cases, responsibility and blame seem sufficiently clear that widely accepted moral judgments have been made. After Pol Pot and the Khmer Rouge took power in 1975, at least one million people out of Cambodia's total population of seven million were killed, including virtually anyone perceived by the Khmer Rouge leadership to have Western connections, training, language, or even eyeglasses. Idi Amin, formerly a Ugandan army sergeant, took over the Ugandan government in 1971, initiating a reign of terror believed to have claimed more than 300,000 lives before Tanzanian troops, supported by Ugandan exiles, invaded that country in 1979 and drove Amin from power.

However, even (perceived) villainy—or, at least, the extent of villainy—is open to dispute. The traditional, mainstream Anglo-American interpretation of the causes of World War II, for example, lays particular stress upon Hitler's aggressive designs plus, in a supporting role, British and French appeasement. But at least one revisionist historian, A. J. P. Taylor, has refused to heap all the blame on Hitler, viewing World War II instead as a continued pattern of German expansionism and militarism traceable back at least as far as Bismarck in the second half of the 19th century. Also to blame in Taylor's view were the highly punitive Versailles Treaty that terminated World War II and faulty calculations by Hitler and the Western leaders.

Regardless of the specific historical details, there may be some validity to placing substantial blame for many and perhaps most wars on a limited number of individuals. This view, however, must reconcile itself with the likelihood that even with a different cast of major characters, the outcome might have been fundamentally the same. Much of this blame should also go to what has been called the "military mind," which, according to the influential American political scientist Samuel Huntington,

> emphasizes the permanence of irrationality, weakness and evil in human affairs. It stresses the supremacy of society over the individual and the importance of order, hierarchy and division of function. It accepts the nation state as the highest form of political organization and recognizes the continuing likelihood of war among nation states. . . . It exalts obedience as the highest virtue of military men. . . . It is, in brief, realistic and conservative.[6]

# Crisis Decision Making

Stimulated in particular by the close call of the Cuban Missile Crisis, psychologically minded students of international relations have directed considerable attention to the process whereby decisions are made—often focusing on issues of perception and misperception, communication and miscommunication, or understanding and misunderstanding—and the effects of crisis conditions and of small-group processes on decision making.

## Small Groups

Major governmental decisions, especially regarding war or warlike actions, are often made by small *ad hoc* groups—that is, groups that may have been convened for that specific purpose. During the crisis at the beginning of the Korean War, for example, 14 people participated in the emergency deliberations of the U.S. government; during the Cuban Missile Crisis, the committee convened by President Kennedy had 16 members. The Politburo, the core unit of decision making in the former Soviet Union, normally consisted of 14 full members. In this context, it has been suggested that the United Nations Educational, Scientific, and Cultural Organization (UNESCO) charter should be rewritten to read, "Since wars begin in the minds of men in the core decisional groups of the nation-states, it is in the minds of those men that the defenses of peace must be constructed."[7]

It is often hoped that a group will temper the enthusiasm and impetuosity of a leader. However, studies initiated by social psychologist Irving Janis suggested that the opposite is more likely: Group members tend to egg each other on, reinforcing tendencies present in the most dominant individual(s). Social psychologists have also found that risk taking tends to be more pronounced in groups than in individuals, because no one person must (or can) take responsibility for the outcome. Janis coined the word "groupthink" to identify this tendency for groups to be no more rational than individuals, and often less so. Janis also emphasized that groupthink "is likely to result in irrational and dehumanizing actions directed against out-groups."[8]

Following General Douglas MacArthur's success in repelling the North Koreans early in the Korean War, the United States made the fateful decision to unify all of Korea by force of arms. This soon resulted in China crossing the Yalu River into Korean territory and 3 years of stalemated war, with hundreds of thousands—perhaps more than one million—additional casualties. This decision was taken by a small group of American officials, strongly influenced by MacArthur's overconfidence. Discussion within the group shared and reinforced an illusion of invulnerability based in part on racial stereotyping of the enemy—the North Koreans—and the potential enemy, the Chinese. Experts with dissenting views were excluded from the decision-making process. Something similar appears also to have been the case in the governments of both the United States and Great Britain during the run-up to the 2003 invasion of Iraq, which may provide a case study in how *not* to decide whether to initiate a war.

## Excluding Bad News

During the Korean War, General MacArthur's commitment to conquering (he claimed, "liberating") North Korea made him insensitive to reports that would counsel caution to someone more open-minded. As a result, subordinates—eager to ingratiate themselves with their commander or, at least, to avoid antagonizing him—slanted intelligence reports to reinforce what they believed to be MacArthur's perception of the situation.

This is a widespread and dangerous phenomenon in crisis decision making: The fact that it may be based on incorrect information because the information sources have been hesitant to send bad news. There are two useful lessons here: (1) When the bearer of bad tidings is likely to fare poorly, he or she may well doctor the message, and (2) people—including state leaders—often exhibit selective attention, so if they are already committed to a course of action, they tend to disregard what they do not want to hear, focusing only on information that confirms their preexisting beliefs. Thus, Stalin actually ordered the execution of a Czech agent who warned in April 1941 (correctly, it turned out) that Nazi Germany was preparing an attack on the Soviet Union. At the time, Stalin maintained that the spy must be a British provocateur, so convinced was he of British animosity toward the Soviet Union and of the reliability of his alliance with Hitler. It seems increasingly clear that prior to the U.S.-led invasion of Iraq, White House officials not only cherry-picked intelligence information that supported their predetermined insistence on going to war, but they also intimidated Central Intelligence Agency (CIA) and State Department officials who disagreed with them, thereby squelching alternative views.

## Decision-Making Pressures

Political crises may be defined as unanticipated threats to the values and institutions that leaders hold most important and that accordingly impel them to make prompt decisions. Decisions made during perceived crises are likely to be especially crucial for war and peace; unfortunately, it is precisely under such conditions—when stress is unusually high—that decision making is most likely to be flawed.

Crisis decision making is likely to have the following characteristics:

1. *Time pressure.* There is frequently a need (or a perceived need) for leaders to make decisions quickly.

2. *Heavy responsibility.* Most leaders are aware—or, at least, claim to be aware—of the potential costs in human suffering if their decision results in war.

3. *Faulty and incomplete data.* Intelligence about the potential opponent (motivations, alternative options, strengths and weaknesses) is usually limited and inadequate. Under such conditions, there is a tendency for decision makers to rely on simplistic and often inaccurate stereotypes of the opponent.

4. *Information overload.* Many contemporary decision makers are inundated with large amounts of information, and although much of it may in fact be erroneous, decision makers often do not know what information to ignore or believe.

5. *Limited options.* Decision makers frequently see themselves as having only a limited range of potential courses of action (in part because the stress of the situation itself tends to limit creative problem solving); at the same time, the opponent is often perceived as enjoying a wide latitude of possible choices.

6. *Short-term over long-term.* Decision makers' attention tends to be focused on the immediate, short-term effects of a course of action, with relatively little patience for assessing the possible long-term implications of their decision. Their chief desire is then to act in such a way as to relieve the current, pressing crisis.

7. *Surprise.* Although the situation may not be entirely unexpected, an element of surprise is often involved, so most crises appear to the decision makers as needing to be resolved on the spot, without benefit of pre-analyzed scenarios.

8. *Personal stresses.* Decisions of great import must often be made under conditions of sleep deprivation and sometimes under great anxiety, bordering on panic.

All of these factors combine to make it especially difficult for leaders—either singly or in small groups—to render intelligent and rational judgments. Writing of the Berlin Crisis of 1961, the Cuban Missile Crisis of 1962, and the U.S.-Soviet tensions raised during the Arab-Israeli Six-Day War (1967), former U.S. Secretary of Defense Robert McNamara noted that

on each of the occasions lack of information, misinformation, and misjudgments led to confrontation. And in each of them, as the crisis evolved, tensions heightened, emotions rose, and the danger of irrational decisions increased.[9]

## Crisis Management

In view of the importance of such situations, a recent area of investigation, known as *crisis management,* has emerged. The goals of crisis management are not only (1) to prevent a crisis from escalating to war but also (2) to keep the leaders in control of the situation and (3) to gain maximum advantage, whenever possible, from such crises when they occur. When crises involve the danger of war, especially nuclear war, decision makers on each side want to appear strong, fear to seem weak, and are eager to gain some advantage over the other that they would not like to see the other have over them. Crisis behavior then tends to become an exercise in "competitive risk taking." Contrary to the widespread belief that "tough" leadership makes would-be aggressors back down, it seems equally plausible that the likelihood of war increases when leaders are willing to accept a high level of risk.

The leaders on each side are inclined to engage in *one-upmanship,* hoping to induce the other side to back down, in a situation dangerously reminiscent of the game of chicken, whether nuclear weapons are involved or not. For example, a senior aide to President Kennedy recounted that during the Cuban Missile Crisis, former secretary of state Dean Acheson recommended bombing the Soviet missile sites, which had just been discovered in Cuba. When asked what, in his judgment, the Soviets would do in response, Acheson replied, "I think they'll knock out our missile bases in Turkey." "What do we do then?" "Under our NATO Treaty, we'd be obligated to knock out a base inside the Soviet Union." "What will they do then?" "Why, then we hope everyone will cool down and want to talk."[10]

## Psychological Effects of Repetitive Crises

Even when an individual crisis is resolved peacefully (as in the case of the Cuban Missile Crisis), repetitive crises can produce an expectancy of war. For example, during the few years preceding the outbreak of World War I, Germany was embroiled in numerous situations of near war—with Russia over Austria's annexation of Bosnia and Herzegovina, with Britain and France over Morocco—in addition to a naval arms race with Britain and an army arms race with France. Such situations can result in a feeling of fatalism as yet another crisis emerges or an existing one is painfully prolonged and things appear to be leading slowly but irrevocably toward war. Rationality and flexible decision making are often replaced by a sense on the part of leaders that they must accept the ensuing, and apparently inevitable, destruction to come. As a result of their having looked into the abyss of possible nuclear devastation, the U.S. and Soviet decision makers who took part in the Cuban Missile Crisis seem to have been somewhat sobered, leading to a warming of relations the following year, including the signing of the Atmospheric Test Ban Treaty and eventually to a long period of détente, if not friendship.

## Crisis in the Nuclear Age

Prior to World War I, mobilization of the Great Powers was extraordinarily fast, given the immense amount of men and material involved, but it still required several days. In the nuclear age, mobilization requires mere minutes, and entire wars could be fought within hours. The quick-reaction regime of ballistic missiles has resulted in a chronic crisis mentality in leaders, advisers, and military chiefs. Thomas Schelling offers the following metaphor:

> If I go downstairs to investigate a noise at night, with a gun in my hand, and find myself face to face with a burglar who has a gun in his hand, there is danger of an outcome that neither of us desires. Even if he prefers just to leave quietly, and I wish him to, there is danger that he may *think* I want to shoot, and shoot first. Worse, there is danger that he may think that I think *he* wants to shoot. And so on.[11]

In the idealized case, crisis decision making is based on instrumental or strategic rationality. Decision making is seen as a variant of mathematical economics, a process of maximizing the difference between benefits and costs; this approach is especially popular among devotees of nuclear deterrence theory. Nuclear strategist Herman Kahn, for example, developed an elaborate classification of 44 different rungs of nuclear escalation, beginning with precise, low-intensity options such as "slow-motion counterproperty," moving through "augmented disarming attacks," and culminating in "spasm or insensate war."

The assumption that decision makers will remain rational during a full-fledged crisis, carefully picking and choosing among the various options while the bombs are going off all around, is one of the less credible aspects of modern strategic thinking. In 1974, Secretary of Defense James Schlesinger testified to Congress about his judgment as to the feasibility of rationally conducting a "limited" nuclear war:

> . . . in spite of [the claims] that everything must go all out, when the existential circumstances arise, political leaders on both sides will be under powerful pressure to continue to be sensible. . . . Those are the circumstances in which I believe that leaders will be rational and prudent. I hope I am not being too optimistic.[12]

Evidence from history and psychology suggests that, almost certainly, he was.

## The Effects of Crises on Rational Decision Making

What must be decided during a crisis? According to the political scientist Ole Holsti, the tasks include (but are not limited to) the following:

(a) Identify major alternative courses of action; (b) estimate the probable costs and gains of alternative policy choices; (c) distinguish between the possible and the probable; (d) assess the situation from the perspective of other parties; (e) discriminate between relevant and irrelevant information; (f) tolerate ambiguity; (g) resist premature action; and (h) make adjustments to meet real changes in the situation (and, as a corollary, to distinguish real from apparent changes).[13]

There have been numerous cases of crisis decisions made hastily, emotionally, and erroneously. The psychological data are also clear that mild stress tends to facilitate human decision making but that intense stress is likely to be especially disruptive, resulting in actions that are increasingly self-defeating. During severe crises, therefore, good policy decisions become both more important and less likely. Information overload, for example, becomes a substantial problem.

Laboratory studies have also shown that as perceived threat increases, messages sent and received reveal assessments of the situation that are increasingly stereotyped and simplistic. Moreover, during real-life international crises, time pressures are often intensified by the use of deadlines and ultimatums. "Nothing clarifies the mind," according to Samuel Johnson, "like the prospect of being hanged in the morning." This may well be true, but it also seems likely that nothing fogs the mind like the prospect of immediately having to make a potentially catastrophic decision in a stressful environment during a perceived crisis.

Experimental research has also shown that severe stress is particularly likely to impede precisely those decision processes needed during international crises: Verbal and logical performance deteriorates; problem solving becomes more rigid; tolerance for complexity and ambiguity diminishes (this is especially crucial because in the real world of international affairs, issues are rarely simple matters of "either/or"); errors are more frequent; the focus of attention is reduced, both spatially and temporally; and decision makers become less able to discriminate the trivial from the crucial. In short, the decision maker finds him- or herself less able to see the problem clearly and to respond creatively.

Still, it remains uncertain whether simulation studies accurately reflect real experiences. Speaking from his own experience in the Kennedy administration, however, Theodore Sorensen noted that "I saw first-hand, during the long days and nights of the Cuban crisis, how brutally physical and mental fatigue can numb the good sense as well as the senses of normally articulate men."[14]

# Some Issues Regarding Perception and Cognition

It can be argued that most wars begin in error, since each side often feels at the outset that it will win—or else it wouldn't go to war in the first place. Insofar as this is true, the process of war itself is a movement, from error, through agony, to a more accurate appraisal of the situation, since wars usually end when both sides agree which is the stronger. To be sure, some wars take place because one side is attacked or perceives the other as hostile and threatening, and it may fight back not because it expects to win but because it sees no viable alternative: for example, Poland after Germany invaded in 1939; Finland after the Soviet Union attacked in the same year; and Iraq during the Persian Gulf War. But in many other cases, human error—notably perceptual distortions—appears to have a role in causing war. Thus, Horatio, in Shakespeare's *Hamlet,* relates a tale

> Of carnal, bloody and unnatural acts,
>
> Of accidental judgments, casual slaughters,
>
> Of deaths put on by cunning and forced cause,
>
> And, in this upshot, purposes mistook
>
> Fall'n on th' inventors' heads.

Insofar as blunders and misperceptions have an important role in the real world as well, it is advisable to be attuned to these sources of error. "We can never walk surely," wrote the British statesman Edmund Burke, "but by being sensible of our blindnesses."

Even in the absence of a crisis, leaders and decision makers are often prevented from getting a clear, unbiased view of the situation. The result is a range of potential errors, resulting from misperceptions, misunderstandings, and/or miscalculations. Some of these, such as the tendency to disregard information that does not conform to one's preconceptions, have already been touched on. There are two major contending theories of perceptual distortion: cognitive theory, which is concerned with errors in the processing of information, and motivational theory, according to which the emotional needs of the decision makers are paramount. And, of course, in some cases of perceptual distortion, *both* cognitive and emotional factors are present. Here, we focus on the nature of misperceptions rather than on their causes.

## Inaccurate Perception of Others

History is replete with examples of this phenomenon. Thus, Hitler disdained the British as "shopkeepers" and the Russians as "barbarians." Arabs who attacked the fledgling state of Israel with five armies in 1948 were highly (and wrongly) confident of victory over a Jewish nation that had been seen, in modern history, as nonmilitarist. Conversely, the Israeli armed forces came to suffer from a misconception that Arabs were hopelessly incompetent in military matters; as a result, they nearly lost the 1973 October War and achieved, at best, a draw during the 2006 incursion into Lebanon.

Five different U.S. presidents apparently misread the determination of the North Vietnamese and their leader, Ho Chi Minh. All seemed convinced that the North Vietnamese's drive for unification would crumble if only more American military pressure were applied. Iraq, under Saddam Hussein, first apparently underestimated the resilience of the Ayatollah Khomeini and the Iranians and later misperceived the determination of President George H. W. Bush to undo Iraq's invasion of Kuwait as well as President George W. Bush's desire to topple Hussein's regime. (On the other hand, Bush misperceived the resilience of the Taliban in Afghanistan and woefully underestimated the insurgency in Iraq.) The list is very long; many decision makers have persistently underestimated their opponents. Of course, it may also be the case that we only become acutely aware of such errors because the results can be glaring. When, by contrast, decision makers correctly assess a would-be opponent or overestimate its strength, the resulting *inaction* doesn't make headlines.

Decision makers commonly misjudge the strength of allies as well. U.S. political leadership misjudged the precarious status of the shah of Iran in 1979, until it was too late. According to one expert on the role of misperceptions in international affairs, American officials were so slow in recognizing the Iranian revolution because it went counter to many preexisting and reinforcing beliefs:

> Not only were the Shah and his regime perceived as strong, but also the specific image was supported by the general belief—based on good historical evidence—that leaders who control large and effective internal security forces were not overthrown by popular protest. These preconceptions were reinforced by several others that were more peculiarly American: the menace to pro-Western governments comes from the left; modernization enjoys the support of the strongest political elements of society, and those who oppose it cannot be serious contenders for power; religious motives and religious movements are peripheral to politics.[15]

As a result, American decision makers not only misinterpreted events in Iran but also made inappropriate decisions based on those misperceptions. This difficulty was enhanced by the anguish associated with making difficult decisions: The harder it is to make a decision and to set a policy, the greater the resistance to reversing that decision once it has been made.

Many preconceptions are self-serving. Hawks, for example, tend to see an opponent as unrelentingly hostile and aggressive, so even conciliatory moves are interpreted as clever maneuvers to make the other side let down its guard—thus further proving the correctness of the original impression. Doves tend to emphasize the role of perceptions, thereby sometimes excusing an unacceptably aggressive act as a consequence of misunderstanding or misperception. These "motivated errors" include, for example, the tendency among British leaders during the 1930s to underestimate German hostility. Some promilitary conservatives fear that a similar process may be occurring with regard to Western perceptions of Iran, with antiwar sentiment ostensibly blinding many people in the West to Iran's alleged pursuit of nuclear weapons. (At the same time, there is the risk that motivated misperceptions on the part of promilitarists might precipitate another unnecessary war in the Middle East.)

## Misreading History

Decision makers' perceptions are often modified to minimize psychological distress and to provide a congenial, often simplistic, view of current events. There is also an understandable yearning by many leaders to avoid repeating past errors and instead to repeat past successes. Following the Franco-Prussian War, for example, two assumptions were widespread among many European politicians and generals: (1) The next war would be intense and brief, because (2) a long war would ruin a state's economy. The result was a desire to strike first and decisively; this contributed, in turn, to plans for total mobilization, with disastrous consequences: namely, World War I.

Past successes can also overshadow present realities. For example, NATO's history of inaction during the Bosnian War in the early 1990s emboldened Serbian president Milošević to assume he would have a comparably free hand in subduing the rebels in Kosovo, but history did not repeat itself. Che Guevara's success during the Cuban revolution led him to believe that history would repeat itself in Bolivia; it also did not.

Professional "security managers" generally give special attention to cases that suit their own, often aggressive goals. For example, Argentine forces took over the Falkland Islands in 1982, with the Argentine military looking as a historical analogy to the Indian takeover of Goa, a small colonial enclave on the Indian mainland that had been forcibly retaken by India and whose loss was quickly accepted (without bloodshed) by the Portuguese government. To the British, however, the relevant metaphor was Hitler and the origins of World War II, and they responded not as Portugal did in 1961 but rather as they wished they had done in 1938.

States such as the United States, which have relatively limited historical experience in world affairs, may be unusually susceptible to drawing inferences from the small number of international events that have been significant for them. And the more recent the event, the more likely it is to be salient in memory, even if it may not be especially relevant.

## The Double Standard of Hostility

In 1970, during the Vietnam War, the United States bombed and invaded Cambodia, claiming that because Cambodia was providing haven and supply routes to the Viet Cong and the North Vietnamese, it could legally be attacked, even though it was a sovereign, nonbelligerent state. In 1988, however, after Nicaraguan forces pursued *contra* rebels to their staging and supply areas inside of neighboring Honduras, the Reagan administration decried what it called an "unjustified invasion" and dispatched 3,000 U.S. troops to Honduras.

In the late 1950s, the United States placed medium-range missiles, capable of reaching the Soviet Union, in Turkey and Great Britain; this was considered (by the United States) to be a defensive and justified action. But when, shortly afterward, the Soviet Union sought to place medium-range missiles capable of reaching the United States in Cuba, this was deemed by the American government to be a dastardly, offensive, and unjustified act, and the Kennedy administration was willing to go to the brink of nuclear war to get them removed.

The principle sounds absurd but is widely followed: When *we* (Russia, the United States, Iraq, Iran, whoever) do something, it is acceptable—often, laudable—but if *they* do the same thing, it is not. What is involved here, in part, is a profound absence of empathy, a failure to recognize that there is more than one way to look at a problem, and a refusal to consider that the motivations and actions of one side may be perceived quite differently by the other side. Historian Herbert Butterfield attributed much of this widespread misperception to "Hobbesian fear":

> You yourself may vividly feel the terrible fear that you have of the other party, but you cannot enter into the other man's counter-fear, or even understand why he should be particularly nervous. For you know that you yourself mean him no harm, and that you want nothing from him save guarantees for your own safety; and it is never possible for you to realize or remember properly that since he cannot see the inside of your mind, he can never have the same assurance of your intentions that you have.[16]

During a 1989 speech at an East-West conference on reducing conventional forces in Europe, then–secretary of state James Baker asserted, "Those in the West should be free of the fear that the massive forces under Soviet command might invade them. Those in the East should be free of the fear that armed Soviet intervention . . . would be used again to deny them choice."[17] Another, possibly more sensitive statesman might also have added something like "Those in the East should be free of the fear that the forces of the West will invade them, as they have so often in the past," and perhaps even "Those in the West should be free of the fear that their own military forces might precipitate a war, which, although ostensibly fought on their behalf, would destroy them."

Among psychologists, three related theories have sought to explain this tendency to perceive the other as hostile, while holding oneself blameless and to minimize or misconstrue the concerns of others:

1. *Ego defense.* A theory of ego defense emphasizes that individuals would find it troublesome to admit that their activities threaten others; hence, they protect their self-images by maintaining their own innocence and benevolent intentions. When others then respond aggressively, this is regarded as "evidence" of their hostility, since it couldn't possibly have been evoked by us, "the good guys."

2. *Attribution.* Attribution theory suggests that individuals are intensely aware of the various external constraints on their behavior, including economic factors, the need to placate others, and so on. Any threat or actual harm to others is therefore unintended. By contrast, it is much more difficult to understand the complex forces acting to produce the behavior of others, which is often attributed to unreasoning hostile intent.

3. *Projection.* Projection is the phenomenon in which people take certain unacceptable tendencies of their own, displace them onto another person, and then identify those traits in the other instead of in themselves. Finding it painful to recognize nastiness, aggressiveness, and the like in themselves, many people project such characteristics onto an opponent.

Not surprisingly, wars fought because of the perception that an opponent is hostile, allied with an enemy, or bent on conquest tend to make that opponent hostile, allied with an enemy, and/or bent on conquest. Such wars vindicate the assumptions on which they were based. For example, the Vietnam War was presented by presidential administrations to the American public as a result of North Vietnam's (alleged) invasion of South Vietnam; this came to pass after U.S. bombing of North Vietnam triggered massive movement of North Vietnamese units into South Vietnam. Similarly, Soviet repression of reform efforts in Hungary and Czechoslovakia, out of the Kremlin's fear they were anti-Soviet, only increased anti-Soviet sentiment throughout Eastern Europe. The double standard of hostility prescribes not only that one's own actions are blameless but also that one's opponents are relentlessly hostile.

Similarly, to many Israelis, their country seems small, isolated, and vulnerable. To many Arabs, and especially to Palestinians, Israel is a dagger wielded by Western imperialists, stabbing right into the midsection of the Arab world. The Sandinistas in Nicaragua saw the Reagan administration as an imminent threat to their survival; at the same time, Nicaragua was rhetorically branded by President Reagan as an imminent threat to the security of the United States, located merely "two days' drive" from Harlingen, Texas.

## Miscommunication

Some communication errors occur simply because people speak different languages and come from different cultures. For example, consider the "*mokusatsu* affair." In the early summer of 1945, the Allies, meeting in Potsdam, issued a surrender ultimatum to Japan. The official Japanese response was to *mokusatsu* the ultimatum, which was translated into English as "ignore." The Truman administration saw this as an outright rejection, whereas in fact it should more accurately have been rendered as "withhold comment, pending deliberation." It is at least possible that with better communication between Japanese and American decision makers, American atomic bombs might not have been dropped on Hiroshima and Nagasaki shortly thereafter.

In many other cases, and for diverse reasons, communication may result in what the French call *un dialogue des sourds,* "a dialogue of the deaf." Senders typically assume that if they spend much time and attention designing a message calibrated to convey a particular meaning, the receiver will necessarily understand it. Often, however, "messages" are not read as intended, whereupon warnings are not heeded, and the sender may even blame the receiver (unjustifiably) for intransigence or hostility.

Similarly, in 1950, Secretary of State Acheson testified to Congress that Korea was outside the United States' Pacific defense perimeter; the North Koreans, not understanding that these words were intended more for domestic consumption than as an international signal, felt emboldened to attack the South Koreans. Later, when U.S. forces were pushing far north of the 38th parallel (dividing North and South Korea), China sent numerous signals indicating that it would intervene if U.S. troops continued their military operations near the Chinese border. The United States, however, apparently did not pick up on these warnings. Furthermore, in seeking to reassure the Chinese that it did not wish to expand the Korean conflict, the United States referred frequently to long-standing friendship between the American and Chinese people. At the same time, Chinese authorities had a very different perception of Sino-American relations, viewing the United States with deep distrust, as merely one of many imperialist exploiters of China during the 19th century and, more recently, as the inheritor of Japan's goal of an Asian empire. Similarly, Saddam Hussein may have felt emboldened to invade Kuwait in 1990 because he misinterpreted the statements of a high-ranking American diplomat then stationed in Baghdad, who indicated that her government "does not take a stand" on Iraqi territorial claims to Kuwait; Saddam apparently thought this meant that the United States would not respond to Iraq's invasion, whereas it meant that the United States wasn't taking sides in the existing dispute, not that it would sit idly by if either side attempted to resolve the matter militarily.

## Overconfidence

Many people have a habit of hearing what they want to hear and believing that something is true simply because they wish that it were so. Military leaders tend to be "can-do" people; it is their job to take an aggressive, problem-solving approach to their mission. Often there is no lack of intelligence (either data or IQ) but rather a reluctance to draw unpleasant conclusions.

For example, prior to the 1962 Sino-Indian War—a stinging defeat for India—Indian leaders evidently assumed that the Chinese leadership was timid and that their military forces were superior to the Chinese, simply ignoring evidence to the contrary. The same kind of unwarranted self-confidence led the United States into the quicksand of Vietnam, with most American decision makers confident that there was "light at the end of the tunnel." In 1965, President Johnson was told by his joint chiefs of staff that "the communists" would be defeated in Vietnam within 2 years, if only sufficient additional military pressure was applied. In 1971, the Pakistani leadership—ignoring all evidence that India enjoyed clear superiority—nonetheless attacked its archrival, seeking, unsuccessfully, to destroy the Indian Air Force on the ground, as Israel had succeeded against Egypt at the onset of the Six-Day War in 1967.

When the risks are high, one might expect that an uncompromising, self-critical honesty—if only for self-interested reasons—would develop. But the opposite occurs at least as frequently: Self-delusion is rampant in the events before a war and in its early stages. For example, Lord Asquith, British prime minister in the early days of World War I, claimed that the War Office "kept three sets of figures: one to mislead the public, another to mislead the Cabinet, and a third to mislead itself." On the eve of their attack on Pearl Harbor, Japanese leaders realized that Japan could only hope to prevail over the United States in a brief and limited war, so they convinced themselves that this is what would probably happen, especially if the United States were sufficiently shocked and crippled militarily at the outset. And U.S. vice president Dick Cheney claimed—and may even have believed—that the Iraqi people would welcome American invaders/liberators with "flowers and chocolates."

Overconfidence has often cost states and leaders dearly. In the autumn of 1914, the Kaiser promised Germany that its sons would be back "before the leaves had fallen from the trees." Hitler did not even have his quartermasters issue winter uniforms to his troops attacking the Soviet Union, so confident was he that the campaign would be over before winter (as it happened, many German soldiers died of exposure in Russia). In fact, most wars have been initiated on a note of confident optimism; in many cases, this optimism may itself have been a reason for the war. Only rarely have soldiers marched off to war in a mood of grim determination and resignation—those emotions usually come after hostilities have begun.

But it can also be argued that what is unintentional about most wars has not been the decision to fight but the outcome. Wars have often turned out to be longer or costlier than expected at their outset. Above all, they typically result in the defeat of half the participants, virtually all of whom had initially expected to win.

## Wishful Thinking

Wishful thinking is hardly a recent phenomenon. The defeat of its Armada, in 1588, marked the end of Spain as a global power. Before sailing, one Spanish commander "reasoned" as follows:

> It is well known that we fight in God's cause. So when we meet the English, God will surely arrange matters so that we can grapple and board them, either by sending some strange freak of weather, or more likely, just by depriving the English of their wits. . . . [Unless God helps us by making a miracle, the English, who have faster guns and handier ships than ours, and many more long-range guns, and who know their advantage as well as we do, will . . . blow us to pieces with their culverins, without our being able to do them any serious hurt. . . . So, we are sailing against England in the confident hope of a miracle.][18]

Military adventures are often launched on something more than the "confident hope of a miracle." Nearly three-quarters of all wars in the past 150 years have been won by the initiator, suggesting some tendency for accurate planning. However, there have been notable exceptions, including the American Civil War, World War I, World War II, the Korean War, the 1973 October War, the Falklands War, the Iran-Iraq War, and the Persian Gulf War all of which were initiated by the side that ultimately was defeated. Others become unanticipated quagmires, despite the initial appearance of success. The United States and the former Soviet Union became embroiled in their disastrous Vietnam and Afghanistan wars, each confident of relatively easy victory against a small, impoverished, Third World state. Not surprisingly, brief interventions by powerful states into much weaker states (such as the United States in Panama in 1989) are more likely to be successful, at least in the short term. The long-term consequences of these invasions, however, are more difficult to predict.

## Negative, but Sometimes Accurate, Perceptions

The biases of certain leaders may well have contributed to dangerous and costly misperceptions. But one should beware of assuming that international conflict arises solely from psychological errors and misperceptions. In some cases, negative perceptions are, regrettably, all too accurate. Conflict may occur not because the adversaries misunderstand each other but rather because they understand each other all too well. In short, we must at least admit the possibility that sometimes states and their leaders are nefarious and war seeking. To seek peace and harmony or to strive for mutual understanding and confidence-building may not necessarily imply that one is naive or duped by the other side. But similarly, to be distrustful or to recognize danger or enmity is not necessarily to misperceive an adversary.

## A FINAL NOTE ON DECISION MAKING

The making of war, and of peace, is the responsibility of human beings, typically of men (and, increasingly, women) who find themselves in positions of political and military leadership. To some degree, therefore, we are all at the mercy of those leaders whose decisions may be crucial for our survival. We thus have an interest in maximizing the quality of their decision making and of the information available to them. Nonetheless, even with perfect perception of all current issues, leaders are necessarily plunging into darkness.

For example, some influential members of Spain's aristocratic military tradition believed, in 1898, that a war with the United States was necessary, in order to lose Cuba gracefully; they hadn't counted, however, on losing Puerto Rico and the Philippines, too, to America. "The future," wrote the eminent historian A. J. P. Taylor, "is a land of which there are no maps, and historians err when they describe even the most purposeful statesman as though he were marching down a broad highway with his objective already in sight."[19] It is of the greatest importance, then, especially in the nuclear age, that leaders be as free as possible from emotional and perceptual blinders in making the crucial decisions related to war and peace.

## NOTES

1. Leo Tolstoy. 1942. *War and Peace.* New York: Simon & Schuster.

2. E. Stilman & W. Pfaff. 1964. *The Politics of Hysteria.* New York: Harper & Row.

3. Desiderius Erasmus. 1936. *The Education of a Christian Prince.* New York: Columbia University Press.

4. Woodrow Wilson. 1965. *A Day of Dedication.* New York: Macmillan.

5. Herodotus. 1910. *History of Herodotus.* New York: E. P. Dutton.

6. Samuel P. Huntington. 1964. *The Soldier and the State.* New York: Vintage.

7. R. Falk and S. Kim. 1980. *The War System.* Boulder, CO: Westview.

8. Irving L. Janis. 1972. *Victims of Groupthink.* Boston: Houghton Mifflin.

9. Robert McNamara. 1986. *Blundering Into Disaster.* New York: Pantheon.

10. Quoted in Theodore Sorensen. 1965. *Kennedy.* New York: Harper & Row.

11. Thomas C. Schelling. 1960. *The Strategy of Conflict.* Cambridge, MA: Harvard University Press.

12. James Schlesinger. In John G. Stoessinger. 1985. *Why Nations Go to War.* New York: St. Martin's.

13. Ole Holsti. 1971. "Crisis, Stress and Decision-Making." *International Social Science Journal* 23 (1).

14. Theodore Sorensen. 1964. *Decision-Making in the White House.* New York: Columbia University Press.

15. Robert Jervis. 1985. "Perceiving and Coping With Threat." In R. Jervis, N. Lebow, and J. G. Stein, eds., *Psychology and Deterrence.* Baltimore: Johns Hopkins University Press.

16. Herbert Butterfield. 1951. *History and Human Relations.* New York: Macmillan.

17. Quoted in the *New York Times,* March 7, 1989.

18. Quoted in B. Brodie and F. Brodie. 1962. *From Crossbow to H-Bomb.* New York: Dell.

19. A. J. P. Taylor. 1955. *Bismarck, the Man and the Statesman.* New York: Knopf.

## QUESTIONS FOR FURTHER REFLECTION

1. In today's international context, which leaders do you perceive as "strong" or "weak," and why? Are there really "good" and "bad" guys?

2. Give some recent examples of "groupthink" at the decision-making level of nations embarking on recent military adventures. How did their peer groups influence these decisions for better or worse?

3. What were some of the pressures that may have affected the decision by the administration of President George W. Bush to invade Afghanistan and Iraq? Conversely, what factors may have influenced the decision by Islamists to attack the United States on September 11, 2001?

4. How have (mis)perceptions and (faulty) cognitions influenced the conflicting parties in the "Global War on Terror"? Would more accurate perceptions and cognitions make a significant difference?

5. Taking a specific example of crisis management in the nuclear age, what factors led to the crisis and to its more or less successful management? Could the crisis have been managed better?

## SUGGESTIONS FOR FURTHER READING

Irving Janis. 1982. *Groupthink: Psychological Studies of Policy Decisions and Fiascoes.* Boston: Houghton Mifflin.

Lionel Tiger. 2004. *Men in Groups.* New York: Transaction Books.

R. Jervis, R. N. Lebow, and J. G. Stein, eds. 1985. *Psychology and Deterrence.* Baltimore: Johns Hopkins University Press.

Robert F. Kennedy. 1999. *13 Days: A Memoir of the Cuban Missile Crisis.* New York: Norton.

Williamson Murray. 2011. *Military Adaptation in War: With Fear of Change.* Cambridge, UK: Cambridge University Press.

Thomas C. Schelling. 2007. *The Strategy of Conflict.* Cambridge, MA: Harvard University Press.

# CHAPTER 10

# THE IDEOLOGICAL, SOCIAL, AND ECONOMIC LEVELS

Adolf Hitler giving the Nazi salute at a Nazi Party rally in Nuremburg, Germany, around 1928.

*Source:* © 2008 Corbis Corporation.

*Theories and schools, like microbes and corpuscles, devour one another and by their warfare assure continuity of life.*

—Marcel Proust

Wars are caused not only by individuals, groups, states, and leaders but also—at a less tangible level—by underlying ideological, social, cultural, and economic factors. We first consider some ideological and social reasons for wars and then turn our attention to cases in which economic issues figure prominently. Then we briefly examine some of the social and economic effects of war and preparations for war. This is followed by a look at the contemporary notion of "the clash of civilizations."

# Conflicting Ideologies

An ideology is an integrated but often unarticulated network of ideas upon which social and political actions are often explained, justified, and implemented. Ideologies are usually characterized by a certain number of rigidly held and often implicit central propositions, a degree of comprehensiveness and systematization, and commonly a feeling of urgency on the part of the ideologues about the need for and desirability of pursuing the favored approach. Ideologies are belief systems that pull together information, underlying assumptions, and global viewpoints that are generally not amenable to rational refutation. That is, differing ideologies weave together patterns of beliefs and basic premises that make up a self-contained thought system. Once accepted, such a belief system normally leads to only one admissible set of conclusions.

Ideologies can be organized around religious traditions or around such secular belief systems and social organizations as capitalism, Marxism-Leninism, democracy, aristocracy, conservatism, liberalism, ethnocentrism, and nationalism. They can be powerful engines of human behavior, and when ideologies conflict, they can contribute to war.

Ideologies are not necessarily bad in themselves; nor is the word *ideology* necessarily pejorative, although the term *ideologue*, a person who strongly adheres to a particular ideology, generally conveys negative connotations of rigidity and close-mindedness.

Because they are deeply and reflexively held, ideological differences can contribute to wars of extraordinary brutality, with little or no quarter asked or given. The 18th-century wars of monarchical succession, for example, were fought among states that all accepted the same ideologies; hence, they were relatively brief and limited. By contrast, wars of religion, including the Crusades and the Thirty Years' War, involved passionately held conflicting ideologies and were exceptionally bloody.

## Marxism, Capitalism, and Fascism

Among contemporary Western ideologies, Marxism in particular has addressed itself to the reasons for war and peace. According to orthodox Marxism (or Marxism-Leninism), modern capitalism results in two major antagonistic classes, the proletariat (workers) and the bourgeoisie or ruling class that owns the means of production and controls the government. War is the external manifestation of this class struggle: War will therefore be abolished when communism has triumphed worldwide over capitalism, following a possibly violent "transition" known as "the dictatorship of the proletariat," after which the state will "wither away."

By contrast, mainstream Western capitalist ideology, of which current neo-liberalism is a major component, implies that individual "success" and social well-being are greatest in a situation of maximum economic freedom for markets and freedom of thought, speech, and property ownership for individuals. Wars are caused by many factors but most notably by perceived threats to human freedom, such as those allegedly posed by "communist-inspired" revolutionary social and political movements, as well as by "antidemocratic militants," often considered by many influential Western decision makers to be "terrorists."

Although Fascist ideology has not been as clearly articulated as its Marxist-Leninist and capitalist counterparts, it can be viewed as a far-right-wing, nationalistic/militarist extension (or distortion?) of capitalism, a worldview that places great reliance on social rigidity and respect for hierarchy. It glorifies patriotism, the state, and militarism, harking back to a "golden" and typically very romanticized past. Big business and conventional church-centered religion typically enjoy a prominent place in Fascist states, so long as the former cooperates with the regimes especially in the production of war material and so long as the latter espouses doctrines that emphasize obedience to secular authorities (including the promise of heavenly reward for patriotic loyalty to the state), while demonizing any opponents of Fascist rule. Racist appeals have also been important to most Fascists, largely to buttress claims about the appropriateness of dominating other "inferior" peoples and achieving the nation's legitimate "place in the sun."

## Ideologies and Wars

Ideologies can lead to perceptions, institutions, and activities that contribute to war making. For example, those American decision makers who saw the Sandinista government in Nicaragua as a manifestation of international communism were likely to consider it a threat to the peace and stability of the Western Hemisphere, whereas those who saw it as an example of revolutionary nationalism were more likely to recommend accommodation and coexistence, maybe even friendship. Similarly, rigid Communist Party ideologues within the former Soviet Union were quick to brand reform efforts within such former Eastern European bloc nations as Poland, Hungary, and Czechoslovakia as part of the global capitalist and counterrevolutionary offensive against socialism.

World War II had clear ideological underpinnings: The Axis powers saw it as a crusade in defense of their nation-states and racial purity and in opposition to "the red peril" of godless communism, while the West saw it as the equally holy defense of democracy against Nazi Germany (whose National Socialist ideology can be seen as an extreme form of fascism), as well as Fascist Italy and Japan.

Although similar sentiments were expressed by political leaders before World War I, that conflict was not really an ideological war—until it began. World War I evolved into a kind of ideological conflict, especially on the part of the United States, not only "to make the world safe for democracy" but also as "the war to end all wars" (in the words of President Woodrow Wilson). Before 1914, however, few people in the United States, Great Britain, or France had advocated war against Germany or Austria-Hungary simply because the Central Powers were autocratic and monarchic. Moreover, Russia under the czar (and then in World War II under Stalin) was extremely undemocratic. For the Germans, Austrians, and Turks, World War I became an ideological conflict in defense of monarchy and—more important—their national homelands.

The following is part of an address in 1917 by President Wilson, in which he requested a congressional declaration of war:

A steadfast concern for peace can never be maintained except by a partnership of democratic nations. We are glad . . . to fight thus for the ultimate peace of the world and for the liberation of its peoples, the German peoples included; for the rights of nations great and small and the privilege of men everywhere to choose their own way of life and of obedience. . . . America is privileged to spend her blood and her might for the principles that gave her birth and happiness and the peace which she has treasured . . . the world must be made safe for democracy.[1]

In the contemporary world, ideologies may make crosscutting demands. For example, although the state of Iran is Shiite-Islamic, its populace is ethnically Persian and not Arab, whereas Iraq is largely Arab and Sunni. During the Iran-Iraq War, therefore, many Shiite Arabs were forced to choose between their religious ideology and their secular ideology (Arab nationalism). In most cases, they opted for the latter and supported Iraq over Iran.

Many wars, on the other hand, have been nonideological: communist Vietnam against communist China in 1979 or right-wing capitalist Great Britain under Margaret Thatcher against right-wing capitalist Argentina under General Galtieri in 1982. And largely because of *Realpolitik* considerations, states that one might expect to be ideological enemies have become allies instead: officially communist and atheist China and right-wing, Islamic Pakistan, for example.

Although ideologies are undoubtedly important, the distinctions between them are not always clear. Twenty-first-century Chinese "communism," for example, is increasingly capitalist; Russian "democracy" under Vladimir Putin became distinctly authoritarian; "right-of-center" governments in Europe typically follow social policies that are to the "left" of the Democratic Party in the United States; and Venezuelan "socialism" under President Hugo Chávez is avowedly Catholic as well as "anti-capitalist," even while its economy is largely based on oil sales to capitalist nations.

## Capitalism and War

It has been widely thought (except by Marxists) that capitalism would discourage war. This is because capitalism favors trade over the forcible seizure of land and political stability over instability.

Capitalist-industrial states have been no less warlike than others, although previously the pressure for war has come from classes besides the bourgeoisie. In the 19th century, for example, American agitation for the War of 1812 and the Civil War came primarily from the agrarian South and West rather than the mercantile East or North. In Britain, liberal merchants and industrialists were less supportive of imperialism than was the landed aristocracy. Japanese militarism was similarly spearheaded by the army and the peasantry rather than the capitalist classes, and in the lead-up to World War I, German militarism came primarily from the aristocratic Prussian *Junkers* rather than from the business community. But since World War II, the behavior of leading capitalist states, in their search for energy, new markets, land, and cheap labor, may undermine the notion that inherently expansionist capitalist enterprises would contribute more to peace and global security than to war and insecurity (as in the Middle East and elsewhere).

# Population Pressure and Other Social Stresses

Some scholars have argued that internal social stresses make war more likely, even though there is at present little evidence to support this contention. The Vietnam War was clearly associated with an increase in domestic conflict within the United States, but just as clearly, this increase was a *result* of that war rather than a reason for it. No strong and enduring correlations have yet been established between war proneness and population density, homicides, suicides, alcoholism, or urbanization. The role of population pressure, however, has repeatedly drawn attention.

The simplest claim is that expanding population drives a state to conquest, much as Hitler claimed that his conquests in Poland and the western Soviet Union were a result of the German need for *Lebensraum* (living space). Japan was, by many standards, overpopulated in the 1930s, when it was very aggressive. Today, however, it is even more crowded, and yet its aggressiveness is limited to foreign trade. Nor is this a recent phenomenon. Between the 3rd and 8th centuries CE, for example, the population of Europe fell, yet this was a time of Roman imperial wars followed by smaller "barbarian" wars and the end of the *Pax Romana*. Later, the European population was reduced drastically, by perhaps 30% to 60%, during the Black Plague (14th century), and yet this period was characterized by the Hundred Years' War and an uneasy transition from the religious wars of the Crusades to feudal wars among opposing princes. Moreover, rapid population growth in the ancient and more recent past was associated not with increased war but rather with the *Pax Romana* and *Pax Britannica*.

At the same time, smaller states have often worried that they were at risk of being attacked by larger, more populous ones: Belgium's fear of France, France's fear of Germany, Germany's fear of Russia, Vietnam's fear of China, Cambodia's fear of Vietnam, many nations' fear of the United States, and the United States' concern about the military potential of China are notable cases. Yet when they are not provoked, larger states seem if anything to be more inclined to overconfidence and complacency. Nevertheless, high unemployment, homelessness, mass poverty, starvation, and general social dissatisfaction, whether in industrial regions or in rural societies in which population growth has exceeded available land, may lead to a dangerous kind of national restlessness.

The peace that typically follows a war may simply occur because there is nothing left to fight about, at least for a time. In other cases—when there was something to fight about—wars have followed hard upon one another, with no breathing space. For example, after fighting Japanese invaders during the early 1940s, the Viet Minh continued battling the French forces that reoccupied Vietnam (prior to World War II, Vietnam had been imperially dominated by France). Then, they fought the Americans. As soon as their devastating war with the Japanese was finished in 1945, the Chinese communists resumed, with scarcely a pause, their comparably devastating civil war against Chiang Kai-shek's right-wing and American-backed government. If wars necessarily lead to national exhaustion and therefore to peace (or at least to a cease-fire), one might expect that periods of peace would lead to a lower threshold for war, as the immunizing effects of painful memories wear off. But states such as Switzerland and Sweden, which have enjoyed centuries of peace, do not seem any more war prone than others, such as Afghanistan, Israel, Iraq, Sudan, and Ethiopia, which should rightly be tired of war.

Following the Vietnam War, by contrast, the United States went through a period when it was hesitant to engage in other military adventures; American conservatives in particular criticized this as the "Vietnam syndrome." It did not, however, appear to be a weariness with war in general so much as a determination to avoid "bad wars." And the Vietnam syndrome was short-lived, as evidenced by America's military involvements against Iraq, Serbia, and other perceived foes during the 1990s, as well as the current "war against terrorism." The former Soviet Union, following its extremely unpleasant military episode in Afghanistan, underwent a parallel "Afghanistan syndrome," which was also shed as Russia has battled "terrorists" in Chechnya from the mid-1990s to the present.

# Poverty as a Cause of War

According to orthodox Marxist thinking, wars are caused by class struggles, including conflicts within societies as well as those between the upper classes of different societies for control over other countries.

In *The Communist Manifesto*, Marx predicted that "in proportion as the antagonism between classes within the nation vanishes, the hostility of one nation to another will come to an end." But one doesn't have to be a Marxist to see that poverty can breed dissatisfaction, which in turn can lead to war. In 1962, for example, President John F. Kennedy, referring specifically to Latin America, warned, "Those who possess wealth and power in poor nations must accept their own responsibilities. . . . Those who make peaceful revolution impossible will make violent revolution inevitable."

Socioeconomic deprivation was a major factor in generating popular support for Fidel Castro's successful revolt against Cuban dictator Fulgencio Batista in 1959 and for the overthrow of Nicaraguan dictator Anastasio Somoza in 1979. Right-wing violence has also been spawned by economic conditions, as witnessed by the Central Intelligence Agency (CIA)-sponsored over-throw of the democratically elected, socialist president of Chile, Salvador Allende on September 11, 1973, as well as the coming to power of Adolf Hitler during the early 1930s, a time of severe economic stress in Germany. U.S. students might note that whereas "September 11" immediately conjures thoughts of the terrorist attacks of September 11, 2001, for millions of Chileans—and others in Latin America—it implies the anniversary of the coup that installed neo-Fascist General Augusto Pinochet. In contrast, September 11, 1906, is the date ascribed to Gandhi's formulation of his nonviolent doctrine of "satyagraha." Efforts to destabilize a given regime by creating economic and social chaos testify to the widespread assumption that governmental stability can be diminished when domestic economic conditions are difficult.

Some of history's most notable revolutions (France in 1789, Russia in 1917, Italy's fascistic one in 1922, Iran's Islamist revolution in 1979, Haiti and the Philippines in 1986, the "Velvet Revolution" in Czechoslovakia and elsewhere in Eastern Europe in 1989, as well as the Tunisian and Egyptian revolutions during "The Arab Spring" of 2011) have not involved lengthy civil wars but rather an array of strikes, demonstrations and other mass actions, in which the government lost the ability to control its own armed forces as a result of the disaffection of the people. More recently, military governments have feared their own people more than an external enemy; accordingly, police expenditures in less economically advanced countries have increased much more rapidly than have expenditures for externally directed military forces. The large "defense" budgets of many Latin American, South Asian, and African countries, in particular, are aimed almost entirely against their own populace rather than against some threatening, external enemy.

## Poverty and Domestic Unrest

Poverty does not, however, inevitably breed war or even revolution. The decade preceding the American Revolutionary War (1765–1775), for example, was a time not of poverty and deprivation but rather of prosperity and expansion: Business was booming, and the number of ships in New York's harbor had nearly doubled in a decade. Even the French Revolution—long considered a classic case of hunger leading to violence—in fact took place at a time when conditions, although bad, were improving. According to Alexis de Tocqueville, "It is a singular fact that this steadily increasing prosperity, far from tranquilizing the population, everywhere promoted a spirit of unrest." Tocqueville also noted that "those parts of France in which the improvement in the standard of living was most pronounced were the chief centers of the revolutionary movement."[2] Misery within a country, in short, does not necessarily lead to war. Germany was not belligerent during a period of runaway inflation in 1923 but rather in 1914, at a time of unparalleled prosperity. Hitler may indeed have been aided in his rise to power by the Great Depression of the early 1930s, but by the time of German expansionism (the late 1930s), prosperity was already returning.

"The revolution of rising expectations," rather than declining conditions, may in fact be especially likely to lead to social violence. Some theorists have proposed that the crucial point at which a society becomes unusually violent depends less on so-called objective conditions than on a gap between prevailing conditions and a public *expectation*—that is, when the "want-to-get ratio" is high. Propaganda and agitation can, of course, intensify the effect of this gap.

Frantz Fanon, apostle of anticolonial revolutionary violence in post–World War II Africa, maintained that "violence is a cleansing force. It frees the native from his inferiority complex and from his despair and inaction; it makes him fearless and restores his self-respect."[3] "Why does the guerrilla fighter fight?" asked Che Guevara, comrade-in-arms of Cuba's Fidel Castro.

> We must come to the inevitable conclusion that the guerrilla fighter is a social reformer, that he takes up arms responding to the angry protest of the people against their oppressors, and that he fights in order to change the social system that keeps all his unarmed brothers in ignominy and misery.[4]

## Wars and Social Change

Civil wars may occur when a disparity exists between the forces of socioeconomic change and the ability of existing political structures to accommodate these changes. Thus, the wars heralding the breakup of the Hapsburg and Ottoman empires occurred when nationalist sentiments could not be satisfied within those existing imperial systems. This is, however, a relatively new phenomenon: Prior to the late 18th century, wars had resulted largely from elite decision makers' ambitions for empire and conquest, from dynastic disputes and squabbles over state power and influence, as well as from messianic impulse, or for perceived self-defense. There had always been sporadic uprisings, such as that of the ill-fated Wat Tyler in 14th-century England or, before that, the Spartacus-led slave revolt against ancient Rome. But with the U.S. War of Independence and even more so the wars of the French Revolution, organized violence between large armed groups came to be seen as a potential instrument for social change. Prior to the Napoleonic Wars, which were to convulse Europe in the early 19th century, the newspaper *Patriote Français* exulted over the coming "expiatory war which is to renew the face of the world and plant the standard of liberty upon the palaces of kings, upon the seraglios of sultans, upon the chateaux of petty feudal tyrants and upon the temples of popes and muftis."

Although economic and social deprivations appear to have been important in unleashing rebellions, such as the civil wars in China and Cuba, they seem less likely to have produced war *between* states. In many cases, economic gain was a major motivating factor, especially the prospect of booty obtained by looting the defeated side. For example, the successes of the Macedonians under Alexander the Great, the Huns under Attila, and the Mongols under Genghis Khan, and the remarkable advances of the armies of Islam during the 7th and 8th centuries CE all were due at least in part to the lure of obtaining the "spoils" of successful conquest. However, these armies were not so much driven by desperation about their personal well-being as by the hope of obtaining yet more booty.

Poverty may drive war in unexpected ways. In 1966, President Johnson sought to justify the presence of so many U.S. troops overseas (including, notably, those in Vietnam at the time).

"There are 3 billion people in the world," he said while reviewing U.S. troops in Korea, "and we have only 200 million of them. We are outnumbered 15 to 1. If might did make right they would sweep over the United States and take what we have. We have what they want." Thus, when it comes to violence between states, poverty may be less influential in motivating the poor than in activating the wealthy to defend what they already have by taking measures ranging from "police actions" abroad to suppressing "civil disturbances" at home.

Economic conditions, however, can serve as an indirect cause of international war, as other states become nervous at the success of recently established revolutionary regimes. The French Revolution was stimulated in part by the outright physical hunger of a significant part of the French people. In turn, the new republican government was seen as a threat to the established monarchies of Europe, and efforts were therefore made to invade France and suppress that revolution. The resulting French Revolutionary Wars led to the ascension to power of Napoleon Bonaparte and to the much larger Napoleonic Wars that engulfed Europe.

## Poverty as a Restraint on War

Overall, the correlations between poverty and war are unclear. Poor people are more likely to seek food and land than overseas conquests. In the contemporary world, impoverished peasants may occasionally pose a threat to their own governments but not to their wealthy, well-armed neighbors. No one seriously believes that the poor *campesinos* of Mexico, for example, are going to invade the United States (at least not militarily). But they have been largely responsible for an ongoing low-level insurgency against the Mexican government. It can be argued that, if anything, poverty has been more likely to restrain the military adventuring of states than to encourage it. Wars are expensive; it is costly to equip soldiers, navies, and air forces and to supply them in the field.

Truly desperate conditions, more often than not, reduce rather than enhance an army's motivation for fighting. For example, the terrible food, medicine, and supply situation (as well as despair over the high casualties and lack of battlefield success) led Russian forces to seek to end their war against Germany and Austria-Hungary from early 1917 onward. This was pursued with even greater determination following the Bolshevik Revolution later that year.

When England introduced the world's first nationwide income tax in the early 19th century, it was to pay the costs of the Napoleonic Wars. Only rarely has poverty pushed a country to war; more often, leaders have hesitated to make war unless their economies were strong enough to withstand the strain. By contrast, a degree of prosperity can make leadership pushy and dangerously self-confident. (It can also make them relatively peace loving—although highly militarized—like modern-day Switzerland, Norway, and Sweden.)

# Imperialism

Imperialism refers to the policy of extending a city- or nation-state's rule over other, foreign peoples. It has an ancient history, beginning with the first efforts to conquer and subdue a foreign people. The Roman historian Tacitus commented, "Worldwide conquest and the destruction of all rival communities or potentates opened the way to the secure enjoyment of wealth and an overriding appetite for it."

Until the early 20th century, imperialism was widely accepted and even lauded—at least by the leadership of major imperialist states. At the same time, imperialism may have contributed directly to war and suffering—that is, by generating not only the direct violence of war but also the indirect, structural violence of colonial oppression. By the end of the 20th century, it seemed to many mainstream Western scholars that the world had passed into a postimperialist era. Therefore, suggestions that imperialism causes war may appear outdated. However, imperialism still occupies an important place in Marxist and postcolonialist thinking on war and even among some American conservatives and neo-liberals who argue the United States should be celebrating and securing, rather than bemoaning and diminishing its "democratic empire." Hence, imperialism can be very resilient, cropping up in many different forms.

Lenin argued that imperialism necessarily led to war, especially when it was wedded to capitalism, which, in the Leninist view, inevitably generates overproduction and, in turn, competition for new markets. Even today, "anti-imperialists" both in the less economically developed counties (especially in Latin America) and in advanced industrial nations (particularly in France, Italy, Spain, and Greece) decry what they perceive to be the economic and cultural imperialism of Western multinational corporations and American mass media, as well as the continuing American and Israeli occupations of Arab lands.

## A Brief History of Modern Imperialism

During its heyday from the 15th century through the end of World War I, overt imperialism had many backers, notably among such conservatives as Benjamin Disraeli, Lord Curzon, Rudyard Kipling, and Cecil Rhodes in England; Jules Ferry in France; and Theodore Roosevelt, William McKinley, and other "manifest doctrine" supporters in the United States. Imperialism was lauded as helping "modernize and Christianize" the savage, benighted peoples of the Earth, whose improvement and care were "the white man's burden." Moreover, advocates were generally unapologetic about the value of imperial conquests in providing raw materials for domestic, Anglo-American industrial production and overseas markets for manufactured goods, as well as the prestige that befits a Great Power. "The issue is not a mean one," wrote Benjamin Disraeli, conservative prime minister of Great Britain during the 1870s. "It is whether you will be content to be a comfortable England, molded upon Continental principles, and meeting in due course an inevitable fate, or whether you will be a great country, an imperial country."[5]

But imperialism has had numerous critics as well, especially from the political left. In 1902, in his influential book *Imperialism*, the liberal English economist John Hobson argued forcefully that imperialism was a social and economic wrong, indicating a defect in capitalism. In this view, imperialism results when nations enter the machine economy, with its advanced industrial methods, whereupon manufacturers, merchants, and financiers find it increasingly difficult to dispose profitably of their products. This in turn generates pressure for access to undeveloped overseas markets as well as to sources of raw materials.

Hobson's line of reasoning seemed especially cogent, coming as it did after such events as the Boxer Rebellion and Opium Wars in China, which in large part signified Chinese protests against Western economic domination of China and the insistence of the European imperialist powers (especially Great Britain) on opening China to the lucrative opium trade. The major intra-European conflict of the 18th century, the Seven Years' War (known in North America as the French and Indian War), was in some ways the first world war, brought about by worldwide colonial competition between England and France, a rivalry that was extended to India, the Caribbean, the west coast of Africa (over the highly profitable slave trade), Canada and the upper Ohio Valley, and the eastern Atlantic of colonial America. In addition, the Crimean and Boer wars, as well as the Moroccan crises of 1905 and 1911, lent further weight to Hobson's critique of imperialism as a cause of war. "As soon as one of our industries fails to find a market for its products," we read in Anatole France's novel *Penguin Island,* "a war is necessary to open new outlets. . . . In Third Zealand we have killed two-thirds of the inhabitants in order to compel the remainder to buy our umbrellas and braces."

## Modern Manifestations of Imperialism

Undoubtedly, imperialism can lead to war between the imperial government and the local population: Examples include wars of occupation and conquest, such as the Maori wars in New Zealand, the Zulu wars in southeast Africa, and the Indian wars in the United States. These were followed in turn by wars of national liberation—for example, the Huk rebellion against the United States in the Philippines, the Mau Mau rebellion in Kenya, the Algerian War of Independence, and so on.

Even though states do not directly compete for colonies these days, they are likely to engage in various conflicts, by intervening on behalf of their own nationals or by competing with local forces or the nationals of another country in some economically impoverished arena or over economic, political, or ideological influence. Of the frequent U.S. interventions in Latin America, many occurred on behalf of private U.S. investments, notably those of the United Fruit Company. For example, in 1954 the Central Intelligence Agency organized the overthrow of the democratically elected Arbenz government in Guatemala. Arbenz, a leftist, had sought to nationalize the United Fruit holdings in his country, distributing them to landless peasants and insisting that the company accept, as fair compensation, the value it had declared for tax purposes to the U.S.-supported Guatemalan government that preceded him.

The United States' conflicts with Sandinista-led Nicaragua in the 1980s and with Hugo Chávez–led Venezuela since the presidency of George W. Bush, by contrast, seemed motivated largely by fear of a kind of ideological/social/economic domino effect: If a small, poor state such as Nicaragua, or an oil-rich nation like Venezuela, were to escape from the U.S. orbit and to prosper as a consequence, perhaps this would encourage others to do likewise. This is also consistent with the single-minded insistence by the Reagan administration on destroying the Nicaraguan economy, since by this strategy, even if the Sandinistas were not overthrown, their revolution could be discredited if Nicaraguan society could be sufficiently damaged. If nothing else, the suffering of the Nicaraguan people would serve as an object lesson for what will befall any other client state that might seek to go against the United States. A similar interpretation might apply to the persistent hostility by the government of the United States toward Castro-led Cuba, although in this case the political power of Cuban Americans, particularly in southern Florida, has also been key. As for Venezuela, as long as Hugo Chávez or one of his supporters decrees policies, its oil wealth permits it to extend its economic and political influence in a way not possible for either Nicaragua or Cuba—hence the greater perceived threat to American regional hegemony.

## Neo-Imperialism and Dependency Theory

By the 1960s and 1970s, European imperial powers had dissolved their empires, and virtually all former colonies had gained political independence, even while their economic dependence on the West continued unabated. Contemporary neo-imperialism is now seen to operate more subtly, not through outright colonial control and only rarely via war. Rather, it typically manipulates the economic, political, and sociocultural structures of less developed economies, maintaining them in a condition of dependency, by a process that Lord Lugard, British governor of Nigeria, called "indirect rule": control via indigenous ruling classes. For example, consider the roles of the United States in Central America, France in western Africa, and Britain in its former colonies in eastern Africa and the Caribbean.

Previous colonial masters no longer rule by naked military power. Rather, they exercise control over local economies—and, often, sources of communication and information as well, such as the mass media and Internet access—typically relying on homegrown political allies recruited from the dominant socioeconomic classes. The emphasis here is not so much on war as on the structural violence found when one state dominates another and when the indigenous elites within a state exploit the rest of the population.

Particularly influential in the development of what has become known as dependency theory are the Brazilian economist Andre Gunder Frank, the American global systems theorist Immanuel Wallerstein, and the Norwegian peace researcher Johan Galtung. Wallerstein and Galtung have developed models in which both the neo-imperial state and the neo-colony are divided into *center* (elites) and *periphery* (peasants and workers). According to this analysis, the neo-imperial system involves a connection whereby the center in the neo-imperial state is closely allied with the center in the neo-colony, with antagonism between center and periphery in the neo-colony, and a perceived disharmony of interest between peripheries in the neo-colony and the neo-imperium. Instead of physical occupation, the imperial state provides limited economic aid, relatively abundant military aid, and intellectual underpinning and legitimacy to a colonial center that actively oppresses its own people, for the benefit of the two centers, both colonial and imperial.

But it is difficult to argue, for example, that participation of the United States in the Vietnam War was primarily motivated by economic factors. Thus, Vietnam's teak, tungsten, and modest offshore oil deposits paled by contrast with the cost of that war for the United States: 50,000 U.S. lives and about $150 billion. In addition, the stock market fell whenever it appeared that the Vietnam War would be prolonged, further suggesting that it was not good for American business. On the other hand, the invasion and occupation of Iraq and Afghanistan by the United States and its "coalition of the willing," as well as the continuing presence of American military bases throughout the Middle East and central Asia, are clearly not unrelated to the advanced industrial world's dependency on the oil resources and minerals in that region. The role of "oil-lust" in generating the Iraq War has also been disputed, however. Thus, whereas Iraq's oil reserves (variously estimated as third, fourth or fifth largest in the world) were used to buttress the Bush administration's internal arguments that the war's expense would be paid for by Iraqi oil, the war itself was likely caused by factors other than a yearning for "petro-dollars" as such.

# The Military-Industrial Complex

The link between economics and war is often a real one, particularly as this connection operates in contemporary capitalist societies through money making, the global reach of multinational corporations and the Internet, and the "military-industrial complex." Although this phrase has become especially popular among its left-wing critics, it was first introduced by the relatively conservative American president Dwight Eisenhower in his 1961 Farewell Address:

> We have been compelled to create a permanent armaments industry of vast proportions. . . . This conjunction of an immense military establishment and a large arms industry is new in the American experience. The total influence—economic, political, even spiritual—is felt in every city, every statehouse, every office of the federal government. . . . In the councils of government, we must guard against the acquisition of unwarranted influence, whether sought or unsought, by the military-industrial complex. The potential for the disastrous rise of misplaced power exists and will persist.[6]

This alliance of military, economic, and political interests, sometimes called "The Iron Triangle," has been joined by scientists and technologists, research universities, mainstream labor unions, the mass media, and government. And it is more firmly entrenched than ever.

## Forerunners of the Military-Industrial Complex

The American military-industrial-science-labor-academic-government complex since World War II is not totally new in human experience. Those with a financial and social interest in making war have long had a disproportionate influence on the policies of governments. In the days of warrior-kings, they *were* the government. During ancient times, soldiers were rewarded with a proportion of the spoils of a sacked city. Mercenary armies, by definition, fought for pay and/or a share of the booty. Much of the martial enthusiasm that marked the Muslim conquests of much of Europe and the Mediterranean world during the Middle Ages, for example, has been attributed to fact that Islamic warriors were fighting not only for their faith but also for personal enrichment. In the late 16th century, Spanish soldiers—fighting the Dutch effort at independence—sacked Antwerp (then the richest city in northern Europe), when Philip II of Spain went bankrupt and could not make good on their back pay.

"The orientation toward war," wrote the economist Joseph Schumpeter, "is mainly fostered by the domestic interests of ruling classes, but also by the influence of all those who stand to gain individually from a war policy, whether economically or socially."[7] From early in the industrial age, the great armaments manufacturers—Krupp in Germany, Vickers and Armstrong in England, Remington and Colt in the United States, and more recently Dassault in France—all profited when their countries went to war. They even profited when other countries did the same, by selling arms to the belligerents—often to both sides.

During the 1930s, a U.S. Senate committee, chaired by Senator Gerald Nye, investigated the charge that U.S. arms manufacturers were responsible for American entry into World War I. Although the Nye Committee was unable to prove these allegations, the "merchants of death" theory gained credibility. On the other hand, popular pressure in opposition to military spending has also influenced government decisions: Britain and France, for example, found it very difficult to maintain large military forces during the early 1930s because of popular antimilitary sentiment. And during the 1990s, the United States and Russia succeeded in restricting at least certain aspects of their nuclear competition, a kind of "peace dividend" due to the end of their long Cold War (1945–1991). Since 2001, however, both American and Russian defense expenditures and bellicosity have increased, as have Chinese, and tensions between the West and resurgent Russia and China have increased, partially due to differing attitudes toward ballistic missile defense, nuclear proliferation, the perceived anti-Russian thrust of North Atlantic Treaty Organization (even after the end of the Cold War), and the perceived antidemocratic and antihuman rights conduct of Russian president Vladimir Putin and current Chinese political elites.

## The Contemporary Military-Industrial Complex

Military expenditures and those who profit by them remain significant forces in the world today: Arms sales have been the number-one export for France and Israel and have been growing rapidly in Brazil. With the exception of Japan, arms comprise a major proportion of the exports of every industrialized state, with the United States, Russia, and France leading all the others in absolute terms (and with the United States by far the largest arms peddler to the world).

Huge amounts of money are made on armaments, both through domestic weapons programs and in sales to other nations. Within the United States, during the latter part of the 20th century, about 10% of all business derived from military-related production—more yet for large corporations such as Lockheed, General Dynamics, Boeing, and Northrop, which in some cases derive up to 50% of their profits from military-related production. In certain regions of the United States, such as California and parts of the Southeast, military spending has accounted for upward of one-third of all jobs.

In addition, influential politicians have often succeeded in bringing extraordinary amounts of military business, sometimes under the rubric of "earmarks," to their local districts. Not only has this continued, but a growing trend for the "privatization" of war-related matters has resulted in an enormous growth of mercenary forces. This has also benefited such large private corporations as Halliburton and Blackwater, which has sought to obscure its nasty reputation by repeatedly changing its name: first to Xe, and more recently, to Academi. These and other private corporations have emerged as "military contractors" that handle—and make enormous profits from—security arrangements, food, sanitation, and other logistics both domestically and abroad (notably in Iraq and Afghanistan, where local leaders hold them responsible for many civilian deaths).

There has long been a Soviet, and now a Russian and a Chinese counterpart, to the Western military-industrial complex. Nikita Khrushchev called them the "metal eaters," the alliance of industrial bureaucrats and military leaders in the former Soviet Union. In a society that long valued heavy industry and national defense over civilian goods, military production received highest priority in the former Soviet Union until Gorbachev came to power in 1985 and initiated *glasnost* and *perestroika*. Gorbachev's political liberalization policies have largely been reversed since then, however.

Instead, a somewhat different "military-industrial" complex, largely financed by Russia's immense oil, natural gas, and mineral resources, has emerged with the accession to power of Boris Yeltsin in 1991 and during the presidency of Vladimir Putin since the beginning of this century. The recent process of capital accumulation in Russia is primarily based on the acquisition—at bargain prices—of former state enterprises by onetime government cronies and newly enriched "oligarchs." Loyalty to the Kremlin has resulted in extremely lucrative contracts for these "New Russian" businesspeople. Perceived disloyalty, on the other hand, can result in Siberian imprisonment, voluntary or involuntary exile, or untimely death.

The emergence of Russia as an economic power is also inducing a revived Russian nationalism, which sometimes expresses itself as xenophobia. Accompanying this has been a revival of Russian aspirations to "Great Power" status, which include a strong army with modernized nuclear weapons and delivery systems. Such developments could conceivably lead to a new "Cold War" between Russia and the West.

There is also growing concern in many Western strategic quarters that the booming economy of China may result in increased Chinese competition with American, European, and Japanese corporations for global markets, profits, and political dominance. Whether this also results in cold, or even hot, military conflicts between or among the West, Russia, and/or China remains to be seen. The wars between European empires during the 17th, 18th, and early 19th centuries were largely caused by competition for natural resources, political domination, profits on investments, and overseas markets. The global economic and energy conflicts of the 21st century between old (the United States and Europe) and emerging (Russia, China, South Asia) great powers sooner or later may also accelerate arms races and lead to armed conflicts.

Since wars themselves typically impoverish countries, whereas preparing for them results in substantial – albeit concentrated – wealth, a key issue is not so much war profiteering as war-preparation profiteering. In limited cases, wars can help stimulate an economy; the Great Depression of the 1930s ended with the onset of World War II. However, peace researcher Lewis Richardson concluded that fewer than one-third of wars from 1820 to 1949 were generated by economic causes, and these were limited to small wars rather than large ones. Economic considerations clearly influence military spending levels as well as specific procurement decisions, such as the purchase of one weapons system over another. The profit motive may contribute indirectly to war by supporting arms races and by creating important constituencies with an interest in the maintenance of international tension, which in turn makes it difficult to achieve disarmament or even arms control. Although it appears that the military-industrial complex does not always directly cause war, it is clear that wars have dramatic economic effects.

## The Economic Effects of Wars

The location of the war is crucial: A war on one's own territory can be devastating; on someone else's, it is much less painful and can even help an economy. The Napoleonic Wars, for instance, put a special premium on iron, which in turn hurried along Britain's entry into the Industrial Revolution.

There is another view, however; namely, war has done little to stimulate industrial progress, whereas industrial progress has done much to stimulate war and to make it more horrendous when it occurs. Wars rely heavily on peacetime scientific and economic achievements, such as advances in metallurgy, transportation, chemistry, medicine, communication, information technology, robotics, mathematics, and even food processing and preparation. War is very often a parasite on civilian economies, taking much and contributing little. During the 1980s, declines in American economic productivity and trade deficits were due largely to the Reagan administration's investment of substantial national resources—both human and material—in the military economy. By contrast, during the "economic boom" (for the affluent) in America during the 1990s, defense spending and investment were held relatively constant. This "boom" continued during the early 21st century for the Western financial and corporate elites, if not for most members of the working and middle classes or for impoverished people globally.

As to the alleged spin-offs from military technology, if governments and corporations had really wanted no-stick frying pans or computer miniaturization, they would have been able to create these things much more rapidly, and cheaply, by investing directly in such technology. Moreover, military research and development is typically insensitive to cost while very demanding as to performance. As a result, advanced weaponry tends to be very expensive but not useful in the civilian marketplace. Consumers, for example, don't need toasters that will operate at 80 degrees below zero or megacomputers that can perform "Star Wars" calculations in nanoseconds; rather, they need reliable, inexpensive items that benefit their lives.

In the majority of less economically developed nations, wars have contributed little of benefit to the local economy, whereas the physical, economic, and social effects of wars have been horribly destructive. Wars lay waste to nations not only by the direct detonation of weapons but also by the disruption of economies, especially in those areas least able to afford it, such as Central Africa and Central America.

Likewise, during its occupation by Western forces, as Iraq increased expenditures for its nascent army and police, it experienced a precipitous deterioration in its infrastructure, as the provision of water and electricity fell dramatically below pre-invasion levels, domestic morbidity and mortality rates greatly exceeded those during the dictatorship of Saddam Hussein, and millions of Iraqis emigrated or internally migrated to perceived safe havens. These conditions may have been somewhat ameliorated by the apparent cessation of active war-making by U.S.-led occupation forces. On December 15, 2011, U.S. defense secretary Leon Panetta officially declared the Iraq War over, and the last U.S. combat troops left Iraqi territory a few days later (many of them headed to Afghanistan). But tens of thousands of contractors and other forces remain in Iraq, which is still torn by factional and sectarian violence.

Furthermore, emergency and relief efforts—difficult enough to mount successfully in peacetime—can be lethally disrupted. During 1984 and 2000, Ethiopia suffered serious famines in which hundreds of thousands starved and millions were malnourished. In 1988, Ethiopia received $534 million from abroad for famine and development aid; at the same time the government was spending $447 million on military forces to fight its civil wars in Eritrea and Tigre, as well as the Ogaden. Also, relief convoys conducted by the Red Cross were unable to make deliveries of needed food to people in the rebellious areas of Eritrea and Tigre. The Ethiopian government claimed that such convoys would not be safe, while critics accused it of withholding food as a weapon against the rebels and of spending three-fourths of the national budget on arms and internal security when poverty and hunger remain Ethiopia's most pressing needs. Likewise, since 2004, the situation in the Darfur region of war-torn Sudan has continued to deteriorate, despite tepid emergency and relief efforts by the West, the United Nations, and some African states.

# The Effects of Military Spending

Some claim that military spending is economically beneficial, providing jobs, permitting federal governments to target areas needing financial investment, and generating demand that can stimulate a lagging economy. On the other hand, many experts agree that in the long run military spending is economically damaging. (Of course, the primary justification for military spending is not economic but rather that it supposedly enhances national security; economic arguments are generally seen as secondary.)

Economic criticisms of military spending focus on five areas:

1. *Employment.* Although military spending creates jobs, it almost invariably results in fewer jobs than would be generated by the same funds spent for civilian purposes. This is especially true for high-tech military procurement, notably for aerospace and nuclear weapons. Such expenditures are capital-intensive—that is, they cost a lot of money but hire relatively few people—as opposed to such labor-intensive expenditures as education, health care, and construction.

2. *Inflation.* Military spending is perhaps the most inflationary way for a government to spend money. By using up major resources without producing consumable goods, military spending reduces supply while also increasing demand for raw materials, thereby contributing doubly to inflation. Moreover, costs tend to rise yet further when the supply of money and credit increases without corresponding increases in productivity. The result is the classic inflationary process: too much money chasing too few goods.

3. *Deficits.* Governments typically obtain military forces by paying for them. The immense federal deficits of the Reagan and George W. Bush administrations, for example, occurred largely because the U.S. government chose to lower taxes while dramatically increasing military expenditures and cutting taxes for "the 1%."

4. *Productivity.* Industrial productivity is strongly influenced by the availability of scientists and engineers to provide innovative technologies and the ability of federal governments to invest in civilian research and development as well as the renovation of aging industrial plants. Military economies tend to dominate scientific and research and development activities, thereby robbing the civilian economy.

5. *Unmet social needs.* Resources spent on the military are not available to be spent in other ways. A "substitution effect" tends to operate, whereby expenditures for submarines, missiles, and machine guns, for example, are deleted from money available for hospitals, day-care centers, and schools. One half of 1% of 1 year's world military spending would purchase enough farm equipment, according to the Brandt Commission on North/South Issues, to permit the world's low-income countries to reach food sufficiency within a decade.

Military spending is also a serious problem in such nations as the United States, Israel, and Russia. During most of the 1990s, Russia acknowledged the need to reduce military spending so as to address its inadequate domestic productivity; more recently, however, Russian politicians, led by President Vladimir Putin, have expressed their desire for Russia to resume Great Power status, which is usually acquired through military posturing. The problem is even more acute in many developing countries. In the 1990s, for example, military spending in Africa increased by 7.0% per year, while economic growth was only 0.3%. Taken as a proportion of Gross National Product (GNP), military expenditures of the world's richer states have actually declined since 1960, whereas those of the poorer states have increased; countries that cannot meet the basic social needs of their people have been spending a larger share of their meager incomes on weapons and soldiers than the richer states spend of their much more abundant income.

"Every gun that is made," said President Eisenhower,

every warship launched, every rocket fired signifies, in the final sense, a theft from those who hunger and are not fed, those who are cold and are not clothed. The world in arms is not spending money alone. It is spending the sweat of its laborers, the genius of its scientists, the hopes of its children.[8]

# Cultural Conflicts and the "Clash of Civilizations"

Cultures have always differed, and civilizations have clashed, on and off, since premodern times. "Western" (or "occidental") and "Eastern" (or "oriental") city-states and empires have coexisted peacefully and have also had violent interactions for millennia. Anthropologist Margaret Mead defined culture as "the systematic body of learned behavior which is transmitted from parents to children."[9] It may be understood as a kind of "second nature," in which we are immersed from cradle to grave and which we usually take for granted—until we enter another, "foreign" culture or our own culture clashes with another.

Cultures differ in many ways, especially by language, religion, and social customs; nonetheless, they usually manage to get along with one another. However, when one culture lacks important natural resources, such as grain or oil, it may invade another to get what it needs. And agglomerations of cultures that are urban-based, sometimes called "civilizations," may also clash violently, especially when their differences involve significant ideological distinctions, such as religion, or badges of identity, such as different languages. In many conventional texts, the history of human civilization reads like a story of civilizational conflicts.

For example, after centuries of relatively peaceful coexistence between the Greek city-states and their "barbaric" neighbors to the east and south, the Persian emperor Xerxes attempted to invade continental Europe but was defeated by the Greeks at the beginning of the 5th century BCE. (Interestingly, the word *barbaric* derives from the Greek insistence that anyone not speaking Greek was babbling incoherent nonsense that sounded to them like "bar-bar-bar.")

In 1993, the American political scientist Samuel P. Huntington wrote an article titled "The Clash of Civilizations." This was published in the mainstream journal *Foreign Affairs* and is one of the most cited and controversial pieces in the history of international relations. The following year, he expanded his argument in a book of the same name. The "Huntington thesis" regarding the rise, clash, and fall of civilizations is worth considering in some detail, both because of its intrinsic interest and because of its implications for the analysis of war and the prospects of peace in the multipolar world of the early 21st century.

According to Huntington, in the 1920s, there was a bipolar (political) world: "the West and the Rest," the latter consisting of nations/cultures "actually or nominally independent of the West." During the 1960s—the peak of the Cold War—there was a tripolar world: the Free World, led by the United States and also consisting of America's allies in the Western and Eastern hemispheres; the "Communist Bloc," mainly the Soviet Union and China; and the "unaligned" nations, comprising most of Latin America, Africa, and South Asia. Since 1990, according to

Huntington, there has arisen a multipolar "World of Civilizations," composed of nine centers: Western; Latin American; African; Islamic; Sinic (mainly Chinese); Hindu; Orthodox (mainly Slavic); Buddhist; and Japanese. In this new post–Cold War world, Huntington claims that "local politics is the politics of ethnicity; global politics is the politics of civilizations. The rivalry of the superpowers is replaced by the clash of civilizations.[10]

"In the post–Cold War world," according to Huntington,

> for the first time in history, global politics has become multipolar *and* multiciviliza-tional. . . . In the late 1980s the communist world collapsed, and the Cold War international system became history. In the post–Cold War world, the most important distinctions among peoples are not ideological, political or economic. They are cultural. The central and most dangerous dimension of the emerging global politics would be conflict between groups from differing civilizations . . . clashes between civilizations are the greatest threat to world peace.[11]

Huntington claims that Islam has long had "bloody borders" and that conflict between Islam and the West was renewed after the fall of the Soviet Union. Moreover, the Soviet Union and Russia have had their own internal and "near abroad" conflicts with restive Muslim minorities within its borders and with *mujahideen* outside, most notably in the Caucasus, Afghanistan, and Iran. The centuries-long rivalry between Christendom and Islam has been over power and cul-ture. Europe, not just the United States, is now on the front line of this conflict, as evidenced by the terrorist bombings in London, Istanbul, and Madrid; plots, assassinations, and conspiracies in Germany, Denmark, and the Netherlands; and the uprisings of Muslim youth and recent immigrants in France and elsewhere. For some Muslims, the struggle between Islam and the West is rooted in Western colonialism. For others, the clash is between "the Judeo-Christian Western ethic and the Islamic revival movement, which is now stretching from the Atlantic in the west to China in the east."[12]

Huntington focuses on the aftermath of the "Free World's defeat" of Soviet Communism in 1990. Perhaps unexpectedly, Western universalism in general and American triumphalism in particular have *not* led to a period of unparalleled Western military, cultural, and political domi-nance. Thus, non-Western cultures have not rushed to adopt such Western values as free markets and democracy.

Huntington observes that "all civilizations go through . . . processes of emergence, rise, and decline,"[13] and he claims that the greatest danger in our time is "major intercivilizational war between core states," a war that "could lead to defeat of the West." Although he argues that such a conflict is "highly improbable," should it occur, it would most likely involve "Muslims on the one side and non-Muslims on the other."

The other possible "global civilizational" war in Huntington's view would be between the United States and China. A Sino/American military conflict could readily escalate to the use of weapons of mass destruction delivered by intercontinental ballistic missiles. Although a global conflict between the West and Islam would likely be mutually devastating as well, it would not necessarily be catastrophic for the West in the long run. On the other hand, an "occidental/ oriental" or Western/Sinic intercivilizational war would likely be cataclysmic. Such a cataclysm would probably be initiated by the intervention of what Huntington calls a "core state," such as the United States, in the conflict of another civilization (for example, a local war between China and Taiwan, if the latter were to claim total political independence).

To avoid major intercivilizational wars, Huntington posits three rules. The first is "the abstention rule," which he defines as the requirement that "core states" (the United States, Russia, China, etc.) abstain from intervention in the conflicts of other civilizations. The second prerequisite for the avoidance of war in our multipolar, multicivilizational post–Cold War world is what Huntington calls "the mediation rule," which requires core states to negotiate with each other to halt or contain wars between states or groups within their civilization. And the final "rule for peace" (more precisely, for negative peace) in the world today is what Huntington calls "the commonalities rule," according to which

> peoples in all civilizations should search for and attempt to expand the values, institutions, and practices they have in common with peoples of other civilizations. This effort would contribute not only to limiting the clash of civilizations but also to strengthening Civilization in the singular. . . . The singular Civilization presumably refers to a complex mix of higher levels of morality, religion, learning, art, philosophy, technology, material well-being, and probably other things.[14]

While much of this analysis seems realistic, or even prophetic in light of the events since he penned these words, it is also necessary to consider the implications of Huntington's prescriptions. For instance, if one civilization were to follow strictly the "non-intervention" rule, it would entail, for example, that the West was wrong to intervene in Islamic "internal affairs" (such as in Iraq and Iran). But it would also imply that it would similarly be wrong to intervene in the intracivilizational genocide in Rwanda or to stop the ethnic cleansing in the former Yugoslavia in the 1990s. Nonintervention in the "internal affairs" of another civilization would seem to preclude "humanitarian intervention" as well as "spreading democracy." The latter seems increasingly beyond the reach, and motivation, of Western power, especially insofar as it would require wars against Islamic and/or Sinic cultures; the former, on the other hand, might amount to a politically and ethically painful "hands-off" toleration of some of the worst atrocities in human history.

Furthermore, Huntington claims that whereas pluralism and multipolarity are increasingly relevant to the post–Cold War world, not all civilizations are created equal. On the contrary, "Western civilization is valuable not because it is universal but because it is *unique*." And to "preserve Western civilization in the face of declining Western power," Huntington argues, "it is in the interest of the United States and European countries" not merely to adhere rigorously to his "three rules"—especially not to intervene "in the affairs of other civilizations"—but also "to encourage the 'Westernization' of Latin America . . . ; to restrain the development of the conventional and unconventional military power of Islamic and Sinic countries . . . ; [and] to maintain Western technological and military superiority over other civilizations."[15]

Not surprisingly, many advocates and practitioners of peace studies are unenthusiastic about the Huntington thesis. Although some components, such as nonintervention and elaboration of supra-civilizational commonalities, seem largely desirable, others are extremely troublesome, not least the explicit claim that all civilizations are equal but that some are more equal than others. Specifically, Huntington believes that Western civilization and Occidental culture are and should be dominant. But to maintain its dominion over rivals (such as Islam) and upstarts (such as orthodox and Sinic cultures), Western civilization, led by the United States, must, according to Huntington, maintain its "superiority" over other civilizations in the areas that have always had the greatest geopolitical weight—the military and the technological dimensions of "hard power." More insidiously, the "clash of civilizations" threatens to become a self-fulfilling prophecy, by which the diagnosis of a problem, if taken seriously, risks creating its own reality: If countries act as though in the grip of civilizational conflicts, they are likely to exacerbate and/or generate precisely such conflicts.

The "clash of civilizations" thesis is thus a recipe for the preservation and continuation of American/Western hegemony, one that risks generating yet more conflict even as it seeks to identify the sources of such conflict. It claims that in a multipolar, multicivilizational world, the "peaceful" solution to civilizational clashes is for the West not to intervene in the internal conflicts of other civilizations but to maintain its hard power superiority in case "soft power" (such as mediation and negotiations) should fail. This sounds like a post–Cold War version of "containment," with Islamic and Sinic civilizations substituted for the former Soviet Union.

But in the nuclear age, if one prepares for war and a war between nuclear-armed civilizations occurs, neither is likely to prevail, because no civilization is likely to survive. In today's multipolar world, where the major civilizations have nuclear weapons and the means to deliver them, a hot war between civilizations would likely incinerate all conflicting parties, as well as everyone and everything else. So, although the "Huntington thesis" is a cogent diagnosis of our current global predicament, it is also an atavistic effort to resolve it in accordance with the "rules" of conventional power politics. And in our age of nuclear terror, these rules may need to be rewritten if any civilization is to be preserved. That will likely entail the realistic consideration of multilateral, multicivilizational, cross-cultural *dis*armament, instead of rearmament, as a way to de-escalate the clash between civilizations and to build a durable peace among differing and sometimes conflicting cultures.

"The real 'clash of civilizations,'" according to philosopher Martha Nussbaum,

> is not between 'Islam' and 'the West,' but instead within virtually all modern nations— between people who are prepared to live on terms of equal respect with others who are different, and those who seek the protection of homogeneity and the domination of a single 'pure' religious and ethnic tradition. At a deeper level, as Gandhi claimed, it is a clash within the individual self, between the urge to dominate and defile the other and a willingness to live respectfully on terms of compassion and equality, with all the vulnerability that such a life entails.[16]

## A FINAL NOTE ON THE REASONS FOR WARS AND PEACE

Wars—and the preparations for wars—take place within contexts that usually transcend individuals and their group affiliations. These contexts include such diffuse but extremely important factors as ideologies, economic forces, sociocultural conditions, leadership, and perceptions of power.

Accordingly, there are no simple cause-and-effect relationships in this realm. Rather, war, like other forms of violent human conflicts and human behavior more generally, is an overdetermined phenomenon: Multiple factors, some short term and relatively easy to discern (such as an assassination) and others that are long term and harder to pinpoint (such as cultural antagonisms), lead people and countries to go to war.

A somewhat useful mnemonic device for remembering some of the multiple factors leading to wars is the acronym EGGIEs: ego, greed, groups, ideologies, and extenuating circumstances (of which the two most significant historical variables have been leadership and technology). From this perspective, wars are fought because powerful and influential individuals (political decision-makers), usually in search of personal aggrandizement or revenge ("ego") and often motivated to increase their or their nations' wealth and/or power ("greed"), persuade, manipulate, and/or command their compatriots ("groups") to pursue their personal and national agendas ("ideologies") by force of arms—despite the opposition of other individuals in different groups and/or nations, who would oppose them by violent means if necessary. Leadership, both good and bad, and technology (including the never-ending search for "the winning weapon") can sometimes make the difference between winning and losing any particular war. And even deeper underlying factors, such as possible hormonal imbalances and/or brain and genetic abnormalities, may also predispose certain individuals to commit excessively aggressive and violent actions (thus possibly adding another *G*—"gonads"—to the acronym).

Although wars are extremely complex phenomena, often eliciting the entire range of human motivations and conduct, they are, like all human artifacts, modifiable and preventable. In the remainder of this book, we consider ways to reduce the incidence and virulence of wars (building negative peace) and to lay the groundwork for a world "beyond war" (building positive peace).

## NOTES

1. Woodrow Wilson. 1965. *A Day of Dedication*. New York: Macmillan.

2. Alexis de Tocqueville. 1955. *The Old Regime and the French Revolution*. New York: Doubleday.

3. Frantz Fanon. 1963. *The Wretched of the Earth*. New York: Grove.

4. Che Guevara. 1968. *Guerrilla Warfare*. New York: Monthly Review Press.

5. Quoted in Michael Howard. 1978. *War and the Liberal Conscience*. New Brunswick, NJ: Rutgers University Press.

6. Dwight D. Eisenhower. 1961. *Peace With Justice: Selected Addresses*. New York: Columbia University Press.

7. Joseph Schumpeter. 1955. *Imperialism and Social Classes*. New York: Meridian.

8. Eisenhower, op. cit.

9. Margaret Mead. 1934/2005. Preface. In Ruther Benedict. *Patterns of Culture*. New York: Houghton Mifflin.

10. Samuel P. Huntington. 1997. *The Clash of Civilizations and the Remaking of World Order*. New York: Touchstone, 28.

11. Ibid., 311.

12. Ibid., 320.

13. Ibid., 311–312.

14. Ibid., 320.

15. Ibid., 311–312.

16. Martha C. Nussbaum. 2007. *The Clash Within: Democracy, Religious Violence and India's Future*. Cambridge, MA: Harvard University Press.

## QUESTIONS FOR FURTHER REFLECTION

1. What are some principal ideological motivations for and inhibitions against the initiation of wars?

2. To what degree does imperialism still exist and operate as a war-making system?

3. Does the existence of a "military-industrial complex" in the United States and elsewhere necessitate wars? Are there realistic alternatives?

4. What are the strengths and weaknesses of the "clash of civilizations" thesis? Is a reconciliation among conflicting cultures possible?

5. In assessing the reasons for wars, do you consider any particular level of analysis and explanation (the economic, political, ideological, etc.) as most helpful in understanding contemporary international conflicts? Why or why not?

## SUGGESTIONS FOR FURTHER READING

Bernard Lewis. 1994. *Islam and the West.* New York: Oxford University Press.

Ian Buruma and Avishai Margalit. 2004. *Occidentalism: The West in the Eyes of Its Enemies.* New York: Penguin Books.

Jerome Frank. 1968. *Sanity and Survival: Psychological Aspects of War and Peace.* New York: Vintage.

Samuel P. Huntington. 1997. *The Clash of Civilizations and the Remaking of World Order.* New York: Touchstone.

Seyom Brown. 1987. *The Causes and Prevention of War.* New York: Macmillan Education.

# PART III

# Building "Negative Peace"

Throughout history, people have recognized the absurdity and horror of war, even as they have engaged in it. There has been no shortage of proposed solutions to the problems posed by war. The simplest solution, perhaps, can be derived from the failed "war on drugs": Just say no. But this turns out to be no solution at all, if only because it has been tried many times, yet war persists. Although seemingly straightforward moral judgments and outright condemnation undeniably are appealing to many people, most nations have been no more able to go "cold turkey" on war than individuals have on drugs. Mark Twain once noted that it was easy to stop smoking—he had done it many times! Similarly it may seem easy to prevent war; many different solutions have been proposed, and some have even been implemented (to varying degrees).

Perhaps these solutions are not sufficiently innovative, forward thinking, or creative. Others may not be practical or even feasible. Perhaps the problem is that no one solution has been pushed hard and far enough. Or perhaps war is still with us because these various solutions have not been attempted in the right combination or with the right variation or nuance. Perhaps they actually are working, only slowly, so that peace—like President Herbert Hoover's claim about prosperity during the Great Depression—is just around the corner. On the other hand, maybe they have not and will not, and something else is needed. If so, let us hope that by considering humanity's efforts to prevent war, we can at least save peacemakers of the future from repeating the errors of the past. And, maybe, we can inspire greater efforts, and achieve greater success, in the days to come.

"War is waged," wrote St. Augustine, "so that peace may prevail. . . . But it is a greater glory to slay war with a word than people with a sword, and to gain peace by means of peace and not by means of war."[1] In the following chapters, we shall examine efforts to gain peace by peaceful means. It is no easy quest. As General Omar Bradley put it:

> The problem of peaceful accommodation in the world is infinitely more difficult than the conquest of space, infinitely more complex than a trip to the moon. . . . If I am sometimes discouraged, it is not by the magnitude of the problem, but by our colossal indifference to it. I am unable to understand why . . . we do not make greater more diligent and more imaginative use of reason and human intelligence in seeking . . . accord and compromise . . .[2]

What, then, do human reason and intelligence have to offer by way of preventing war and creating peace? Maybe this question is inappropriate, and peace requires a fundamental change in the human mind-set rather than specific plans and protocols. "There is no way to peace," wrote the noted pacifist A. J. Muste, "peace is the way." But if we are to follow it, the route must at least be discerned, even if dimly. Like the blind men and the reasons of war, the causes of peace are also multifaceted. Just as no one body part defines an elephant, if there is no one way to peace but instead many, some of them might lead down blind alleys, some to dangerous cliffs, and others to yet more paths, each with additional branching points and an unending series of twists and turns. In Part III, we shall walk a short way down some of the most prominent of such paths.

## NOTES

1. St. Augustine. 1950. *The City of God.* New York: Modern Library.

2. Quoted in Alan Geyer. 1982. *The Idea of Disarmament.* Elgin, IL: Brethren Press.

# CHAPTER 11

## PEACE MOVEMENTS

Peace movement demonstration in England.

*Source:* © 2008 Getty Images.

> *Peace is patriotic.*
>
> —Popular slogan

S ince virtually any war is an odious tarnishing of the human record, the work of peacemaking is not only essential but woefully unfinished. By many measures, wars have become more destructive, thus making the work of the peacemaker all the more urgent. There have been, nonetheless, numerous efforts at building peace, raising many possibilities and opportunities, some long-standing and others quite recent. There have also been hints of success; although paradoxically, whereas the toll of war can be tallied, it is impossible to assess how many wars—or how much destruction during wars—have been prevented by the efforts of people seeking peace—that is, the various "peace movements."

# Popular Attitudes Toward Peace

One difficulty faced by would-be peacemakers is that although most people claim to be in favor of peace, a considerable number seem to be more interested in war. At present, all too many people find peace boring and war exciting. We can readily identify a war novel, a war movie, a war song, a war painting, or a war toy; by contrast, how many of us can identify clearly a *peace* novel, movie, and so on? When war is mentioned on the daily newscasts, people prick up their ears; when peace is mentioned, they are more likely to yawn. The journalistic credo for attracting a wide audience reads "If it bleeds, it leads...."

On the other hand, a distinct peace culture exists in the form of antiwar poetry (notably the works of Wilfred Owen and Siegfried Sassoon after World War I), novels (such as *All Quiet on the Western Front* and *Catch-22*), films (including *Platoon, Gandhi,* and *The War Game*), and folk and pop music, including but not limited to Pete Seeger, John Lennon, and, more recently, Steve Earle. Opposition to war, interestingly, seems easier to express than is commitment to peace. Thus, not surprisingly, most peace movements have been fundamentally antiwar movements.

# Attention, Success, and Failure

Human beings tend to use a variety of different terms to identify things in which they are particularly interested. The Inuit peoples of the far north, for example, are said to have 11 different words for what in English is known simply as "snow," and the Bedouins have 100 distinct words for "camel," depending on an animal's age, sex, health, and temperament. Similarly, we assign titles to our different wars (e.g., the War of the Roses, the Seven Years' War, the Balkan War, the Iraq War). By contrast, *peace* is a generic term, used only in the singular, even though the "peace" obtained, say, in Europe between World Wars I and II differed markedly from that of the 1950s or from the period just after the defeat of Napoleon. Perhaps when our interest in peace equals our interest in war, we shall begin to identify not only "wars" but also "peaces," as something more meaningful than simply the intervals between those things that "really matter" to many people and especially to the mass media: namely, wars.

Peace entails more than the absence of war. However, a defining characteristic of peace movements has long been their antiwar stance. Efforts to achieve ecological balance, economic fairness, social justice, and human rights are crucially important, and they certainly belong within the purview of peace and conflict studies, but they are only just beginning to be integrated into what has generally been meant by a "peace movement."

Significantly, there are virtually no "war movements"—at least, none that would identify themselves as such! A notable exception is fascism, which has often glorified war as necessary for the fullest expression of individual strength, racial purity, and national identity. For the most part, however, a wide variety of doctrines and organizations espouse various (often contradictory) ways of achieving peace. Advocates of "peace through strength," for example, claim that it is in the interest of peace that states must maintain large military forces, along with a willingness to employ them if necessary. In this book, we shall consider "peace movements" as they are more traditionally identified—that is, as sources of popular opposition to war and to militarism and for the creation of structures and cultures of peace.

Many 21st-century students of peace agree that war has reached its nadir: It has become less useful and less desirable than ever before. Virtually every modern war has been unacceptably wasteful, destructive, and cruel. Moreover, in many cases, the state initiating a given war has not achieved its aims. For example, during the 20th century, many aggressors were either defeated or stymied in their goals: the Central Powers in World War I, the Axis in World War II, North Korea in the Korean War, Pakistan in the India-Pakistan Wars, Iraq in its war with Iran and its venture into Kuwait and the resulting Gulf War, and Serbia in Bosnia and Kosovo. Similarly, it appears that Israel's brief wars with Hezbollah in Lebanon (2006) and with Hamas in the Gaza Strip (2008–2009), and the U.S. invasion and occupation of Iraq (2003–2011), have left the initiating country worse off than before. As of this writing, the U.S.-sponsored overthrow of the Taliban government in Afghanistan appears to be less than successful; only time will tell whether it, too, will eventually be judged a tragic failure.

At the same time, there have been some politically successful wars, notably those of national liberation, such as those for independence in Indonesia, Algeria, and Kenya, as well as NATO's war against Serbia. The Vietnam War can also be seen as a successful war of unification for the Vietnamese, with distinctly anticolonial overtones as well, since it represented the culmination of struggles with France, Japan, and, last, the United States.

# Historical and Current Perceptions of War

Although contemporary readers may be surprised, until recently war has not generally been recognized as a serious human problem, nor has it been widely or deeply deplored. Indeed, war has not even been considered particularly unseemly. Rather, it was long accepted as an instrument of statesmanship, to be used under appropriate circumstances. Several factors seem to be involved in the recent public perception that war is a problem and that peace is not only a desirable goal but one that is—or must be—attainable:

1. *The potential for global destruction.* The development of increasingly destructive weapons, including various forms of conventional explosives, chemical and biological substances, and most especially nuclear weapons, has given all people a stake in the permanent abandonment of armed hostilities.

2. *The social, economic, and environmental toll.* The enormous economic, social, and environmental costs of war and war preparations have induced many people to call for a reduction of the role of the military in daily life.

3. *The evolution of the Earth into a "global village."* The increased means and speed of communications and transportation have enhanced the interconnections among human beings: economically, socially, and emotionally. More than ever before, people are directly affected by the experiences of others, such that peace has become indivisible: There is no real peace on Earth so long as war is raging anywhere.

4. *The increase in political involvement.* With the growth in literacy and the spread of more democratic forms of government, people are more likely than ever before to accept personal responsibility for the actions of their country. To an extent not seen in the past, war is no

longer considered a visitation of some god or an acceptable consequence of a monarch's whim. Likewise, peace is increasingly seen as everyone's business, something that is attainable, if enough people want it and are willing to work for it.

Before 1914, states were relatively unashamed to acknowledge their own offensive goals in starting a war. But since 1945 in particular, aggression without a self-justifying, "national security" rationale has become rare, with national leaders feeling obliged to proclaim their defensive and peace-loving *motivations*; even if their *behavior* is not dramatically different, this difference in emphasis may be meaningful. Prior to 1947, for example, the United States had a War Department; its name was subsequently changed to the Defense Department. Indeed, the military branch of government of virtually every state in the world employs the word *defense,* rather than *war.* Perhaps this switch is merely cosmetic. But even so, it reflects a significant change of attitude: Defense is acceptable to policy makers and to most of the public; offensive war is not. Hence, to paraphrase former president George W. Bush, "We make war for the sake of peace."

## Movements: Theory and Practice

In English, the noun "movement" refers to a move, a change of place or position or posture; a tactical or strategic shifting of a military unit, a maneuver; to an action or activity—usually used in the plural, "movements." A movement also refers to a tendency or trend. And it importantly denotes a series of organized activities working to promote or attain an end, especially such political and social movements as the civil rights movement, the antiwar movement, and the peace movement.

With reference to peace, the distinction between "theory" and "movement" is somewhat arbitrary, since peace denotes *both the idea* of peace *and the action* needed to bring it about. This "unity" of theory and practice is exemplified by the life and work of Mohandas K. Gandhi, for whom peace, or individual and collective nonviolence, was religious, philosophical, psychological, legal, and political at the same time. Gandhi, in turn, was deeply influenced by spiritual and secular theories and traditions, both those indigenous to India (Hinduism) and Western. A political movement is a social movement in the political arena. Social movements are a type of group action. They are large, often informal groupings of individuals and/or organizations focused on specific political or social issues, on carrying out or resisting a social change or a political state of affairs.

A political movement may be organized around a single issue or set of issues, or around a set of shared concerns of a social group. In contrast with a political party, a political movement is usually not organized to elect members of the movement to government office; instead, a political movement aims to convince citizens and/or government officials to take action on the issues and concerns that are the focus of the movement. They are often represented by non- or even antistate groups. A political movement may be local, regional, national, or international in scope. Some aim to change government policy, such as the antiwar movement, the ecology movement, the antiglobalization movement, and the peace movement.

# History and Taxonomy of Peace Movements

One of the problems confronted by antiwar activists is that peace plans, almost invariably, are far less specific and detailed—and typically less immediately workable—than a military staff's plans for war. Peace campaigns, even the best organized and most generously funded, have rarely come close to rivaling the organization and funding behind even the smallest or most confined war campaigns. Nonetheless, peace movements have a long and noble history.

In considering this history, an important distinction must be made between the proposals of specific individuals and the history of peace movements in general. Mass-mobilized peace movements as we understand them today are relatively recent developments, dating from the early 19th century. But they draw on a vast reservoir of popular discontent with war and have been nourished, in large part, by a belief in *universalism,* an idealist cosmopolitan ethic that sees a common interest in peace and in shared humanity as trumping the political and ethnic distinctions between peoples.

## Early History

Perhaps the first organization specifically devoted to achieving lasting peace was the Amphictyonic League, organized among a number of city-states in ancient Greece; the members agreed not to attack one another or to cut off one another's water supply. The Olympic Games also served a peacemaking function in ancient Greece. Every 4 years, any ongoing hostilities were halted by a 1-month truce, during which Greeks were prohibited from bearing arms or making war and instead supported the athletic competition at Olympus.

The initial Christian church apparently was entirely pacifist. During the first few centuries BCE, Christians were persecuted by the Roman Empire for refusing to serve in the Roman legions. Renunciation of arms was inspired by the teachings of Jesus, notably as presented in the Sermon on the Mount. In addition, early Christian writing rejected service in the Roman legions as "idolatry." Pacifism also seemed especially appropriate to many early Christians because it involved renunciation of the secular world, in anticipation of the Second Coming of Christ. Subsequently, with the conversion of Emperor Constantine, Christianity also experienced a dramatic conversion, toward a state-supportive view of the legitimacy of war and of military service. Earlier pacifist views came to be considered heresy by the so-called Christian realists, who believed that Christians must come to terms with the world of power and politics, as in the biblical injunction to "render unto Caesar that which is Caesar's." Christian realists, including St. Augustine, the founder of Just-War theory, granted a certain legitimacy to the secular world of military force.

Traditions of absolute pacifism nonetheless reemerged during the Middle Ages, most of which carried a strong antistate flavor as well: The Waldensians of the 12th century and the Anabaptists of the 16th century (both of them minority Christian "heretic" sects that briefly flourished in Europe) were notable in this regard and were aggressively persecuted by both church and state. Such vigorous, if small-scale, groups as the Quakers, the Mennonites, and the Brethren—sometimes known as the "prophetic minorities"—nevertheless maintained religiously oriented peace traditions. Much of their activity was centered on individual statements of religious and ethical conscience, an individual refusal to participate in war often referred to as "personal witness."

## Secular Peace Movements

By contrast, secular peace movements, as we know them today, are less than 2 centuries old. Numerous organizations sprang up during the 19th century. The New York and Massachusetts peace societies, for example, were both founded in 1815, and other organizations were established on both sides of the Atlantic, including the American Peace Society and the Universal Peace Union in 1866. Many international peace conferences were held during the mid-19th century, including gatherings in London (1843), Brussels (1848), Paris (1849), and Frankfurt (1850).

These efforts were largely political fringe events. Other than legitimizing the concept of peace and spreading hope among those attending, they had virtually no concrete political successes. Later, the Hague Peace Conferences of the late 19th century had more influence with government leaders, generating widespread expectations among many citizens as well. Although measurable successes were rare, it can be argued that by placing the concept of international peacemaking on the world agenda and keeping it there, international peace meetings helped set the stage for such peace-oriented multinational organizations as the League of Nations after World War I and the United Nations after World War II. They also gave voice to a growing international mood in which war was seen as uncivilized, and recourse to war became increasingly unpopular.

Probably the first organized efforts by any peace group to *prevent* a war took place in the United States, prior to the Mexican-American War (1845). Although they failed to prevent this war, peace groups did succeed in getting the antagonists to negotiate their differences, and a pro-peace viewpoint was forcefully expressed. During that war, the famous American writer Henry David Thoreau was jailed for refusing to pay a poll tax, which, in his judgment, indirectly supported that conflict. His essay *Civil Disobedience* has been enormously influential ever since. In it, Thoreau argued that citizens of a democracy have a higher obligation than to the policies of their government. He maintained that the conscientious citizen is obliged to do what is right and to refuse personal participation in wrongdoing—even if the wrongdoing is sanctioned by the legal authority of government and even if defiance leads to government retribution. When Thoreau was imprisoned for failure to pay his taxes (which helped fund the Mexican-American War, which he strongly opposed), he was visited by his close friend, Ralph Waldo Emerson. The story goes that Emerson asked "Henry, what are you doing in *here*?" whereupon Thoreau responded "Ralph, what are you doing out *there*?"

The idea of civil disobedience has been greatly enlarged upon by modern practitioners of nonviolence. Within the past 100 years, the dominant periods of peace movement activism within the United States, and the primary theme of each, can be identified as follows:

- 1890–1914: Alarm about such modern armaments as accurate, breech-loading artillery, machine guns, and heavily armed naval vessels
- 1916–1921: Opposition to World War I and to Western interventionism in the Soviet civil war
- 1920s: A variety of movements based on revulsion to World War I
- 1930–1939: Concern about a second world war and anxiety about the risks of aerial bombardment
- 1957–1963: Opposition to nuclear weapons, notably atmospheric nuclear testing with its resulting radioactive fallout
- 1965–1972: Opposition to the Vietnam War
- 1980–1985: Opposition to nuclear weapons, military bellicosity, and the growing danger of nuclear war; support of a nuclear freeze
- 1986–1990: Opposition to military involvement in Central America, concern regarding underground testing, deployment of "new generation" weapons, and the militarization of space

- 1991–1999: Concerns centering on military use of depleted uranium, child soldiers, and proliferation of small arms; greater emphasis on humanitarian intervention in such intrastate wars as Bosnia and Kosovo
- 2003–present: Opposition to the Iraq and Afghanistan wars (the former most especially), increasing worry about possible future wars with Iran and North Korea

The worldwide antiwar movement was probably at its peak after World War I. This was because, despite mutual distrust among the great powers of the time and the long history of military and economic competitiveness that preceded that war, before that conflict the European antagonists had no grudges that justified the immense slaughter that ensued. No nation was obviously aligned with "good" or "evil," and, indeed, World War I appears to have been largely a consequence of blunders by all major belligerents. Hence, it has widely been labeled "the war nobody wanted," which in turn gave momentum to the current Anglo-American understanding of "pacifism." People who considered themselves peace loving but who supported President Wilson's "war to end all wars" began calling themselves internationalists; they placed their long-term hopes on agreements between states. Strict, or absolute, pacifists were (and still are) associated with a firm personal refusal to fight in *any* war, a stance that typically is based on individual religious and/or moral convictions. In contrast, according to the noted peace scholar David Cortright, "pragmatic pacifism can be understood as a continuum of perspectives, beginning on the one hand with the rejection of military violence and extending across a range of options that allow for some limited use of force under specific conditions." [1]

In the United States, the antiwar movement of 1917 was eventually dismantled by wholesale arrests, brutal police raids (most notorious were the Palmer Raids in 1919, named for the attorney general at the time), and vigilante mobs. Many leaders were given long prison terms or expelled from the country.

## Peace Movements in Historical Context

Historically, wars have been followed by periods in which peace is espoused with particular vigor. This is apparently due to potential adversaries' physical, economic, and social exhaustion, as well as to the literal inability of devastated societies to mobilize the resources—emotional and material—necessary to prosecute a lengthy war. The Greek historian Herodotus, called the "father of history" for his masterful treatment of the Greco-Persian Wars (500–479 BCE), pointed out that "in peace, children bury their parents; war violates the order of nature and causes parents to bury their children."[2] Insofar as such experiences are what psychologists describe as *aversive stimuli,* people are especially peace prone in the immediate aftermath of war.

For example, after the Peloponnesian War, Greece experienced an upwelling of pacifist sentiment, as also occurred following the chaotic civil and imperial wars toward the end of the Roman Republic. Later, during the Middle Ages, the Crusades, as well as the various wars among dynastic rivals, including the murderous Hundred Years' War between England and France, partially induced the pacifism of humanists such as Erasmus, as well as numerous suggestions for doctrines of international law.

The Thirty Years' War ended in 1648 with the establishment of the modern state system, which was in large part motivated by widespread revulsion at how devastating that war had been. But the new system of states did not prevent war, at least not for long. The ruinous Napoleonic Wars, 150 years later, led not only to the so-called Holy Alliance and the "balance-of-power peace" of mid-19th-century Europe but also to an increased interest in international prohibitions on war and in the various peace conferences of that century.

The wars of nationalism, especially the Franco-Prussian War (1871), led to renewed popular concern with the structure of international law. And, of course, the horrors of World War I were directly responsible for creation of the League of Nations and various disarmament efforts during the 1920s and 1930s, just as World War II led to the establishment of the United Nations as well as renewed interest in world government. The threat of global thermonuclear war, which intensified during the U.S.-Soviet Cold War, was responsible for unprecedented concern about limiting and, if possible, abolishing a whole class of weapons. With the end of the Cold War, such "nuclear abolitionism" is now a much less prominent concern for both the public and politicians than it was during the Gorbachev/Reagan era (1981–1991) and before, which had been characterized by a vigorous nuclear arms race and conspicuous saber rattling.

Unlike World War I, popular support for World War II was much more widespread. To some extent, in fact, World War II legitimized war in the minds of many and led to a lull in peace movement activity. In part, World War II was widely viewed as having occurred because the Western democracies had been unwilling to confront Germany and Japan strongly and early enough (the so-called lessons of Munich). In addition, because the aggressive militarism of Germany and Japan had represented such a threat to the West, pacifism became widely discredited as a way of coping with international "evil." Moreover, during the decades following World War II, anticolonial liberation movements gave further credence to the legitimacy of organized violence, so long as it was for a "good cause," while the growth of Stalinism in the Soviet Union and Maoism in China served to justify militarism on the part of the United States and its NATO allies.

The resurgence of the peace movement during the 1950s and 1960s was due largely to growing popular anxiety about nuclear weapons, as well as opposition to specific wars, as in Korea and—to a much greater extent—Vietnam. The peace movement also was influenced by activity in the so-called Third World, notably the nonviolence of Gandhi and antinuclear awareness in the aftermath of the atomic bombings of Hiroshima and Nagasaki.

Following the Vietnam War, promilitary commentators worried that the United States had developed a "Vietnam syndrome," whereby Americans would be especially reluctant to wage war. Thus, President George H. W. Bush announced with pride following the first Iraq War—which evicted Iraqi forces from Kuwait in 1990—that the United States had overcome this syndrome. This might help explain the support of Congress and most of the U.S. public for the second Iraq War, which began in 2003, at the prodding of President George W. Bush, British prime minister Tony Blair, Australian prime minister John Howard, and other members of a supposed "coalition of the willing." Given the consequences of that endeavor, it will be interesting to see if it leads to a return of the Vietnam syndrome and, if so, whether this particular disinclination will be considered beneficial rather than worrisome.

## A Typology of Peace Movements

Peace movements may be divided into three categories:

1. Movements to eliminate war in general

2. Movements to stop particular aspects of war (e.g., conscription) or particular weapons (e.g., landmines or nuclear weapons)

3. Movements to stop particular wars (e.g., wars in Vietnam or Iraq)

Of course, it is easier to stop specific wars than to stop war in general; hence, efforts to banish war altogether are also most likely to be associated with efforts to reshape public opinion and to establish firm structures of positive peace. These struggles are also more likely to persist, in contrast with opposition to particular wars or to specific means of waging war, which typically end along with the war in question or with the banning (or deployment) of the contested weapons.

Movements to eliminate war generally have spawned secular groups such as the Peace Pledge Union in England and the Women's International League for Peace and Freedom,[3] as well as various religious organizations and traditions, such as the Fellowship of Reconciliation, Pax Christi, the Quakers, and numerous advocates of nonviolence. Movements to stop particular aspects of war have included opposition to poison gas, to specific weapons delivery systems (Euromissiles, the MX missile, depleted uranium), to nuclear weapons themselves (SANE, the Freeze campaign, the British Campaign for Nuclear Disarmament), and to conscription (War Resisters League), as well as campaigns in support of converting military industries to civilian production (the Ploughshares Fund) and opposition to specific wars.

The following list, modified from Nigel Young's pioneering work on these matters, suggests a more detailed typology of peace movements, identifying some of the major traditions, and an example of each:[4]

| Tradition | Example(s) |
|---|---|
| Religious pacifism | Conscientious objection: Society of Friends (Quakers), Pax Christi (Catholic), Fellowship of Reconciliation |
| Liberal internationalism | Associations, national peace councils, world disarmament campaigns |
| Anticonscription | War Resister's League, Amnesty International |
| Socialist internationalism | No exact contemporary equivalents, but active until World War I, including the International Workers of the World ("Wobblies") |
| Feminist antimilitarism | Women for Peace, Women's International League for Peace and Freedom |
| Ecological pacifism | Greenpeace, Green Party (especially in Germany) |
| Communist internationalism | World Peace Council |
| Nuclear pacifism | Europe: CND (Campaign for Nuclear Disarmament), END (European Nuclear Disarmament); United States: SANE/Freeze, Physicians for Social Responsibility, and many others |

# Interconnections Between Peace and Other Social Movements

There have been many interconnections between peace movements and other popular social movements. For example, feminist antimilitarism, which emerged in the early years of the 20th century, was strongly infused with energy and leadership from the women's suffrage movement.

Opposition to nuclear power—in the late 1960s and throughout much of the 1970s—contributed to broader antinuclear sentiment in the 1980s and later. Many people active in feminist, socialist, gay and lesbian rights, religious nonviolent, and other social justice movements participate in peace movement activities as well. Environmental organizations, such as Greenpeace and Friends of the Earth, have found themselves increasingly involved in antinuclear protests. Such groups express their antiwar and antinuclear concerns because of the threat of environmental destruction arising not only from nuclear war but also from the ongoing radioactive contamination emanating from nuclear weapons facilities, even while "nuclear peace" (or, more accurately, nuclear terror) prevails.

Other groups, which focus primarily on economic justice, have been drawn to the peace movement agenda as a result of their recognition of the social and economic costs of military expenditures. The era of avowedly conservative U.S. government policies, ushered in with the election of Ronald Reagan and followed by both Bush administrations, resulted in massive federal budget deficits, a reluctance to raise taxes, and thus belt tightening with respect to social expenditures. American activist groups, accordingly, became more aware of the *opportunity costs* of military spending—that is, the degree to which military expenditure diminishes a country's opportunity to invest money in ways that are socially more productive. During much of the 1990s, those who believed that the end of the Cold War would result in the end of peace movements were proven to be incorrect. (At the same time, those who believed that these developments would result in greater domestic investment—the much hoped-for "peace dividend"—were also disappointed.) A more accurate portrayal of peace movement life is one of a brief hiatus followed by regeneration around revised issues.

## The United States

Despite the interconnections between peace and other social justice movements, contemporary peace-related movements in the United States have often been accused of being excessively a concern of middle-class white people. The reenergized antinuclear movement of the 1980s made efforts to reach out to progressive social justice groups organized by the poor and by people of color, to broaden its appeal and deepen its commitment to social justice. Nevertheless, antinuclear protesters as well as feminists and environmental activists were largely drawn from the relatively well-educated and well-to-do sectors of American society.

By contrast, opposition to U.S. intervention in Central America and to apartheid in South Africa, as well as support for civil and gay rights, may well have derived from a wider socioeconomic cross section of society. Such organizations as Committee in Solidarity with the People of El Salvador (CISPES) and others seeking more peace-affirming policies toward Nicaragua regularly underwent Federal Bureau of Investigation (FBI) harassment but nonetheless persevered and grew. Contemporary American and European opposition movements—especially those opposing the Iraq and Afghanistan Wars—also appear to have undergone similar scrutiny by federal governments, especially with various restrictions on civil liberties (notably the abolition of *habeas corpus* and the imposition of warrantless wiretaps in the United States) initiated by the administration of George W. Bush in association with the "war on terror."

Peace movements (and left-of-center movements within the United States in general) have tended to focus largely on one issue at a time, as earlier concerns are abandoned and the latest issue—cynics would say, the most recent fad—attracts most of the energy and outrage. Thus, in the late 1950s, it was opposition to McCarthyism; in the early 1960s, protests against atmospheric testing and fallout shelters and in favor of arms control; in the mid-1960s, the civil rights movement; in the late 1960s and early 1970s, opposition to the Vietnam War; in the mid-1970s, defense of the environment; in the late 1970s, affirmation of feminism and human rights generally; in the early to mid-1980s, opposition to nuclear weapons and nuclear war fighting; in the late 1980s and early 1990s, protests against South African apartheid and U.S. interventionism in Central America; in the late 1990s, support of humanitarian intervention, economic conversion, and strategic nonviolence through various social movements, along with opposition to economically oppressive and environmentally destructive components of "globalization"; and during the first part of this century, opposition to the Iraq War and the economic hegemony of "the 1%."

To some extent, it can be argued that these shifting priorities have been appropriate, reflecting changing global threats to peace. It should come as no surprise that the Reagan administration, for example, with its verbal bellicosity and cavalier attitude toward nuclear war, generated the most vigorous antinuclear peace movement in U.S. history, just as the Iraq War, with its accompanying doctrine whereby the United States announced itself prepared to invade other countries at will—"preemptive war"—has eventually produced considerable political opposition around the world.

Often, however, peace movements have been motivated by a surge of popular anxiety regarding a perceived threat that quickly subsides, even though the underlying problem remains as serious as ever. For example, the antinuclear movement of 1958–1963 diminished rapidly after the Partial Test Ban Treaty was signed, although nuclear testing and the nuclear arms race simply went underground, increasing the number of such tests—and the intensity of the arms race itself—rather than diminishing either. In other cases, peace movements that were narrowly focused around opposition to something specific tended to disband—perhaps appropriately— when "their issue" was resolved. A good example is the resistance to the war in Vietnam, which ended when U.S. ground forces eventually withdrew. European opposition to the deployment of nuclear missiles by the North Atlantic Treaty Organization sparked a virtual firestorm of antinuclear protest during the early 1980s. With the signing of the INF (Intermediate-Range Nuclear Forces) Treaty of 1988, which banned the deployment by both NATO and the Soviet Union of such missiles, the European antinuclear movement became much more quiet.

At the same time, by exposing the absurdities of various war-fighting, war-surviving, and war-winning doctrines, the antinuclear movement succeeded in delegitimizing nuclear weapons to such a degree that even the Reagan administration eventually found itself proclaiming that "a nuclear war can never be won and must never be fought" and rescinding (at least for public consumption) its earlier bellicosity and pronuclear stance. In this way, the path of the U.S. antinuclear movement has been similar to that of the environmental movement of the early 1970s, many of whose goals and ways of thinking have progressed from radical to mainstream. The withdrawal of American combat forces from Iraq and Afghanistan will likely be a similar consequence of peace movement activism having both stimulated mainstream political opinion and become absorbed into it.

## Europe

Several important peace movement traditions have also developed in Europe. One is the Green Party (*Die Grünen*), which originated in what was then West Germany. In the reunified

Germany, the Greens gained political prominence, at one time forming part of a coalition government with the left-leaning Social Democrats. The Green movement also gave rise to other Green parties throughout Europe. The movement's underlying philosophy is a synthesis of ecology, feminism, political decentralization, community and workplace democracy, antiauthoritarianism, and antimilitarism.

Like their American counterparts, European peace movements have long been dominated by direct opposition to war, a trend that continued through the last decades of the 20th century. Anticonscription advocates, especially the Berlin Appeal, became popular in both East and West Germany. Nearly 20% of those eligible for military service applied for conscientious objector status in West Germany, while the evangelical Lutheran churches of the German Democratic Republic (the former East Germany) also helped consolidate antimilitary sentiment. These church groups were particularly influential in organizing opposition to the former East German government, resulting in the dramatic events of late 1989 and 1990, when it (and other East European governments dominated by the Soviet Union) was toppled and the hated Berlin Wall dismantled.

Also in Europe, the Campaign for Nuclear Disarmament (CND), founded in the United Kingdom in 1958, was stimulated initially by British opposition to nuclear testing. During the 1980s, largely in response to the intensification of the Cold War during the early Thatcher and Reagan years, the CND expanded dramatically as a broad-based, populist movement. In 1981, massive street demonstrations involving hundreds of thousands of people convulsed Bonn, Brussels, Athens, London, Rome, Madrid, and Amsterdam, largely in opposition to nuclear weapons policies. These demonstrations were part of a peace movement revitalization that united antinuclear protesters with antinuclear power activists. They included the women's and ecological movements, gay and lesbian rights supporters, and socialists and internationalists of a variety of orientations, including supporters of the United Nations, a sprinkling of pro-Kremlin peace fronts, and advocates of world government.

Although numerous peace movements exist in less developed countries, they are almost always concerned with domestic issues. These typically focus on opposition to a government's oppression of its own indigenous people (e.g., Guatemala), political dictatorship (e.g., many African and Middle Eastern regimes), or its socioeconomic policies (e.g., Zimbabwe). It is mostly in the wealthier northern countries that peace movements respond to government actions in *other* parts of the world.

In early 2003, major European cities experienced huge demonstrations opposing the forthcoming U.S.-led invasion of Iraq. For partisans of peace movement activism, these events offer both hope and disappointment: hope, because they were unprecedented in human history, the first example, ever, of massive public opposition to a war *before* it began . . . but disappointment because they failed to prevent it.

## Some Internal Debates Within Peace Movements

Peace movements are not homogeneous. They have fluctuated substantially in tactics, as well as in goals. They have periodically been galvanized by opposition to especially atrocious wars (Vietnam) or weapons (poison gas, nuclear, depleted uranium-tipped shells), only to recede somewhat when the war is terminated (Vietnam, the Cold War) or when especially provocative actions have been removed (aboveground nuclear testing, Euromissiles, etc.). One observer of the European peace movement during the 1980s suggested that peace movements were like whales, which periodically break the surface and then disappear under the waves. "When the whale disappears in a dive, those on the right believe the movement no longer exists. Supporters of the movement, on the other hand, see the leaping whale and claim it can fly."[5] The truth is somewhere in between.

In addition to their inconstancy, peace movements are notorious for their ideological hetero-geneity and occasional combativeness. Ironically, peace activists fight a lot (not actual violence, but often with substantial verbal and conceptual aggressiveness), at least with each other! Certain sources of debate and tension have persisted within "the movement," which is actually much more plural than singular. In part, this may be because movements advocating social change tend to attract adherents who are antiestablishment, strong-willed, and inclined to rebel against authority. In any event, here are some of the major controversies that have caused substantial splitting within peace movements but have also contributed to the vibrancy that comes from vigorous internal debate.

## State-Centeredness

Since states (and multinational corporations, whose interests are usually closely aligned with those of the major states) are the primary actors on the international war-peace arena, some claim that it is essential to reform the way states behave toward one another—for example, by encouraging trade, democracy, disarmament conferences, and agreements on the rules of war; the abolition of certain weapons; and the establishment of international agencies such as the League of Nations and the United Nations. On the other hand, critics of the state-centered approach claim that focusing on the behavior of states merely perpetuates such behavior by exac-erbating rather than alleviating nationalist biases. They think that states are the problem, not the solution, and that, accordingly, genuine solutions must be less state-centered.

Following the breakup of the Warsaw Pact in the 1990s, NATO's move to fill the Eastern European strategic vacuum and employ its military muscle in the former Yugoslavia and in Afghanistan prompted new divisions in the peace movement. Some praise the international cooperation implicit in NATO's new interventionist role as a welcome challenge to state sover-eignty and superpower policing of the world. Others see the same actions as an attempted exten-sion of Western hegemony and of inordinate American influence.

## The Use of Military Force

Within the European peace movement, the same internal divisions over NATO's role arose over bombing raids in Serbia and, later, its use of "boots on the ground" in Afghanistan. Some defended military action as a means of assisting humanitarian causes, such as defense of the Kosovars and the (possibly temporary) violent removal of the Taliban from power in Afghanistan. Opponents of any use of military force (*absolute pacifists*) disagree with those we might call *relative pacifists,* who believe that a "good," "just," or permissible war or military action (such as, arguably, those in Afghanistan, Kosovo and Libya, the first Gulf War, the Spanish Civil War, or World War II) may still be possible but who often oppose specific wars, as in Vietnam, Central America, and Iraq. Even with so-called good wars—about which there is considerable debate—the question must be posed: Is the "evil" to be overcome (e.g., Slobodan Milošević's ethnic cleansing, Saddam Hussein's alleged weapons of mass destruction, Nazism in World War II, slavery in the Civil War) greater than the "evil" of a war waged to overcome the malignancy? (An analogy with cancer may be apt, since some "cures" for this disease can be at least as devastating as the illness.)

A similar debate attends to the use of smaller military forces. Was the "liberation" of Grenada worth the loss of life that resulted from the 1983 invasion of that island by the United States? Did the removal of Panama's former dictator Manuel Noriega warrant another American invasion in 1989, or did the end of the Gadhafi regime require the NATO bombing of 2011? Did American Marines move too quickly into Somalia and then conduct a too-hasty retreat when American lives were threatened by local tribal warlords? Some self-styled realists argue that under certain conditions, the use of force is appropriate; others—equally realistic—maintain that violence is ultimately self-defeating and also filled with unintended negative consequences for those who retaliate violently against an attack (so-called blowback).

## Centralization Versus Grassroots Organization

One antiwar tradition favors the development of strong peace movement leadership and central authority. The other prefers local, grassroots organizing and "leaderless" or at least decentralized organization (e.g., "The Occupy Movements" of 2011–2012).

It is unclear whether peace movements historically had greater success when they were composed primarily of large numbers of people mobilized as "objects" or of relatively fewer but more strongly motivated individuals, who saw themselves as "subjects" of their own intense actions and protests. Thus, the peace movement mobilization of 1 million people in New York City in June 1982 had an undeniable impact on the Reagan administration but so did the handful of Buddhist monks, who, a decade or so earlier, immolated themselves to protest the Vietnam War (and who have been the basis of much nonviolent resistance to the junta in Burma/Myanmar). U.S.-based opposition to the Iraq and Afghanistan Wars has been largely at the grassroots level, with peace proponents deeply impatient of political leadership in both the Democratic and Republican parties. Despite a proliferation of antiwar organizations, antiwar activities in the United States have not coalesced around any particular one. In much of Europe and Latin America, there is massive popular as well as selective elite political opposition to continuing Israeli occupations of Arab lands.

## Single-Issue Versus Broader Social Agendas

Many peace groups have opposed specific aspects of war (such weapons as the MX missile and Trident submarines in the United States or neutron bombs and cruise missiles in Europe; conscription; war taxes; or specific wars, as in Vietnam or Iraq), whereas others have emphasized the importance of broadening their agenda to embrace economic aspects of social justice (employment at decent wages, economic equity, medical care, affordable housing, and child care), environmental concerns (clean air and water, preservation of open space, wildlife conservation, renewable energy sources, protection of tropical forests, mitigation of global warming), support for gay rights, and opposition to racism and sexism in the United States and apartheid in South Africa.

In some cases, peace movements have become closely associated with a single political party, such as Labour in Britain or the former Communist Party in Italy. In the United States, the Democratic Party has traditionally shied away from being too closely associated with peace, fearing that it would be tainted with an image of being "weak on national security." Supporters of the single-issue approach emphasize that by concentrating on a small number of manageable concerns, they are more likely to have a demonstrable effect, which will also provide them with successes upon which to build. Supporters of a broader agenda counter with the argument that specific issues come and go and that the peace movement can actually be weakened whenever a single issue is resolved, no matter what the outcome. In addition, peace advocates are increasingly aware of the importance of pointing out the linkages between various "single issue" considerations. For example, the Nuclear Freeze campaign in the United States during the 1980s received relatively little support from African Americans, at least in part because the U.S. underclass was more concerned with economic and social justice.

Single-issue politics offers the advantage of bringing sharp, substantial pressure to bear on a narrow point. However, such thrusts are also susceptible to being turned aside by mainstream opposition. Broad, programmatic, consensus-building blueprints for social change, by contrast, bring pressure across a much wider societal front but often with less visible impact in any one area.

## Practicality Versus Idealism

How high should peace movements aim? Is there danger that by setting their sights too high, they will make "the best an enemy of the good"? On the other hand, don't peace movements have an obligation to be above normal politics, which bills itself as the "art of the possible"? At times of unique danger and opportunity, perhaps peace movements should, as some peace advocates put it, "be realistic—demand the impossible." Thus, there can be a disadvantage in being too timorous: "Realism" on the part of the U.S. Nuclear Freeze campaign, for example, appeared to be a step backward to many in the European peace movement, many of whom had long demanded substantial reductions in nuclear weapons, while others called for nuclear abolition.

Another dilemma of practicality versus idealism may be observed in Germany, where the Green Party has enjoyed such electoral success that at the beginning of this century the elected Green Party members became insiders rather than protesters outside parliamentary politics. Earlier, the party had generated two factions within the Green movement: the "Fundis" ("fundamentalists"), who held out for ideal goals such as the total abolition of nuclear weapons and refused to form coalitions with more conservative parties, and the "Realos" ("realists"), who were willing to make certain practical concessions in the interest of achieving immediate, although incomplete, political goals.

One view of peace movements is that they serve as grit in the cogwheels of the world's war machines, preventing them from running smoothly and perhaps eventually causing them to break down altogether. Another analogy—and a more positive one—compares peace movements to bread yeast, helping dough rise. Perhaps states are by their nature unqualified to promote creative transformations and are dependent on changes that emerge only from protest groups. In any case, peace movement activists remain divided as to whether they ought to compromise their principles in the interests of real but ambiguous "progress."

## Civil Disobedience

Supporters of civil disobedience maintain that when the government is engaging in ethically unacceptable behavior—often counter to international law—it is acceptable and even essential to oppose these practices, even if opposition of this sort involves breaking domestic law. Opponents of civil disobedience worry about the morality and consequences of law breaking and also about the possibility that such acts may alienate the majority of the citizenry and ultimately prove counterproductive. This is actually part of a broader debate about tactics, especially between those who advocate grassroots activism "in the streets," by as many people as possible (as in the "Occupy Movement"), and those who favor a more top-down approach that focuses on working within the political system to influence decision makers. In turn, the debate about tactics is part of an even larger issue: whether to *oppose* war through the electoral process, by writing, speaking, organizing and attending meetings, and passing resolutions, or actively to *resist* it, by strikes, tax resistance, and nonviolent civil disobedience or even by violent confrontations.

# Some Criticisms of Peace Movements

Although public opinion is often mobilized by peace movement efforts, sometimes it has also been alienated by them. In some cases, wars have been made more unpopular by peace movements but in others they may actually have been prolonged. Peace movement efforts nearly always have unseen, latent consequences as well as visible, immediate ones. This makes it difficult to pronounce a specific peace campaign—or the movement as a whole—a success or failure.

In the famous (some say, infamous) Oxford Peace Pledge Union during the 1930s, many students in England declared that they would not "fight for king and country," which, according to some observers, emboldened Hitler by suggesting that his aggression might not be resisted. Similarly, it can be argued that the other vigorous European peace movements of the 1930s not only may have made Nazi and Fascist aggression more likely but diminished the degree of Allied preparedness when war finally did come. In addition, peace movements, by excessive wishful thinking, may sometimes blind their fellow citizens to the provocative and dangerous behavior of others. "Nothing is more promotive of war," writes peace researcher Quincy Wright, "than diversion of the attention of the prospective victims from the aggressor's preparations."[6]

However, as previously noted, there are many reasons for wars; of these, the occasional counterproductive effects of peace movements seem quite insignificant. Few things are more disruptive of peace, we might conclude, than blaming well-intentioned peace movements for the war-prone behavior of states and their leadership.

Peace movements often have a difficult time. During war, they are typically denounced and often banned or even attacked as unpatriotic, cowardly, or traitorous for giving "aid and comfort to the enemy." And during times of peace, they often are hard-pressed to make a dent in public complacency. A sociopsychological view of peace movement activism puts special emphasis on the personal needs presumably being met by such activity: "acting out" youthful rebellion, opposing authority as a predictable "age appropriate" stage in personal development, and exercising the opportunity of behaving outrageously while still relatively free of social or family responsibilities. This line of argument can readily be overused, especially by right-wing critics eager to discredit peace movement activists. But it would also be a mistake to ignore the diverse personal motivations of such activists, who in fact represent a wide cross section of ages; many are peace movement veterans, some of whom may have "dropped out" for a while, to develop careers or to start families, only to return when the issues appear especially acute, when time allows (the children are grown, retirement is at hand), or when their conscience beckons.

Another question arises: How vociferous should peace activists be in criticizing their own governments? Most devotees of peace studies point out that world peace, demilitarization, and an end to violence are not *zero-sum games,* in which one side must lose if the other wins. Rather, all sides stand to come out ahead if a peace agenda is actually realized. It is a fact of life, however, that citizens are usually most able to influence the polities of which they are members: For U.S. citizens, this is the government of the United States, just as for Russians it is the Russian government, and so on. In most cases, governments are all too happy to have their citizens—whether members of a peace movement or not—criticize and demonstrate against rival foreign powers. But in doing so, they are unlikely to have much impact on the conduct of their own governments.

Peace movement activists generally operate on the assumption that people—especially, perhaps, those fortunate enough to be living in a democracy, which is supposed to respond to their will—have a special responsibility to evaluate critically and, if necessary, to seek to reform the behavior of their own government. In this respect, they have much to do.

## Maintaining the Momentum of Peace Movements

It is all too easy for peace activists to fall victim to personal fatigue, despair, and cynicism. But, in fact, peace workers worldwide have accomplished a great deal. In the 20th century, for example, conscientious objection became widely recognized in most Western countries as a basic legal right, although exercising that right was sometimes perilous. Interestingly, within peace movements themselves, even anticonscription was not universally accepted as an appropriate goal. Historically, a segment of socialist antiwar activists actually applauded conscription, hoping it would create a "people's army," whereas others feared that it would simply contribute to an "army against the people." The Vietnam War was terminated in large part because of American discontent with the war, fueled by immense pressure from the domestic peace movement.

Similarly, in the 1980s and 1990s, nuclear weapons underwent a rapid process of delegitimation, much to the dismay of militarists and cold warriors. At the same time, many professed liberal internationalists supported NATO military engagement in Serbia and Afghanistan and even the Iraq War, justified at the time in the name of humanitarian intervention, peace, and ending the dictatorship of Saddam Hussein. The same debate has arisen over armed assistance to anti-Gadhafi and anti-Assad forces in Libya and Syria, respectively. Not surprisingly, peace advocates of good conscience have found themselves on different sides of these conflicts. It is also interesting to note that many American "paleoconservatives" (as contrasted with the so-called neoconservatives) joined traditional peace movement leftists in opposing the Iraq War and, in 2011–2012, supporting armed intervention in Libya and Syria.

It remains to be seen whether contemporary peace movements can sustain their momentum when and if immediate, readily perceived threats no longer exist and when governments modulate their rhetoric but not their policies or co-opt various peace movement agendas by showy but relatively trivial concessions. More specifically, it is uncertain whether antiwar sentiment in the United States will outlast current crises in the Balkans, Africa, and the Middle East. Also in doubt: whether the antinuclear movement will resume its previous fervor or be co-opted or "pacified" by political rhetoric that equates nuclear weaponry with patriotism and security.

Contemporary peace movements may well profit by developing alternative foreign policy concepts, alternative defense strategies, a pragmatic view of social goals, broader motivations beyond single-issue rallying points, a workable model of a disarmed (or, at least, substantially demilitarized) economy, and staying power. In addition, successful peace movements should be more realistic in confronting the power of the state while also, when possible, breaking out of a strictly state-centered model of politics.

The overriding goal of many peace movement activists is not so much the elimination of states as their transformation from warfare states to peace-promoting agencies of social justice. Specifically, demilitarization could serve not only as a goal but also as a method of such change. And demilitarization, as such, is independent of specific weapons or particular "hot spots" around the world.

The peace movement of the 1980s and 1990s called for the denuclearization of military policy as well as the demilitarization of defense policy. It called into question the fundamental rationality of "national security" based on military means alone. In addition, it called not only for widespread participation but also for empowerment of ordinary citizens. Early 21st-century peace movements appear to have a full agenda, especially given the threats posed not only by subnational terrorists from below but also by the often violent responses of certain countries—including but not limited to the United States and Israel—to these threats.

Peace movements are sometimes depicted as quixotic, hopeless quests, peopled by refugees from the 1960s and 1980s. Yet evidence abounds that the movements of the past, with all their peculiarities, often influenced national policy, nearly always for the better. Both supporters and opponents of the war in Vietnam, for example, agree that the United States terminated its involvement in that conflict because of an ebbing of political will to continue prosecuting the war. In addition, the Reagan administration, during its latter years, grew increasingly less pronuclear due to peace movement pressure that was widespread, vocal, and highly visible. National policy in New Zealand was also strongly influenced by domestic peace movement sentiment. The result was a ban on all nuclear facilities, including visits by nuclear-armed or nuclear-powered naval vessels, much to the consternation of the U.S. government at the time. And the United States' withdrawal of its occupation forces from Iraq and Afghanistan is probably a result of domestic political pressure, felt keenly by elected officials in Washington, D.C.

Moreover, history offers many examples of successful movements that initially appeared to be facing impossible odds: support for women's suffrage; opposition to monarchy; and opposition to the institution of slavery, which was an ancient and firmly rooted practice, at one time virtually worldwide and considered by many to be an immutable and irrevocable part of human society. As recently as the last few decades of the 20th century, few people would have imagined that

1. decades-old Fascist dictatorships in Spain and Portugal would give way to modern parliamentary democracies;

2. bloody tyrannies in the Philippines or Haiti could have been overthrown peacefully;

3. the Soviet Union would renounce its Stalinist heritage and institute massive democratic restructuring (*perestroika*) and political/ideological openness (*glasnost*) and, moreover, disappear as a political entity;

4. the "captive nations" of Eastern Europe would throw off their shackles and emerge as fledgling democracies eager to embrace free-market economic reforms;

5. the apartheid regime of South Africa would end, with remarkably little bloodshed given its violent past and consistently oppressive governments; or

6. dictatorial regimes in Tunisia, Egypt, and Yemen would have been overthrown, and once again, with very little violence.

And this is just a partial list.

Maybe sometime in the future, people will look back wonderingly at the 21st century, noting with amazement that in such a war-prone world, persistent, widespread peace movements could mount so successful a campaign against war itself.

## A FINAL NOTE ON PEACE MOVEMENTS

What if they had a war and no one came? This old question seems never to go away—at least in part because it has never been tested. People always show up for wars. But what if "they" had a war and no one objected? What if no one protested the plans for future wars?

The alternative to vigorous peace movement activism is to continue "business as usual" in a world of war, injustice, and deprivation. Many people have long recognized that the old way of international power politics and warfare is unacceptable, a perception that has become even more widespread with the advent of weapons of mass destruction. Yet progress toward a different and more peaceful world has been painfully slow. With the end of the Cold War—and especially with the prospect of an unending "war on terrorism"—it seems that we have been, as Matthew Arnold put it,

> Wandering between two worlds, one dead,
>
> The other powerless to be born.[7]

There is no simple agreement among activists as to what, specifically, peace movements should strive for: an end to specific wars or to particular weapons or governmental policies and/or various aspects of the complex tapestry of positive peace that we discuss in Part IV. Regardless of the goals favored by each individual, the special hope of peace movements is that they might serve as midwives for a newer and better world, providing it with the impetus to be born at last.

## NOTES

1. David Cortright. 2008. Peace. *A History of Movements and Ideas*. Cambridge and New York: Cambridge University Press: 1–21.

2. Herodotus. 1910. *History*. G. Rawlinson, trans. New York: E. P. Dutton.

3. For a brief history of women's peace activism and movements, see Joshua Goldstein. 2010. *War and Gender*. Cambridge and New York: Cambridge University Press: 322–331.

4. Modified from Nigel Young. 1984. "Why Peace Movements Fail." *Social Alternatives* 4: 9–16.

5. Philip P. Everts. 1989. "Where the Peace Movement Goes When It Disappears." *Bulletin of the Atomic Scientists* 45: 26–30.

6. Quincy Wright. 1964. *A Study of War.* Chicago: University of Chicago Press.

7. Matthew Arnold. April 1855. "Stanzas from the Grande Chartreuse." *Fraser's Magazine.*

## QUESTIONS FOR FURTHER REFLECTION

1. Make some specific suggestions for how peace movements ought to organize themselves in order to achieve general goals. Do the same for goals that are more narrowly focused.

2. Suggest at least one classification of peace movements other than that proposed in this text.

3. Analyze current peace movements in Burma/Myanmar, Guatemala, Zimbabwe, Nepal, or Israel. How do they compare with those in the United States or Europe?

4. Describe your personal position regarding the various controversies within modern peace movements, supporting that position with examples.

5. Make the argument that, on balance, peace movements do more harm than good. Take the opposite position.

## SUGGESTIONS FOR FURTHER READING

April Carter. 1992. *Peace Movements in International Protest and World Politics Since 1945.* London: Longman.

Pam Solo. 1988. *From Protest to Policy.* Hagerstown, MD: Ballinger.

Robert Cooney and Helen Michalowski. 1987. *The Power of the People.* Philadelphia: New Society Publishers.

Scott Ritter. 2007. *Waging Peace: The Art of War for the Antiwar Movement.* New York: Nation Books.

Simon Hall. 2006. *Peace and Freedom: The Civil Rights and Antiwar Movements in the 1960s.* Philadelphia: University of Pennsylvania Press.

Ted Gottfried. 2004. *The Fight for Peace: A History of Anti-War Movements in America.* New York: 21st Century.

# CHAPTER 12

# DIPLOMACY, NEGOTIATIONS, AND CONFLICT RESOLUTION

President Anwar Sadat of Egypt (left), President Jimmy Carter of the United States (center), and Prime Minister Menachim Begin of Israel (right) celebrating the signing of the Camp David Accords in 1978.

*Disagreements must be settled, not by force, not by deceit or trickery, but rather in the only manner which is worthy of the dignity of man, i.e., by a mutual assessment of the reasons on both sides of the dispute, by a mature and objective investigation of the situation, and by an equitable reconciliation of differences of opinion.*

—Pope John XXIII, *Pacem in Terris*

One way of achieving peace is for the contending sides in a dispute to reach a mutually acceptable agreement among themselves. When such agreements or understandings are obtained among states, through the efforts of trained government representatives, often employing stylized communication, we say that "diplomacy" has taken place. People who practice this art are known as diplomats. (There is also a more cynical view of diplomats, who have been defined as "men [and, increasingly, women] sent abroad to lie for their country.")

Peace researcher and political scientist Anatol Rapaport has usefully distinguished among fights, games, and debates. In a fight, the intent is to defeat the opponent, sometimes even to destroy him or her. Rules may exist, as in a prizefight, but they may also be ignored—as in a street fight or a particularly vicious war—and the means are nonetheless violent. In a "game," by contrast, each side tries to outwit the opponent, playing strictly within certain rules. And in a debate, the goal is to persuade the opponent of the justice or correctness of one's cause. The process of conflict resolution and management, ideally, is closest to a debate, just as wars are fights, although conflict resolution bears some aspects of a "game" as well. However, even diplomacy and negotiations involve elaborate rules and, not uncommonly, the threat of fighting as well.

Although ways of fighting have changed through history, basic techniques of negotiation scarcely have. Usually, negotiators have two things that they can offer: threats and promises. These can be backed up by varying degrees of good or ill will and a continuum from blind trust to ironclad verification. Negotiations, however, can only succeed if there is a set of outcomes that each party prefers to no agreement. Admittedly, dispute participants (especially if they are governments) occasionally engage in negotiations just to appear virtuous. But there is good reason to think that, in most cases at least, a negotiated settlement is preferred over either a failure to agree or the use of violence to force an outcome. The trick is to find a peaceful settlement acceptable to both sides.

Techniques for successful negotiations—often involving trained third parties—can contribute greatly to the peaceful resolution of conflicts. We must also consider the phenomenon of conflict resolution and transformation more generally, not only in the international sphere but also with respect to domestic antagonisms and even interpersonal as well as intrapsychic efforts at resolving conflict.

# Human Conflict

Within the human realm, a conflict may occur within a person, between two or more individuals or groups, or within or between large social organisations, most notably nation states.[1] Hence there are many different kinds of conflicts, ranging from the intrapsychic to the international.

Conflicts within and between individuals may occur for a number of reasons. As noted earlier, for Sigmund Freud, we are torn between our innate drives for love and self-preservation on the one hand and aggression and destruction on the other hand. Contemporary conflict theorist Johan Galtung tends to eschew such overarching explanations, instead claiming that human conflicts are largely due to a real or perceived incompatibility, or contradiction, between conflicting parties' attitudes, behaviors, interests, needs, positions, and/or values.

## Modes of Conflict Analysis

There are two dominant, and sometimes "conflicting," models of addressing conflicts: the "realist" and "peace oriented" perspectives.

From a "realist," "security-oriented" perspective, actions taken to address conflicts include such bellicose measures as wars, espionage, and sanctions, often in tandem with diplomacy. The goal is to defend one's perceived interests and to defeat or "neutralize" the "enemy," preferably by "managing" a conflict so that it does not spiral out of control, and by "resolving" it through a mixture of violent and nonviolent means, such as mediation, arbitration, cease-fires, and treaties. The Cuban Missile Crisis is a classic example of international conflict *management*. But since the underlying reasons for the conflict are not addressed or resolved, hostilities may resume at a later time.

If conflicts are not addressed or "managed" at an early stage in the dispute, they may escalate, to the degree that the conflicting parties will deploy whatever means they choose, including threats, legal reprisals, and direct or indirect violence, to "defeat" the other and "win" the conflict. This happens frequently between such parties as couples in the process of a nasty divorce, as well as between nations (India and Pakistan, for example), existing states and nascent nation-states (Israel and Palestine), and states and nonstate adversaries (the United States and al-Qaeda).

A peace-oriented perspective, in contrast, stresses the *prevention* rather than the management of conflicts, and *nonviolent* conflict transformation as the preferred means of conflict resolution. Since violence rarely works to control violence, nonviolent strategies and tactics must be utilized if conflicting parties are to transform their attitudes and behavior from enmity to tolerance. Gandhi's campaign for Indian independence, Martin Luther King's struggle for civil rights in the United States, and the "Velvet Revolution" of 1989 are examples of nonviolent conflict resolution.

Conflict appears to be inherent in human relations and is therefore unlikely to be eliminated. Hence, the mission of nonviolent conflict transformers and peace workers is not to end conflict, but as peace and conflict researcher Kenneth Boulding said, to "make the world safe for conflict." This means to reduce the likelihood that social/political conflict erupts into violent combat and war.

## Conflict Outcomes and Solutions

Conflicts have different outcomes. One side may "win" and the other "lose" (but not be eliminated), as in divorce settlements involving contested assets or child custody, or in many international disputes. Both sides may withdraw temporarily from the conflict, but because one or both parties may not believe its interests/needs were satisfactorily addressed, they might resume the conflict later. Many international conflicts fit this profile, and historians argue that World War II resulted in part from the failure to address successfully long-simmering resentments by Germany against the "victors" of World War I. Israel's ongoing conflicts with its Arab neighbors and many insurrections and "terrorist" actions against governments, especially against occupying powers, also conform to this model.

A conflict may infrequently result in the real or perceived total elimination of the "enemy," as with the destruction of the Nazi regime in 1945. In contrast, the Sri Lankan government, for example, claims to have "eliminated" the Tamil Tigers as of 2011. But since the Tamil people assuredly have *not* been eliminated, it remains to be seen whether the Sinhalese-Tamil (Buddhist-Hindu) conflict in Sri Lanka will persist, possibly breaking out in another, less lethal form. This situation provides a model for appreciating the difference between mere conflict management and true conflict resolution.

## Negotiating "Solutions" to Conflict via Peacemaking

It is important to realize how often we negotiate solutions to conflict, typically on the interpersonal level. Disagreements among siblings over who gets to sit in a given chair, within families over what television program to watch, or between coworkers over whether or not to have an office party—such disputes are typically resolved, nearly always short of violence. This highlights the many routes available for dealing with conflict; it is something we do every day.

And yet, one of the most pervasive myths of our current culture of militarism is that war and preparation for war are "natural," unavoidable phenomena, whereas peace and conflict resolution strategies are hopelessly unrealistic. We are surrounded with subliminal messages to the effect that peacemaking is an impossible dream, whereas war making—or at best deterrence or a kind of armed standoff—is the only realistic option. Hence, it is important to affirm and make visible the peacemaking that happens all around us, most of the time. Often, peacemaking receives society's attention only when it takes place at the highest government level.

# Summitry

In ancient times, leaders were themselves often renowned warriors and, not uncommonly, would meet person-to-person, to settle their disputes via individual combat. At other times, at least according to folklore, champions would be selected, one from each side, to fight it out: The classic example is David versus Goliath. Today, leaders are more likely to be political figures, and their meetings are intended to help establish or cement relationships or to engage in personal resolution of disputes between their countries (while also playing to their domestic constituencies).

When the leaders of two major groups meet, this is referred to as a summit meeting. There have been many; for example, President Richard Nixon's meeting with Chinese leader Mao Tse-tung in 1972 was especially dramatic, as was Egyptian president Sadat's journey to Jerusalem and his meeting with Israeli prime minister Begin, which led to the Camp David Accords of 1978–1979. In both cases, the states involved had previously been bitter enemies, so antagonistic, in fact, that they were not even communicating with each other. Hence, the mere fact that political leaders were meeting and talking amicably sent a powerful signal about the possibilities of peaceful coexistence.

During the Cold War, the term *summit* was largely reserved for meetings between leaders of the United States and the Soviet Union. Here, too, it was widely thought that if only the leaders could meet and talk over their disagreements, as intelligent and concerned human beings, peace between longtime adversaries might be possible. Unfortunately, there is no reason to expect this. In some cases, summit meetings were merely cosmetic, perhaps improving the international atmosphere but offering few if any specific changes, thereby often disappointing those who had hoped for more. At other times, minor progress was achieved, largely by signing agreements that the diplomats had laboriously worked out in advance: a 1972 summit between Richard Nixon and Leonid Brezhnev, for example, at which the Strategic Arms Limitation Talks (SALT I) agreement was signed or a 1987 meeting in Washington, D.C., between Mikhail Gorbachev and Ronald Reagan at which the Intermediate Range Nuclear Forces (INF) agreement was signed. More recently, American president Barack Obama and former Russian president Dmitri Medvedev signed the new Strategic Arms Reduction Treaty (START) in April 2010 in Prague.

Occasionally, however, summit meetings made things worse, resulting either in feelings of ill will or in dangerous misjudgments by one or both parties. For example, a summit meeting between John F. Kennedy and Nikita Khrushchev in Vienna during 1961 appears to have been a personal embarrassment for Kennedy (who was younger and less experienced than his Soviet counterpart), and it led to Khrushchev's inaccurate estimation that the U.S. president could be pushed around, which in turn set the stage for the Cuban Missile Crisis. It also evidently contributed to Kennedy's determination that he would be especially tough in the future.

With the end of the Cold War, meetings between world leaders have rarely carried the same emotional freighting as in the past and have generally received less public attention. Also contributing to their lowered visibility is the fact that such meetings have become more frequent, at least on a multilateral basis, with regular convocations of the world's major industrial states (the so-called Group of Eight, which includes Russia), as well as frequent trade and other ministerial meetings.

Summit meetings notwithstanding, it isn't necessarily true that closer relations and greater communication among world leaders will make war less likely. Kaiser Wilhelm of Germany and Czar Nicholas of Russia, for example, were first cousins, and on the very eve of World War I, they sent each other a flurry of telegrams signed "Willy" and "Nicky"! Summit meetings and personal relationships, in short, can be helpful, but they can also cause problems, depending on the issue and the personal dynamic between the leaders, or provide only an illusion of warmth and mutual understanding.

Probably the most dramatic example of successful summitry occurred during the Camp David meetings in 1978, which resulted in a historic agreement signed in 1979. Hosted by then–U.S. President Jimmy Carter, who served as facilitator, Israel's prime minister Menachem Begin and Egypt's president Anwar Sadat spent 13 days at the rustic presidential retreat in Maryland. The meetings took place without the formalities, protocols, and rigid negotiations characteristic of traditional summit meetings or bargaining sessions. Rather, there was no formal agenda, no intrusive press, and—perhaps as a result—some highly emotional interchanges. Although the Camp David meetings did not solve all Middle East problems, or even all areas of Egyptian-Israeli dispute, they did turn out to be highly productive and led to the first example of diplomatic recognition between Israel and one of its Arab neighbors, as well as a treaty.

The result has been a historic peace—although a "cold" one—between Israel and Egypt, followed in the late 1990s by a similar treaty between Israel and Jordan.

# A Brief History of Diplomacy

Until recently, diplomats were usually drawn from the same social and economic class (upper), and in most cases they spoke the same language, literally: French. Although there is a long history of monarchs sending ambassadors to the courts of other rulers, it is generally agreed that the current system of diplomatic protocol was established by Cardinal Richelieu, the chief minister—some would say, chief manipulator—of the early-17th-century French king, Louis XIII. Although there has always been a peculiar stiffness to official diplomatic discourse and protocol, such formalities have evolved over many years so as to enhance precision of communication and, whenever possible, to reduce the chances that personalities will interfere with formal and goal-oriented communication between governments.

Historically, ambassadors were the personal representatives of one sovereign to the court of another, and this polite fiction is still maintained, even in the case of democracies: Upon their arrival, ambassadors typically present their credentials to the head of state of the host country. In modern times, electronic communication has largely supplanted the individual diplomat when it comes to the establishment of important international agreements, but the role of person-to-person contact, even at the highest levels, remains important.

Ironically, states communicate with each other least frequently and least clearly during war—precisely when such communication is likely to be the most needed. At such times, and occasionally when interactions become severely strained during peacetime, diplomatic relations are broken off, and each state recalls its ambassador. Otherwise, officials are available to correct possible misunderstandings, to clarify positions, and, when all else fails, to simply buy time, occasionally in the hope that tense situations will eventually blow over.

A point of contention is whether the prospect of negotiations itself should be used as a diplomatic lever. Most governments are adamant about not negotiating with "terrorists," a position that initially might appear reasonable insofar as doing so appears to be rewarding violent and unacceptable behavior. On the other hand, by foreclosing the option of negotiations, this stance runs the risk of foreclosing a potential avenue of nonviolent conflict resolution. During the administration of George W. Bush, the United States, in addition, refused to "sit down at the table" with the governments of North Korea or Iran, although it did participate in multiparty talks. However, this posture proved notably unavailing and was to some extent replaced by an eventual willingness to discuss policy differences (especially regarding nuclear proliferation) with North Korea and Iran.

To some extent, summit meetings—especially if conducted one-to-one—are seen as conveying political legitimacy. For most people devoted to peace, diplomacy and negotiation are not synonymous with capitulation; nor are they favors extended to the other side. Rather, they are important components of any serious attempts to resolve conflict short of violence. As we shall see, diplomacy has nonetheless failed in many cases; however, there have also been successes.

## Some Diplomatic Successes in Averting War

In 1987, Greece and Turkey exchanged threats over Turkish plans to prospect for oil near several islands in the eastern Aegean that were under Greek ownership but very close to the Turkish mainland. These two states have a long history of antagonism and warfare: Greece was once dominated by Turkey, as part of the Ottoman Empire, and the two states have engaged in threats as well as fighting over the fate of the Greek and Turkish communities on the island of Cyprus. Tensions have gradually been reduced, however, even though the Greek part of Cyprus is now part of the European Union and the long-term status of the Turkish enclave is still uncertain. This is at least in part because both sides fear antagonizing their NATO ally, the United States, with the possible cutoff of military aid that might ensue.

In many cases, multilateral diplomacy has negotiated an end to fighting—for example, termination of the wars in Bosnia, Kosovo, southern Sudan, and Northern Ireland. It may be overly optimistic, however, to consider these straightforward diplomatic successes, since they may also be examples of diplomatic failures that resulted in war, followed eventually by diplomacy-assisted termination once one or both sides tired of the war's costs. Even in this minimal sense, however, diplomacy can be profoundly useful, as a means whereby warring sides eventually achieve peace.

## Some Diplomatic Failures

Sometimes, diplomats make things worse. Perceived slights among rulers and diplomats have occasionally endangered the peace. Late in the 17th century, France and Spain nearly came to blows when a coach carrying the Spanish ambassador to England cut in front of the French ambassador on a London street. In 1819, the Dey of Algiers, angered about the failure of the French government to make good on a debt, struck the French consul three times with a fly swatter. This insult precipitated a naval blockade by the French and ultimately served as an excuse for what became the longtime occupation of Algeria.

Even at its best, diplomacy breeds a certain deviousness and social artifice that most people find laughable, if not downright unpleasant. During the protracted negotiations leading to the Treaty of Paris after Napoleon's defeat, the famed Austrian diplomat Metternich was told that the Russian ambassador had died. Story has it that he responded, "Ah, is that true? I wonder what he meant by that."

Efforts at diplomatic clarification sometimes backfire: For example, in late July 1914, Sir Edward Grey, the British foreign secretary, warned Kaiser Wilhelm that if a general war occurred, Britain would enter it on the side of France and Russia. Rather than deter Germany (as Grey had intended), this was seen as a threat, which made Wilhelm more belligerent, convinced of a plot against him by the Triple Entente.

Sometimes, statements by diplomats, intended for domestic consumption, have had serious international repercussions. In 1950, for example, Secretary of State Dean Acheson gave a speech in which he outlined the United States' "defense perimeter" in the Pacific; this appeared to exclude Korea, which gave the North Korean government the false impression that the United States would not forcibly resist an invasion of South Korea. Shortly before invading Kuwait, Iraqi leader Saddam Hussein met with the U.S. ambassador to Iraq, who responded to a query by stating that the United States "takes no position" on Iraqi territorial claims to Kuwait. This was taken by the Iraqis, incorrectly, to mean that the United States would not become involved in the event of an Iraqi invasion. Of course, the United States did intervene and forcibly ejected Iraq from Kuwait.

Sometimes, ironically, war can be made more intense by the fact that diplomats are striving to bring the fighting to a close, as each side seeks to make gains on the battlefield that might influence the ultimate peace settlement. Middle East diplomats noticed that the proposals put forward by Count Bernadotte, the first UN negotiator sent to settle the 1948 Israeli-Arab War, closely reflected the immediate battlefield situation; as a result, both sides paid less attention to him and put more effort into achieving military gains so as to influence the negotiations in their favor. During the end stages of the Bosnian War in the early 1990s, all sides tended to initiate offensives, hoping to improve their bargaining position in the eventual postwar settlement. For this reason, it is generally recommended that the first step in negotiating peace is an immediate cease-fire.

On occasion, diplomacy has even been consciously employed by leaders eager to initiate war. The most famous example of this was the Ems Telegram, which was craftily edited by Prussian chancellor Otto von Bismarck to make it appear to the French that Kaiser Wilhelm was snubbing the French ambassador. In Bismarck's own words, he "waved a red flag in front of the Gallic bull." The bull charged, as Bismarck had calculated, and ran into a Prussian steel wall in the ensuing Franco-Prussian War. In this case, Bismarck could have simply declared war on France, but he wanted to goad the French into appearing to be the aggressor.

Before the second half of the 19th century, European diplomacy often served to make peace in ways that tended to avoid excessive humiliation of the loser, so as not to foment grievances that would lead promptly to additional war. Some territory would be transferred; fortresses would be surrendered and frontiers adjusted; indemnities might be required and reparations exacted. But more recently, especially with national wars replacing sovereign's wars, concessions have often been cause for lasting resentment, which have in turn sowed the seeds for subsequent wars. Thus, France's loss of Alsace and Lorraine during the Franco-Prussian War—and its national fervor for reclaiming these lost regions—did much to bring about World War I. The German anger and humiliation associated with the Treaty of Versailles (which ended that war) led in part to World War II. By contrast, the diplomatic settlements at the end of World War II, although imperfect, have had greater staying power.

Critics often note, however, that diplomacy is often not so much a means of avoiding war as it is an adjunct to national hostilities. "Diplomacy is a disguised war, in which States seek to gain by barter and intrigue, by the cleverness of wits, the objectives which they would have to gain more clumsily by means of war," wrote Randolph Bourne. "Diplomacy is used while the States are recuperating from conflicts in which they have exhausted themselves. It is the wheedling and the bargaining of the worn-out bullies as they rise from the ground and slowly restore their strength to begin fighting again."[2]

Accordingly, let us turn to the relationships between diplomacy and military force.

# Diplomacy and Military Force

According to one influential viewpoint, diplomacy is only as effective as the military power available to each side, the threats that underwrite courteous diplomatic interchanges. "Diplomacy without armaments," according to Frederick the Great, "is like music without instruments."

There have been many examples of diplomatic intimidation, some successful, some not. Shortly after taking office in 1992, President Clinton sent diplomatic representatives to the Haitian colonels who had kept democratically elected Jean-Bertrand Aristide from assuming power in that country. At the same time, a military invasion force was readied; only when reports reached Port-au-Prince that U.S. aircraft were en route did the junta agree to step down . . . peacefully.

Also during the Clinton administration, after years in which NATO dithered and thousands of Bosnians died, the Serbs of Yugoslavia and Bosnia finally agreed to a settlement of the Bosnian War only after NATO actually initiated bombing of Serb positions. This is not a precedent that gladdens the hearts of peace advocates, but its reality must be acknowledged. Serbs claim, however, that they had already planned their exit from Bosnia and that the bombing did less to hurt

Serb forces than to kill civilians, including Chinese diplomats, whose embassy in Belgrade was severely damaged by NATO bombs. (On the other hand, the lack of U.S. and Western intervention in Rwanda during its genocidal civil war in 1994, leading to the murder of perhaps 800,000 Rwandans, is often cited as a major failure of military resolve, especially by former president Clinton himself.)

Otto von Bismarck, the 19th-century chancellor of Prussia and architect of German unification, was hardly a pacifist. Yet, while he freely employed military force, he also understood its limitations. During the Austro-Prussian War, for example, in 1866 the Austrians were badly defeated at the Battle of Königgrätz, far more soundly than anyone had expected. At this point, political pressure within Prussia called for a wider victory over Austria, including the dismemberment of the Austrian Empire itself. But Bismarck insisted on limiting Prussian demands to the provinces of Schleswig and Holstein, thereby preventing war with France and possibly Russia and Britain. As the arch-diplomat Metternich once put it, "Diplomacy is the art of avoiding the appearance of victory."

In contrast to Bismarck's sensitivity to the dangers of pushing one's victories too far, during the Korean War General Douglas MacArthur and President Harry Truman underestimated the costs of similarly pressing the North Koreans and Chinese. After a surprise landing of U.S. forces at Inchon resulted in dramatic gains in the autumn of 1950, UN (mostly U.S.) troops advanced deeply into North Korea. This led in turn to large-scale Chinese involvement and massive bloodshed on both sides, ending 3 years later in a stalemate, which could have been achieved with much less suffering had the Western leaders shown greater farsightedness and restraint. The lesson of Königgrätz—that military restraint can often lead to greater diplomatic and long-term success—had not been learned.

Another kind of bargaining has occasionally been useful in diminishing levels of violence. Often termed "tacit bargaining," this entails that conflicting parties reach agreements without actually spelling out the terms of the understanding. Because threats are strongly implied in such tacit bargains, they have most commonly taken place in close association with conditions of war or other violence. For example, during the Korean War, a tacit bargain existed on both sides: The Chinese would refrain from attacking U.S. aircraft carriers, supply lines, and bases in Japan, while similarly there would be no bombing of North Korean supply lines in China. In the Middle East today, there is another tacit bargain: Israel will not flaunt its stockpile of nuclear weapons, and Arab states will not repeatedly and publicly call attention to them. To some extent, this understanding serves the interests of both sides: The Israelis would rather not acknowledge their nuclear capability, and some Arab states would rather not have to respond publicly to its existence. This example is not particularly satisfying to students of peace, since it involves at best a kind of standoff. Skilled diplomats and negotiators generally hope for better.

# Diplomacy and *Realpolitik*

In *Poetry and Truth,* the great German writer Goethe acknowledged, "If I had to choose between justice and disorder, on the one hand, and injustice and order, on the other, I would always choose the latter." Many others—notably Metternich in the 19th century and one of the 20th century's best-known students of Metternich, Henry Kissinger—followed suit and made social and political stability a goal in itself, often tolerating repression and social injustice in the pursuit of a state's self-interest, so-called *Realpolitik*.

Hans Morgenthau,[3] one of the 20th century's most influential advocates of *Realpolitik* in international relations, proposed numerous rules for diplomacy, which, he hoped, would help states resolve conflicts short of war while also pursuing their own self-interest in international affairs. Morgenthau's rules included the following:

- Do not be a crusader. Avoid "nationalistic universalism," the insistence that the goals of one's own nation are appropriate as universal goals for all nations. As the 19th-century French Foreign Minister Talleyrand put it, *pas trop de zèle* ("not too much zeal"). Such excessive zeal was shown in the enthusiasm of U.S. National Security Council aides to assist the *contra* rebels in Nicaragua, even at the cost of illegal activities and, ultimately, at great harm to U.S. influence and prestige. Ditto for neo-conservative enthusiasm about overthrowing Saddam Hussein and "remaking the Middle East."
- Employ a narrow definition of vital national interests—namely, the survival and maintenance of socioeconomic well-being. Morgenthau emphasized that in the nuclear age, states cannot afford war—or the risk of war—for anything short of their most supreme security interests.
- Be willing to compromise on all national interests that are not truly vital. Of course, there is disagreement about what is "vital."
- Try to see the other side's point of view, recognizing that all participants have vital national interests, and no one should be pushed into compromising them.
- Distinguish between what is real and what is illusory; do not allow considerations of honor, credibility, or prestige to override issues of real national security.
- Never paint yourself into a corner; always retain avenues of retreat (or advance).
- Do not allow an ally (especially a vulnerable one) to make decisions for you. As a corollary, do not allow yourself to be drawn into someone else's fight.
- Always keep military factors subordinate to political ones.
- "Neither surrender to popular passions nor disregard them."

Following Napoleon's defeat in 1815, Western Europe entered into a period of relative stability, based in large part on the system established by the victors at the Congress of Vienna. Some of this "success" was because all the major players accepted the agreed system as legitimate, and everyone felt about equally rewarded and equally slighted by the outcome.

In contrast to Morgenthau's conception of value-free diplomacy is the notion that issues of right and wrong lie at the heart of international disputes. Unfortunately, states generally find it easier to look dispassionately at conflicts in which they are not themselves embroiled; once physically and emotionally involved, the process of moralizing often becomes intense, leaving only victory as a tolerable outcome. U.S. president Woodrow Wilson urged the participants of World War I to seek a "peace without victory" and "a peace between equals" . . . until the United States entered that war. Then, even the American Peace Society declared, "This is not a war of territory, of trade routes or of commercial concerns, but of eternal principles. There can be no end of war until after the collapse of the existing German government."

Historically, many of the crucial aspects of diplomacy have been carried out largely in secret. Secrecy was subsequently blamed, by many, for the errors and miscalculations that led to

World War I, and President Woodrow Wilson accordingly called for "open covenants openly arrived at." On the other hand, although secret diplomacy sounds inherently unpalatable, especially to a democratic society, it remains true that when conducted in public, diplomatic negotiating isn't usually conducive to compromise. Each side fears appearing soft or a dupe and is inclined to play to domestic public opinion, making arguments and advancing proposals that may be politically popular, even if it knows that other solutions may be fairer and even more desirable. So, there is much to be said for diplomacy that is carried out not so much "in secret" as under a mutual understanding that not every offer and counteroffer will be leaked to the waiting world. It may not be coincidental that some of the noteworthy diplomatic successes of recent years, such as the Oslo Accords that brought a measure of peace (or, at least, hope) to the Middle East, the Dayton Accords that ended the Bosnian War, and the termination of fighting in Kosovo, all followed secret negotiations.

# Track II Diplomacy

Since the late 1970s, there has been growing interest in so-called Track II diplomacy, also sometimes called unofficial or "encounter group" diplomacy. Track II diplomacy is unofficial in that it need not involve formal negotiations between representatives of different states; rather, it revolves around relatively informal interactions among representatives of opposing groups. It contributes largely to laying the social and political groundwork needed in order for government leaders to act. It also can be seen as representing a way of solving problems independent of the nation-states themselves.

In Track II diplomacy, people are brought together, typically in the presence of an experienced third party or facilitator, for the purpose of achieving mutual understanding, exploring their commonalities as well as differences, and establishing interpersonal relationships despite the political disagreements between their "home" groups.

This has been attempted, sometimes with considerable success, in groups of Catholics and Protestants from Northern Ireland, Greek and Turkish Cypriots, Israelis and Palestinians, and Tutsis and Hutus in East Africa. Typically, the individuals in question are relatively influential in their communities: doctors, lawyers, professors, journalists, midrange politicians, and military officials. Success is never guaranteed, and there is typically substantial distrust and, often, numerous minor incidents, especially at the outset. Over time, however, most of these "encounter groups" have produced very positive results and have increasingly involved students participating in international exchange programs.

# Third-Party Involvement

Consider a married couple who has been squabbling, for example, over how to divide household chores. Left to themselves, the partners may be unable to reach agreement, in part because each individual sees only his or her viewpoint. Moreover, each may hesitate to give in, even partially, for fear that any concession might be seen as an admission that he or she has a weaker case. Similar deadlocks arise in other situations of conflict, such as disputes between labor and management. In such cases, disputes between contending parties—whether individuals, organizations, or states—are sometimes more readily resolved if a third party is brought in. For domestic disputes, marital counselors may be helpful; for labor disputes, trained mediators or arbitrators, often provided by the government, might work well. A similar process can apply to international disputes.

An outside expert may be called in to help clarify the issues, resolve misunderstanding, and suggest areas of compromise and common ground. A third party—unbiased and trusted by both sides—can sometimes help reach agreements for which everyone may be grateful but which (for a variety of reasons) neither party could suggest or even accept if it was proposed by the other. Imagine, for example, that two adjacent states are disputing the location of the border in a strip of land 100 kilometers wide, between them. If A proposes placing the border right down the middle, giving 50 kilometers to each side, B might use this "opening" to bargain further, "splitting the difference" between them and proposing a border so that B gets 75 kilometers and A, 25 kilometers. In such a case, the side that first proposes a compromise finds itself at a disadvantage. One obvious solution, therefore, is for a third state, C, to propose independently that A and B agree to 50 kilometers each. (Unfortunately, international disputes are rarely this simple, given historical backgrounds, social factors, political passions, military alliances, and economic considerations, as well as such geographic factors as marshes, rivers, or mountains, and so forth). It is also important to bear in mind that disputes always occur on at least two levels: the specific issue under dispute and also the underlying questions of who wins, who is more powerful, and what this portends for subsequent interactions.

## Go-Betweens

There are several ways in which third parties can be helpful to disputants. First, they can serve as go-betweens, providing what is known as their "good offices," which may simply involve making a meeting place available on neutral ground. The Scandinavian states, as well as Austria and Switzerland, have often provided this service; when in doubt about a "neutral ground," international diplomats typically meet in Geneva. Go-betweens can also be crucial when participants on one side (e.g., the Arab states excepting Egypt and Jordan) do not officially recognize the existence or legitimacy of another (Israel). In the early 1990s, the Norwegian foreign minister was influential in facilitating the Oslo Accords between Israel and the Palestinians, and in 1999, the president of Finland served as go-between when NATO forces and Yugoslavian president Slobodan Milošević ended the war in Kosovo.

Of course, when the third party is a high-ranking representative of a major power, he or she presumably does not merely act as a messenger but also can engage in various forms of arm twisting—for example, threatening to cut off economic or military aid unless some proposed compromises are accepted. This further suggests why some forms of diplomacy are best conducted in secret: It may be politically unacceptable, for example, for a state to appear to buckle under such pressure, although it may be better for everyone concerned if it does so. At the same time, powerful countries are able to "sweeten the deal," as with the United States providing billions of dollars in aid to both Israel and Egypt in the aftermath of the Camp David agreements. The promise of similar assistance also underlines the prospects of further Arab-Israeli peace deals.

Third parties, if they have the respect of the contenders, can also serve a valuable role as "fact finders," ascertaining, for example, whether a disputed border was crossed, how many political prisoners are held in specified jails, how large the military forces involved are, or what the economic situation is in a particular region. International organizations, notably the United Nations, have been especially helpful in this respect, establishing various "commissions of inquiry" to evaluate conflicting claims. In certain cases, basic facts are in dispute, but in others the disagreement is not over numbers or other data but rather over values—over not what is true but what is right.

## Mediation and Arbitration

Aside from providing a place to meet, facilitating communication, and occasionally twisting a few arms, third parties can basically fulfill two diplomatic functions: mediation and arbitration. Mediators make suggestions that might be agreeable to both sides. Like marriage counselors, mediators try to resolve disputes, but adherence to their suggestions is voluntary. By contrast, in arbitration both sides agree in advance to accept the judgment of the arbitrator. Mediation therefore involves less of a threat to sovereignty; it is accordingly less radical and more often acceptable to contending states. A third procedure, adjudication, involves making decisions with reference to international law.

There is nothing new in the practices of mediation and arbitration. They were especially frequent and successful in Europe during the late Middle Ages, from about the 13th to the 15th centuries. The success of third-party involvement at this time was apparently due to several factors: Family ties among diverse political leaders were frequent (not uncommonly, heads of state were cousins or even closer). The economic costs of war were widely recognized as exceptionally high, and local treasuries often teetered on the edge of bankruptcy. Finally, a powerful third party was available to aid in the settling of disputes—namely, the Catholic Church and its emissaries.

Conflicting governments often face a dilemma: Even when a compromise is feasible, both sides want to project an image of power. Accordingly, the mediator or arbitrator can suggest something that, privately, both sides want but that neither is willing to propose. During the Geneva Conference of 1955—which formally ended the French occupation of Indochina—Britain, China, and the Soviet Union mediated between France and its primary Indochinese adversary, the Viet Minh. In this case, as with many others, it can certainly be argued that mediation did not resolve the dispute; it only postponed it. But even apparent failures may sometimes be helpful: As Winston Churchill once noted, "Jaw, jaw, jaw is better than war, war, war." Sometimes, moreover, there can be a real advantage in postponing war, if, over time, passions cool and peaceful solutions eventually become possible. And sometimes, of course, mediation is altogether successful. American president Theodore Roosevelt, for example, won a Nobel Peace Prize for his successful mediation between Russia and Japan, which ended the Russo-Japanese War.

When both sides agree to abide by the judgment of a third party, we say that the dispute has been submitted to arbitration. One of the most important historical cases is the so-called *Alabama* claim, known for a Confederate warship that had been purchased (illegally) in Britain, a neutral country, during the U.S. Civil War. The U.S. government subsequently demanded reparations for the damage done to U.S. shipping by the *Alabama* and other similar ships, and in 1872 both sides consented to arbitration. An independent panel eventually awarded the United States more than $15 million in damages, which Britain paid, thereby lowering tensions between the two countries. In fact, the now-close relationship between Britain and the United States can be counted as beginning with this successful arbitration.

# Negotiating Techniques for Resolving Conflict

Numerous techniques are available to arbitrators. One promising example is the so-called last best offer. Imagine two sides disagreeing over the amount of money to be paid for ownership of a disputed island. Rather than making offers and counteroffers, each side is told to give the arbitrator its last best offer, from which the arbitrator will choose the one that seems the most fair. The arbitrator cannot decide to split the difference, since this would only encourage each side to be intransigent. In the last-best-offer technique, by contrast, each side is nudged to be as conciliatory as possible, in hopes that its offer will be the one accepted.

## Resolution Versus Dominance

In 1964, conservative American policy analyst Fred Charles Iklé wrote an influential book titled *How Nations Negotiate.* It focused on how one nation (the United States) can prevail over the other side, concluding that a good negotiator must, above all, "maintain the will to win."[4]

This view would probably still be endorsed by the majority of diplomats and negotiators today. However, if negotiations are to help resolve conflict, rather than to become arenas for yet more, another perspective is needed, one that views negotiations as a means whereby contending parties seek to resolve their differences, not to prevail over each other. It suggests that to be fruitful, negotiations must be seen as non-zero sum solutions, interactions in which my gain is not necessarily balanced by your loss, or vice versa. It aims to achieve "win-win" solutions in which all sides are better off than they were before.

## Compromise

The most obvious and, in some cases, the most common negotiating technique is to compromise—that is, to reach an agreement that is in some sense intermediate between the demands of both sides. There are, however, several disadvantages to this method. For one, a compromise may leave both sides dissatisfied. In some cases, this may actually be desirable so that a "fair" decision may be defined—only somewhat tongue in cheek—as one that leaves everyone equally unhappy. This is happens because although the immediate conflict has been "managed," the underlying reasons for the conflict have not been addressed or resolved, thus increasing prospects for the conflict's resumption at a later time.

In some cases, in fact one side's claim may in fact be just and the other's unjust; in such a case, a compromise simply rewards the unjust side while penalizing the just one. Compromise assumes that both contenders are equally worthy so that "splitting the difference" between them will produce a fair settlement. But what if state A arbitrarily insists on imposing a 50% tariff upon all imports from state B but refuses to allow B to tax its imports? Clearly, a "compromise" that allows a 25% unilateral tariff would not be fair and is unlikely to be acceptable to state B.

In other cases, however, one side can "win" without the other "losing." For example, Franco-German relations were bedeviled through the first half of the 20th century by a dispute over ownership of the Saar region, a rich industrial sector of the Rhineland. Following World War I, occupation and mining rights to the Saar were ceded to France; French control was reasserted after World War II. But the region's population was (and still is) overwhelmingly German, and the governments in Paris and Bonn eventually cooperated to resolve this issue: After a plebiscite in 1955, France permitted the Saar to rejoin what was then West Germany. This negotiated agreement, in which France ostensibly "lost," served everyone well, since it proved to be a cornerstone for subsequent Franco-German cooperation and friendship.

## Positional Versus Integrative Bargaining

Compromises are often the outcome of what has been called "positional bargaining," in which each side stakes out a position and then holds to it. Positional bargaining clearly does not encourage flexibility and reasonable stances or attitudes; rather, intransigence is rewarded, and willingness to compromise (or even to suggest compromise) is penalized. Thus in positional bargaining, the participants are rewarded for staking out a "hard" position and sticking to it, and they are penalized, in turn, for being "soft." As a result, "good" bargainers are those who remain relatively intransigent—that is, who make it difficult or unlikely that an agreement will be reached, except on their terms.

Fortunately, there is another way, known as "integrative" or "principled negotiating." It tries, among other things, to separate the actual dispute from the underlying interests of each side. The goal is to focus on the latter and avoid getting bogged down in the former.

As negotiators Roger Fisher and William Ury recount,[5] consider the story of two sisters who quarreled over an orange; they decided, finally, to compromise, each getting one half. One sister then proceeded to squeeze her half for juice while the other used the peel from her portion to flavor a cake. By compromising—an old and honorable solution—they overlooked the integrative solution of giving one all the peel and the other all the juice.

Or imagine once again that two states disagree over a boundary. The real dispute may not be over territory as such but rather over one state's desire for access to certain transportation routes, along with worry by the other that granting such access would diminish its military security. In such a case, integrative bargaining would seek to identify the underlying issues and solve them directly, perhaps reaching an understanding in which the needs of both sides are integrated into one solution: for example, access to the desired transportation routes for an agreed annual fee, along with a bilateral treaty specifying strict limitations on the nature of the vehicles or number of personnel permitted to travel along them. (Earlier in this century, an agreement of this general sort permitted Palestinians living in the West Bank and the Gaza Strip to go back and forth, with Israel in between.)

Numerous tactics may be employed by negotiators seeking to bridge differences between contending sides. They include focusing on the shared interests of both sides, rather than on the demands as such, diminishing the role of personalities—that is separating the people from the problem—and "fractionating" the conflict—that is separating a dispute into resolvable and intractable components and then working on the former in the hope of building confidence between the antagonists before tackling the latter. Such tactics also contribute to a process of confidence building, which increases the probability that more difficult issues will be solved in the future. In fact, researchers in this area have become increasingly interested in enumerating possible confidence-building measures (CBMs) as better than ICBMs at keeping the peace. The idea is that having made some degree of progress, disputants will likely try all the harder for additional success and be less inclined to resort to violence.

Certain disputes—such as the story of the oranges—have a high "integrative potential" in that they inherently lend themselves to agreements that leave all parties entirely satisfied. Others are more difficult, as when, for example, buyer and seller disagree over the price of a house. Even here, however, there is room for integrative agreements: modifications in the interest rate, the date of occupancy, the amount of principal to be paid off by certain dates, and so on. In such cases, it may be possible to integrate the interests of both sides, essentially by reaching agreement on other dimensions aside from those initially in dispute (in this case, the purchase price).

# Methods of Integrative Bargaining

Let us now examine five different methods[6] by which integrative agreements might be reached, taking as an example a hypothetical dispute between a husband and wife over where to spend their 2-week vacation: The wife wants to go to the seashore, the husband to the mountains. One solution is to compromise and spend 1 week at each; they would like, however, to find some more satisfactory settlement.

## 1. Expanding the Pie

Sometimes, solutions can be achieved by increasing the amount of a resource in short supply. Perhaps the couple could arrange to take 4 weeks of vacation, thereby spending 2 weeks at each location. This is not as utopian as it may seem, since expanding the pie need not necessarily involve getting something for nothing. Thus, if they value their vacation enough, it might be possible, for example, to work overtime during the rest of the year so as to pay for it. For such solutions to work, however, each party must not find the other's preferred outcome to be aversive; that is, it could work if neither has an intrinsic objection to the other's preference but simply a stronger desire for his or her own choice. In our example, the husband must be able to tolerate going to the seashore, and the wife to the mountains. Solutions of this sort are largely based on efforts to help each side get what it wants and to do so by increasing the amount of a limited resource (time, money, land, people, security, hard currency, and so on).

## 2. Nonspecific Compensation

In this case, one party "gives in" but is repaid in some other way. The husband, for example, may agree to go to the seashore but only if he is relieved of housecleaning chores for the next 4 months. By extension, a country may permit a neighbor to flood its markets with exported goods if the exporting country agrees to provide a certain number of jobs for citizens of the importing country. Solutions of this sort require information about what is particularly valued by both parties and what one party may be able (and willing) to provide to another in return for getting its way. An important factor is whether some form of compensation exists that may be of low cost to the donor and high value to the recipient: Perhaps the wife doesn't particularly mind doing the husband's share of the housecleaning, at least for a few months, and perhaps the exporting country actually needs the labor skills of the importer.

## 3. Logrolling

If both parties differ on issues within the main ones under dispute, and if they differ in their priorities regarding these issues, the possibility exists for creative "logrolling," which is, in a sense, a variant of nonspecific compensation. For example, perhaps the husband-wife disagreement over vacations also involves differences of opinion about the preferred accommodations. Let us say that the wife favors simple, rustic beach cottages, whereas the husband is looking forward to an elegant mountain resort. Perhaps, then, the husband will be quite happy going to the seashore, so long as the wife agrees that they stay in a fancy seaside resort. For successful solutions based on logrolling, it helps to identify potential concessions and especially to ask, "Are some of my low-priority issues of high priority to the other?"

## 4. Cost Cutting

Solutions based on cost cutting are those in which one party essentially "wins" but the costs to the other party are reduced or eliminated. Thus, cost-cutting solutions are more one-sided than those discussed above but are nonetheless feasible and potentially stable if the side that "gives in" truly does not suffer any disadvantage from the agreement. In the case of the husband-wife vacation dispute, perhaps the husband had resisted going to the seashore because he feared being lonely and isolated while his wife was windsurfing; in this case, a cost-cutting solution— and one that could be entirely satisfactory to the husband—might be for the couple to agree to go to the seashore but to do so along with some of their friends, who could provide company for the husband.

## 5. Bridging

Bridging occurs when the two parties agree to a solution in which neither side wins or loses but rather both agree to a different option from whatever each originally favored. This solution must address the primary interests that actually underlie the specific issues in dispute. Thus, if the husband wanted to go to the mountains to hike and the wife wanted to go to the seashore for the sun, perhaps it would be possible to find a beach resort near hiking trails (or a vacation site where the mountains are dry and sunny). Successful bridging requires that the parties refocus their negotiations from an insistence on their *positions* to an examination of their underlying *interests*. Why are they pushing for their particular position? Is there some alternative outcome that would meet their actual needs? Is it really the mountains or the seashore that they want, or do these simply provide a means of achieving some other goal, such as sunshine, exercise, comfort, adventure, or simplicity?

# Additional Negotiating Techniques

Apparently trivial details can become surprisingly influential in the negotiating process. In some cases, for example, attention to the physical arrangement of participants may be important: Thus, it can even be helpful to seat the contenders on the same side of a table—opposite the negotiator, whose job is to articulate the disagreement—thereby literally facing the problem together, rather then contentiously facing each other. This can encourage both sides to cooperate rather than compete, to concentrate on solving the problem rather than defeating each other. In other cases, a wise conflict resolver will simply ignore uncooperative statements, rather than allowing them to derail an agreement. During the Cuban Missile Crisis, for example, the U.S. government received two communications from Nikita Khrushchev, Soviet premier at the time, one conciliatory and the other contentious. At Robert Kennedy's suggestion, the United States simply ignored the latter and responded to the former, thereby avoiding a possible nuclear conflict.

Clarity is generally a virtue; negotiated agreements can unravel or become a source of irritation when they are interpreted differently by the different parties. For example, Britain and the United States felt that at the Yalta Conference toward the end of World War II, the Soviet Union had agreed to allow pluralistic democracy in postwar Poland. Soviet diplomats (and some U.S. participants), on the other hand, argued differently. It is also possible, however, that if the expectations and intentions of each side had been spelled out in detail, an even greater falling out would have occurred. Part of the negotiator's art may therefore include recourse to equivocal and imprecise language. Nobel Prize–winning Canadian diplomat Lester Pearson noted that he has sometimes used language "not so much to record agreement as to conceal a disagreement" that it was desired to play down and which, it was hoped, would disappear in time.[7]

On the other hand, imprecise diplomatic language can impede action. An important current example is United Nations Resolution 242, passed after the Six Day War in 1967, in which Israel captured the Gaza Strip (from Egypt), the Golan Heights (from Syria), and the West Bank (from Jordan). Resolution 242 calls for a classic "land for peace" swap between Israel and its Arab neighbors, including "withdrawal of Israeli armed forces from territories occupied in the recent conflict." Note that the wording specifies "withdrawal . . . from territories" rather than "withdrawal . . . from *the* territories." As a result, diplomats have argued for more than 40 years about whether Israel is obliged to remove its forces from all of the occupied territories or just some.

To avoid misunderstandings, a negotiator might also request that each side state, as clearly as it can, the arguments of the other side. This can help build empathy, a deeper awareness and appreciation of the other's perspective and of the constraints felt by the other. (Remember that in serious disputes, each side is often intensely aware of the limitations on its own behavior while imagining that the opponent has great latitude; failure to reach agreement is then likely attributed—by each side—to the other's intransigence.)

Adequate empathy can lead to another helpful exercise, the "yesable proposition." In this case, each party to a dispute is asked to consider formulating a proposition that the *other* side is likely to accept. This is a subtle but important shift: In most cases, each side makes demands—indeed, the nature of the negotiating process encourages them to do so—that are likely to be outrageous and unacceptable. In the search for "yesable propositions," both sides are more likely to uncover shared interests.

In the course of seeking an agreement, it can be helpful to make proposals through an intermediary—often a low-ranking one—so that the proposals can be disowned if the other rejects them out of hand. This avoids the embarrassment that could result from acrimony and ridicule; by having the capability of denying that any such opening was ever made, either side may be more willing to make an initial attempt. For example, during the Cuban Missile Crisis, Premier Khrushchev chose a low-ranking Soviet embassy official to convey his proposal: removal of Soviet missiles from Cuba in return for a U.S. pledge not to invade that island. In addition, this message was sent to a news broadcaster rather than directly to U.S. officials.

Additional suggestions include the following: avoid ultimatums, do not impugn the motives of the other side, try to keep from playing to the crowds, be flexible but not spineless, avoid ad hominem (personal) attacks, avoid nonnegotiable ploys, and do not be so desperate for agreement that you sacrifice future peace for short-term palliatives.

What counts, in the long run, is reaching agreements without either side giving in or resorting to violence. Sometimes it may be possible, even desirable, to paper over disagreements so as to buy time for new events to unfold or for old disputes to grow stale. And, of course, there is no guarantee that all disputes can be resolved by negotiations. A positive outcome, for example, requires a degree of goodwill and a genuine desire to reach an agreement. It also requires willingness to "bargain in good faith." There have been cases in which good faith was not shown. For example, in 1939 the Soviet government was openly negotiating with Britain and France for a mutual defense pact against Nazi Germany while at the same time secretly organizing the now-infamous nonaggression pact that briefly allied Stalin with Hitler and paved the way for Germany's invasion of Poland. Similarly, Japanese diplomats were negotiating with their U.S. counterparts on December 7, 1941, when Japanese forces attacked Pearl Harbor. And when, in 1955, Soviet negotiators accepted U.S. disarmament proposals, complete with international verification procedures, the U.S. delegation promptly withdrew them . . . having never thought they would be accepted!

Fortunately, there is good reason to believe that such cases are exceptions. The desire for nonviolent resolution of conflicts appears to be strong and widespread—although it is always possible that governments make such claims, wishing to appear to be "on the side of the angels," while actually planning (even, sometimes, hoping) for a failure of negotiations in order to justify recourse to arms. Nonetheless, other factors—domestic opinion, international law, international organizations, the shared costs of violence—frequently combine to make nonviolent conflict resolution an attractive alternative to the use of force, so long as the participants (including the mediator if there is one) are both skillful and persistent.

## A FINAL NOTE ON CONFLICT RESOLUTION

Ultimately, belief in the feasibility of nonviolent conflict resolution—whether by diplomacy or negotiation, between two parties, or with the assistance of a mediator or arbitrator—is just that, an exercise of faith: faith in the underlying goodwill of most people and in their fundamental rationality. Such faith or trust may or may not be warranted. Certainly, the human species has long displayed a penchant for irrational acts, personal as well as collective. But skeptics might consider that the alternative—war—is usually no more rational.

Moreover, if it seems unrealistic to rely on the rationality of one's opponents, bear in mind that the fundamental peacekeeping strategy of great powers during the nuclear age—deterrence—relies precisely on just this kind of instrumental rationality and mutual dependence. It is much better, therefore, to employ tactics for the pursuit of conflict resolution than to resort to conflict prolongation or, worse yet, violence as the final arbiter of disputes.

## NOTES

1. See the special issue "Human Conflict: Winning the Peace." 2012. *Science*, Vol. 336, May 18.

2. Randolph S. Bourne. 1964. *War and the Intellectuals, Collected Essays 1915–1919*. New York: Harper & Row.

3. Hans Morgenthau. 1978. *Politics Among Nations*. New York: Knopf.

4. Fred Charles Iklé. 1964. *How Nations Negotiate.* New York: Harper & Row.

5. R. Fisher and W. Ury. 1981. *Getting to YES.* Boston: Houghton Mifflin.

6. Derived from Dean G. Pruitt. 1983. "Achieving Integrative Agreements in Negotiation." In M. H. Bazerman and R. Lewiski, eds., *Negotiating in Organizations.* Beverly Hills, CA: Sage.

7. Lester B. Pearson. 1949. *Diplomacy in the Nuclear Age.* Cambridge, MA: Harvard University Press.

## QUESTIONS FOR FURTHER REFLECTION

1. Identify some factors common to diplomatic successes in averting war; do the same for failures.

2. Analyze an interpersonal conflict you have experienced or observed. Who were the key actors; what were their interests and positions; which methods were used to "manage," "resolve," or "transcend" the conflict; and what were the outcomes for the parties involved? What, if anything, might have been done differently to produce a more "satisfactory" outcome?

3. Distinguish between positional and principled bargaining, giving some examples of each.

4. Choosing examples other than those in this chapter, illustrate the following negotiating techniques: expanding the pie, nonspecific compensation, logrolling, cost cutting, and bridging.

5. Apply Morgenthau's rules for diplomacy to a contemporary international conflict, such as the U.S.-led war in Iraq, to international attempts at stopping genocide in Darfur (Sudan), or to efforts to prevent Iran from acquiring nuclear weapons.

## SUGGESTIONS FOR FURTHER READING

D. G. Pruitt. 1981. *Negotiation Behavior.* New York: Academic Press.

G. R. Berridge. 2005. *Diplomacy: Theory and Practice*, 3rd ed. London: Palgrave Macmillan.

Oliver Ramsbotham, Tom Woodhouse, and Hugh Miall. 2005. *Contemporary Conflict Resolution.* Cambridge, UK: Polity.

Roger Fisher and William Ury. 1981. *Getting to YES.* Boston: Houghton Mifflin.

Roy J. Lewicki, David M. Saunders, and Bruce Barry. 2005. *Negotiation.* New York: McGraw-Hill.

Peter Wallensteen. 2012. *Understanding Conflict Resolution: War, Peace and the Global System,* 3rd ed. Los Angeles and London: SAGE.

# CHAPTER 13

# DISARMAMENT AND ARMS CONTROL

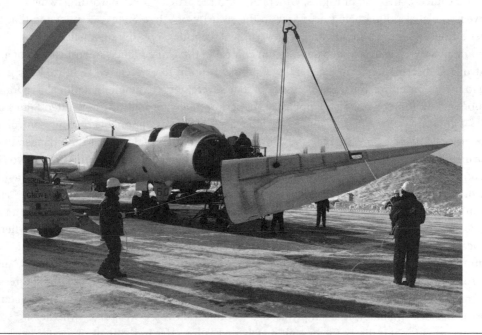

Workers in 2006 cutting off the nose of the last of Ukraine's "Backfire" bombers originally designed to carry nuclear weapons.

*Source:* © 2008 Getty Images.

> *You cannot simultaneously prevent and prepare for war.*
>
> —Albert Einstein

No one—not even the most ardent advocate of disarmament—claims that doing away with weapons will solve the problem of war. So long as the underlying causes of personal, group, and state conflict remain, and so long as human beings possess the capacity and inclination to resort to violence under certain circumstances, war will continue to haunt us. Nonetheless, advocates of peace often favor eliminating weapons or, at least, exercising strict control over them. In this chapter, we examine some aspects of disarmament and its close cousin, arms control.

# Different Visions of Disarmament

## Arms Control and Gun Control

There have been many different visions of disarmament. Perhaps the simplest is General and Complete Disarmament, or GCD (General = all countries; Complete = all weapons). Not surprisingly, there are problems with this proposal, one of which is how to define a weapon. Dynamite, for example, can make an effective weapon, but it is also used for seemingly legitimate commercial purposes, such as mining or demolition.

And what about firearms? Many citizens of the United States, for example, fervently maintain that "the right of the people to keep and bear arms shall not be infringed," as stated in Article 2 of the United States' Bill of Rights. Others point to the article's precise wording, which begins, "A well-regulated militia being necessary to the security of a free State . . . " inferring that this constitutional guarantee applies only to governmental entities, not to individuals.

In many ways, the heated debate over gun control in the United States mirrors issues of arms control and disarmament more generally: Opponents point to a perceived right (to keep guns) and to the supposedly comparable necessity of state sovereignty (to maintain national weaponry). Opponents of gun control also emphasize that crime rates are high in the United States and that "if guns are outlawed, only outlaws will have guns," just as opponents of arms control and disarmament point to the anarchy prevailing in international affairs and to the danger that a disarmed country will be at the mercy of aggressive armed states. At the same time, advocates of gun control emphasize that the easy availability of firearms contributes mightily to the high rate of violence, just as advocates of arms control and disarmament note the widespread "security dilemma," whereby the multilateral pursuit of military power tends to make everyone less secure. Opponents of gun control argue that "an armed society is a polite society," whereas advocates point to the rate at which members of armed societies tend to kill one another. Even as gun control opponents are fond of suggesting that "guns don't kill people; people do," arms control opponents emphasize that the problem is not military hardware but the aggressive designs of certain malevolent leaders . . . while to proponents of gun control as well as arms control and disarmament, it is simply absurd to think that more weapons—whether personal firearms or national military forces—ultimately makes for safer individuals or a safer world.

Once a society is heavily armed, control and elimination of personal weapons might indeed make disarmed individuals especially vulnerable to those who cheat by retaining their weapons; a similar concern is expressed with regard to the disarmament of states. In both cases, the possession of weaponry is like riding a tiger: Not only dangerous, it requires great care in extricating oneself! And many studies indicate that the folks most likely to be injured by firearms are their owners and/or their kith and kin. Just as most contemporary proposals for gun control in the United States involve elimination of those firearms that are especially lethal (e.g., automatic weapons) or likely to fall into the wrong hands (e.g., "Saturday night specials") and generally call for careful monitoring rather than total elimination. A parallel can once again be drawn with proposals for arms control.

## Maintenance of National Security Capabilities

A less ambitious goal than general and complete disarmament was proposed at the end of World War I by President Woodrow Wilson in his Fourteen Points, which he recommended as international goals. Wilson called for national disarmament "to the lowest point consistent with domestic safety." This suggests that states would be allowed to retain police forces but nothing capable of threatening other states. A police force adequate for China, however, might be quite threatening to Korea or Vietnam. And a Russian police force could threaten Ukraine, Bulgaria, and its other eastern and southern neighbors.

At the Versailles conference, Wilson's proposal was watered down to "the reduction of national armaments to the lowest point consistent with *national* safety," [italics added], terminology that leaves much open to interpretation. A state like Poland, for example, located on the wide plains of Europe and surrounded by large and potentially threatening neighbors, might seem to require a larger military force than does Switzerland, which has many natural mountain barriers. And the United States, with friendly neighbors north and south and oceans east and west, would appear to need relatively little in the way of military force . . . unless (as has the case for many decades) it considers that its national "safety" requires a military presence—via bases, advisers, and/or the capacity for intervention—in countries overseas.

Disarmament is not uniquely applied to sovereign governments. Among the most contentious issues arising between governments and insurgent movements are typically those involving potential disarmament of the latter. Governments often refuse to negotiate with armed opponents; it is equally easy to see why revolutionary and other insurgent groups—especially those deemed "terrorist organizations"—typically resist being disarmed! This can readily lead to a kind of "chicken and egg problem," in which each side refuses to budge until the other does so. For decades, for example, the Israeli government refused to negotiate with the Palestine Liberation Organization, considering them armed terrorists, just as "decommissioning" (disarming) of the Irish Republican Army was long a precondition set by the British government in Northern Ireland before any peace plan could be implemented.

## Selective Disarmament

Another possibility is to disarm selectively, focusing on offensive weapons. This was the goal of the Geneva Disarmament Conference of 1932; it failed because of inability to reach agreement on exactly which weapons are defensive and which are offensive (states typically define their own armaments as the former and those of their opponents as the latter). When the United States initially ended its occupation of South Korea in 1949, it removed airplanes and tanks, seeking in this way to ensure that South Korea would not be emboldened to attack North Korea. One result was that North Korea, instead, attacked South Korea, which found it very difficult to mount an effective defense after being deprived of these "offensive" weapons. In response, the United States, under UN authorization, sent thousands of troops to the Korean peninsula, where they remain to this day.

Probably the most popular version of selective or qualitative disarmament is the enthusiasm that countries have for disarmament of the other allegedly more aggressive nations but not for themselves. This was especially notable during the U.S.-Soviet arms race, when many observers concluded that the two superpowers essentially colluded in creating a "duopoly," whereby the two superpowers excluded others from being major players on the world stage. There is a fable that describes a disarmament conference held among the animals. The eagle, eyeing the bull, recommends that all horns be cut off. The bull, looking at the tiger, suggests that sharp teeth and claws should be pulled. The tiger, sizing up the elephant, urges that tusks be filed down. The elephant, looking at the eagle, insists that all would be well if only wings and beaks were clipped. Then the bear, speaks up in tones of sweetness and reason: "Come now, my friends, let us abandon these halfway measures and agree to abolish all weapons, and simply resolve any disagreements with a great, friendly hug."

## Weapons of Mass Destruction

The possibility exists for mutually-agreed restrictions on obviously offensive weapons, such as bombers, motorized artillery, and the like. Perhaps the greatest prospect—as well as the greatest need—for selective disarmament concerns atomic, biological, and chemical weapons ("weapons of mass destruction," or so-called ABC weapons) because of the unique threats they pose. In addition, nuclear weapons—especially when combined with fast and highly accurate delivery systems—are unusual in potentially generating their own instability, because they arouse fear of a preemptive strike. This makes enforceable and monitored selective disarmament agreements regarding weapons of mass destruction especially important and perhaps even of incalculable value.

## Military Budgets

Reductions and restrictions in military budgets have often been discussed. Not surprisingly, there have been problems. For example, if all states are restricted to a maximum total expenditure, the same national defense would be purchased for Luxembourg, which has a small border and few enemies, as for Russia, which has an immense border and much greater legitimate need for defense. But if larger states are permitted larger military budgets (such as an agreed percentage of area, population, or their Gross National Product [GNP]), they might pose a threat to smaller states. In addition, difficulties arise in determining the actual military expenditures of many states that do not publish reliable figures. Even the budget for the U.S. Department of Defense is misleading: It does not include the costs of nuclear bombs and warheads, for example, which are included in the Department of Energy budget. Together, U.S. military expenditures annually total more than a half-trillion dollars, exceeding that of all other military budgets in the world, combined. . . .

## Weapons-Free Zones

The idea here is to agree on the elimination of weapons within a designated geographic area. For example, under the Treaty of Tlatelolco (named for a suburb of Mexico City), most of the states of the Western Hemisphere agreed not to develop or deploy nuclear weapons. Similar suggestions, especially for nuclear-free zones, have been made for Africa, the Middle East, Australasia, the Balkans, and Scandinavia. Agreement to forgo all weapons within a designated zone, or even just those of a certain type, can help diminish anxiety that a local rival is seeking to gain superiority. Consequently, such agreements could diminish pressure to push ahead with armaments that—when matched by the opponent—would ultimately diminish the security of all concerned. Thus, they offer the prospect of emerging from the Prisoner's Dilemma.

For example, the Rush-Bagot Treaty of 1817, which arranged for the demilitarization of the U.S.-Canada border, helped set the stage for good relations between these two North American neighbors. This was no merely cosmetic treaty. It called, among other things, for a 3,000-mile unfortified border and for the actual dismantling of a number of naval vessels, which had been built on the Great Lakes and were too large to be sailed out. It is also worth noting that this agreement was reached only 2 years after the United States and Britain—then governing Canada—had fought a war, including several naval battles on the Great Lakes. Looking at U.S.-Canadian relations today, we blithely take peace for granted, but at the time of the Rush-Bagot Treaty, things were very different. Even the treaty itself did not immediately lead to peace; rather, distrust and several near wars characterized the ensuing several decades. Undeniably, however, in this case, a serious disarmament agreement hastened a genuine peace. If threatening naval vessels had been allowed to continue patrolling the Great Lakes, and if military fortifications had been constructed along the U.S.-Canadian border, relations between the two countries would probably have gone quite differently.

Another type of disarmament agreement, similar to the establishment of a weapons-free zone, occurs when all parties agree to the establishment of political neutrality (nonalignment) of a particular country. Following World War II, for example, the victorious allies occupied Austria. By the Austrian State Treaty of 1955, all sides agreed to end that military occupation, signing an accord whereby the state of Austria was essentially demilitarized and pledged to Cold War neutrality.

# A Brief History of Disarmament

## Self-Serving Plans

Governments have on occasion tried to reduce armaments, and sometimes they have even succeeded. But the history of such efforts is largely one of failure. After the Napoleonic Wars, for example, Czar Alexander led an (unsuccessful) effort to save governmental funds via multilateral disarmament. Later, Czar Nicholas II convened the first Hague Peace Conference in 1899, once again in an effort to stave off an arms race that threatened to lead to bankruptcy. But political motivations—especially the desire to appear peace loving—have also been important. After taking office in 1981, for example, President Reagan showed himself to be not only uninterested in disarmament but antagonistic to it, especially during his first term in office. Later, the U.S. government begrudgingly entered into arms negotiations with the Soviet Union, almost certainly as a response to mounting political pressure, both within the United States and in Europe, and also as a result of the efforts of Soviet leader Mikhail Gorbachev and his advisers.

Other practical concerns have motivated disarmament efforts as well. For example, when Nicholas II suggested a freeze on all military budgets in 1899, Russia already had the largest army in Europe; a freeze would have perpetuated that asymmetry. Churchill proposed a naval building "holiday" to the Germans during 1912 to 1914, when Britain was ahead, especially in battleships. Immediately following World War II, the United States proposed the Baruch Plan, which would have required that all states abandon the possibility of producing their own nuclear weapons, *after which* the United States would place its nuclear facilities under international supervision. This would have left the United States the only state with the knowledge and ability to produce nuclear weapons in the future. The Soviets countered with a plan whereby the United States would dispose of its nuclear facilities first, after which other states would join in. (It was argued in the West that the Soviet Union, as a vast and secretive society, would have had a greater opportunity to cheat if it sought to do so.) The United States objected, and an arms race between the United States and the Soviet Union ensued. In short, disarmament negotiations and conferences have often served as a forum for advancing the interests of each state and prosecuting interstate rivalry, rather than as a means of diminishing those rivalries.

During nuclear arms negotiations in the 1980s, the Soviet Union tried to restrict cruise missiles, forward basing of nuclear forces, and most new technological developments in the arms race: all areas in which the United States was ahead. The United States, in turn, urged reductions in large throw-weight intercontinental ballistic missiles, or ICBMs, (where the Soviets were ahead), while zealously protecting bombers and submarine-based missiles (where the United States has long been particularly strong).

Germany disarmed briefly after World Wars I and II; ditto for Japan after World War II. But in these cases, the victors simply imposed disarmament on the losers; there is no evidence that the people of Germany and Japan suddenly came to appreciate the merits of disarmament. Shortly afterward, the United States encouraged its new ally, West Germany, to rearm during the 1950s and eventually to join the North Atlantic Treaty Organization, much to the dismay of the Soviet Union. U.S. government officials have long urged Japanese leaders to devote a larger share of Japan's national budget to its military. (By tradition, since World War II this had always been less than 1% of its GNP, and by its postwar constitution, Japan pledged never to maintain offensive military forces, which has been called into question by the country's contributions to the U.S.-led wars in the Middle East.)

## Unsuccessful Attempts

At a disarmament conference held in 1931, great excitement ensued when several Afghans were found to be in attendance; the conference organizers were delighted that the idea of disarmament had spread so far and was being so widely accepted. But when asked why they were attending, the Afghans replied, "If these nations really are going to disarm themselves, perhaps we can pick up some weapons cheaply."

Disarmament policies have often served simply to demonstrate to public opinion that efforts are being made in a noble direction and that any failures are due to the stubbornness of other countries. Attempts at renouncing war by treaty have also been notably unsuccessful. By the early 1920s, the Treaty of Versailles appeared to be unraveling, with Germany refusing to pay its obligatory World War I reparations and France responding by sending troops to occupy Germany's Ruhr Valley. The German foreign minister then organized a peace conference involving the major European powers, hoping to head off the establishment of a new anti-German alliance. At a meeting in Locarno, Italy, numerous agreements were reached, including demilitarization of the Rhineland and a mutual defense treaty linking France to both Poland and Czechoslovakia. Enthusiasm ran high for the outlawing of war altogether, and shortly thereafter, French foreign minister Aristide Briand proposed to U.S. secretary of state Frank Kellogg that, on the 10th anniversary of the U.S. entry into World War I, France and the United States sign an agreement outlawing war between the two states.

The U.S. government responded with unexpected enthusiasm, urging that the proposed instrument be expanded to a worldwide renunciation of "war as an instrument of national policy," in addition to further agreement that "the settlement or solution of all international disputes or conflicts . . . shall never be sought except by peaceful means." Unfortunately, the Kellogg-Briand Pact of 1928 was unenforceable, and—along with the "Spirit of Locarno"—may have unwittingly done more harm than good, since it gave a false sense of security to states that were already peace loving and a smokescreen behind which aggressive states were able to pursue their ambitions. The Kellogg-Briand Pact became a prototype of meaningless and often misleading "statements of principle." On the other hand, agreements of this sort may be important in affirming a widespread multinational yearning for dramatic reductions in armaments; violations of the Kellogg-Briand Pact were also used against former Nazi officials in the Nuremberg Trials, after World War II.

## Modest Successes

When Albert Einstein was asked his opinion of the Geneva disarmament conference of 1926, he responded: "What would you think about a meeting of a town council which is concerned because an increasing number of people are knifed to death each night in drunken brawls, and which proceeds to discuss just how long and how sharp shall be the knife that the inhabitants of the city may be permitted to carry?"[1] There have, however, been some modest examples of successful disarmament. The Washington Naval Conference resulted in a 1922 treaty that caused the United States, Britain, and Japan to scrap 40% of their capital ships (battleships and aircraft carriers). Certain minor restrictions have been obtained, such as the elimination of expanding ("dum-dum") bullets, prohibitions against the use of poison gas, and a ban on landmines (unfortunately ignored or evaded by many countries, including the United States). Poison gas was used, however, by the Iraqi government against rebel Kurds during the late 1980s.

## Arms Control

In the aftermath of World War II—widely seen as not only a "good war" but also one that was hastened by the West's reluctance to arm adequately in the 1930s—public enthusiasm for disarmament waned significantly. The two emerging superpowers—the United States and the Soviet Union—each proposed plans for disarmament, but these were almost certainly a mixture of propaganda ploys and efforts to achieve a unilateral advantage over the other. By the late 1950s, governments began to turn their attention from disarmament to a more modest and attainable goal, especially regarding nuclear weapons—namely, "arms control."

There were many reasons for this shift. Following Stalin's death, under Khruschev and Eisenhower, the Cold War thawed somewhat. Improvements in technology permitted verification with higher confidence, especially by satellite surveillance. The ongoing arms race had heightened citizen anxiety and pushed the West in particular to recognize the growing dangers posed by radioactive fallout from aboveground nuclear testing. And, finally, with its acquisition of ICBMs and a growing nuclear arsenal, the Soviet Union achieved essential strategic parity with the United States, thereby permitting both superpowers to negotiate seriously, from a position of more or less equivalent strength. (It has been said that there are two rules for negotiators: Don't negotiate when you are behind, and don't negotiate when you are ahead. Hence, the best opportunity for progress often comes when two sides are functionally equal.)

To many dovish critics, arms control is a mere smokescreen, a thinly veiled excuse for continuing to accumulate weapons, all the while quieting the public with claims that "progress" is being made. Moreover, arms controllers are concerned with managing and stabilizing the arms race; disarmers, by contrast, do not seek to stabilize the arms race but rather to *destabilize* it and end the arms race (which physicist Herbert York called "the race to oblivion") altogether.

To hawkish critics, arms control is only somewhat more acceptable than unilateral disarmament (which is utterly anathema); it is considered a snare and a delusion whereby a nation allows itself to be outmaneuvered at the bargaining table by its adversary. Their presumption is that the other side is untrustworthy and will cheat, as well as that the other side will settle only for victory—or, in the case of an arms race, remaining continually ahead. To some extent, a free-for-all arms race, unfettered by international agreements, also reflects the economic free market, beloved by political conservatives and "market fundamentalists."

These, then, are some of the hidden, unpeaceful goals of arms control: gain a unilateral advantage either by ending competition when you are ahead or by steering competition into an area of one's advantage, establish a monopoly that effectively subjugates other states, and create the false impression of progress, thereby quieting domestic dissatisfaction. The official, legitimate goals of arms control are as follows:

1. *Reduce the likelihood that war will break out, by removing some of the more threatening situations or weapons.* For example, World War I might have been averted if some agreement could have been reached that dampened competition for early mobilization on both sides. The de-alerting of nuclear missiles has somewhat diminished fears of a surprise attack, thereby also reducing the danger of war being provoked by error or false alarm.

2. *Prevent competition that could be not only financially ruinous but also destabilizing.* The Anti-Ballistic Missile Treaty of 1972, by which the United States and the Soviet Union agreed not to develop or deploy significant antimissile weapons, headed off a strategically futile and economically intolerable spiral of competition between the offensive and defensive weapons of each side. In the early 21st century, this treaty was unilaterally abrogated by the Bush administration in 2001, producing significant tension with Russia, which at the end of 2007 withdrew from the restrictions of a conventional forces treaty in Europe.

3. *Create an environment of increasing trust and confidence.* By reaching agreements—even over trivial issues—contending parties can progressively gain greater confidence in each other, as they become increasingly familiar with their counterparts, comfortable with their motivations, and thus more willing to engage in serious agreements in the future. Of course, this also presupposes that the participants are well-meaning and that the agreements in question will be adhered to.

4. *In the event that war breaks out, arms control can still have been helpful if, because of preexisting arms control agreements, the war is less destructive than it otherwise would have been.* The major powers appear to have destroyed biological warfare agents, following an international agreement in 1972, and chemical weapons stocks as called for in an international agreement in the late 1990s. One hypothetical danger here is that in making war less destructive, it might also be rendered more tolerable and, therefore, a more acceptable instrument of national policy. After all, deterrence generally rests on the proposition that by making the costs of war intolerable, it will be prevented.

## Some Current Treaties

Many arms control treaties have been signed since 1945, most of them related to nuclear weapons. Although the list is long, it is not impressive, because countries were generally willing to restrict only those arms-related activities that they were not interested in pursuing. For decades, arguably, the real arms race was not between the United States and the Soviet Union but rather between arms builders and arms restrictors. If so, there is no question who won, most of the time, as evidenced by the tens of thousands of weapons and delivery systems that were and are still being constructed. But the arms controllers have had some successes.

## Basing and Testing Treaties

Nuclear weapons have been banned from the Antarctic continent, from planetary orbit, and from the seabed. In 1963, the Partial Test Ban Treaty, or PTBT (1963), capped many years of public protest against rising levels of worldwide fallout from atmospheric nuclear tests. Signatories agreed to refrain from atmospheric, outer space, or undersea testing of nuclear weapons, although testing was not stopped altogether. Testing of new nuclear weapons systems moved to underground sites or to controlled simulations in laboratories, and the governments of China, France, India, and Pakistan refused to sign and persisted in testing above ground (China) and beneath the ocean (France). India and Pakistan detonated relatively low-level nuclear explosions in 1998.

The United States hasn't tested nuclear weapons since 1992 and has no plans to do so, based on the argument that this country has already conducted more than 1,000 nuclear tests (more than any other state), and that as a result, has accumulated sufficient information plus the capacity for computer-based simulations to render actual explosions unnecessary. The real goal of most antitesting advocates was—and continues to be—a Comprehensive Test Ban Treaty (CTBT), which would constrain all nuclear testing, underground as well as aboveground. A CTBT was signed in 1996 and ratified by the Russian Duma (legislature) in 2000. As of late 2012, 157 countries had ratified the CTBT, but the treaty will not enter into force until 44 states that have been deemed "nuclear capable" have also ratified it, including China, Egypt, India, Iran, Israel, North Korea, Pakistan, and the United States. Such a move forward on the part of the United States might well establish the leadership needed to bring other countries along. China, for example, has announced that it will ratify the CTBT if the United States does.

On the positive, pro-CTBT ledger, during the Obama administration, the United States canceled plans to develop and deploy a new, "Reliable Replacement Warhead," electing to rely on a highly sophisticated "stockpile-stewardship program," and thus keeping the door open for an eventual worldwide CTBT. However, conservatives have thus far prevented Congressional ratification by the United States, continuing to claim that (1) such a ban could not be satisfactorily verified and that (2) even if it could, continued testing is necessary to ensure the reliability of the existing nuclear arsenal. This rejection has done much to deprive the United States of any pretense of leadership in promoting nuclear disarmament or even arms control. It also raised the dangerous proposition that other countries, notably Pakistan and India, will continue to develop their own nuclear arsenals and has left the door open for Israel to further develop its existing arsenal and for Iran to pursue the possible development of a nuclear arsenal, perhaps as a means of "deterrence" of a possible Israeli or American attack or perhaps for other reasons.

U.S. president Ronald Reagan famously pronounced with respect to nuclear arms negotiations with the Soviet Union: "trust, but verify" (a translation of the Russian proverb *"doveryai, no proveryai,"* perhaps ironically, a favorite expression of Lenin). In this regard, it can be argued that the capacity of the United States to monitor nuclear testing unilaterally, as well as the capabilities of the International Monitoring System (IMS), both substantially exceed what had been predicted in 1999, such that any state attempting to cheat by testing a nuclear weapon would probably be detected. Only one state has conducted a nuclear test since 1998: North Korea in 2006 and 2009. Both times, the IMS—although less robust than it is at present—successfully detected both of these rather feeble ("fizzle yield") tests.

A 2011 report by the nonpartisan U.S. National Academy of Sciences in consultation with senior scientific and military officials concluded with respect to the CTBT that the "United States is now better able to maintain a safe and effective nuclear stockpile and to monitor clandestine nuclear-explosion testing than at any time in the past," and that a strong case can thus be made that worry over the maintenance of the U.S. nuclear stockpile and about verification of a CTBT are no longer compelling arguments; the issue is currently one of political will rather than technological capability or strategic vulnerability.

This new study concluded that "if sufficient resources are dedicated to the task, the United States has the technical ability to maintain a safe, secure, and reliable stockpile of nuclear weapons into the foreseeable future without nuclear explosive tests." In particular, a global test ban would make it much more difficult—and perhaps impossible—for China, India, and Pakistan to deploy multiple warheads, since doing so would require extensive testing to validate the reliability of new, more compact warhead designs. It is further suggested that "[o]ther states intent on acquiring and deploying modern, two-stage thermonuclear weapons would not be able to have confidence in their performance without multi-kiloton testing. Such tests would likely be detectable (even with evasion measures)." States such as Iran or North Korea deprived of the opportunity of nuclear testing, couldn't perfect a new generation of sophisticated two-stage thermonuclear warheads suitable for delivery by long-range missiles.

## Communications Agreements

The "Hot Line" agreement (1963) established an emergency communications link between Washington and the Kremlin. This was subsequently updated and modernized, with the addition of satellite links and so-called crisis control centers in each capital. In the Nuclear Accidents Agreement (1971), the two superpowers agreed to notify each other in the event of accidental or unauthorized nuclear detonations, and a High Seas Agreement (1972) sought to establish rules of conduct to minimize the chances of oceanic collision and misunderstandings during naval maneuvers. In 1975, nearly all European states agreed to the Final Act of the Conference on Security and Co-operation in Europe (CSCE, better known as the Helsinki Accords), which essentially ratified the post–World War II map of Europe and also arranged for advance notification of large military exercises.

## Biological and Chemical Weapons

The Biological Weapons Convention (1972) committed the signatory states to refrain from developing, producing, or stockpiling biological weapons (primarily viruses and bacteria). Chemical weapons, however, were not included. The Environmental Modification Convention (1977) prohibited the alteration of the environment, including climate, of an adversary, and the Chemical Weapons Agreement of the 1990s has led to reductions—but not complete elimination—in major powers' chemical arsenals.

## Strategic Nuclear Weapons

The first set of Strategic Arms Limitation Talks, or SALT I, resulted in an Interim Agreement (1972) that established numerical limits for American- and Soviet-guided missile submarines, submarine-launched missiles, and ICBMs. SALT II established various additional restrictions on strategic weaponry but fell victim to domestic U.S. politics, having been strongly opposed by influential right-wing groups. Under the Reagan administration, the United States unilaterally breached certain terms of SALT II and then belatedly began negotiations on a replacement, known as START (Strategic Arms Reduction Talks). Critics maintained that these talks were begun with no serious expectation of success but only to quiet the U.S. peace movement. A START I treaty was eventually signed and ratified by the U.S. Senate as well as the Russian Duma. It called for, among other things, a complex mix of reductions in missile launchers and in numbers of warheads to about 6,500 on each side.

In 2000, the Russian Duma ratified the START II agreement, by which the two sides agreed to a maximum of 3,500 strategic warheads each by 2007. This treaty also bans multiple-warhead missiles, long considered dangerously destabilizing. Russia—eager to reduce the cost of maintaining such expensive arsenals—has urged that START III, the next step, ought to decrease the number of strategic warheads to 1,500, although during the Bush administration in particular, the United States resisted such reductions while also agitating for a new generation of warheads, including earth penetrators or "bunker busters."

## New Start

Under this treaty, which was approved by the U.S. Senate in late 2010, the United States and Russia have agreed to significantly limit the numbers of deployed strategic weapons 7 years from when the treaty enters into force. Under the terms of New Start, each country can determine the structure of its own strategic forces but within the aggregate limits specified by the treaty: 1,550 total strategic warheads, whether deployed ICBMs or submarine-launched ballistic missiles (SLBMs), with each deployed heavy bomber equipped to carry nuclear weapons counting as one warhead toward this limit.

This number permits each side essentially one-quarter the strategic armament level allowed by the 1991 START Treaty and only about one-third of the deployed strategic warhead limit allowed by the 2002 Moscow Treaty. Under the New Start agreement, thousands more warheads can be kept in storage as a backup force; in addition, its restrictions do not apply to hundreds of short-range nuclear weapons in the American and Russian arsenals.

New Start mandates a combined limit of 800 deployed and nondeployed ICBM launchers, SLBM launchers, and heavy bombers equipped for nuclear arms. The treaty also establishes a verification regime that mandates 18 on-site inspections per year, replacing a long-standing mutual inspection regime that lapsed in 2009. In addition, it mandates data exchanges and advance notification of any tests related to strategic offensive arms while also granting both countries unrestricted unilateral use of Earth-orbiting satellites and mandating noninterference with each other's satellites. Data exchanges are also organized with respect to the number, locations, and technical characteristics of all weapons systems and facilities subject to the treaty.

Unique among arms control treaties, New Start provides each ICBM, SLBM, and heavy bomber with an identifying number that allows its presence or absence to be confirmed during every inspection. Both the United States and Russia have agreed to a mutual annual exchange of telemetric information normally obtained to monitor missile performance during ICBM and SLBM test flights. The treaty also establishes a Bilateral Consultative Commission that will meet at least twice per year to iron out any difficulties in compliance. Part of the expressed motivation for supporting New Start is the Obama administration's recognition that it cannot expect other countries to reduce or limit their weaponry unless the United States demonstrates its willingness to do the same.

As described above, however, in order to generate political approval, treaties that limit nuclear weapons must often be associated with certain compromises demanded by the "hawks" within each country. In this case, a "Resolution of Advice and Consent" was certified by President Obama in early 2011 in which the Obama administration undertook to "... *modernize or replace* the triad of strategic nuclear delivery systems: a heavy bomber and air-launched cruise missile, an Intercontinental Ballistic Missile (ICBM), and a nuclear powered-ballistic missile submarine (SSBN) as well as a new Submarine-Launched Ballistic Missile (SLBM)."

## Policy Modifications

Certain policy decisions, although not strictly treaty based since they are taken unilaterally, constitute important modifications of nuclear policy. In particular, every 5 years the U.S. government undergoes a "Nuclear Posture Review." During President Obama's initial term, this strategic doctrine was revised, with the declaration that "the fundamental role" of nuclear weapons is to "deter nuclear attacks on the United States, allies or partners," which constitutes a narrower policy statement than had existed in the past. This modified policy also eliminates much of the deliberate ambiguity that in the past had surrounded the possible use of nuclear weapons, in that for the first time, the United States has explicitly committed itself to *not using* such weapons "against nonnuclear states that are in compliance with the Nuclear Nonproliferation Treaty," even if they attacked the United States with other weapons of mass destruction such as biological or chemical weaponry. In addition, the U.S. government renounced the development of any new nuclear weapons—part of an avowed policy first announced in a presidential speech in Prague, Czech Republic in the spring of 2009, which explicitly embraced the goal of eventually making nuclear weapons obsolete worldwide.

Toward this end, there have also been some revealing changes in the nuclear weapons component of the U.S. military budget from fiscal year 2010 to fiscal year 2011: There was a notable increase in funds allocated for "fissile material disposition" (safely isolating and when possible disposing of plutonium and highly enriched uranium within the United States) as well as in projects concerning global and cooperative "Threat Reduction Programs," focused primarily on securing fissionable material worldwide, sponsoring reactor conversions, and a variety of anti-smuggling initiatives aimed at combating prospects of such material falling into the hands of terrorists or "rogue governments."

There is a growing consensus that nuclear weapons are simply not the security priority they once were, with many, including such former avowed nuclearists as Henry Kissinger, believing that the opposite is true: That world security would be enhanced by verifiably reducing U.S. and Russian nuclear arsenals, which are largely relics of the Cold War. Thus, there is widespread interest in verifiably reducing these excess U.S. and Russian strategic nuclear arsenals. Even the Pentagon's January 2012 strategy document "Sustaining U.S. Global Leadership: Priorities for 21st Century Defense" stated that "It is possible that our deterrence goals can be achieved with a smaller nuclear force, which would reduce the number of nuclear weapons in our inventory as well as their role in U.S. national security strategy." It seems increasingly clear that the major threats facing the world today—including but not limited to proliferation, terrorism, cyberattacks, environmental degradation, energy shortages, and so forth—cannot be addressed by nuclear arms.

# The Nuclear Non-Proliferation Treaty (NPT)

There is a widespread consensus that nuclear proliferation constitutes a real danger. International efforts to prevent horizontal proliferation are known generally as the "nonproliferation regime," the centerpiece of which is the Non-Proliferation Treaty (NPT). The original impetus for the NPT came from several nonnuclear nations, in appeals to the United Nations in 1960. The two superpowers were interested but not very enthusiastic. A major stumbling block consisted of plans by the United States to develop a "multilateral force" within NATO, which would give the various NATO members joint control over nuclear weapons maintained by the alliance. The Soviet Union was especially upset at the prospect of German hands on the nuclear trigger and the plan was eventually dropped, after which an NPT was negotiated without too much difficulty—largely because both superpowers felt that their security interests were enhanced by such an agreement.

The NPT took effect in 1970. It basically divides the world into "have" and "have not" countries with respect to nuclear weapons. Its most significant nonproliferation items are that

1. nuclear weapons states agree not to transfer nuclear weapons to nonweapons states or to help nonweapons states make their own weapons; and

2. nonweapons states agree not to receive and not to manufacture their own. They also agree to accept inspection safeguards on their nuclear facilities to be monitored by the International Atomic Energy Agency (IAEA), under the auspices of the United Nations.

Not surprisingly, some of the nonweapons states objected to the NPT, feeling that it was discriminatory: They were being asked to give up the possibility of acquiring nuclear weapons without receiving any tangible benefit in return. As a result, they insisted on the additional provisions of

1. weapons states agree to share peaceful nuclear technology with the nonweapons states; and

2. the weapons states agree to begin serious bargaining to end their arms race and to undertake efforts at nuclear disarmament.

The NPT is to be reviewed every 5 years (1975, 1980, 1985, etc.). At these review conferences, the nonweapons states have consistently expressed anger at what they initially saw as the superpowers' failure to live up to their agreement to work seriously to end their arms race and, more recently with the end of the Cold War, to make active efforts toward nuclear disarmament. Critics, led by Swedish disarmament expert (and Nobel Peace Prize winner) Alva Myrdal criticized the United States and the Soviet Union as constituting a "duopoly" while insisting that the rest of the world do as they say, not as they do. Exhortations by the United States and the Soviet

Union that other countries refrain from going nuclear tended to ring hollow while those two nuclear superpowers essentially clung to their own arsenals.

Despite an understandable tendency for public attention to focus on cases of real or suspected proliferation, the NPT is generally considered to have been successful in halting and preventing horizontal nuclear proliferation. Whereas during the 1960s and 1970s authorities worried that dozens of nations would shortly acquire nuclear weapons, the nuclear club has actually grown rather slowly in recent decades, certainly more slowly than most experts had feared. As of 2012, three states that developed nuclear weapons—India, Pakistan, and Israel—never signed the NPT, and North Korea renounced the treaty in 2003. Iran remains a signatory, but the United Nations Security Council has repeatedly found it in violation of its obligations, because it has hidden nuclear plants and refused to answer questions about evidence that it was working on a warhead.

In addition, critics of the NPT point out that a would-be proliferator can ratify the NPT, receive substantial assistance (including reactors, fuel, and the necessary technological expertise) and then, when it is on the threshold of building bombs or warheads, withdraw from the treaty and construct its arsenal. Despite its successes, the NPT clearly is not foolproof and proliferation-resistant.

As noted, the NPT is an explicit bargain by which the nuclear nations have committed themselves to provide civilian nuclear technology to the nonweapons signers. According to its supporters, this is the only possible way to restrict proliferation, since states desiring nuclear technology will somehow acquire it. Under the NPT, such acquisition will at least be supervised and therefore less likely to result in new nuclear arsenals. According to critics, however, there is no such thing as nonmilitary nuclear technology: Every reactor is a potential bomb factory. Moreover, the inclusion of reprocessing technology as "nonmilitary" further blurs the line between civilian and military.

Even aside from the problem of nonsigners, who are not bound to the NPT in any way, the nonproliferation regime has a number of weaknesses:

1. The nuclear safeguards overseen by the IAEA are of questionable reliability, since they include no means of enforcing compliance or of preventing diversion of plutonium for military use. Rather, IAEA inspectors are empowered to report any possible violations they happen to detect. The intent is that a negative inspection report will constitute "timely warning," after which it is up to the international community to respond as it sees fit, possibly with sanctions.

2. IAEA inspectors may examine only nuclear facilities that have been "declared" by the host country. They may not search for undeclared or secret facilities. Hypothetically, a state could be maintaining both safeguarded and unsafeguarded facilities at the same time.

3. Compliance is verified by allegedly tamperproof remote-control cameras, fuel components with special seals, and accounting checks, procedures that may nonetheless offer loopholes for would-be violators. It has been estimated that the "annual detection threshold" for plutonium may be as high as 18 pounds: That is, it may be possible to divert as much as 18 pounds (about one bomb) per country per year without being detected.

4. Although a nation's nuclear facilities are to be open for inspection at all times, IAEA inspectors typically must announce their visits weeks in advance, giving the host operators ample opportunity to prepare for such events. Moreover, host countries can veto inspectors from nations they consider unfriendly.

These weaknesses derive from a reluctance on the part of host nations to give up the perquisites of national sovereignty. They do not necessarily indicate an intent to circumvent the terms of the NPT. However, it rankles many nonweapons states that the requirements of inspection are asymmetric and discriminatory: The nuclear weapon states are not obligated to have their facilities inspected. Supporters of the safeguards and inspection system, while acknowledging its weaknesses point out that it is better than no system at all. And although many people are alarmed about nuclear proliferation, its rate has in fact been relatively modest.

Nuclear supplier states (including such technologically sophisticated countries as Canada, Holland, Australia, Germany, and Japan, which possess well-developed civilian nuclear programs but no nuclear weapons) tend to favor stricter safeguards than recipient nations deem appropriate. The IAEA was also charged with the job of promoting peaceful uses of nuclear energy, a role many critics feel poses a conflict of interest with its job as watchdog and proliferation.

In 1978, the U.S. Congress passed the Non-Proliferation Act, which required strengthening of safeguards and the seeking of agreements among supplier nations to reduce the prospects of nuclear proliferation, as well as further investigation into nonnuclear ways of meeting the world's energy needs. It also forbids U.S. vendors from dealing with other countries, whether or not they are signatories to the NPT, whose nuclear facilities have not been placed under "full-scope" IAEA inspections and safeguards. (Under full-scope conditions, all a nation's nuclear facilities are included, whether they were produced indigenously or acquired via outside assistance.)

The various nonproliferation strategies currently discussed and available (excluding preemptive military attack) include the following:

1. Assume that nuclear proliferation, especially to one's allies, is in many states' national security interest and should be encouraged.

2. Nuclear proliferation should be neither encouraged nor discouraged; rather, states should be free to avail themselves of any commercial opportunities to profit from nuclear exports. After all, states wanting nuclear technology are likely to buy it from somewhere.

3. Nuclear proliferation should be stringently minimized, which would be enhanced if the nuclear states develop a record as reliable suppliers. As a result, nations will be able to meet their energy needs without relying heavily on Middle East oil or developing their own reprocessing or enrichment operations.

4. Nuclear proliferation will be minimized if all prospective nuclear supplier states insist on rigorous IAEA safeguards, with stringent enforcement consequences for noncompliance.

5. Nuclear proliferation will be minimized if nuclear states do everything within their power to see that nuclear technology is not spread to other nations. This can and should include economic and social sanctions, and if necessary, various undercover methods such as industrial espionage, targeted assassinations, and so forth.

## The ABM Treaty and Star Wars

The Anti-Ballistic Missile (ABM) Treaty, signed in 1972 as part of SALT I, was a watershed in strategic doctrine in that both sides essentially pledged themselves to mutually assured destruction: an agreement that nuclear deterrence between the United States and the Soviet Union would be based on the mutual vulnerability of each state. It was unilaterally abrogated by the United States in 2001, so as to permit development, testing, and deployment of a form of Ballistic Missile Defense (BMD), or Star Wars (initially designated by the Reagan administration as the Strategic Defense Initiative).

Initially proposed as a "defensive" shield against Soviet nuclear missiles, a BMD system has been touted post–Cold War as offering possible protection against a terrorist attack or one launched by a fledgling nuclear state, such as Iran or North Korea. Critics question whether it could work, given that offensive countermeasures appear to have the advantage, especially since only a small number of warheads would have to penetrate such a BMD. In addition, a system of this sort runs the risk of making other nuclear powers nervous, since it could conceivably be paired with a first strike, as follows: Suppose that a surprise attack eliminated a large portion of another country's missiles. A BMD system, incapable of defending against a first strike, could in theory nonetheless be effective against the "ragged retaliation" that would take place if the victim sought to strike back with its limited remaining forces. The result of such a "defensive" system—even one of limited effectiveness— could therefore be to encourage its possessor to strike first, confident that the victim could not retaliate. Hence, a system described as defensive could also appear offensive, and therefore pro- vocative, to a potential opponent, such as China, for instance, which fields between one and two dozen ICBMs and might well feel a need to increase its arsenal in response. The Russian govern- ment has long been very critical of U.S. plans to deploy a BMD defense system (previously planned by the Bush administration in Poland and Czechoslovakia), ostensibly to "shield" European and U.S. forces stationed there from an accidental or limited attack by terrorists or a "rogue" state, such as Iran, even though such a system's capability would be so questionable that it seems unlikely to threaten an arsenal as large as that of Russia. Nonetheless, deployment would likely encourage nationalists and militarists to resist any further decrease in Russian nuclear forces.

## Euromissiles

The so-called Euromissiles provide a notable example of limited but genuine nuclear disarma- ment. The emplacement of U.S. limited-range missiles in Germany, Italy, and the United Kingdom was a very contentious issue during the period from 1979 to 1989, beginning with the Soviet deploy- ment of medium-range, SS-20 missiles in Eastern Europe, which NATO insisted upon matching with Pershing II and ground-launched cruise missiles. The ensuing situation was potentially dangerous, since the Euromissiles on both sides not only were highly accurate but also had very short flight times, which threatened to precipitate a "hair-trigger" pattern of mutual anxiety. Fortunately, the Euromissile crisis was resolved when just before the dissolution of the Soviet Union both sides accepted the "zero option," whereby the INF Treaty eliminated this entire class of nuclear weapons.

## Future Prospects

Most of the above events occurred in the context of the Cold War, a period of antagonism, dis- trust, and overt geopolitical, military, and ideological competition between the United States and the former Soviet Union. By contrast, the current post–Cold War world would seem to offer an opportunity to abolish nuclear weapons and other weapons of mass destruction (WMDs). Admittedly, the "genie cannot be put back in the bottle"—that is, the knowledge of how to make nuclear weapons cannot be undone—but the weapons themselves can be dismantled and fissile materials recycled or otherwise disposed of (though significant technical and political challenges stand in way of the latter).

Numerous specific suggestions have been made for dramatic reductions in nuclear stockpiles of the major nuclear states, as well as for physically separating warhead and missile components so that no country can quickly make use of whatever weaponry it may retain. With long-range (satellite) and on-site verification, there is no question that such developments are technically feasible; lacking is political will.

Ironically, at a time when it is most attainable, the future of nuclear disarmament is very much at risk. On the positive side, the total number of deployed warheads in the combined Russian and American nuclear arsenals has declined significantly from a peak of around 65,000 in 1985 to about 8,000 active weapons in 2010 (with another14,000 in storage). Yet the Bush administration opposed formal negotiations on further START-type reductions, while the collapse of the Soviet Union generated worry about the control of nuclear weapons and materials in Russia and in other parts of the former Soviet Union (the problem of "loose nukes"). Most ominously, perhaps, political and military developments in the two countries have regularly threatened to halt, if not reverse, progress made in nuclear disarmament. A major contributor has been pursuit by the United States of a series of policies that threaten to undermine American-Russian relations. These include the expansion of the NATO alliance, including former Soviet allies/satellites (such as Poland, Hungary, the Czech Republic, and the Baltic states), which moved NATO's borders closer to Russia and look offensive (at least to wary Russian nationalists), terminating the ABM Treaty while insisting on deploying missile defenses, insistence on preserving the capability to rapidly expand the U.S. strategic nuclear arsenal, aggressively sponsoring research on new nuclear weapons designs, and the U.S. Senate's refusal to ratify the CTBT. Under both the Clinton and George H. W. Bush administrations, the U.S. government was lacking in creativity or even, perhaps, interest in pursuing nuclear disarmament, a hesitation that has long bedeviled all post–World War II U.S. governments: fears of being considered "soft on defense." These uncooperative American military policies, meanwhile, provided Russian hard-liners with further justification for resisting nuclear disarmament and even arms control.

Nonetheless, numerous opportunities still exist to take advantage of the (possibly fleeting) window of opportunity opened by the collapse of Soviet communism. These include a "consolidate-monitor-dismantle" initiative that would encompass the thousands of tactical nuclear warheads (not covered by the strategic arms control reduction process) and place them under secure control, in preparation for dismantlement. U.S. and Russian forces could take thousands of strategic nuclear warheads off alert, which would reduce the risks of accidental nuclear war. Retraining, conversion, and alternative employment opportunities can be made available for nuclear weapons designers, to ensure that their expertise is not diverted to nuclear "wannabe" nations. Global and domestic security can be most effectively achieved by bilateral and multilateral initiatives designed to reduce and dismantle threatening weapons, rather than insisting on "going it alone."

One much-discussed option is a Fissile Material Cut-Off Treaty, which would prohibit the production of weapons-capable highly enriched Uranium (U)-235 or Plutonium (Pu)-239 but that would also allow lower level enrichment U and separation Pu for purposes of nuclear power generation. During 2004, under the Bush administration, the United States cast the only

"No" vote in the United Nations General Assembly against a resolution calling for negotiation of such a treaty. However, in 2009, U.S. president Barack Obama reversed this position and proposed negotiating "a new treaty that verifiably ends the production of fissile materials intended for use in state nuclear weapons." Certain "newly nuclear states," notably Pakistan, have opposed such a treaty.

# Some Conventional Arms Abuses and Opportunities

## Exporting Weapons

The United States is the major purveyor of arms to other countries of the world, supplying more weaponry to other nations than the rest of the world combined. Russia and France also export large numbers of weapons, especially to developing countries and other nations undergoing violent internal conflicts. A proposed modification of the current arms export regime would involve adoption of a legislatively mandated code of conduct governing weapons transfers, requiring that arms would be made available only to regimes that are democratic, that respect human rights, that are not engaged in aggressive military policies, and that make their military plans and activities "transparent"—that is, available for public scrutiny. If enacted, this would limit the likelihood of possible tragedies, such as the use of U.S.-supplied weapons to the Indonesian government during its army's slaughter of East Timorese, as well as the use of millions of cluster bombs, provided to Israel as U.S. military assistance and scattered indiscriminately among civilian areas during the brief war between Israel and Hezbollah in Lebanon in 2006.

In 1999, President Clinton, for the first time in American history, apologized for the U.S. role in training and arming Guatemalan troops who committed acts of genocide against the indigenous population. It is unresolved whether, or to what extent, U.S. or UN forces should become involved in cases of within-country genocide or "ethnic cleansing." Nonetheless, the United States can act unilaterally to limit its own culpability by refusing to provide weapons and training to regimes likely to engage in such outrages.

## Prohibition of Landmines

There are more than 100 million antipersonnel landmines lurking underground in over 40 countries, notably Cambodia, Angola, Mozambique, Bosnia, and Kosovo. Tens of thousands of persons—nearly all of them civilians, especially farmers working their fields or children at play—are maimed or killed by these devices every year. In 1997, the International Campaign to Ban Landmines and its coordinator, Jody Williams, were awarded the Nobel Peace Prize for their efforts toward the elimination of landmines. Representatives from more than 100 countries gathered in Ottawa, Canada, to sign a comprehensive landmine treaty that would prohibit the "use, stockpile, production, and transfer of anti-personnel landmines." This treaty entered into force in 1999, by which point it had been signed by 135 countries and ratified by 71. Although the United States has promised increased funding for humanitarian demining, it has refused to sign the Ottawa Treaty, maintaining that military necessity requires it to retain the option of using landmines on the border separating North and South Korea.

# Pitfalls of Arms Control Agreements

It sometimes seems as though the threat of weaponry can be ended via treaties and appropriate negotiated agreements. But even aside from the problem of underlying hostilities, there are numerous pitfalls lurking along the road of negotiated arms control.

## Numerical Obsessions

Arms reduction treaties usually involve things that can be counted, which in turn gives greater importance to quantitative than qualitative factors. For example, the actual count of warheads or missiles can be misleading and distracting, especially since asymmetries in force structures make it possible for partisans on either side to point selectively to certain measures, thereby making it seem that their side is unacceptably behind. By focusing on the need for nuclear parity, excessive "bean counting" tends to discourage interest in "sufficiency," in which states would assess what they need for their legitimate defense needs, rather than seeking to match their opponent in every category.

## Slowness

Arms control negotiations are almost always slow. It took 3 years for the United States and the Soviet Union to agree on SALT I, 7 years for SALT II, and another 7 years for the INF Treaty. Moreover, for reasons of pride and ideology, new presidents tend to discard what their predecessors have accomplished, insisting on starting afresh. It is also more difficult to reach the political consensus needed to ban or even restrict a weapon than to meet the engineering requirements of designing and constructing it; as a result, by the time negotiators wind up banning a weapon, it may be virtually obsolete, while new weapons are being planned and produced. (On the other hand, when political will is present, agreements can be made quickly; the Partial Test Ban Treaty, for example, was negotiated in a matter of weeks.)

## "Leveling Up"

It is easy to decide to build more weapons; such decisions are *unilateral.* It is much harder, by contrast, to decide on a *bilateral* or *multilateral* halt, or even a ceiling, because such decisions must be made in concert with others. There is also a reluctance to destroy expensive weapons that have already been deployed. So, rather than accept a limit below one's current level, negotiators are inclined to accept—as a limit for all—the level of the side that is currently higher. Often, treaty limits are even set above those of either side, whereupon they become production goals.

## The "Balloon Principle"

When a weapon is constrained, states tend to put effort into another system, one that is unconstrained and which then expands, like a balloon that is squeezed in one place and pops out somewhere else. For example, after the PTBT was ratified, the rate of nuclear testing (underground) actually *increased.* After SALT I, which did not restrict the number of warheads per missile, there was a great increase in the strategic arsenals of each side, as both sides proceeded with MIRVing.

## Bargaining Chips

It is widely held that bargaining should proceed from a "position of strength"—that is, lots of weapons. At a time, for example, when even its advocates agreed that the MX missile was not supportable on its merits, it was promoted as a way of buttressing the ongoing strategic arms negotiations. Often, weapons, originally justified as bargaining chips, tend to be retained when the negotiations fail. And governments sometimes begin negotiations so as to build support for the procurement of weapons, ostensibly as bargaining chips. National governments also sometimes find themselves having to bargain with their own military-industrial leadership. For example, the vast increase in underground testing that followed the PTBT took place because President Kennedy had to agree to it in order to garner support within the joint chiefs of staff for the PTBT.

## Linkage

Arms control skeptics often claim that agreements should be held hostage—"linked"— to other aspects of the other side's behavior. This suggests that such treaties are favors extended to the other side, whereas in fact if they are of any value, it is as positive-sum game developments that are beneficial to both.

Moreover, as President Kennedy pointed out,

A sea wall is not needed when the seas are calm. Sound disarmament agreements, deeply rooted in mankind's mutual interest in survival, must serve as a bulwark against the tidal waves of war and its destructiveness. Let no one, then, say that we cannot arrive at such agreements in troubled times, for it is then that their need is greatest.[2]

## Legitimating an Arms Race

Only rarely (e.g., the INF Treaty, the ABM Treaty) have treaties actually stopped weapons competition. More often, they are consistent with continuing trends and have in effect ratified arms races themselves, providing government leaders with a touchstone by which they can assure their citizenry that even escalations in weaponry are consistent with treaty obligations. The presence of arms control agreements sometimes allows leaders to claim that they are pursuing an end to a given arms race, while actually managing and channeling it.

## False Confidence

In the 21st century, nuclear weapons have become so reviled in many places that their very legitimacy has once again been questioned. In the past, however, popular revulsion at such weapons came largely from signs that governments were not sincere about trying to restrain or abolish them. By providing occasional arms control "successes," all the while ensuring that weapons regimes remain fundamentally undiminished, governments may succeed in quieting public opposition while essentially maintaining a dangerous status quo. Hawks, by contrast, tend to worry that arms control agreements produce a false sense of confidence in the other direction.

## The Paradox of Small Arsenals

By the peculiar logic of deterrence, there can be a kind of safety inherent in relatively large nuclear arsenals. This is because when a country has many potential weapons available for retaliation, an opponent would likely be especially reluctant to initiate a first strike, knowing that some of the victim's weapons would likely survive and be available for devastating retaliation. At the same time, countries with a large arsenal would presumably be aware of such reluctance by would-be attackers and would therefore be less nervous and less likely to misinterpret false alarms or crisis conditions as indicating an imminent attack against themselves. Alternatively, a comparatively small arsenal is necessarily more vulnerable to a preemptive attack, both because such an attack might theoretically succeed in eliminating any capacity to retaliate (thereby undermining deterrence), and also because a country possessing a small arsenal might be especially worried that such a preemptive attack might occur, as a result of which it could be tempted to preempt the opponent's preemption!

# Benefits of Arms Control Agreements

We live in a real world, not an ideal one. Just as a *Realpolitik* argument is regularly used to justify the presence of armed forces, it also explains efforts to control them. There are enormous risks in permitting uncontrolled arms races; hence, it seems essential that non-zero sum game solutions to humanity's shared dilemma be identified and acted upon, since nothing less than the fate of the Earth is at stake.

In this regard, it appears that arms control and continued efforts at disarmament have a crucial role to play. Good agreements can inhibit wasteful competition (e.g., the ABM Treaty), reduce worldwide pollution (the PTBT), diminish the chances of accidental war (the Hot Line), and even eliminate dangerous weapons (the INF Treaty).

## Verification

Successful arms control (and disarmament) must rely on something more than trust. Specifically, compliance must be verifiable. During the Cold War, the Soviet Union, largely a closed and secretive society, was consistently averse to on-site verification, which it long considered unacceptably intrusive and a license for spying. So, just as the Soviets once disingenuously pressed for widespread (and unverifiable) disarmament schemes, the United States also disingenuously would insist on iron-clad verification procedures it knew would be vetoed by the Soviets. These issues are no longer likely to block agreements, and, in fact, Russia has in many ways been more open to U.S. arms inspectors than have some U.S. military contractors, who periodically object to what they fear might be industrial espionage. At the same time, verification has on occasion been hotly contested, notably in the aftermath of the Gulf War, with Iraq's resentment of UN arms inspections and its periodic refusal to permit on-site monitoring of Iraqi weapons facilities. On several occasions, indeed, this issue was used by the United States as a reason to bomb Iraq and also delayed the lifting of UN economic sanctions.

Verification is not simply an excuse for avoiding arms control or disarmament; it is important in its own right. No one should expect that a country will tolerate substantial cuts in its own arsenal unless it can be confident that others are abiding by their share of such agreements. Certain reductions in arms—even if made unilaterally—will not diminish a state's security. So long as hundreds of warheads remain in a country's arsenals, it would not matter if the other side squirrels away a few hundred more than are called for in any build-down agreement. Even in this case, however, verification may well be helpful, and perhaps necessary, if the reductions are to be acceptable to the hard-liners on each side.

## Techniques and Prospects

A useful distinction can be made between "absolute" or legalistic verification, by which *any* violation will be detected with absolute certainty, and "functional" or realistic verification, according to which some violations may be missed, but any that could be of strategic significance will be detected. With the advent of spy satellites and other detection techniques, functional verification can generally be ensured; insistence on absolute verification, by contrast, is tantamount to insistence on no agreement at all.

A variety of verification procedures are available. Most treaties provide for verification by "national technical means," which refers to a variety of long-range reconnaissance procedures that do not directly intrude on the side being monitored. Of these, satellite observation is the most powerful and important, while infrared imaging can even penetrate cloud cover and detect changes in work patterns inside factories.

Governments have additional sources of information. Radar, for example, provides for accurate detection, tracking, and monitoring of missile tests, thereby assessing compliance with treaty restrictions. Seismic instrumentation has become so sensitive that nuclear explosions as small as one kiloton reportedly can be distinguished from such natural events as earthquakes; this appears to hold even for so-called decoupled explosions, detonated in sites designed to absorb the blast effects. An array of tamper-proof black boxes, installed within national territory, can provide a very high level of reassurance that no one is conducting nuclear tests. National technical means of verification also include the capability of electronic signal interception, whereby one country listens to the communications of another.

As a general rule, verification of military *capabilities* has been remarkably reliable, a notable exception having been U.S. and British intelligence reports that the Iraqi government, under Saddam Hussein, had stockpiled weapons of mass destruction. It remains controversial, however, whether this represented a genuine breakdown in intelligence or a political ploy by the Bush and Blair administrations, which apparently had decided to invade Iraq for other reasons and then cherry-picked intelligence that supported their contention. Most often, intelligence failures have been in a "softer" area, notably political and military *intentions*. The West was caught off guard, for example, by the rapidity of the Soviet Union's disintegration, by the rampage of Hutus against Tutsis in Rwanda, by Serbian ferocity toward Kosovar Albanians, and by the sudden "Arab Spring" uprising against several dictatorial regimes.

# Economic Conversion

The economy of the United States is heavily militarized, as was that of the Soviet Union; indeed, the ruinous economic pressure of keeping up an arms race appears to have contributed substantially to the Soviet Union's disintegration. The economies of such other states as Israel, Iraq, North Korea, and South Korea are even more heavily oriented toward military expenditures and production, as measured by the proportion of GNP devoted to military purposes. Converting such economies from military to civilian functions poses special challenges and opportunities.

It had been expected in many Western progressive political circles that the end of the Cold War would generate a substantial "peace dividend," as military spending was redirected toward the civilian economy. This has not happened in the United States, largely because of the "war on terror," such that current military spending in the United States is about 150% of its earlier Cold War levels. It is unclear whether this change is a justified response to terrorist threats or if international terrorism has been used as an excuse to ramp up military investment in the absence of the Cold War. In any event, it seems clear that economic conversion—from a military to a civilian economy—deserves a place in the U.S. national agenda, both to generate political pressure for the process itself and to ensure that, if and when it happens, it is carried out intelligently.

## Challenges

Large military expenditures tend to create their own constituency, which in turn makes disarmament—and even arms control—politically difficult. When big corporations and their many employees make large amounts of money based on current market demands, the result is powerful pressure to continue business as usual, even if the military/strategic justification for such "business" has evaporated. Moreover, whole regions now rely on military spending, and many U.S. politicians attribute their election and reelection to success in bringing some of the Pentagon "bacon" home to their constituents. Disarmament—even if it is partial—can thus appear to threaten the livelihoods of many people. Not only do economic factors make disarmament politically unattractive to many government leaders (in many countries besides the United States), but large-scale demilitarization of an economy would in fact require a major overhaul of existing economic arrangements, in some cases generating real hardships, at least until funds and priorities are rearranged. Thus, the closing of only a relatively small number of military bases in the United States during the 1990s generated heated political opposition.

## Opportunities

On the other hand, military spending is, on balance, more hurtful than helpful to a national economy. In the long run—and aside from its presumed benefit in diminishing the likelihood of war—restructuring from a military to a civilian economy offers the promise of (1) reducing inflationary pressures, (2) increasing employment, (3) lowering the deficit, (4) improving productivity, and (5) freeing up resources—human as well as financial—for needed social programs. Although skeptics may bemoan the problems posed by economic conversion, it is at least as plausible to consider economic conversion as an opportunity yielding a potential "disarmament dividend" that provides yet another reason for moving toward a demilitarization of security.

Economic conversion has been achieved in the past. Following World War II, the U.S. military budget plummeted from nearly $76 billion in 1945 to less than $19 billion in 1947. As part of this postwar demobilization, the armed forces went from 11 million troops in 1945 to 2 million 2 years later, yet unemployment never exceeded 4% during this period. Skeptics point out, however, that successful post–World War II conversion in the United States was based in part on conditions that would probably not be repeated in the event of comparable conversion today. For example, many women who had been recruited into the workforce in the early 1940s returned home to raise families, thus making room in the workforce for demobilized servicemen. In addition, a large pent-up consumer demand had accumulated during the war years, when new automobiles, for example, were not produced, since factories had been retooled to make jeeps, tanks, and other military hardware. On the other hand, the U.S. economy is far larger today than it was in 1945, and the number of people to be "demobilized" is far smaller. If substantial government expenditures are ever redirected away from the military, these funds will not simply evaporate; rather, they will be available for use in other areas (except for some portion left unspent, to diminish the federal deficit).

And on balance such expenditures actually produce *more* jobs, per dollar spent, than does military spending, since the latter is "capital intensive," using large amounts of money to employ relatively few people. Moreover, national and global needs are immense and include funding for education, health, renewable energy, pollution abatement, housing, environmental protection, disaster emergency preparation and relief (as in New Orleans), and public transportation; rebuilding roads, bridges, and other structures; retooling the industrial base for the production of affordable consumer goods; reconstructing blighted cities; reforestation and other types of land reclamation; providing drug treatment and rehabilitation; establishing more humane penal institutions; and so on. Many billions of dollars and millions of workers would be released as resources were redirected from destructive to constructive purposes. It would seem to indicate a stunted imagination to consider this a calamity to be avoided rather than an opportunity to be embraced.

## Conversion Planning

Most people employed in today's military-industrial complex could be retrained for productive work in the domestic economy within about 6 months. Mid- and upper-level managers and engineers would require somewhat more extensive retraining, since they have generally specialized in making narrowly focused, cost-insensitive products, rigidly defined within certain bureaucratic guidelines. In short, they are accustomed to pleasing the Pentagon, not the public.

But there is no reason to think this cannot be changed. The United States already maintains an Office of Economic Adjustment, concerned with helping local communities mitigate the effects of plant and base closings. Such work could readily be expended on a national scale. Some industries and labor unions have (in most cases begrudgingly) begun making contingency plans for converting their activities to domestic and civilian purposes, although peace groups have thus far done the bulk of the work. Careful conversion planning could yield several payoffs: (1) In the event of a transition from a military to a genuinely nonmilitary economy, dislocation would be greatly reduced; and (2) the existence of realistic, mutually beneficial plans would make the disarmament process itself more feasible politically (which might help explain the reluctance of government, industry, and some communities to engage in such planning!).

Economic conversion is important not only as a positive consequence of disarmament but also as a necessary prerequisite for movement in that direction. It is discouraging, therefore, that despite the immense opportunities afforded by the end of the Cold War, the U.S. government remains resistant to the concept of economic conversion and averse to planning for it.

## GRIT

In his book, *An Alternative to War or Surrender* (1962), psychologist Charles Osgood proposed a practical strategy whereby states might achieve substantial progress in reducing tensions and the level of armaments. He called it GRIT, for "Graduated and Reciprocated Initiatives in Tension Reduction." The idea is simple: Just as individuals, or states, increase tension by a series of unilateral escalations, it is also possible to proceed down the tension ladder by a series of unilateral initiatives in the opposite direction. Arguments between two people, for example, often escalate through a series of annoyances, insults, and affronts to each other, with increasing distrust and animosity. However, people also often "make up," and this generally requires a reaching out from one to the other; that is, it begins with some sort of unilateral initiative.

Comparable initiatives can be applied to international affairs, quite possibly with comparable results. These initiatives are not intended as appeasement. Rather, Osgood points out that when individuals, or states, make conciliatory gestures, substantial pressure builds up in favor of matching gestures from the other side. It is possible—even likely—that the initial phases of GRIT will encounter skepticism. Over time, however, assuming that the initiatives are maintained and (better yet) intensified, powerful psychological and social pressure build up to reciprocate . . . which, in turn, contributes to a process of mutual tension reduction that can be as real as the process of tension escalation that preceded it. Osgood recommends that a national policy of GRIT follow certain basic rules:

1. Each step should be small so the initiator does not at any time run risks with its military security.

2. Each initiative should be taken in the interest of reducing tension; initiatives should not be accompanied by threats or efforts at coercion, which tend to harden the opposition.

3. Each initiative should be publicly announced and carried out with maximum publicity.

4. Each action should be real and meaningful, not something that would be done in any case, like retiring an obsolete weapons system or withdrawing from territory already known to be indefensible.

5. The GRIT initiatives should be continued, and if necessary repeated several times, in the hope of generating a like response. If it fails, a GRIT strategy could always be abandoned, with little loss and no diminution to national security.

The United States and the Soviet Union apparently used a GRIT-like strategy of progressive mutual disengagement to defuse a highly tense situation during the Berlin crisis, when U.S. and Soviet tanks were literally facing each other. President Kennedy apparently was aware of GRIT in the summer of 1963, when he initiated a series of outreaches to the Soviet Union, beginning with the announcement that the United States would stop atmospheric testing and not resume unless the Soviets did so first. Premier Khrushchev responded positively and announced a decrease in production rates for strategic bombers. Numerous tit-for-tat benefits followed, including the Hot Line agreement, a large wheat sale, the PTBT, and overall a dramatic lowering of East-West tensions. (The Soviets liked the interaction so much that they coined their own phrase to describe it, "the policy of mutual example.")

There are many possibilities for GRIT-ty initiatives in today's world. If there is any benefit to being overarmed, perhaps it is that it provides an opportunity for all parties to initiate substantial reductions—in both armaments and tension—without diminishing security. GRIT could also be usefully applied to the many conflicts between adjacent rivals, such as India and Pakistan, Israel and its Arab neighbors, North Korea and South Korea, and so forth. In such cases, it appears that the limiting factor is less likely to be national security than local public opinion. This makes peace-related education and outreach all the more important.

## A FINAL NOTE ON DISARMAMENT AND ARMS CONTROL

In 1981, when he received the Albert Einstein Peace Prize, diplomat/historian George F. Kennan assessed the nuclear arms race as follows:

> We have gone on piling weapon upon weapon, missile upon missile, new levels of destructiveness upon old ones. We have done this helplessly, almost involuntarily: like the victims of some sort of hypnotism, like men in a dream, like lemmings heading for the sea, like the children of Hamlin marching blindly along behind their Pied Piper. And the result is that today we have achieved . . . in the creation of these devices and their means of delivery, levels of redundancy of such grotesque dimensions as to defy rational understanding.[3]

He concluded by noting that

> We are confronted here, my friends, with two courses. At the end of the one lies hope—faint hope, if you will, uncertain hope, hope surrounded with dangers, if you insist. At the end of the other lies, so far as I am able to see, no hope at all. Can there be—in the light of our duty not just to ourselves (for we are all going to die sooner or later) but of our duty to our own kind, our duty to the continuity of the generations, our duty to the great experiment of civilized life on this rare and rich and marvelous planet—can there be, in the light of these claims on our loyalty, any question as to which course we should adopt?

Disarmament is a long-standing, traditional value, to which—like peace, Mom, and apple pie—many people pay lip service, yet efforts at disarmament typically bog down when it comes to the specifics of implementation. Human beings have used weapons and war in efforts to resolve their differences for thousands of years; it is not reasonable to expect that such ancient habits will be overturned in a matter of years or even decades. And whereas the goal of absolute disarmament may at the present time seem unattainable, short-term disappointment should not blind us to the benefits to be obtained from various arms-reduction accomplishments along the way. Most of all, we must recognize that disarmament is a *process,* not an *event,* more a verb than a noun, more a way of progressing than a finished and concluding masterpiece to be unveiled to the admiring world with a grand *"voilà!"* Like perfect grace, disarmament may never be altogether achieved, but that doesn't mean that it is not a valid goal or even a route toward possible short-term salvation.

## NOTES

1. Albert Einstein. 1960. *Einstein on Peace.* New York: Meridian.

2. Quoted in A. Geyer. 1982. *The Idea of Disarmament.* Glencoe, IL: Brethren.

3. George F. Kennan. 1981. *The Nuclear Delusion.* New York: Pantheon.

## QUESTIONS FOR FURTHER REFLECTION

1. What, in your opinion, have been some of the most important disarmament and/or arms control agreements since World War II. Why?

2. Distinguish between arms control and disarmament. What are some similarities?

3. Identify one or more current areas of tension or actual violence in the world, and show how arms agreements have either helped diminish or actually exacerbated the problem. Alternatively, describe how an agreement—not currently in force—might be helpful.

4. Look into current prospects for enhanced verification of arms agreements or for economic conversion.

5. How does GRIT differ from traditional ways of reaching negotiated agreements?

## SUGGESTIONS FOR FURTHER READING

Charles Osgood. 1961. *An Alternative to War or Surrender.* Urbana: University of Illinois Press.

Helen Caldicott and Craig Eisendrath. 2007. *War in Heaven: Stopping the Arms Race in Outer Space Before It's Too Late.* New York: The New Press.

Scott Ritter. 2010. *Dangerous Ground: America's Failed Arms Control Policy, from FDR to Obama.* New York: Nation Books

SIPRI Yearbook (revised each year). *Armaments, Disarmament, and International Security.* New York: Oxford University Press.

Thomas Graham. 2002. *Disarmament Sketches: Three Decades of Arms Control and International Law.* Seattle: University of Washington Press.

Waheguru Pal Singh Sidhu and Ramesh Chandra Thakur. 2006. *Arms Control After Iraq: Normative And Operational Challenges.* New York: United Nations University Press.

Lawrence Wittner. 2009. *Confronting the Bomb: A Short History of the World Nuclear Disarmament Movement.* Stanford, CA: Stanford University Press.

# CHAPTER 14

# INTERNATIONAL COOPERATION

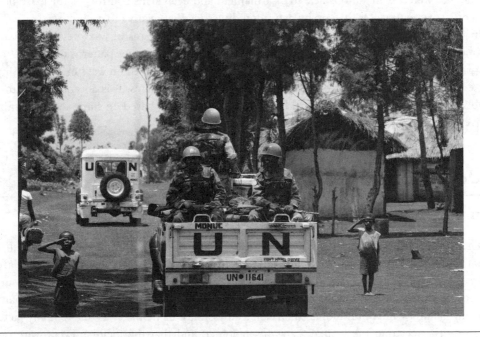

Members of an Indian battalion of the United Nations peacekeeping force in the Democratic Republic of the Congo.

*Source:* © UN Photo.

*Nothing will ever be attempted if all possible objections must be first overcome.*

—Samuel Johnson

*Everything will be all right—you know when? When people, just people, stop thinking of the United Nations as a weird Picasso abstraction and see it as a drawing they made themselves.*

—Dag Hammarskjöld

Most people have experienced something like this: Trouble develops between two individuals, whereupon others step in and help resolve the matter short of violence. They may restrain one or both of the rivals, or perhaps merely their presence helps "cool" the situation. Maybe the contending parties will simply be urged to separate from each other, or perhaps some sort of genuine accommodation will be reached. In any event, conflict situations between countries can often be resolved by separating or connecting, and, in either case, the involvement of others is often crucial.

Peace researcher Kenneth Boulding identified two contrasting options: "associative" and "disassociative." The latter involves reliance on military strength and political separation, based on the notion that "good fences make good neighbors." Associative solutions, on the other hand, are efforts to tear down walls, to join together. As we have seen, prominent among the reasons for war—as well as a major obstacle to disarmament and even arms control—is the existence of bellicose, sovereign states that are by definition disassociative relative to each other.

In the next few chapters, we shall examine possible mechanisms of war prevention that go beyond the current state-centered world system and look toward larger patterns of international integration. In this chapter, we consider associative possibilities based on ways of ameliorating—and even perhaps eliminating—the often troublesome role of states. It is an ancient dream: to establish world peace via international brother- and sisterhood, based on some sort of administrative system that unites people rather than dividing them.

# The United Nations

## From the League of Nations to the United Nations (UN)

The most dramatic and notably unsuccessful effort in the 20th century to create a multinational global organization was the of the League of Nations (1919–1946). Founded in the aftermath of World War I, the League was intended as a worldwide guarantor of collective security. But the League of Nations proved unable to successfully address aggression by Japan in Manchuria and by Italy in Ethiopia (then called Abyssinia). Its demise was due to many factors, including the fact that the United States never joined and that the major powers were more interested in pursuing their perceived national interests than in banding together to prevent distant wars.

As World War II drew to a close, the victorious allies—once again traumatized by war and disillusioned at the failure of the state system to prevent it—decided once more to establish an international body that would work toward human benefit generally and especially the abolition of war. They also hoped that this new organization, known as the United Nations, would avoid some of the pitfalls that had doomed the League of Nations. The formal idea of an international organization for preserving world peace was approved by Roosevelt, Churchill, and Stalin during a conference in Teheran in 1943. Specific plans for such an organization were drawn up at the Dumbarton Oaks Conference, outside Washington, in late 1944.

It was agreed that all governments would be welcome, with membership in a large General Assembly, but that primary enforcement power would lie in a Security Council, with the United States, the Soviet Union, Britain, France, and China being permanent members, with each permanent Security Council member having a veto. Finally, in the spring of 1945, delegates from 50 countries met in San Francisco at the United Nations Conference on International Organization, which established a Charter for the United Nations. The Preamble to that Charter reads as follows:

> We the peoples of the United Nations determined to save succeeding generations from the scourge of war, which twice in our lifetime has brought untold sorrow to mankind, and to reaffirm faith in fundamental human rights, in the dignity and worth of the human person, in the equal rights of men and women and of nations large and small, and to establish conditions under which justice and respect for the obligations arising from treaties and other sources of international law can be maintained, and to promote social progress and better standards of life in larger freedom, and for these ends to practice tolerance and live together in peace with one another as good neighbors, and to unite our strength to maintain international peace and security, and to ensure, by the acceptance of principles and the institution of methods, that armed force shall not be used, save in the common interest, and to employ international machinery for the promotion of the economic and social advancement of all peoples, have resolved to combine our efforts to accomplish these aims.

## The UN's Basic Structure

There are several major differences between the United Nations and its predecessor, the League of Nations. For one, whereas the United States remained aloof from the League of Nations, it became a charter member and, in many ways, the most important single actor in the United Nations. For another, the United Nations, unlike the League of Nations, was constituted to have many other important functions beyond those dealing strictly with the avoidance or termination of wars. A branch of the United Nations, the Economic and Social Council, was established, with many specialized agencies concerned with various economic, educational, health, scientific, and social issues—such as the Food and Agriculture Organization (FAO), the World Health Organization (WHO), the World Bank and International Monetary Fund (IMF), the United Nations Children's Fund (UNICEF), and United Nations Educational, Scientific and Cultural Organization (UNESCO), as well as a number of globally focused organizations, such as the International Civil Aviation Organization, the International Telecommunication Union, the World Meteorological Organization, and so on. The major organs of the UN and their prime missions are as follows:

- The Security Council: issues of war and peace
- The General Assembly: the main parliamentary, budget, and decision-making organ
- The Economic and Social Council: quality of life worldwide
- The International Court of Justice (also known as the World Court) located at The Hague, Netherlands: adjudication of international legal disputes
- The Secretariat: essentially the executive organ of the UN, led by one individual, the Secretary-General

## The UN and the State System

To understand the United Nations and assess its actual and potential contributions to peace, it is important to realize what it is *not*. Thus, it is not a world government or even an effort at establishing one. It does not offer an alternative to state sovereignty; in fact, the United Nations was established with a number of guidelines to ensure that, if anything, state sovereignty supersedes it. Accordingly, although the United Nations often proclaims high-minded goals and resolutions, its decisions and actions are not above the more parochial interests of the states that comprise it. It is not a substitute or cure-all for the current state system; rather, the United Nations is in large part a *reflection* of that system: a mirror, not a panacea. It is not a solution to problems of personal aggressiveness, poor decision making, nationalism, oppression, or ethnic strife, and it did very little to ameliorate or end the Cold War. It is limited to the actions of states and can solve only problems those states want to solve, in ways that are approved by the existing states. Whatever one's disappointments in how the United Nations has functioned, it cannot fairly be said that the United Nations has failed its member states. Rather, if there has been failure, it is the states—especially the permanent members of the Security Council—that have failed the United Nations.

Shortly after the United Nations was founded, it became apparent that the United States and the Soviet Union were not going to cooperate very much. In fact, the Cold War quickly began. In the early years after the United Nation's founding, the United States had a number of allies in the General Assembly and was thus able to use the United Nations to prosecute its side of the Cold War. The Soviet Union, in turn, was isolated and used its veto in the Security Council on numerous occasions. However, UN membership expanded rapidly, due largely to an influx of newly independent former colonies. In 1946, there were only 55 members of the United Nations; by 1960, there were 99, and by 1982, 157. Now there are more than 200, including other entities, such as the Palestinians, who have "observer" status. By the late 1950s, the United States could no longer count on an automatic two-thirds majority in the General Assembly, as most of the new states considered themselves nonaligned, and in 1966, the United States cast its first veto in the Security Council. For decades, during which the United States refused to recognize the Communist government of mainland China, that country was excluded from the United Nations. By 1971, however, a watershed was reached when—over U.S. objections—China was seated in place of Taiwan (whose presence as a Security Council member had been something of a farce since 1949). UN security operations had earlier ceased to be a means whereby the United States prosecuted the Cold War, and the United Nations entered more clearly into a phase of limited peacekeeping and peacemaking.

## Attitudes Toward the UN

Many conservatives in the United States have long been uncomfortable with the United Nations, seeing it as—at minimum—an infringement on national sovereignty. "Get the U.S. out of the UN," read bumper stickers and the occasional roadside sign, "and get the UN out of the U.S." (Perhaps ironically, many less-powerful nations today have adopted these slogans in large part due to their anger at what they perceive to be undue influence of the United States over the United Nations.)

As economically developing countries have become a numerical majority in the United Nations, right-wing opposition to it has intensified. Annoyance with the organization has been especially fueled by the fact that every state has one vote in the General Assembly, no matter how small it may be or how despotically governed. Moreover, the UN General Assembly has voted for numerous resolutions that many Americans have found distasteful, such as one in 1975 stating that Zionism (support for the establishment of Israel) is a "form of racism." Moreover, the United Nations tends to embrace concerns that U.S. conservatives generally oppose—namely, disarmament, economic and social equality, environmental protection, and women's rights. And finally, conservatism and nationalism tend to be tightly linked, and many conservatives oppose any organization, such as the United Nations, that they see as threatening the absolute national sovereignty of their country. As a result, for a long time the United States lagged behind in paying its dues, while regularly threatening to provide even less support unless various demands—for organizational rearrangement as well as greater compliance to U.S. wishes more generally—were met.

From a peace studies perspective, the major failing of the United Nations has been its inability to achieve global disarmament, to prevent wars, and to end quickly those armed conflicts it could not prevent. On the other hand, the United Nations offers a vision of superordinate goals: The coming together of sovereign states because of a commitment—albeit sometimes a modest one—to planetary concerns. It may also help legitimize the idea of world government. Meanwhile, the United Nations does good work in bettering the social, economic, educational, medical, scientific, environmental, and cultural condition of humanity. This is desirable in itself, and it also helps create conditions more conducive to "positive peace." In addition, the United Nations has had some (admittedly limited) success in acting directly to make peace and to keep it.

## Peacemaking Efforts

In the immediate aftermath of World War II, it was hoped that the "grand alliance" that defeated Germany and Japan would hold together and that the major powers, acting in concert, would fashion a truly functional system of collective security. The Security Council was empowered to identify an aggressor and then, to request various member states to provide military force as necessary to enforce the peace. To keep disagreements from escalating and possibly even causing war between them, the permanent members of the Security Council were each given veto power over any such decision: This meant, in effect, that the United Nations would be paralyzed if any one of its permanent Security Council members opposed a given action. Although this feature has prevented UN involvement in many cases where it might have been helpful, the Security Council veto has also acted as a circuit breaker, preventing the multinational system from overloading and possibly blowing itself apart when it faced situations that were especially contentious. As a result, the United Nations is virtually powerless to resolve disputes in which any of the permanent members feel that they have a high stake. But on the other hand, it has been able to function much longer than its predecessor, the League of Nations, and—especially in issues involving the less powerful member states—more effectively as well. The United Nations has been involved in a wide array of armed disputes, and its roles have varied from brokering peace to active *peacemaking* (which has sometimes been distressingly close to war fighting!) to peacekeeping.

UN-sponsored commissions have arranged cease-fires between Indonesian independence fighters and their Dutch colonial occupiers, as well as between India and Pakistan during two of their wars over Kashmir. The United Nations supervised successful elections in a number of war-torn countries, including East Timor, El Salvador, Cambodia, and the Democratic Republic of Congo. The United Nations has also been involved as an armed intermediary, supervising cease-fires on Cyprus, Angola, Namibia, and Mozambique, among other trouble spots. Although the United Nations was not formally a belligerent in Bosnia, in Kosovo, during the Gulf War, or the brief Libyan civil war (military operations in these cases were carried out by the North Atlantic Treaty Organization, often with leadership by the United States), it was called in afterward, to help monitor cease-fires and achieve a degree of subsequent "nation-building." The United Nations also played a key role in ending the civil war in Sudan and in assisting the millions of displaced refugees from the Darfur region of that country. It may also be called upon to assist efforts to rebuild Iraq in the aftermath of that country's devastating war, and quite possibly, to oversee negotiations between the West-supported government in Afghanistan and the Taliban, after NATO and U.S. forces leave.

More controversially, the Korean War was officially prosecuted by the United Nations (although, in fact, the United States provided the overwhelming majority of forces) in opposition to North Korea and China. The United Nations, as well, held sway in the Congo during the 1960s. Perhaps the most prolonged UN involvement, however, has been in the Middle East, which provides a case study of both success and failure.

## The Arab-Israeli Wars

Over Arab opposition, the General Assembly approved a British plan in 1947, dividing Palestine into a Jewish and an Arab state, with Jerusalem to be governed under UN auspices. When Israel was declared an independent state, in 1948, it was invaded by armies from Egypt, Syria, Lebanon, Iraq, and Transjordan (now Jordan). The General Assembly and Security Council tried vainly to stop the fighting; a Swedish diplomat, sent to the Middle East as a potential mediator, was assassinated by Jewish extremists. Eventually, U.S. diplomat and UN mediator Ralph Bunche established an armistice in 1949, for which he received a Nobel Peace Prize. However, the issue was resolved not so much by UN diplomacy as by force of arms—that is, the defeat of Arab armies in the field. Indeed, the underlying issues were not resolved.

By the end of the fighting, Israel had expanded its borders over those earlier approved by the United Nation, and hundreds of thousands of Arab refugees (stateless Palestinians) fled to neighboring Arab states, where they remain today, largely unassimilated and demanding a homeland. In 1956, Egypt blockaded Israeli shipping in the Gulf of Aqaba and nationalized the Suez Canal, whereupon Britain and France, in coordination with Israel, invaded Egypt and captured the Sinai Peninsula as well as the Suez Canal. Britain and France vetoed action by the Security Council; the General Assembly then called for a cease-fire, which was finally achieved several months later. In this case, UN pressure was relatively unimportant; however, Britain and France were pushed to withdraw by the vigorous opposition of their close ally, the United States. But the General Assembly arranged for UN troops to guard the border between Egypt and Israel, which agreed to pull back to the 1949 cease-fire line.

This UN presence, the United Nations Emergency Force, represented a very important and innovative step, first proposed by Canadian premier Lester Pearson (for which he won a Nobel Peace Prize) and administered by Secretary-General Dag Hammarskjöld: a new system that came to be known as "peacekeeping." The idea was not to favor either side but to enforce the peace by interposing a lightly armed UN presence between the belligerents. By what Hammarskjöld called "preventive diplomacy," UN peacekeepers help patrol and maintain otherwise shaky cease-fires. At minimum, this prevents further bloodshed; at maximum, it gains time and helps create conditions under which creative diplomacy might help resolve the conflict. In Hammarskjöld's conception—which has been retained ever since—the United Nations seeks to isolate local conflicts from big power involvement, in part by recruiting peacekeepers largely from smaller states.

# Limitations on the UN's Use of Force

The UN's ability to serve as an active peacemaker and peacekeeper has been severely limited. For one thing, member states have never been able to agree on maintaining an independent UN force with sufficient military strength and political independence to deter would-be adversaries.

In the case of many large-scale conflicts, the United Nations was uninvolved or ineffective, reduced to making futile pleas for peace or—worse yet—failing even to make any statement at all. Moreover, the United Nations has been especially hamstrung when it comes to conflicts involving the permanent members of the Security Council. The United Nations played no part, for example, in ending the struggle between Algeria and France—in which 10% of Algerians perished before their country ultimately won its independence—because France, as a permanent Security Council member, wielded a veto. In response to the Iranian hostage crisis in 1979 to 1980, the Security Council toothlessly requested that Iran release the U.S. hostages, but the Soviet Union vetoed a recommendation for economic sanctions. The United Nations also did essentially nothing to end the Vietnam War, the Soviet involvement in the civil war in Afghanistan, U.S. subversion of Nicaragua, Soviet incursions into Hungary and Czechoslovakia, Chinese oppression in Tibet, or Russian military excesses in Chechnya.

The United Nations was also unable to intervene and prevent ethnic warfare in Bosnia and Kosovo, because Russia—ethnically and historically linked to Serbia—threatened to veto any such actions. (Eventually, NATO intervened militarily, with the United Nations subsequently enlisted to assist peacekeeping after the heavy fighting was over.) The United Nations eventually helped end disastrous famines in Somalia, but after U.S. forces suffered a small but humiliating military defeat, UN activities in the country ceased. Shamefully, the United Nations (like the United States) did nothing to prevent genocide by the Khmer Rouge in Cambodia during the 1970s or by Rwandan Hutus against Tutsis in 1994. The U.S.-led invasion of Iraq in 2003 was undertaken after it was clear that the United Nations would not support such an action, so the United States did not attempt to get a UN resolution to authorize the invasion. At the time, such unilateralism on the part of the George W. Bush administration appeared to weaken the United Nations or, at least, to underscore its inability to prevent war; later, once the devastating effects of the Iraq War became clear, UN opposition to such adventurism may well have enhanced its prestige. The merits of concerted, multilateral intervention (assuming, of course, that any such intervention is warranted) may also have become more apparent as a result of the Iraq debacle. At the same time, the United Nations' refusal to intervene in the Syrian bloodletting, because of vetoes by Russia and China did not—as of late 2012—generate much confidence in its willingness or ability to prevent future violent conflicts in which the major powers have differing interests.

## The Promise of Peacekeeping

The fact that the United Nations hasn't prevented or stopped most wars does not mean that it has not been effective and useful in certain cases. Although the United Nations has not been a cure-all for the disease of war generally, it has achieved some notable successes: The United Nations has negotiated more than 200 different peaceful settlements, helping bring about an end to the Iran-Iraq War, as well as the civil wars in El Salvador and Namibia, and administering withdrawal of Soviet troops from Afghanistan. It also supervised elections in Angola and East Timor.

Peacekeeping troops—lightly armed, blue-helmeted "soldiers without enemies"—currently serve as valuable buffers between contending forces in many hotspots worldwide (including Bosnia and Cyprus). They have also been important in monitoring compliance with cease-fires, supervision of disengagement lines, the maintenance of a "no man's land" between belligerents, and so forth. When neutral forces are interposed between armed adversaries, suspicious events are less likely to be misinterpreted as a provocation, and intentional provocations themselves are less likely.

UN operations in the Golan Heights, for example, have been especially fruitful. This elevated region along the Israeli-Syrian border has great strategic value, since it constitutes a high spot from which one can look down on either Damascus or Jerusalem. Under UN supervision, the Golan Heights was effectively demilitarized, setting the stage for negotiations that might eventually lead to it being returned by Israel to Syria, presumably as part of a more comprehensive peace agreement in the region.

However, in many cases the United Nations has only been "effective" after the guns have spoken, and/or depleted treasuries and popular impatience has forced governments to seek some kind of settlement as a result. A peacekeeping regime helps produce an atmosphere of calm, in which a just and peaceful solution can be negotiated. But even successful peacekeeping can have drawbacks. Although it may save lives at the time, UN-sponsored peacekeeping may also help perpetuate a crisis, by reducing the urgency of the conflicting parties reaching a political solution. By taking the edge off a conflict, UN peacekeeping prolongs the unresolved situation, making it more tolerable and even part of the way of life in the affected region.

Another disadvantage to peacekeeping is that, occasionally, UN forces have been inserted when there is no peace to keep. In addition, these forces may be inadequately trained, equipped or provided with guidelines for military engagement that render them ineffective. For example, outgunned UN forces were unable to prevent the slaughter of thousands of Bosnian Muslim men and boys in Srebrenica during Bosnia's struggle for independence from the former Yugoslavia, and several hundred UN peacekeepers were taken hostage by Sierra Leone rebels in 2000. And, in at least one case, UN peacekeeping forces in West Africa were accused of engaging in rape and other atrocities.

Despite its occasional failures and disappointments, international peacekeeping is not merely an altruistic endeavor. Thus, peacekeeping directly serves the security, political, and commercial interests of most countries. But although the United Nations is often a first line of crisis response overseas, the United States (and, to a much lesser extent, a few other states) consistently fall behind in paying dues and peacekeeping assessments. These overdue bills limit the United Nations' ability to respond rapidly to crises and implement needed reforms. Ironically, given its reliance on the United Nations as a potential means of preserving peace and preventing genocide, the United States has often balked at paying its UN bill of more than $1 billion, which represents *less than one quarter of 1%* of planned U.S. annual military budgets. If the United States—and, indeed, any country—is to avoid the costs and dangers of a unilateral role as world policeman, it would seem that, if anything, greater—and certainly not less—reliance on the United Nations is in order.

## A Troublesome Example: Darfur

The two largest current UN peacekeeping missions are both in Africa: in the Democratic Republic of Congo and in Darfur (Sudan). Since 2003, thousands of activists and celebrities have urged support of the UN mission there, confident (or at least hoping) that peacekeepers could end (or at least reduce) the violence, most of it initiated by the Sudanese government in Khartoum, which has displaced nearly three million people, fully half that region's population. And the UN peacekeeping force in Darfur has undoubtedly done much good in mitigating the human suffering in Darfur, mostly by providing and distributing humanitarian aid and by restraining violence on the part of nomadic government-sponsored militias known as the *janjaweed*.

These accomplishments, however, required that the UN team make substantial concessions to the Sudanese government and its murderous military. As of 2010, mortality rates in Darfur had diminished to prewar levels, but rather than solving the Darfur problem, UN involvement seems to have formalized it, converting refugee camps into "instant city-slums" that threaten to become permanent, while the Sudanese government has acted as though the United Nations has relieved it of the responsibility to clean up the mess it has largely created. In short, rather than facilitating the return of displaced Darfurians to their former lives, or actively participating in pushing the Sudanese government in Khartoum to make needed social and economic adjustments, UN peacekeepers, while pursuing a humanitarian agenda have also found themselves supporting a new and regrettable status quo. In addition, the UN peacekeeping force in Darfur is under-funded, underequipped, and continues to suffer casualties inflicted by organized bandits. However, this outcome—although admittedly undesirable—is probably preferable to the full-scale genocide and human catastrophe that preceded UN involvement. The UN's total peace-keeping budget is about $10 billion, of which about one-third has been spent on Darfur and Congo. Up until the 2008 financial crisis, Western countries had been willing to shoulder this cost (seeing this as preferable to ignoring a preventable disaster or sending in their own troops); it is now uncertain however, how much longer this will continue.

# Other Functions of the United Nations

## Third-Party Mediation

UN mediators have occasionally served as valuable third parties, helping belligerents reach acceptable and face-saving agreements. Former secretary-general Javier Pérez de Cuéllar and other UN diplomats were instrumental in helping reach an agreement whereby Soviet troops began leaving Afghanistan in 1988; the secretary-general and his deputies have also served as intermediaries in many conflicts, helping achieve long-desired cease-fires. (As of this writing, former UN secretary-general Kofi Annan is at the center of efforts to establish a cease-fire and eventual peace agreement between the Syrian dictator Bashar al-Assad and rebels seeking to overthrow him; the outcome—typical for such cases—is uncertain.) Nonetheless, on balance, the world has benefitted mightily from the work of the United Nations.

Before his death, Dean Rusk—secretary of state during the Cuban Missile Crisis—revealed that President Kennedy had prepared a memo to be proposed by then–secretary-general U Thant in the event that the United States and the Soviet Union appeared irreconcilably headed toward war. This memo suggested a "compromise" that the U.S. government had already decided would be acceptable . . . but only if it came from a disinterested third party, not the Soviet Union. The compromise—that the United States would remove its land-based missiles from Britain and Turkey in return for the Soviets dismantling their Cuban missiles—proved unnecessary, since Premier Khrushchev subsequently agreed to Kennedy's terms. It does, however, show the value of a respected and disinterested third party.

Even if the United Nations had only prevented one nuclear war—and done nothing else—this would have been more than enough to justify its existence.

## A Forum for Debate

On occasion, the United Nations is derided as a mere debating society. But, in fact, debating societies can be very useful, providing opportunity for government representatives to meet each other and exchange views, often without the glare of publicity. (In the words of one observer, the United Nations "has become indispensable before it has become effective.") There have also been cases in which outraged domestic public opinion has pressed a government to respond to some international event, while at the same time peace has been best served by a government's inactivity. "Blowing off steam" is generally less harmful than blowing up weapons. In such cases, the United Nations provides an opportunity for states to confront their adversaries symbolically rather than through bloodshed.

For example, U.S. authorities judged (correctly) that it would be unwise to intervene militarily when the Soviet Union invaded Hungary in 1956; so, its delegates roundly condemned the Soviets in the United Nations, thereby giving American public opinion the impression that something was being done on behalf of the Hungarian resistance. The Soviets had comparable opportunities when the United States unilaterally dispatched troops to Lebanon in 1958 and to the Dominican Republic in 1965. Similarly, Arab delegates castigate Israel regularly, attacking it verbally while Arab armies generally refrain from doing so militarily.

## Prevent Major Power Conflicts

The United Nations has largely moved away from its original function of providing collective security. Peacekeeping, on the other hand, has emerged as a partially successful UN innovation, not only in itself but also as a means of defusing the likelihood that the major powers might intervene in conflicts between other nations and thereby further inflame the situation.

Originally, it was hoped that concerted military action by the major powers would keep the peace; now, the United Nations operates under an opposite assumption—namely, that peace will be enhanced by excluding the major powers from crises and instead recruiting peacekeepers from smaller, neutral states. Former secretary-general Dag Hammarskjöld admitted in 1961 that the United Nations could not overcome superpower rivalry, such as during U.S./USSR disputes over Berlin or regarding nuclear weapons. But it could work, he maintained, to localize disputes in which the superpowers did not have an overriding interest. By bringing in the small powers, the United Nation's preventive diplomacy has generally kept the major states out, thereby averting a dangerous confrontation while also working to defuse local crises. In Hammarskjöld's words, the job of the United Nations was "not to bring mankind to Heaven, but rather, to save it from Hell."

## Constraints on the Use of Force

In theory, the United Nations has the authority, through its Charter, to raise military forces and interject them into a conflict without the permission of the conflicting parties. Article 42 of the

UN Charter authorizes the Security Council to call for military operations against aggressors, and Article 43 calls on member states to provide such forces as requested. Moreover, Article 39 of the UN Charter says that the Security Council shall

> determine the existence of any threat to the peace, breach of the peace, or act of aggression and shall make recommendations, or decide what measure shall be taken . . . to maintain international peace and security. . . . Such action may include demonstrations, blockade, and other operations by air, sea, or land forces of Members of the United Nations.

A buildup of forces, an oppressive social system, or even the ascension to power of a militaristic government could plausibly be defined as a "threat to the peace." In theory, therefore, the United Nations has substantial discretionary powers for the use of force. In practice, however, it has been very cautious. Not only has it generally kept out of Big Power affairs; it has studiously avoided involvement in most civil wars as well. If the United Nations were to take its original mandate literally and squash any threat to peace, in the process it might well be squelching any hopes for national liberation on the part of Eritreans, Kurds, Basques, Kosovars, and so on. For better and worse, the United Nations operates under numerous constraints.

The weaknesses of the United Nations are more a reflection of the weakness of the world system as a whole: The fact that the world has been divided into contending and sovereign states, each of which nearly always evaluates a policy through the lens of national rather than international benefit.

## Sensitivity to State Sovereignty

The United Nations attempts to be sensitive to issues of national sovereignty, trying not to force choices between allegiance to the state on the one hand and allegiance to the world body on the other. For example, since the Korean War and the United Nations' controversial Congo intervention in the early 1960s, prospective host countries have had the option of forbidding any UN peacekeeping presence; the United Nations can send observers into a country only if it is specifically invited to do so, or under a direct mandate from the Security Council. And the United Nations usually withdraws its forces when the host country so requests (as happened in Egypt in 1967). "The umbrella was removed," complained Israeli diplomat Abba Eban, "at the precise moment when it began to rain." As a result, the United Nations has been less forceful than it might otherwise be, but it has also been able to exist in a changing world of self-interested states. This flexibility and adaptability has generally served the United Nations well and has kept it available for those cases in which it has been able to make its mark.

At the same time, rival superpowers have usually decided to handle their own controversies by themselves (e.g., the Berlin and Cuban Missile crises or the various strategic arms negotiations, in which the United Nations has had essentially no part). Similarly, the major powers continue to vigorously rebuff what they see as UN interference in their own foreign policy goals: The United States did not consult with the United Nations before sending troops to the Dominican Republic in 1965 or to Grenada in 1983. The U.S.-led invasion of Iraq in 2003 occurred in the face of explicit UN objections, although this clear breach of international peace was framed by the George W. Bush administration, in part, as an effort to enforce earlier UN resolutions directed against the regime of Saddam Hussein. Increasingly, the United Nations has become a forum for addressing the tension between the industrialized, mainly wealthy North and the largely impoverished South, as well as for confronting worldwide, transnational environmental challenges. To some extent, the various economic and social agencies of the United Nations also have addressed the long-standing North/South economic imbalance.

# Functionalism

When we consider the possible role of the United Nations in promoting peace, we are most likely to think about disarmament conferences and such relatively direct measures as international peacekeeping and mediation. But according to advocates of another approach—"functionalism"— the long-term prospects of peace are enhanced more by other, humanitarian activities that cut across state and national borders.

## Doing Good

Functionalism can best be understood by reference to such so-called functional agencies as the WHO, the FAO, and the Universal Postal Union, which are often given short shrift in popular discussions of the United Nations. The aims of these organizations do not include the establishment or maintenance of peace as such; rather, they include such goals as eradicating malaria, providing protein to undernourished children, and seeing to the fair exchange of international mail. Here is a small sample of some of the humanitarian efforts and successes of the United Nations:

1. A 13-year effort by the WHO eradicated smallpox worldwide in 1980. The WHO also helped wipe out polio from the Western Hemisphere. In 1974, only 5% of children in developing countries had been immunized against these "preventable plagues": polio, tetanus, measles, whooping cough, diphtheria, and tuberculosis. By 1995, as a result of the efforts of UNICEF and the WHO, the immunization rate was close to 80%, saving the lives of over 3 million children each year.

2. The UN has provided famine relief to millions of people. The International Fund for Agricultural Development, for example, provides economic credit for poor and marginalized groups, benefiting over 230 million people in nearly 100 developing countries, while building the potential for long-term hunger relief. In 1996 alone, 27 million refugees— mostly women and children—received food, shelter, medical aid, education, and repatriation assistance from the UN High Commissioner for Refugees.

3. Through sponsorship of several international treaties, the United Nations has been a leader in efforts to protect the ozone layer and curb global warming.

4. UN forestry action plans help limit deforestation and promote sustainable forestry practices for 90 countries.

5. The United Nations has also been active in providing safe drinking water for 1.3 billion people in rural areas and maintains ongoing efforts to help prevent overfishing and clean up pollution.

6. UN programs have helped raise the literacy rate of women in developing countries from 36% in 1970 to 56% in 1990 and 68% in 2000.

## Deemphasizing the Role of States

For its proponents, functionalism is way of deemphasizing the role of states and even, to some extent, undermining states' sovereign authority. Functionalism pins its hopes on a three-pronged strategy:

1. By reducing human misery through eradicating diseases, developing new strains of food crops, disseminating technological know-how, promoting literacy, and so forth, it is hoped that war will be made less likely.

2. By showing that institutions other than the state can attend to human needs—sometimes much better than states do—it is hoped that state sovereignty will gradually be undermined. (This is a goal of many "functionalists" but not one that is explicitly endorsed by the United Nations itself!)

3. By providing opportunities for interactions across political borders, it is hoped that mutual understanding, tolerance, and respect will be enhanced.

It is difficult to evaluate the success, or the future prospects, of functionalism. Although many people think that misery leads to war, no clear evidence supports this claim, at least with regard to international war. And prosperity often seems to have made violence more likely, not less, because strong and wealthy states, flushed with self-confidence, may be more inclined to engage in military adventures, while weaker ones—being less able—tend to be more cautious. On the other hand, making a better life for people might well decrease the chances of rebellions and civil wars, which constitute the great majority of recent armed conflicts. And, certainly, the humanitarian goals of functionalism are worthwhile in themselves, regardless of whether they result in fewer wars.

When it comes to undermining the authority of states, functionalism may be on stronger footing. Thus, some social scientists (stemming from the political philosophies of Hobbes, Locke, and Rousseau), emphasize the so-called social contract whereby loyalty of citizens to the state is supposed to result from a kind of exchange: The state provides certain benefits (most notably, security from violent attacks) to the populace, and in return, the people support the state by, for example, going to war when told to do so. But if inoculations are provided by doctors from the WHO, new tractors are provided by technicians from the FAO, or literacy programs are provided by teachers from UNESCO, it is possible that in subtle ways the state's claim to the loyalty of its citizens will be diminished. Many functionalists also hope that by experiencing the benefits of cooperation across traditional national and state boundaries, citizens could be weaned away from narrow, nationalistic concerns and gradually be imbued with an ethos that is cooperative and transnational.

Proponents of functionalism should be cautioned that states have historically insisted that patriotic loyalty supersedes other affiliations, often obtaining the cooperation and the lives of their subjects while providing little in return. States jealously guard their sovereignty and resist permitting activities that might subvert the loyalty of their citizens. One difficulty impeding the worldwide campaign against AIDS, for example, has been the refusal of some states to admit that they have a problem, for fear that it will result in a loss of international prestige and tourist dollars.

Nonetheless, by accepting the authority of certain functional international agencies, states are in fact accepting certain limitations on their sovereignty—probably a healthy step. For example, the use of airspace and sea lanes is now increasingly governed by decisions made by the

International Civil Aviation Organization and by the International Maritime Organization respectively. In these dimensions of international behavior, a given state no longer follows its own rules and procedures without regard to others. Also, in international telecommunications, the best frequencies are not simply preempted by the most powerful broadcasters; rather, it is universally recognized that to be legitimate, broadcasting frequencies must be allocated by the International Telecommunication Union.

Finally, communication and interactions of the sort provided by UN agencies are clearly beneficial. In his correspondence with Albert Einstein, Sigmund Freud declared, "Anything that creates emotional ties between human beings must inevitably counteract war. . . . Everything that leads to important shared action creates such common feelings." However, most wars have occurred between neighbors, who often know each other quite well. Close contact can breed greater resentment.

Nonetheless, the possibility exists that positive experiences among different and sometimes conflicting individuals and governments will lead to a snowballing, positive-feedback effect, which in turn can lead to improved relations at the official level. There have doubtless been gains from sister-city relationships or even international pen pals, which serve to break down the political, geographical, and ideological barriers between states. Turkey and Greece, for example, have a long history of hostility. In 1999, both countries experienced disastrous earthquakes in rapid succession, and in each case aid was provided to the victims. The resulting "earthquake diplomacy" appears to have thawed relations between these old rivals, although Turkey and Greece still disagree about the status of the Turkish part of Cyprus.

For some, a dramatic shared threat—such as an invasion or asteroid from outer space—might be needed to get many other feuding countries to put their antagonism and mistrust aside. Meanwhile, others have proposed multinational efforts to send a manned mission to Mars, to eradicate illiteracy and such diseases as malaria and tuberculosis, and so forth. While it is important not to be so idealistic as to lose touch with real limitations, it is equally important to recognize that certain advances hold the prospect of benefiting humanity.

# Regional Organizations

Competing military alliances, such as NATO and the former Warsaw Pact, were directed *outward* against potential aggressors and were not designed as collective security organizations intended to protect all members against an aggressor from *within* the region. By many accounts, NATO has been among the most successful cooperative military alliances in history, originally founded to oppose the Soviet Union and having emerged "victorious" when the Soviet Union fell apart. Even during the Cold War, however, there were substantial strains within NATO, concerning plans to deploy intermediate range nuclear weapons, as well as over details of the command structure and which circumstances justify a response by the organization as a whole. Major disputes, continuing to the present day, concern the "rules of engagement" (as in Afghanistan, where the United States resented the insistence of many NATO member states that their troops refrain from direct combat) as well as relative military budgets of member states; in 2011, for example, the United States devoted 4.6% of its Gross Domestic Product to its military, whereas the other NATO states averaged less than 1.8%, leading to the complaint by some influential Americans that these other states were "not doing their share."

Although not strictly collective security systems, other regional organizations include the Organization of African Unity (OAU), the Organization of American States (OAS), the Association of Southeast Asian Nations (ASEAN), the Arab League, and the Organization of Islamic Cooperation, consisting of 57 members, making it the largest international organization outside the United Nations. In some cases, these organizations have helped maintain the peace, providing for third-party pressure to be brought to bear against member states that might otherwise go to war.

When the "Soccer War" broke out between El Salvador and Honduras in 1969, the OAS was able to arrange a cease-fire and to provide independent observers to supervise its details. The OAU helped facilitate the settlement of border disputes between Morocco and Algeria and among Kenya, Somalia, and Ethiopia, and it played a major role in coordinating African opposition to South African apartheid. A military force from various West African states, notably Nigeria, helped stabilize the chaotic postcivil war situation in Liberia. The UN Charter explicitly endorses regional peacekeeping organizations. After an African Union Mission in Sudan was unable to end the genocide and keep the peace, the United Nations replaced it in 2008; prospects of success, however, are uncertain since Sudan and the newly independent South Sudan have fought over oil fields in the south, access to which requires pipelines running through the north.

In other cases, the United Nations has taken a backseat to regional organizations, as evidenced by the role of NATO military forces in enforcing peace in Bosnia, Kosovo, and Afghanistan after the U.S.-led "coalition" overthrew the Taliban in 2001. In the former Yugoslavia, the United Nations was initially unable to act because of Russian and Chinese opposition to UN intervention. Both countries were concerned that a precedent of UN intervention within a country's territorial borders might eventually have implications for their treatment of some of their own rebellious provinces, notably Chechnya and Tibet. So, the military action in Kosovo was carried out by NATO, in an extension of its traditional role, and represented a kind of collective security action, even though the former Yugoslavia is outside the territory of any NATO member. NATO activities in Afghanistan occurred after the United States found that its resources were stretched thin in Iraq. Similarly, NATO air power backed the ultimately successful Libyan rebels who overthrew the dictator Muammar Gadhafi.

On balance, however, regionalism has not been especially successful, for the same reason that the United Nations has been limited in its peacemaking: State sovereignty restricts UN effectiveness. In addition, regional organizations have in the past become vehicles for superpower domination. OAS members, for example, were largely coerced by the United States into supporting sanctions against Cuba and into approving the 1983 U.S. invasion of Grenada.

# IGOs, NGOs, TNOs, and MNCs

States also cooperate by forming so-called intergovernmental organizations (IGOs), such as the Organization of Petroleum Exporting Countries (OPEC). If, as Mao said, power once grew out of the barrel of a gun, it can also grow out of a barrel of oil: The oil revenues of the Middle East OPEC members in 1970 totaled $4 billion; just 4 years later, following price increases by the oil cartel, the figure was $60 billion. Today, it is approaching $1 trillion.

International cartels can be effective in raising certain prices; although this helps states exporting these commodities, it often hurts other states, which have to pay more for the products in question. Moreover, increases in international prices do not always help the poor, even in exporting countries. For example, unroasted coffee rose from $0.60 per pound in the mid-1970s to over $3 per pound in the late 1970s. As a result, the price to growers rose from $10.09 per pound to $0.14 per pound, which did not even keep up with inflation. And the pay raise to laborers was even less. The OPEC oil embargo of 1973 was particularly painful to oil-poor developing countries, whose economic growth was strangled by having to pay increased prices for petroleum. There is, accordingly, no clear evidence that monopoly cartels by producers, exporters, importers, and so forth will further world peace, except perhaps indirectly by weakening the traditional, state-centered world system. They seem as likely to foster war by generating intolerance, resentment, and further inequities of wealth.

Another notable IGO is the European Coal and Steel Community (ECSC), established in 1950 to integrate the industrial economies of West Germany, France, Italy, and the Benelux countries (Belgium, the Netherlands, and Luxembourg). By 1958, the ECSC had become a larger, more integrated entity, the European Economic Community, also known as the Common Market. Today, its successor, the European Union, comprises 25 states (and counting) with a total population and Gross National Product (GNP) exceeding that of the United States. Most trading and transportation barriers throughout Western and Central Europe have been eliminated, and 11 states are members of the European Monetary Union, employing a common currency, the euro. This process of transnational integration could ultimately lead to eventual political union, a kind of United States of Europe.[1]

However, transnational integration of the sort experienced by Europe can include distinct downsides, such as a lack of flexibility on the part of member states to deal with specific needs and crises. For example, the severe economic downturn experienced in 2012 by Greece and Spain was precipitated, at least in part, by the fact that these countries were spending more than they were taking in. In the "old days," when Spain had its own currency, the *peseta*, and Greece had its *drachma*, it would have been possible for these two countries to respond by devaluing their currency, which would have made their goods more affordable worldwide, and accordingly, improved their financial balance sheets by encouraging exports. However, since the euro is a single currency for much of Europe, individual countries with struggling economies no longer have this option.

## NGOs and MNCs

Finally, connections across international borders do not require the direct action of governments. There are many different kinds of nongovernmental organizations (NGOs),[2] including many of the world's religions (e.g., the Roman Catholic Church, the Society of Friends, Mennonites, etc.) and other groups whose affiliations cut across political boundaries, such as Rotary International, the International Physicians for the Prevention of Nuclear War (winner of the 1986 Nobel Peace Prize), CARE, the International Olympic Committee, Amnesty International, and a wide array of scientific, educational, business, and other professional organizations. Some of these groups seek as part of their agenda to break down the traditional barriers between states; most commonly, however, the various NGOs simply go about their affairs, which, as it happens, are best served by cutting across state boundaries. Thus, they are often subtly—benevolently— subversive of state authority. Whereas international organizations embody the principle of national sovereignty, transnational organizations try to ignore it.

One of the most important transnational phenomena of the 20th century is the emergence of powerful multinational corporations (MNCs). Such companies as General Motors, Microsoft, Toyota, Exxon, General Electric, Shell Oil, Ciba/Geigy, McDonald's, Philips, Lukoil, Google, Sony, and so on typically have commercial operations spread across many nations, as well as transnational communication links such as Facebook, Twitter, and so forth. Controversy surrounds the role of these multinational phenomena. On the one hand, given the size of these businesses—many of which have annual earnings larger than the GNP of a midsize country— they might be powerful actors on behalf of transnational integration. And since profitable operations generally require a smooth international environment, it would seem that the influential multinationals might act to reduce the probability of war. Furthermore, it can be argued that by entangling different countries in a web of economic interdependence as well as rapid communication across state boundaries, multinational corporations and linkages make war less likely, exemplifying a kind of benign functionalism—although one that is oriented more toward profits than toward altruistic deeds.

On the other hand, war has in the past been precipitated by economic entanglements; for example, during the 1930s, Japan was dependent on the United States for oil and iron ore, and this dependence led to competition, resentment, and fear that the United States intended to contain further Japanese expansion . . . which was true and which, in turn, contributed to the Japanese decision to attack Pearl Harbor in 1941. As to the multinationals themselves, their pursuit of profits rather than peace can sometimes involve the fomenting of disorder via revolution or coup (e.g., Kennecott Copper and ITT in Chile, in 1973) or counterrevolution (e.g., the influence of United Fruit in inducing the United States, through the Central Intelligence Agency, to overthrow the democratically elected Arbenz government in Guatemala in 1954).

In 1935, the U.S. Marine Corps Commandant General Smedley Butler (winner, incidentally, of three Congressional Medals of Honor) offered this first-person testimony to the role of multinational corporations in generating military intervention:

> I spent 33 years in the Marines, most of my time being a high-class muscle man for big business, for Wall Street and the bankers. In short, I was a racketeer for capitalism. I helped purify Nicaragua for the international banking house of Brown Brothers in 1910–1912. I helped make Mexico and especially Tampico safe for American oil interests in 1914. I brought light to the Dominican Republic for American sugar interests in 1916. I helped make Haiti and Cuba a decent place for the National City [Bank] boys to collect revenue in. I helped in the rape of half a dozen Central American republics for the benefit of Wall Street. In China in 1927 I helped to see to it that Standard Oil went its way unmolested. I had a swell racket. I was rewarded with honors, medals, promotions. I might have given Al Capone a few hints. The best he could do was to operate a racket in three city districts. The Marines operated on three continents.[3]

Charles Wilson, U.S. defense secretary during the Eisenhower administration, once announced that "what's good for General Motors is good for the country." In many cases, government officials have apparently acted on this presumption, deploying military forces worldwide in support of various multinational corporations, especially in the developing world. There is nothing new about this: The British East India Company, for example, was one of the guiding forces behind English colonial expansion during the 18th and 19th centuries, just as the Hudson's Bay Company and the large railroads (such as Union Pacific) helped finance the unpeaceful expansion of Canada and the United States throughout North America.

Furthermore, although the multinationals do provide (usually low-paying) jobs, they also extract resources, paying the lowest possible prices for raw materials and labor. In the process, they may contribute to the long-term environmental degradation of host—that is, exploited—countries, while also keeping these countries economically and often politically dependent on the multinational corporation. The resulting *dependencia* relationship (from the Spanish word for dependency) can be seen as a kind of neocolonialism that brings economic and social enslavement and neither prosperity nor peace.

In this regard, the World Trade Organization (WTO), founded in the mid-1990s to replace the international economic structure known as GATT—the General Agreement on Tariffs and Trade—also deserves mention. It exemplifies the complexities of multinational economic integration, widely known as "globalization." Essentially, this refers to the fact that worldwide communication and transportation have created what is increasingly a single, global economy. The WTO is especially devoted to establishing "free trade," by eliminating tariffs and opposing—by economic sanctions if need be—national policies it perceives as being in restraint of unfettered international trade. As a result of globalization, multinational corporations have been increasingly free to move factories to countries offering the lowest wage scales and minimal protection for human rights and the environment.

On the positive side, such activities offer jobs to impoverished people in developing countries who might not otherwise be employed. On the negative side, union rights and worker safety laws are frequently nonexistent in countries where foreign corporations are active, and the WTO has been roundly criticized as being a tool of the MNCs, simply fostering a "race to the bottom," when it comes to wages, human rights, and environmental stewardship. Thus, under globalization, MNCs often move their operations to those countries offering the lowest wages and the fewest worker and environmental protections. A major challenge for the WTO and for multinational corporations is to expand their concerns to include sustainable development for all people, not just for a privileged few.

# World Government?

It is increasingly clear that most of the problems afflicting our planet and our species transcend the boundaries of the nation-state. The notable exception, war, is itself in part a *product* of the nation-state, which leads to the question: What about the ultimate in "international cooperation"—namely, world government? Many informed people have long sought for alternatives to the nation-state system; not surprisingly, in an age of diminishing resources, shrinking distances, and ever-more-devastating weaponry, advocates of world government speak with a particular urgency.

Ever since the Tower of Babel, people have been plagued by their own political disunity. A potential solution, proposed in one form or another for literally thousands of years, has been to erase the existing political boundaries and to replace them with government structures at the largest, most inclusive level. This suggestion has been raised most urgently with regard to war and its prevention, since when it comes to war, nation-states have been only haltingly part of the solution; in the eyes of many, they are much of the problem. War-making has fractured the human community along ideological, social, and geopolitical lines. The prevention of war, accordingly, may well require that this community be reforged on a global scale.

## Pre- and Post-Westphalian Worlds

In medieval times, most Europeans owed their allegiance to a feudal lord, who in turn may have been subject to the secular authority of the Holy Roman Emperor and the religious power of the Pope. Then came the so-called Wars of Religion, culminating with the Thirty Years' War and the signing, in 1648, of the Treaty of Westphalia, which inaugurated the European state system that was eventually extended into the modern network of nation-states. For citizens in pre-Westphalian medieval times, concerns were overwhelmingly bounded by day-to-day events taking place in local surroundings, nearby towns, and the closest castle with its protector (or oppressor) nobility. The Westphalian world expanded the allegiance of state and national subjects to include lands and people more distant than one's immediate surroundings. In addition, technological advances, especially in transportation and communication, made it unavoidable for individuals to become involved with other places and people beyond their closest neighbors.

It can be argued that we now live in a post-Westphalian world, one in which the state or nation-state system is as obsolete as its feudal antecedents. Our mounting problems—notably pollution, poverty, resource depletion, and the destructive effects of war—supersede the old traditional political boundaries, making it imperative that we think as planetary citizens. The world, in short, has become functionally integrated, even while it remains politically fragmented.

## An Idea Whose Time Has Come?

The appeal of world government is basically that political and legal authorities ought to be able to force quarreling subordinates to refrain from violence, to respect larger common interests, and to solve their disputes peacefully. When two individuals disagree about something, they are expected to resolve the issue in a law-abiding manner; they are generally not permitted to start shooting each other. Settling disputes by a duel, popular in previous centuries, is analogous to nation-states "settling" today's disputes by war. The former has been universally outlawed; the latter has not—or rather, to put it idealistically, not yet. Similarly, individual households are not "sovereign." They do not have the right to dump toxic chemicals into "their" stream, thereby poisoning their neighbors' water supplies; why, then, should "sovereign" states be permitted to do this?

International organizations, such as the United Nations, offer frameworks for transcending political boundaries, but they operate within the present system of sovereign states, which are free to disagree, overrule, or simply ignore these organizations if they choose, because there is no larger authority that can impose restraint on the states themselves. In modern times, the parts (states) claim to be greater than the whole (humanity and the planet Earth). With a just and globally recognized world government, this would likely change: States would be prohibited from imposing themselves on their neighbors, whether economically, ecologically, or militarily, just as domestic governments now prevent individuals from overstepping their bounds and as federal governments keep the peace among their smaller constituent parts.

# A Brief History of Plans for World Government

By the 17th and 18th centuries, there were many proposals designed to establish worldwide political restraints on war making. William Penn, in 1693, wrote *An Essay Towards the Present and Future Peace of Europe,* which included a general parliament with military force to compel observance of its decrees. In 1713, the Abbé de Saint-Pierre, in his *Project for Perpetual Peace,* called for a "Senate of Europe" consisting of one representative from each European state, a plan that received much attention—and criticism. Voltaire, for example, noted that the states in question would overwhelmingly be monarchies and maintained that for peace to be preserved, democracy was necessary . . . and, at that time, democracy was unthinkable as a practical matter, just like world government.

Notable among such proposals, in addition to Jeremy Bentham's *Plan for an Universal and Perpetual Peace* (1789), was one advanced by the philosopher Jean-Jacques Rousseau (1712–1778). In his *Discourse on the Origin of Inequality,* Rousseau claimed that ownership of private property was the underlying cause of war and that to achieve world peace, it would therefore be necessary to abolish private property worldwide. His work, in turn, leads to an interesting—if currently unanswerable—question: If war is a result of a specific form of social organization, is this reason to condemn society per se or to justify certain wars? Thus, many political theorists have argued that the defense of property is a legitimate reason for war.

In *The Spirit of Laws* (1748), the French political philosopher Montesquieu maintained that war was not caused by human nature but by flaws inherent in the system of political states: "As soon as man enters a state of society . . . each particular society begins to feel its strength, whence arises a state of war between different nations."[4] Like Montesquieu, Rousseau argued that war could be prevented by severing the bonds by which the state held people together: "It is only after he is a citizen," noted Rousseau in *The Social Contract,* "that he becomes a soldier." Rousseau also maintained that "conquering princes make war at least as much on their subjects as on their enemies" and that "all the business of kings . . . is concerned with two objects alone; to extend their rule abroad or make it more absolute at home."

Probably the most ambitious design for a potentially workable form of world government was put forth by the great German philosopher Immanuel Kant. In *Perpetual Peace* (1795), Kant made the first major effort to focus specifically on the dangers of arms races and armaments, rather than just proposing yet another kind of world parliament. He also argued strongly for "republican" governments—that is, democracies—as being most likely to keep the peace and that people would necessarily act upon a rational understanding of what is in their shared best interest.

Kant's views should be contrasted with those of Thomas Hobbes, who, 150 years earlier, emphasized that sense perceptions are individual and personal, rather than universal, and that, because of this, individual viewpoints are bound to diverge, often violently. Accordingly, agreement among different and contending agents requires enforcement by fear of and obedience to an overarching power. Whereas Hobbes's emphasis on conflicting interests served to justify the existence of a powerful political state (the "Leviathan"), Kant was concerned with preventing the excesses of state power, especially when states interact militarily with one another. Kant proposed a worldwide organization that would be bound by international law and composed of a federation of free states. His work represented a tendency toward what may be called "optimistic internationalism" among peace theorists and devotees of world government. Rather than focusing on the problem posed by the state's very existence, Kant identified the cause of the problem in what he called the "lawlessness" of how states interact with one another. For Kant, some form of "external coercion" is therefore necessary to establish peace between states.

Shortly after Kant's book appeared, the Napoleonic Wars convulsed Europe. For some, this showed the impossibility of peace; for others, it emphasized its necessity.

## The Early 20th Century

The 19th century was not notable for important proposals concerning world government, at least in part because the post-Napoleonic Concert of Europe did a reasonably good job at keeping the fragile peace. After World War I, however, and the subsequent failure of the League of Nations, there was a flurry of renewed interest in world union, led by such groups as the United World Federalists. In fact, some tension arose between supporters of the United Nations and world federalists, who believe that international organizations of this sort tend to enhance state authority rather than transcend it. Some argue that so long as international organizations are structured around the preservation of state sovereignty, they are not so much steppingstones to world government as threats and impediments to its implementation.

## The Clark-Sohn Plan

The most elaborate and detailed scheme in the past half-century for world government was developed in 1966 by the legal scholars Grenville Clark and Louis Sohn.[5] It called for transforming the United Nations into a world peacekeeping unit, whereby states would retain their sovereignty *except* in matters of disarmament (which would be mandatory) and war (which would be prohibited). Clark and Sohn proposed to increase the power of the General Assembly and to change its voting procedures, making decision making largely proportional to population. Under the Clark-Sohn Plan, the four largest countries (China, India, the Soviet Union, and the United States) would have 30 votes each, the next eight largest would have 15 votes each, and so on. An Executive Council would be authorized to intervene militarily worldwide, so as to prevent war. Unlike the present UN Security Council, however, there would be no veto, although a clear majority (12 of 17 members) would have to approve any armed action, and this vote would have to include a majority of the largest states. An Inspection Commission would ensure that disarmament is total; after a 2-year census of each country's military forces, it would supervise 10% annual reductions, across the board. A World Peace Force, under UN auspices, would consist of 200,000 to 600,000 professional volunteers, initially using supplies and weapons obtained as the member states disarmed themselves. Nuclear weapons would not be supplied to this force, but they could be accumulated if needed—from a Nuclear Energy Authority—to deter the use or threatened use of nuclear weapons by any state that illegally retained a small cache.

The Clark-Sohn Plan, although very detailed and specific, does not offer any suggestions as to the means of achieving its major goal, of getting from "here" to "there." It does illustrate, however, that there is no shortage of precise ideas about possible future world governments. Whatever the strengths or weaknesses of any particular plan, the point is that world government has not been stymied by a shortage of good ideas but rather by a lack of political will.

# Pros and Cons of World Government

## The Maintenance of Peace

The argument for peacefulness under world government is derived largely from analogy: Since domestic governments enforce peace (e.g., between New York and Pennsylvania in the United States) or attempt to do so (Armenia and Azerbaijan from the former Soviet Union), a world government would presumably do the same, treating nation-states much as municipal governments now treat their citizens or as federal governments now treat their subordinate provinces or constituent republics. But analogies do not always hold. Moreover, federal governments do not always create or maintain peace: Civil wars are common and often highly destructive. Europe during the 19th century, for example, was composed of feisty sovereign states, while the United States was a single, ostensibly united country. Yet, the war casualties suffered by the "United" States during its civil war (about 600,000) were almost precisely equal in number to the casualties suffered by Europe during the entire period between 1815 and 1913.

Perhaps if they were not held forcibly within a larger state, independent republics would be freer to work out their ethnic conflicts in peace. Alternatively, maybe they would go to war: Ethnic antagonisms within the former Yugoslavia, for example, were kept from erupting into violence because of the inhibiting and unifying influence of the central government in Belgrade, under a widely respected leader, Josip Tito (a Croat). With that central force removed, the constituent republics (notably Serbia, Croatia, and Bosnia) were vulnerable to violence appeals to previously submerged nationalistic passions. A similar situation developed in post–Saddam Hussein Iraq, with many Shiites, Sunnis, and Kurds resisting a transnational identity as Iraqis.

## The Danger of Oppression

To some people, the prospect of a world government is truly frightening. These include many persons—notably in the United States—associated with various self-styled "militia" and "patriot" movements, who believe that an oppressive world government, most likely under the auspices of the United Nations, is ready to swoop down in fleets of black helicopters and deprive them of their civil liberties (notably, their guns).Notwithstanding such fantasies, the claim that, as a cure, world government might be worse than the disease (state anarchy) needs to be taken seriously.

If large political units tend to be unresponsive to the needs of their citizens and are sometimes oppressive, imagine the danger inherent in government by a worldwide "super state" with the power to enforce its decrees on everyone. (The Clark-Sohn Plan carefully envisioned that the armed forces of several countries, combined, would exceed those of the world force, thereby hedging against centralized despotism.) But why, critics ask, should we expect better government from a world authority than we now get from national governments? And, it is worth noting, many states today do not enjoy functioning representative democracies. So what, if anything, guarantees that a world government would not be a worldwide tyranny? Most of us want to have our cake and eat it too: peace *and* freedom, international order *and* national sovereignty. But perhaps these goals are conflicting. If so, and if we have to choose, which is preferable? Or perhaps we can hope for a compromise, maybe along the lines of the Clark-Sohn Plan, something that offers restrictions on the state's ability to make war, without impinging on other aspects of domestic life.

This may be easier said than done, however. For one thing, powerful states are usually not just uninterested but often vigorously opposed to world government, since it would require that they give up some of the influence and power that they exercise today. It might also make them subject to certain basic principles of equality and fairness, from which they are at present largely exempt. In some cases—notably that of the United States—state sovereignty combined with military/ economic/scientific/political might has been a means of achieving and maintaining what many people believe to be inequitable access to the world's riches. What if, having surrendered its military autonomy, the United States is faced with a demand from the economically less developed states that it cease consuming scarce resources and polluting the planet out of proportion to its population or that it redistribute its wealth? Would world government mean a responsibility to share? If so, many in the wealthy West might prefer autonomy and gluttony, even at the risk of occasional war.

Critics of world government also point to what they see as an inconsistency. World government is supposed to be necessary because the ferocious Hobbesian world of independent nation-states is simply too violent and irresponsible to continue unchecked. But what supports the assertion that fierce competitors and vicious inclinations can be rendered peaceful by a kind of world government modeled after the ideals of John Locke and other Euro-American liberals: a limited, mild, and democratic authority that is based largely on mutual consent? Such a "Lockean" government might indeed be more palatable than its Hobbesian alternative, but if the problem is so grave, the proposed solution might simply be inadequate. In short, a Hobbesian world may require a Hobbesian government, and the problem is that a Hobbesian government is likely to be very unpleasant. It might be even more unpleasant—and more difficult to reform—if its resources and authority were global rather than merely national.

On the other hand, there is no reason why a functioning world government could not allow current national governments to continue exercising autonomy and sovereignty in their internal affairs. But rather than worrying about what the various states would have to surrender, perhaps we should focus on what they would be gaining. World government could then be viewed not so much as requiring us to give up something that we now have (state sovereignty and the ability to threaten and wage offensive war) but rather as offering the opportunity to gain something now lacking and desperately needed: Extending the peaceful rule of law to international affairs and, with it, a massive increase in genuine national and global security.

As to criticism that world government would deprive states of one of the most important perquisites of state sovereignty—deciding whether or not to go to war—it is sobering to realize that such independence as the nation-states now cherish is in part illusory. The Soviet Union, for example, had no choice about entering World War II; when it was attacked by Germany in June 1941, it was forced to respond. Similarly, the United States was propelled into World War II not so much by a declaration of war by the U.S. House of Representatives as by decisions made by the Imperial War Council in Tokyo. And would it have been disadvantageous to world peace, not to mention to the United States, if it had not been "free" to invade Iraq in 2003?

Advocates of world government emphasize that any viable world authority would have clear enforcement powers but that these powers would also be carefully circumscribed and limited. As with the U.S. federal government, rights not specifically granted to a world authority would be reserved for its constituent states. Similarly, in our private lives, we cherish certain personal rights while also accepting restrictions on them: One person's freedom to swing his or her arm ends, for example, where someone else's nose begins. Under minimalist world government, nation-states would have to accept just two restrictions circumscribing their freedom: They would be obliged (1) not to maintain armed forces beyond police capacities needed to deter and prosecute criminals and (2) not to behave aggressively against other states.

Similarly, there need be no anxiety that world government would necessarily mean the homogenization of national identities. Within the United States, Florida is still recognizably distinct from Alaska, and Maine from Arizona, just as national cultures within Russia range from urban Muscovites to tundra-dwelling indigenous people of Siberia and from industrialism to seminomadic Islamic pastoralism. As Israeli prime minister Golda Meir once pointed out: "Internationalism doesn't mean the end of individual nations. Orchestras don't mean the end of violins."

# The Dream of World Government: A Waste of Time?

There is one other potential problem of world government: By focusing on it, devotees may lose touch with the world and its serious problems as they now exist. Or these problems may simply be ignored by the self-styled "realists" who run today's states and, by extension, the world. Lost in dreams of utopia, hungering after what may turn out to be nothing more than "globaloney," proponents of world government run the risk of being marginalized, considered irrelevant to "serious" discourse on issues of war and peace. If advocates of peace studies withdraw into musings over ideal but impractical solutions to real problems, they essentially give over the reins of power to those willing to deal instead with current reality. And time itself is critical, since world government will certainly not happen tomorrow, while wars are happening today. Even Freud, who supported the idea of world government, also warned (in his famous correspondence with Albert Einstein) about unrealistic dreams that "conjure up an ugly picture of mills which grind so slowly that, before the flour is ready, men are dead of hunger."

But no partisan of peace or devotee of world government recommends putting all of one's eggs in the one distant basket of global political union. It is not necessary to choose between nuclear arms reduction and world government, between peace in the Middle East and global disarmament, or between ecological harmony and transnational thinking and acting. In addition, even while addressing immediate, practical, pressing issues, isn't there also a need to focus on ultimate goals, even if they seem—at the moment—to exceed our grasp? As General Omar Bradley once pointed out, "It is time we steered by the stars and not by the lights of each passing ship."

Accordingly, we might ask the self-styled realists—the practical, hardheaded men (and, occasional female militarists notwithstanding, they are still largely *men*) if it is truly realistic to believe that the state system, with its divisions and contradictions and its history of repetitive warfare and state-centered selfishness, can be relied on to keep the peace and create a decent and humane planet into the indefinite future? Clearly, world government is unlikely to be perfect, but in view of the current state system's imperfections, it seems unlikely to be worse, or more dangerous, than our current plight. The dangers of a world with some form of centralized, war-suppressing government seem to pale in contrast to the dangers of a world without it.

# The Prospects for World Government

## A Penchant for Separating?

Despite the attractiveness of the idea of world government, the fact is that most people—once organized into relatively large units—show far more eagerness for splitting off than for joining together. There have been virtually no examples of the successful merging of states. The union of

North and South Vietnam might be one such case, although it was only achieved via appalling violence—and despite substantial resistance from many of the South Vietnamese themselves. Moreover, Vietnam had previously been a single country, so the outcome was not so much the merging of different states as the reunification of a state that had been artificially separated. The same can be said of the reunification of Germany in 1989 after its post–World War II separation into West and East.

At one time, Egypt and Syria attempted a peaceful merger, establishing the United Arab Republic, but that union was quickly disbanded. The former Yugoslavia now consists of separate, independent states: Slovenia, Croatia, Bosnia, Serbia, Montenegro, Macedonia, and the partially recognized Republic of Kosovo. The former Czechoslovakia broke up into Slovakia and the Czech Republic, and of course, what had been the Soviet Union now consists of numerous independent states, ranging from the Baltic republics of Latvia, Lithuania, and Estonia to the "stans" (Kazakhstan, Turkmenistan, and so forth) of central Asia.[6]

When consolidation has occurred, a smaller unit is typically swallowed up by a larger one, often against its will: Tibet was incorporated into China, Goa into India, and the Baltic states into the Soviet Union after World War I. A major reason, indeed, for the breakup of the Soviet Union was the fact that it was an artificial entity, composed of numerous republics, many of which maintained a national ethnic identity that resisted decades of domination and efforts to subordinate local loyalty to a larger Soviet whole. Furthermore, much of the tension in the world today is generated specifically by regions desiring not to submerge their identities into a larger whole but rather to *separate* themselves from control by a larger whole: Catholics in Northern Ireland, Basques in Spain, Tamils in Sri Lanka, Kurds in Iraq, Turkey, Iran, and Syria, and so on.

Despite its flaws, dangers, and difficulties, world government may well be essential. However, just because something is desirable—even necessary—does not mean that it will come to pass. Thus, it is not sufficient simply to state that world government ought to emerge because it is a prerequisite for survival. Maybe we will not survive with or without a world government. But given the current and likely future tensions among nuclear-armed states, it is hard to imagine a world government doing any worse!

## Commitment to States

The pressures against world government are strong. People retain a deep loyalty to their nation-states and also a powerful distrust of large, centralized systems. In addition, like so many proposals for dramatic reform (for example, disarmament), the "devil is in the details." How do we get from here to there?

In 1712, the French Abbé de Saint-Pierre proposed his pan-European Union, complete with a Senate of Peace, which would have authority over military forces sufficient to compel any recalcitrant ruler to submit to the will of the larger unit. Interestingly, the French foreign minister at the time, André Hercule de Fleury did not question the desirability of such a system, but he pointed out to Saint-Pierre: "You have forgotten an essential article, that of dispatching missionaries to touch the hearts of princes and to persuade them to enter into your views."

If state leaders agreed to a world government, it might be roughly equivalent to slaveholders banding together to outlaw slavery. But slavery has in fact been outlawed worldwide, sometimes (as in the United States) only after much bloodshed. It might also be worthwhile to examine in greater detail how certain nation-states (e.g., Sweden, Holland, Portugal, Spain) have made a seemingly healthy transition from world power to secondary status in international politics. This might serve not only to prepare the United States for the possibility of future decline in a world of continuing nation-states but also perhaps to suggest how the state system itself might be afforded lesser prominence and perhaps eventually eased out of existence.

At present, no powerful country seems prone to relinquish sovereignty and embrace world government; in most respects, such states remain fiercely independent. Western capitalist nations in particular tend to be particularly jealous about guarding their political autonomy. And whereas Marxist theory calls for the eventual "withering away" of the state, the former Soviet Union and its allies were equally unreceptive to world government—unless it were under Soviet control!

When the state is taken to embody the needs and aspirations of its citizens, there is little reason to surrender the state's power. Even "peace groups" were described as unnecessary in most Soviet bloc states, since the state itself was purported to be everybody's collective "peace group." (*It* was not the problem; *other* states were the problem!) Traditionally, the political right wing has engaged in relatively more militaristic flag-waving patriotism, while accusing the left of being part of, or duped by, various "international conspiracies," generally communist inspired. However, the heyday of socialist internationalism, as we have seen, was in the late 19th and early 20th centuries; in recent decades, many leftists have shown as much adherence to their own nation-state as have partisans of the political right. And in much of the developing world, militant nationalism is even more pronounced than in the industrialized North.

## Examples of a Wider Identity

Although we do not know whether people are capable of acting as part of a united planet, the prospects may not be all that bleak. The United States of America, for example, is a very diverse country, made up of Caucasians, African Americans, Native Americans, Asian Americans, Catholics, Protestants, Jews, Buddhists, Muslims, and so on—and yet, the country as a whole enjoys a reasonable degree of coherence despite long-standing prejudices, ethnocentrism, and racial enmities. Although some may say that U.S. citizens are united by shared fear of "the other"—Chinese or North Korean communists, Islamic terrorists, international Mafia-style gangsters—the United States also has achieved its unity from a shared cultural and social identity, a shared history, and shared ideals. Certainly, the human species is capable of establishing even wider affiliations than those between Maine and Hawaii, if feelings of connection are encouraged from birth and are reinforced by teaching, symbols, slogans, and a range of appeals, to emotion as well as reason. We are all subjected to vast amounts of pronational and prostate propaganda. Even more desirable would be education for a psychology of world citizenship.

Take another example: People calling themselves "Germans" and "French" have long been at each other's throats, via their respective governments, the nation-states we identify as Germany and France. Yet, quite near these perennially warring states, several million very "French" people live—and have lived for centuries—peacefully with about three times as many equally "German" people. The difference is that in the former case, a sovereign state of Germany has confronted an equally sovereign France, whereas in the latter, "French" and "German" have submerged war-making authority under the sovereignty of a third shared entity, known as Switzerland (which also contains a third large subpopulation that is Italian speaking). Similarly, English and Irish, Italians and Austrians, Vietnamese and Chinese, and Arabs and Jews all have waged brutal wars across the globe . . . but when they become citizens of the United States of America, they submit themselves to a common identity and live together peaceably, at least for the most part. Clearly, it can be done.

# The Case of the United States of America

Consider again the United States of America as it is now constituted: When California, for example, has a dispute with Arizona regarding water rights, the two governments do not call up their militias and fight it out. The "law of force" is subordinated to the "force of law," and both sides submit arguments, if need be, to the U.S. Supreme Court. Then, they abide by the ruling. The states of the United States do not walk about like gunslingers from the Wild West, revolvers on their hips, ready to settle disputes by the fastest draw.

Following the Revolutionary War, the United States under the Articles of Confederation was a loose amalgamation of states, headed toward disaster because of its virtual anarchy. Maryland and Delaware fought an undeclared "oyster war" over fishing rights to the Potomac River; nine states had navies of their own; state militias were separate and distinct armies; seven of the states even printed their own currency; New York placed a tariff on wood from Connecticut and on butter from New Jersey; Boston boycotted grain from Rhode Island; various states imposed taxes on shipping from other states; and so on. Things were a mess, just as they are in the world today.

With the writing of the U.S. Constitution, however, a strong federal system was created, out of whole cloth. Advocates of world government point to this transition from pluralism to unity that gave birth to the United States of America as "the great rehearsal" for world federalism, a transition that the world system can also make if and when the need is widely recognized. Just as some people today fear a potential world "super state," the delegates to the Constitutional Convention also feared to establish a potential despotic dictatorship. Yet, the framers of the Constitution recognized that the semi-independent 13 states were threatened with war and chaos, so they successfully designed a workable federal union, one that preserved the rights of states in regulating their internal affairs while establishing a strong federal system capable of providing unity and ensuring the peace. They did this by establishing a careful, democratic system of checks and balances. At present, the politically independent nation-states of Europe, with all their similarities and all the benefits of federation, have moved haltingly and erratically but with increasing confidence toward a limited and fragile form of economic and legal union.

Most European states recognize the euro as a common currency; furthermore, within most countries of Europe, passports and visas are now entirely unnecessary, and passage through international borders—previously heavily controlled and guarded—is now usually very fast and no more consequential than going from Texas to Oklahoma, despite a history of major wars and a present reality of numerous distinct and cherished linguistic and cultural traditions.

The reality of what the United States accomplished—in the face of grave doubts—suggests the magnitude of what can be achieved. The problem in 1787 was for people to learn to think nationally about the United States, rather than locally. It wasn't until after the Civil War that this was actually achieved: Prior to 1865, Americans were likely to discuss the "United States" as a plural noun. Only by the late 19th century, was it consistently employed in the singular. Now, a major challenge is for people to learn to think internationally, about the planet, rather than nationally.

Must world government then wait until humanity has achieved a higher level of spiritual development? It is true that the "founding fathers" are currently revered in the United States, but they were human beings, just like us. It is also true that the U.S. Constitution was not perfect (although it was certainly better than what preceded it). Moreover, no one in the late 18th century claimed that a strong federal government could not be enacted until all the inhabitants of North America had first become saints.

# Toward World Government?

Several transgovernmental movements have sought to go beyond the current state system by establishing links that intentionally defy present political boundaries. Thus, a number of international tribunals have worked toward delegitimizing certain warlike actions of states, trying to apply principles of international law, even though such proceedings have lacked enforcement capability. For example, the Russell Tribunal in the 1960s excoriated the U.S. wars in Vietnam and the rest of the former Indochina; in 1982, at a meeting held in Nuremberg, another tribunal of international legal experts heard testimony and condemned the existing nuclear weapons regime. The MacBride Commission in Britain investigated Israel's 1982 invasion of Lebanon and pronounced it a violation of international law. Such tribunals and peace movements generally are unpopular with the governments of affected nation-states, because they seek to restrict war-making capacity and also because they represent a budding transnational sensitivity, which might one day undermine state authority more generally.

If these activities truly threaten the current system of state sovereignty, it is an example of the important sociological principle that "if people define situations as real, they are real in their consequences." If we define ourselves as bound irreparably to the current state system, we are so bound, by a kind of self-fulfilling prophecy. But the more we look beyond the states—and the more we find when we do so—the more we may find ourselves liberated from our customary allegiances.

Indeed, one of the things that keeps us prisoners of the state system is our difficulty in envisioning alternatives to it. Few people, as recently as 1990, would have predicted a 21st-century world in which South Africa has become a democratic, multiracial state or in which the Soviet Union has dissolved and, with it, the Cold War. Two futures are easy to imagine: this world ending with the "bang" of nuclear war or with the "whimper" of continued degradation (ecological, economic, social) plus ongoing conventional wars. Both of these are plausible but undesirable extrapolations of the status quo. World government—in whatever specific form—offers a potential third way.

Recently, there has been a proliferation of planetary gatherings, reflecting and dramatizing the fact that as advances in communication and transportation make the world smaller, the costs and responsibilities of technology—no less than its benefits—require attention on a global scale. Such conferences include those on world population, women's rights, food, pollution, the status of indigenous people, the fights against racism and against AIDS, linkages between disarmament and development, problems of global warming, ozone depletion, destruction of the world's rainforests, and the need to protect biodiversity. With or without world government, it is clear that worldwide problems may not be solved if governments remain stiffly within their traditional state boundaries.

Not surprisingly, the new social movements tend to be either local, community based, or region centered (and thus below the level of the state) or transnational and global (above the level of the state). Moreover, states themselves have already begun to surrender some aspects of sovereignty, as in the case of certain international organizations, as well as the general acknowledgment of—if not universal obedience to—international law. Perhaps this is a foot in the door. Or perhaps it simply reflects a defensive strategy by the states themselves: Make a few trivial concessions to "the common good" while at the same time remaining as unwilling as ever to permit any meaningful challenge to their authority. But more subtly, many nation-states have already surrendered some aspects of their autonomy: The U.S. government, for example, is not politically "free" to declare war on Canada. A kind of *de facto* (in fact) restriction of state sovereignty has thus already come into effect, even though it is not yet *de jure* (in law). War is currently extremely unlikely between such historical rivals as Britain and France, Finland or Turkey and Russia, France and Germany, and Japan and the United States.

Interest in world government tends to increase after major world wars—notably, immediately following World Wars I and II. Then, just as predictably, when memories of the horrors of the last war fade, so do impassioned cries of "Never Again! No More War!" So, unfortunately, perhaps another major war, or a close brush with nuclear obliteration, will be necessary for people to rise up and demand a dramatic reworking—if not a surrender—of state sovereignty. Meanwhile, "futurism" need not be limited to technological panaceas and derring-do, a world of genetic engineering, cyborgs, and Star Wars. It can also include moving beyond the state and national security to global human security.

It is also important not to discount the role of vision and visionaries. Before we can ever establish a better world, we must first imagine it. This is not to deny the importance of dealing with the world as it is. It simply emphasizes that to "accept" current realities is not necessarily to accept them as God-given, engraved in stone, or immune to challenge and change. The world system of states, no matter how firmly entrenched, is nothing more than a human creation—and a relatively recent one at that. There is no reason to think that it is so perfect, or so powerful, as to be a permanent part of the human condition. "The dogmas of the quiet past," wrote Abraham Lincoln, "are inadequate to the stormy present. We must think anew and act anew." Only if we think, plan, dream, and act for a future world that is better than today's or yesterday's can we have any hope of attaining such a future.

## A FINAL NOTE ON INTERNATIONAL COOPERATION

Although their record has not been perfect, the many of the activities of international organizations should be commended. Some of these organizations—especially the United Nations and its many branches—promote human and planetary betterment in numerous ways, including but not limited to the keeping of "negative peace." International organizations also represent a partial step in the progression from individualism through nationalism to globalism, a transition that may well be essential if we are ever to give peace a realistic chance. As such, international organizations can be seen as possible halfway houses toward the establishment and solidification of international law and perhaps even world government. And world government, although easily derided as impossible and unrealistic, warrants serious consideration.

## NOTES

1. Although as of 2012, with Europe reeling because of an extended economic crisis—especially among the Mediterranean states (Greece, Portugal, Spain, and to some extent Italy as well) and Ireland—the future of the euro and of European political and economic integration remains somewhat shaky.

2. Peace researcher Johan Galtung has pointed out that the phrase *nongovernmental organizations* is regrettable, since defining such organizations with respect to governments gives too much importance to the latter; analogously, consider replacing "nongovernmental organizations" with "nonpeople organizations"! In place of NGOs, therefore, Galtung suggests using *interpeople organizations* or some equivalent phrase.

3. Smedley Butler. 1935. Untitled article. *Common Sense*.

4. Charles L. de Montesquieu. 1949. *The Spirit of Laws*. New York: Hafner.

5. Grenville Clark and Louis Sohn. 1960. *World Peace Through World Law*. Cambridge, MA: Harvard University Press.

6. At one point during the disintegration of the USSR, it was referred to as the UFFR: The union of fewer and fewer republics.

## QUESTIONS FOR FURTHER REFLECTION

1. What can be learned from the failure of the League of Nations? Is the United Nations similarly at risk?

2. In what way does the United Nations differ from world government? How is it similar?

3. Sketch the positive and negative effects of multinational corporations on the maintenance of peace.

4. Assess the realistic prospects for world government, paying particular attention to people's fears and hopes.

5. Describe how current and recent international events have impacted the feasibility and/or the desirability of world government.

## SUGGESTIONS FOR FURTHER READING

Kelly-Kate S. Pease. 1999. *International Organizations: Perspectives on Governance in the Twenty-First Century*. Saddle Hill, NJ: Prentice-Hall.

Linda Fasulo. 2009. *An Insider's Guide to the UN*, 2nd ed. New Haven, CT: Yale University Press.

Richard Falk. 1975. *A Study of Future Worlds*. New York: Free Press.

Shamima Ahmed and David Potter. 2006. *NGOs in International Politics*. Bloomfield, CT: Kumarian Press.

Thomas G. Weiss and Sam Daws, eds. 2009. *The Oxford Handbook on the United Nations*. New York: Oxford University Press.

# CHAPTER 15

# PEACE THROUGH STRENGTH?

South Korean military forces engaging in a public show of strength during 2005.

*Source:* © 2008 Getty Images.

> *Have you walked up and down upon the earth lately? I have; and I have examined Man's wonderful inventions. And I tell you that in the arts of life man invents nothing but in the arts of death he outdoes Nature herself . . . his heart is in his weapons. . . . Man measures his strength by his destructiveness.*
>
> —The Devil, in George Bernard Shaw's *Man and Superman*

> *To say that force is sometimes necessary is not a call to cynicism—it is a recognition of history, the imperfections of man, and the limits of reason.*
>
> —Barack Obama

When asked about the most important way of maintaining peace, most people today—including governmental leaders—point to military strength. The slogan of the Strategic Air Command (SAC) unblushingly proclaims, "Peace Is Our Profession." (Below this sign at SAC headquarters, someone once scrawled, "Mass Murder Is Our Specialty"!) Not surprisingly, advocates of peace studies and peace activists generally look askance at the traditional reliance on military force to maintain peace, viewing armed force as part of the problem, not the solution.

Like it or not, and agree with it or not, "Peace Through Strength" has probably been the most politically potent and influential concept of war prevention in recent times. It is also one of the most perilous. Whether or not it "worked" in maintaining peace in the past, and whether it will work in the 21st century, "Peace Through Strength" undoubtedly succeeds in one sense at least: It directs the expenditure of vast quantities of national wealth, and virtually all major governments adhere to its precepts. Accordingly, a major challenge for peace studies and the peace movement is to break away from the existing war system—which includes reliance on peace through strength—and to establish a viable ecology of peace whose strength does not derive from violence or the threat of violence.

The motto "Peace Through Strength" is a modern version of the Latin *si vis pacem, para bellum* ("if you want peace, prepare for war"), which has been taken as axiomatic by entire generations of conventional politicians and military leaders. In all fairness, we should at least consider that this perspective may be more than a rationalization for the maintenance of large and threatening armed forces, which exist for other reasons that are rarely acknowledged (such as economic gain, career benefits, distracting the populace, and/or the satisfaction of personal psychological needs to feel potent and powerful, to have clearly defined enemies, and so on). There have been, and still are, many people who sincerely believe that the only way to achieve peace is by the ability and willingness to employ military force.

# Balance of Power

Generally, a geopolitical "balance of power" is obtained when contending states are roughly equal in their military strength. It is intimately associated with the assumption of "peace through strength" and has often been used as an argument in favor of military forces. The argument, in short, is that weakness invites aggression and so the power of one side must be balanced by that of others. Hence, what international relations theorists have called "bipolar" and "multipolar" worlds are more stable and less prone to war than "unipolar" ones.

Thus, peace through strength relies fundamentally on deterrence, the expectation that a would-be aggressor would refrain from attacking opponents who are more powerful than it or who are capable of inflicting unacceptable damage if attacked. Hence, adherence to balance of power implies a continuing arms race or, possibly, mutual agreements to keep the system stable by keeping the mutual threat symmetrical. To some extent, the Cold War involved maintaining a balance of power (more accurately, perhaps, a balance of terror) between the nuclear forces of the United States and those of the Soviet Union. Before that, and especially during the 18th and 19th centuries, balance of power referred less to arms races than to a constantly shifting system of alliances whereby states arranged themselves to keep any one from being too powerful.

Until the end of World War II, Great Britain saw itself as the "balancer" in Europe, consistently aligning itself with weaker powers so as to prevent the emergence of stronger ones that might threaten its supremacy. Wars have often been fought in order to "maintain the balance," although in some cases countries have refrained from war so as not to upset a presumed balance. For example, at the conclusion of the first Gulf War in 1991, the United States avoided overthrowing Saddam Hussein's government by seizing Baghdad in part out of concern that a stable, even if dictatorial, Iraq served as a useful counterbalance to the power of Syria and Iran.

Following World War II, the United States and the Soviet Union emerged as the two dominant states, initiating a "bipolar" balance of nuclear power, with each seeking to buttress its position by the establishment of competing alliances and courting the favor of neutral countries. With the end of the Cold War, that situation changed dramatically, and the United States emerged as the undisputed single great power, or unipolar "hegemon," especially in military terms. It remains to be seen whether other countries will come to fear and/or resent such an imbalance and whether international fear and resentment of an unbalanced "unipolar world" will precipitate new alliances seeking to reestablish a new balance.

The emergence of China, India, Brazil, Russia and Japan (along with the "Asian tigers" of South Korea, Thailand, Malaysia, Singapore, and Taiwan), as well a united Europe, has created a kind of "multipolar" balance, especially in the economic sphere. Some authorities claim that multipolar systems are more stable and less warlike than bipolar systems, because they involve (1) more cross-cutting loyalties, (2) less attention directed to any one state by another, and (3) the fact that increased armaments by one state (an incipient arms race) has less impact on the security of any other state. On the other hand, other authorities point out that satisfactory balances may be more difficult to achieve with the many different actors of a multipolar system and also that the greater diversity of interests and demands provides more opportunities for conflict.

# Problems With Balance of Power

Advocates of balance of power often assume and sometimes assert that such a balance deters war. It remains uncertain, however, whether wars are more or less likely during conditions of balance. Thus, the Peloponnesian War presumably would not have occurred if Athens and Sparta had not been so close in strength as to constitute a threat to each other. This may also have been the case for the Punic Wars between Rome and Carthage. During the *Pax Romana,* Rome was supreme in the Mediterranean world; there was no balance of power, yet there was comparative negative peace. Similarly, there has never been a war between the Soviet Union and Bulgaria or between the United States and Canada or Mexico (at least not recently!), in part because of the *imbalance* of power in these cases.

## Promoting War

Wars often occur when rival states disagree about their relative strength and they end when both sides agree: The stronger side is defined by having won, and the weaker by having lost. Looking at postwar distributions of power, we can conclude that indecisive wars, which resulted in a relative balance of forces, were more likely to result in another war shortly thereafter, whereas decisive victories led more frequently to periods of peace. For example, many Germans felt that they had not been clearly defeated in World War I, attributing their loss to treason and insufficient governmental willpower (a "stab in the back"). World War II followed, barely two decades later. By contrast, World War II was an undisputed defeat for the Axis Powers and has led to a much more firmly established regime of peace, at least among the great powers that fought World War II.

## Slight Imbalances and Their Effects

Evidence suggests that wars tend to break out when there is a slight imbalance, especially if one side has grown rapidly but has not yet reached the power of its opponent. In this situation, the status-quo power (the one seeking to maintain things as they are) feels threatened that the balance is about to tip against it, sometimes calculating that war now is preferable to waiting for the upstart to become stronger. States actively committed to a balance of power, in short, have an incentive to attack their neighbors if they perceive an adverse shift in that balance. Whether that attack is justified as preventive (to forestall gradual change and eventual war) or preemptive (jumping the gun to short-circuit an attack that is considered imminent), states sometimes jump through a "window of opportunity" and begin a war, lest it become a "window of vulnerability" through which they are attacked. This happened to Germany, for example, in 1914. In July of that year, General Helmuth von Moltke, the German chief of staff, wrote:

> "Basically, Russia is not at the moment ready for war. Nor do France or England want war now. In a few years, on all reasonable assumptions, Russia will be ready. By then it will overwhelm us with the number of its troops."[1]

Balance-of-power theories contain an important and often unstated assumption: Given the opportunity, a stronger state will attack a weaker one. This, presumably, is why severe imbalances must be prevented. Whereas there have been cases of aggression by very strong against very weak states (e.g., the Soviet Union attacking Finland in 1939, China attacking Vietnam in 1979, the United States attacking Iraq in 2003) it is also true that the world abounds in unbalanced power relationships, many of them even involving neighboring countries, which have not resulted in war. Brazil, for example, does not seem poised to invade Uruguay; nor is India about to attack Bhutan (but India may attack, or be attacked by, China or Pakistan, which are also nuclear powers). The fact that power imbalances do not necessarily produce war has not, however, diminished the cogency of the concept for those who believe strongly in it.

Upsetting a balance—or threatening to do so—may lead to war, even when the intent may have been to prevent it, as during the Cuban Missile Crisis of 1962. Thus, although power-seeking nations seek *imbalance* in their own favor, such actions may backfire, generating a crisis and possibly leading to war.

## Military Alliances

In his Farewell Address, George Washington reflected a widespread distrust when he urged the United States to avoid "entangling alliances." Of course, alliances—crucially important to any balance-of-power system—do not always promote war. It has been argued that NATO, balanced by the Warsaw Pact, promoted peace and stability in Europe for 45 years after World War II. Immediately prior to World War I, Kaiser Wilhelm sought to restrain his Austrian ally from attacking Serbia; had he succeeded, such textbooks as this might now be extolling the benefits of balanced alliances in preventing war! The fact remains, however, that military alliances have often led to war, with the major participants sometimes drawn in through the actions of their proxies and out of fear that inaction would mean a loss of national honor (today referred to as "credibility").

# The End of U.S. Hegemony and the Rise of the BRICS

The United States has long seen itself as the "leader of the Free World," especially after World War II and during the Cold War. By contrast, the United Kingdom long used to be in the habit of proclaiming its imperialistic success—noting proudly, for example, that "the sun never sets on the British Empire." By contrast, to a great extent the United States has been reluctant to overtly embrace the role of imperial power or world "hegemon." This did not stop the United States, however, from establishing military bases around the world, including such far-off spots as Okinawa, Guam, Britain, Germany, Bahrain, Saudi Arabia, the Philippines, and so forth. But direct occupation was not typically part of U.S. foreign policy; rather, its claim to international dominance relied more on social, economic, cultural, and political example (so-called "soft power," the force of alliances, financial inducements, and behind-the-scenes influence).

Just as World War II marked the end of the British Empire and 1989 to 1991 saw the collapse of the Soviet Empire, the Great Recession that began in 2008 may be one indicator of a gradual decline in the American Empire, due to a complex mix of internal financial strains and a reduction in international economic competitiveness, combined with the immense cost of wars in Iraq and Afghanistan. Some would argue that for all its faults, the United States contributed positively to worldwide peace and stability, such that its decline signals real peril. Others welcome such a shift in international influence, pointing out that although the United States didn't maintain an empire in the classic sense of British imperial control, it used economic pressure plus the adherence of local despots and the threat of military intervention to maintain a system in which the United States and its closest allies enjoyed asymmetric benefits.

There is currently little doubt, however, that regardless of how, when and/or whether the world economy rebounds from the Great Recession of 2008, the relative role of the United States will be diminished internationally compared to its high point during the 1990s and early 2000s, when the Soviet Union collapsed, leaving the United States. as the world's sole superpower, sometimes calling itself, in the words of former U.S. secretary of state Madeleine Albright, the "indispensable nation." It is possible—perhaps likely—that even without having been militarily chastised in Iraq and Afghanistan, the United States would never again be as preponderant in the world as it recently was. On the other hand, after the humiliating retreat of the United States from Vietnam in 1975, it was widely assumed that the United States would not again commit itself to employing land forces abroad . . . and especially not in Asia. Such assumptions often require revising.

The U.S. military interventions in Iraq and Afghanistan, taken together, cost (in addition to thousands of lives) hundreds of billions of dollars, or by some estimates, trillions. All the while, other countries notably Brazil, Russia, India, China, and South Africa (the "BRICS") have collectively been the most rapidly growing large emerging economies, having become regional superpowers and, at least in the case of China, on track to equal and perhaps eventually surpass the United States in total economic output.

As the first decade of the 21st century ended, it was clear that after briefly bestriding the world, the United States is no longer the planet's sole undisputed superpower. In fact, there has been a tectonic shift of growth and economic vitality from the developed world to certain states in the developing world, notably the BRICS. India, for example, is more dynamic and has a Gross Domestic Product (GDP) greater in absolute, though not in per capita terms, than its earlier colonial overlord, the United Kingdom. Similarly, the contemporary importance of Brazil far outstrips that of its western colonizer, tiny Portugal. This diffusion of power from the "West to the rest" has been accelerated by ill-advised military adventures on the part of the former, as well as deindustrialization and outsourcing of manufacturing, combined with fiscal imbalances in trade: Importing more than one exports, as a result of which money flows out rather than in.

As testimony to this both Brazil and India (along with Germany, Japan, Nigeria, South Africa, etc.) have been agitating for seats on the United Nations Security Council, a recognition of geo-political, economic, and military reality that might soon be coming. And China has already replaced Japan as the world's second largest economy, which in turn has generated worldwide interest in "state capitalism" as an appealing model for countries focused on the desirability of economic growth, often at the cost reductions in human rights and environmental values.

Although each of the BRICS has its own problems, notably widespread corruption as well as state-specific concerns, such as Russian worries about its rapidly depopulating eastern regions, India's chaos and pervasive poverty, and so forth, it is estimated that Brazil, India, Russia, and China alone accounted for nearly 40% of all the new investment money raised globally in 2007. China has been especially resurgent. Historically, China perceived itself as the "Middle Kingdom" (because it occupied a special place in the middle of the world). Just as much of the rest of the world—especially the European Union and the United States—has been retrenching financially and economically post 2008, China has experienced a spectacular rise in its GDP, China has also experienced a very favorable balance-of-payments (a great excess of goods exported over goods purchased), which in turn has resuted in a huge accumulation of wealth—a large proportion of which has been invested in U.S. treasury notes and bonds, thus financing much of the U.S. national debt. In addition, this immense in-flow of money has been used by China to invest heavily in energy and resource extraction ventures overseas, especially in Latin America, Africa, and Southeast Asia, and even in some parts of Europe. At the same time, because of its huge population—around 1.4 billion—China remains relatively impoverished on a per capita basis, although this is scarce comfort for those who worry that China will overtake the United States as the world's largest economy.

A significant source of friction between the United States and China has been the Chinese reluctance to raise the value of their currency, the remninbi, or at least, allow it to fluctuate on the open market. If they did, and if the remninbi went up, Chinese products would in turn be more expensive, which would mean less U.S.—and other countries—purchase of them, which in turn, would reduce the purchasers' trade imbalances and foreign debt. As countries' economies get shakier, it becomes harder for them to borrow money—that is, what they obtain is only available at higher interest rates, which adds to the borrowers' debt.

Thus far, Chinese foreign policy has been notably cautious, focused on obtaining raw materials from developing countries disinclined to engage directly (and not at all militarily) in their internal affairs. At the same time, however, China has greatly expanded its military of late, notably producing new generations of fighter aircraft and a growing "blue ocean navy," which will soon be capable of "projecting power" world-wide . . . although not nearly on the scale of the United States. Classical balance-of-power considerations would suggest that the other emerging Asian states (Thailand, Burma/Myanmar, Malaysia, Indonesia, Singapore, the Philippines, and South Korea) should be structuring their international relationships so as to counter growing Chinese economic, military, and political influence. However, these countries have, if anything, tended to ally themselves increasingly with China. To some extent, this is out of pan-Asian pride, but even more so, it acknowledges the new geostrategic reality that China in particular is a nation-state to be reckoned with and that globalization is no longer synonymous with Americanization.

China has an additional advantage compared to the United States and some of the other BRICS states: It isn't viewed with particular apprehension, since it lacks a modern history of being a colonial exploiter. Current Chinese efforts at "exploitation" are limited, instead, to achieving access to raw materials and energy, the development of which is often eagerly sought by rising nations such as those in sub-Saharan Africa and South America. China's chief goal—foreign and domestic—has long been stability at all costs, and not conquest.

One astute observer, noting the transition of world influence toward the BRICS, commented that

The self-deluding universalism of the American imperium—that the world inherently needs a single leader and that American liberal ideology must be accepted as the basis of global order—has paradoxically resulted in America quickly becoming an ever-lonelier superpower. Just as there is a geopolitical marketplace, there is a marketplace of models of success for the second world to emulate, not least the Chinese model of economic growth without political liberalization (itself an affront to Western modernization theory). As the historian Arnold Toynbee observed half a century ago, Western imperialism united the globe, but it did not assure that the West would dominate forever—materially or morally. Despite the "mirage of immortality" that afflicts global empires, the only reliable rule of history is its cycles of imperial rise and decline, and as Toynbee also pithily noted, the only direction to go from the apogee of power is down . . .

What makes America unique in this seemingly value-free contest is not its liberal democratic ideals—which Europe may now represent better than America does—but rather its geography. America is isolated, while Europe and China occupy two ends of the great Eurasian landmass that is the perennial center of gravity of geopolitics. When America dominated NATO and led a rigid Pacific alliance system with Japan, South Korea, Australia and Thailand, it successfully managed the Herculean task of running the world from one side of it. Now its very presence in Eurasia is tenuous; it has been shunned by the European Union and Turkey, is unwelcome in much of the Middle East, and has lost much of East Asia's confidence. "Accidental empire" or not, America must quickly accept and adjust to this reality. Maintaining America's empire can only get costlier in both blood and treasure. It isn't worth it, and history promises the effort will fail. It already has.[2]

In a world increasingly interdependent and sharing numerous problems, from terrorism and rogue states to human-induced climate change, energy and food insecurity, as well as resource depletion, it should be clear that globalization isn't only a fact of economic life but of political and military survival, too. Although some people (not all of them Americans) worry about a future world in which the United States is no longer the sole undisputed superpower, it isn't clear that there is any reason to worry about the rise of the BRICS generally or of China in particular. It will be interesting, however, to see whether the United States—which during the Obama administration announced a "strategic pivot" toward Asia—will come to function as "balancer" vis-à-vis China, like Great Britain did toward Europe during the 19th century.

In summary, let us imagine a world of rising BRICS in which the United States is no longer the undisputed global heavyweight: Will this make the planet less safe and less peaceful? Or more so? How will the United States respond to its perceived/real loss of hegemony? If it behaves like such declining empires as Rome and "The Third Reich," there is much to fear. But if it accommodates itself to a new postimperial, multipolar world, as Great Britain did during its waning days as empire, perhaps collective security will be enhanced and not undermined.

# Collective Security

## Advantages

Closely related to the notion of balance of power, but nonetheless distinct, is the concept of collective security. In systems of collective security, states promise to refrain from using force against other members of the "collective," except that they agree to band together against any member who attacks any other within the group. Collective security differs from balance of power in that it relies on the participation of each state as an individual, nonaligned entity, as opposed to a balance of unstable, constantly shifting alliances. The North Atlantic Treaty Organization and the former Warsaw Pact do not count as examples of collective security, since they were established as mutual defense pacts against a potential aggressor from *outside* each alliance, whereas collective security pacts are specifically directed at defense against any aggression from *within* the pact. Early in NATO's history, some statesmen hoped it might exemplify collective security and might even include the Soviet Union. However, the system of post–World War II alliances degenerated from collective security to "selective security," a series of bilateral and regional arrangements that—in the case of NATO and the Warsaw Pact—set themselves up as competing, opposed alliances.

## Disadvantages

There are problems with collective security. For example, it is debatable whether NATO and the Warsaw Pact prevented war or simply maintained nearly two generations of hostility. In addition, collective security agreements are only as good as the will of the participants to abide by them. Given the extreme destructiveness of war, states may be understandably reluctant to meet their treaty obligations if it entails their going to war to defend an ally. This is especially true unless their populace strongly supports the military action that is called for. And finally, given the social and economic interdependence of modern states, even responses short of war—for example, boycotts and trade embargoes—may cause real hardship, thereby making political leaders hesitant to take such steps.

Also, collective security arrangements, when they involve states with large and powerful friends, can give rise to highly destructive and interminable wars. If North Korea and South Korea had been left to themselves, for example, the Korean War would probably have ended quickly. But instead the United States and China became deeply involved, and the conflict was therefore greatly prolonged and intensified. A similar process occurred in the struggle between

North Vietnam and South Vietnam and between the *contra* rebels and the government of Nicaragua. The Middle East was kept simmering, if not boiling, in part by assistance from the United States and the Soviet Union, primarily to the Israelis and the Arabs, respectively. By contrast, wars between India and China and between Britain and Argentina have been comparatively brief and decisive, in part because they were fought without significant military involvement by allies on either side of the conflict.

# National Security via Military Force

Given the uncertainties of maintaining peace through balance of power or collective security, many government leaders opt for going it alone—not necessarily avoiding alliances but, rather, placing their primary emphasis on being sufficiently strong to deter war by the military power of the state, standing by itself. Just as balance of power and collective security systems depend ultimately on a contest of strength, "peace through strength" is similarly committed to military force.

Richard Perle, a famously hawkish assistant secretary of defense during the Reagan administration, also known as "The Prince of Darkness," once said, "Those who believe that the way to maintain peace is by being weak are over and over again shown by history to be wrong." Here, the political right wing is in agreement with some more violence-prone elements of the far left. Mao Tse-tung wrote that "we do not desire war, but war can only be abolished through war—in order to get rid of the gun, we must first grasp it in hand." In fact, the lessons of history are more equivocal. Diplomatic historian George Kennan suggests that "modern history offers no example of the cultivation by rival powers of armed force on a huge scale that did not in the end lead to an outbreak of hostilities," adding that "there is no reason to believe that we are greater, or wiser, than our ancestors." Moreover, there is every reason to believe that in the nuclear age, the consequences of worldwide hostilities could be far more severe than they have ever been in the past.

Accordingly, strong states are far more likely than weak ones to be involved in wars, especially if the weak ones maintain a position of neutrality, and even more so if their "weakness" is really a refusal to provoke or threaten others. Thus, Switzerland and Sweden have been war free for centuries, and although they appear weaker than their larger, more belligerent neighbors, they are militarily rather strong. In other cases, small, weak countries have indeed been conquered or absorbed by their more powerful neighbors: Latvia, Lithuania, and Estonia were annexed by the Soviet Union just prior to World War II; Hawaii was incorporated within the United States; Tibet was similarly overrun by China; and the Portuguese enclave of Goa was swallowed up by India.

## Military Strength and Failure

There is a kind of logic to the notion that one is better off being strong than weak. Yet, overwhelming military strength has often resulted in failure. The United States, for example, was victorious in virtually every direct major military engagement of the Vietnam War. It dropped 8 million tons of bombs (making more than 20 million craters) and nearly 400,000 tons of napalm, killing approximately 2.2 million Vietnamese, Cambodians, and Laotians; maiming and wounding about 3.2 million more; and leaving more than 14 million homeless—but was defeated. Israel is more than a military match for all its Arab neighbors combined and is infinitely more powerful than the lightly armed Palestinians inhabiting the West Bank and Gaza, yet Israeli security (and even control of the occupied territories) is by no means ensured. Many Israelis now argue that their overwhelming military defeat of Egypt, Syria, and Jordan during the Six Day War in 1967—as a result of which Israeli territory expanded then to include Gaza, the West Bank, and the Golan Heights—actually reduced Israel's security in the long run, because it enhanced anti-Israeli sentiment while placing Israel in the difficult position of being overlord to millions of oppressed and resentful Palestinians.

Similarly, the Soviet Union was enormously more powerful, militarily, than the Afghan rebels who eventually compelled it to retreat. As with the United States in Vietnam, the Soviets were almost always victorious on the battlefield but eventually had to withdraw. And a similar situation appears to be playing itself out for the United States in Afghanistan: After stunning military successes that overthrew the Taliban government in 2002, and even following the Obama administration's decision to institute a military "surge" in 2009, U.S. armed forces and a much smaller NATO contingent are pledged to depart Afghanistan in 2014, after which it isn't at all clear that a pro-Western Afghan government will survive in that country. In addition, although the U.S. military quickly and easily defeated its Iraqi counterpart in 2003, subsequent instability, violence, and civil war kept U.S. military forces in that country until 2011, when its direct combat role was finally concluded, although Iraq remains in a simmering civil war between its Sunni and Shi'ite factions; the duration of the Iraq War, from 2003 until 2011, exceeds that of any previous U.S. war, and implies that overwhelming military strength, even when it leads to "victory" in nearly every battle, may often diminish a country's security and internal stability.

Pyrrhus was a king in ancient Greece. During the 3rd century BCE, he lost nearly all his men in the Battle of Asculum, at which the Romans were defeated. Upon being congratulated for his victory, he replied, "One more such victory and we are utterly undone"—hence, the phrase, *a Pyrrhic victory*. This paradox—that military force, even military victory, does not necessarily lead ultimately to political success or even enhanced national security—is especially true with respect to nuclear weapons. Part of the irony is that by committing a state's existence to military success, leaders paradoxically place its security in the hands of their opponents, and the ultimate outcome of a war—even a seemingly "successful" one—is not only impossible to predict but can often be counterproductive. For a recent example, as of the year 2012, it appears that a primary beneficiary of the American-led invasion of Iraq has been the state of Iran, a country that by some accounts is more threatening to the security of the United States than Iraq ever was under Saddam Hussein.

## Security Through Superiority?

Many government leaders argue that their prime responsibility is the maintenance of *national security,* a phrase that is readily invoked but only rarely scrutinized. It is easy to equate strength with safety and weakness with danger. Fearing to be seen as weak, accommodating, or easily pushed around, government leaders are prone to using threats of military force in efforts to coerce an opponent or to inhibit adventuring by potential adversaries.

Sometimes this works; at other times, the bluff is called. After the Iraqi invasion of Kuwait in 1991, President George H. W. Bush demanded a withdrawal, and the United States did in fact achieve this goal, through military force. At other times, preemptive saber rattling may discourage unwanted actions by other parties; China, for example, has made it clear that it would respond militarily to any unilateral assertion of independence on the part of Taiwan, which the Chinese maintain is an integral part of "one China." The United States has similarly threatened to respond with military force if China seeks to reunite with Taiwan by force, and so far, Taiwan has not formally declared itself independent from China and China has not sought to annex Taiwan.

During times of international tension, participants are likely to be acutely suspicious that the other nation is aggressive, dangerous, and likely to probe for weakness, being deterred only by strength. In the early days of the Korean War, and again during the Cuban Missile Crisis, White House aides argued that the Soviets were following the Leninist maxim, "If you strike steel, pull back; if you strike mush, keep going." And, of course, so long as each side is determined to meet the other with steel rather than mush, each can justify its policy by pointing to the other's policy, as well as its steel.

The inherent logic of forever seeking superiority crumbles when one considers its role in generating the security dilemma, which is that in pursuing their own perceived security, individual nation-states often diminish the security of their competitors, as a result of which these other countries seek to re-establish their security by building up their own forces . . . whereupon, in the end, everyone is less secure and worse off. Nonetheless, thinking of this sort has long dominated the national security managers of many states. Through much of the 19th century, for example, Britain proclaimed the "two-power standard," by which the Royal Navy ought always to be at least equal, and preferably superior, to the combined navies of the next two most powerful states. This was considered necessary to guarantee British national security. The British sought absolute security, despite the fact that, as former secretary of state and national security adviser Henry Kissinger has put it, "the desire of one power for absolute security means absolute insecurity for all the others."

Hence, it is not surprising that the British and German naval establishments competed vigorously during the first decade or so of the 20th century or that the tension generated by this competition contributed to the outbreak of World War I. This Anglo-German arms race also exemplifies another difficulty in trying to achieve peace through strength: the fact that new manifestations of "strength" can undermine a state's preexisting security. It is a classic case, worth exploring a bit further. Thus, the Royal Navy was quite far ahead of its German counterpart when in 1906 the British Admiralty introduced a new class of extra-large, heavily armed, and armored battleships, known as "Dreadnoughts," after the name of the first such ship. At a stroke, this unilateral act—which was the logical culmination of seeking to maintain peace through strength—made much of the Royal Navy obsolete and forced Britain to engage in a more intense competition with Germany, from a position of reduced advantage once the Germans began constructing their own Dreadnoughts, which quickly led to the construction of "super-Dreadnoughts."

The nuclear arms race also illustrated Kissinger's contention: The United States, the consistent leader and innovator, routinely introduced new delivery systems and warheads, only to find the Soviet Union following suit, after which both sides were less secure than they were before each escalation.

## Military Interpretations of National Security and the Security Dilemma

As noted, national security is usually seen by conventional strategists and political decision makers as deriving from military strength. Such security is therefore very scarce and a "zero-sum game," in that the more one side gets, the less there is for the other. A peace studies perspective emphasizes the following, however:

1. *Military strength is often a two-edged sword, evoking less security rather than more.* The security dilemma is important enough to warrant being repeated: States, trying to enhance their security via military forces and alliances, often succeed only in making other states less secure. These other states, in turn, respond militarily themselves, as a result of which everyone is less secure and worse off. The United States may well offer the most dramatic example: It is highly prosperous and surrounded by two great oceans, prosperous Canada to the north, and impoverished Mexico to the south. Not since the War of 1812 has the United States had to worry seriously about invasion by a foreign power. Yet, nuclear weapons in particular (as well as risks of terrorism, whether nuclear, chemical, biological, or conventional) have given Americans substantial reasons to worry about "national security," as well as personal security.

2. *The tendency is to think of security as an exclusive, competitive accomplishment, in which security for one party can only be purchased at the cost of insecurity for all other parties.* In fact, however, national security can be a positive-sum game, in which all sides win. Indeed, in a world of growing interdependence, as well as the shared danger posed by weapons of mass destruction, true and enduring national security can only be achieved multilaterally.

3. *In their quest for national security, government leaders may—intentionally or not— actually create "enemies" so as to justify their continuing position of power and authority with their own society.* This is an ancient pattern. For example, during the latter stages of the Roman republic, the populace was wantonly exploited and pillaged by its own leadership in the name of "security." Enemies were created to justify ruinously high taxes, the appropriation of private holdings, and the abridgement of personal liberties. Economist and historian Joseph Schumpeter unsparingly criticized "that policy which pretends to aspire to peace but unerringly generates war, the policy of continual preparation for war." He described these excesses on the part of Rome's rulers, which should serve as a warning to the excessively enemy prone in the 21st century:

> There was no corner of the known world where some interest was not alleged to be in danger or under actual attack. If the interests were not Roman, they were those of Rome's allies; and if Rome had no allies, then allies would be invented. When it was utterly impossible to contrive such an interest—why, then it was the national honor that had been insulted. . . . The whole world was pervaded by a host of enemies, and it was manifestly Rome's duty to guard against their indubitably aggressive designs.[3]

With the end of the Cold War and the dissolution of the Soviet Union, contemporary American purveyors of new "enemies" have been challenged to fill the gap, employing, by turns, Cuba, Libya, Iraq, North Korea, Iran, international terrorism, fundamentalist Islamic extremism, and, when all else fails, a generalized worldwide "unpredictability." At the same time, notwithstanding an egregious tendency for political leaders to exaggerate threats—especially for domestic political gain—to some extent such threats can also be genuine. The terrorist attacks of 9/11 in the United States and subsequent episodes in Madrid, London, Ankara, Bali, and elsewhere have demonstrated this all too clearly. Or as the sardonic saying has it: "Even paranoids have enemies."

## Other National Security Considerations

Although there is often a legitimate military dimension to national security, it must be emphasized that national security cannot be measured by military parameters alone. It is also a function of economic strength, political cohesiveness, social equity and integration, cultural outreach, racial harmony, and environmental soundness. National security is diminished if one's own populace is inadequately housed, fed, educated, and also if medical care is insufficient.

Historian Paul Kennedy has developed the thesis that great powers tend to rise and fall in a predictable cycle, as their world ambitions make excessive demands on their domestic productivity:

> A nation projects military power according to its economic resources but eventually the high cost of maintaining political supremacy weakens the economic base. Great powers in decline respond by spending more on defense and weaken themselves further by directing essential revenues away from productive investment.[4]

Examples of this cycle include the rise and fall of Hapsburg Spain, the British Empire, and the collapse of the Soviet Union, whose economy was unable to sustain a continuing 14% expenditure on the military sector. It also suggests that the United States might be experiencing a similar decline, especially as it increases its absolute level of military spending far beyond Cold War levels, such that it now exceeds the military spending of the rest of the world combined. According to the Stockholm International Peace Research Institute's report on 2011 military spending, countries worldwide spent at least $1.7 trillion, with the United States accounting for more than any other country, with military expenditures of $711 billion (approximately $2 billion per day). The next highest spender was China ($143 billion), followed by Russia ($72 billion).

In contrast with the United States, whose military expenditures comprise about 7% of its immense Gross National Product (GNP), military spending in Japan has been only about 1% of its GNP, which freed money to help finance its remarkable post–World War II economic boom. Postwar Germany is a similar case. Significantly, about 10% of Japanese government investment in research and development goes into military production, whereas the analogous figure for the United States is 70%. The Japanese were pioneers in developing and marketing VCRs, automobiles, cameras, and so forth, which they sell to the world economy, and despite some economic difficulties beginning in the 1990s, they continue to enjoy an enormous financial surplus and have the world's third largest economy. By contrast, by becoming the world's leading producer of high-tech military gadgetry, the United States has specialized in items that are typically purchased by U.S. taxpayers, contributing to inflation, a large trade deficit, and national debt.

"The problem in defense," said President Eisenhower in 1953, "is how far you can go without destroying from within what you are trying to defend from without."

There is yet another problem with excessive reliance on peace through strength: In addition to running the risk of undermining one's security at home, there is also the danger that by focusing on military considerations abroad, long-term stability in those countries as well is sacrificed for short-term gains. Thus, as of 2012, the United States was spending 12 times more money supporting the military forces of Afghanistan and Pakistan than on all of its diplomatic and aid missions in those countries combined. To be sure, physical security is to some extent a prerequisite for domestic security, but "collateral damage" to civilians often generates alienation and hatred toward the perpetrators, while local populations resent the fact that their other needs—jobs, clean water, education, health care—are to a large extent ignored.

## Bargaining Chips

"We arm to parley," said Winston and indeed, political leaders have long maintained that one of the benefits of armaments is that they provide leverage in disarmament or arms control negotiations with the other side. Generally, whenever two sides agree to divest themselves of weaponry (something that happens very rarely) or to refrain mutually from acquiring certain military forces—either by qualitative or by quantitative restrictions—both sides are expected to forgo something comparable. If one side is militarily weak and the other strong, what incentive is there for the latter to build down? One answer is for both sides to make themselves comparably strong at the outset of any serious disarmament discussions.

Thus, joint efforts at nuclear arms control gathered momentum only in the late 1960s, when the Soviet Union essentially achieved military parity with the United States. At the same time, weapons originally justified as bargaining chips are often never cashed in. Rather, armaments tend to develop a powerful constituency—civilian contractors who build them, military commanders who deploy and command them, politicians in whose district they are constructed and/or sited—so they have often become part of the arsenal, whether needed or not. Significantly, such considerations do not apply only to nuclear weapons, whose constituency may be declining. Rather, they are alive and well with respect to such "big ticket" military procurement projects as destroyers ($2 billion apiece), ballistic missile submarines ($7 billion and more, apiece), aircraft carriers (more than $10 billion each), for a U.S. Navy that is currently larger than that of the next 13 countries combined—11 of which are U.S. allies! Another example: The United States is projected to spend an estimated $323 billion for development and procurement of nearly 2,500 F-35 air combat fighters, making it the most expensive defense program ever. The total lifecycle cost for the entire American fleet is estimated to be $1.51 trillion or $618 million per plane. One problem, however: There is no other country that even comes close to possessing comparable weapons, thus making it difficult to justify such expenses, especially in an atmosphere of diminishing resources as well as security threats that no longer involve a major competing military power.

Military historian and retired U.S. Army colonel Andrew Bacevich described the situation as follows:

> The Pentagon presently spends more in constant dollars than it did at any time during the Cold War—this despite the absence of anything remotely approximating what national security experts like to call a "peer competitor." Evil Empire? It exists only in the fevered imaginations of those who quiver at the prospect of China adding a rust-bucket Russian aircraft carrier to its fleet or who take seriously the ravings of radical Islamists promising from deep inside their caves to unite the Umma in a new caliphate. What are Americans getting for their money? Sadly, not much. Despite extraordinary expenditures (not to mention exertions and sacrifices by U.S. forces), the return on investment is, to be generous, unimpressive. The chief lesson to emerge from the battlefields of the post-9/11 era is this: the Pentagon possesses next to no ability to translate "military supremacy" into meaningful victory.[5]

On the other hand, most American conservatives recoil at any possible diminution in U.S. military expenditures, pointing to the alleged impact of the Reagan-era military buildup in "defeating" the Soviet Union. They suggest that continued overwhelming U.S. strength will provide immediate security and also discourage other would-be rivals from increasing their military power to the point of eventually threatening the status of the United States as the world's superpower. Nonetheless, military pressure most commonly undercuts conciliators on the opposing side and leads to a corresponding military buildup in return. If, for example, the military had been in charge of negotiating the Montreal Protocols, which established standards for ozone protection, we might all be stockpiling chlorofluorocarbons as bargaining chips, all the while competing to be not only number one in the production of atmospheric pollutants but also to generate more than the rest of the world put together.

# Appeasement, Provocation, and Deterrence

Just as doves point to the dangers of overarming and provocation—referring especially to the "lessons" of World War I—hawks point to the dangers of underarming and appeasement, citing the "lessons of Munich" and World War II. Similarly, supporters of deterrence claim that being strong (including the possession of nuclear weapons) has deterred war; others take a very different view.

## World Wars I and II

The security dilemma is not unique to modern times or the nuclear age. In the decade before World War I, for example, German and British naval leaders each worried that the other might be planning a preemptive attack on the other's fleet. In addition, leaders in Germany and Russia were acutely aware that it would take a week or more to mobilize their ground forces using existing railroad lines, and each feared that if the other mobilized first, that side would have a potentially lethal advantage. The result was pressure on both sides to do so before the other. More generally, a would-be defender, seeking to achieve peace via strength, must walk a narrow line between, on the one hand, provoking the war it wants to prevent (the experience of both sides in World War I) and, on the other hand, failing to prevent war by being perceived as too weak or lacking in resolve (the "Munich syndrome" in 1938).

## Does Deterrence Work?

Supporters of "peace through strength" like to point to the fact that no U.S.-Soviet war took place in the nuclear age, even during periods of intense rivalry and antagonism. But this claim cannot be assessed. Perhaps peace prevailed between the two superpowers simply because they had no quarrel that justified fighting a terribly destructive war, even a conventional one. It is not at all clear, for example, that the Soviet leadership was ever itching to invade Western Europe, restrained only by the other side's nuclear arsenal. Such *post facto* arguments—especially negative ones, purporting to show why something has *not* happened—are in fact impossible to prove. (If a dog barks in the night, we might be able to say with confidence that it did so "because" someone walked by. If it does not bark, however, we may never know "why.")

In addition, it should be pointed out that in the context of world events, the 45 years from World War II to the end of the Cold War was not really all that long. More than 20 years separated World Wars I and II; before that, there were more than 40 years of peace between the end of the Franco-Prussian War and World War I; and 55 years had elapsed since the previous major war, which ended with Napoleon's defeat at Waterloo in 1815. The point is that periods of peace have not been all that rare, even in war-prone Europe. And furthermore, when peace ended and the next war began, it was fought with the weapons available at that time—which, for the next major war, might well include nuclear weapons.

In short, it may be inaccurate—even premature—to congratulate ourselves, or our weapons, for keeping the peace. The story is told about the man who sprayed perfume on his lawn every morning. When his perplexed neighbor asked about this strange behavior, the man replied, "I do it to keep the elephants away." The neighbor protested, "But there aren't any elephants within 10,000 miles of here," whereupon the man triumphantly announced, "You see, it works!"

There is also a logical fallacy at work here: If nuclear weapons had failed to keep the peace and we had a nuclear war, there might be no one around to argue about their effectiveness as peace-keepers! Moreover, although it is possible that the post-1945 U.S.-Soviet peace was achieved "through strength," it is also possible that it has occurred *in spite of* the provocations of deterrence rather than because of them. Thus, the presence of nuclear weapons on hair-trigger alert capable of reaching each other's homeland has certainly made both sides nervous and edgy. The Cuban Missile Crisis—when by all accounts the world came closer to nuclear war than at any other time—was hardly testimony to the effectiveness of deterrence, since it was itself brought about by the provocative nature of nuclear weapons themselves. Thus, it can be argued that we haven't been spared nuclear war because of deterrence but in spite of it.

There have also been many cases in which the possession of strong military forces—including nuclear weapons—has not deterred war. The Chinese, Cuban, Iranian, and Nicaraguan revolutions all took place despite the fact that the United States was allied with the governments previously in power and possessed nuclear weapons. Similarly, the United States lost the Vietnam War, just as the Soviet Union lost in Afghanistan, despite the fact that both countries were not only nuclear armed but also much stronger than their opponents. Nuclear weapons also did not aid Russia in its unsuccessful war against Chechen rebels in 1994 to 1996 and again from 1999 to 2000; nor have they helped the United States achieve its goals in occupied Iraq or to insulate the United States from terrorist threats—which are more likely to be made via nuclear weapons than deterred by them. It was a nuclear-armed United States that "lost" China in 1949 and a nuclear-armed Soviet Union that "lost" China once again, in the early 1960s. (It may seem odd, incidentally, that such a huge nation can have been so frequently misplaced!)

One of the most unstable world regions has long been southern Asia. Unlike the United States and the Soviet Union during the Cold War, India and Pakistan share a common border and have fought four wars; by contrast, the United States and the Soviet Union were global and ideological competitors without a history of direct bloodshed or conflict over specific real estate. Since 1998, India and Pakistan have also been nuclear armed. Although it is possible that the mutual possession of nuclear weaponry will induce both countries to be more cautious than they might otherwise be, most observers do not derive comfort from the fact that nuclear deterrence is potentially operating in this case.

Arms races in general can be criticized as a kind of action-reaction sequence, in which an action by one side leads to a reaction by the other, which generates, in turn, yet another action. Closely related are "worst-case analyses," in which the military establishment of each side—seeking to be prudent—assumes the worst of the other's capabilities and intentions. The result is a process of "threat inflation," in which each side takes an alarmist view of the threat that the other poses and, as a result, overreacts, thereby further escalating the competition and nervousness on both sides.

# The Use and Abuse of Threats

The most extreme example of attempted peace through strength and threats has involved nuclear weapons. Arguments in their favor rely, as we have seen, on the concept of deterrence, as well as on the presumption that, in the absence of immense destructive power, the United States would be susceptible to attack, blackmail, and/or domination. Supposedly, we are made safe by our super-weapons. In *Realpolitik* terms, it may not be the best of all imaginable worlds, but perhaps it is the best of all realistically possible worlds in that it keeps our enemies at bay. As we read in Shakespeare's *Henry IV, Part I*, "Out of this nettle, danger, we pluck this flower, safety." And as Winston Churchill proposed, referring specifically to nuclear deterrence, "Safety will be the steady child of terror, and survival, the twin brother of annihilation."

## Fear, Stubbornness, and Opportunity

When a nation seeks to maintain peace through strength, it relies on the effectiveness of threats. In *The Strategy of Conflict*, economist and strategic analyst Thomas Schelling distinguished between "compellent" and "deterrent" threats: The former are more aggressive, forcing the opponent to *do* something, surrender something of value, and so forth. The latter are intended to *prevent* the opponent from acting in a way that the threatener finds undesirable: deterring aggression, dissuading the opponent from subverting another state, and so on. Schelling also pointed out that force can be used for its punishment or shock effect, aside from its military usefulness: Examples include Sherman's march through Georgia, General Sheridan's genocidal tactics against the Comanches, German use of V1 and V2 weapons against Britain in World War II, and the atomic bombings of Hiroshima and Nagasaki. States also tend to employ force when they see a need to shore up their credibility.

Deterrence theory and the assumptions of "peace through strength" can have a pernicious effect. Nuclear deterrence in particular depends on a mutually threatening posture, as each side seeks to impress the other with its toughness and willingness to use force if provoked. Thus, conflicts that may in themselves be of no intrinsic importance for either side and that may even occur far from the borders of either country become imbued with a peculiar significance: Indicating the credibility, reliability, toughness, and hence security of one side (or both). It then becomes vital to intervene in virtually any struggle, just to prove that "we" will not be pushovers and to ensure that our "national will" is not about to be tested or doubted in the future. For example, concern about avoiding the image of the United States as a "pitiful, helpless giant" served as a major motivator for U.S. perseverance in the Vietnam War and may motivate a long-term U.S. military presence in the Middle East as well.

It is possible that deterrence made the superpowers cautious in their provocations of the other. However, deterrence also encourages a kind of "competitive risk-taking," in which the bolder, tougher, more violence-prone player appears likely to win. When two sides collide, each determined to be the tougher, peace through strength can succumb to war through stubbornness, as with World War I.

Moreover, a cogent argument can be made that when they are assessing whether or not to go to war, political leaders do not necessarily follow the expectations of deterrence theory, which assumes that states regularly assess their potential prospects vis-à-vis one another and are likely to leap through any "windows of vulnerability" that might reveal themselves. Thus, advocates of peace through strength assume that military weakness relative to another state invites attack, whereas strength deters it. But wars have often been precipitated by *fear* (of the other side being stronger or—even more often—that it will shortly become stronger) rather than by overconfidence. Thus, at the eve of World War I, Germany and Austria feared being encircled and outmaneuvered by the Triple Entente (France, Russia, and Great Britain), just as the Israeli attack on Egypt and Syria in 1967 was brought about by fear that its Arab neighbors were getting too strong.

States are more likely to be influenced by their own internal political needs than by their objective military strength vis-à-vis an opponent. Thus, Argentina clearly was militarily inferior to Britain when it attacked the Falkland Islands in 1982, just as India clearly was militarily inferior to China when it provoked the brief and (for India) disastrous Sino-Indian War over the disputed Himalayan region of Ladakh in 1962. (It is also noteworthy that in both these cases, the unsuccessful attacker was not deterred by the fact that the "victim" possessed nuclear weapons.) Similarly, the deteriorating political fortunes of India's ruling Hindu fundamentalist party were revived after India's nuclear testing in 1998 and its successful repulsion of Pakistan in Kashmir in 1999, just as the election of Russia's Vladimir Putin in 2000 was facilitated by his vigorous promotion of the comparatively popular Second Chechen War in 1999 to 2000. Although it eventually proved to be an immense political liability for President George W. Bush and his administration, in the early stages of the Iraq War, when the government of Saddam Hussein was quickly overthrown, the Bush administration's political popularity and prestige (as well as its electoral prospects) were greatly enhanced; indeed, it seems likely that the expectation of a positive domestic political outcome loomed large in the Bush administration's decision to invade Afghanistan and Iraq in the first place. And during those wars' initial phases, when it appeared that the Taliban had been defeated in Afghanistan and Bush declared, "Mission accomplished" following the overthrow of Saddam Hussein, his administration's popularity and his party's electoral prospects reached a new high. When quick and relatively bloodless U.S. victories in those countries were not forthcoming, however, American public opinion shifted against the Bush administration.

Finally, reliance on threat as an arbiter of victory may also lead to a false estimate of the other's threshold, which can be dangerous in the extreme if both sides engage in a game of chicken, each determined that the other must be the one to swerve.

# The Prisoner's Dilemma

Advocates of peace through strength often maintain that states have no choice: They must maintain and even increase their armaments—as well as a credible threat to use them if called upon to do so—because if they relied less on military force, they would be at the mercy of another state that continued to arm heavily. Hence, each state may find itself forced into a warlike posture that neither wants but that both are unable to escape. This situation has long been recognized and modeled mathematically as the so-called Prisoner's Dilemma. Analyses based on the Prisoner's Dilemma have a prominent place in mathematical game theory, strategic analysis, social psychology, and even evolutionary biology—fields that sometimes attempt to model various competitive interactions. Understanding the "rationality" of the choices made by decision makers is therefore important, not only for the light it might shed on threats, competition, and the problems of cooperation but also for what it reveals about the mind-set of people whose opinions are influential in shaping military and political doctrine and decisions.

The Prisoner's Dilemma is also a model for the evolution of cooperation versus competition. In its very simplified thought-experimental world, individuals (or states) have two options: "cooperate" (or disarm) and "defect" (or arm). If both cooperate, both receive payoff (R), the reward for cooperation; if both defect, both receive payoff (P), the punishment of mutual defection. But if one defects and the other cooperates, the defector receives T, the temptation to defect, and the one who cooperates (disarms, etc.) while the other takes advantage of the situation receives S, the sucker's payoff.

Basically, a Prisoner's Dilemma occurs when the payoffs are in the following relationship: T > R > P > S. In this case, the "players" are tempted to get T and fearful of getting stuck with S, so they wind up getting P (a punishing arms race) when the best mutual payoff would have been R, the reward for cooperation or mutual restraint.

The Prisoner's Dilemma is a useful way of modeling the dilemma of thinking that one must be "nasty" for fear that anyone who is "nice" is at the mercy of others who persevere in being nasty. On the other hand, it may well be unduly pessimistic in that it assumes only two choices, whereas in reality individuals or states have a variety of options. They can try a mix of tactics: disarm in one respect, build up in another, delay a modernization program, and so on. The simplified model also requires that there is only one possible payoff and that "games" are one-time affairs. In reality, states interact many times in succession, and they can vary their behavior depending on what happened the previous time. And if both sides have an interest in generating a sequence of cooperative interactions, as political scientist Robert Axelrod has demonstrated in his book, *The Evolution of Cooperation,* cooperative outcomes can yield the highest payoff.

In short, the Prisoner's Dilemma can be useful in clarifying our decision-making thinking, and, indeed, variants of it are used extensively by analysts in the promilitary strategic community. But it should be remembered that such an approach carries many hidden assumptions and that individuals—and states—must avoid becoming prisoners of their own narrow-minded dilemmas.

# Sanctions

Violence and the threat of violence are, by definition, coercive. Another way, ostensibly nonviolent, to influence the behavior of states is to rely on sanctions. These typically involve economic and cultural restrictions and boycotts, sometimes outright refusal to trade with the targeted country and punishments aimed specifically at political leaders: The latter include restrictions on their international travel, appropriation of foreign bank accounts, and occasionally even indictment by international legal tribunals. International sanctions of this sort often seem appealing since they do not include overt violence. To some extent, therefore, they have become a preferred means of international "arm-twisting," as with efforts to induce North Korea and Iran to rethink their nuclear programs by isolating these countries diplomatically, economically, and, when possible, socially and even intellectually.

It is uncertain whether such a "sanctions regime" has ever succeeded, although it appears that the apartheid government of South Africa was financially injured by persistent international boycotts. Moreover, the South African white population in particular—which has long valued athletic prowess—felt painfully isolated from international sports competition. There is reason to think that the government of Libya, under Muammar Gadhafi, succumbed to a "carrot-and-stick" approach—combining economic pressures with the lure of financial incentives—when it agreed in 2003 to suspend its nuclear program and open its borders to inspectors. On the other hand, there is no currently enforceable or consistent "sanctions regime," in part because countries like Sudan or Iran, with a valuable resource (petroleum), can usually induce other countries to defy sanctions and trade with them regardless of their transgressions. Moreover, sanctions typically exert their most painful effects on the poorest inhabitants of the target country, thereby enhancing any existing structural violence while having little impact on its wealthy, powerful rulers. It has been estimated that during a dozen years of rigorous international sanctions against the regime of Saddam Hussein (from 1991 until 2003), as many as 500,000 Iraqi children may have died as a result of poverty and malnutrition. It must therefore be concluded that international sanctions aren't nearly as nonviolent as their admirers like to claim and that their efficacy remains in dispute.

# Nonprovocative Defense

Finally, having considered the major traditional doctrines related to peace through strength and found them wanting, we turn now to another concept, one that is perhaps congenial to military-minded seekers after peace. It is variously known as "alternative defense," "transarmament," and "nonprovocative defense." This approach seeks to make war less likely through a substantial restructuring of strategic planning and the actual disposition of armed forces.

Although most countries describe their military as "defense" forces, they almost always have a large offensive component, which leads, as we have seen, to the "security dilemma." By contrast, under a regime of nonprovocative defense, states would emphasize weapons that are defensive, and they would reconfigure their forces so as not to threaten other states. The goal would be to establish a regime in which defense dominated offense, in which states felt secure in their ability to repel an aggressor but insecure in their ability to successfully attack another nation.

## How It Might Work

Tanks would be prohibited, but antitank defenses permitted; bombers prohibited, but antiaircraft batteries and short-range fighter-interceptors permitted; heavily armored mechanized forces prohibited, but lightly armed, mobile infantry units permitted; supplies would be prepositioned, and defensive networks constructed throughout the countryside. Such arrangements are not suitable for attack but can help contribute to a formidable defense. U.S. military thinking has not been especially receptive to nonprovocative defense, although some European planners have shown substantial interest.

One difficulty with implementing nonprovocative defense is the problem of distinguishing unambiguously between defensive and offensive forces. Fighter aircraft, for example, can be used to supplement offensive operations, as well as to defend against invaders. Armored personnel carriers can be either aggressive or defensive, as can destroyers or submarines. Even fixed defensive fortifications can serve the offense: The Siegfried Line, built by Germany along its border with France, made it less likely that France would assist its Polish ally while the Nazis made war in Eastern Europe. Of more current relevance, a Ballistic Missile Defense system (derided as "Star Wars"), although touted as defensive by its advocates, alarms other nations, especially Russia, who see it as possibly offensive, since it might encourage its possessor to initiate an attack with confidence (whether or not well founded!) that it will be immune to retaliation.

In other cases, the distinction is more clear-cut: Minefields and immobile tank traps are unambiguously defensive, while nuclear weapons are offensive (even if they ostensibly provide deterrence).

Nonprovocative defense would require a substantial change in doctrine, compelling war planners to abandon existing plans for "forward-based defense," "deep strikes," and the like, tactics that call for "defending" a country by carrying the fight deep into opposing territory. Instead, countries would concentrate on "defense in depth," emphasizing small mobile units trained to mount disruptive partisan operations, if necessary deep within their own borders. Certain states—notably the United States—specialize in "projecting power" far from their shores. These forces—aircraft carriers, long-range fighter-bombers, mobile artillery, amphibious assault units—are not used for defending one's own borders; rather, their purpose is overwhelmingly to intervene (or threaten to intervene) in other countries, generally far from home. Nonprovocative defense would require states to forgo such activities.

A world in which interstate war is significantly less likely would be a potential advance on most Western strategic war planning. In this regard, the prospects for nonprovocative defense, although cloudy, are not altogether bleak. The idea of confining each state's "defense forces" to real defense, thereby making war less likely, reducing tensions, and saving money to boot, has practical appeal. Importantly, nonprovocative defense would not offer any less defense than current military postures; in fact, by being less threatening to would-be opponents, it should reduce the likelihood of armed hostilities between disputing nations, thereby providing *more* defense for all sides. In addition, unlike most arms control or disarmament proposals, the transition to nonprovocative defense does not require complex bilateral or multilateral negotiated agreements; any state that wishes can make the shift unilaterally.

Several have already done so; a number of countries, notably the European states that practice "armed neutrality," are examples of successful nonprovocative defense. For example, Switzerland requires that all men between 20 and 50 years of age participate in the Swiss Army, which emphasizes antiaircraft systems, tank traps, and other unambiguously defensive capabilities, as well as a high degree of mobility, keyed to the mountainous Swiss homeland. Supplies have been cached throughout the country; thousands of strategic demolition points have been identified and prewired, so as to slow any invader; and the Swiss Air Force features short-range fighter-interceptors, deliberately excluding long-range heavy bombers. In addition, a network of well-stocked, fortified underground bunkers has been built beneath the Alps to shelter Swiss citizens in case of attack. The net result is a robust military capability but one that is distinctly nonprovocative and also oriented toward deterrence by dissuasion rather than by threat.

Sweden and Norway are other contemporary examples of affluent modern states that have achieved a kind of peace through strength, by emphasizing defensive and nonprovocative strategies. Norway and Sweden have enhanced their own national security by promoting disarmament—especially nuclear disarmament—as a major issue on the world agenda. Thus, Swedish and Norwegian politicians have long been prominent in disarmament efforts, and their governments fund what are probably the preeminent peace institutes, the Stockholm International Peace Research Institute and the International Peace Research Institute, Oslo, home—not coincidentally—of the Nobel Peace Prize.

## A FINAL NOTE ON PEACE THROUGH STRENGTH

In today's world, the pursuit of security clearly must be deepened beyond military strength and widened beyond current conceptions of "national security." Specifically, security must be recognized as encompassing economic, political, social, and environmental considerations, and national security can no longer be achieved by any country acting alone; that is, real security must be mutual or, better yet, collective or global. With the Cold War fading into memory, the inability of most people—notably, the United States, the richest and most powerful country on

Earth—to articulate a nonmilitary, nonconfrontational vision of peace and global security must count as one of the great failures and most profound opportunities of the 21st century.

It is lamentable that in an age of unparalleled technological and scientific achievement, most influential political decision makers still rely more on weapons than on peacemaking to prevent war. Writer Calvin Trillin penned this bit of cynical doggerel:

> It seems so familiar to me:
>
> They know one more tank, one more gun'll
>
> Allow best and brightest to see
>
> The light at the end of the tunnel.[6]

## NOTES

1. General von Moltke, quoted in Richard Ned Lebow. 1981. *Between Peace and War*. Baltimore: Johns Hopkins University Press.

2. P. Khanna. 2008. "Waving Goodbye to Hegemony." http://www.nytimes.com/2008/01/27/magazine/27world-t.html?pagewanted=all

3. Joseph Schumpeter. 1988. "The Sociology of Imperialism." In *Two Essays by Joseph Schumpeter*. New York: Meridian.

4. Paul M. Kennedy. 1987. *The Rise and Fall of the Great Powers*. New York: Harper & Row.

5. Andrew Bacevich. 2011. "Cow Most Sacred: Why Military Spending Remains Untouchable." http://www.huffingtonpost.com/andrew-bacevich/cow-most-sacred-why-milit_b_814888.html

6. Calvin Trillin. 2000. In *The Nation*, February 17.

## QUESTIONS FOR FURTHER REFLECTION

1. What is the relationship between balance of power, peace through strength, and the motto *si vis pacem, para bellum?*

2. What are some advantages of the Prisoner's Dilemma model in conceptualizing matters of cooperation and competition? What are some disadvantages?

3. Describe some merits and demerits of defining national security in strictly military terms.

4. It can be argued that for all its liabilities, "peace through strength" remains the most widespread conception of how to achieve negative peace. Why?

5. Discuss "nonprovocative defense" in the context of "the use and abuse of threats" as well as deterrence theory.

## SUGGESTIONS FOR FURTHER READING

Paul M. Kennedy. 1987. *The Rise and Fall of the Great Powers: Economic Change and Military Conflict 1500–2000*. New York: Harper & Row.

Rebecca Moore. 2007. *NATO's New Mission: Projecting Stability in a Post–Cold War World*. New York: Praeger.

Richard Rhodes. 2007. *Arsenals of Folly: The Making of the Nuclear Arms Race*. New York: Knopf.

Stuart Kaufman, Richard Little, and William C. Wohlforth. 2007. *Balance of Power in World History*. New York: Palgrave Macmillan.

Thomas Schelling. 1966. *Arms and Influence*. New Haven, CT: Yale University Press.

# CHAPTER 16

# INTERNATIONAL LAW

Members of Adolf Hitler's Third Reich sit in the defendants' box during the International Military Tribunal's war crimes trial in Nuremberg, Germany, in November, 1945, after the end of World War II.

*Source:* © 2008 Getty Images.

> *The international community should support a system of laws to regularize international relations and maintain the peace in the same manner that law governs national order.*
>
> —Pope John Paul II

Governments are supposed to operate by laws, the rules of conduct that specify what is permissible and—more commonly—what is not. Even in our current system of separate states, a legal framework undergirds the relationship of states to one another. It is known as international law and is reviewed in this chapter.

# The Sources of International Law

We are all familiar with domestic law, with its prohibitions against such violent crimes as murder, robbery, or assault, as well as the way laws regulate the nonviolent conduct of daily living, from the flow of traffic to the work of businesses and the standards of licit conduct in private and public life. Less familiar, by contrast, is international law, the acknowledged principles that guide the interactions between states and that set limits on what is and what is not permissible.

People live within societies, not between them, so more has been done to encourage *intra*national law than *inter*national law. Yet, international law does exist; in fact, the current body of international law is very large. Just as most daily life among individuals within a society is peaceful, most interactions among states on the world scene are also peaceful, in accord with expectations, and thus, in a sense, "legal."

Unlike domestic law, which in the United States is codified in constitutions, amendments, and the specific laws passed by federal, state, and municipal law-making bodies, the body of international law is relatively diffuse and generated in many different ways. There are four major sources of international law: (1) classical writings that have become widely accepted, (2) custom, (3) treaties, and (4) the rulings of international courts.

## Classical Writings

In the 16th century, the Spanish legal scholar Francisco de Vitoria developed the thesis that war must be morally justifiable and could not simply be fought over differences of religion or for the glory of a ruler. He also maintained that soldiers were not obliged to fight in unjust wars, even if so commanded by their king. But the best-known and most influential example of classical international law was the work of the Dutch legal scholar Hugo Grotius. In his treatise *On the Law of War and Peace* (1625), Grotius maintained that there was a fundamental "natural law," which transcended that of nations and that emanated from the fact that people were ultimately members of the same community. Grotius argued strongly for the sovereignty of individual states, within their own realms. From this, he concluded that states must avoid interference in the internal affairs of other states. Grotius pointed to the agreements that states had made among themselves and which proved to be durable: peace treaties, decisions as to the allocation of fishing and navigation rights, commonly accepted boundaries, and so on.

The Grotian tradition thus derives the legitimacy of international law from the legitimacy of states themselves. But it goes further in seeking to derive principles whereby the behavior of one state toward another can be regulated, arguing that "natural right" must govern the interactions among states and that this supersedes the authority of the states themselves. As Grotius saw it (and subsequent international law has affirmed), international "society" exists, which requires certain norms of conduct among states, including rules governing what is acceptable during war itself. For Grotius, war was not a breakdown in the law of nations but rather a special condition to which law still applies.

One of the earliest and most effective examples of international law in action was the European battle against international piracy, during the 16th through 18th centuries. It was widely agreed at the time—even by England and France, for example, which were bitter enemies and which often outfitted or tacitly supported pirate raids against the other country—that all states had jurisdiction over acts of piracy on the high seas; such unanimity permitted concerted and successful action against a growing threat to international trade and exploration. It is noteworthy, however, that pirates were apprehended by the military forces of individual, sovereign states and tried by domestic courts, rather than by some international legal body.

The term *international law* first appeared in 1783, with the publication of Jeremy Bentham's *Principles of International Law*. Accordingly, whatever its shortcomings, international law has taken shape in just a few hundred years; in fact, things have really gathered steam in the last 50 years. Beginning around 2009, piracy has once again emerged as a significant threat, this time to shipping in the waters off the Horn of Africa, especially Somalia, where the absence of an effective government combined with extreme poverty has induced many Somalis to take up a modern form of piracy, in which cargo ships are taken over by small groups of armed pirates, who then demand ransom for ship and crew. Although responses to this situation has generated a degree of cooperation from navies as diverse as those of the European Union, the United States, Iran, Russia, and China, it also poses a dilemma for international law, since there are no clear venues or existing systems of international law under which apprehended modern-day pirates can be tried and, if convicted, punished.

## Custom

Custom is one of the most important and least appreciated sources of international law. For example, consider the "rules of diplomatic protocol," whereby diplomats from one country are considered immune to arrest or detention in another. This is clearly in the interest of all countries, since if the representatives of opposing states could legally be harassed, communication between them would quickly cease, to the disadvantage of all sides. Diplomats are occasionally expelled from a host country, usually for "activities incompatible with their diplomatic status" (that is, for spying), in which case some of the other side's diplomats are typically expelled in retaliation. But normally—that is, customarily, and thus by international law—diplomats are allowed substantial leeway, including guarantees that they will be able to communicate freely with their home government. (The strength of this presumption is shown by the outrage generated when the custom of diplomatic immunity is violated, as when U.S. diplomats were held hostage in Iran during 1979 to 1980 or when, during its attack on Serbia, NATO bombed the Chinese Embassy in Belgrade, killing Chinese diplomats.)

Another example of international law derived from custom is the emerging concept of "Common Heritage of Mankind" (CHOM). This developing notion has figured in the Law of the Sea and Antarctic treaties, as well as the Montreal Protocols directed at reducing the production of chemicals (especially chlorofluorocarbons) implicated in destroying the Earth's ozone layer. According to CHOM, the fact that certain entities—the ocean bed, Antarctica, the ozone layer—transcend state sovereignty means that individuals or states may not simply exploit or despoil them as they wish. Rather, as part of the common heritage of mankind, these terrestrial resources (and, presumably, others as well) are entitled to protection under international law. At present, CHOM is of uncertain but growing status as an established principle of international law. It also exemplifies the important concept that international law, no less than domestic law, must be flexible and responsive to change and growth in accepted standards. Insofar as it has been successful, CHOM has thus far applied only to areas that are not within the accepted jurisdiction of existing states; the approach has not yet been effective, for example, in preserving tropical rainforests, whose ownership is zealously insisted upon by each state in question.

## Treaties

International treaties are analogous to contracts among individuals. And of course, there have been many treaties, covering not only the termination of wars but also agreements about boundaries, fishing and navigation rights, and mutually agreed restrictions as to permissible actions during war. Treaties are not always honored, but in the vast majority of cases, they have been. Backing away from treaty obligations results in substantial loss of face, and once branded a treaty breaker, a state may subsequently have difficulty establishing useful, reliable relationships with other states. Through treaties as well as customary practice, international law provides "rules of the road" by which international interaction, beneficial to each side, can be conducted. As a result, states have an interest in abiding by them. According to the U.S. Constitution, international treaties are to be considered part of the "supreme law of the land," although in practice they are often accorded considerably less respect.

## Courts

Finally, international law—like domestic law—requires courts to hear disputed cases and render decisions. For example, the European Court of Human Rights, at Strasbourg, hears human rights cases involving citizens of any of its 47 signatory states. The International Court of Justice located in The Hague, the Netherlands, is administered by the United Nations. Also known as the World Court, this institution consists of a rotating membership of world jurists. It issues decisions about international law that are generally considered authoritative, although often unenforceable.

An International War Crimes Tribunal was convened during the 1990s and has held trials against individuals accused of participating in genocide in Bosnia and Rwanda. This tribunal has tried some prominent government leaders—once they were out of power—notably Serbian president Slobodan Milošević for war crimes in Bosnia and Kosovo. (Milošević died of natural causes before a verdict could be rendered.) A new International Criminal Court (ICC) entered into existence in 2002, with 121 signatory countries, as of mid-July 2012, including all of Latin America, nearly all of Europe, and about one-half of African states. Its purpose is to prosecute individuals indicted for genocide, crimes against humanity, war crimes, and orchestrating international aggression. Primary responsibility for such prosecutions is nonetheless left to sovereign states, and the ICC is empowered to act only when these states refuse to do so. Nonetheless, many prominent states—including India, China, Russia, and the United States—have opposed this court and refused to sign on to the activities of the ICC. (The United States has objected to the possibility that its nationals might be brought before such a court but seems quite willing to support the indictment, trial, and imprisonment of citizens of other countries.)

As of mid-2012, former president Laurent Gbagbo of the Ivory Coast awaits trial at the ICC, where a warrant for the arrest of President Omar Hassan al-Bashir of Sudan is still outstanding. Nearly two decades after the wars in Bosnia and Kosovo, which were notable for numerous human rights violations as well as genocide especially against Bosnian and Kosovar Muslims, the major perpetrators were finally captured and brought to trial. Former Serb dictator Slobodan Milošević died before his trial was completed, and the trial of Ratko Mladic, the former Bosnian Serb military commander, had just begun (these trials take a very long time: literally years). Another Serb leader, Vojislav Seselj, has been indicted for numerous offenses including orchestrating murder, rape, and looting on the part of gangs of Serbian irregulars he mobilized in 1991 to fight in Croatia and Bosnia. As of mid-2012, however, the most significant prosecution and conviction was that of Charles Taylor, who, while dictatorial "president" of Liberia, sponsored a brutal civil war in neighboring Sierra Leone, in which "blood diamonds," mined in Sierra Leone, provided much of the financing for such atrocities as the amputation of the arms and legs of civilians, most of whom were caught in the middle between opposing armies.

As we have already noted, the wars of the 21st century have thus far taken place overwhelmingly within states rather than between them, a situation that seems likely to persist. Such wars—as in Bosnia, East Timor, Kosovo, Darfur, the Democratic Republic of the Congo, Libya, and Syria—although typically involving relatively light weapons, have been characterized by extreme brutality toward civilians. More and more, international courts have been called upon to see that the rule of law applies to the perpetrators, especially those in command (whether military or civilian) who violate basic codes of conduct.

Former Obama administration State Department official Anne-Marie Slaughter points out that

> When a government charged with making and enforcing laws systematically violates those laws by a deliberate decision to torture, murder, "disappear," or detain citizens without legal justification, domestic law gives way to international human rights law, and increasingly to international criminal law. When those citizens fight back in an organized fashion, or otherwise organize themselves against the state in a sustained military confrontation, then international human rights law gives way to the patchwork of international rules developed to apply to conflicts within states.

> The boundaries between all these categories are very blurred, witness the ongoing dispute over the past decade as to whether to try terrorists as criminals in a domestic court or as unlawful combatants under the laws of war. It will probably take many years to sort out when "the state" should be treated as one unit under international law, as a government accountable to its people under domestic constitutional and statutory law, or as a group of individuals responsible for their actions under domestic and international criminal law.[1]

Until recently, it was very rare for major political or military leaders to be held criminally liable for their actions; more commonly, defeated heads of state, for example were either executed by the victors or they escaped or were driven into exile in other countries. As the various international criminal tribunals multiply, however, the legal decisions of these courts seem likely to have increasing influence as international law evolves. Thus far, however, the verdict on international courts is mixed. On the one hand, states are gradually becoming more accustomed to forgoing enough sovereignty to settle disputes in court instead of in combat. But on the other hand, adherence to the dictates of the various international courts is entirely "consensual," whereas adherence to domestic law is obligatory. Moreover, even as individuals are increasingly held accountable for international crimes—including but not limited to war crimes, genocide, and the like—there is currently no widely accepted legal framework for indicting, trying, and punishing transnational corporations. Imagine a community in which accused lawbreakers could only be brought to trial if they agreed that the laws applied to them, and further imagine that they could decide whether or not to abide by any ruling of the courts!

# Enforcement of International Law

The major problem with international law, therefore, aside from its diffuseness, is enforcement. Because enforcement provisions are generally lacking, some people contend that in fact international "law" is not, strictly speaking, law at all but rather a set of acknowledged customs, or norms, of behavior. The importance of norms alone should not be underestimated; in fact, most human behavior occurs with regard to widely shared norms, not formal law. Nonetheless, domestic law is the last resort (short of violence, which domestic law typically prohibits), and law is effective at least in part because, if worse comes to worst and a lawbreaker is apprehended and found guilty of violating the law, he or she can be held accountable, suffering fines, prison terms, and so on. In the case of domestic law, individuals acknowledge, whether overtly or not, that they are subordinate to the state and its machinery of enforcement: the police, court bailiffs, the national guard, and so on. When it comes to relations among states, by contrast, "individual" states insist on their sovereignty; they emphatically do not recognize that there is an authority that supersedes theirs. The major problem with international law, therefore, is that individual states insist on a kind of latitude that they would never allow their own citizens.

Consider the role of sanctions (punishments for noncompliance) in law more generally. There are three primary incentives for obeying any law, domestic or international: self-interest, duty, and coercion. For example, most individuals stop at red lights not because they fear getting a traffic ticket but rather because they know that, otherwise, they are more likely to have an accident. Rules may therefore be followed out of purely utilitarian concerns—in this case, citizens' interest in personal safety. Laws provide a way of regulating human conduct, ideally for the benefit of all: You can proceed with reasonable safety through an intersection when the light is green, because you know that opposing traffic has a red light, and you have some confidence that other drivers will respect this law, just as you do.

In addition, individuals may follow the law because they feel duty-bound to contribute toward an orderly society that functions with respect for authority. As members of society, who benefit from orderly behavior, individuals assume a responsibility to behave accordingly. That is, some people are influenced by "normative" considerations, or a kind of Kantian categorical imperative to do what is right and good because this is part of being a rational and responsible member of society. Finally, some people are induced to be law abiding by fear that "violators may be prosecuted" and forced to succumb to the state's authority if they are found guilty. Although the role of such coercive factors cannot be denied, coercion by the state apparatus is not the only reason most people are law abiding. Similarly, the absence of such coercion or mechanisms for enforcement does not invalidate international law or render it toothless.

States have numerous incentives, both positive and negative, for abiding by their legal obligations to other states. If a state abrogates its legal responsibilities, adversaries may well retaliate, friends and allies are liable to disapprove, and world opinion is likely to be strongly negative, leading to ostracism and possible economic, political, and cultural sanctions.

Moreover, governments themselves have a strong stake in their own legitimacy, and—even in totalitarian states—adherence to law is fundamental to such legitimacy. Furthermore, a strong case can be made that enforcement per se is less important in inducing compliance with any law—domestic or international—than is the moral aura that surrounds law. Thus, in a law-abiding society, police forces do not make law respectable; rather, it is underlying respect for the law that enables police forces to function effectively. According to this view, what is primarily lacking in international law is not so much a mechanism for enforcement as a deeply felt sense that such law carries its own moral imperative.

# Conflict With State Sovereignty

It simply isn't true that all is anarchy in the international arena any more than everyone is law-abiding in the domestic sphere. States generally obey the law—out of a combined sense of duty and self-interest—even though coercive sanctions, as understood in domestic law, are often absent. States engage in nonviolent commerce—exchange of tourists, diplomats, ideas, trade—according to certain regulations and usually with good will and amity. Moreover, states usually do not enter into treaties unless they intend to abide by them, and they only acquiesce to customary norms of behavior when they anticipate that over the long run they will benefit by doing so. But at the same time, they typically cling to various aspects of sovereignty. Most treaties include a provision permitting signatories to withdraw within a set period of time, typically 3 or 6 months, if their "supreme national interests" are jeopardized. And who makes this decision? The state itself.

States can be defined (following Max Weber and Lenin) as those political entities that claim a monopoly of "legitimate" violence within their borders. When they engage in what they claim is lawful violence outside their borders, states typically maintain that (1) they are acting in self-defense (the Soviet Union in World War II, Israel in the Six Days' War, the United States after 9/11 when it invaded Afghanistan), (2) they are fulfilling treaty obligations (France and Britain in World War II), (3) they are intervening on the side of legitimate authority (the United States in Vietnam, the Soviet Union in Afghanistan), (4) the situation is anarchic and lacks a legitimate authority (the United Nations in the Congo or Somalia, the United States in Iraq), (5) the conflict is within the realm of international legal obligations (the United Nations in Korea), or (6) the conflict presents an overriding moral imperative, such as the prevention of genocide and the "responsibility to protect" civilian noncombatants (NATO in Kosovo, Libya and the Congo, the United States briefly in Somalia). In short, state sovereignty continues to reign—at least when it comes to the interveners. And, usually, a semblance of international law is invoked as well. States have been especially hesitant, moreover, to circumscribe their day-to-day authority. Whereas the Hague Peace Conferences, for example, produced a few halting restrictions on the waging of war, they were unable to establish any significant binding rules for peace.

States are also selective even when it comes to accepting the jurisdiction of international courts, a process known as *adjudication*. Adjudication is very similar to arbitration in that the decision of the third party is binding. The only difference is that in adjudication, the decision is based on international law and rendered by a world court, rather than made by an independent and agreed-upon arbitrator. When, in 1946, the United States formally agreed to refer all of its international disputes to the International Court of Justice, the U.S. Senate attached an amendment, known as the Connally Reservation, stipulating that the court's authority does not include anything within the domestic jurisdiction of the United States of America as determined by the United States of America. With this loophole, the United States is free to "determine" that any dispute is essentially within its domestic jurisdiction, thereby avoiding international adjudication whenever it wishes.

This stance is not unusual. France, for example, refused to acknowledge jurisdiction of the World Court when it tested nuclear weapons on French possessions in the Pacific, despite complaints of international illegality from New Zealand, Australia, and other Pacific states. And when the World Court ruled against the United States and in favor of Nicaragua in a case involving U.S. mining of Nicaraguan harbors during the "Contra War" of 1983 and 1984, the United States simply shrugged aside this verdict, claiming that in this instance it did not recognize the court's authority.

## Law, Power, and Social Change

Law is an important part of human life; some would even say that it is crucial to civilization. Despite many people's concerns about enforcement—and anxiety when, as in the case of international law, enforcement powers are lacking—law is in many ways the antithesis of rule by brute force. Might does not make normative right; law should reflect what is right. As a result, most decent people are presumed to be law-abiding, and in fact, rule by law is almost inevitably seen as preferable to rule by force. However, law can be an instrument of oppression. Laws are made by those in power, and as such, they can serve to perpetuate that power and to prevent social and political change. Thus, laws—international as well as domestic—serve best in a conservative, relatively unchanging environment. Developing and revolutionary states often point out that international laws were established by Western powers in support of their domination. One of the earliest and clearest examples is the Treaty of Tordesillas (1494), following Columbus's "discovery" of the New World, whereby the pope "legally" divided that world into Spanish and Portuguese domains—without any regard for the peoples already living there.

Similarly, Western international law relies heavily on the basic principle that *pacta sunt servanda* (treaties should be honored). But consider cases in which a puppet ruler, imposed by a foreign colonial power, signs a treaty granting economic privileges to that power: If an indigenous, representative government eventually replaces the colonial authorities, should the new government be obliged to fulfill those obligations? For example, the establishment of a U.S. naval base at Guantánamo, Cuba, derives from an agreement reached by the U.S.-backed Batista dictatorship that was overthrown in the Cuban revolution. Nonetheless, the power of previous treaties (plus, in the case of Guantánamo, the power of the United States) has generally been such that even treaties negotiated by a previous regime are typically continued in force. When the Soviet Union dissolved, its major successor state—Russia—not only acceded to the previous Soviet Union's seat in the United Nations but also undertook to meet the Soviet Union's treaty obligations.

Not surprisingly, however, economically developing and, to a lesser extent, revolutionary nationalist states are often inclined to repudiate *pacta sunt servanda* and to rely instead on an opposing doctrine, also recognized under law: *rebus sic stantibus* (circumstances have changed). This principle states that international laws must be living documents, subject to modification and, if necessary, annulment whenever conditions become substantially different from those obtained when an agreement or treaty was reached. By the same token, agreements made under duress—like contracts signed with a gun to one's head—are not generally considered valid.

International law must be flexible, if only because of the march of technology. For several centuries, for example, since a Dutch ruling in 1737, *territorial waters* had been considered to extend 3 miles from shore; this distance was based on the effective range of shore-based cannons at the time. New guidelines, however, established by the Law of the Sea Treaty after decades of wrangling, call for 200-mile limits. This treaty—known as the United Nations Convention on the Law of the Sea, or UNCLOS—also created mechanisms of dispute resolution, waste disposal, and navigation procedures. But under the Reagan administration, the United States refused to sign, maintaining that the treaty's call for an intergovernmental body to supervise mining on the deep-sea bed constituted "international socialism." This highlights, once again, the susceptibility of international law to asserted claims of state sovereignty, as well as the growing pressure of North-South cleavages. (The United States eventually signed this treaty, but the U.S. Congress has yet to ratify it.)

# Hidden Strengths of International Law

## Governmental Respect for Law

Most governments do not routinely flout the law, not even their own domestic statutes, over which they have complete control. In most democratic countries, governments accede to legal decisions, even those that go against them. Citizens of the United States, for example, often take for granted the fact that in many cases, they can, if they wish, bring legal action against their own government. And if the courts—which are themselves organs of the government—rule against the government, citizens can receive compensation or other redress for their grievances, even though governments, not the courts, have the strong-arm potential of enforcing their will. This emphasizes the primacy of law over force (except in such cases as the indefinite detainment of "enemy combatants" at Guantánamo Bay, Cuba, and the Central Intelligence Agency's "renditions" of purported "terrorists," when the executive branch of a government acts "extralegally" and later seeks court and/or congressional ratification of its actions).

During the Korean War, following a labor strike that supposedly threatened U.S. war production at a critical time, President Truman sought to nationalize the U.S. steel industry. The Supreme Court, however, overruled this action, and the government obeyed the law, albeit reluctantly. Because democratic governments have a long-range interest in settling disputes amicably, an interest that supersedes its short-term interest in winning a given dispute, they usually tend to accept legal rulings, even those that they dislike. On the other hand, such acceptance is generally less likely in international affairs, unless the opponents are so mutually balanced that the costs of losing a case are less than the costs of further wrangling and possible war.

## Tacit Acceptance and Expectation

International law often appears weaker than it really is. This is because violations, when they occur, are often sensational and dramatic, whereas compliance is taken for granted and hence goes largely unnoticed. When a domestic law is broken by individuals, only rarely are citizens moved to question the legitimacy of the law itself and almost never do they doubt its existence. But a different standard is often applied to international law: When states violate international law, they may or may not be condemned by public opinion, but almost invariably, the law *itself* is called into question, and the purported weakness of international law is once again lamented. Just as we are not told about the vast majority of people who obey domestic law every day, we do not see headlines proclaiming, "Paraguay today complied with its treaty obligations regarding its border with Bolivia, and therefore no invasion took place."

Virtually the entire civilized world was shocked, by contrast, when in the early days of World War I, Chancellor Theobald von Bethmann-Hollweg justified the German invasion of Belgium by describing the international guarantee of Belgian neutrality as a "mere scrap of paper." On the one hand, this announcement—and, even more so, the brutal invasion itself—showed the truth of the chancellor's assertion: Belgian neutrality was in fact "only" an international agreement, lacking any guarantee and incapable, by itself, of keeping out the invading German divisions. But on the other hand, the level of international outrage showed that international law, even when it lacks a means of enforcement, is nonetheless real in its effects on public perception. In addition, we should note that the immediate reason for Britain entering the war against Germany was in fact the German violation of Belgian neutrality; so, in a sense, international treaty law was ultimately enforced in this case. Had Germany respected the law, Britain could well have stayed neutral, and Germany might have won World War I.

# The Law of War

War can be seen as the antithesis of law, whose goal after all is the ordering of relations without recourse to violence. Cicero first wrote that *inter arma silent legis* (in war the law is silent). This is taken to mean that the justifiability of any given war is outside the purview of international law, since states are sovereign authorities unto themselves and are thus free to make war or not, as they choose. Under this view, since there is no higher authority than a state, no one can claim that a state is making war *unlawfully*.

Nonetheless, a body of law is widely thought to apply to states under conditions of war. Legal scholar and war historian Quincy Wright has even defined war itself as "the legal condition which equally permits two or more hostile groups to carry on a conflict by armed force." Therefore—at least according to some experts—war is a highly formalized interval when violence may *legitimately* be practiced between two opposing groups. Enough agreement exists within the community of nations that belligerents and neutrals alike recognize the existence of certain accepted standards: "Although war manifests the weakness of the community of nations," Wright claimed, "it also manifests the existence of that community."

On occasion, members of that community coalesce in opposition to acts that are sufficiently outrageous. For example, international conscience has been deeply offended by the use of children—some as young as 8—in military engagements. In Geneva in 2000, the UN Convention on the Rights of the Child was revised, raising the minimum age for participation in armed conflicts from 15 to 18 and defining recruitment of soldiers under the age of 15 as a war crime. The United States eventually signed the convention, after having long objected to such a provision, insisting on its "right" to recruit 17-year-old volunteers and even to send them into combat. At the same time, rebel groups, especially in sub-Saharan Africa, rather than national armies, are especially likely to employ grossly underage child soldiers, and such groups generally show relatively little inclination to abide by the international laws of war.

## The Nuremberg Principles

States that are party to international treaties may find themselves subject, even against their will, to the legal restraints of these treaties. The losers in World War II, for example, were tried—and many convicted—for having waged aggressive war in defiance of their obligations under the Kellogg-Briand Pact of 1928 (which has also served as the partial legal basis for the notion of "Crimes Against Peace"). These trials, conducted in the German city of Nuremberg, were unique for having developed the legal doctrine that individuals are personally liable to criminal prosecution for crimes against international law. This includes illegal resort to war as well as violations of accepted restraints as to appropriate conduct during war—notably, the treatment of prisoners and the waging of genocide.

Telford Taylor, the chief Allied prosecutor at Nuremberg, wrote that

> war consists largely of acts that would be criminal if performed in time of peace—killing, wounding, kidnapping, destroying or carrying off other people's property. Such conduct is not regarded as criminal if it takes place in the course of war, because the state of war lays a blanket of immunity over the warriors. . . . But the area of immunity is not unlimited and its boundaries are marked by the laws of war.[2]

Some critics objected to these proceedings, claiming that the Nuremberg Trials were simply examples of "victors' justice" and not real international law. Nevertheless, the so-called Nuremberg Principles have served as a benchmark in efforts to introduce humane and reasoned limits to acceptable wartime behavior. Thus, the international military tribunal that convened in Nuremberg specified a series of international crimes. Article 6 of the Nuremberg Charter identified the following:

1. Crimes against the peace—namely, planning; preparation; initiation or waging of a war of aggression or a war in violation of international treaties, agreements, or assurances; or participation in a common plan or conspiracy for the accomplishment of any of the foregoing

2. Crimes against humanity—namely, murder, extermination, enslavement, deportation, and other inhumane acts committed against any civilian population, before or during the war, or persecutions on political, racial, or religious grounds . . . whether or not in violation of the domestic law of the country where perpetrated

3. War crimes—namely, violations of the laws or customs of war. Such violations shall include, but not be limited to, murder; ill treatment or deportation to slave labor or for any other purpose of civilian population of or in occupied territory; murder or ill treatment of prisoners of war or persons on the seas; killing of hostages; plunder of public or private property; wanton destruction of cities, towns, or villages; and devastation not justified by military necessity

Article 7 specified that "the official position of defendants, whether as Heads of State or responsible officials of Government departments, shall not be considered as freeing them from their responsibility or mitigating their punishment." And according to Article 8, "The fact that the defendant acted pursuant to orders of his Government or of a superior shall not free him from responsibility."

Whereas the German defendants at Nuremberg were tried for crimes they committed that were subsequently ruled to have been against international law, a series of lesser-known trials was conducted in Tokyo, of Japanese officials accused in large part of crimes of *omission*—that is, illegal failure to act—as contrasted with the crimes of commission with which the Nuremberg Tribunal was concerned. For example, Kōki Hirota, Japanese foreign minister from 1932 to 1937, failed to insist on an end to Japanese atrocities against civilian Chinese during the "rape of Nanking." Several decades later, when U.S. Army lieutenant William Calley was tried and found guilty for his role in the slaughter of hundreds of old people, women, and children—known as the My Lai Massacre—during the Vietnam War, it appears to have been the first time a state had accused one of its own soldiers of war crimes. Calley's higher-ranking commanding officers were not tried, however, despite the fact that parallels can be drawn between the actions of senior U.S. military and political leaders and those high-ranking Japanese officials who were tried and convicted after World War II. So again, whereas international laws exist and have been enforced, such enforcement has been highly selective.

## Military Necessity?

The treaties that were violated by the Nuremberg defendants, originating from the Geneva and Hague conventions, specified limitations on naval and aerial bombardment. But they also made allowances for "military necessity," which can be stretched to permit nearly any act in wartime, however brutal. Similarly, even the unenforceable Kellogg-Briand Pact, which officially outlawed war, was interpreted by many as permitting "wars of self-defense," as does the current UN Charter: Article 51 grants states the "inherent right of individual or collective self defense." Self-defense would clearly have justified Poland's attempt to resist the German invasion in 1939, but what about France's response: declaring war on Germany? (France was bound by treaty to help defend Poland.) And what about the Israeli invasion of Egypt in 1967, in which Israel clearly struck first but in which it was argued that Egyptian behavior constituted a real provocation as well as an imminent threat that justified a "preemptive" attack by Israel? Similarly, the "Brezhnev Doctrine," by which the Soviet Union justified its invasion of Czechoslovakia in 1968, was described at the time as simply "self-defense by socialist people against Western-inspired counterrevolutionaries."

And the "Reagan Doctrine," under which the United States assisted right-wing revolutionaries seeking to overthrow leftist governments in Angola and Afghanistan, was also described by its supporters as aid to people seeking to defend themselves.

Although the Bush administration showed very little respect for or patience with international law, apologists for wars have usually been able to find loopholes in international treaties. And when it comes to governments using force against their own citizens—such as Serbia in Kosovo or Sudan's persecution of its own citizens in Darfur—obligations and restraints of international law are murkier yet.

In short, when states considered that their security interests required it, violations of international law have occurred, and this situation can be expected to continue. Many scholars argue, incidentally, that the very possession of nuclear weapons runs counter to international law, because it involves preparations for genocide. It seems likely, however, that if these and other undiscriminating weapons of mass destruction are to be abolished, it will be for reasons other than their "illegality."

## A FINAL NOTE ON INTERNATIONAL LAW

International law has many imperfections. It appears to have exerted some useful restraints on illicit state conduct in some cases while being woefully inadequate in others. The major powers give it less credence than do the militarily weaker states, in part because the former have recourse to their military strength, whereas the latter are generally more invested in the rule of law, which offers them the possibility of a "level playing field" in contests with larger, stronger opponents.

Some legal and political authorities recommend only a modest role for international law in the future, avoiding "the Charybdis of subservience to state ambitions and the Scylla of excessive pretensions of restraint" and recognizing that "it is in the interest of international law itself to put states' consciences neither to sleep nor to torture."[3] Another view is that international law is a good beginning, something on which to build a world without boundaries or, at least, one in which the sanctity of state sovereignty is curtailed in the greater interest of human survival.

## NOTES

1. Anne-Marie Slaughter. 2011. "War and Law in the 21st Century: Adapting to the Changing Face of Conflict." *Europe's World.* http://www.europesworld.org/NewEnglish/Home_old/Article/tabid/191/ArticleType/ArticleView/ArticleID/21912/language/en-us/Warandlawinthe21stcenturyAdaptingtothechangingface ofconflict.aspx

2. Telford Taylor. 1970. *Nuremberg and Vietnam.* Chicago: Quadrangle.

3. Stanley Hoffmann. 1971. "International Law and the Control of Force." In K. Deutsch and S. Hoffmann, eds., *The Relevance of International Law.* New York: Anchor.

## QUESTIONS FOR FURTHER REFLECTION

1. It has been said that to the extent that law is law, it is not international, and to the extent that it is international, it is not law. Analyze this contention.

2. How does the question of enforcement in international law differ from that of domestic law? How is it similar?

3. Are there any weaknesses of international law other than the problem of enforcement? If so, describe them.

4. In what sense can international law be seen as revolutionary? In what sense can it be seen as conservative?

5. What relevance, if any, do the Nuremberg Principles have to international events occurring today? Your answer could be framed in general principles or specific examples.

## SUGGESTIONS FOR FURTHER READING

Christian Reus-Smit. 2004. *The Politics of International Law*. New York: Cambridge University Press.

Christopher C. Joyner. 2005. *International Law in the 21st Century: Rules for Global Governance*. Lanham, MD: Rowman & Littlefield.

Jack L. Goldsmith and Eric A. Posner. 2006. *The Limits of International Law*. New York: Oxford University Press.

Sean Murphy. 2006. *Principles of International Law*. Eagan, MN: Thomson West.

Malcolm Shaw. 2008. *International Law*. New York: Cambridge University Press.

Simon Chesterman. 2002. *Just War or Just Peace?: Humanitarian Intervention and International Law*. Oxford: Oxford University Press.

# CHAPTER 17

# ETHICAL AND RELIGIOUS PERSPECTIVES

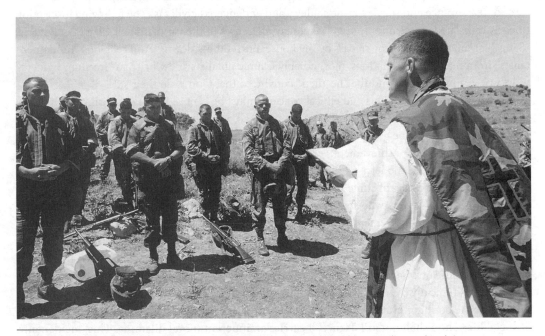

United States Marines in Iraq attending Catholic Mass conducted by a military chaplain.

*Source:* © 2008 Getty Images.

*The God of peace is never glorified by human violence.*

—Thomas Merton

Killing another human being, except by accident, in self-defense, or because of insanity, is condemned in modern societies—unless done during war or by the state against criminals within and enemies outside, in which case it is not only permitted but also frequently applauded. In fact, in war, particularly good killers are often accorded high honors. Not surprisingly, therefore, war has received substantial attention from ethicists and theologians. However, the relationship between ethical teachings and war has long been ambiguous and its message ambivalent; advocates of peace have often derived inspiration and strength from such teachings, while at the same time, the war prone have also turned to religious and moral authorities (sometimes the same ones) to support their arguments.

It may be that a concerted opposition to war will ultimately derive considerable impetus from ethical and religious sources; nonetheless, it remains true that some versions (or perversions) of ethics and religion have also fueled much warfare in the past and may continue to do so in the future.

Unfortunately, many of the world's organized moral and theological preachers historically have been more likely to support militarism than to oppose it. Sometimes, religious authorities have been among the primary cheerleaders for war making. At other times, their stance has been passive acquiescence. In czarist Russia, for example, Russian Orthodox priests traditionally said a funeral mass for peasants when they were inducted into the army. Commonly, religious and ethical values were limited to self-protective and self-serving doctrines, such as immunity for the clergy and mixtures of reassurance and solace for the soldiery and endangered civilians. The following inscription (loosely translated) is commonly seen even today on houses in the various small villages of Bavaria: "Saint Florian, protect our town, pass by my house, burn others down"! And religious "fundamentalists" from many denominations, most notably Islamic jihadists and Christian "freedom fighters," wage war against civilians and the "heathen," convinced that God is on their side.

On the other hand, religious and ethical concerns must be central to the establishment of peace. Moral decisions cannot be avoided: There was, after all, virtually nothing technically wrong with Auschwitz, Dachau, or the bombings of Dresden and Hiroshima. (The latter, especially, was a major scientific and technical achievement.) Criticism, or condemnation, must come—in moral and spiritual terms. In the modern world, religion in particular has been transformative: Examples include the respective roles of Shiite Islam in post-shah Iran, Catholicism in Poland, Episcopal bishop Desmond Tutu and others who fought apartheid in South Africa, and Protestant Christianity in fueling the civil rights movement in the American South during the 1960s. Numerous American churches opposed the war in Vietnam, and during the 1980s church-led movements were instrumental in calling for the abolition of nuclear weapons and the end of East-West hostilities. The Berlin Wall fell in part because of nonviolent mass protests by Evangelical Christians in the former East Germany.

Warfare is typically overlain with numerous rules and elaborate structures of permissible and impermissible conduct. But fundamentally, it is an inversion of one of the most basic strictures of social life: Thou shalt not kill. Hence, it carries an inherent moral dilemma. This, incidentally, may also be why war is so often the midwife of social change. Having broken out of the prescriptions of what is permissible and what is not, situations of war occasionally open up possibilities for rearranging the social order. Any meaningful turnabout in fundamental attitudes regarding the acceptability of war will almost certainly involve ethical and religious formulations; conversely, no such turnabout will be possible if it is not somehow anchored in ethical and religious precepts. This, plus the support now provided by ethics and religion to peace workers and war boosters alike, makes it all the more important that close attention be paid to these issues.

# Ethics

Ethics, also known as moral philosophy, studies the groundwork of morality. Morality is concerned with the nature of right and wrong, good and bad actions, often from within a particular set of cultural and social norms and customs. Applied ethics seeks an understanding of the moral dimensions of specific, real-life controversies and their potential solutions. It assesses how moral outcomes can be achieved in specific situations. It attempts to apply ethical theory to real-life situations. The discipline has many specialized fields, such as business ethics, bio-ethics, medical ethics, environmental ethics, government or military ethics, and the ethics of war and peace.

## Two Influential Western Ethical Traditions: Deontology and Utilitarianism

Deontology, or the theory of ethical duties and obligations, argues that the morality of an act is determined by an actor's good will—the *intent* to fulfill a moral duty or obey an applicable moral rule. Immanuel Kant's moral and political philosophy is closely identified with deontology. From a Kantian deontological perspective, a rule is ethical when: 1) it is *categorical*—there are no exceptions to its application, 2) it exhibits *universality*—when the rule is applied to one person or group, the resulting good must equal the good obtained when the same rule is applied to any other persons or groups, and 3) it does not use persons as a means to an ends—it respects all persons as "ends" in themselves.

According to Kant, war involves an inevitable moral descent. It deprives the enemy of the respect that is fundamentally due to all persons by virtue of their humanity. Kant emphasized that we should treat people as rational agents intrinsically deserving respect (i.e., as *ends*), whereas war often compels the combatants to see each other as mere *means*, as objects, numbers, or targets. Frequently, commanders even treat their own soldiers as cannon fodder. Because this underlying depersonalization runs counter to deep-seated humanistic moral precepts, there is a widespread need, especially on the part of aggressors, to justify their actions in moral terms. But overall, deontology tends to deem virtually all violence, especially warfare, as unethical.

Utilitarianism is probably the dominant moral philosophy in the Anglophonic world and is a version of consequentialism. Consequentialism is the view that the morality or rightness of an act or belief depends only on the consequences of that act or of something related to that act, such as the motive behind the act or a general rule requiring acts of the same kind. The paradigm case of consequentialism is utilitarianism, whose classic proponents were Jeremy Bentham (1789), John Stuart Mill (1861), and Henry Sidgwick (1907).

For utilitarians, the morality is determined by an act's utility (efficacy) in producing the greatest good for the most people. Good ends justify the means. The efficacy of an act has greater moral significance than the actor's intentions. Utilitarianism also places particular value on the balance of benefits and costs (also called the "utility") associated with any act.

For example, many sensitive and thoughtful people maintain that violence—even war—can be justifiable if it occurs in pursuit of some lofty goal, such as human freedom. More than 2,500 years ago, when the invading Persians called for their opponents to surrender, the greatly outnumbered Greeks responded as follows: "A slave's life thou understandest, but, never having tasted liberty, thou canst not tell whether it be sweet or no. Ah! Hadst thou known what freedom is, thou wouldst have bidden us fight for it."

From a utilitarian or consequentialist perspective, the morality of an act is dependent upon how the outcome criteria are defined; for example, a drone attack may be judged a success by the nation that launched it because it met its criterion for killing alleged enemy combatants, while the villagers where the attack took place may judge it an immoral act because civilians were killed. The same would be true for judging the ethics of using nuclear weapons and other weapons of mass destruction—the outcome might be judged a success by the attackers, but the survivors and other members of the global community probably won't agree. Additionally, judgment of results often depends upon the length of time between the act and the evaluation of its consequences. For example, in the case of the drone attack, immediately afterward it may be judged a success because it killed the targeted group of alleged terrorists, but over a period of several years it may be judged a failure because many of the family, friends, and community of those killed subsequently supported or joined terrorist groups or failed to cooperate with the nation that launched the drone.

Critics claim that once the door is opened to official sanction for violence, arguing that consequentialist or utilitarian ethics can rapidly become apologies for mass murder. The deliberate killing of civilians, for example, can be deemed permissible if enough perceived benefits can be gained by it. The alternative, deontological ethics, would include such stances as absolute pacifism. In this view, no killing is permissible, no matter what immediate good is achieved or what evil is averted thereby.

## *Realpolitik,* Just War, and Pacifism

Specific applications of ethics to war usually encompass three applied ethical traditions: realism/*Realpolitik*, just war, and pacifism, each relevant to ethical analyses of war and peace. All three traditions presume that an individual has a "natural" right to life; however, they differ in the extent to which war is acceptable as a moral means of protecting lives designated as innocent and of preserving "national security."

Realism or *Realpolitik* argues that the political behavior of nations and their adversaries is based, not on civilian private morality, but on pragmatic considerations of national self-interest and power. An alternate version is that the moral duty to protect the greatest number of innocent persons from harm justifies using virtually any means necessary, including total war. In realism, it makes no sense to fight under rules that might give an advantage to the enemy and thereby prolong the war, when unrestricted military action might end the war more quickly and efficiently. Universality is not a consideration, since the only obligation is to the nation's defense of its own real and perceived interests, but often at the expense of the lives of its own and other nations' citizens.

The ethical criteria of the Just War Tradition, which we discuss later in this chapter, presume that it is in the interests of all nations to restrict war within certain limits that will minimize harm to persons, especially civilians and other noncombatants. It seems, unfortunately, that Just War criteria have failed to reduce the frequency or destructiveness of war, in part due to the ease with which nations can interpret them in favor of their own interests. (At the same time, it can never be concluded with certainty that a given set of restraints upon war have failed altogether, since we don't know how things would have turned out if they hadn't been in place.)

Pacifism is an ethical system that tends to be absolutist about the inviolable sanctity of human life—war is never defensible as a moral exception to society's fundamental prohibition against killing. Designating groups of persons as innocent or guilty is irrelevant because all persons have a natural right to life that is not dependent upon fallible determinations made by human authority.

## War, Ethics, and Religion

Mainstream Western ethical and religious thought typically condones war in particular cases; occasionally, as in Fascist doctrine, war is even enthusiastically embraced. But when considering war in general, ethical judgment by and large is critical. Approval—when it comes (and, sooner or later, it usually does)—is largely restricted to *specific* wars, in which people are confronted with particular conflicts and identifiable enemies who typically are also perceived as threats. One might argue that the specifics are what count: Just as there is no "war" in the abstract, but rather particular wars, it is of little help if ethicists and religious leaders condemn war in general but lend their approval to each individual war as it comes along. But this misses a potentially important characteristic of most ethical thought: a predisposition *against* violence and killing. This fundamental and often unspoken precept may contribute importantly to the eventual delegitimation of war.

## Presumptions Against War

Like the presumption of innocence in legal proceedings, a widespread moral orientation presumes that the way of peace is better than the way of war. For war to be justified, therefore, the burden of proof must lie on those who make war.

In addition, many reasonable citizens recognize that might does not make right. When trial by combat became legal in Burgundy in 501 BCE, the clergy at the time objected, whereupon King Gundovald replied: "Is it not true that the event of national wars and private combats is directed by the judgment of God, and that his providence awards the victory to the juster cause?" Times have changed, and dramatically so: No modern state currently condones the settling of private disputes by violent combat between the contending individuals. When state or national disputes are settled by war, however, it is analogous to settling personal disputes by individual combat, with the outcome presumably a function of strength, not of individual merit or justice. Hence, violent procedures employed to try to resolve conflicts are difficult to justify.

One of the most dramatic and famous exceptions to the Western moral injunction against the politics of "might makes right" occurred in the ancient Athenian campaign against the residents of the island of Melos. The Melians had favored Sparta during the Peloponnesian War (in the 5th century BCE, between Athens and Sparta) but sought to maintain neutrality since they were geographically close to Athens, which was far stronger than tiny Melos. After a lengthy siege, the Athenians delivered an ultimatum to the inhabitants of Melos: Surrender and be enslaved, or be destroyed. The Melians protested the unfairness of this choice, arguing that they had not given Athens any cause for such violence. According to Thucydides, the great historian of this war, the Athenian spokesman answered in a speech that is renowned for its brutal honesty: "Right only comes into question when there is a balance of power, while it is might that determines what the strong extort and the weak concede." Ultimately, all Melian males were killed, and the women and children were taken as slaves.

The Athenian disregard for our conventional civil morality is shocking, and the fact that it is so upsetting is part of the reason why blame for the causation of war is nearly always heaped on the opponent. It is almost unheard of for a belligerent to announce: "We have decided to make war on our neighbor, not because of any misdeeds on their part, or for any righteous cause, but because we desire to plunder their resources—including their women—settle on their territory, enhance our prestige, enrich our arms manufacturers, provide amusement and occupation for our dissatisfied young men, and/or deflect domestic criticism." Even when the aggressive design is transparent, the other side is typically blamed; such convenient fictions provide a shred of moral legitimacy to which the aggressor state's populace may cling and behind which the leadership may hide.

## Blaming the Other Side

Wars are often preceded by efforts of antagonists to emphasize the perfidy of the other side or, if necessary, to create "incidents" that make the war more acceptable. Many historians suspect, for example, that the sinking of the U.S. battleship *Maine* in Havana harbor in 1898 generated great national anger and led to the United States declaring war on Spain. Today, most historians agree that this *casus belli*, cause of a war, was actually an accident or a deliberate provocation, initiated by persons hoping to goad the United States into war. Similarly, Hitler repeatedly claimed that ethnic Germans within Czechoslovakia and Poland were being criminally maltreated, and prior to the invasion of 1939, German forces even staged a phony "attack," ostensibly by Polish troops against a German radio station near the border.

The Gulf of Tonkin Incident (1964) was essentially manufactured by President Lyndon Johnson as a successful ploy to paint North Vietnam as an aggressor against the United States and to get Congress to approve direct U.S. military intervention in the conflict in Southeast Asia. The second Russian war in Chechnya (1999–2000) was justified domestically as a response to the bombing of several apartment houses in Moscow—terrorist acts that were never proven to have been undertaken by Chechens and that some critics even suggest were initiated by the Russian government as an excuse for mobilizing public opinion in favor of crushing a troublesome, independence-minded republic. The U.S.-led invasion of Iraq in 2003 was preceded by claims that the government of Saddam Hussein was somehow involved in the terrorist attacks of 9/11 (it was not) and that the Iraqis were accumulating "weapons of mass destruction" for use against the United States (it was not). It is clear that the Bush administration wanted to invade Iraq for other reasons—the specifics of which will doubtless be debated for a long time—and that purported links to terrorism and weapons of mass destruction were justifications for initiating war and thus, ways of mobilizing initial popular support, not actual reasons.

Government leaders are only rarely as direct as the Athenians who destroyed Melos. In addition to concocting justifications, often phony ones, statesmen almost invariably describe their wars as moral, often as crusades. Thus, for many in the United States, the Vietnam War was a crusade to defend the "democrats" of Saigon against the "butchers" from Hanoi, even as the murderous *contras* in Nicaragua were likened by President Reagan to the American founding fathers. For Hitler, expansion of the Third Reich was "required to save the world" from Jews and communists. For the Soviet Union, interventionism was justified to protect the human rights of Afghans (especially the women, oppressed by Muslim fundamentalism) and to liberate Hungary from the horrors of counterrevolution. For China, occupation of Tibet was explained as necessary to banish Tibetan feudalism. For India, its long-sought goal of dismembering Pakistan was clothed in the high moral purpose of aiding the persecuted Bengalis in East Pakistan. The U.S. insistence on driving Iraq out of Kuwait during the Gulf War was presented as a high-minded pursuit of international justice, whereas in all likelihood it was primarily driven by worry about securing Kuwaiti oil, as well as domestic political needs.

NATO's war in Kosovo may well have been driven by desire to prove its relevance in a post–Cold War world but was publicly justified as purely moral in purpose: to prevent genocide by Serbia against native Kosovars. And so it has gone.

On the other hand, ethical outrage serves many purposes, not all of which are cynical. It is all too easy to criticize the ease with which moral indignation is aroused in support of organized killing. After all, politics is a difficult and messy occupation, and nowhere is it more difficult or messier than when it comes to decisions about war.

In the view of some distinguished theologians, such as Reinhold Niebuhr, the necessity for tough, practical choice and action in a world of moral ambiguity transforms politics into nothing less than tragedy: "Politics will, to the end of history, be an area where conscience and power meet, where the ethical and coercive factors of human life will interpenetrate and work out their tentative and uneasy compromises."[1] An alternative view, however, is that especially when it comes to issues of war and peace, death and life, there is no room for compromises or moral equivocation. Under such circumstances, it is not enough to choose the lesser of two evils. One must choose to do what is right.

# Religious Attitudes Toward War

Religious intolerance has led to many wars; in addition, religions have often contributed to war making directly, by their own internal demands and expectations, thereby disturbing the peace rather than promoting it.

## Judaism

Like most religions, Jewish doctrine is inconsistent with respect to war. Whereas many modern European Jews have traditionally been strongly peace oriented, the ancient Israelites were notable warriors, and indeed, the Old Testament is replete with bloody accounts of the so-called commanded wars, in which God urged his people to destroy others: "When the Lord your God has given them over to you, and you defeat them, then you must utterly destroy them; you shall make no covenant with them, and show no mercy to them" (Deuteronomy 7:2). However, after its domination by the Romans, for many centuries Jewish tradition emphasized pacifism, only to be overcome by a renewed warlike ethos in association with the founding of the state of Israel and in the aftermath of the Holocaust of the late 1930s and early 1940s, when approximately 6 million European Jews were slaughtered. Today, the Israeli army (technically known as the Israeli Defense Forces) is widely considered one of the most effective fighting forces in the world (although this vaunted reputation has been somewhat called into question by Israel's unsuccessful foray in 2006 into Lebanon as part of its conflict with Hezbollah, and by the inconclusive outcome of its 2008 to 2009 and 2012 battles with Hamas in the Gaza Strip).

## Islam, Hinduism, and Buddhism

Other religious traditions have also intermittently displayed a positive attitude toward war. Best known among these is the *jihad,* or holy war, among Muslims, in which fallen warriors are considered to be guaranteed entry into heaven. Islamic scholars maintain a distinction between the "greater *jihad*," which applies to internal struggle, a personal "war" against one's own disobedient and thus ungodly inclinations, and the "lesser *jihad*," involving war in the more traditional sense, emphasizing the "glory" of dying in defense of Islam. Just as Christianity is divided into numerous denominations (notably Protestant, Catholic, and Orthodox), Islam is similarly diverse, with the major distinction between Sunni and Shiite. And just as Christianity has been riven by violence between Catholics and Protestants (the "Wars of Religion" in Europe during the late Middle Ages), armed struggle between Sunnis and Shiites has a long history, most recently reflected in what is essentially a civil war in Iraq following the destabilization of that country by the U.S.-led invasion.

Hinduism (and Jainism) contributed to Gandhian nonviolence, but it has also had a rigorous military tradition. The great Hindu texts emphasize the duty of devout Hindus to fight even for a cause with which they may disagree: In the *Bhagavad Gita,* the hero Arjuna is enjoined to kill even his friends and relatives, if his duty so demands. Moreover, battle is seen as a kind of divine, selfless action (*karma yoga*), and Arjuna, the man and warrior, is advised by Krishna, the warrior-god, to cease all personal striving on behalf of a greater goal.

Peace has long been a central doctrine for Buddhism, but it has traditionally been more inward—than outward—looking. Resistance to particular wars, as a self-conscious Buddhist goal, has historically been rare; moreover, some Zen Buddhist practices in Japan strongly supported Japanese militarism during World War II. Notable exceptions were the Unified Buddhist Church of Vietnam and elsewhere in Indochina, especially during the 1960s, when some Buddhists committed self-immolation (suicide by burning themselves) as a means of personal protest against the Vietnam War and, more recently, in Burma (Myanmar), protesting a dictatorial military junta. Subsequently, an intentional Buddhist peace tradition has emerged, emphasizing "engagement" in the world, especially under the influence of the Vietnamese Zen teacher Thich Nhat Hanh.

## Christianity

Christianity, too, has a complex relationship to war. Although many of its founding principles emphasize pacifism, turning the other cheek, and loving one's neighbor, Christianity (along with Islam, Hinduism, and Shinto, the predominant religious tradition of Japan) constitutes one of the great warrior religions of history. The fundamental Christian ambiguity toward war is reflected in attitudes toward the cross. On the one hand, it is supposed to be the ultimate symbol of God's peace and love, divine grace with which to replace violence and sin. But on the other hand, the cross has long been seen as a new and more effective sword with which to smite the forces of evil. Thus, Saint Paul warned that "if thou dost what is evil, fear, for not without reason does it [government] carry the sword. For it is God's minister, an avenger to execute wrath on him who does evil" (Romans 13:4).

Christendom was the eventual heir to the dying Roman Empire, and as such, many of its early wars were unsuccessful, although fought with increasing fervor. The "holy war" tradition in Christianity is a direct descendant of the commanded wars of the Old Testament and was especially influential during the Middle Ages, most dramatically during the Crusades. Saint Bernard of Clairvaux, in the 12th century, delivered the following sermon in support of Christian efforts to drive Muslims from Palestine:

A new sort of army has appeared. . . . It fights a double war; first, the war of the flesh and blood against enemies; second, the war of the spirit against Satan and vice. . . . The soldier of Christ kills with safety; he dies with more safety still. He serves Christ when he kills. He serves himself when he is killed.[2]

In 1215, the Catholic Church forbade participation of priests or bishops in trials by combat. God, it was claimed, was not concerned with such demeaning matters; nonetheless, the tendency to see wars as divine judgment and retribution continued, in part as a carryover from the time when various Old Testament prophets warned that the sinning city of Babylon would be punished by God, via war. From the 16th to the 18th centuries, many Christians adhered to a similar perspective; war was widely seen as "God's beadle," chastising the ungodly, the sinners, those who were insufficiently devout and righteous. Not only did war represent God's vengeance on the wicked; it also served as a hair shirt, a kind of penance for the war maker, a chastisement for people who had been backsliding, who needed its miseries to remind them of their wickedness and smallness and of God's almighty power. At other times, religious zealotry served to legitimize the Christian conquest of nonbelievers.

Although "conversion by the sword" was a stimulus for the expansion to Islam from 700 to 1450 CE, it was also prominent among Christian war makers. Even as recently as 1914, the Bishop of London urged his countrymen to "kill Germans—kill them, not for the sake of killing, but to save the world, to kill the good as well as the bad, to kill the young men as well as the old. . . . As I have said a thousand times, I look upon it as a war for purity, I look upon everyone who dies in it as a martyr."[3] And of course, bellicose German priests and ministers were simultaneously reassuring their countrymen that *Gott mit uns* (God is with us).

War is bad enough; when religious zealousness adds the conviction of absolute certainty of one's righteousness, it becomes even worse. "Men never do evil so completely and cheerfully," noted Blaise Pascal in his 17th-century *Pensées*, "as when they do it from religious conviction."

## Religious Support for the Status Quo

Religious leaders and traditions have not only been accused of serving as cheerleaders for war but have also been condemned for hindering human freedom by serving as a bulwark in favor of the status quo. Christian doctrine in particular has been criticized for legitimating the oppression of women, blacks, sexual minorities, and the impoverished. The faithful have frequently been called upon to support law and order (often favored code words for government-sponsored repression), as a way of keeping human "sinfulness" under control. In short, religion has often served to keep people submissive, accepting of their oppression. Not surprisingly, therefore, revolutionary socialist doctrine has generally been antagonistic to organized religion, consistent with Karl Marx's famous observation that "religion is the opiate of the masses." During World War II, Joseph Göebbels—the minister of propaganda in Nazi Germany—suggested to German religious leaders, "You are at liberty to seek your salvation as you understand it, provided you do nothing to change the social order." Similarly, the Russian Orthodox Church was permitted to operate more or less freely in the former Soviet Union, so long as it did not challenge the political dominance of the Communist Party.

In fact, however, Christian doctrine is not inevitably wedded to entrenched power, supportive of government-sponsored war making, or consistently opposed to social betterment. "Liberation theology," which originated in Latin America, proclaims a vigorously *social* gospel, emphasizing the social sensitivities of Christ and the need for the modern-day Catholic Church to align itself on the side of the poor, the despised, and the disenfranchised. The General Conference of the Bishops of Latin America in Puebla, Mexico, in 1979 issued the following statement: "From the heart of Latin America, a cry rises to the heavens ever louder and more imperative. It is the cry of a people who suffer and who demand justice, freedom, and respect for the fundamental rights of man. . . . We identify, as the most devastating and humiliating scourge, the situation of inhuman poverty in which millions of Latin Americans live."[4] With a few exceptions, however—notably John XXIII—this approach has not been particularly welcomed by popes in Rome.

# Christian "Realism"

To some extent, each Christian denomination has its own tradition with respect to war; often, in fact, the same church has differing, conflicting approaches. Thus, there are pacifist Baptists and highly militarist Baptists, nonviolent Lutherans and Lutheran paratroopers. Undoubtedly, the most carefully enunciated and influential Christian doctrine with respect to war has been a middle-of-the-road approach known as Just War doctrine. Certainly, there is nothing new in seeking to provide ethical underpinnings for the initiation and conduct of war.

## The Late Roman Empire

Substantial evidence suggests that the early Christian Church was pacifist; indeed, pacifism seems to have distinguished early Christianity from both the warlike Roman Empire and the equally violence-prone Old Testament Jewish tradition (including the "terrorist" Zealots). Many early Christian martyrs died for refusing service in the Roman legions. By the 4th century CE, the secular fortunes of Christianity improved, and with the conversion to the faith of the Roman emperor Constantine, Christianity became the official religion of the Roman state. Almost overnight, Christianity went from a persecuted minority and prophetic movement to the prime defender of Roman government and society. Its transformation was such that soon *only* Christians were permitted to serve in the Roman army! (It was in the context of taking up secular—especially war-related—burdens that the Catholic Church became the *Roman* Catholic Church.) When the Roman Empire was threatened by such "godless barbarians" as the Goths, Vandals, and Huns, Christianity quickly developed a more practical and accepting view of organized violence, a middle ground between the bloodthirsty commanded wars of the Old Testament and the uncompromising pacifism of the early Christian Gospels. The result was a series of careful rules by which a Christian could engage in a "just war."

## The Augustinian View

The main contributor to Christian Just War theory was St. Augustine, Bishop of Hippo in the 4th century CE. Augustine was primarily concerned with justifying Christian participation in the defense of Rome. In *The City of God*, Augustine wrote that "it is the wrong-doing of the opposing party which compels the wise man to wage just wars" and that "war with the hope of peace everlasting" to follow was preferable to "captivity without any thought of deliverance."

To Augustine, and the large tradition of "Christian realism" that followed him, peace was "tranquility in order." Augustine thus prefigured the tension between the devotees of order (often represented in modern times by the political right wing) and of justice (typically represented by the political left). In the Augustinian view, peace often requires violence against evildoers, and the soldier who goes to war in defense of right—and order—does not violate the commandment against killing.

War, in Augustine's view, must be based ultimately on "Christian charity"—that is, the defense of a neighbor who has been unjustly attacked. Nonetheless, a Christian was expected to go to war, if at all, with a heavy heart, and only after carefully examining his conscience, because the presumption was at all times supposed to be in favor of peace. Thus, Augustine emphasized that when the Christian goes to war, he must do so with anguish and deep regret. Whereas the City of God is founded on an act of loving grace, the City of Man, in Augustine's view, is founded on war: Since evil exists, the Christian is obliged to struggle against it. Much debate has arisen, however, over whether this is really a necessity, a permission, or an excuse. In certain hotly contested cases, wars themselves seem to be the greater immorality. Opposition to the Vietnam War in the United States, for example, was fueled by a passionate sense that this war was unjust in its origins and also unjustly fought, which raises the painful but unavoidable question of personal responsibility, especially when one's society is perceived to be prosecuting an immoral war.

## Just War Doctrine

There are two major components to Just War doctrine. The first refers to the justification of fighting a particular war—known by its Latin phrase, *jus ad bellum,* or the justice *of going to* war. It spells out the requirements that must be met in order for a Christian to identify a particular war as acceptable. The second major component of Just War doctrine is *jus in bello,* or justice *in* a war. Whereas *jus ad bellum* concerns whether or not a war ought to be fought (the rules for selecting war versus peace), *jus in bello* deals with the manner in which such a war may be engaged (the rules for conducting any given war). Thus, a just war, one that meets *ad bellum* criteria, may be fought unjustly (if it fails to accord with *in bello* restraints), and similarly, an unjust war can be prosecuted justly.

## Jus ad Bellum

The generally acknowledged criteria for *jus ad bellum* are as follows (it is a worthwhile exercise to examine various specific wars with these principles in mind):

1. *Last resort:* War must not be entered into with undue haste or unseemly enthusiasm but only if all other means of resolution have been explored and found inadequate.

2. *Legitimate authority:* The decision to go to war cannot be made by disgruntled individuals or self-appointed groups; it must come from duly constituted state authority.

3. *Right intention and just cause:* War is unacceptable if motivated by aggression, revenge, or the hope of gain; it must be consistent with Christian charity and/or self-defense. (Interestingly, Augustine himself specifically excluded self-defense, arguing that it was acceptable only to wage war in defense of *others.*)

4. *Chance of success:* Futile resistance cannot be justified; only when there is reasonable chance of a beneficent outcome may the Christian consider that a war is justifiable.

5. *Goal of peace:* Looking ahead to the war's conclusion, it must be possible to envision a peace that is preferable to the situation that would prevail if the war were not fought.

Conditions 3 through 5 are sometimes summarized as the "principle of proportionality," which states that for a war to be just, its overall moral benefits must exceed its costs. Thus, proportionality recognizes that war is inherently evil and can therefore be justified only if it leads to an even greater overall good. In practice, once a state's leadership decides on war, many of its religious figures pronounce it to be just, whereupon the average citizen or soldier goes along (often literally). But at the same time, the requirements for *jus ad bellum* arguments provide—at least in theory—a yardstick whereby "good" Christians can personally evaluate the legitimacy of a state's call to arms.

## Jus in Bello

Once a war is under way, it can, in Just War doctrine, be fought justly or unjustly. The generally acknowledged *in bello* restraints can be summarized in two principles: double effect and discrimination. The principle of double effect is a specific application of the *ad bellum* doctrine of proportionality. Just as wars can be seen to have good and bad overall effects, the principle of double effect states that specific *in bello* actions—those taken during a war—typically have two effects: a "good" effect in bringing the war to a successful conclusion and a "bad" one in causing pain, death, and destruction to combatants and often noncombatants as well. According to the principle of double effect, therefore, such actions as bombings and invasions can be countenanced only if the good effect outweighs the bad. Military means and the cost of war must be proportional to a moral end and its presumed benefits.

The second component of *in bello* restraints, the principle of discrimination, is synonymous with "noncombatant immunity." It states that civilians must not be the direct, intentional object of military attack. This principle recognizes that civilians will often be killed during hostilities, but the direct targeting of noncombatants is prohibited. In practice, however, the principle of discrimination further acknowledges that noncombatants will often be targeted "indirectly," and such activities, so long as they are inadvertent, are generally condoned. For example, when strategic bombardment seeks either to destroy war-production facilities or to diminish the other side's morale, as in the firebombing of German and Japanese cities during World War II, the practical effect has been the incineration of hundreds of thousands of noncombatants.

Various attempts have been made to establish *in bello* restraints on the conduct of war. The medieval "Truce of God" defined certain days as unacceptable for fighting, and the "Peace of God" prohibited direct attack against certain persons: travelers, merchants, clergy, and farmers. The "code of chivalry" established rules concerning who may fight with whom and regarding the treatment of prisoners (if members of the nobility). The Second Lateran Council, in 1215, even banned the use of certain weapons, notably the crossbow. Significantly, however, these prohibitions applied only to use against Christians; the crossbow could still be employed against Muslims, during the Crusades for example. But even this prohibition eventually faltered, and in fact, there have been very few examples of weapons that have been effectively banned because their use was judged immoral.

Chemical weapons appear to be an exception. Although used widely during World War I, they were also universally condemned and hardly employed at all during World War II. On the other hand, this restraint may have been more a function of deterrence than of moral considerations, since each side knew that the other was capable of retaliating with comparable weapons. Moreover, chemical weapons were used during the 1980s, notably by the Iraqis against the Iranians and also by Saddam Hussein's forces against Kurdish rebels in northern Iraq. Biological weapons are universally condemned and have been essentially banned, although stockpiles are still maintained in certain cases, supposedly so as ostensibly to facilitate the design of countermeasures.

## Violations of Noncombatant Immunity

Perhaps the most notable feature of *in bello* restraint, however, and its most tragic failures, involve violations of noncombatant immunity, a trend that has been increasing since 1914. For example, although military casualties were roughly comparable during World Wars I and II, civilian casualties were substantially higher in the latter. This seems due to two factors: (1) the greater involvement of entire populations in a nationwide war effort, thereby blurring the distinction between military and civilian and (2) the invention of increasingly more destructive and less discriminating weapons, most of which also operate at great distance. Nuclear weapons represent a culmination of this trend.

Strategic bombing of cities became increasingly frequent during World War II. There had been great public outcry at the Fascist bombing of Guernica during the Spanish Civil War, the Japanese bombing of such Chinese cities as Nanking, and the German bombing of Rotterdam and Warsaw. By the time of the London blitz and the subsequent Allied bombings of civilian populations in Germany and Japan, however, countercity (or "countervalue") targeting was virtually taken for granted. Night bombing was safer than daytime raids for the attacking side but was substantially less accurate than bombing by day; hence, it was virtually impossible to conduct precision attacks on specific military (or "counterforce") targets or even on war industries, so whole cities became targets. Hundreds of thousands of civilians died during American and British firebombings of Dresden, Hamburg, Tokyo, Osaka, and other German and Japanese cities. Munitions were specifically designed to increase the probability of creating firestorms, and bombing patterns were employed to create a ring of fire, trapping civilians within.

Lewis Mumford denounced the Allied saturation bombing of German civilian targets in World War II as "unconditional moral surrender to Hitler," and David Lilienthal, later the first chairman of the Atomic Energy Commission, warned, "The fences are gone. And it was we, the civilized, who have pushed standardless conduct to its ultimate." Others argued that strategic bombing in general and the atomic bombings of Hiroshima and Nagasaki in particular were morally justified under the doctrine of double effect, claiming that the good effect (hastening the end of the war) overrode the bad (killing hundreds of thousands of civilians). In any event, ethical standards were not abandoned altogether. It is interesting to note, for instance, that a plaque in Westminster Abbey commemorates the Royal Air Force pilots of Fighter Command who died defending Britain against German bombers, whereas there is no comparable recognition of the (equally brave) fliers of Bomber Command who died while attacking German cities.

Such an ethical principle as noncombatant immunity has been influential in the propaganda associated with war, with each side typically accusing the other of causing civilian casualties.

President Truman even described the first atomic target, Hiroshima, as "an important military base," whereas it definitely was not. (By late summer of 1945, U.S. bombers had been striking targets throughout Japan at will; all targets of military significance had already been attacked, most of them many times.) Rather, Hiroshima was chosen specifically because its military irrelevance had caused it to escape prior attacks, and as an intact city, it could provide a clear demonstration of atomic destruction.

The principle of noncombatant immunity is sometimes accused of being a dangerous and misleading nicety that makes war seem civilized and, therefore, acceptable. Why, one might ask, is it considered an atrocity to throw a human being into a fire but a legitimate military activity to throw fire on a human being? The firebombing of Dresden, moreover, took place during the last days of World War II, when its outcome was already known and when the city itself was swollen with thousands of refugees and in the middle of a children's carnival.

Since unethical behavior seems inherent in war itself, perhaps it is hypocritical to introduce restraints once organized violence has commenced. Yet, the horrors of unrestricted warfare are so great that it is only natural to be grateful for whatever *in bello* restraints may exist, however imperfect or frequently violated in practice. During the U.S.-led bombing of Kosovo and, later, Afghanistan and Iraq, serious efforts apparently were made to minimize civilian casualties, the exact number of whom may never be known but is probably in the hundreds of thousands. Efforts to win "hearts and minds" (a phrase from the Vietnam War) of the people to be "liberated" are hobbled in direct proportion to the amount of death and destruction rained upon noncombatants.

# Religious Pacifism

Neither holy wars nor Just War doctrine constitute Christianity's unique contribution to the ethics of war: Holy wars trace their ancestry to the warlike traditions of the Old Testament, and Just War doctrine is essentially a reworking of Greco-Roman ethics. It is in the doctrine of organized *pacifism*—at least in the sense of doctrinal refusal to participate in military service—that Christianity stands out in the Western religious tradition.

The Second Commandment calls us to love our neighbor as ourselves, but the New Testament, especially the Gospel according to John, goes further by having Jesus enjoin his disciples and followers to *love* their *enemy* and actively to return good for evil. Among modern Christian churches, the historic "peace churches," including the Society of Friends (Quakers), the Mennonites, and the Church of the Brethren, are notable for their literal adherence to pacifist doctrines as enunciated, for example, in Christ's Sermon on the Mount: "You have heard that they were told, 'An eye for an eye and a tooth for a tooth.' But I tell you not to resist injury, but if anyone strikes you on your right cheek, turn the other to him too. . . . You have heard that they were told, 'You must love your neighbor and hate your enemy.' But I tell you, love your enemies and pray for your persecutors" (Matthew 5:38–46).

Many Christian religious traditions have had a clear conception of peace, although relatively few have specifically elevated it to central position in their dogma or practice. A notable exception is the Society of Friends (also known as the Quakers), established by George Fox in the mid-17th century. Quakers have maintained a tradition of peacemaking, opposition to military conscription, and resistance to taxes for military purposes.

Pacifist traditions have also persisted as minority views within most mainstream Christian churches, including Catholicism, via such organizations as Pax Christi. The Fellowship of Reconciliation is an ecumenical effort to unite and coordinate religious pacifists of all faiths. In addition to opposing military policies, pacifists refuse personal participation in wars, most directly by resisting conscription. They often practice tax resistance as well, which frequently takes the form of refusing to pay the proportion of national taxes that goes toward the military. Some governments, including that of the United States, have reluctantly accepted the legitimacy of conscientious objectors, so long as some form of alternative service is available; on the other hand, war resisters have traditionally been persecuted and sometimes killed, and even today they are often imprisoned for their views.

Many pacifists agree with G. K. Chesterton's sardonic observation that "the Christian ideal has not been tried and found wanting. It has been found difficult and left untried." Mennonite theologian John Howard Yoder was one who tried:

> Christians whose loyalty to the Prince of Peace puts them out of step with today's national-istic world . . . are not unrealistic dreamers who think that by their objections all wars will end. The unrealistic dreamers are rather the soldiers who think that they can put an end to wars by preparing for just one more. . . . Christians love their enemies not because they think the enemies are wonderful people, nor because they believe that love is sure to con-quer those enemies. . . . The Christian loves his or her enemies because God does, and God commands His followers to do so; that is the only reason, and that is enough.[5]

Religious pacifists, such as Yoder, emphasize that people were created in God's image and that Christ died for all humanity. Hence, they maintain that the Christian has no choice: He or she must follow Christ's injunctions and model, refusing to do violence against others, especially if this might entail refusing to take another's life—regardless of what the secular authorities might demand. Noted pacifist A. J. Muste made numerous impassioned calls for noncompliance with the military draft, which he termed an act of "holy disobedience." In Western religious traditions, disobedience is widely considered to be the primary human sin (witness Satan's disobedience to God or Adam and Eve's alleged transgressions in the Garden of Eden). And yet a case can be made that, throughout human history, far more harm has been done by obedience to authority than by disobedience.

# Nuclear Ethics

Although considerable debate surrounds religious and ethical approaches to war, when it comes to *nuclear* war, the issues may appear clear-cut. And despite the end of the Cold War, there continue to be thousands of nuclear weapons maintained in different countries, and their use—by "terrorists," "rogue states," newly proliferated nuclear powers, or even the declared nuclear weapons states—cannot be precluded so long as they exist.

Most religious and ethical authorities agree that a nuclear war could never meet Just War criteria. Noncombatant immunity could not be maintained, although some hawkish ethicists argue that civilians might legitimately be killed in such a war so long as they are not targeted directly. In 1966, the Second Vatican Council concluded that "any act of war aimed indiscriminately at the destruction of entire cities or of extensive areas along with their populations is a crime against God and man itself. It merits unequivocal and unhesitating condemnation." In their pastoral letter in 1983, the American Catholic bishops added that "this condemnation, in our judgment, applies even to the retaliatory use of weapons striking enemy cities after our own have already been struck."

It is difficult to imagine what kind of "good effect" could balance the "bad effect" of killing millions of people, possibly billions, and maybe even threatening the continuation of life on Earth. Moreover, nuclear war would seem to fail each of the various *ad bellum* considerations listed previously. Accordingly, the U.S. Catholic bishops concluded that "our No to nuclear war must, in the end, be definitive and decisive."

## Ethics and Nuclear Deterrence

Although there is general (but by no means universal) agreement among civilians that nuclear war would be altogether unethical, much debate surrounds the question of whether nuclear *deterrence* is equally unacceptable. The question is, can a country legitimately threaten something that would be unethical if carried out? Protestant ethicist Paul Ramsey used this metaphor to describe the dilemma: "Suppose that one Labor Day weekend no one was killed or maimed on the highways, and that the reason for the remarkable restraint placed on the recklessness of automobile drivers was that suddenly every one of them discovered that he was driving with a baby tied to his front bumper! That would be no way to regulate traffic even if it succeeds in regulating it perfectly, since such a system makes innocent human lives the direct object of attack and uses them as a mere means for restraining the drivers of automobiles."[6]

Ramsey's point is that moral error lies first in the intention to do wrong and only later in the act itself. This is why intended wrong (such as attempted homicide) is considered more serious than accidental wrong (such as manslaughter) or doing the right thing for the wrong reason is nonetheless considered an ethical transgression. To rework Ramsey's metaphor, imagine that society decreed that, in the event of murder, punishment would befall not only the murderer but also all his friends and relatives. This would clearly be an unethical system, *even if it worked.*

Nonetheless, Ramsey ends up defending the legitimacy of nuclear deterrence, so long as it is limited to counterforce targeting. He admits that an adversary might be restrained by fears of collateral effects—the practical awareness that nuclear retaliation, even if ostensibly aimed at military targets only, would cause enormous destruction to the country and civilian populace at large. But so long as this is a by-product of the intended, discriminate targeting, defenders of nuclear deterrence deem it acceptable.

Other thinkers justify nuclear deterrence with the argument that sometimes it is necessary to commit an evil (threatening nuclear war) in order to prevent an allegedly greater one. On the other hand, the paradox remains that only by making credible threats can nuclear deterrence possibly work, and only by meaning these threats—that is, deploying weapons and using strategies that are intended to be used—can they be effective. So the effectiveness of deterrence varies directly with the likelihood that, if one's bluff is called, nuclear war will follow, yet, should this happen, the outcome would be profoundly unacceptable.

In a speech at Hiroshima, Pope John Paul II said that "in current conditions, deterrence based on balance, certainly not as an end in itself but as a step on the way toward a progressive disarmament, may still be judged morally acceptable." As time goes on, however, ethicists may well ask whether deterrence has truly been used as a step toward disarmament, or as an end in itself, and also as a means of justifying yet more weaponry (e.g., "modernization" typically being justified as a means of "enhancing deterrence.") Thus, the Council of Bishops of the United Methodist Church went further than their Catholic counterparts and refused to condone nuclear deterrence: "The moral case for nuclear deterrence, even as an interim ethic, has been undermined by unrelenting arms escalation. Deterrence no longer serves, if it ever did, as a strategy that facilitates disarmament. . . . Deterrence must no longer receive the churches' blessing, even as a temporary warrant for the maintenance of nuclear weapons."[7]

Supporters of deterrence have argued that nuclear weapons are ethical and acceptable because they preserve the essential values of Western, Christian civilization. By attributing the collapse of Soviet communism to the West's perseverance in maintaining and adding to its nuclear arsenals, nuclear supporters justify the continued maintenance of such arsenals as a deterrent to other states and ideologies, as well as a hedge in case Soviet-style communism should reappear in Russia, China, or elsewhere. Moreover pro-nuclear thinkers do not discount the possibility that limited nuclear wars could be fought and even won.

On the other hand, opponents maintain that nuclear weapons are themselves profoundly unethical and that willingness to employ these weapons is simply unacceptable. In the words of diplomat/historian George Kennan,

> The readiness to use nuclear weapons against other human beings—against people whom we do not know, whom we have never seen, and whose guilt or innocence it is not for us to establish—and in doing so to place in jeopardy the natural structure upon which all civilization rests, as though the safety and the perceived interests of our own generation were more important than everything that has ever taken place or could take place in civilization; this is nothing less than a presumption, a blasphemy, an indignity—an indignity of monstrous dimensions—offered to God![8]

## A FINAL NOTE ON ETHICS AND RELIGION

It remains unlikely that ethical and religious precepts and courageous leaders alone will someday abolish war. Absolute prohibitions—against killing, for example—have rarely been followed with absolute fidelity. And given that human beings have often used alleged moral or religious certainty as a justification for repression, intolerance, and cruelty, there is some reason to be distrustful of any form of ethical absolutism.

On the other hand, it may be that at this stage of human history, revulsion against organized violence is as much a necessity as a hope. Such remarkable recent changes as the collapse of the Soviet Union and the end of the Cold War, as well as the end of apartheid in South Africa, offer exciting possibilities for redirecting human endeavors toward life instead of the mechanisms of oppression and death.

Having now completed our analysis of negative peace—that is, of the prospects and proposals for preventing war—let us bear in mind that, in the long run, such prevention will be a shallow victory if it does not include the establishment of positive peace as well. Hence, in Part IV, we turn from preventing war to building peace.

## NOTES

1. Reinhold Niebuhr. 1932. *Moral Men and Immoral Society.* New York: Scribner.

2. Saint Bernard of Clairvaux. 1980. *Sermons.* Geneva, Switzerland: Slatkine Reprints.

3. Quoted in Roland Bainton. 1960. *Christian Attitudes Toward War and Peace.* Nashville, TN: Abingdon.

4. Quoted in Penny Lernoux. 1982. *Cry of the People.* New York: Penguin.

5. John Howard Yoder. 1982. "Living the Disarmed Life: Christ's Strategy for Peace." In J. Wallis, ed., *Waging Peace.* New York: Harper & Row.

6. Paul Ramsey. 1968. *The Just War.* New York: Scribner.

7. Council of Bishops of the United Methodist Church. 1986. *In Defense of Creation: The Nuclear Crisis and a Just Peace.* Nashville, TN: Graded Press.

8. George F. Kennan. 1982. "A Christian's View of the Arms Race." *Theology Today* 39:2.

## QUESTIONS FOR FURTHER REFLECTION

1. Compare and contrast arguments that religion in general has largely contributed to war with those maintaining that it has largely been a force for peace.

2. Agree or disagree with the proposition that ethical support for war is necessarily an oxymoron—that is, a self-defeating or logically inconsistent proposition.

3. Pick a current war and assess its morality according to Just War criteria. Do the same for some other violent conflict currently under way.

4. Make a case for why the prospect of nuclear war requires a rethinking of ethics and/or religious teaching as it has traditionally been applied to war. Alternatively, make a case for why it does not—that is, for why the implications of nuclear weapons are quantitatively different but not qualitatively unique.

5. Pick a specific religious or ethical tradition and assess its strengths and weakness regarding its doctrines concerning war and peace.

## SUGGESTIONS FOR FURTHER READING

Joseph Fahey. 2005. *War and the Christian Conscience: Where Do You Stand?* Maryknoll, NY: Orbis Books.

James Turner Johnson. 1984. *Can Modern War Be Just?* New Haven, CT: Yale University Press.

Paul Ramsey. 1978. *The Just War.* New York: Scribner.

Gregory M. Reichberg, Henrik Syse, and Endre Begby. 2006. *The Ethics of War: Classic and Contemporary Readings.* New York: Wiley-Blackwell.

Michael Walzer. 2006. *Just and Unjust Wars: A Moral Argument With Historical Illustrations.* New York: Basic Books.

# PART IV

# Building Positive Peace

*We travel together, passengers on a little spaceship, dependent on its vulnerable reserves of air and soil; all committed for our safety to its security and peace; preserved from annihilation only by the care, the work and the love we give our fragile craft, and, I may say, each other.*

—Adlai E. Stevenson

Preventing war is a necessary condition for establishing real peace, but it is not sufficient. A world without war is certainly desirable, but even this would not really produce a world at peace. It is not enough to be against something—namely, war. We need, as well, to be in favor of something, and that something should be positive and affirmative—namely, peace. Of necessity, therefore, positive peace must be part of a broader, deeper effort to rethink the relationship of human beings to each other and to their planet. As difficult as it will be to obtain negative peace—the prevention of war—it may be even more of a challenge to achieve positive peace, since a world without violence would be a significant challenge to our basic way of living, not just our ways of occasionally dying and killing.

The study of peace and conflict is unusual not only in its transdisciplinary approach to the understanding and prevention of war but also in its efforts to envision and help establish a desirable and attainable peace. But if war seems difficult to define—as evidenced by disagreement about the role of formal declarations, number of casualties, nature of the combatants, level of violence, and so on—peace can be even more elusive. Nonetheless, it is possible to sketch the outlines of a just and sustainable peace, recognizing that in a world that relies on violence and on the structures of violence, efforts toward such a peace may be not only visionary but also what conventional society may deem "radical."

It is increasingly clear that ideologically based political and military competition is outdated, dangerous, and also irrelevant to humanity's fundamental needs. Ardent militarists seem more and more to be ideological dinosaurs, formidable but dated, moving clumsily and even stupidly across a rapidly changing landscape. Militarized competition should cease, but we must not stop there. Conflicts that have so preoccupied the post–World War II world need to give way to planetary issues (many of which reveal tensions along a North-South axis) concerning human rights, poverty, the environment, and fundamental principles of nonviolence in politics and in personal life.

Much importance has been attributed to the "Just War" doctrine. The conditions for a "just peace" are no less important. For many in the West (at least, those who are relatively affluent and well educated), hope for a peaceful world is often equated with continuing the status quo, with some improvements around the margins, such as guaranteed health care, children in college, and an ever-increasing stock portfolio; whereas for many in the lesser developed countries, it is reflected in basic aspirations for human rights, national autonomy, and economic well-being. For a growing number of people around the globe, just peace also entails achieving a viable relationship with the natural environment.

Whereas the absence of war is relatively easy to define—but still susceptible to dispute— reasonable people are even more likely to disagree about what constitutes positive peace. It brings up what we might call the "car-canine problem": Imagine a dog that has spent years barking and running after cars. Then one day it catches one. What does it do with it? Analogously, what would devotees of peace *do* with the world if they had the chance?

# CHAPTER 18

## HUMAN RIGHTS

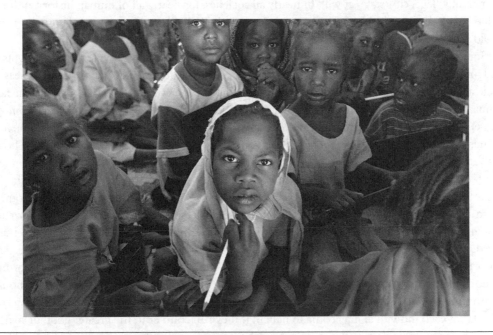

Children at an internally displaced persons camp run by the United Nations in Darfur, Sudan, in 2007.
*Source:* UN Photo.

> *Injustice anywhere is an affront to justice everywhere.*
>
> —Martin Luther King, Jr.

Like Mark Twain's celebrated remark about the weather, we can say that many people talk about human rights but relatively few do anything about it. Yet, a great many human beings are denied some of the most basic human rights: Nearly one-half of the world's people are denied democratic freedoms and political participation; about one-third face severe restrictions on their right to own property; over one-half of Asians and sub-Saharan Africans do not have access to safe water; jails are filled with political prisoners, many of them held without trial and victimized by torture; child labor is widespread; women are often deprived of the economic, social, and political rights that men take for granted; many workers are not only nonunionized but prohibited even from forming unions; the right of conscientious objection to military service is not recognized in most countries; censorship is widespread; and billions of people are illiterate, chronically sick, without adequate shelter, and hungry.

# A Brief History of Human Rights

It is tempting to claim that human rights are as old as the human species, but the truth is quite different. Even if human rights are God-given, inalienable, and fundamental, the conception of human rights as such—and respect for them—is relatively new. Rights and privileges have traditionally been considered the province of society, to be bestowed or revoked by the larger unit (band, tribe, monarch, village, city, state) at will. In nearly all societies, for nearly all of human history, ultimate values have been derived from the social order, not the individual. Hence, a single human being could not claim entitlement to very much, if anything, simply because he or she existed.

Some representatives of traditional cultures support the concept of individual human rights as wide-ranging and universally derived. Confucius, for example, argued that "within the four seas all men are brothers," and Buddhists believe in "compassion for every sentient being." But, in fact, human rights as currently understood are largely a Western tradition, deriving especially from the works of the English philosophers John Locke and John Stuart Mill. Locke maintained that the fundamental human right was the right to property, primarily the right to the security of one's own body; civil and political rights flowed, in his view, from this. Thus, there is some truth to the criticism that Westerners advocating human rights may occasionally be guilty of moral arrogance, seeking to export their own rather culture-bound ideas, especially their emphasis on civil/political freedom.

In addition, Western political thought coexists with respect for—and, occasionally, virtual worship of—the state. According to such influential German political theorists as Hegel and Herder, rights are enlarged and created for individuals only through the actions of the state. And for orthodox Marxists, value derives only from the social order: There is no meaning, according to doctrinaire Marxist analysis, to individual rights prior to those granted by society. Although communist societies were supposedly designed to maximize the benefits of every person, the "rights" of each individual may come to naught if they run counter to the greater good of society as a whole. Individuals can expect to receive benefits from a community only insofar as they participate in it and further its goals. And, even today—with communism largely a memory and ever-increasing agreement on the meaning and desirability of human rights—there continues to be substantial disagreement as to priorities.

## Human Rights in Modern Times

There was little concern with human rights until after World War II. Despite the Enlightenment, modern capitalism's emphasis on individual property rights, and Western democracy's emphasis on individual political rights, state sovereignty has long taken precedence over human rights. When the modern state system was established in the mid-17th century, governments agreed—ostensibly in the interest of world peace—not to concern themselves very much with how other governments treated their own citizens. Within its own boundaries, each state was supreme and could do almost as it wished.

Gradually, however, human rights law developed, initially out of concern with protecting persons during armed conflict. The Geneva Convention of 1864, for example, sought to establish standards for treatment of wounded soldiers and of prisoners. (It is ironic that war—one of the most inhumane of human situations—should have led to the first organized recognition of shared humanitarian values.) The International Committee of the Red Cross is a nongovernmental organization long concerned with international human rights; it was organized by a group of Swiss citizens who had attended the 1864 Geneva Convention. The Red Cross remains active today, as does its Islamic equivalent, the Red Crescent, seeking especially to ensure fair treatment of people during armed conflict; it has also participated in several modifications and revisions of the Geneva Convention, most recently in 1977.

Following World War I, there was widespread recognition that one cause of that conflict was the denial of national rights within such large empires as Austria-Hungary's. Hence, human rights received explicit attention from the League of Nations, which emphasized that minorities must be respected by larger federal governments. Labor rights—to organize, to obtain decent working conditions and wages, restrictions on child labor—were the focus of the International Labour Organization, which later became part of the United Nations and also won a Nobel Peace Prize. Opposition to slavery catalyzed numerous early human rights organizations, such as the Anti-Slavery League. (Many people do not realize that in certain countries slavery was only abolished during the 1950s; some claim that it is still being practiced today, notably in Mauritania, Pakistan, Haiti, and Sudan.)

Organized worldwide concern for human rights did not really coalesce until after World War II, perhaps in part as a reaction to the devastating denials of rights that occurred during that conflict. In the aftermath of the Nazi Holocaust, the world's conscience was finally activated—partly out of regret for those who had suffered and partly out of enlightened self-interest. Martin Niemöller put it memorably: "First they came for the Jews and I did not speak out—because I was not a Jew. Then they came for the communists and I did not speak out—because I was not a communist. Then they came for the trade unionists and I did not speak out—because I was not a trade unionist. Then they came for me—and there was no one left to speak out for me."[1] (In fact, Pastor Niemöller himself became a victim of the Nazis.)

## Liberalism

In traditional liberal thought, human rights exist not only because of their contribution to human dignity but also because human beings naturally possess such rights. "The object of any obligation in the realm of human affairs," according to philosopher Simone Weil, "is always the human being as such. There exists an obligation toward every human being for the sole reason that he or she is a human being, without any other condition requiring to be fulfilled."[2] Or, in Thomas Jefferson's phrase, people have certain "inalienable rights," which may not be denied.

States with long traditions of social equity, including Scandinavian nations and New Zealand, are also constructed along liberal lines but with a dose of economic egalitarianism. Thus, while the classical liberalism of the United States stresses equal civil and political rights with freedom of socioeconomic competition, egalitarian liberalism such as Sweden's (and, to a lesser extent, that of Canada, New Zealand, and much of western Europe), places greater emphasis on the right to a certain degree of social welfare as well.

## Conservatism

Traditional Anglo-American conservatism has little to say today with respect to human rights, because conservatism is in part a philosophy of *unequal* rights and privileges. But the unspoken tenets of conservatism are nonetheless influential in practice. Classical Western conservatism can be said to have originated with Plato, who argued in *The Republic* that all people are not equal and that the best form of government is therefore not democracy but rule by philosopher-kings. More than two millennia later, this belief in unequal rights underpins many right-wing governments, from the "classical conservatism" of the military juntas that ruled Brazil and Greece to the various U.S.-sponsored Central American governments through most of the late 20th century (Guatemala, Honduras, Panama), to the neofascist dictatorships in Chile, Paraguay, Indonesia, and the Philippines, in which rights were reserved only for the most powerful.

## Collectivism

Finally, the third branch of human rights philosophy might be called "collectivist." It can be subdivided into two streams, Marxist and nationalist. For Karl Marx, individuals were not fully independent actors; rather, they were largely controlled by economic forces engaged in a relentless class struggle. In the Marxist view, the liberal emphasis on individual rights is therefore a misplaced bourgeois luxury, ideological form without social substance. Instead, rights are conferred by society and theoretically belong exclusively to the proletariat or working class. Such an approach leads automatically to an embrace of socioeconomic rights and economic equity, with a downplaying of civil/political rights. Thus, in Marxist-oriented societies, freedom of speech and opinion are permitted insofar as they do not conflict with the stated goals of group advancement and welfare. The state, ideally as the embodiment of the working class, typically becomes paramount.

The second version of collectivist human rights has a leftist flavor but is not, strictly speaking, Marxist. It derives instead from national liberation movements, and it places special emphasis on the right to national self-determination and economic development, from which all other rights are then derived. Believers in the human right of national self-determination downplay the individual, although they remain committed to equal rights. Emphasis instead is on the rights of a national grouping. This approach lay behind the Universal Declaration of the Rights of Peoples, which grew out of an influential 1976 meeting of highly regarded, nongovernmental spokespeople from the developing world. Its concern with "people's rights" clearly distinguishes this approach from the Western focus on "individual rights."

## Choosing the Appropriate Philosophy

Not surprisingly, there is substantial debate over which human rights model is most appropriate for any given country. The two major contending Western systems of the past—capitalism based on classical liberal principles and Soviet-style Marxism based on a particular collectivist philosophy—historically have produced deep structures of oppression. Thus, although Marx himself explicitly claimed that the state will eventually disappear, Marxist state structures showed no tendency to do so; in fact, they became notably oppressive in their own right, until, as in the case of the Soviet Union, they simply crumbled (which is very different from Marx's original conception, under which the ideal workers' state would wither away by mutual consent only after all its goals had been achieved). Even more than liberal capitalist states, Marxist governments have tended to be super-states, abusing power via ossified bureaucratic structures that were generally insensitive to personal civil and political liberties.

By contrast, the supposedly "minimal states" envisioned by some Western liberal philosophers and established especially in Northern Europe and North America have been primarily concerned with balancing the various political powers of government, as well as balancing governmental and popular sovereignty. Social and economic "rights" are generally treated as secondary, as capitalist/democratic societies rely on market mechanisms and an ethos of individual competition. Only begrudgingly have many capitalist/democratic states recognized a social responsibility toward their populace.

On balance, capitalist democracies give insufficient attention to socioeconomic rights, while state socialist governments take inadequate account of civil/political ones. Economic development is generally more rapid under capitalism, especially the "state capitalism" of China and Russia today, and, indeed, the economic stagnation of most state-socialist countries contributed mightily to their dramatic political decline.

At the same time, relatively little benefit from economic development actually reaches the poorest citizens of most capitalist states. The rapid transition to a primitive kind of capitalism on the part of Russia and some of its former satellite states has been accompanied, in most cases, by immense wealth for a small minority of successful entrepreneurs (and more than a few outright crooks and beneficiaries of rampant cronyism, as state assets were sold off at extremely low prices). Simultaneously, living conditions for the majority may have actually worsened. In some cases, political freedoms have expanded dramatically across the board, along with economic opportunities, while most people formerly living under Soviet-style communism and now experiencing Western-style "freedom" have also experienced deterioration in their socioeconomic rights.

## Individual Liberty and Socioeconomic Rights

Individual liberty is not unidimensional. It involves many things—notably, bodily freedom from torture, unjust imprisonment, and execution; as well as intellectual freedom to speak, write, and worship; and various political freedoms, including the right to peaceful assembly, freedom of association, and the right to vote by secret ballot. Similarly, "socioeconomic rights" include the right to work, decent housing, education, medical care, and adequate food. To some extent, the United States and most other economically advanced capitalist states associate human rights with the first category, whereas state-socialist and many impoverished, Third World, undeveloped, "underdeveloped," or "developing" states have long given greater weight to the second.

Those who are wealthy and privileged characteristically favor maximum individual freedom (especially freedom of economic competition) and a minimal role for government, which at least in the United States often leads in turn to opposition to the "welfare state." Those lacking in wealth and power are typically more in need of protections ensured by society. Hence, there is a tendency among some Western governments to describe socioeconomic rights as not really "human rights" at all but rather as goals or aspirations for society.

A global consensus has been developing that incorporates not only the traditional American concern with political liberty but also an additional concern with socioeconomic rights, as well as other values that are difficult to pigeonhole. In some cases, alternative visions of human rights are different indeed: the "right to life" (of a fetus) versus a woman's "right to choose" (whether to have an abortion). Many other asserted rights are not quite as controversial—states' rights, consumer rights—but to claim that something is a "human right" is to claim something particularly fundamental and weighty. It should not be done lightly but might well include the right to security from mass destruction and to a safe natural environment. One simple categorization parallels the famous French motto "liberty, equality, fraternity": (1) political and intellectual rights, (2) economic and social rights, and (3) the right to peace and to a safe natural environment. Of these, the third ("fraternity") is the most unsettled—and, for some, unsettling—of all.

Many people, especially in developing countries, attribute great importance to socioeconomic rights. In the words of Léopold Senghor, former president of Senegal, "Human rights begin with breakfast." Without such an awareness, it is all too easy for relatively well-off Westerners to sneer at the poor "rights" records of other countries, oblivious to their own shortcomings in the eyes of others, and thus to miss the intimate connection between political and socioeconomic rights. If structural violence is such that people die from malnutrition and poverty, are poorly educated, and lack medical care or if such a society imprisons and tortures its political opponents, then either way, it is an abuser of human rights. In addition, if Westerners were to recognize the validity of socioeconomic rights, such governments as Libya under Gadhafi or Cuba under Castro—which to many in the West are failures because of their lack of representative government, widespread censorship, and other civil-political inadequacies—could at the same time be acknowledged as admirable in other domains, such as public health or literacy. This is not to claim that success in some dimensions of human rights cancels outrages in another; rather, it helps permit a more balanced perception of systems that might otherwise seem unidimensionally evil and whose high level of local domestic acceptance is otherwise difficult for Americans to understand.

## Indigenous People and Others

There are about 300 million indigenous people worldwide, representing national majorities in Guatemala and Bolivia, for example, and notable minorities in Brazil, Australia, Russia, and the United States. Regardless of their numbers, indigenous people are generally in dire straits, sometimes—as in Guatemala and Brazil—having suffered genocide even in recent times. For example, a UN investigation concluded in 1999 that three former Guatemalan presidents had been involved in genocide, state terrorism, and torture as part of a brutal counterinsurgency campaign conducted by the Guatemalan military during the 1970s and 1980s; this resulted in the deaths of more than 200,000, most of them Mayan Indians.

In other cases, indigenous people are severely maltreated and/or they enjoy dramatically fewer opportunities and privileges than their nonnative counterparts:

- Australian aborigines are on a per capita basis the most imprisoned people on Earth, with an incarceration rate 16 times that of the Caucasian population.
- Even aside from being the targets of government-inspired atrocities, the life expectancy of Mayan Indians in Guatemala is 11 years shorter than that of the nonindigenous population.
- The average per capita income of Native Americans is half that of the rest of the U.S. population.

- Large dams have devastated the homelands of indigenous peoples in Canada, China, Brazil, Norway, the Philippines, and India, depriving them of an arguably crucial human right: to live in their ancestral homelands. And there are other cases as well.

Other groups can also be identified as having particular human rights claims and vulnerabilities: mentally ill persons, children, homeless persons, racial and sexual minorities, handicapped persons, convicts, unskilled workers, migrant laborers, refugees, political dissidents, the elderly, and so on. Ideally, human rights, such as civil freedoms, economic opportunity, protection from mass destruction, and the right to a safe and clean environment, will be equally shared by all people. In practice, these rights must often be defended most vigilantly for those groups that have been the most victimized.

# Women's Rights

Women comprise slightly more than 50% of the world's population, yet for centuries women have suffered from patriarchal social structures that devalue their personhood and deny many of their basic human rights. This includes a diverse array of abuses, such as foot binding in precommunist China; the forced seclusion and isolation of women in certain contemporary Hindu and Muslim societies; sexual mutilation, as currently practiced on millions of young women in numerous African societies; polygamy; restricted or nonexistent choice as to marriage; substantial discrimination as to educational opportunities, especially in some conservative Islamic countries, and—even in such ostensibly liberated societies as that of the United States and Great Britain—restricted economic and professional opportunities along with underrepresentation in political life. In can be argued that whatever the sources of well-being in the world, women as a group consistently enjoy fewer of them; this includes intangibles, such as opportunity and the expectation of a fulfilling and freely chosen life, as well as such physical assets as property.

As noted previously, even though there are virtually no significant differences between men and women when it comes to their attitudes toward war, it is noteworthy that individuals who support gender equality are less likely to support war as a solution to international problems. Moreover, when civil wars break out, societies characterized by relative gender equality are more likely to lead to successful UN peacekeeping than are societies in which males and females had more rigidly defined roles.

## Some History

In the West, concern with women's rights dates from the Enlightenment. These rights were set out clearly, for example, in Mary Wollstonecraft's *A Vindication of the Rights of Woman*, published in England in 1792. This powerful book emphasized the importance of providing education for women equaling that available to men. (Even in the 21st century, however, illiteracy rates remain consistently higher for women than for men, especially in developing countries.) During the late 19th and early 20th centuries, crusaders for women's rights were especially concerned about obtaining "suffrage," the right to vote and to hold political office.

By the mid-20th century, something of a shift occurred, with growing awareness in Western liberal circles of the degree to which women were also oppressed in the domestic sphere.

Especially influential were these milestone books: *The Second Sex,* by Simone de Beauvoir, which raised "feminist" consciousness by pointing out the extent to which men were tradition- ally considered the "subjects" of modern life whereas women were merely "others" and second- ary "objects"; *The Feminine Mystique,* by Betty Friedan, which identified the deadening domesticity to which women were typically relegated; and *The Female Eunuch,* by Germaine Greer, which castigated the sexual passivity to which many women were traditionally forced. Added to this were innovations in birth control technology (especially the development of con- traceptive pills), as well as the U.S. Civil Rights Movement, which raised public awareness about the need to reevaluate and reconfigure the role of women in the home, the workplace, and the public sphere.

## In the West

Although women's suffrage is essentially universal in the West, women's participation in the political process or in the business and professional world is nonetheless often constricted by the traditional idea that "a woman's place is in the home" (which is not that far removed from the Nazi motto for women: *Kinder, Küche, Kirche*—children, cooking, and church). Advocates for women's rights point out that women are typically paid 80% of what men receive and they demand, instead, "equal pay for equal work." The number of women in executive-level positions in the U.S. corporate world remains very low. The effort to expand women's social and political options involves a continuing effort to challenge social stereotypes of women as dependent, weak, passive, and hyper emotional, compared with most men. Although some countries (Great Britain, Norway, Israel, India, Sri Lanka, Pakistan, Chile, Argentina, and Germany) have had female prime ministers, the U.S. Congress has not passed an equal rights amendment. Women's reproductive rights remain especially precarious, as evidenced by ongoing efforts on the part of social conservatives to restrict access to birth control and abortions and to roll back affirmative action programs that benefit women as well as minorities.

In addition, a continuing debate within the Western women's rights movement revolves around the degree of change to be sought: Whether society (ranging from private domestic rela- tionships to the sinews of our public life) should be radically restructured or whether change should be incremental within the basic social structures that currently exist. Such debate is not necessarily a weakness of the women's rights movement; rather, it reflects the vigor and hetero- geneity of its devotees, paralleling ongoing discussion within other social justice movements.

## In Developing Countries

In most economically developing countries, the goals of the women's movement tend to be more basic: increased literacy, health care, and an end to polygamy and bride price (whereby men literally purchase a wife). Women often cannot own property and typically may not obtain a divorce without their husband's consent. In many traditional societies, especially in Africa, millions of women are subjected to genital mutilation, which is often justified as a legitimate cultural practice but that causes immense suffering, as well as diminished sexual pleasure, not to mention high mortality rates. Many Muslim countries insist on very restrictive dress codes for women, legally sanctioned violent—often lethal—responses to sexual infidelity, and frequently the denial of educational, social, and economic opportunities. Women are prohibited from driving a car in Saudi Arabia, for example, while the fundamentalist Taliban government of Afghanistan denied even basic education to women and prohibited them from working outside their houses. Indeed, women were not even permitted to go outside at all unless accompanied by a male relative.

## Feminism and Peace

Women's rights have also become increasingly tied to an integrated peace agenda. This reflects, among other things, the fact that whereas men are the primary wagers of war, women have long been among those most likely to suffer. Feminists also point out a connection between patriarchy (male dominance) and war making, as reflected in what is (dubiously) claimed to be a greater male propensity for violence, in hierarchical structuring of systems of power, and in the use of threats and physical force over consensus building. Feminist scholar and peace educator Betty Reardon also emphasizes that "traditional gender roles have assigned the main functions and maintenance of quotidian ["daily, and domestic"] security to women while excluding them from participation in the exercise of power over national and global security" and that "this arrangement has made women more vulnerable to the violent consequences of militarized security," an arrangement that is especially unfair given that "the substance of daily life, the domestic and social chores upon which everyday human life depends, the functions that make all other human activities possible are women's work. Public decisions of life and death are not." In Reardon's view—and that of a growing number of feminist peace workers—this must change: "The feminist challenge is becoming a challenge to the war system itself."[4]

Ever since the classical Greek dramatist Aristophanes wrote *Lysistrata* (in which women ended the Peloponnesian War by refusing sexual relations with their husbands until they stopped killing each other), women have taken part in efforts to end war and violence . . . although, to be sure, many have also participated in such activities or even instigated and—rarely—led them. Many women have also engaged in direct action in support of an avowedly feminist peace agenda. Women in Black, composed of Israeli and Palestinian women, have been urging an end to Israeli military occupation of the West Bank and Gaza, as well as to terrorism. The Argentinean Mothers of the Plaza de Mayo, beginning in the 1970s, protested the "disappearances" (the kidnapping, torture, and murder) of their children, raising consciousness about crimes against humanity on the part of their government and shaming political leaders into action. Similar courageous and effective actions were taken by the Chilean Association of the Relatives of the Detained and Disappeared. The Soldiers' Mothers' Movement in Russia actively disrupted the drafting and brutalization of Russian conscripts—especially in the Soviet Union's war in Afghanistan and Russia's war in Chechnya—in the process becoming an important political force. It is noteworthy that these and other groups have carried their message via direct actions and nonviolent public protest rather than by mere lamentation.

The 2011 Nobel Peace Prize was given to three women for their efforts on behalf of nonviolent political change on behalf of human rights generally, and women's rights in particular: Tawakkol Karman of Yemen, and Leymah Gbowee, and Ellen Johnson Sirleaf of Liberia. Here is an extended excerpt of Ms. Johnson Sirleaf's Nobel acceptance speech:

There is no doubt that the madness that wrought untold destruction in recent years in the Democratic Republic of Congo, in Rwanda, in Sierra Leone, in Sudan, in Somalia, in the former Yugoslavia, and in my own Liberia, found its expression in unprecedented levels of cruelty directed against women. Although international tribunals have correctly declared that rape, used as a weapon of war, is a crime against humanity, rapes in times of lawlessness continue unabated. The number of our sisters and daughters of all ages brutally defiled over the past two decades staggers the imagination, and the number of lives devastated by such evil defies comprehension.

Through the mutilation of our bodies and the destruction of our ambitions, women and girls have disproportionately paid the price of domestic and international armed conflict. We have paid in the currencies of blood, of tears, and of dignity. However, the need to defend the rights of women is not limited to the battlefield, and the threats to those rights do not emanate only from armed violence. Girls' education, seen far too often as an unnecessary indulgence rather than the key investment it is, is still under-funded and under-staffed. Too often girls are discouraged from pursuing an academic training, no matter how promising they may be.

As we celebrate today, we are mindful of the enormous challenges we still face. In too many parts of the world, crimes against women are still under-reported, and the laws protecting women are under-enforced. In this 21st century, surely there is no place for human trafficking that victimizes almost a million people, mostly girls and women, each year. Surely there is no place for girls and women to be beaten and abused. Surely there is no place for a continuing belief that leadership qualities belong to only one gender.

Yet, there is occasion for optimism and hope. There are good signs of progress and change. Around the world, slowly, international law and an awareness of human rights are illuminating dark corners, in schools, in courts, in the marketplace. The windows of closed chambers where men and women have been unspeakably abused are being opened, and the light is coming in. Democracies, even if tentatively, are taking root in lands unaccustomed to freedom.

As curtains are raised and as the sun shines upon dark places, what was previously invisible comes into view. Technology has turned our world into one interconnected neighborhood. What happens in one place is seen in every corner, and there has been no better time for the spread of peace, democracy and their attending social justice and fairness for all. Today, across the globe, women, and also men, from all walks of life are finding the courage to say, loudly and firmly, in a thousand languages, "No more." They reject mindless violence, and defend the fundamental values of democracy, of open society, of freedom, and of peace.

So I urge my sisters, and my brothers, not to be afraid. Be not afraid to denounce injustice, though you may be outnumbered. Be not afraid to seek peace, even if your voice may be small. Be not afraid to demand peace.

## Some Human Rights Controversies

It seems unavoidable that various rights will conflict. In a famous opinion, U.S. Supreme Court Justice Oliver Wendell Holmes concluded that the right to free speech did not extend to yelling, "Fire!" in a crowded theater. The "right" to a drug-free society may conflict with the "right" to privacy, just as the "right" of people in developing countries to healthy babies has already been found to conflict with the "right" of the Nestlé company to market infant formula in poor countries. In fundamentalist Islamic states, women's "rights" are often subordinated to the "rights" of people (especially men) to practice the religion of their choice in the way they interpret it. A woman's "right" to control her own body, including an abortion if she desires, runs contrary to the perception of many that the fetus has a "right" to life; the "right" of religious freedom can conflict with a child's "right" to necessary medical care, as when fundamentalist-Christian parents refuse lifesaving treatment for their child; the public's "right" to safe air travel appears to have trumped individual "rights" not to be searched without a warrant; and the list goes on.

Many human rights are essentially claims against the authority of governments. As such, they are freedoms *from* guarantees that governments will refrain from behaving badly toward their own people. These can be distinguished from freedoms *to* the asserted obligations of society to help its members achieve a better life. It is a distinction that somewhat parallels the one between negative and positive peace: between those rights asserted *against* governments (no war, no intrusions into personal freedom) and those expected *of* them (establish positive peace, provide for basic human needs). In most cases, the first category (negative rights) seems easier for governments to achieve; certain states may simply lack the financial resources to make substantial improvements in socioeconomic conditions, but they all can stop torturing, murdering, and oppressing their people in other ways.

Although human rights constitute a diverse and sometimes confusing array of causes, from peace, women's rights, environmental protection, and penal reform to national independence, they share a common humanizing focus, placing individuals at the center of public policy.

# The Legal Status of Human Rights

## UN-Related Agreements

Although the UN Charter serves as a kind of international constitution, it lacks a binding Bill of Rights, specifying which human rights are to be protected. The UN-sponsored Universal Declaration of Human Rights (UDHR) was passed unanimously in 1948, enumerating these rights. The United States was a major contributor to the UDHR; much of its impetus came from Eleanor Roosevelt, at the time the widow of U.S. President Franklin D. Roosevelt.

The UDHR consists of 30 articles, of which the first 21 are primarily civil/political, prohibiting torture and arbitrary arrest and guaranteeing freedom of assembly, religion, speech, and emigration and even the right to vote by secret ballot. The remaining articles are concerned with socioeconomic and cultural rights, including the right to work, to an "adequate" standard of living, to education, to some form of social security, and even to vacations with pay.

The UDHR is not technically binding in the sense of an international treaty; it is a recommendation only, with no provisions for enforcement. Nonetheless, it has had substantial impact on thinking worldwide, is widely respected, and has legitimated widespread concern with human rights; it has even been incorporated into many national constitutions.

To some degree, the UDHR has become part of customary international law and, accordingly, many judicial scholars argue that it has the literal force of law, although it is often violated. Numerous worldwide legal instruments have built on the UN Charter and the UDHR, including an array of covenants, conventions, treaties, and declarations of diverse legal meaning but all helping further define the concept of human rights. Of these, the most important are probably the Convention on the Prevention and Punishment of the Crime of Genocide (1948) and the International Convention on the Elimination of All Forms of Racial Discrimination (1965).

There have also been two UN human rights covenants, signed in 1966, which entered into force in 1977, when they were ratified by a sufficient number of national governments but not by the United States. These are the International Covenant on Civil and Political Rights and the International Covenant on Economic, Social and Cultural Rights. There are also two 1977 Geneva Protocols on Armed Conflict, both of them controversial and not universally in force, in addition to various instruments concerned with specified rights, such as those of refugees and children, as well as denunciations of apartheid and numerous declarations that were less formal in character.

Scholars and political decision-makers dispute precisely what obligations member states undertake when, in the UN Charter, they agree to "promote universal respect for and observance" of human rights. Nonetheless, an underlying consensus has emerged that governments may not participate in a "consistent pattern of gross violations of human rights." Thus, whereas isolated incidents are unlikely to generate worldwide outrage, "gross violations," if they recur, merit condemnation and, ultimately, such actions as censure, economic boycott, and possibly even military intervention. Abuses of this sort could include widespread torture, mass arrests and imprisonment without trial, genocide, vicious policies of racial segregation and debasement, and forced relocation of entire populations.

## Human Rights and the Nation-State

Some halting progress has been made as *national* courts have begun ruling to enforce *international* norms with respect to human rights. For example, in a celebrated legal case, *Filártiga v. Peña-Irala* a U.S. court ruled in 1980 that politically inspired torture and murder were so clearly prohibited by international agreements on human rights that the United States had jurisdiction to prosecute a Paraguayan national for events occurring within Paraguay. In 1998, the British government arrested former Chilean dictator Augusto Pinochet and nearly put him on trial for thousands of cases of torture and the "disappearance" of political prisoners while he had been dictator of Chile (Pinochet narrowly avoided legal action because he was judged too old and feeble to stand trial; he was deported to Chile, where he died before the legal process had run its full course). Nonetheless, this case constitutes an important precedent, one that might well be expanded to allow prosecution of the many ex–heads of state—typically living in comfortable exile—who ordered or condoned murder and torture while in office. The ultimate significance of such prosecutions would likely go beyond the satisfaction of justice, notably by putting current rights violators on notice that they may well have to answer for crimes committed on "their watch."

As controversial as was the Pinochet case, there is nothing new about governments criticizing human rights abuses in *other* states, although it is novel for them to place national leaders under arrest for human rights violations committed while they were heads of state. Governments have long found it useful to complain loudly about the actions of foreign governments—especially those to which they are not allied—while turning a blind eye to their own misbehavior. The real tension between states and human rights concerns the degree to which a state is willing to forgo part of its own sovereignty and permit its own human rights practices to be the subject of international scrutiny, judgment, and influence—if not control.

## Resistance to Western Intervention

Although many Western citizens often assume that people from other cultures would necessarily applaud their actions on behalf of worldwide human rights, sometimes the response is less than enthusiastic. Partly, this is because of the perceived moral arrogance with which the primarily Western concept of human rights is exported to other societies. Partly, it is because people from developing countries remain very aware of Western imperialism and the fact that, in the past, the West's legitimate promotion of human rights has often been used as a moral pretext in connection with colonial conquest: for example, bringing an end to "barbarous" practices, such as the Indian custom of *suttee* (burning a widow on her deceased husband's funeral pyre), foot binding, and female infanticide. In addition, many developing countries are intensely committed to socioeconomic rights, and they believe that progress in this respect may require that governments exert some restrictions on civil and political rights.

Following World War II, more than 80 former Western colonies won their political independence, liberating more than 1 billion people in the world's most massive transfer of political power. But national independence does not necessarily guarantee the rights of individuals. In some cases, quite the opposite takes place, especially when the newly established government is shaky; threats to the security of the nation serve as a handy excuse for denying individual rights, and in fact many newly independent countries are politically insecure, for a variety of reasons. There is, accordingly, a strong tendency for such states to be run by dictatorial, often military governments and for such governments to be especially repressive of human rights.

## The Primacy of State Sovereignty

The greatest underlying conflict between human rights and the nation-state is one that is characteristic of virtually all governments. It derives from the very nature of state sovereignty, since a call for human rights is often a claim on behalf of individuals *against* the state. Whether demanding that states refrain from mistreating their people (negative rights) or that they commit themselves more aggressively to their betterment (positive rights), claimants for human rights typically push governments in directions they would not otherwise choose.

International standards of human rights may represent claims against state power and sovereignty by restricting what a state can do (and, sometimes, telling it what to do), even within its own borders. This could include disapproval by the international human rights community of a country's internal policies, notwithstanding that such policies may be fully "legal" according to its own domestic laws. For example, South African apartheid laws were not internationally acknowledged as legitimate, despite the fact that they were duly passed by that country's parliament. NATO's brief but violent air war in Kosovo was largely a response to the widespread perception that the Serbian government was abusing the human rights of Kosovars, and international intervention occurred despite the fact that Kosovo at the time was legally part of Yugoslavia. (This intervention derived in part from an earlier human rights failure, insofar as it was a Western effort to compensate for the fact that other countries did nothing to prevent genocidal slaughter in Rwanda 5 years earlier.) NATO's successful air support of Libyan rebels in 2011 was similarly justified by dictator Gadhafi's brutal treatment of his own people.

Perhaps surprisingly, a concern for human rights may actually enhance state sovereignty, or at least, stability. States that by and large adhere to international standards of human rights (the Western democracies generally) normally experience a higher level of legitimacy and security than those that routinely trample on them. No informed observer of the United States, Western Europe, Australia, or Japan worries that any of these governments will be overthrown by coup or revolution—unlike others that abused human rights, such as the regimes of Duvalier in Haiti, Somoza in Nicaragua, Ceaușescu in Romania, or Gadhafi in Libya. At the same time, when governments, such as the United States, trample on accepted norms of human rights—as by torturing suspected terrorists or incarcerating so-called enemy combatants indefinitely and without providing basic *habeas corpus* rights (the right to be confronted with evidence of a crime)—they clearly diminish their international standing.

## The Role of Politics

Governments are often asked to report on the status of human rights within their own borders. It can be argued, however, that allowing states to report on their own human rights situation is like having the fox report on the status of the chickens. The assessment by outside experts, including dissidents, is generally much more critical and believable than judgments made by official representatives about their own government's behavior.

The United Nations has also played politics with human rights. Thus, the UN Commission on Human Rights has generally been willing to criticize such "pariah" states as Israel and (during its apartheid regime) South Africa but not the major powers. On the other hand, such organizations as the Red Cross, the International Labour Organization, United Nations Educational, Scientific and Cultural Organization (UNESCO), United Nations Children's Fund (UNICEF), the Food and Agriculture Organization (FAO), the World Health Organization (WHO), and the High Commissioner for Refugees have done much to improve human rights within offending states. Private nongovernmental organizations (NGOs), notably Amnesty International (which won a Nobel Peace Prize in 1977), have sometimes been effective in improving conditions for specific political prisoners and, on many occasions, even winning their release. But such groups have typically focused on individual cases, avoiding the more troublesome, general issue of state sovereignty versus human rights.

## The Problem of Enforcement

Faced with the sovereign power of states, it can seem that the international human rights regime is woefully inadequate, based as it is on legalisms or exhortations, devoid of enforcement mechanisms. But legal systems always have difficulty controlling powerful actors: For example, labor unions in France and large corporations based in the United States. Ultimately, most international human rights regimes rely on voluntary compliance. And some states have in fact complied voluntarily with international human rights norms, largely to achieve international legitimacy as well as to avoid ostracism.

Frustration with the rights-denying policies of states occasionally spills over into individual and group efforts to transcend or undermine state authority. Individuals of high moral and international standing have on occasion gathered together to fill what they see as a vacuum in the protection of human rights. So-called people's tribunals have periodically convened to draw attention to various human rights abuses. Most notable of these was the Russell Tribunal, which during the 1960s criticized U.S. policy during the Vietnam War. The League for the Rights of Peoples, established in Rome in 1976, has held numerous sessions, condemning political repression under Ferdinand Marcos in the Philippines and offering retrospectives on Turkish genocide against Armenians from 1915 to 1916 and on the Brazilian government's treatment of its indigenous Amazonian population. It has also criticized Indonesia's strong-arm tactics in East Timor, U.S. intervention in Central America, and Soviet intervention in Afghanistan, and it has questioned the legitimacy of nuclear weapons. Such actions are of uncertain effectiveness, but they do attract public attention and undercut the presumption that only state-centered approaches are relevant in dealing with violations of human rights.

## Human Rights Policy and the United States

Americans think of their government as being especially supportive of human rights. After all, the Declaration of Independence states: "We hold these truths to be self-evident, that all men are created equal, that they are endowed by their Creator with certain inalienable Rights, that among these are Life, Liberty and the pursuit of Happiness—That to secure these rights, Governments are instituted among Men, deriving their just powers from the consent of the governed."

The right to "Life" presupposes the right to self-defense and protection against unwarranted attack and unjust government; the right to "Liberty" includes freedom of speech, of public association, of religion, and to establish a government of one's own choosing; the right to "pursuit of Happiness" includes the right to own property and to enjoy the fruits of one's labor. The U.S. Constitution was later amended to include a much-cherished Bill of Rights, which specifically guarantees freedom of religion, speech, the press, and peaceable assembly; the right to petition the government for redress of grievances; the right to keep and bear arms (arguably, the right of state militias to do so); freedom from unwarranted search and seizure and from self-incrimination; the right to a fair and speedy trial; and protection against excessive bail.

On the other hand, the behavior of the early government of the United States was not exactly a paragon of human rights: Slavery was practiced in the South, and women were denied the vote. Even today, racial discrimination is widespread, and the United States still has not passed an equal rights amendment, explicitly guaranteeing equal rights and legal protection to women, including such a basic guarantee as equal pay for equal work.

Moreover, many other nations frequently see the United States as an opponent of human rights. In the past, this widely critical attitude derived from the U.S. government's military intervention in Vietnam and Central America, its long-standing association with an array of oppressive right-wing dictatorships, American corporations' economic exploitation of many developing countries, U.S. coddling of apartheid in South Africa, tacit support for Israeli oppression of Palestinians in the occupied territories, and vigorous initiation and furtherance of the nuclear arms race. In addition, the United States is widely perceived to pursue a single-minded sponsorship of free-enterprise capitalism as the sole acceptable solution to the world's ills, officially encouraging civil and political liberties while in fact opposing most efforts at promulgating socioeconomic rights. More recently, the use of torture in its "War on Terror(ism)" has alienated many people throughout the world and threatened to make a mockery of overt U.S. commitment to human rights even in its Western version that traditionally focuses on civil liberties.

## Messianic Zeal

One of the more pernicious doctrines under which human rights are violated is the notion that one's ideas are so good, pure, correct, and universally applicable that virtually anything is justified in pursuit of them. Totalitarian states, fascist and communist alike, have justified violent repression of their own population in the name of a "greater good," either the glory of the fatherland (fascist) or the dictatorship of the proletariat (communist). And the United States has not been immune to a dose of messianic ideology, beginning early in its history, when the fledgling country viewed itself as a "shining city on a hill" and a self-proclaimed "light unto the nations."

For example, U.S. National Security Council directive no. 68, issued in 1950 at the dawn of the Cold War, noted that "the integrity of our system will not be jeopardized by any measures, covert or overt, violent or nonviolent, which serve the purposes of frustrating the Kremlin design." This directive has never been rescinded. In effect, it gives the U.S. government license to intervene—both domestically and overseas—in ways destructive of human rights so long as such activities are aimed at "frustrating" the goals of its opponents—in the past, the Soviet Union and, more recently, "international terrorism" and various "rogue nations." These actions included a range of interventions abroad, as well as the toppling of governments; attempts to assassinate Fidel Castro; and apparent collaboration in the murder of Vietnam's Ngo Dinh Diem, the Congo's Lumumba, and Chile's Allende, as well as bombing a presumed chemical warfare factory in Sudan, subsequently shown to be a pharmaceutical plant.

U.S. concern with human rights has sometimes had a messianic quality. Thus, the U.S. entry into both World Wars I and II was facilitated by the argument that both wars were in defense of liberty and democracy. Nonetheless, U.S. foreign policy—like that of other countries—has not always been directly influenced by concern about human rights abroad. More important has usually been concern for national power and profit. When democratically elected leftist governments threatened to practice something less than their predecessors' anticommunist zeal and/or when such governments threatened to restrict the profits of U.S. companies abroad, the United States often intervened to replace them with other regimes more friendly to U.S. corporate interests, as happened in Guatemala, Iran, and Chile. Typically, the human rights records of these new governments were far worse than their predecessors'.

At other times, the export of human rights seems more like outright chicanery, as in George W. Bush's announcement, during his second inaugural address in 2005, that "it is the policy of the United States to seek and support the growth of democratic movements and institutions in every nation and culture, with the ultimate goal of ending tyranny in our world." These words might have had greater credence if they had not occurred in the context of an increasingly failed war in Iraq, which was then explained—in retrospect—as part of a purported effort to export human rights, in the form of democracy, to the Middle East. It seems likely that such policies, because they are ultimately destructive of human rights, also feed anti-Western anger and may well contribute to terrorism more than they oppose it.

## Traditional National Self-Interest

Despite its avowed commitment to human rights, U.S. policy has long been influenced by traditional self-serving Great Power concerns. Shortly before the outbreak of World War II, for example, the U.S. government refused to permit the immigration of tens of thousands of German Jews attempting to flee growing Nazi persecution. Motivated in part by anti-Semitism, as well as by concern to avoid the economic and social stresses immigration might produce, the United States chose to adhere strictly to its narrowly written laws governing immigration and naturalization rather than to a broader conception of human rights.

The Truman administration gave some initial support to human rights, through the UN Charter and the UDHR, but as the Cold War heated up, things changed, and during the second half of the 20th century, U.S. human rights policy was subsumed into a foreign policy based largely on anticommunism and containment of the Soviet Union. This in turn produced alliances with a large number of repressive governments, which were said by the U.S. government to constitute part of the "free world," regardless of the degree of their own human rights violations, so long as they professed anticommunism. Despite a respite during the presidency of Jimmy Carter, when human rights briefly became a genuine touchstone of foreign policy, the U.S. government generally downgraded human rights, a tendency epitomized by the Reagan administration, which largely ignored socioeconomic rights and human rights violation by right-wing, anticommunist military dictatorships.

The selectivity of recent U.S. human rights policy is exemplified by antagonism toward Cuba and its accommodation with China, although both violate civil/political rights, with China's offenses more egregious than Cuba's. Considerations of *Realpolitik* appear to be paramount: Unlike Cuba, China is a major economic power and trading partner, while anti-Castro Cuban exiles represent a potent force within U.S. politics, especially in the key state of Florida.

Nor is the United States unique in this regard. For example, China has trampled on the religious and political rights of Tibetans and looked the other way with respect to Sudanese genocide in Darfur (China imports oil from Sudan). The presumed Kurdish right to self-determination has been ignored by NATO countries more concerned about not alienating Turkey. In fact, often when a country's "national interest" conflicts with its avowed concern for human rights, the latter loses.

## Human Rights and Peace

Human rights and peace are inextricably connected. First, the denial of human rights is itself a denial of positive peace. A world in which there is no armed conflict but in which fundamental human rights are thwarted could not in any meaningful sense be considered peaceful. Speaking at the United Nations, Pope John Paul II explicitly linked human rights and war: "The Universal Declaration of Human Rights has struck a real blow against the many deep roots of war since the spirit of war in its basic primordial meaning springs up . . . where the inalienable rights of men are violated."

Not all dictatorships are aggressive: Fascist Spain stayed neutral during World War II, and neither neofascist Paraguay nor neo-Stalinist Albania was an international aggressor. Similarly, for all its size and power, as well as political despotism, China has remained largely unthreatening to its neighbors (with the notable exception of Tibet!). On the other hand, there is also a connection between the way a state treats its own population and its behavior toward other states. And as we have seen, democratic states have rarely made war against other democracies.

To some extent, the foreign policies of states reflect their domestic tendencies. While it existed, the Soviet Union often denied political freedoms to its own people. Likewise, the relative disinterest of the United States in promoting economic justice at home has long paralleled its opposition to any substantive efforts at democratizing the international economic system.

The denial of human rights can also provoke breaches of international peace, if other states become involved. Humanitarian intervention may be legal; there is precedent in some classical writings of international law. In Vattel's *The Law of Nations* (written in 1760), for example, the author claimed that "nations have obligations to produce welfare and happiness in other states. In the event of civil war, for example, states must aid the party which seems to have justice on its side or protect an unfortunate people from an unjust tyrant." Great Britain, France, and Russia intervened in 1827 when Turkey used inhumane means to put down Greek aspirations for independence, and much of the world cheered. U.S. intervention in the Cuban civil war of 1898, which was intended, according to the congressional resolution at the time, to put an end to "the abhorrent conditions which have existed for more than three years in the island of Cuba, have shocked the moral sense of the people of the United States, and have been a disgrace to Christian civilization."

On the other hand, claims of humanitarian intervention have often been used as an excuse for aggression (of which the Spanish-American War may well be an example). Violations of Nicaraguan human rights, for example, were cited by the United States as justification for its efforts to overthrow the Sandinista government, although no comparable justifications were ever used by the United States to overthrow rightist regimes, including the earlier Somoza dictatorship, which had been far more abusive of human rights.

Finally, one of the widely recognized human rights—specified in the first article of both 1966 human rights conventions—is that of national self-determination. Abuses of this right often lead directly to war, especially civil war. The pursuit of human rights may lead more to violence than to peace, since human rights often are won by struggle and confrontation. Furthermore, it is not obvious whether all claims for national self-determination are worthy of success: For example, should there be independent states of Kurdistan, Baluchistan, Chechnya, and/or Kosovo? And what about the national aspirations of Basques, Welsh, Scots, Québécois, native Hawaiians, Okinawans, and Puerto Ricans? The UN Security Council has determined that in certain cases, such as anticolonial struggles, a continuing denial of human rights constitutes a threat to international peace. (This was applied, for example, to apartheid South Africa but not to China's oppression of Tibet.)

In summary, the connection between human rights and peace is complex and multifaceted; it well may be that the most useful connection is the claim that such a connection exists, which in turn can serve as an argument in favor of human rights, regardless of whether this actually promotes peace.

## Competing Conceptions of Human Rights

It is clear that human rights will continue to be controversial, with different conceptions competing with each other, while the very notion of human rights competes with the basic inclinations of states to engage in *Realpolitik*. What should a state do, for example, when confronted with this choice: It desires a particular strategic relationship with another state, but that other state engages in human rights abuses. Which should be sacrificed: national strategy or a commitment to human rights?

Theologian Reinhold Niebuhr argued that "group relations can never be as ethical as those which characterize individual relations." Similar thinking inspired some Marxist-Leninist leaders to rationalize the power politics by which their states generally function, as well as their failure to "wither away," as Marx had originally predicted. During the Renaissance, Niccolò Machiavelli, in *The Prince*, wrote that "a man who wishes to make a profession of goodness in everything must necessarily come to grief among so many who are not good." This may have been largely an excuse, justifying a ruler's amorality, but it also expressed a genuine political dilemma.

Perhaps, on the other hand, the "natural law" school is correct, and support of human rights is simply the right thing to do—period—regardless of its practical consequences. Consider this observation from German philosopher Karl Jaspers, who addressed himself to the question of "metaphysical guilt," following the Holocaust. Jaspers (1961) wrote,

There exists a solidarity among men as human beings that makes each co-responsible for every wrong and every injustice in the world, especially for crimes committed in his presence or with his knowledge. If I fail to do whatever I can to prevent them, I too am guilty.[5]

There is yet another possibility, a middle ground between the amorality of *Realpolitik* and the absolutism of inflexible ethical norms. Some argue that power (or, at least, security) can readily be reconciled with human rights. After all, the United States has found that brutal, oppressive regimes—Somoza's in Nicaragua, the shah's (emperor's) in Iran, Marcos's in the Philippines—do not always make reliable allies. And Mikhail Gorbachev's policies of *glasnost* and *perestroika* in the Soviet Union between 1985 and 1991 reflected in part the fact that, in the long run, national security may be enhanced, not diminished, by allowing human rights to flourish, even at the cost of traditional measures of national power.

Former secretary of state Cyrus Vance once offered the following similar observation: "We pursue our human rights objectives, not only because they are right, but because we have a stake in the stability that comes when people can express their hopes and find their futures freely." In short, when it comes to human rights, our ideals and our interests coincide.

## The Responsibility to Protect

A new and important concept has recently been articulated in the arena of human rights, known as the "responsibility to protect" (R2P or RtoP). Former UN secretary-general Kofi Annan raised the following question in the aftermath of the international community's failure to intervene during the 1994 mass murder of an estimated 800,000 people in Rwanda: "Under what circumstances, if at all, is the international community entitled—or even obliged—to intervene in a state's sovereignty, especially when that state is perpetrating genocide?" In response, the Canadian government established the International Commission on Intervention and State Sovereignty in 2000, to which was added the phrase "responsibility to protect" (which was thought better than "right" or "obligation" to intervene). The basic idea of R2P is that under certain circumstances, other states—ideally in conjunction with the UN or some other international grouping—have a duty to protect civilians if their own sovereign state fails to do so. It is a radical doctrine, basically because it asserts that a sovereign state that engages in mass atrocities has by this behavior sacrificed some or all of its otherwise legitimate sovereignty.

R2P became a formal UN initiative in 2005, structured around the concept that sovereignty is not supreme; rather than being simply an unlimited right of governments, sovereignty carries with it a responsibility toward those being governed. R2P is especially concerned with preventing—or if that fails, halting—four crimes: ethnic cleansing, crimes against humanity, war crimes, and genocide. It is thus rather conservative and limited, in that it does not include a governmental responsibility to protect people from disease, illiteracy, social injustice, or to protect the environment. Instead, it focuses on the four most egregious insults to a populace, which are identified as mass atrocity crimes. R2P is currently an emerging global norm, not an established part of international law, although in various forms it has been included in several international treaties. The R2P is generally acknowledged to consist of three pillars:

1.  Each state has a responsibility to protect its population from mass atrocity crimes.

2.  If the state is unable or unwilling to carry out pillar #1 on its own, the international community has a responsibility to assist that state in doing so.

3.  In the initial stages of such intervention, coercive but nonviolent measures such as economic sanctions are appropriate; if such efforts fail, however, military intervention is justified.

Not surprisingly, "responsibility to protect" has been controversial, mostly because of its challenge to traditional conceptions of state sovereignty. In the UN report *Implementing the Responsibility to Protect,* Secretary General Ban Ki-moon responded to this concern by pointing out that if a state is allowing mass atrocities to occur, it is committing what are widely recognized under international law (and affirmed in the Nuremberg Principles) as crimes of omission; similarly, if the state is directly committing these acts it is guilty of crimes of commission. Either way, it has abrogated its responsibilities as a sovereign, making corrective action from outside the state appropriate and legal.

It remains to be seen whether R2P will be abused. It is conceivable, for example, that in the future a state will insist upon intervening militarily in the domestic affairs of another state, claiming a responsibility to protect some of its inhabitants, analogous to Adolf Hitler's bogus claim in 1938 that Germany was annexing the Sudetenland because German inhabitants there were being abused by the Czech government. More likely, if R2P fails in the future, it will be because of failure at the other end of the spectrum, with the international community proving reluctant to enforce its responsibility against powerful states when they abuse their own people. For example, there has been no consensus as to an international obligation to restrain China from abusing the people of Tibet, or for Russia to treat its restive Chechen population more kindly.

R2P is also unconvincing when governments maintain (sometimes with good reason) that they are confronting violent internal rebellion which the state has a responsibility to suppress, not to protect! Furthermore, in an age greatly marked by terrorism, governments under internal threat are especially prone to describe their opponents—whether violent or nonviolent—as "terrorists"(as the Assad regime has done in Syria), and therefore not entitled to protection. On the other hand, R2P was raised as a justification for NATO's support of the anti-Gadhafi rebels in Libya, and it is being considered with regard to the brutal repression of antigovernment activities in Syria.

# Promoting Human Rights

It is difficult to imagine exactly what a foreign policy—for any country—would be if it were organized primarily around the promotion of global human rights. However, the following specific actions, which have already been taken at different times in support of human rights, suggest the benefits to be gained from a continuation of such policies:

*Subtle diplomacy.* Quiet, persistent pressure applied to offending governments has the advantage that the government in question need not worry about losing face if and when abuses are corrected. There may, however, be a disadvantage beyond the possibility of simply being ignored—namely, that a government may claim to be employing subtle diplomacy while actually doing nothing.

*Public statements.* This involves drawing world attention to specific abuses and to governments that violate human rights. It may include publicly dissociating one's own government from the unacceptable behavior of another. Human rights compliance can be promoted by publicizing violations through the publication of reports conducted by respected, impartial investigative commissions; in a world climate committed to human rights, most governments seek to avoid the embarrassment that comes with being branded a violator of these rights.

*Symbolic acts.* Sending support to dissidents, either by words, contact with opposition figures, or otherwise indicating disapproval of abuses, is a way of emphasizing to both the offending government and its people that human rights violations are noticed and rejected.

*Cultural penalties.* By isolating offenders at international cultural events, including athletic exhibitions and other exchanges, such governments may be made to feel like pariahs. National pride and the universal desire to be accepted add weight to such actions.

*Economic penalties.* Applying trade embargoes, renouncing investment in the offending country, and refusing development loans and other forms of foreign aid: These actions can hurt the economy of offending countries, thereby putting pressure (often on the more wealthy and influential citizens) to modify policies and/or oust the government. Both cultural and economic penalties were applied, with some success, to the apartheid regime of South Africa, and, more recently, to Iran.

*Immigration.* Human rights activists, dissidents, and those being deprived of their human rights can be permitted to immigrate to receptive countries. In the past, the United States applied this "right" selectively, facilitating immigration by people fleeing leftist-governed countries whose human rights policies the United States wished to criticize while making it very difficult for refugees from rightist-led countries that were allied to the United States and whose human rights policies it was inclined to ignore or whitewash.

*Legal approaches.* International law can be applied more vigorously by identifying, indicting, and, when possible, arresting and trying violators of human rights overseas, just as people involved in the international drug trade have occasionally been indicted and, when possible, extradited for trial. Such actions could serve as a substantial deterrent to future outrages.

*Multilateral approaches.* Countries can commit themselves to the various human rights organizations now active worldwide, especially the UN Commission on Human Rights. There are many other possibilities, such as the regular publication of a UN-sponsored catalog of human rights abuses, subject to international scrutiny. Regimes with disproportionately large military spending tend generally to be the worst human rights abusers, in part, perhaps, because such states recognize their own instability and, accordingly, they invest in military power as a hedge against domestic unrest or civil war. At the same time, such spending drains funds that might otherwise be available to help secure socioeconomic rights. Thus, the ratio of military to domestic national spending could be publicized for each state, and governments could be expected to explain and justify their priorities.

*Destabilization and regime change.* In the past, the United States actively sought to destabilize the governments of certain countries—for example, Nicaragua—because of their alleged human rights abuses. This remains an option, although of questionable legality or morality, unless the abuses are sufficiently flagrant and unless the policy is applied even-handedly to all regimes, regardless of ideology. The human rights abuses of Nazi Germany and imperial Japan may have facilitated the U.S. decision to make war, although these abuses actually became more serious *after* war was declared. The Tanzanian invasion of Uganda, which ultimately toppled the government of Idi Amin, won widespread support because Amin's human rights record was particularly atrocious.

## A FINAL NOTE ON HUMAN RIGHTS

In the short run, attention to human rights can be destabilizing, as the last Soviet administration discovered, and repression can also clamp a lid on human rights abuses. But, in the long run, political stability—either within a state or between states—can be maintained only by the institutionalization of all human rights, socioeconomic as well as political. Thus, human rights not only are compatible with genuine security (of individuals and governments) but also are necessary for it.

In the face of human cruelty, frailty, and misunderstanding and the power of states, securing human rights may appear to be extremely difficult, conjuring up the Greek myth of Sisyphus, who was condemned to spend eternity pushing a boulder up a hill, only to have it roll back again. Yet, as the existential philosopher Albert Camus pointed out in a famous essay, "The Myth of Sisyphus," there may be no greater testimony to human dignity than the struggle to achieve such apparently "hopeless" goals.

## NOTES

1. Quoted in J. Bentley. 1984. *Martin Niemöller*. New York: Free Press.

2. Simone Weil. 1952. *The Need for Roots*. New York: Putnam.

3. Betty Reardon. 1985. *Sexism and the War System*. Syracuse, NY: Syracuse University Press.

4. Testimony to the Senate Committee on Foreign Relations, 1980.

5. Karl Jaspers. 1961, *The Question of German G Guilt*, trans. by E.B. Ashton, New York: Capricorn.

## QUESTIONS FOR FURTHER STUDY

1. To what extent can human rights be seen as being an "umbrella concept" including most of the social/political agenda of a peace activist?

2. Compare a "natural law" approach to human rights (in which these rights are seen as inhering, naturally, to all human beings) with the "positivist" approach, which states that rights are those specified by common law.

3. What should states do when support for human rights appears to conflict with "national security"? Be specific with regard to one or more current world issues.

4. The United States has consistently been inclined to define human rights in political rather than socio-economic terms. Why? Agree or disagree with the wisdom of this policy.

5. In 2002, British prime minister Tony Blair stated in a speech to a Labour Party conference, "Our values are not Western values. They are human values, and anywhere, anytime people are given the chance, they embrace them." Agree or disagree.

## SUGGESTIONS FOR FURTHER READING

David P. Forsythe. 2012. *Human Rights in International Relations,* 3rd ed. New York: Cambridge University Press.

Jack Donnelly. 2002. *Universal Human Rights in Theory and Practice*. Ithaca, NY: Cornell University Press.

Lynn Hunt. 2008. *Inventing Human Rights: A History*. New York: W. W. Norton.

Paul Gordon Lauren. 2011. *The Evolution of International Human Rights: Visions Seen,* 3rd ed. Philadelphia: University of Pennsylvania Press.

Samuel Moyn. 2012. *The Last Utopia: Human Rights in History*. Cambridge, MA: Belknap Press.

Philip Alston, Ryan Goodman, and Henry J. Steiner. 2007. *International Human Rights in Context: Law, Politics, Morals*. New York: Oxford University Press.

# CHAPTER 19

# ECOLOGICAL WELL-BEING

Livestock grazing in the National Tapajos Forest, Brazil. Millions of acres of formerly species-rich tropical rainforest such as this have been burned and replaced with cattle pastures.

*Source:* UN Photo.

> *When we see land as a community to which we belong, we may begin to use it with love and respect.*
>
> —Aldo Leopold

The word *ecology* comes from the Greek *oikos,* meaning "house." It refers to the interrelations between living things and their environments, which include other living things (plants, animals, and microorganisms), as well as such inanimate factors as climate, rocks, water, and the atmosphere. Despite widespread dreams of space travel, and the recent discoveries of hundreds of exoplanets outside our solar system, some of which are possibly life-bearing, good planets are hard to find. For the foreseeable future at least, human beings have only one home, Earth, which also houses millions of other species (many of which are becoming extinct), virtually all of them intimately connected to each other and, ultimately, to us.

# Enhanced Environmental Awareness

Environmental awareness has emerged fitfully over many centuries. Within the United States, it did not begin to achieve widespread public attention until the last third of the 20th century, in large part as a result of a number of worries that seemed to surface more or less simultaneously: increased public dismay about air and water pollution, the effects of persistent pesticides, worldwide reduction in biodiversity, anxiety about climate change, overpopulation, diminishing energy supplies, and so forth.

For a time, many social activists saw environmental concern as a distraction from socioeconomic needs and even, in some cases, as a plot by Western economic elites to ensure continued underdevelopment of impoverished countries. Now, the dependence of human beings on their planetary environment is undeniable, such that both human happiness and human survival depend on the maintenance and proper functioning of natural systems. In addition, many people working closely with social movements in developing countries are convinced that environmental/ecological/resource issues are at the heart of their struggle. The web of life has been fraying; positive peace requires that it be rewoven or, at least, allowed to regenerate on its own.

## From 1980 to the Present

By the 1980s, substantial progress in raising ecological awareness had been made in the United States—both in legislation and in public attitudes—but the environment itself continued to deteriorate, at least in part because of political policies that prized short-term economic growth over the natural environment. As part of their strong commitment to free enterprise, most political conservatives have remained opposed to active government intervention on behalf of environmental protection, preferring to leave markets as free as possible, regardless of the environmental impact. (Others argue that they are no less committed to sound environmental stewardship than is anyone else, but that this goal will most effectively be achieved by relying on unfettered free-market mechanisms.)

Environmental concern has become quite widespread in other countries as well. The Green Parties of Europe periodically make strong showings in national elections, especially in German-speaking and Scandinavian countries and in elections to the European Parliament. The environment has been very much on the front pages: Heat waves and droughts alternating with occasional severe flooding, validate concern about human-induced climate change. Fires have ravaged the American West, including Yellowstone National Park, as well as huge tracts in Mexico, Brazil, Greece, and Indonesia. The Earth's protective ozone layer has been thinning, perhaps dangerously. Nuclear accidents at Three Mile Island in the United States (1979), Chernobyl in the Soviet Union (1986), and Fukushima in Japan (2011), combined with the revelation that U.S. nuclear weapons plants had secretly and recklessly fouled thousands of acres with radioactive waste, have tarnished the image of nuclear power as a "pollution-free" energy panacea. Waste disposal has become a worldwide problem, along with toxic contamination and floods exacerbated by forest destruction. Famines scourge Africa, soils are increasingly degraded, and the human population has surged to more than 7 billion. The world's rain forests have diminished rapidly, and biodiversity has been drastically reduced, with many "charismatic" species (giant pandas, tigers, rhinos, gorillas, and even elephants), as well as a host of lesser-known ones, pushed to the edge of extinction.

## The Environment and National Security

In the final analysis, a world at peace must be one in which all living things are "at home." This does not require a state of perfect, unchanging harmony; indeed, the world has never known an extended period of static immobility. Life itself involves change: consumption, synthesis, metabolism, locomotion, reproduction, competition, disintegration, and evolution. But life also depends on a kind of fundamental, underlying stability, at least in the long run—that is, in hundreds, thousands, or even millions of years. In recent times, some of the crucial relationships among the world's species and between those species and their environments have become increasingly tenuous, and this in turn has begun to threaten the quality of life, both human and nonhuman. It also threatens to undermine the integrity of our fundamental life-support systems: The air we breathe, the water we drink, the food we eat, and the diverse fabric of life that provides emotional and spiritual sustenance.

One of the most important shifts in human thinking noticeable in the early 1990s was the growing realization that national security must be defined in broader terms than strictly militarily. As our planet becomes increasingly interconnected politically, economically, and socially—and also increasingly endangered—the health, well-being, and security of every individual becomes inseparable from the health, well-being, and security of the Earth itself. In his famous "strategy of peace" speech, delivered at American University in 1963, President Kennedy noted, "We are devoting massive sums of money to weapons, that could be better devoted to combating ignorance, poverty and disease. . . . We all inhabit this same small planet. We all breathe the same air. We all cherish our children's future. And we are all mortal."

Our connectedness—to each other and to other forms of life—is rapidly emerging as something beyond rhetoric or metaphor. Observing the growing numbers of species pushed to extinction, increasing numbers of people feel a sense of foreboding for the future. In the looming threats to clean air, clean water, and the integrity of the Earth's atmosphere, and in an era of diminishing resources, many people are recognizing threats to their own well-being that are as real as any military threat emanating from an armed opponent. Ecological thinkers maintain that human beings have an obligation to be something other than a predatory and destructive species. Rather, we must exercise wise stewardship over the planet's wild things and wild places, not just for our own benefit but as an ethical imperative. Environmentalists also see the connection between despoiled, depleted, and polluted lands and human misery. We cannot fully make "peace" until we make peace with our planetary environment.

Moreover, in responding—albeit belatedly—to the various environmental threats, we will not be running the risk of anything like the "security dilemma," in which military "preparedness" actually threatens to bring about the danger it is intended to surmount. Environmental sensitivity and protection seem likely to be largely win-win propositions, although there are also economic, social, and political conflicts to be faced. Nonetheless, environmentalism, once considered an indulgence of the rich, is increasingly recognized as fundamental to a decent life for everybody.

In the absence of dramatic environmental disasters, public attention rarely focuses on the continuing plight of a silently deteriorating planet. Many of the most serious and adverse environmental effects (including climate change, resource depletion, and overpopulation) will not become fully apparent until sometime later in this century, but if we wait until then before acting, we may well have foreclosed the opportunity to intervene effectively. As with the prevention of war, the prevention of ecological disaster requires that we intervene *before* catastrophe actually takes place, after which effective responses may well be virtually impossible.

## The Tragedy of the Commons

A model—first described in a much-noted scientific article by ecologist Garrett Hardin[1]— helps us understand one of the major social factors underlying environmental problems. It considers the sort of situation that long existed in Britain, in which some grassland was privately owned and another part, the "commons," was shared property of the community at large. Various citizens owned livestock, which they could graze on their own private lands or on the public commons. Overgrazing was harmful to the productivity of the grassland, so shepherds generally avoided overgrazing their own property. But they treated the commons differently: The shepherds recognized that a healthy commons benefited everyone, but each also reasoned that if he refrained from grazing his animals on the commons, others would probably take advantage of this restraint and fatten their flocks on the public lands. As a result, tendencies to be prudent and ecologically minded were suppressed because individuals reasoned that if the commons was going to be degraded anyhow, they may as well be in on the profit. The result was deterioration of the commons, until it was no longer fit to support sheep or shepherds.

The tragedy of the commons, then, is that individuals—each seeking to gain personal benefit—find themselves engaging in behavior that hurts everyone. It can also be generalized to other situations whenever short-term perceptions of self-interest conflict with long-term public good. For example, there may be immediate, selfish benefit for a factory owner to use the atmosphere as a public sewer; after all, even though his effluents pollute the air, the cost is borne more or less equally by everyone who breathes, whereas the owner personally is saved the expense of having to install pollution control devices. Similarly with overuse of resources, if it is inconvenient to recycle and easier for individuals simply to throw their garbage away or to use more than their share of scarce commodities, they may derive some personal gain or enhanced convenience by doing so, while the cost—in overcrowded dumpsites or worldwide resource shortages—is diffuse and generally borne by all. Besides, if they don't abuse the environment, surely someone else will (which is just what the flock owners told themselves about the commons).

The tragedy of the commons has global dimensions: Scandinavian forests and lakes were polluted by acid rain because of the effluents of English smokestacks while Britain benefited. Japan and Norway periodically defy international outcry while hunting the world's great whales to the verge of extinction. Brazil benefits economically from the Amazon rain forest, even though such "benefit" is rapidly destroying the Amazon jungle.

# Some Major Environmental Problems

## Pollution

Modern life produces large amounts of by-products, many of them toxic. These include pesticides, herbicides, nitrates, phosphates, heavy metals, petroleum products, and numerous other poisons, including contamination from military uses and abuses of the air, water, and soil.

For many years, the atmosphere, fresh waters, and the oceans have been considered publicly owned (which is to say, unowned) and thus suitable for dumping all manner of unwanted substances. Automobiles spew out vast quantities of additional air pollutants, as do power generators and the widespread, large-scale burning of forests and grasslands, especially in the developing world. The American Lung Association estimates that air pollution alone is responsible for $40 billion in annual damage, counting medical expenses as well as damage to crops and buildings. And this is just in the United States, where air-quality standards are among the highest in the world.

Even though industrialization generates much air and water pollution, wealthier countries still tend to have cleaner air and water, on average, than poorer ones. Since pollution control devices can be costly, they are often unattainable for those already poor. Environmental protection has thus become a luxury that most developing countries cannot afford—although, in the long run, they cannot afford *not* to protect the environment. At present, however, multinational corporations preferentially establish factories in countries where poverty and politically pliant leadership have resulted in low standards of environmental protection. The air in Mexico City, Manila, Beijing, and Mumbai, for example, is among the worst on Earth. Major rivers in such regions are often little more than open sewers.

The problem is not intractable, however. Industrial pollution can be greatly diminished, not only by end-of-the-pipe treatment of effluents but also by reducing the waste stream itself. The nations of the world do not have to wallow in their own toxic waste, polluting the air and water and poisoning those—especially the poor—who usually cannot afford to live in safer, cleaner environments. A modest tax on carbon and other emissions can go far toward stimulating conservation and pollution reductions, although domestic industries—and many developing countries—object vigorously, complaining that such a tax would inhibit their ability to compete internationally. Therefore, innovations of this sort would probably be most acceptable if adopted by many states simultaneously.

Attempts to respond in this manner have been bedeviled by demands by developing countries that they be given special dispensation when it comes to curtailing toxic emissions—since, after all, the developed countries attained their status largely without worrying about such constraints, while developed countries tend to insist that all states, rich and poor alike, should be treated equally. At the same time, wealthy countries (notably the United States) argue that poorer countries should not be granted special privileges, especially when, as in the case of India and China, they have become huge mega-industrial states. As of 2011, China exceeded the United States as the world's number one emitter of greenhouse gases, especially carbon dioxide. China, however, argues that since it is still comparatively "underdeveloped" on a per capita basis, it shouldn't be held to the same standards as the countries of Western Europe and the United States.

Pollution is not only hurtful but also wasteful. In a resource-limited world, mercury belongs in thermometers, not in fish; sulfur belongs in matches and pharmaceutical drugs, not as sulfuric acid in dead lakes; and so on. Environmental protection can thus be good economics as well as good ethics, with beneficial consequences in terms of diminished cost for health care and enhanced opportunities for fisheries, forestry, hunting, "ecotourism," and so forth. Thus, a thorough cleanup of air and water has practical benefits as well as ethical advantages.

There are signs of international cooperation in cleaning up the planet, along with growing public awareness of the problem. International protocols have been signed restricting emissions of nitrogen, sulfur, and chlorofluorocarbons (which eat away the ozone layer) and reducing the production of greenhouse gases, notably carbon dioxide. Progress in this respect, however, has been frustratingly slow, such that despite a worldwide scientific consensus as well as increasing political recognition of the problem, much-ballyhooed international meetings have accomplished little except for setting laudable goals and guidelines. A Law of the Atmosphere, comparable to the Law of the Sea, would be immensely helpful, but does not seem likely in the near future—especially so long as many of the world's economies continue to struggle in the aftermath of the 2008 Great Recession.

Nuclear energy constitutes one of the most pernicious environmental problems, even for economically developed nations (including France and Japan), which have come to rely on it for a significant percentage of their energy needs. Despite claims of the nuclear power industry, military contractors, and the government, nuclear power is not "clean." In the United States alone, more than 100 commercial reactors plus a handful of weapons reactors (as well as several hundred naval power plants) produce an average of 30 metric tons of nuclear waste per reactor per year. To this environmental risk must be added nuclear power's potential for weapons proliferation. Many experts fear that Iran, for example, has been developing a nuclear weapons capability under the guise of civilian nuclear power. In addition, there are the as-yet-unresolved problems related to the permanent disposal of nuclear waste.

In the aftermath of a huge tsunami in 2011, and the resulting destruction and partial meltdown of Japan's Fukushima nuclear power plant, Japan temporarily closed all of its nuclear reactors, and Germany has pledged to end entirely its reliance on nuclear energy by 2022. This is especially notable for a country with advanced technological capacity that had been considered a world leader in the generation of "safe" electricity from nuclear power, and, moreover, one notably lacking in indigenous energy resources and that accordingly had been expected to be in the forefront of civilian nuclear power reactors. It speaks profoundly about nuclear energy's likely future.

## Global Warming

Since the middle of the 20th century, scientists have warned that human technology and economic "progress" have been disrupting the worldwide carbon cycle, one of many fundamental processes on which life on Earth depends. Then came the 1980s and 1990s, during which the 14 warmest years of the past century occurred.[2] It became increasingly apparent—even to indifferent citizens, antagonistic industrialists, a small handful of financially compromised and/or contrarian scientists, and obtuse politicians—that the "greenhouse effect" had already begun.

Global warming begins with the sun's energy striking the Earth. This energy is most familiar to people as visible light. However, the Earth then radiates heat back, largely in the form of infrared radiation. This is readily absorbed by the atmosphere, much of it by "greenhouse gases," notably carbon dioxide. If it were not for the atmospheric absorption of this heat reradiated by the Earth, our planet would become lifelessly cold. But as the quantity of these gases has been increasing, the atmosphere has become a heat sink, absorbing so much warmth that the Earth's climate has begun to change. (A similar principle keeps greenhouses substantially warmer than their surroundings, relying in this case on the structural characteristics of glass rather than the chemical properties of carbon dioxide: Light passes easily through the glass of a greenhouse—as solar energy passes readily through a carbon dioxide-rich atmosphere—but the reradiated infrared energy is trapped inside, since glass, like carbon dioxide, absorbs this energy rather than allowing it to escape. The same thing happens when an automobile is left in the sun.)

Under natural conditions, a certain amount of carbon is released into the atmosphere as a result of the respiration of animals and the burning or decomposition of organic materials. At the same time, carbon is removed from the atmosphere and "fixed" in the bodies of plants via photosynthesis. Since the industrial revolution, this cycle has been unbalanced, with much more carbon released to the atmosphere than is being fixed in plants. The combustion of fossil fuels (coal and oil) has been especially responsible, but the burning of forests and grasslands has also added substantially to the atmosphere's carbon load. About two-thirds of the planet's excess carbon comes from fossil fuels (emitted especially by automobiles and trucks, power generation, and heavy industry) with about one-third coming from burning and rotting vegetation (especially savanna fires in Africa and burning of the Amazon and other tropical forests, notably in the Democratic Republic of Congo and Indonesia). In addition, the steady destruction of the world's remaining forests—for fuel and to clear land for cultivation and/or grazing—not only adds carbon dioxide directly but also destroys the major means by which carbon is naturally removed from the atmosphere.

If left unchecked, increasing carbon dioxide levels could well result in an increase in world temperatures by 3 °F to 9 °F by the year 2050. Such a worldwide temperature increase would represent a rate of climate change 100 times faster than at any time in recorded history, with possibly catastrophic results: Agriculture would be profoundly disrupted; many species would almost certainly die (polar bears, for example, are currently drowning in the Arctic when their ice floes melt); and droughts (because of higher evaporation rates) would add to the calamity. As the oceans expand because of the higher temperatures and some melting occurs in the polar ice caps, sea levels would rise, causing potentially devastating floods to low-lying terrain. Many of the world's great cities are coastal and at sea level, including Los Angeles, San Francisco, New York, Rio de Janeiro, Mumbai, Tokyo, and Manila, as is nearly the entire population of Bangladesh.

There is also the problem of positive feedback, or "vicious circles." Because of their white color, snow and ice have a high "albedo," or reflectivity, by which energy from the sun is dissipated away from the Earth. Following substantial loss of this natural reflective covering, global warming would likely increase yet more. Similarly, forests absorb large quantities of carbon dioxide; the logging and burning of tropical rain forests in particular not only releases vast quantities of carbon dioxide but also diminishes the ability of the Earth's natural ecosystems to sequester it, thereby increasing the rate of warming.

Carbon dioxide is not the only greenhouse gas. Others are nitrogen oxides, methane (produced in landfills, termite mounds, and the digestive processes of cattle), and chlorinated fluorocarbons (CFCs), also implicated in the destruction of the ozone layer. Per molecule, in fact, these chemicals are far more heat absorbing than carbon dioxide, but they are much less abundant.

There seems no way to reverse worldwide climate change in the short run. However, it can be ameliorated, essentially buying time for future generations. One practical series of solutions is the adoption of a triad: renewable energy sources (wind, solar, etc.), strict conservation, and reforestation. These suggest many possibilities for action; for example, a tax on carbon emissions could exert economic pressure for the development and use of noncarbon energy sources. Another example: Increasing automobile fuel economy standards from an average of 25 miles per gallon (in 2007) to 35 miles per gallon would save 2.3 million barrels of oil per day in the United States alone, approximately the number currently imported from the Persian Gulf. As with the prospects for world government, the challenge of climate change isn't so much a lack of specific options as a lack of political consensus.

We don't know the exact dimensions of the climate change threat, but comparable uncertainty has never stopped human beings when it came to other threats, such as those posed by international aggression. The threat posed by climate change may be just as great or greater; thus far, however, the human response has been much more restrained.

The major culprits—that is, the major carbon emitters—are the United States, China, India, and Russia. However, any state, once it becomes heavily industrialized or highly dependent on coal (such as China), will contribute more than its share to the Earth's carbon load. After much controversy, more than 150 countries—including the United States—signed the Kyoto Protocols in 1997, which committed them to cut their carbon dioxide emissions by 2010; the Bush administration refused to comply, however, instead calling for more research, while at the same time minimizing and even misrepresenting the established conclusions of existing studies. When it comes to acknowledging climate change and its anthropogenic (human-caused) nature, there is a broad-based scientific consensus. Doing something about it, however, is another story.

## Energy

As population increases, and industrialization along with it, the demand for energy rises exponentially. Although technological innovation (coal, oil, hydropower, nuclear) has to some extent enabled economic development to continue despite the extraordinary increase in demand, it is undeniable that the Earth's energy resources are limited. Moreover, all standard sources of energy employed thus far carry significant environmental downsides. Wood burning, for example, is prominent throughout much of the world as a means of cooking and heating; however, it produces immense quantities of pollutants, including carbon dioxide, while also contributing to the planet's tragic deforestation.

Nor is coal any better, even the supposed "low sulfur" variety. In addition to the overt destructiveness of coal mining, the burning of coal generates huge amounts of carbon dioxide emissions, and although so-called "clean coal" is trumpeted as being on the horizon, the reality is that cost-effective carbon dioxide sequestration technology has yet to be developed, never mind implemented. The burning of oil, too, releases large quantities of greenhouse gases, while oil wells, pipelines and supertankers regularly pollute the oceans.

In 2010, a devastating oil spill in the Gulf of Mexico from the BP Corporation's Deepwater Horizon offshore well was a dramatic example of just how costly energy extraction can be. The explosion killed 11 workers and spilled upward of 5 million barrels of oil into the Gulf of Mexico. This disaster exposed serious structural flaws in federal oversight of offshore drilling, including a cozy relationship between the oil industry and its ostensible regulators in the Interior Department. BP has subsequently paid $14 billion in cleanup costs, $6.3 billion in damages to individuals and businesses, and has pledged another $7.8 billion in additional payments, once subsequent claims are evaluated. This corporation is also likely to owe several billion dollars for damages to natural resources under the Oil Pollution Act, and between $5 billion and $20 billion in penalties under the Clean Water Act, depending on the level of negligence yet to be established. The devastation from this spill was enhanced by the fact that prior to the event Gulf Coast wetlands and barrier islands were already seriously compromised by rampant industrialization and mismanagement of the Mississippi River as well as by Hurricane Katrina. It is also worth noting that Arctic conditions are such that a spill in the far

North would be even more difficult to control and to remediate, although pressure for Arctic oil exploration and drilling continues, especially in the Arctic National Wildife Refuge.

Relatively abundant oil is believed to occur in the "tar sands" of north central Canada. However, extracting this resource is extremely energy intensive and produces immense amounts of greenhouse gases. Similarly, although natural gas has been touted as a relatively "clean" energy course, it, too, produces carbon dioxide when burned, and whereas "hydraulic fracturing" or "fracking" promises to release large quantities of natural propane gas from formations in the United States and elsewhere around the world, this technique threatens to cause significant chemical pollution of the same underground aquifers that are increasingly being tapped for domestic, agricultural, and industrial use. Nuclear power plants also seem poor candidates for meeting the world's energy needs: In addition to the risk of facilitating the proliferation of nuclear weapons, the Fukushima nuclear power plant disaster in Japan emphasized just how vulnerable such operations are to catastrophic failure.

At the same time, and on the "glass half full" side of the world's energy ledger, there remain several possible routes toward energy independence via renewable sources. The amount of energy reaching the Earth via sunlight is more than enough to meet all imaginable future demand . . . if and when efficient, affordable photovoltaic systems can be designed and employed. Prospects are similarly encouraging for eventually harnessing the energy of wind, tidal, and even photosynthetic sources. In the short term, great energy savings—equivalent to putting a whole new generation of coal and oil-fueled power plants—could be generated by such simple and low-tech solutions as improving household and industrial insulation, lowering thermostats by just a degree or two, mandating higher automobile fuel efficiency standards, and so forth.

## Ozone Depletion

When near the ground, ozone—$O_3$, a molecular form of oxygen—contributes to air pollution, especially photochemical smog. But in the upper atmosphere, it has a beneficial effect, absorbing dangerous ultraviolet radiation and preventing it from reaching the ground. (Excessive ultraviolet exposure can cause sunburn, skin cancer, and blindness.) Several decades ago, atmospheric scientists noted that the ozone layer, especially above the Antarctic, was rapidly thinning. Major culprits were CFCs—chemicals that have been widely used in industry, such as aerosol propellants and refrigerants, and in the manufacture of polystyrene.

The precise causes of ozone depletion have been difficult to track down, and even its effects are diffuse. Unlike wars, epidemics, and famines, atmospheric deterioration generally does not photograph well or lend itself to dramatic 30-second "sound bites." But for all its subtlety, it is no less real. This is once again a kind of tragedy of the commons, in that individuals, or individual industries, have little motivation to behave responsibly toward the atmosphere unless others are persuaded or coerced into behaving similarly. The same applies to countries: Unless all states can be persuaded to act together, there is little motivation for anyone to act separately. Thus, there is an immediate economic cost, for example, in forbidding the use of CFCs (or, for that matter, taxing carbon emissions).

This makes it especially heartening that in the case of ozone depletion, at least, substantial cooperation has been achieved. In a success for the United Nations Environment Programme, most of the world's heavily industrialized countries agreed to the Montreal Protocols, pledging themselves to a dramatic cut in CFC production. Although it affects only one of the many environmental problems that require attention—and, in the opinion of most experts, overall levels of ozone in the atmosphere will recover to pre-1980 levels only by about 2060 to 2075—it represents an important victory for environmental consciousness and planetary hygiene.

Even in this case, however, the situation remains less than satisfying. Thus, even though the Montreal Protocols have greatly reduced the rate at which the ozone layer is deteriorating, by substituting other chemicals for ozone-destroying CFCs, the new substances—known as HCFS—are literally several thousand times more active than greenhouse gases! And the use of air conditioning, which requires large quantities of HCFS, has skyrocketed in recent years, especially in India and southern China, warm regions that are also experiencing very rapid economic growth. Fortunately, other environment-friendly chemicals do exist, but their introduction has been slowed by patent disputes, government inertia, and political pressures.

## Threats to Tropical Rain Forests and to Biodiversity

The world's tropical rain forests are the greatest repositories of biological diversity—sheer numbers of species—on Earth. Also among the most endangered, they cover only about 7% of the Earth's surface but are home to 50% to 80% of all plant and animal species. Of the estimated 5 million to 30 million species on Earth, fewer than 2 million have even been identified. It is difficult to assess their value to *Homo sapiens.* Seen as entities in themselves, each is irreplaceable and priceless. In addition, rare species often prove to be of direct human benefit—for example, providing raw materials for treatment of cancer and other diseases.

More than one-third of all plant and animal species (excluding fish and invertebrates) live exclusively on 1.4% of Earth's land surface. These "hot spot" regions are concentrated in the tropics: notably Madagascar, Brazil, the Congo, Borneo, Sumatra, a few other Southeast Asian islands, the tropical Andes, and the Caribbean. This concentration underscores the risk of extinction but also suggests that by focusing on protection of a relatively small total area, substantial amounts of the world's biodiversity can yet be protected.

However, hunger by agricultural interests for land, combined with government eagerness for "development," has resulted in the destruction of vast amounts of tropical rain forests, notably in South America, Africa, and Indonesia. Regions that are especially threatened include the island of Madagascar (home to many unique, "endemic" species) where more than 90% of the original vegetation is gone, the eastern slope of the Andes, the monsoon-prone rain forests of the low Himalayas, the Atlantic coastal forest of Brazil, and much of Malaysia. Less than 5% of the world's tropical forests are under any protection whatsoever, and those that are often are protected on paper only: They remain subject to extensive poaching, lumbering, grazing, and so on, largely because of human poverty and locally dense population.

Tropical rain forests lie mainly in economically developing countries, which are often desperately poor and thus eager for economic improvement, even if the "gains" are only short-lived. Moreover, these countries tend to suffer from high national debt and lack funds to make interest payments. Some Central American countries, for example, clear their remaining rain forests to raise beef so as to earn money from U.S. fast-food restaurants, and many Southeast Asian states export teak and mahogany, similarly destroying their own countryside, in return for short-term gains (which tend to benefit only a small proportion of the local population).

About 11 million hectares of tropical forests—roughly the area of Virginia—are cleared annually. More than 8 million hectares of Brazilian rain forest are burned every year to clear land for cattle ranching. In his book *Earth in the Balance,* former U.S. vice president, and Nobel Peace Prize winner Al Gore asked, "If, as in a science fiction movie, we had a giant invader from space clomping across the rain forests of the world with football field-size feet—going boom, boom, boom every second—would we react?"[3] His point is that the equivalent of this is happening right now.

As awareness of the plight of the rain forests has increased, so has international pressure on those states that are currently devastating theirs. But this too raises difficulties. For example, having abused their own environment (also making themselves rich in the process), North Americans are on poor moral ground lecturing Brazilians to refrain from doing to the Amazonian "frontier" what they have done to their own. A major environmental and social challenge in developing countries is to emulate the prosperity of the industrial states without repeating their mistakes. Conservation efforts must also contend with fierce nationalism, often evoked when the wealthy North lectures the impoverished South about what the latter should do with its land.

Brazil, for example, has its ancient battle cry, *A Amazonia e nossa* (the Amazon is ours). Following centuries of destructive ecological and political imperialism worldwide, Europeans have little moral basis for urging the Indonesian government to spare its watersheds. Imagine the response if the British government had sought to prevent the United States from slaughtering its own indigenous bison herds during the 19th century. Accordingly, it will not be easy to persuade inhabitants and governments in poor countries—or the rest of us, for that matter—that the Amazon, the upper Congo watershed, the New Guinea lowlands, and, indeed, all of the planet belong to all of us.

Global trends have been worrisome. According to the 2012 "Living Planet Report" produced by the highly regarded, World Wildlife Fund, the world's biodiversity (the number of different species of plants, animals, and other organisms) has declined by about 30% since the 1970s. Although temperate species are doing relatively well, tropical species have declined by 60% since the 1970s, with freshwater tropical species being the hardest-hit, having declined by 70% in that time period, and terrestrial species have declined worldwide by 25% between 1970 and 2008.

But there is also cause for hope. Worldwide awareness of the plight of the rain forests has increased greatly. Funds have been established to help preserve these irreplaceable regions. The field of "restoration ecology" has also gathered momentum, investigating ways to restore previously devastated lands. Local governments have begun to realize that their own economic, social, cultural, and political health requires that they preserve a healthy environment. And some organizations have been experimenting successfully with "debt for nature swaps," in which the external debt of certain developing countries is purchased at a substantial discount (say, 50 cents on the dollar) and then used, in turn, to purchase nature reserves. In this way, countries like Ecuador and Bolivia have been able to retire some of their debt while also preserving some of their natural environment—to everyone's benefit.

The relatively new field of ecotourism has also been blossoming, giving countries that are wildlife-rich but cash-poor a financial incentive to preserve their living resources. Rwanda, for example, has been able to reap substantial income by providing opportunities for wealthy nature-loving tourists to observe free-living gorillas. (The alternative is to clear the forests, and destroy the gorillas, for short-lived subsistence farming, which is also less remunerative.) More than 20% of Costa Rica's land is now protected, much of it in national parks, and if the worldwide environmental movement continues to show political vitality, other countries can be expected to follow suit. Significantly, Costa Rica has been able to lead the way in this regard in part because that country constitutionally abolished all of its military forces—retaining only police and a modest coast guard—and has been able to use the money saved to preserve its environment (as well to provide subsidized education and health care for its citizens).

## Renewable Resources

A fundamental principle of environmental stewardship is that we must respect the natural cycles on which all life depends. There is simply no viable alternative to some form of global balance: between carbon emissions and carbon fixation, between soil erosion and soil formation, between tree cutting and burning and tree planting and growth, and between births and deaths. In the long run, we cannot take more away from the land than we—or nature—put back. Moreover, we must plan for the long run. A commitment to positive peace recognizes that it is ethically unacceptable, and ultimately impractical as well, to purchase short-term gratification and growth while robbing future generations. Whereas it is relatively easy for most people to see the foolishness of "mining our capital" when it comes to nonrenewable resources, it is less obvious—but no less important—to behave responsibly with regard to renewable resources.

Forests and soils are especially worrisome cases of renewable resources that are being disrupted. Over geological time, for example, soils were formed more rapidly than they eroded, which bequeathed all of us a life-sustaining layer of topsoil averaging about 6 to 10 inches deep worldwide. But deforestation, erosion, overgrazing, and the like have dangerously degraded this natural legacy. It may be difficult to believe today, but in ancient times, Northern Africa was the granary of Rome. Now, much of Northern Africa is desert, and *desertification* is advancing south across Africa at a frightening pace. This must be distinguished from drought. Desertification—a major threat to soil—is not a natural event but rather the consequence of human mistreatment, whereby the rich organic material is washed or blown away, leaving relatively coarse rocky materials that cannot retain moisture and sustain plant life, which in turn contributes to yet more erosion and further degradation. The resulting sand dunes or gullies are nonproductive and very difficult to reclaim, even for wildlife habitat.

In the United States today, farmers lose 6 tons of topsoil for every ton of produce grown. Atmospheric sensing stations in Hawaii can detect when spring plowing begins in China because of the increased particulate matter as airborne soil lost to the land! Worldwide, approximately 25 billion tons of topsoil are lost to erosion every year; this is nearly equivalent to the amount covering the wheat lands of Australia.

As population increases—especially in the poorest countries—marginal land is brought under cultivation, leading to further erosion by wind and water, desertification, and additional loss of long-term productivity. Up to the middle of the 20th century, worldwide crop production increased at least in part because additional lands were brought under cultivation. Then, further increases in agricultural yields were achieved during the 1950s and 1960s through the "green revolution," which combined improved genetic varieties and fertilizer use with the cultivation of new land. But the limits of such advances are rapidly being reached: Per capita productivity in much of Africa, for example, has actually begun *declining,* and there are no major new regions—anywhere—that can be brought under cultivation, at least not for long. In addition, overuse of existing croplands can exact a heavy price. In addition to erosion, millions of acres of cropland are being destroyed by salinization: When underground soil drainage is insufficient, irrigation water—loaded with fertilizer and other salts—puddles up and evaporates, leaving an implacable manmade saline desert, which already covers vast areas of previously productive land and is expanding rapidly.

The World Bank has introduced the concept of "food insecurity," which refers to those people who lack enough food for normal health and physical activity. Central African states— notably Ethiopia, Congo, Uganda, Chad, Somalia, Sudan, and Mozambique—are especially food inse-cure. Moreover, developed states may not be immune. Thus, by the end of the 20th century, the U.S. grain harvest fell below consumption for the first time in recent history.

The destruction of productive soil is very difficult to reverse but not impossible. Overgrazed and overcultivated land should be allowed to lie fallow, sometimes for many years. Land that is especially vulnerable should be taken out of active production. The United States has led the way in this regard; the Food Surplus Act is intended to shift millions of acres of highly erodible land into meadows or forests. (This does not actually represent a sacrifice, since such land is not highly productive, and, moreover, it cannot produce worthwhile yields for very long before being seriously degraded.)

The principle of sustainability applies to forest growth and regeneration as well. If we destroy more than is created, we are cutting into the productive substance of the planet. And such imbal-ance cannot continue for long: If we cut and burn more than grows in that same period, forests (or other resources) are diminished, weakened, and ultimately destroyed.

In most developing countries, forest cover is declining dangerously, through logging, land clearing, and firewood gathering. In a mere 8 years, for example, India lost 16% of its forest cover; as a result, fuel wood prices in India's 41 largest cities increased by nearly one-half, exacting a painful toll on that nation's poor. It doesn't take a higher degree in mathematics or forestry to see that such trends cannot continue for very long and that ecological degradations must inevitably have devastating effects on wildlife, soil formation and maintenance, water quality, atmospheric equilibrium, and—not least—human well-being. In Central Europe and North America, acid rain generated by industrial air pollution, especially coal-fired power-generating plants, has already damaged up to 25% of the forests and rendered thousands of lakes uninhabitable to fish and other aquatic life. Forest destruction, in turn, leads to soil erosion, degradation of water qual-ity, and increased runoff; for example, years of forest destruction in the Himalayan foothills above Bangladesh have contributed to devastating floods, which take an enormous toll in lives and property.

There is also the little-understood problem of acidification of the oceans. About 25% of anthropogenic carbon dioxide dissolves in the oceans, where—among compounds—it repro-duces carbonic acid, which lowers the pH of seawater. It is estimated, for example, that over the past two-and-one-half centuries, the acidity of the oceans has increased by nearly one-third, and at the current rate, is expected to increase to 150% by the year 2100. The exact effects of ocean acidification are unclear, but increased acidity is known to decrease the amount of carbonates dissolved in seawater, which in turn has an effect similar to that of osteoporosis in human beings: It softens and weakens bone and shells produced by animals such as corals, mollusks, and vertebrates.

## Some Environmental Principles

These and other tragedies exemplify several important environmental themes:

1. *Political boundaries are virtually irrelevant to the world's ecology.* Forest cutting in northeastern India, Nepal, and Bhutan results in widespread destruction downstream, in Bangladesh.

2. *Environmental issues are the legitimate worry of not only the affluent.* Poor people—and often poor countries—are typically located where the environment has been most severely abused and are liable to suffer most seriously from environmental disasters.

3. *Environmental abuse can generate short-term profits but invariably at the cost of long-term declines, both environmental and economic.* Natural systems underpin all national economies; as the former deteriorate, so will the latter. As a result, sensible policies must reflect environmental wisdom no less than economic, social, and political realities.

4. *Natural processes must be respected.* Human beings can intervene in those processes—we can unbalance them and sometimes even restore them—but we cannot transcend them. Francis Bacon (1561–1626) wrote that "Nature, to be commanded, must be obeyed," a useful warning . . . with the addition that it is questionable whether in the long run, nature can be commanded at all.

It is possible, fortunately, to turn the tide on forest loss. Tree planting on a massive scale will help overcome anthropogenic climate change, reverse erosion, and improve water and air quality while also providing fuel and wildlife habitat. South Korea has begun to do just this, China is on the verge, and India at least has developed a forward-looking plan to reclaim its forests. Trees grow back, and reforestation is generally feasible, so long as the money is available and people understand the long-term need while restraining their short-term greed.

One of the most important renewable resources involves the production of food itself. Nontechnological farmers obtain small yields, and they are often thought to be inefficient compared with modern high-tech agriculture. In fact, however, much of the productivity of agro-industry is achieved by using vast amounts of energy. On average, every calorie expended by nontechnological farmers (as human and animal labor) yields 5 to 50 calories of food energy. By contrast, the intensive mechanized farming practiced in the United States expends 5 to 10 calories of energy (mostly as petroleum, some as fertilizer and pesticide), to produce just a single calorie of food. We grow a lot of food, but we do so by expending even more energy, which not only contributes to global warming but also depletes our most important nonrenewable resource, fossil fuels.

# Environmental Activism

## In the United States

Within the United States, environmental activism is largely expressed through legislation and direct citizen participation. Legislative environmentalism involves the passing of laws designed to protect environmental values, to preserve wild and open space, to restrict pollution by establishing air or water standards to which states and local municipalities are required to comply, to prohibit the sale of materials derived from endangered species, to punish toxic polluters, and so forth. A landmark piece of legislation passed in the early 1970s requires that before the government expends federal funds on any project likely to produce adverse environmental impacts, an Environmental Impact Statement must first be prepared and evaluated; this statement must employ scientific studies to evaluate the extent of the impact and whether adverse effects can be diminished and provide impartial information as to whether the project should be permitted to go forward.

Legislative remedies are often incomplete, in part because governments are frequently hesitant to enforce regulations they see as harmful to business interests, which include mining, oil drilling, grazing, and manufacturing. In such cases, citizens may have access to legal procedures, such as obtaining court injunctions to prevent illegal actions and, in some cases, to force governments to enforce their own laws. The field of environmental law has grown rapidly, and such groups as Environmental Defense, the Natural Resources Defense Council, and the Center for Biological Diversity bring polluters and habitat despoilers to court; there has also been some progress in identifying environmental values (the right to clean air, clean water, and an environment with wildlife) as having legal standing comparable to personal property rights or the right to privacy.

Finally, there is the question of direct action, analogous in many ways to nonviolent antiwar resistance. Such groups as Greenpeace have blockaded whaling ships and sewage outfalls and, by a variety of dramatic and often courageous acts, including boycotts and sit-ins, called public attention to other environmental abuses, such as the clubbing of baby seals or improper disposal of nuclear waste. Such actions often include civil disobedience and can be controversial. The radical environmental organization Earth First! sometimes resorts to ecological sabotage ("ecotage"), by vandalizing land-clearing equipment or "spiking" trees (hammering large nails into them, thereby making it dangerous to log them). Governments have occasionally responded with violence and outright terrorism, as when French intelligence agents blew up the Greenpeace vessel *Rainbow Warrior*, which had been protesting French nuclear weapons testing in the South Pacific. Nonetheless, the environmental movement in the United States continues to be strong, although there seems little immediate prospect for electoral success of a United States Green Party modeled from the European experience. There is also a risk that some of the energy and enthusiasm for environmental protection will be co-opted by corporate activities that are environmentally destructive but are misleadingly presented as beneficial: so-called "greenwashing."

## In Other Countries

Grassroots environmentalism has, if anything, developed more strongly in certain other countries, especially those less imbued with an ethos of predatory capitalism and the Western-inspired credo that human beings are "created" independent of the natural world. One of the most remarkable is the Chipko, or "Hug-the-Tree," movement of India. Beginning in the 1970s, Chipko developed in remote villages in the southern foothills of the Himalayas. It arose spontaneously, based on a cultural heritage that holds a deep respect for the region's lofty mountains, magnificent forests, and clear streams. A series of disastrous floods, resulting from extensive deforestation, induced local activists to literally hug the great trees and, in time-honored Gandhian fashion, to lie down in front of logging operations. The Chipko strategy has since been used to save other natural areas in India, and it has also spread to other countries, where environmental concern is often most strongly developed among the poor, who rely most deeply on the land.

Another struggle has pitted indigenous Amazonian tribes, rubber-tappers (who earn their living extracting latex sap from free-growing rubber trees), anthropologists, and environmentalists against land development interests, especially in Brazil. There, ecological exploitation has been intimately connected with violence—notably genocidal extermination of whole villages and indigenous tribes—by private "armies" hired by landowners and abetted by the military.

Small-scale grassroots organizing is occurring worldwide on behalf of the environment and its people. There are tens of thousands of community development groups in India alone, and their focus, increasingly, is on ecologically sensitive, sustainable development. Similarly, more than 100,000 "Christian base communities" have sprung up in Brazil while Africa and Asia have been especially prominent in struggling for local reforestation, soil preservation, and the like. The 2004 Nobel Peace Prize, for example, was awarded to Wangari Maathai, a Kenyan who founded the Green Belt Movement, an environmental organization that combines women's rights with a commitment to sustainable development and countrywide tree planting. The 2007 Nobel Peace Prize was awarded to former U.S. vice president Al Gore in conjunction with a United Nations agency, in recognition of their joint role in raising public concern about global warming.

It cannot be concluded, however, that the tide has turned. Every year, the planet seems on balance to be losing rather than gaining ground in the struggle for its preservation. Beyond this, there has been a worldwide trend for environmental activists—often allied with human rights workers on behalf of indigenous peoples—to be persecuted by governmental authorities, who stand to make large amounts of money by permitting destructive land-use and resource-extraction policies.

# Struggling for Sustainability

It has been suggested that some of the world's great civilizations—Sumerian, Mayan, and Roman—may have declined in part because they were destabilized internally by depletion of their underlying resource base. Today, very few knowledgeable people question the ultimate desirability, even the necessity, of a sustainable world economy. There is considerable debate, however, over the best route to sustainability and even about when the limits to growth must be faced. Some people retain faith that technology will somehow save us, as it often has in the past. And indeed, it is always possible that some break-through is waiting just around the corner, which—like faxes and the Internet—will dramatically change our current way of life, leading to truly clean energy and a sustainable future. Others maintain that the Earth is blessed with abundant resources—natural as well as human—sufficient to see us through any crisis that will arise, at least for the foreseeable future, especially since as resource shortages arise, prices increase, which tends to lead to diminished resource use along with a more vigorous search for alternatives.

## Faith in Technology

The argument goes that as resources are used up, the ensuing shortages will serve as incentive to (1) find new reserves; (2) reduce the rate of consumption, for example, by increasing efficiency; and (3) substitute abundant resources for those in short supply, such as making telephone lines out of fiber-optic tubes instead of copper. Necessity (or, more precisely, reduced supply and resulting higher prices) may be the mother of invention as a resource-poor world finds new solutions to old problems. In the recent past, fossil fuels largely replaced wood and animal power in providing energy for heavy industry, and aluminum has to some degree supplemented iron as a construction material. New resources, new forms of energy, and new ways of replenishing the Earth may be just over the horizon.

The difficulty with such thinking is that innovations cannot be counted on, whereas the depletion of known resources is certain. Moreover, even when they do prove successful, "solutions" often carry a new array of problems along with them: Fossil fuels pollute the atmosphere, high-technology mining operations are often energy-intensive themselves, and so on. A starry-eyed confidence that technology or inventiveness will always save us may well become a tragic disappointment. At the same time, fuel-efficient hybrid cars are current realities, just as hydrogen technology may be on the horizon, as well as enhanced use of biofuels.

## Thresholds

Many environmental experts fear that there may well be key thresholds in the planetary environment that, once crossed, could permanently impair the Earth's ability to meet our needs in the future. If the atmospheric load of greenhouse gases becomes too high, the ozone layer too sparse, soils too eroded, air and water pollution too severe (or some combination of these and other factors), or if forest clearing and desertification go too far, at some point the planet may simply become incapable of nurturing life, regardless of later attempts to remedy things. Thus, it could be that the current generation has the responsibility of determining the habitability of our planet, not just for ourselves but for other species as well. In this regard, time is not on our side: Soil, once eroded away, can take centuries to be replenished; certain forms of contamination (plastics, nuclear waste, and long-lived pesticides) will probably be around longer than human history has thus far endured; the atmosphere, once warmed, may be impossible to cool, and species, once extinct, cannot be recreated.

## Human Perception

Many dramatic human achievements require that a perceptual threshold be crossed. Before this happens, relatively few people have deep dissatisfactions with the status quo; the result is business as usual. Then, charismatic leaders, catastrophic events, and/or successful education campaigns may combine to force a dramatic perceptual shift, after which the world appears transformed, and sometimes people then transform it in reality, too. These events often have a distinct ethical/religious component, but self-interest may also be effective: Consider the abolition of slavery and of hereditary monarchies and—increasingly—worldwide revulsion against nuclear weapons. It may be that with the various combined threats to the worldwide environment and the intense publicity they have generated in recent years, ecological wholeness will finally receive the attention and action that it warrants.

## Interconnections

A world at peace is one in which environmental, human rights, and economic issues all cohere to foster sustainable growth and well-being. Ecological harmony cannot realistically be separated from questions of human rights or economic justice. The right to a safe and diverse environment, clear air, and pure water is no less a human right than the right to freedom of expression or dissent, equal employment opportunity, and participation in the political process.

Environmental degradation is also intimately connected to poverty: Wealthy states are often able to export their most odious environmental abuses (sometimes literally, as in the case of toxic materials), and impoverished states are often forced, by their poverty, to accept the situation. The plowing of steep, erosion-prone slopes (which permanently destroys soil) and large-scale intrusions onto wildlife habitats (which contribute to species extinction) are in large part a response to land hunger in rural countries, where a small minority of wealthy people own the great majority of the arable land, thereby pushing less-affluent people to environmentally abusive behavior, simply to survive. In addition, wealthy people are able to purchase environmental amenities, while the poor find themselves living in polluted, degraded surroundings.

Ecological well-being cannot be achieved piecemeal. The rain forests will continue to be abused so long as there are too many people on too little land; indeed, overpopulation has an impact on most environmental issues. Poverty often leads to land degradation as hungry desperate people are likely to clear and cultivate regions that should be left untouched. The burning of fossil fuels produces air pollution as well as greenhouse gases. Global warming will increase food insecurity by reducing agricultural productivity, perhaps catastrophically; accordingly, solutions of these and other problems must be intimately tied to providing adequate, safe energy.

Environmental problems are integrated in another sense as well. Many of the most severe ecological threats are worldwide in scope, such as global warming. Others, although occurring within national boundaries, affect the world economy and/or the global quality of life, such as the loss of species diversity. Deforestation in Nepal causes flooding in Bangladesh; water overuse by the United States deprives Mexico of the Colorado River; pollution of the Rhine by Swiss and German chemical industries makes its water toxic for the Dutch who live downstream; whaling by the Japanese and Norwegians destroys these magnificent animals for everyone; and so on.

Finally, environmental and social issues are interlocking: Population stabilization will likely occur only when poverty is reduced; developing countries will be able to devote themselves to the preservation of their unique wild resources only if their debt burden is relieved; energy use will be sustainable only if it does not burden the air and water with additional pollutants. World cooperation on issues concerning the environment is as necessary as cooperation on economic matters or on issues of global security and war prevention.

## Tension Between Economics and the Environment

In the long run, there should be compatibility between economic needs and ecology, because what destroys the environment also destroys economies. But economic planners typically look to the near future, and, in the short run, the push for jobs, profits, and development often conflicts with environmental preservation. Air and water pollution controls cost money, and installing such controls may make an industry uneconomic, hence leading to plant closings and loss of jobs. A sound environment may demand that wetlands be preserved (to absorb variations in the water table and to control floods, as breeding grounds for fish and other aquatic organisms, etc.), but such preservation may come at the cost of restrictions on development (fewer new shopping centers, housing sites, and industrial parks).

Ultimately, however, economic development and environmental protection are not antagonistic. Vast numbers of people rely directly on the natural surpluses produced by a healthy environment: harvesting fish from wild populations in oceans, rivers, and lakes; hunting game from the land; and obtaining fuel from the forests. A Mauritanian cattle herder does not need advanced training in ecology to know that "the land is tired"; nor does a Philippine fisherman require a degree in marine biology to recognize that fish don't thrive where the ocean is polluted.

Guatemalan peasants know the consequences of plowing land that is too steep, and it is not only wealthy, amateur bird-watchers who mourn the loss of such dazzling animals as the quetzal bird, which has a prime place in Central American cultural identity.

But it is not only distant "primitives" who are immersed in the environment: We all depend on stable hydrological cycles for water, on atmospheric processes for air, on a stable world climate, and on the productivity of world's organic soils. Nonetheless, battle lines still continue to be drawn between those who see themselves as defending the environment and those who champion jobs and economic development. China, which has seen spectacular economic growth in the last 20 years (correlated, at least in part, with its enthusiastic embrace of a unique form of state-sponsored, free-market capitalism), has also experienced some of the world's most horrible environmental problems—notably air and water pollution. For example, as of 2010, only 1% of China's more than 500 million urban residents had access to clean air that met UN standards.

All too often, there is conflict between economic growth and environmental values. In the Pacific Northwest of the United States, for example, a major controversy erupted between conservationists and the timber industry. A rare bird, the northern spotted owl, nests only in relatively large, undisturbed tracts of old-growth forest. But the timber in these forests is also coveted by loggers. It remains to be seen whether a lasting accommodation can be reached in this and other acute conflicts between economic demands and ecology. In the long run, however, a successful timber industry requires a continuing supply of trees, just as the spotted owl does. Accordingly, it seems not only possible that a win-win solution can be achieved but also necessary, because neither the economy nor the environment can survive if the other is defeated. In this regard, the promise of "green jobs"—substantial employment generated by a switch to more efficient, less polluting, sustainable resource use and energy production—is encouraging but more a future hope in the United States than a current reality.

## Political Ideologies

Some Western critics of environmental policies assume that capitalism is largely to blame; after all, a system that exalts profits above everything seems unlikely to prize environmental values. Without doubt, the industrialization of capitalist states was—and continues to be— intimately connected to their many environmental abuses. But socialist states have been at least as insensitive to environmental issues. Often, rigid adherence to production goals—regardless of environmental consequences—combined with state ownership of the "means of production" made the tragedy of the commons even more widespread within the former Soviet bloc than in market-oriented societies. A significant difference between traditional economics (whether market-oriented or centrally planned) and sustainable economics is that the former is concerned with how to produce what for whom whereas the latter expands the definition of "for whom" to include future generations.

Within the former Soviet Union, the once-majestic Aral Sea dropped 40 feet because of destructive, short-sighted dam and irrigation projects. The Neva River, which runs through the heart of historic St. Petersburg, Russia, is befouled with oil. Swimming is regularly curtailed at Black Sea resorts, due to typhoid and dysentery contamination. Environmental restrictions on the development of Siberia are almost nonexistent and are ignored when present. Forest destruction in the former East Germany, the Czech Republic, Slovakia, and Hungary is among the most severe on Earth, and many regions of Poland are drastically polluted by chemical and other toxic waste.

It has been said, "The difference between capitalism and communism is that in the former, man exploits man, whereas in the latter, it was the other way around!" In both cases, it is the environment—and, ultimately, everyone—that loses.

## Making Environmental Peace

A world of increasingly scarce and endangered resources might be one in which people are motivated to cooperate for everyone's benefit. But it could also be one in which conflict and violence are intensified, as wealthy states seek to achieve continuing access to raw materials and to hold onto their advantages while poor ones attempt to translate their existing resources into power or simply to retain them in the face of growing demands from the "have-nots." It would be tragic if a world made tense by ecological scarcity slides into war, which, in addition to its human toll, destroys yet more of the environment, nonhuman as well as human. The prospect of "resource wars"—over water, oil, natural gas, mineral deposits, and so on—looms as a very real threat. As of 2012, Sudan and the newly formed South Sudan have come to blows over oilfields controlled by the South, Yemen teeters on the brink of becoming the first country to run out of water, and limited water availability (from the Jordan River) has been emerging as a major source of tension between Israel and Jordan as well.

The future can still, however, be reclaimed, although doing so requires not only the prevention of war but also an active commitment to peace. This calls for measures that include public as well as private commitments to invest heavily in environmental protection and restoration. Such investments require time, effort, and money. The following goals are minimal but also achievable:

1. Reforesting the Earth and stopping current deforestation

2. Slowing and eventually stabilizing population growth

3. Increasing energy efficiency

4. Developing renewable energy sources

5. Retiring Third World debt

6. Protecting topsoil from erosion, desertification, and salinization

7. Preserving representative, adequate-sized samples of the planet's pristine ecosystems and its wildlife

8. Protecting the air, water, and land from harmful, persistent pollution

Such accomplishments will not come cheaply. Some estimates suggest that they would require annual expenditures, over the next few decades, in the range of $200 billion per year. (The Government Accountability Office estimated in 2010 that it will cost about $200 billion just to clean up the mess already existing at U.S. nuclear production facilities.)

It is difficult to argue that the goal—a habitable, sustainable planet—isn't worth such a cost. Moreover, even a price tag of $200 billion annually is only about one-fifth of the world's annual military expenditures, which currently exceed $1 trillion per year (more than half of which is spent by the United States alone). If national security is eventually redefined in broader terms than mere military security, such a transformation may well be possible. After all, the Netherlands currently spends about 6% of its Gross National Product (GNP) defending itself from floods originating from the Atlantic Ocean, a far greater expenditure for its national security than it spends on its NATO obligations.

Citizens of all countries can begin now to make a major contribution toward correcting the sad state of the world's environment. There are certain key states, which, by acting decisively, could greatly mitigate our current environmental difficulties. For example, the United States, China, and the states that comprised the former Soviet Union produce fully 50% of the world's carbon dioxide emissions; Brazil, Indonesia, and Congo hold 48% of all virgin tropical rain forest; China and India together account for 35% of the world's annual population increase; and the northern tier of industrial states is responsible for virtually all of the world's acid rain production.

Just as some people claim that "peace begins with me," strides toward environmental peace can begin with the actions of individual countries as well, not only to showcase what can be done but also to get results. Otherwise, it is possible that before the physical and biological limitations of the Earth take a more direct toll, a period of Hobbesian strife may ensue; chaos and war—with all its profoundly anti-ecological effects—would then add to the devastation. It remains to be seen whether environmental threats, even when shared, result in a viable political mass movement of the inhabitants of our shared and endangered planet.

## Environmental Ethics

This chapter—like the others in this book—has been partially motivated by a need to identify real-world problems and to suggest real-world solutions. However, just as there is an underlying ethic to peace studies itself (including the virtues of peace, negative as well as positive, and the iniquity of violence), we can also identify deep-seated ethical aspects to environmental sensitivity.

In Hindu culture, for example, human activity is guided by three values of life: *artha* (which is essentially resources), *kama* (the needs and desires of human beings), and *dharma* (right conduct, or what people *ought* to do as opposed to what they *want* to do). *Dharma* also involves the proper utilization of resources, restricting their use to the satisfaction of one's primary needs and not appropriating the resources of others. To do otherwise is to steal from others and from the world. In this worldview, *dharma* consists of mediating skillfully and thoughtfully between desires and resources; there is therefore a close link between justice and ecological and social harmony.

As historian Lynn White pointed out in an influential essay,[4] Judeo-Christian tradition is quite different, emphasizing a separation between human beings on the one hand and the rest of the biological world on the other. Human beings are seen as having been created in the image of God, in sharp contrast with the nonspiritual material world. Christians and Jews have been told to "go forth and multiply" and to "subdue the Earth." Having emphasized these distinctions between people and the natural world, Judeo-Christian teaching established a context for destruction and exploitation, providing the intellectual and emotional underpinnings to what has since become the planet's ecological crisis. Nonetheless, White concludes his essay by describing an alternative tradition in Western theology: the gentle, nature-centered, and compassionate ministry of Saint Francis of Assisi; he proposes Saint Francis as the patron saint of ecologists.

Other thinkers have also proposed the establishment of ethics on a less human-centered and more diversity-oriented basis. If human beings saw themselves as part of the life process rather than its most powerful rulers, the result would likely be a kinder, more tolerant, and gentler way of living. Moreover, a growing trend in liberal Judeo-Christian theology has been emphasizing the human responsibility to act as reliable stewards on behalf of "the creation."

The great environmental struggles, on which the future viability of the world's ecology depend, will probably be played out during the first half of the 21st century. For the planet and those who depend upon it to win, humanity will have to see itself as part of planetary processes, not set apart from the Earth. Scholars and scientists should study the rate of soil erosion as closely as the rate of inflation, expending at least as much concern keeping up with air- and water-quality standards as keeping up with the stock market, reconsidering basic questions about common benefit versus individual rights. Individuals may be able to afford two automobiles, for example, or a large family, but can the planet?

To expand this example, consider that China's current population is 1.4 billion, many of whom used to rely on bicycles as their primary means of transportation. Along with China's rapid economic growth has come a sky-rocketing increase in automobile ownership, along with a corresponding decline in bicycle use. Given the immense environmental costs of automobiles compared to the comparatively benign impact of bicycles, it is challenging, to consider the ecological impact if per capita Chinese automobile ownership begins to approach that of the United States or Western Europe.

Environmental ethics seeks to respect the natural world as having value in itself, not simply because of its possible utility or threat to human beings. It emphasizes that peace may ultimately require a much broader view of the human community, in which people are responsible not only for their own actions, the actions of other people, and their effects on other people but also for their effects on all other life forms. The West has long had a code of religious ethics, the Ten Commandments. As of the 18th and 19th centuries, it developed ideological systems of societal ethics: capitalism, democracy, liberalism, conservatism, and socialism. Perhaps what is needed from the 21st century is a code of environmental ethics.

## A FINAL NOTE ON ECOLOGICAL WELL-BEING

The fundamental lesson to be derived from a search for ecological well-being may well be the idea of underlying planetary unity. All things, quite literally, are linked to all others. As poet Francis Thompson wrote, "All things . . . near and far, hiddenly to each other connected are, that thou canst not stir a flower, without the troubling of a star." Accordingly, any striving for peace must take account of this connectedness: of living things to the soil and the atmosphere, as well as to all other living things; of people to their natural environment, as well as to their man- and woman-made social systems and each other; of the past to the future of this planet; and of risks to opportunities for everyone and everything.

## NOTES

1.  Garrett Hardin. 1961. "The Tragedy of the Commons." *Science* 162: 1243–1248.

2.  This trend has continued, such that the 13 warmest years for the entire planet have all occurred since 1998, according to data that stretches back to 1880.

3.  Al Gore. 1992. *Earth in the Balance: Ecology and the Human Spirit.* Boston: Houghton Mifflin.

4.  Lynn White. 1967. "The Historical Roots of Our Ecologic Crisis." *Science* 155: 1203–1207.

## QUESTIONS FOR FURTHER REFLECTION

1. How do environmental/ecological concerns qualify as matters of security?

2. Explain how the following serve as examples of the Tragedy of the Commons: deforestation in India, the slaughter of whales, and global warming.

3. It has been said that ecological awareness is a luxury to be indulged by the middle and upper classes. Agree or disagree.

4. Demonstrate the connection—or, alternatively, the disconnection—between ecological wholeness and socioeconomic processes, considering a current issue of environmental controversy, either in the world or in your local community.

5. It has been suggested that there may well be "resource wars" in the future; describe some possible examples. It has also been suggested that there have already been numerous wars over resources; describe some possible examples.

## SUGGESTIONS FOR FURTHER READING

Al Gore. 2006. *An Inconvenient Truth: The Planetary Emergency of Global Warming and What We Can Do About It*. Emmaus, PA: Rodale Press.

Aldo Leopold. 2001. *A Sand County Almanac*. New York: Oxford University Press.

Jay H. Withgott and Scott R. Brennan. 2006. *Essential Environment: The Science Behind the Stories*. Saddle Brook, NJ: Prentice-Hall.

Lester Brown. 2009. *Plan B 4.0: Mobilizing to Save Civilization, Third Edition*. New York: W. W. Norton.

Peter H. Raven, Linda R. Berg, and David M. Hassenzahl. 2009. *Environment*, 7th ed. New York: Wiley.

# CHAPTER 20

# ECONOMIC WELL-BEING

Lacking modern machinery, farm workers in the Philippines till their rice field with water buffalo.
*Source:* UN Photo.

> *If a free society cannot help the many who are poor, it cannot help the few who are rich.*
>
> —John F. Kennedy

Peace implies a state of individual and collective tranquility and satisfaction. But it is very difficult to be tranquil or satisfied when denied such basic needs as food, clothing, shelter, education, heat, and medical care. It is even difficult to establish ethical guidelines—let alone to abide by them—when fundamental necessities are not available. Bertolt Brecht said it clearly (if cynically) in his play *The Threepenny Opera*:

> First feed the face, and then tell right from wrong.
>
> Even noblemen may act like sinners,
>
> Unless they've had their customary dinners.

Moreover, even if their bellies are filled, people are rarely peaceful when they perceive that their economic conditions are far inferior to those of others. Not surprisingly, therefore, there is little peace in a world characterized by painful differences between the haves and the have-nots. Poverty may not lead directly to war, but it certainly is not conducive to peace. Revolutions in particular have been incited and maintained by grinding economic privation. And it seems likely that one of the most important but rarely acknowledged reasons why the rich states maintain large military forces is that they are concerned with preventing any fundamental reorganization in the worldwide distribution of power and wealth. St. Francis, commenting on the "plight" of the wealthy, noted that "he who has property also needs weapons and warriors to defend it."

But most of all, inequality in resources and opportunities is a direct burden on the poor themselves (poor *people* as well as poor *countries*). When poverty is persistent, degrading, miserable, life-shortening, life-threatening, and life-denying, it is an affront to human dignity. The search for peace must accordingly include a search for human economic and social betterment. At the same time, it must be recognized that not all economically "poor" people feel miserable and abused, especially in some Buddhist countries, for example, where material condition is tradi-tionally considered less important than spiritual well-being.

Most of the world's people are so preoccupied with their own immediate problems (of which poverty looms especially large) that such wider preoccupations as nuclear weapons, peace and war, or the condition of the natural environment seem almost irrelevant. Political imagination is typically constrained by such immediate issues: in Latin America, debt, democratization, and poverty; in Africa, famines, displaced persons, debt, epidemics, racial and religious vio-lence; and so forth. The concrete day-to-day struggles of average people to lead tolerable lives occupy most of the energies of most of humanity. Many Americans, by contrast, know what it is to be *hungry* on occasion but have had blessedly little experience with *hunger*.

Efforts to eliminate poverty or—not necessarily the same thing—to maximize wealth have stimulated some of the major socioeconomic ideologies of modern times, notably capitalism and communism. Accordingly, we shall not attempt here to reinvent the wheel by drafting blue-prints for a preferred world economy. We instead try to sketch out some of the primary issues, identify some of the major controversies, and point toward possible courses of action.

Like war, poverty is not an abstraction, although we often speak of it in general terms. Just as there are specific wars, there are specific, flesh-and-blood people and particular regions of especially bleak poverty, even in so-called wealthy countries. As with war, there are also questions of definition and identification: What is poverty? How do regions and countries differ? Is it getting better or worse? Not surprisingly, as in efforts to understand war, there are many different explanations, some of them conflicting in their interpretations and their recommendations.

# The Problem of Poverty

In its simplest terms, poverty exists when people do not have sufficient access to the "good life"; however, this may culturally be defined. Of course, one person's good life is another's luxury. For a middle-class American family, the good life may require two cars, color TVs, at least one satisfying vacation annually, and the ability to send one's children to a college of their choice.

For a resident of Manila's Tondo slum, it may be regular meals, a sewer system, one day off per month, and the ability to keep one's children from dying of diarrhea. The official "poverty level"—in terms of annual income—in the United States would be considered luxury in much of the developing world. (At the same time, consider the following figures for the technologically advanced countries: 80% of global suicides, 74% of heart attacks, 75% of "television zombies," 56% of sexual dysfunction, 98% of illicit drug consumption—out of only 10% of the world's population.)

Despite the favored economic position of the United States, moreover, it does quite poorly on numerous comparative measures of overall "quality of life." In 2011, for example, the United States placed 82nd (below Gabon and ahead of Bangladesh) in *The Economist* magazine's Global Peace Index of 121 nations. This ranking was based on such considerations as percentage of population that is incarcerated, potential for terrorist acts, access to dangerous weapons, crime rates, indicators of citizens' mutual trust, and so on. The top 10 were Iceland, New Zealand, Japan, Denmark, Czech Republic, Austria, Luxemburg, Finland, Canada, and Norway. Just behind the United States was Iran, at 97, and in last place, Somalia, preceded by Iraq, Sudan, Afghanistan, North Korea, Democratic Republic of the Congo, Russia, Pakistan, Israel, and the Central African Republic.

The most dramatic examples of clear-cut poverty on a global scale concern underindustrialized states of the South. Variously labeled "Third World," "underdeveloped," "developing," "have-nots," "lesser developed countries" (LDCs) and so on, it remains clear that these states are significantly poorer than their Northern industrial cousins. It is also clear that they have generally, although not universally, been subject to colonization and exploitation by the wealthier states, at least in the past.

## Physical and Psychological Effects of Poverty

One of the most important, if least recognized, aspects of poverty is its psychological effect, the bitter pill of perceived injustice and inequality that must be swallowed by those who observe the affluence of others while mired in poverty. With increased communication and transportation, even the most isolated people, living traditional and impoverished lives, are exposed to examples of affluence. The results are often deep mental suffering: envy, shame, and either despair or anger. (Moreover, along with "development" in previously impoverished countries, there seems to be an inevitable widening of the gap between rich and poor, as has notably been the case—in the United States as well since the early 1980s.)

Beyond the psychological phenomenon of envy, there is the painful physical fact of deep, absolute poverty. Hunger is the most obvious manifestation. Other deficits usually accompany poverty: Poor housing and inadequate sanitation contribute to disease, as does malnutrition. Health care is minimal or nonexistent. Educational opportunities are very limited, because areas of extreme poverty frequently have few and typically inadequate schools and also because the very poor often need their children to work, so they are denied whatever limited education might otherwise be available. The result is a deepening cycle of poverty, making it even more difficult for such people or their descendants to escape. Not surprisingly, life spans are significantly shorter among the very poor than for the more affluent.

The worldwide economic crisis beginning in 2008 and dubbed the Great Recession has impacted the developed world as well. Thus, a 77-year-old Greek retiree became a national symbol of economic despair when he shot himself in 2012. Even as the U.S. economy began to climb slowly out of this recession—the worst since the Great Depression from 1929 to the late 1930s—it became an increasingly widespread problem in Europe. Countries suffering most acutely from the prolonged economic crisis (notably Greece, Spain, Italy, Ireland, and Portugal)—have experienced a sharp rise in suicides. The suicide rate among Irish men, for example, increased more than 16% from 2007 to 2009, while among Greeks it rose nearly 25% and in Italy, 52%. A similar problem has long been reported among impoverished farmers in India, whose debts have come to exceed their incomes.

## National and Global Inequalities

Poverty may be measured in absolute terms—sheer deprivation of food, poorer health, shortened life expectancy, and so on—or in comparative measures: inequality in the distribution of wealth, such that a small proportion of the population monopolizes more than its share of wealth, leaving the majority with less income and fewer assets per capita. In addition, trends in poverty are also important. The per capita income in most LDCs was lower in 2010, for example, than in 1995. But relative inequality in wealth is perhaps even more appalling, even in the wealthy United States, where the top 20% of the population receives more than 50% of the annual Gross National Product (GNP), while the lowest 40% gets less than 15%. Interestingly, even Soviet-bloc states were not substantially more egalitarian: In Bulgaria, for example, the top 20% earned 33%, and the bottom 40% earned 27%. (States of the former Soviet bloc were actually more equitable than appears from these statistics, however, since health care, education, housing, and some degree of employment were typically guaranteed.)

Within most newly democratizing, fledgling capitalist countries, disparities in wealth have become extraordinarily wide: In Russia, for example, the newly ascendant top 1% of the population controls more than 20% of that country's wealth, while those at the bottom—notably, elderly people on pensions, rural residents, and children—have seen their standard of living plummet as the communist-era socioeconomic safety net has been frayed almost to the point of nonexistence. Russia and many of the now-independent former Soviet republics have a flat income tax, with everyone, regardless of personal wealth or poverty, paying the same percentage of their income; by contrast, tax systems in Europe and—to a lesser extent—the United States are more graduated or "progressive," with wealthier individuals taxed at proportionately higher rates.[1]

The developing world is one of widespread and appalling contrasts, gleaming high-tech development alongside unremitting poverty. Moreover, the absolute gap between global rich and poor is widening. In many cases, the degree of deprivation is hidden by governmental manipulation of statistics. In Chile, for example, instead of assessing malnutrition by considering a child's weight in relation to his or her age, it was long estimated by weight in relation to height; thus, a child whose growth is stunted is declared to be adequately nourished! Examples abound of governmental callousness toward the poor—even in the United States—in part because the poor tend to have very little say in governmental decision making, which generally takes place on behalf of the wealthy and powerful. During the Reagan administration, for example, a notorious effort was made to cut school lunch programs for the poor by declaring ketchup a vegetable.

Although poverty is a worldwide phenomenon, it is not homogeneously distributed. There are poor people living in rich countries (e.g., parts of Appalachia in the United States) and wealthy people in the poorest countries: multimillionaire plantation owners in Bangladesh and the Philippines. Poverty, however, is generally easy to identify, wherever it is found: high unemployment, poor nutrition, inadequate health care and education, little or no savings, high indebtedness, low investment, inadequate housing, and, often, ecologically depleted environments.

A UN Population Fund report for 2011 estimated more than half of the world's population—4 billion people—live in cities. Of these, more than 1 billion live in slums, 90% of them in developing countries; although there is no rigid definition for "slum," it is generally taken to mean an urban area characterized by a lack of sanitation, water, and legal rights to housing. Such areas consistently occupy the worst living places: steep hillsides, riverbanks that periodically flood, and so on. It is also well known that cities concentrate poverty, yet, paradoxically, they also concentrate some of humanity's best hopes of escaping poverty.

Although urban slums are devastating in their impoverishment and typically receive the bulk of public attention, in fact the *favelas* of São Paulo, the *barrios* of Mexico City, and the slums of Cairo, Kinshasa, or Karachi are a relatively recent phenomenon; despite their terrible squalor, the urban poor are generally better off, statistically speaking, than their rural counterparts. This is part of the reason why Third World cities are doubling in size every 10 to 15 years, as impoverished landless peasants flock there, creating situations that become ever more desperate and unmanageable. Even now, however, more than 65% of the world's poor still live in rural villages, in India, China, Africa, Indonesia, and so on. Ten percent of the world's population—more than 700 million people—live in rural India alone. Among the rural poor, illiteracy and the great epidemic diseases—malaria, cholera, and tuberculosis—are at an all-time low, but the good things in life (and some of the necessities, such as an adequate diet) are no more available now than they were before.

Historically, rural interests have been overrepresented in Western democratic republics, notably in England and the United States. By contrast, rural people—especially the very poor—are underrepresented in political and economic decision making in less-developed countries. The rural poor tend to be ignored because their poverty makes them less influential within the "corridors of power" in faraway cities and also because the rural poor are especially likely to be seen as irrelevant as well as an embarrassment to those elite decision makers who look to the wealthy North for material goods, for images of their country's future, and—not least—for their own advancement.

Although the United States is, by many measures, the wealthiest country in the world, it does not rank very high regarding socioeconomic equity: 5th in worldwide literacy rate, 7th in public school expenditures per capita, 8th in public health expenditures per capita, 14th in life expectancy, 16th in percentage of women enrolled in universities, 18th in infant mortality rate (lower than Cuba, incidentally), and 20th in teachers per school-age population. From 2000 to 2007, incomes for the bottom 90% of earners rose only about 4%, once adjusted for inflation. For the top 0.1%, incomes climbed about 94%. In 2010, the top 10% of earners took about half of overall income. There are more homeless people on the streets of the United States than in China, and an estimated 20 million Americans are functionally illiterate. In the richest country in human history, 1 child in 5 lives in poverty.

## Causes of Poverty

"The rich are different from you and I," the eminent American writer F. Scott Fitzgerald is said to have commented to his fellow writer Ernest Hemingway, whereupon Hemingway responded, "Yes, they have more money."

It is not terribly useful to conclude that poverty is caused by an absence of money. But what, then, are its underlying causes? There have been many explanations. In certain cases, the natural resources of a country are so inadequate that wealth is virtually impossible to create. The African state of Chad, for example, is so arid as to be agriculturally unproductive; it also lacks significant mineral resources. By contrast, wealthy countries such as the United States tend to be resource rich. But this argument is not altogether satisfying: Japan, for example, has relatively few natural resources, yet despite recent setbacks it is an economic giant. The same is true of Hong Kong, South Korea, Singapore, and Taiwan, as well as such wealthy but resource-poor European states as Belgium and the Netherlands. In a sense, some can be considered especially resource rich (Venezuela, Norway, Saudi Arabia, and Kuwait), while others are capital rich (Singapore, Luxembourg, Hong Kong, Taiwan, and Japan). Some—notably the United States—are rich in both resources and capital, whereas others—Chad and Bangladesh—appear to be poor in both. Clearly, resources alone do not explain everything.

Roughly 70% of those who are profoundly impoverished—sometimes called the "bottom billion"—live in sub-Saharan Africa. Explosive economic growth in Asia, although certainly not equally distributed throughout the populations of, for example, India, South Korea, Thailand, and so forth, has nonetheless largely outstripped Africa in terms of the availability of inexpensive labor. Average life expectancy for the bottom billion is less than 50 years, among whom 1 in 7 children dies before age 5. What to do? Some progressive Western economists argue that what is especially needed are improved agricultural policies based on widely available, appropriate technology, such as person-operated well pumps, devices for producing fresh water, inexpensive photoelectric systems, antimalarial mosquito nets, and antiretroviral drugs for those afflicted with AIDS. Others continue to blame the legacy of Western colonialism as well as endemic political corruption by which the wealth of LDCs is often skimmed off and deposited in the personal bank accounts of a small number of political and military leaders.

Yet another likely culprit is war, especially civil war. The World Bank has described war as "development in reverse," and in fact nearly three-quarters of the bottom billion either are in the midst of civil war or have only recently emerged from one. War breeds poverty, and poverty in turn makes people more likely to engage in civil war. Moreover, once a civil war has occurred, it is more likely to be repeated. The risks of civil war are also increased by a high proportion of young, uneducated, and unemployed men; by an imbalance of power among ethnic groups; and, ironically, by a supply of natural resources that exempts rulers from investing in their people (e.g., oil in the Middle East and Nigeria or diamonds in Sierra Leone).

## Government Policies

Government policies can also influence poverty, in either direction. Many analysts have attempted to explain the "economic miracle" of Japan (even though the Japanese economy suffered during the 1990s, it remains one of the strongest on Earth). There seems little doubt that social organization—in Japan's case, most notably a powerful work ethic as well as comparatively little defense spending—helped boost economic productivity, as it did in postwar Germany. Alternatively, where poverty is widespread and has existed for thousands of years with little sign of improvement, a kind of fatalistic lethargy often sets in. Government policies can have substantial impact in such cases, either encouraging grassroots self-help or deepening the plight of a country's majority. The Democratic Republic of Congo, for example, is "rich" as measured by natural resources. Yet 80% of Congolese are desperately poor, and real wages are only about one-tenth what they were at the time of its independence in 1960. At least some of the responsibility must be borne by longtime dictator Mobutu Sese Seku, who stole more than $5 billion directly from the national treasury. National wealth was similarly plundered by the likes of Ferdinand Marcos in the Philippines and Suharto in Indonesia.

Fiscal mismanagement and irresponsibility—often bolstered by a rigid adherence to discredited ideology—have also resulted in economic degradation. An example is Romania, a country abundantly endowed with natural resources (notably oil) but that was reduced to poverty by the destructive Stalinist-style policies of the former strongman Nikolai Ceauşescu. Zimbabwe (formerly Rhodesia) suffers from 1,000% annual inflation and an agricultural economy—once vibrant—that can no longer feed itself; it seems undeniable that the predatory policies of dictator Robert Mugabe have been largely to blame. Zimbabwe appears to be an example of economic collapse due to corruption and social and/or economic insensitivity rather than adherence to a clear-cut ideology.

Political leaders frequently take power by promising to advocate for the oppressed and underprivileged. Once in office, however, rulers often find it advantageous to cater to the powerful (i.e., in most cases, the wealthy). There are many reasons for such policy shifts, including keeping the military happy (thereby allowing the government to remain in power), satisfying the demands of foreign bankers, notably the World Bank and the International Monetary Fund, which typically insist on domestic fiscal "austerity" in return for loans or debt relief, as well as the lure of personal payoffs. Short of revolution or the overt threat of it, the very poor generally have a disproportionately small voice in government decision making.

## Political Ideology

Social and political factors can also contribute to income disparities. According to Marxists, capitalism itself is largely to blame: Capitalist societies are stratified by economic class, with the owners of corporations exploiting the workers, thereby keeping them underprivileged, divided, and poor. According to mainstream capitalist economic theory, wealth is most likely to be generated by an unfettered free market and poverty results from lack of effort, will, or ability; from bad luck; or from the allegedly negative influence of government interference. According to the classical economist Adam Smith, private enterprise, if left to its own devices, will act as though guided by an "unseen hand," producing the maximum economic good for the greatest number of people. Implicit in capitalist economic theory is the idea that some people will inevitably do less well than others, a difference that is presumably due at least in part to unavoidable differences between them. From this perspective, it is therefore not the job of society to establish socioeconomic equality. Moreover, if government intervenes to redistribute wealth, this will not only diminish the efficiency with which new wealth is produced, it also constitutes a major blow to individual liberty.

Even most capitalist societies, however, do not subscribe to classic *laissez-faire* theories, in which governments are expected to take a purely hands-off attitude. Various "safety net programs" have been established in the United States—for example, Head Start, Temporary Assistance to Needy Families (TANF, the successor to Aid to Families with Dependent Children), Medicare, Medicaid, and "Obamacare." Most other Western democracies are substantially more involved in their economies, especially at the federal level, seeking to maintain and improve the lot of their poorest citizens. In the past, conservative ideologies attributed poverty to alleged natural individual inferiority; more recently, the scapegoating tends to be more subtle, pointing to cultural circumstances such as single parent families and thereby relieving government of its social responsibility.

It used to be thought that democracy and capitalism inevitably go together—as appeared to be the case with the United States. But in fact, recent experience suggests that neither necessarily sets the stage for the other: China has increasing capitalism and high economic growth but nothing approaching democracy, at least not at the national level. Ditto for Singapore. Other countries, such as Peru, have taken substantial steps toward democracy but have experienced relatively disappointing growth. Whatever its connection to economic growth, capitalism typically leads to increased inequality, which in turn is not conducive to democracy. Similarly, political democracy—as in Ukraine—doesn't necessarily produce capitalist success, widespread prosperity, or even economic equality (as in the United States).

## Poverty and War

The relationship between poverty and war is complex. Preparing for war occasionally yields economic benefits: Many advances in the aircraft and electronics industries, for example, were stimulated by military research and development. But on balance, it is clear that domestic social progress, if such were the goal, would be produced far more effectively by targeting investment explicitly at domestic needs. Moreover, considering the immense destructiveness of war itself, on balance war is impoverishing. It is essentially a parasite, feeding off the economic and social strength of societies. Like most parasites, it weakens its host until either—or both—die. There is also little evidence that poverty leads to war. In fact, the cause-and-effect relationship may well be in the opposite direction, with impoverished countries being less likely to make war, if only because in an age of elaborate military technology, the equipping of strong military forces requires substantial resources . . . unless, as in the case of North Korea, a government is willing to literally starve its population while fattening its army.

# Socioeconomic Development

"Development" has long been seen as the key to LDCs' economic future. As President John F. Kennedy put it, "A rising tide lifts all boats." The idea is to improve the economic situation in the world generally, as a result of which some economic benefits would be enjoyed by everyone, including the poorest countries and the most deprived segments of society. In a bit of U.S. political jargon from 1980s "Reaganomics," a dynamic world economy would generate benefits that "trickle down" to all inhabitants. On the other hand, it must be pointed out that when one is chained to the bottom, a rising tide can be rather frightening! Moreover, famed U.S. labor leader George Meany once noted that during his decades as a licensed plumber, he had seen lots of things trickle down—but money wasn't one of them.

## Growth and Modernization

During its heyday in the 1960s and 1970s, neoliberal development theory, claimed that economic progress would spread from the industrialized states to the LDCs, and foreign aid, as well as enhanced trade and credit provided by the North, would help speed the process. Instead of dividing up the global pie differently, wealthy states would simply help bake a larger pie.

Development theory is closely allied to classical free-enterprise economic models, which espouse the basic theme of "grow now, redistribute later (if at all . . . )." Developing countries, according to this view, should strive to attract foreign capital and to emphasize efficiency and economic growth—not equity—as their goals. There have been some dramatic success stories in such development models, notably the so-called Asian Tigers: Hong Kong, Singapore, South Korea, and Taiwan, as well as the Asian giants of India and China. Moreover, those economies least integrated into the world free-market system, such as North Korea and, until recently, Myanmar (Burma), have been among the least dynamic.

## Disappointments

Development theory still persists in various forms, although the great majority of poor countries have not had positive experiences with growth and development in recent decades. This in turn has led to dissatisfaction and increasingly militant demands for economic equity and redistribution of the world's wealth by many poor people and even by some socialist-led governments, particularly in Latin America.

One of the major disappointments of development has been a phenomenon sometimes referred to as *marginalization,* whereby increases in the size of the middle and upper classes are actually accompanied by deeper poverty on the part of the very poor. It seems there will always be *relative* poverty—with some people at the poorer end of the income spectrum—just as there will always be those who are comparatively wealthy. The tragedy of marginalization is that it involves an increase in *absolute* poverty. In short, the benefits of economic growth in the poorest countries typically do not reach the lowest levels of society, with the poorest of the poor pushed more and more to the margins of subsistence. Whatever its causes and correlates, the distressing fact remains that in many, if not most, cases development has been an abject failure, as the already low-income poor face *declining* incomes.

## Globalization

Dramatic advances in communication and transportation, plus the remarkable growth of computer technology, have provided impetus for the denationalization of economies and the advent of *globalization.* In a globalized economy, a product may be designed in Italy, fabricated in Malaysia using raw materials from Brazil, and then sold in Australia—to the economic benefit of a corporation based in Chicago! Not surprisingly, globalization is a two-edged sword. On the positive side, it offers the prospect of some employment for impoverished people in nonindustrial countries and, thus, a possible "hand up" in their lives. It may connect such people to the world economy and/or to international communication via the Internet, and it may involve them and their government leaders in a web of interconnections that promises to break down parochialism and reduce the likelihood of armed conflicts. But there are also negative aspects to globalization.

For example, in the absence of carefully enforced international standards, multinational corporations are tempted to scour the globe for the lowest-paid workforce, for the most marginal worker safety and health benefits, and for minimal and sometimes nonexistent environmental protections. The ensuing "race to the bottom" benefits such corporations and—in the short run—consumers, since products can therefore be produced cheaply. At the same time, higher-paid, better-protected workers (as in the United States and, increasingly, in Western Europe) suffer in return, as their jobs disappear, while low-paid workers in poor countries are denied basic and essential protections. In addition, excessive focus on the elimination of trade barriers has caused a lowering of environmental standards (since they, like labor standards, have often been judged to be "unfair restraints on trade").

One source of the world's economic dislocation following the 2008 Great Recession has been the integration of billions of low-wage workers (notably in China and India) into the global economy, as well as increases in productivity stemming from the successful application of information technology and robotics to the manufacturing sector. These developments, in turn, have pushed global production capacity much higher than demand, taking a heavy toll on economies in the industrialized West, where formerly high-paying jobs have been replaced by low-paying service sector jobs, or unemployment. In addition, the nature of "production" has had a depressing effect on job-creation. In 2011, for example, Facebook's estimated value was around $70 billion; this company has roughly 2,000 employees. By contrast, General Motors, valued at about $35 billion, has nearly 80,000 employees in the United States and more than 200,000 worldwide. As a result of such disparities, compared to an earlier generation of industry, much of the wealth of U.S. cutting-edge companies has been much less likely to "trickle down" to the middle class, which has been shrinking since the Great Recession, which began in 2008.

From the end of World War II until the early 1990s, the primary vehicle for globalization was GATT, the General Agreement on Tariffs and Trade. Currently, such issues are taken up by the World Trade Organization, which has concerned itself almost exclusively with lowering trade barriers between countries. Globalization has the potential to help alleviate some world poverty while protecting worker rights and the environment; thus far, however, it has not lived up to these hopes and instead has tended to enhance corporate profits over human and environmental values.

Some countries have begun to move away from a simple pro-growth-and-development model. Sri Lanka, for example, succeeded in significantly reducing abject poverty by devoting half of its national budget to free rice, education, and health services and to subsidized food and transportation. As a result, life expectancy there has risen dramatically, approaching that of more "developed" countries. (Tragically, ethnic conflict between Tamil and Sinhalese interfered with and, to some degree, overshadowed these remarkable social accomplishments. With the apparent defeat of the "Tamil Tiger" rebels in 2010—at the cost of tens of thousands of civilian casualties and massive human rights abuses—perhaps Sri Lanka will be able to focus once again on socioeconomic development for all its citizens.)

## *Dependencia* Theory

This alternative perspective on international poverty originally derived from the economic situation in Latin America, a region that has long tended to be economically, politically, and militarily subservient to the United States. Under the influence of progressive economic theorists such as Andre Gunder Frank, the term *dependencia,* based on the Spanish word for dependency, has also been applied to other regions, wherever indigenous peoples and resources are believed by many social critics to be exploited by the wealthier, industrialized states of the North.

The basic idea of *dependencia* is that poverty in what peace researcher Johan Galtung and sociologist Immanuel Wallerstein have called the "periphery" (the less industrialized South) occurs in large part because of affluence by the "center" or "core" (the industrialized North). Poor countries are thus not so much underdeveloped as overexploited, such that their poverty is not a result of neglect by the wealthy North but of too much attention. Such countries as the Democratic Republic of Congo, Indonesia, Brazil, India, and Malaysia are rich; only their people are poor!

According to *dependencia* theory, not only did the North exploit the South overtly during the days of colonialism but such exploitation has continued, covertly, even after outright imperial control was terminated. Even now, the wealthy, powerful North takes advantage of the South by manipulating markets, credit, and trade balances. In the past, repressive control was exerted directly, by armed forces of occupation. Such control is currently indirect, through surrogate local rulers (the so-called *comprador* class), who are clients of the wealthy states and who profit personally by impoverishing their own people while being essentially in league with the Northern powers. As a result, people in most LDCs are victimized directly by their own governments, as well as indirectly by the industrialized states. Unlike the relationship between, say, the United States and France, in which benefits often flow in both directions, exchanges between either of these wealthy Northern powers and Mauritania, for example, are likely to be exploitative and distinctly one-sided.

## The Debt Problem

In addition to poverty, most of the world's nonindustrialized countries have another problem, one that saps revenues, limits domestic spending options, and sits like a troll inhibiting progress along the path of economic betterment: debt. Forced to pay billions of dollars annually out of national economies that barely keep their heads above water, these countries have little hope of achieving prosperity for most of their citizens, since they are literally unable to invest in their own economies.

The debt crisis was precipitated several decades ago, in large part by a widespread recession among the wealthy states. The stage was set during the 1970s, as costs skyrocketed for petroleum, weapons, and food—all of which were purchased by developing countries, in part using funds that Northern banks eagerly made available. By the 1980s, interest rates rose dramatically while commodity prices plummeted, whereupon debtor states found themselves increasingly hard-pressed to meet the interest payments on their loans. Ever since, poor countries have fallen ever farther behind in their capacity to pay; their plight has been like that of the coal workers in the folk song "Sixteen Tons": "You load sixteen tons and what do you get? Another day older and deeper in debt."

Under certain circumstances, the chief international lending agency, the International Monetary Fund, has allowed this crushing debt burden to be rescheduled, but only if the debtor country agrees to "austerity programs," which typically require drastic cutbacks in government subsidies of food, transportation, health care, and education, as well as anti-inflation policies that substantially increase unemployment and underemployment. A related strategy has been to provide new loans to enable debtors to pay the interest on old ones—a "solution" that is unlikely to inspire much long-term confidence.

The human cost of international debt has been staggering. A United Nations Children's Fund (UNICEF) report estimated that approximately 500,000 children die annually because of economic decline or stagnation in the world's poorest states, conditions that generate government cutbacks in basic health services, primary education, and food and fuel subsidies. These reductions have taken place while family incomes for a billion people have been *declining,* especially in Africa and southern Asia. Under these circumstances, some of the most impoverished and indebted states have begun to threaten default on their loans. One alternative—debt forgiveness—has been proposed by several religious institutions (notably the Roman Catholic Church) but with little prospect of widespread enactment.

As a result of the Great Recession that began in 2008, developed countries have also begun to suffer under a burden of debt, which in turn has led to further frictions. For example, a growing source of friction between the United States and China has been the perceived Chinese reluctance to raise the value of their currency, the remninbi, or at least, allow it to fluctuate on the open market. If they did, and if the remninbi went up, Chinese products would in turn be more expensive, which would mean reduced purchase by the United States and other countries, which in turn, would diminish the purchasers' trade imbalances and foreign debt. Disputes have also emerged within developed countries over economic policies, with Western conservatives arguing for "austerity" (less government spending on social programs, reduced pension allowances, and so forth), while progressives argue for an emphasis on growth, to be achieved by government stimulation of demand.

## Ethics and Equity

Amid these conflicting ideologies and attempts, a fundamental question remains: Why should the wealthy states agree to forgive the debt burden of poor countries or, indeed, to any policies designed to reduce worldwide inequality? Do wealthy countries have any obligation toward poor ones? An extension of laissez-faire capitalism and the ideology of "rugged individualism" is that poverty is the unavoidable consequence of differences (among countries no less than among individuals) and that inequality should be not only tolerated but also even celebrated, since it indicates that "merit" is being rewarded. By this argument, it is in fact unethical to redistribute wealth, since such redistribution necessarily involves taking away resources that rightfully belong to someone while conferring it on others who are unworthy; otherwise, they wouldn't be in such need.

But there are many reasons for opposing inequalities in global wealth. One is the notion of distributive justice—that is, the ethical conviction that gross inequity is of itself unfair, even when it might not be the result of unjust practices. Certainly, there is something ethically repugnant about the spectacle of dire, life-threatening poverty coexisting with extreme luxury. For some, it is a moral imperative based essentially on charity: When suffering exists, people have a duty to alleviate it.

Ethicist and political philosopher John Rawls developed a theory of rights, according to which "social and economic inequalities are to be arranged so that they are . . . to the greatest benefit of the least advantaged." In his influential book, *A Theory of Justice,* Rawls proposed that we evaluate any social institution from "behind the veil of ignorance"—that is, that we consider every system as though we have no foreknowledge as to our own specific place within that system: Not knowing whether we would be privileged or not, how would we feel about being part of a given social form? (Our view of the Hindu caste system would probably be affected, for example, if we had a high probability of being an "untouchable.")

Moreover, it is not unreasonable to suggest that the poverty of the many is connected to the extreme wealth of the privileged few. Wealth amidst poverty is often the result of extortion, theft, unmerited good luck, and so on. But beyond the issue of fairness and merit, there looms the question of distributive justice. Should society intervene to ensure equitable distribution of wealth? Alternatively, should certain minimum levels of economic welfare be established? If so, how? And what should they include: housing, education, medical care, guaranteed employment? How, under such systems, could societies make room for individual initiative and ensure that people will contribute their "fair share"?

A classic Marxist maxim is "from each according to his ability, to each according to his need." But in practice, it has proven difficult to assess and reward need and even more difficult to induce people to contribute according to their ability, unless they perceive that a direct personal benefit will flow from their labors. This is one reason for the relatively low productivity of most officially Communist economies. (China, although ostensibly communist and experiencing extraordinarily high rates of economic growth, has in fact become capitalist in many areas of its economy.) Beyond this, is it necessarily true that everyone should be treated equally? With respect to legal entitlements or political rights, most people would agree that the answer is Yes. But in other respects, it is clearly No: Criminals, for instance, are treated differently from law-abiding citizens. What about reward for special effort or skill? Is inequality of compensation in itself unjust? And what about unequal wages between farmer and factory worker, computer entrepreneur and common laborer, villager and city dweller, Eskimo and Polynesian? Is economic inequality any more acceptable between different countries than within a single country?

# Hunger

## The Extent of the Problem

Approximately 15% to 20% of the human population suffers from malnutrition, primarily insufficient protein and/or calories. About 70% of the world's hunger is found in nine countries: India, Bangladesh, Pakistan, Indonesia, the Philippines, Congo, Cambodia, Brazil, and Ethiopia.

The average inhabitant of southern Asia consumes fewer than 2,000 calories per day, as compared with more than 3,000 for the average American. The average Asian consumes about 400 pounds of grain per year, almost all of it directly as grain. The average American, by contrast, consumes an extraordinary 2,000 pounds of grain per year, but of this only about 150 pounds are eaten directly as grain (the most energy-efficient way); about 100 pounds are consumed as alcohol, and most of the remainder is eaten much less efficiently, as meat. When calories are transferred from grain to livestock and the meat eaten by human beings, between three-fourths and nine-tenths of those calories are lost. Approximately 1 billion people are chronically undernourished, while worldwide food imports have increased, reinforcing dependence as well as vulnerability to droughts, hurricanes, floods, earthquakes, and other natural catastrophes.

Unfortunately, per capita food production in many impoverished states, notably in central Africa, actually went *down* in recent decades, at least in part because, being poor, such states cannot afford modern agricultural technology: Rice yields in India and Nigeria, for example, are only one-third of those in Japan. Approximately one-tenth of the world's land surface is now under cultivation, but little increase can be anticipated, since most of the remaining land is desert, mountain, arctic, or otherwise uncultivable. Nonetheless, despite serious problems of desertification, erosion, and pollution, worldwide agriculture raises two-and-a-half times the grain needed for human consumption. The problem is, accordingly, inadequate distribution rather than under-production of foodstuffs. Inequities in such consumption, however, are dramatic.

## A Matter of Distribution

To a large extent, the problem of world hunger is not really so much a production problem as it is a *distribution* problem. In Mexico, for example, where as many as 80% of the country's rural children are undernourished and livestock consumes more grain than the entire rural population, nearly all of which becomes meat then exported to the United States. Throughout much of Africa, land that once grew sorghum and corn—for local consumption—is now owned by multi-national agribusiness conglomerates and used for the production of cotton and coffee for export. Local people are thereby denied native grains even as they are left unable to pay for imported wheat and rice. People may have desperate needs, but, in classical economic terms, this doesn't constitute "demand" unless they can pay for what they want. When poor countries are capable of production, there is a tendency to make luxury goods (for export) to be consumed by the rich instead of necessities for domestic consumption.

Fewer than 3% of the world's landowners—many of them absentee and/or large agribusiness firms—own nearly 75% of all the Earth's cultivatable land. In some areas, this inequity is even greater: 1% of the population of northeast Brazil, for example, owns 45% of the land, much of it used to grow sugar, which generates money for the owners but provides virtually no food for the population. Peasant farmers, desperate to raise their own food, find themselves forced to cultivate erosion-prone hillsides and infertile terrain, which in turn are quickly depleted, leading to ecological ruin and yet more poverty and famine.

Subsistence farmers typically rely on their own seed—derived from this season's crops—to provide for the next season's planting. Agribusiness companies have developed "sterile" plant strains, requiring that new seeds be purchased every year. Although public outrage resulted in recall of these "innovations," they indicate the pervasive and continuing conflict between corporate profit and human need. The politics of scarcity, which dominates the lives of most "Third World" people, have rarely been examined in the overfed "First World." At the same time, even as the wealthy nations have a burgeoning obesity epidemic—particularly among their poorest citizens because of growing consumption of low-quality, high-fat "junk foods" combined with insufficient exercise—a similar public health problem has ironically begun to emerge among many of the world's poorest countries.

## Measuring Wealth, Poverty, and Income Inequality

It is generally agreed that per capita GNP is a useful index of wealth by which different countries or regions can be compared. Alternatively, if the value of imports and exports is omitted, we have Gross Domestic Product (GDP). If we take GDP as a percentage of Total World Product, we get a measure of the extent to which a country or a region enjoys more, or suffers from less, than "its share" of the world total. To be meaningful, this figure should then be adjusted for population in each country or region. When this is done, we obtain the "coefficient of advantage"—the percentage of total world product obtained, per capita, by a given country or region. For example, North America contains about 5.5% of the world's population; it obtains, however, 30.5% of the world's GNP, for a coefficient of advantage of 30.5/5.5 = 5.5. By contrast, Africa has 8.7% of the world's population but only 2.0% of the world's GNP, for a coefficient of (dis)advantage of 2.0/8.8 = 0.23. A coefficient of advantage of 1.0 would indicate an equitable per capita division of the world's resources. (It should be noted, however, that even in this case, divisions of wealth *within* countries or regions could still be extreme.)

Another important index—the Gini coefficient—is widely used to measure degree of inequality within a larger unit, most commonly a country. Although the actual calculation of Gini coefficients is mathematically complex, the basics can readily be understood. It is essentially a measure of dispersion (thus conceptually similar to standard deviation and variance, as used in basic statistics). The lower Gini coefficient, the more equal the distribution, with 0 corresponding to absolute equality in which everyone has exactly the same income. Higher Gini coefficients indicate more *unequal* distribution, with 1 corresponding to complete inequality, in which a single person gets all of the total income and everyone else gets nothing.

The world's Gini coefficient is estimated to be about 0.6 and the Gini coefficient of the United States is around 0.46. European countries generally have lower Gini coefficients, whereas those of Latin America and Africa are considerably higher. Gini coefficients can also be calculated for land ownership, family wealth, and so forth. When this is done, interesting patterns emerge. For example, the Gini coefficient for European land ownership is substantially higher than for annual income, which reflects historical patterns: The concentration of land ownership in Europe is a holdover from the preindustrial, feudal era, when a landed aristocracy held sway. By contrast, income has become more equalized as a result of industrialization and the success of labor unions. In much of Southeast Asia, agriculture is relatively intensive, with large numbers of small private holdings, but also fabulously wealthy princes, merchants, manufacturers, and miserable impoverished landless peasants. In much of Latin America and Africa, land ownership and wealth coincide, largely through ranching, plantations, and/or mines, leaving the vast majority with neither land nor income. One consequence of this inequality, in addition to its manifest unfairness, is the likelihood that many of these countries—especially perhaps those that are comparative newcomers to democracy—may well find themselves politically fragile.

# Population

Positive peace involves a web of interconnected relationships. This is especially true of the population problem. Population—the sheer press of human numbers—makes itself felt in every aspect of the human condition, including many aspects of economics and environmental and human rights.

The negative impact that human beings exert on their environment is largely a function of technology: Compare the relatively slight damage done to a tropical rain forest, for example, by 10,000 indigenous hunters, gatherers, and horticulturists, who have lived in relative balance with the forest for thousands of years, with the massive damage wrought by 10,000 people armed with bulldozers, dynamite, asphalt, and guns, who threaten to destroy whole ecosystems in a matter of years.

Even among nonindustrialized countries using minimal technology, expanding population threatens to destroy major wildlife populations because of habitat destruction (e.g., the fencing and plowing of land otherwise needed for jaguar habitat in Belize) and hunting (e.g., poaching of elephants and rhinos in Tanzania). Too many people in too small a space results in too much consumption, which in turn pollutes the air and water, creates unmanageable quantities of solid waste, and threatens to exceed the productive capacity of any given region—and, ultimately, the entire planet—to provide nourishment, decent living conditions, and an acceptable environment. The Earth's resources are limited; even with extraordinary new technological innovations—which might not materialize—the demands of an indefinitely expanding human population simply cannot be met. Many environmental problems can be ameliorated in the short term by social, political, and technological innovations, but even with the best of policies, there must ultimately be a stabilization of the human population or else no solutions will hold for the long haul.

This is especially true of attempts at economic self-betterment. All too often, countries seem poised to make real gains in their living standards only to have the progress nullified by an exploding population. No country can "pull itself up by its bootstraps" if the weight of the human population is so great as to tear those straps.

## Some Trends in Population Growth

The human species, *Homo sapiens,* is estimated to be at least several hundred thousand years old. World population, however, did not reach the 1 billion mark until about the year 1600. This increase was due largely to the Agricultural Revolution, begun around 8000 BCE with the domestication of plants and animals. This in turn resulted in better diets and more reliable food supplies. After that long journey to the first billion, it took only 300 years to add the next billion, which happened around 1900, stimulated in large part by the Industrial Revolution (which made energy available via mechanization and the use of fossil fuels), as well as advances in public hygiene and vaccination. The third billion arrived in just one-sixth that time, in 1950, and the fourth by 1975. Human population reached 5 billion in the 1980s, 6 billion at the beginning of the 21st century and 7 billion in 2011. It is still climbing. The United Nations estimated in 2011 that world population will stabilize at 10 billion in 2100, assuming that birthrates will decline and eventually yield a global average of 2.1 children per woman. At a rate of even 2.6, that number rises to 16 billion.

In short, not only has the world population been growing but the rate of that increase itself increased, because, as the English economist Malthus pointed out, human population increases geometrically (or exponentially).

This rate of worldwide population increase has slowed in recent years, although because the total population has continued to grow, *the actual number added per year has increased.* In some cases—notably, the developed economies of the West—population levels are stabilizing and even declining, a trend that generates hope in the minds of some while alarming others. It is anticipated, for example, that the U.S. population may decline slightly by the mid-21st century based on birthrates but not counting possible immigration. Similarly, the population of most northern European states is expected to decline by as much as 10% by the year 2025. Some effects of declining birthrate in these countries are already apparent, including the accommodation of increasing numbers of "guest workers" from Turkey, Iran, northern Africa, and Asia, along with attendant ethnic and racial tension and a rise in right-wing, neofascist ideology on the part of some indigenous Europeans.

On balance, however, total world population seems destined to increase dramatically, doubling in another 40 years. About 30% of the world's people live in developed countries, although the percentage of world population increase attributable to these countries is less than 10%. The world adds the equivalent of Mexico—an additional 100 million people—every year, with more than 90% of this growth occurring among the poorest countries. Indeed, "the rich get richer while the poor get children." To maintain a constant population size, women must bear, on average, two surviving children in their lifetime. The U.S. average is 1.8, but in rapidly expanding populations, such as Nigeria and Kenya, the numbers reach a whopping 6.6 and 8.0, respectively. The cause of this increase is an excess of births over deaths, which leads to a deepening of the planetary ecological crisis plus increasing poverty for rapidly growing populations.

Dramatic population growth has had results that are little short of cataclysmic, making a mockery of efforts at economic and environmental self-improvement. For example, in Nigeria, the most populous country in Africa, the population has grown from 43 million in 1950 to 155 million persons, and by 2025 that number is expected to swell to more than 300 million, at which time a population about equal to the present-day United States will occupy an area the size of Arizona and New Mexico. Nigeria's current unemployment rate for people aged 15 to 24 is nearly 50% in its urban areas . . . which in turn has generated increased crime and discontent. It is believed, for example, that increasing numbers of unemployed youth have contributed to the rapid growth of Boko Haram, a radical Islamist group that has recently burned or bombed numerous churches and schools.

Sub-Saharan Africa has been particularly hard-hit by an exploding population. Thus, there are currently about 20 countries in which the lifetime birthrate per woman exceeds five; nearly all are in sub-Saharan Africa. And whereas per capita GDP increased between three- and sixfold in North Africa, Latin America, and Asia, as population numbers began to level off, it has increased only marginally if at all in many African countries, even where economic growth has been rapid overall. The problem is that population growth has been more rapid yet. There is a scene in Lewis Carroll's *Through the Looking Glass* in which Alice is urged by the Red Queen to run—but she doesn't get anywhere. The Red Queen explains that when things are moving so quickly, one must run in order to stay where you are; to get anywhere, it is necessary to run even faster! (In response, the Nigerian government made contraceptives free in 2011; social pressures, however, evidently restrict their use.) There is also this danger: that in countries such as Nigeria, the existing rich-poor inequality will be enhanced as richer families have fewer children, who in turn are granted more per capita advantages, while the poor have many children who grow up to be even poorer adults in turn.

Some people contend that concern about overpopulation—especially when the worried parties are Caucasian—is actually a concealed form of racism; this accusation is at least plausible, since rapid population increases are largely occurring in Africa, Latin America, and parts of Asia. But the costs of overpopulation are borne overwhelmingly by the poor and marginalized people who are already overcrowded and among whom overpopulation relative to social and environmental resources is responsible for much of the distress. Countries in which resources are already stretched to the limit are required, by virtue of their expanding human numbers, to increase demands on water, soil, wildlife habitat, education, and health and other human service budgets, which are already dangerously depleted. Struggling, debt-ridden governments have in many cases already reached or surpassed their abilities to provide even basic services to their people. In 1969, for example, Mexico City had a population of 9 million people; in 2011, there were more than 21 million residents. Other "megacities" include Mumbai, Cairo, Shanghai, São Paulo, Karachi, Jakarta, and Dhaka, all in developing countries.

Continued high population growth in the poorer countries will not only prevent a closing of the economic gap between rich and poor; it also will actually *widen* that gap. The rates of *income* growth in rich and poor countries are roughly comparable; accordingly, it is the different rate of *population* growth that keeps the latter from catching up. This problem is particularly acute in the Indian subcontinent, Africa, and parts of Latin America.

## The Demographic-Economic-Environmental Trap

There is a real danger that some states may never emerge from what might be termed the "demographic-economic-environmental trap." In these cases, rapid population growth contributes to increased demands on natural and socioeconomic systems, which are then overtaxed and begin to collapse. People commonly respond by having more children, in turn leading to increased ecological and socioeconomic pressures, which ultimately further impoverishes the land and the people, leading to increased mortality, notably from starvation and epidemics, and possibly to direct violence as well.

Population levels, ecological factors, and economic conditions are all intimately related. Thus, every environment can be said to have a *carrying capacity*: the number of people who can be supported by the soil, forests, grassland, croplands, water, and other resource supplies of that region. If demand exceeds carrying capacity, the effect is of "mining capital" rather than "living off one's interest." It cannot be sustained for long. For example, in many areas of the world, wood is used for fuel. More people result in more demand for wood, which leads to cutting, often in excess of the amount that grows annually. As forests dwindle, wood becomes scarce and expensive, adding to the misery of the poor who can little afford it, while the deforestation itself seriously diminishes wildlife values, contributes to global warming, and generates erosion and downstream flooding. (Devastating floods in Bangladesh have become commonplace, periodically killing tens of thousands and making hundreds of thousands of people homeless, due to the destruction of forests in the foothills of the Himalayas above that country.)

Another significant consequence of the demographic-economic-environmental trap is the production of large numbers of so-called eco-refugees, people who are forced to leave their ancestral homes because of environmental degradation. Land-hungry farmers are increasingly driven onto wildlife preserves and marginal land that is highly erodible and easily destroyed. The result is *desertification,* a process that is distinct from drought. In this case, overgrazing, overplowing, and deforestation destroy the productivity of the soil, on which whole ecosystems depend. The process is accentuated by natural drought, to which weakened and overcrowded people are especially susceptible. The increasing numbers of eco-refugees congregate in cities and refugee centers, where they rely on government assistance and are highly susceptible to disease and—as has occurred in drought-stricken sub-Saharan Africa—massive starvation when and if relief efforts run into political, economic, or logistic difficulties.

Uncontrolled population growth in subsistence economies threatens not only the country's environment but also its social and economic system. Universal public education becomes virtually impossible when school systems are drowned beneath a tidal wave of youngsters.

When population is constant or declining slightly (as in Germany, Sweden and Switzerland), a 2% increase in economic growth results in increased overall per capita prosperity; when the population increases by 3% or 4%, that same 2% economic growth results in painfully *declining* living standards for most people.

It is difficult to make a cogent case that more people are needed, in any part of the world. Those regions that we generally consider to be "unpopulated" usually possess few people because in fact the land and its climate can support only small populations. Deserts, high mountain slopes, or low-lying marshland or swampland that is regularly inundated by floods cannot—and should not—be heavily populated. There are no Shangri-las on the planet Earth, regions that are currently unpopulated but that could provide idyllic, well-balanced lives for substantial numbers of people.

On the other hand, overpopulation can easily be exaggerated as a cause of human misery. Some of the most impoverished regions of the Earth—such as Sudan or northeastern Brazil—are among the most sparsely populated. Ecologists note that such regions, because of their environmental limitations, should not be heavily populated in the first place; given the extreme susceptibility of tropical soils to destruction and the dryness of northern Africa, it seems likely that the natural "carrying capacity" of such regions for human population is necessarily low. The extreme poverty of India, Pakistan, and Indonesia is often blamed on their high birthrates and population density, yet they have fewer people per square mile than do England, Japan, the Benelux countries, and Singapore. Clearly, then, although population can be a problem and can add to existing problems, it is not the entire problem.

## The Demographic Transition

Many European states—as well as Japan, those formerly comprising the Soviet Union, and the United States—have virtually attained zero or even negative population growth whereas in Latin America, Africa, and Asia the population growth rate is about 2%. However, the demographic-economic-environmental trap may be avoidable, and these high rates of population increase may decline in the future, as women see an improvement in their social and economic status and if developing countries experience social and economic improvements more generally. This expectation is based on one of the most important trends in human population, known as the *demographic transition*: Birthrates consistently decline as a result of industrialization, urbanization, and a general improvement in economic conditions.

For nonindustrial, rural societies, birth and death rates both tend to be high, and the population is therefore relatively stable. Then, with improved public health measures, immunizations, widespread food distribution, and so on, death rates decline while birthrates remain high. In this second demographic stage, population increases dramatically. But in the final stage of the demographic transition, as social and economic conditions continue to improve and infant mortality declines, there typically arises a demand for *smaller* families, as growing numbers of parents realize that they do not need large numbers of children to serve as field hands, to compensate for high mortality, or to serve as a kind of social security in their old age. Moreover, many parents recognize that to provide their children with such benefits as higher education, they must have fewer of them. As a result, in the final stage of the demographic transition, populations eventually level off. In Latin America, for example, requiring girls to finish high school has correlated with a sharp drop in birthrates.

One can conclude, therefore, that there is a double payoff to improving the socioeconomic conditions of developing countries. On the one hand, there is the direct benefit of generating more human lives. In addition, there is the beneficial effect of reducing otherwise catastrophic population growth.

## Efforts at Birth Control

Successful birth control requires more than just appropriate technology; as a matter of public policy, it also requires understanding the social causes and effects of population growth. There are four basic theories correlating population growth with socioeconomic situations:

1. *Reproduction leads to poverty:* People have too many children, forcing them to try to feed too many mouths, to divide their land and resources across too many individuals.

2. *Poverty leads to reproduction:* People have children because they are needed to work and support their families; moreover, among the very poor, infant mortality is high, which generates pressure for high birthrates.

3. *Oppression of women leads to reproduction:* Women would have fewer children if they had greater control over their lives, especially an increase in status and access to inexpensive, reliable family planning techniques. Fundamentalist religious traditions also contribute to the oppression of women.

4. *Male pigheadedness leads to reproduction* (actually a variant of theory (3)): Population growth is due to the influence of men, who equate large families with sexual virility and other "macho" characteristics.

To some extent, all of these theories seem to be true; they are not mutually exclusive. Large families are often a result of poverty and low status of women, but they also generally lead to a vicious circle of yet more poverty and sexism.

At present, about two-thirds of all birth control users live in the industrialized world. In some cases, hesitation regarding birth control can be attributed to cultural factors such as the "macho" tradition in Latin America, which equates manhood with number of children, opposition by the Catholic Church in such countries as Mexico, the Philippines, and Kenya, as well as by Islamic fundamentalists in Egypt, Iran, Pakistan, and India. However, there is reason to believe that birth control technology, if more widely available, would be used: UN surveys, for example, consistently find that one-half of all married women do not want *any* more children. Yet funding for contraceptive research and population assistance has declined in recent decades, in part because conservative politicians in the United States—long antagonistic to family planning, contraceptives, and abortions—are very influential, both domestically and globally. The World Bank estimated that it would cost $8 billion (less than 4 days' worth of U.S. military spending) to make birth control easily available worldwide.

Breast-feeding is a moderately effective means of birth control or, at least, of birth spacing: Lactation tends to inhibit ovulation. (This is one reason why Western corporate campaigns to convince mothers in poorer nations to substitute artificial infant formula for breast-feeding have been especially pernicious.) Approximately 28 million abortions are performed annually in developing countries and about 26 million in industrialized countries—of these, roughly one-half are illegal and, thus, likely to be performed by unskilled people and under unsafe conditions. Abortion is a highly charged issue for many; even its supporters concede that it is less desirable than contraception. Nonetheless, when other means of birth control have failed, access to safe abortions would seem preferable to enforced childbearing.

## Reproductive Rights for Women

The relatively low social and economic status of women worldwide contributes to high birth-rates, so perhaps the most effective way to reduce population growth is to improve the status of women. Thus, married women—who in many developing nations are subordinated to their husbands—are often denied social permission to say "No" to their husband's demands for more children. In much of Africa, for example, social pressures are especially strong, since, at marriage, the husband essentially purchases his wife's labor as well as her future children; each additional child solidifies the mother's place within the household. By contrast, when the government of Bangladesh initiated a program of small-business loans to rural women, contraceptive use among the recipients increased from an average of 35% to 75%.

When large numbers of women are denied access to education and other forms of advancement, childbearing may become the only accepted rite of passage to adulthood. As a result, increased education for young women is likely to help reduce fertility, thereby diminishing poverty and also helping prevent further environmental degradation.

Birth control and family planning are advisable as matters of public health alone. For example, complications arising from pregnancy and childbirth are the leading killers of Third World women in their 20s and 30s. More than 3,000 maternal deaths occur per 100,000 live births in regions of Ethiopia and Bangladesh, as compared with 10 in the United States and only 2 in Norway.

## Government Policies

China began its "one family, one child" program in 1979. The goal—no more than 1.2 billion people by the year 2000—was essentially achieved. Violators were punished by fines and dismissal from government jobs, while better housing and stipends were available to one-child households. The overall results have been mixed: Such coercive policies are often unpalatable to Western conceptions of individual liberty. Moreover, there is reason to believe that female infanticide increased, as patriarchal bias induced parents to make their one child a boy. In addition, Chinese population policy has been concentrated among urban, ethnic (Han) Chinese, whereas ethnic minorities and rural people have been to some extent exempted. Population growth in China, however, has decreased, from nearly 3% to 1.4%, largely because of a recent Chinese tendency to marry and bear children at a later age and because of the active efforts of the Chinese government. (One very effective way of slowing population growth is for women to delay reproduction until later in life—for example, age 32 instead of 17—a cultural tradition that has reduced the population growth of Ireland, for example, a country that is strongly Roman Catholic and where contraception was frowned upon and where abortion was long illegal.)

Although population policies are necessary, for them to be persistent as well as effective, they will likely have to be based on voluntary compliance rather than compulsion; that is, they should educate, provide incentives and technology, and minister to existing demand, without being heavy-handed.

## Unmet Need

There is, in fact, a very large unmet need with respect to family size limitation. For example, women of reproductive age were surveyed in four developing countries: India, Egypt, Peru, and Ghana. The percentages of women who indicated that they did not want any more children were, respectively, 50, 56, 70, and 90, whereas the percentages using contraception were, respectively, 28, 30, 25, and 10. Subtracting the latter from the former, we get the proportion of women who wish to limit their family size but are not employing any form of birth control: 22%, 26%, 45%, and a staggering 80% in Ghana. Clearly, the unmet need for contraception is enormous, and whereas it can be seen as a personal, family, national, and world tragedy, it also provides population planners with an immense opportunity—a chance to reduce the catastrophic increase in human population while at the same time satisfying the desires of those involved.

In the past 20 years, average fertility in developing countries has declined while use of contraceptives has increased; as a result, the rate of world population increase has slowed from 2.1% per year to 1.7%. But, importantly, this is a reduction in the *rate of increase,* not in world population itself. (Analogously, consider a bus hurtling toward a cliff and accelerating as it goes. Even if the *rate* of acceleration may eventually decline, this is likely to convey little comfort to the occupants!) Furthermore, population growth is not evenly spread: Typically, states that are already pressing hard on their economic, social, and ecological resource base are likely to be experiencing the most rapid population growth.

A rational population policy commends itself on financial grounds alone. Mexican studies, for example, indicate that for every peso spent on family planning, 9 pesos are saved (from maternal and infant health care, not even counting education). Although birth control programs are no substitute for investment in education, health care, and economic and environmental betterment, it is clear that fertility reduction is essential if the foregoing are to have any significant chance of succeeding.

## The Developed Countries

Poor countries tend to reduce their rate of population growth as they become wealthier, and wealthy countries (like those in North America and Western Europe) have relatively low rates of population increase. However, this is no reason to be complacent or self-righteous, because the wealthy countries use far more resources per capita than do the poor ones, and they also produce proportionately more pollution as well. The United States is about twice as wasteful as the other developed states—with about 5% of the world's population, the United States consumes more than 30% of the world's resources, six times its "rightful" share. Or look at it this way: The average U.S. citizen consumes about 20 times the resources as does the average resident of a Third World country.

Clearly, population growth in the world's poorest countries is a serious social, environmental, and economic problem, especially for the residents of these countries. But considering its planetary costs, population growth in such economically developed states as the United States is far more serious. The poor, in short, cannot legitimately be blamed for the world's environmental plight, since the rich are a disproportionately large part of the problem.

# Future Directions

If we don't change direction, states an ancient Chinese proverb, we shall end up where we are headed. An overcrowded, overarmed world, increasingly divided between haves and have-nots, is not a desirable prospect, either in terms of basic ethics or in terms of its tangible consequences: misery, disruption, and, perhaps, increased violence. Granted, poor people are unlikely to march aggressively into the rich countries, especially so long as the latter possess abundant lethal weaponry. Unlike a ghetto riot, in which people's poverty and frustration erupt into looting a local department store, poverty is more apt to continue generating its own kind of structural violence, eroding the quality of life. It may also continue to generate political instability, especially in the poor countries.

As with so many other issues in peace and conflict studies, the problem of poverty is easier to diagnose than to cure. It is a major accomplishment just to appreciate the problem, since—like human rights, environmental degradation, or the prevention of war—it is vast and multidimensional. The plight of the poor is not just temporary but it also need not be eternal.

In this respect, one of the greatest impediments to effective action is the inclination of powerful governments—representing people who are essentially satisfied with the status quo—to ignore the problem, minimize it, blame its victims, and, if pressed, give only lip service to its urgency. Among the more general and widespread suggestions for reducing global poverty, the following may have particular merit:

- Recognizing that whereas economic growth is to some degree desirable, growth in itself does not necessarily lead to a greater sharing of prosperity, either between states or within them
- Establishing an internationally accepted floor below which poverty shall not be permitted, analogous to the "safety net" currently in place in most Western democracies
- Making birth control universally available, either free or at minimal cost
- Developing and implementing a worldwide literacy program, plus upgrading of educational facilities and opportunities, especially in the developing world and focused especially on women
- Enhancing the role and effectiveness of local, grassroots activities that promote economic growth along with environmental protection
- Providing massive debt relief for the poorest states, coupled with reorientation of their economies from being export-oriented to satisfying domestic needs
- Making serious efforts toward achieving self-reliant "ecodevelopment," which is neither stagnation nor ecological exploitation but rather respects the cultural heterogeneity of the local inhabitants as well as their need to work *with* nature rather than against it
- Recognizing that resource-guzzling technologies will likely be harmful for many if not most developing countries as well as for the industrialized world, and, similarly, that high-technology procedures don't necessarily create more jobs than they destroy and that unemployment contributes significantly to poverty
- Redirecting a large proportion of planetary resources, currently eaten up by military spending, to upgrading the living conditions of the world's people

# The Case of Costa Rica

Toward the end of the 20th century, it was widely hoped that with the apparent cessation of East-West military competition, resources previously consumed by the military could be released for desperately needed civilian purposes. Although this optimistic hope was not fulfilled at the global level, the experience of Costa Rica may be instructive.

This small Central American state abolished its army, navy, and air force in 1948. Whereas nearby Guatemala and Honduras, by contrast, spend 15% of their GNP on their military, Costa Rica spends less than 3% of its GNP on its police. These savings permit Costa Rica to devote 11% of its GNP to health and education, more than twice the proportional expenditure of Honduras and three times that of Guatemala. As a result, polio and diphtheria have been eradicated in Costa Rica, and whooping cough, tetanus, and measles are nearly gone. Infant mortality has plummeted, as has the birthrate, which declined by nearly 50% from 1960 to 2010. During the 1980s, the U.S. government regularly pressured Costa Rica to reverse its priorities and invest in national armed forces, ostensibly as defense against communism (but, in fact, as part of the Reagan administration's desire to put military pressure on nearby Sandinista-led Nicaragua). It seems clear, however, that the demilitarized, prosocial policy of Costa Rica is a surer path to stability and security than is the traditional neoliberal and militarist model of socioeconomic development. Accordingly, it may be hoped that Costa Rica represents the future.

## A FINAL NOTE ON ECONOMIC WELL-BEING

Despite unparalleled wealth enjoyed by some, the great majority of the world's people are poor, so much so that many lives are shortened or made miserable; even more are prevented from developing their full potential. Indirect, or structural, violence is thus widespread and, to a discouraging extent, increasing. Overpopulation exacerbates this problem as well as the disparity between the haves and the have-nots (who, not surprisingly, are also "want-mores").

Solutions, however, do exist, including various redistribution strategies, programs of genuine development, and family planning. The problem of poverty—like the problems of human rights, the environment, and war itself—is ancient but not necessarily intractable. Enough resources exist to provide a decent material life for everyone, especially if human population is eventually controlled. The greatest obstacle to economic well-being appears to be the possessive social and political inclinations of some human beings, corporations, and nations, usually those with the financial resources to help people in need but who decline to do so. The question is whether these people, and the governments who represent their interests, will acknowledge the aspirations and needs of the "wretched of the Earth" and make the changes needed to improve the lot of their fellow human beings.

## NOTES

1. In reality, the very wealthy typically manage to take advantage of various tax breaks such that they often end up paying a lower rate—although typically a higher total amount—than those whose incomes are considerably lower.

## QUESTIONS FOR FURTHER REFLECTION

1. What is meant by "uneven development" or "increased marginalization despite development"?

2. Discuss the matters of poverty and inequity in ethical terms; also discuss them in terms of state security.

3. Describe several different explanations for why there is so much poverty in the developing world compared with the "developed world." Do the same for inequity within the developed world itself.

4. Why should relatively wealthy people in, say, Sweden or Norway, Canada or the United States, care about starvation in, say, Sudan?

5. It can be argued that poverty and population lead to mutually reinforcing downward spirals. Show how these disturbing trends could be reversed, leading to mutually reinforcing patterns of amelioration.

## SUGGESTIONS FOR FURTHER READING

Harold R. Kerbo. 2005. *World Poverty: The Roots of Global Inequality and the Modern World System*. New York: McGraw-Hill.

Jeffrey Sachs. 2006. *The End of Poverty: Economic Possibilities for Our Time*. New York: Penguin.

John Weeks. 2007. *Population: An Introduction to Concepts and Issues*. Belmont, CA: Wadsworth.

Joseph E. Stiglitz. 2003. *Globalization and Its Discontents*. New York: W. W. Norton.

Joseph E. Stiglitz. 2012. *The Price of Inequality: How today's divided society endangers our future*. New York: W. W. Norton.

Muhammad Yunus. 2003. *Banker to the Poor: Micro-Lending and the Battle Against World Poverty*. New York: Public Affairs.

# CHAPTER 21

## MOVEMENTS TOWARD DEMOCRACY

Egyptian anti-goverment demonstrators wave Egyptian flags in Cairo's Tahrir Square in 2011, during (ultimately successful) protests against President Hosni Mubarak's regime.

*Source:* PEDRO UGARTE/AFP/Getty Images.

*"Revolution is as unpredictable as an earthquake and as beautiful as spring. Its coming is always a surprise, but its nature should not be."*

—Rebecca Solnit

*"Democracy is the worst form of government, except for all those other forms that have been tried."*

—Winston Churchill

Citizens of democratic countries have especially appreciated Churchill's quip, in part because even as it appears to be self-deprecating ("the worst form of government"), it nonetheless makes a clear statement of the overriding merit of democracy, maintaining that it is better than "all those other forms that have been tried." Churchill may or may not have been correct . . . although we admit to being unable to identify a more appropriate candidate for the "best form of government." Perhaps there is no "best form," or perhaps the best form varies with local circumstances, or perhaps democracy really *is* the best (however that is ultimately defined).

In any event, it seems clear that when given the opportunity—and even when such opportunities are severely restricted by state dictatorship—many people yearn for democracy and are often willing to run great risks and to suffer horribly in the hope of establishing democracy in their homelands. Since the aspiration for democracy appears to be deep as well as widespread, such that it has become a conspicuous hallmark of international affairs in the early 21st century in particular, and since movements toward democracy have definite implications for both negative and positive peace, we devote this chapter to a brief review of the phenomenon.

## What Is Democracy?

A simple definition states that a democratic government is one in which supreme political decision-making is ultimately vested in the people (*demos*, in Greek, means "people" and *kratia*, means "rule," as in "technocratic," "meritocratic," etc.), who exercise this power either directly or via decisions made by their chosen representatives. In its classic form democracy was characteristic of ancient Greek city-states (especially Athens) and of the Roman Republic; it still occurs in a small scale among New England town meetings in the United States, or the "jirga" system of many central Asian societies. With increasing local population size, such direct democracy has become more and more unwieldy, so that decision making has typically been the responsibility and privilege of a limited number of individuals expected to represent their constituents; hence, "representative" or "parliamentary" democracy.

Despite widespread use of the term, in reality there are many different forms of democracy and variations on what constitutes the "democratic ideal." Thus, truly competitive elections are often seen as a cornerstone of democracy, and yet, there is substantial diversity when it comes to electoral practice. In most countries, for example, only citizens are permitted to vote, thus disenfranchising large numbers of people who actually constitute an arithmetic majority; in other cases—notably certain Arab states—women are not permitted to vote. In some countries only landowners are "enfranchised," while in others (including, historically, the United States) voters are required to pay a poll tax that effectively disenfranchises the poor, or to prove literacy.

Freedom of association, freedom of the press, freedom of political speech and writing, are often considered prerequisites for political democracy, although many countries that proclaim themselves democratic actually restrict such activities. Similarly, even though it is widely assumed that democracy (a political system) implies free-market capitalism (an economic system), this isn't always the case. China provides a dramatic example, since the Chinese political system—nominally communist—is rigidly authoritarian, whereas its vibrant, rapidly-growing economic system is basically capitalist, with a small number of fabulously wealthy entrepreneurs, a growing middle class, and little or no protection for workers or peasants.

It is also widely assumed that "one person, one vote" is characteristic of democracies, although "vote buying" through various means is not uncommon. In the United States—widely seen as a paragon of democratic political process—political campaigning requires large financial expenditures, leading to well-founded accusations that wealthy people (by virtue of their ability to make campaign contributions and/or purchase media advertising) have a disproportionate influence on political elections as well as when it comes to decision-making and the crafting of legislation.

In some countries (e.g., France) national leaders—"presidents"—are chosen by direct vote of the citizenry, whereas in others (e.g., the United Kingdom, Germany, Israel, and in the world's most populous democracy, India) voting takes place for members of parliament, with the party receiving a parliamentary majority being empowered to "form a government," which not uncommonly involves complex coalitions among disparate parties in the event that no single party achieves an electoral majority of representatives. It isn't clear whether such "parliamentary democracies" are more or less democratic than those in which national leaders are chosen directly, especially since in the United States (considered by many the international showcase of democracy), presidents are not chosen by simple majority vote but rather, via an "electoral college" system that has produced several minority presidents in the past.

The desirability of democracy is rarely questioned by Western nations, despite its diversity in practice. Thus, even notoriously undemocratic governments—notably those of North Korea and the former Soviet satellite states of Eastern Europe—incorporated the word "democratic" in their formal state name, as in "The Democratic People's Republic of _____." In contrast to such verbal commitment to democracy, typically characteristic of communist countries, Fascist and Nazi ideology has a long history of being dismissive of democracy as "degenerate," just as many on the political left criticize the ostensible democracy of right-wing despots as being a sham, whose elections cannot realistically be considered "free."

The most famous philosophical critique of democracy derives from Plato's *Republic*, in which democracy is equated to mob rule, as opposed to a supposedly more just and therefore desirable form of governance: by an unelected aristocracy of "philosopher-kings." For example, at one point in *The Republic*, Socrates refers scathingly to ""Democracy, which is a charming form of government, full of variety and disorder, and dispensing a sort of equality to equals and unequaled alike."

## Participatory Democracy and "Astroturf"

In this chapter, we focus on democracy on the national scale, which typically involves "representative democracy," since as group size increases it becomes less feasible to make political decisions by the direct participation of each citizen. However, a case can be made for the value of direct or "participatory democracy," in which every individual has a say. The appeal of participatory democracy has been especially strong within the political left; it was a major principle underlying the Port Huron Statement (PHS), a manifesto written in 1962 by the young founders of the Students for a Democratic Society. This statement—a now-classic announcement of left-wing goals—called for extending participatory democracy from community organizing to the larger realms of economic and foreign policy.

In the 21st century, echoes of participatory democracy can be heard in a range of "shack-dwellers movements," especially in South Africa, Brazil and India, as well as "landless peasants movements" in South and Central America. It should also be emphasized, however, that right-wing activism has also been energized by a vision of participatory democracy, ranging from the extremes of Fascist and Nazi movements of the 1930s to more "moderate" manifestations of conservative populism such as the Tea Party movement in the United States.

Within participatory democracy, the presumption is that decision making still occurs via some form of democratic voting process, in which one person—regardless of gender, wealth, and so forth—casts one vote. In practice, even in so-called democratic countries, those in positions of power exercise disproportionate influence, via their wealth (which enables them to purchase political advertising as well as influence via lobbyists and campaign contributions) or capacity to intimidate their opponents, by the use of hired thugs. In this regard, a distinction needs to be made between genuine participatory or "grassroots" democracy and its artificial counterpart, sometimes called "astroturf,"[1] whereby wealthy individuals and corporations use their purchasing power to give the appearance of widespread public support, whereas the "movement" is essentially financed and operated by a small minority.

## Social Democracy

Another aspect of democracy (this time, one that is exclusively a phenomenon of left-wing politics) is known as "social democracy." This approach, especially prominent in Europe, is a social movement and political philosophy that advocates decentralized economic democracy, rejecting authoritarian rule as well as violent, revolutionary tactics. The emphasis is on grassroots ("bottom-up") participation rather than the comparatively heavy-handed "top-down" approach of the Soviet Union under Lenin or Stalin.

# A Brief Modern History of Democratization

### A Series of "Waves"

As the Cold War between the United States and the Soviet Union concluded, political theorist Francis Fukuyama proposed that "liberal democracy"—essentially, democracy plus capitalism—had triumphed worldwide. Although not "the end of history," as the title of his book announced, Fukuyama's point was that the competition between democracy and other governmental forms had been resolved, in the former's favor.

Reality has been more complex. Thus, political scientist Samuel Huntington argued that democracy has advanced and receded in a series of "waves." The first began in the early 19th century, with voting rights extended to most white males in the United States and England, reaching its peak in the early 1920s, at which time there were just under 30 democracies worldwide. With the Great Depression came the rise of Fascist, Nazi, and communist dictatorships, along with "strong-man" rule in much of the Balkans, the Baltic States, China, and many countries in Latin America. As a result, according to Huntington, the number of democracies declined to just 12 by the middle of World War II.

Continuing this perspective, a second wave of democratization began with the Allied victory in World War II, associated with decolonization (the breakup of the British, French, Dutch, and Belgian empires most especially) as well as the transition of postwar Germany, Italy, and Japan to democracy. By the early 1960s, there were 36 identified democracies worldwide, although this number then declined slightly until the mid-1970s. Many countries at that time were only nominally democratic, experiencing sham elections and limited actual political freedom.

A third wave of democratization can be considered to have started in 1974, with the "Carnation Revolution" that ended fascist rule in Portugal, followed by democratization in Spain with the death of the fascist dictator Francisco Franco. This third wave picked up steam in Latin America during the 1980s, when military or one-party regimes collapsed in Bolivia, Peru, Uruguay, Honduras, Ecuador, and Paraguay and were replaced by constitutional governments. To some degree, this third wave continued and perhaps even picked up steam after 1989, with the collapse of the Soviet Union and the emergence of numerous former Soviet republics that became independent states. The countries of Eastern Europe—Czechoslovakia (which subsequently split into the Czech Republic and Slovakia), East Germany (which subsequently joined with West German to form a united Germany), Poland, Hungary, Romania, Bulgaria, and even rigidly isolated and Maoist Albania—which previously had been undemocratic Soviet "satellites"—moved rapidly and dramatically toward democracy.

However, with the exception of the Baltic countries (Latvia, Lithuania, and Estonia), the successor states to the Soviet Union—including Russia itself—did not become notably democratic. They typically established official structures for holding free and fair elections, but in reality, one-party rule persisted, often combined with economic instability, a strong military footprint upon ostensibly civilian affairs, governmental control of the media, and so forth. This is especially true of the Asiatic "stans" that emerged from the former Soviet Union (Uzbekistan, Tajikistan, Kazakhstan, Turkmenistan, etc.), as well as Russia itself, and, more recently, Ukraine, where democratic gains a decade or so ago are receding.

The various "waves of democratization" don't necessarily exist as clear-cut entities, since every country must be considered a unique case, with each offering different issues. For example, Switzerland is generally considered an early democracy, and thus part of the first wave, yet Swiss women were not enfranchised (permitted to vote) until 1971. In addition, the exact beginning and ending of each "wave" is subject to dispute. Whereas some scholars consider, for instance, that the third wave of democratization has continued up to the present, others make a distinction between the events concluding with the breakup of the Soviet Union and those associated with the various "color revolutions," which might therefore warrant being labeled the fourth wave, with yet a fifth wave, the so-called Arab Spring, being the most recent. In any event, by most estimates there are currently more than 100 functioning democracies in the world, although not all are equally stable or comparably democratic.

## The "Color Revolutions" (a Fourth Wave?)

Although the 1990s witnessed some expansion of democratic governance (notably in the Republic of South Africa), the most dramatic cases of democratization involved events in a number of different countries, which were similar in several respects: (1) They involved massive, nonviolent street demonstrations and other examples of political (and often economic) protest; (2) they were essentially leaderless, "crowd-sourced" movements, largely involving "bottom up" or "grassroots" protest; (3) participants tended to be middle class, often students as well as professionals (doctors, lawyers, and so forth), but also often included unemployed and otherwise disaffected citizens, with no evidence that their ranks were significantly swelled by extremist ideologues; (4) techniques typically involved substantial use of modern communications technology, including cell phones, Facebook, and Twitter, to coordinate activities as well as to disseminate information—often about recent governmental abuses—that helped mobilize yet more protesters; (5) popular unrest frequently emerged in the aftermath of a disputed election in which there was strong evidence of major fraud and vote rigging by the ruler in power; and (6) in most cases, these prodemocracy protest movements developed characteristic and powerful symbols, often simply involving use of a distinctive color.

These events were foreshadowed and also, to some extent inspired by, the nonviolent protests that toppled the autocratic Marcos regime in the Philippines in 1986, sometimes called a "Yellow Revolution," for the color adopted by Corazon Aquino, widow of assassinated Filipino opposition leader Benino Aquino. This success, in turn, may have helped generate the various Velvet Revolutions of 1989 which ended Soviet control of Eastern Europe and shortly thereafter, led to the dissolution of the Soviet Union itself.

A major event in the history of recent democracy movements was the "Bulldozer Revolution" in 2000, which led to the overthrow of Serbian dictator Slobodan Milošević. Opposition groups rallied around the slogan *Gotov je* ("He's finished"), a campaign that galvanized Serbian discontent with Milošević and resulted in his defeat and eventual trial for war crimes by the International Criminal Court. Next was the Rose Revolution in Georgia, in the aftermath of a disputed election in 2003 and which resulted in a new election in 2004. The Orange Revolution in Ukraine took place after a disputed Ukrainian presidential election in 2004 and led to the annulment of the result and repeat voting, after which the opposition's leader was declared president, defeating the Russian-backed incumbent (who subsequently was returned to power). The Tulip Revolution in Kyrgyzstan (also sometimes called the "Pink Revolution") was more violent than its predecessors; it followed a disputed parliamentary election in 2005.

Now, several years later, the short-term prospects for democracy in much of post-Soviet Eurasia (Uzbekistan, Kazakhstan, Azerbaijan, Belarus, and Russia itself) remain bleak. What initially began as a transition from communism to democracy quickly transitioned back to autocracy, based on family and clan associations of the leader. There may be a general trend toward democracy worldwide, but its failure to take root in such cases (including the world's most populous country, China) shows that movement of this sort is necessarily erratic, with more than a few reversals. Nonetheless, and taking a wider historical view, the number of electoral democracies increased dramatically from about 40 in 1972 to more than 120 by 2007.

In the Middle East, the Cedar Revolution in Lebanon (2005), didn't follow a disputed election, rather it followed the assassination of a highly regarded opposition leader, for which the Syrian government was widely thought to have been involved. One outcome was the departure of Syrian troops from Lebanon, after nearly three decades of semioccupation. The Lawyers Revolution, consisting almost entirely of upper middle class professionals in Pakistan, initially sought in 2007 to reinstate a judge who had been deposed by military strongman Pervez Musharraf; the nonviolent protests eventually resulted in Musharraf's resignation.

Even though dictatorships were generally on the run by the close of the 21st century's first decade, not all popular movements for democracy were successful. In Iran, popular protests known as the Green Revolution, broke out in 2009, following an election widely considered to have been rigged. Unlike many of the other "color revolutions," the Green Revolution was military suppressed and as a result, can be considered a failure . . . at least for the moment. On the other hand, another initially unsuccessful color revolution eventually helped induce the military dictatorship of Burma (aka Myanmar), to ease its repression of that country. This prodemocracy movement became known as the Saffron Revolution because Buddhist monks, who led it, traditionally wear robes of that color.

## The Arab Spring: A "Fifth Wave"?

On December 17, 2010, a young Tunisian man, Mohammed Bouazizi, was in despair because, although he was a college graduate, the economic stagnation and unemployment in his country were such that Bouazizi had been reduced to selling vegetables from a streetcart. The final straw in Mr. Bouazizi's sense of degradation occurred when his wares were confiscated by a policewoman, whereupon he set himself on fire in protest . . . an action that almost literally set much of the Arab world ablaze. Two weeks later, Mr. Bouazizi died, after which street demonstrations erupted in Tunisia against a decades-old tyranny (which had been supported by the West), whereupon protests quickly spread through much of the Arab world, including Libya, Bahrain, Algeria, Yemen, and most notably—because it is the most populous Arab country and in many ways the center of Arab culture, Egypt.

The result became known as the Arab Spring, named in part for its similarity to the "Prague Spring," a short-lived, largely nonviolent democratic uprising in Czechoslovakia, in 1968. But whereas the Prague Spring was quickly suppressed by Soviet tanks, the Arab Spring (aka the "Arab Awakening") seems to have been far more successful. Not since the widespread European revolutions of 1848 have there been so many spontaneous uprisings, although the overthrow of Eastern European communist dictatorships in 1989 offers a similar pattern. In the present case, the protestors' focus was not on Islamic radicalism or antagonism to Israel or to the United States; rather, their demands were limited and clear-cut, directed toward their own oppressive governments, many of which had persisted for decades: In Arabic, these demands were summarized by "Kifaya" and "irhal'"—simply, "enough" and "leave." (Oil-rich Saudi Arabia has thus far been able to "buy off" protests by providing enhanced financial benefits to Arabian citizens, an option that was not available to either Tunisia or Egypt, which lacked oil wealth. And its troops quelled popular resistance to the monarchy in Bahrain.)

Although a yearning for democracy played a consistent role in each of the antidictator movements within the Arab world, as well as in the color revolutions that preceded the Arab Spring, other factors were also involved. Protestors typically objected to deep-seated political corruption and cronyism, the concentration of wealth in the hands of autocrats who had remained in power for literally decades, sexual frustration deriving in part from little or no prospects for economic growth (which doomed many young men to bachelorhood in societies in which it was expected that prospective husbands must have a certain level of wealth in order to marry), and more than anything, perhaps, refusal of youth, the downtrodden, disaffected elites, democracy lovers, and the disappointed to accept the status quo. Rapidly rising food prices may also been a significant factor, in addition to the fact that a large proportion of the Internet-savvy youth of these Arab countries had become increasingly inclined to view absolute monarchs and other despots as anachronisms.

Many decision makers in the West were initially surprised that the Arab world, which had long been considered rigidly hierarchical, indifferent to change, and almost medieval in its outlook and technology, was instead inhabited by serious-minded, democracy-loving patriots with access to the Internet, strong antitotalitarian impulses, and a courageous willingness to take risks and participate in politically sophisticated, nonviolent protest. But an even greater surprise, perhaps, was the fact that several long-standing, highly repressive Arab regimes collapsed as a result. Eventually, the dictators of Tunisia, Yemen, and Egypt relinquished power once it became apparent that they had lost the support of their military in the face of massive and persistent "people power" (a term that dated from the Yellow Revolution that ousted Ferdinand Marcos). Popular uprisings against Libyan dictator Muammar Gadhafi evoked a violent response by loyalists within the Libyan military, with Gadhafi eventually defeated (and killed) after a brief but bloody civil war in which NATO forces assisted the rebels.[2] Similarly, antigovernment protests in Bahrain were brutally suppressed by military force (assisted by Saudi Arabia), and as of 2012, the situation remains uncertain.

Events in Tahrir Square—a prominent meeting place in Cairo, which became the epicenter of ongoing protests against longtime Egyptian dictator Hosni Mubarak—were especially dramatic. The government initially responded with violent repression, in which as many as 300 people may have been killed. But an important pattern emerged: When it was clear that the Egyptian people in large numbers, were willing—even eager —to risk injury and death for their beliefs, the legitimacy of the regime was lethally undermined. Writing of the events in Tahrir Square, one observer noted:

> In Egypt, there were moments of violence when people pushed back against the government's goons, and for a week it seemed like the news was filled with little but pictures of bloody heads. Still, no armies marched, no superior weaponry decided the fate of the country, nobody was pushed from power by armed might. People gathered in public and discovered themselves as the public, as civil society. They found that the repression and exploitation they had long tolerated was intolerable and that they could do something about it, even if that something was only gathering, standing together, insisting on their rights as the public, as the true nation that the government can never be.

> It is remarkable how, people one day simply stop believing in the regime that had, until then, ruled them, as African-Americans and their white supporters did in the American South 50 years ago. Stopping believing means no longer regarding those who rule you as legitimate, and so no longer fearing them. Or respecting them. And then, surprisingly, they begin to crumble.[3]

Significantly, a key factor leading to the dissolution of the dictatorial Mubarak government was the refusal of the Egyptian Army to attack the Egyptian people. By contrast, as of 2012, similar protests against the dictatorial government of Bashar al-Assad of Syria weakened his control, but instead of toppling the government, it precipitated a civil war, since, despite prominent defections, large segments of the Syrian Army remained loyal to the existing government. The United Nations attempted to arrange a cease-fire and negotiations between the contending parties but with only limited success.

Throughout the Arab Spring, it took some time for the United States and other Western powers to distinguish between the people and their oppressors—or rather, to act on a distinction of which they were surely well aware. This may well have been due to worry that these democratic revolutions would produce outcomes equivalent to the Iranian Revolution of 1979, which overthrew the U.S.-backed shah, and then turned toward anti-American Islamic fundamentalism.

As was true of Iran's shah, the Arab dictators thus far overthrown have also been allied to and supported by the West, which initially reacted to grass roots calls for democracy by condemning the "violence on both sides," whereas nearly always, violence was perpetrated overwhelmingly by the governments in power, not the protestors.

Although the future of the Arab Spring is yet to be seen (it is currently a work in progress), it is important to note the courage, tenacity, and nonviolence that has generally characterized the protestors, and to take heart from their successes thus far. In the words of Russian poet Nadezhda Mandelstam, speaking of Josef Stalin's long and bloody rule in the USSR,

> There was a special form of sickness—lethargy, plague, hypnotic trance, or whatever one calls it, that affected all those who committed terrible deeds. All the murderers, provocateurs, and informers had one feature in common: it never occurred to them that their victims might one day rise up again and speak.

Describing the tipping point in nationwide political revolutions of the sort that have characterized the Arab Spring, the philosopher Hannah Arendt noted more than half a century ago that

> The situation changes abruptly. Not only is the rebellion not put down but the arms themselves change hands—sometimes, as in the Hungarian revolution, within a few hours. . . . The sudden dramatic breakdown of power that ushers in revolution reveals in a flash how civil obedience—to laws, to rulers, to institutions—is but the outward manifestation of support and consent.[4]

## Lessons From the Arab Spring

The Arab uprisings that began in Tunisia and spread so rapidly through much of the Arab world focused on corruption, poverty, and lack of freedom, rather than Western domination or Israeli occupation. But the fact that they kicked off against Western-backed dictatorships meant they posed an immediate threat to the strategic order . . . at least, as perceived from the West. And it isn't only the example of Iran that has generated anxiety among some Western elites. Thus, overthrow of the Egyptian monarchy (which had been supported by the previous colonial powers) in 1952 ushered in nearly 60 years of rule by military "strong men" that arrested the growth of promising political institutions and flagrantly disregarded civil rights, culminating in more than 30 years of dictatorship by Hosni Mubarak. It is always problematic to extract lessons from currently unfolding events, since in such cases, only time can provide the necessary perspective—not to mention clarifying outcomes that are presently unresolved. Even so, a few generalities can be hazarded:

1. Just because something is familiar and comfortable when viewed from the outside (e.g., the governments of Libya, Yemen, and especially Egypt prior to the Arab Spring) does not mean that it is stable. Saudi Arabia, for example, is even now seen as an island of stability. A more likely assumption is that dictatorships, absolute monarchies, and so forth may appear stable but are liable to be inherently fragile in the face of democratic yearnings, widespread discontent, and international outrage. Political and social stagnation should not be perceived as stability, and

"outside" governments would be well advised to incorporate an expectation of dynamism and change—insofar as they allow themselves to be involved at all in the internal structural affairs of another country.

2. Insofar as they represent the genuine desire of a significant proportion of a country's population, democracy movements cannot be orchestrated by outside countries, just as their outbreak is typically determined by local internal events. For example, even though NATO's participation was crucial to the overthrow of Libya's Gadhafi, the nature and direction of a new Libyan state will be determined by Libyans. (By the same token, the United States has been forced to learn, from its experiences in Iraq and Afghanistan, that in today's world, outside powers have only limited ability to influence the ultimate governance of another country.) Such a limitation may well be healthy, since the legitimacy—and thus, the longevity and stability—of those social and political systems that eventually emerge from the Arab Spring will depend on whether they derive from authentic domestic processes rather than having been imposed from the outside. Trying to keep a dictator in power who has worn out his welcome is always a big mistake on the part of a great power, as was seen in the case of the Shah of Iran, among others

3. The Arab Spring also vividly demonstrated what appears to be a widespread human desire for dignity, self-expression, and freedom, even though the exact nature of each country's preferred system is likely to vary depending on its history, population makeup, economic practices, religious and ideological preferences, and so forth. One size is unlikely to fit all.

4. Although it seems likely that replacing pro-Western despots with governments that more accurately reflect the political preferences of the "Arab street" will result in greater distance from the West in general and the United States in particular, as has already happened in Egypt with the political ascendancy of The Muslim Brotherhood, this does not necessarily mean that these governments will be violently anti-Western, anti-Israel, and/or proterrorist. Islamist rule is not a victory of jihadism; on the contrary, moderate Islamists, probably including the new president of Israel, undercut the popular appeal of jihadis. Indeed, it is entirely possible—maybe even likely—that insofar as democracy can be achieved in the Arab world, it will serve as a deterrent to violent extremism, which flourishes more readily under dictatorship than in a democracy.

5. Although past examples of revolutionary successes and tragedies are instructive, there are no blueprints or reliable forecasts for the outcomes of new revolutionary movements. What happens in Tunisia and Egypt, for example, may or may not prefigure the outcomes of events in, for example, Syria, and even in Bahrain and Saudi Arabia. Historical and political analysis is not an exact science, and, forecasting future social and even economic events is far from predictable. Accordingly, policy makers and scholars alike are best prepared if they have multilevel and multifactorial explanatory systems as well as contingency plans.

## The "Occupy Movement"

In recent years, Americans have grown accustomed to being the initiators and "exporters" of sociocultural trends, from blue jeans, information technology, and rock and roll to corporate and financial capitalism and even to democracy itself. An interesting exception has been the

"Occupy Movement," a series of homegrown prodemocracy events that were to a large extent inspired by the earlier color revolutions and especially by the Arab Spring, which had been roiling the Middle East for nearly a year previously.

This movement, originally known as Occupy Wall Street, and which subsequently spread to many cities and college campuses, entered public (and the mass media's) consciousness in October, 2011. Unlike the Arab Spring, the Occupy Movement did not seek to overthrow the existing (U.S.) government; hence, its actions—and the reactions it has generated—have been substantially less fraught. In fact, many public opinion polls indicated that a majority of those Americans polled supported what they believed to be the goals of the Occupy Movement, a remarkable indicator of widespread discontent with the status quo!

This movement has especially been motivated by a perception of economic inequality in the United States, and has been notably leaderless and nonhierarchical, functioning via a highly decentralized array of activists, localized in various cities and communities, and making conspicuous use of consensus decision making and participatory democracy, with some anarchist overtones. The "Occupiers" attracted attention to their cause by establishing a variety of symbolic and real encampments, drawing public attention to income inequality and their claim that the political system in the United States is biased in favor of "the 1%" who are wealthy and politically connected, to the detriment of "the 99%." Their popular catchphrase became "We are the 99%."

In its initial stages, the Occupy Movement was denigrated by some observers and media as made up of "hippie malcontents" who "needed to get a job and pay greater attention to their personal hygiene." As with the Arab Spring—notably in Tahrir Square—the Occupy Movement organized around the literal occupation of public spaces, an effective way of gaining attention while italicizing its democratic credentials. Within a few weeks, the Occupy Movement began to resonate with much of the public because of widespread anger that some of the wealthiest Americans, who were largely responsible for the Great Recession that began in 2008, were not punished for their financial misdeeds and, moreover, profited greatly while "the 99%" suffered. As with the Arab Spring, the Occupy Movement is too recent a phenomenon to permit a comprehensive assessment of its success or failure. A preliminary evaluation, however, suggests that if nothing else, the media attention it generated resulted in a shift from previous emphasis on government deficits (a concern voiced especially by conservatives) to a newfound concern with income inequality and how it has increased in the United States in recent decades, such that the economic condition of the lower and middle classes has stagnated and often gotten worse, while that of the upper classes has increased dramatically—a concern voiced especially by liberals and progressives but increasingly on "Main Street" as well, as un- and underemployment rates remain high in the United States and in the West in general.

The Occupy Movement was especially successful in dramatizing economic inequalities rather than pushing a specific policy agenda. Another way of saying this: its political goals have been diffuse and free-form, its "demands" range from reduced college tuition to higher tax rates on the wealthy, to special fees imposed on financial transactions and legislation making it more difficult for banks to foreclose on unpaid mortgages. Its greatest impact may well be in changing the public discourse, impacting what is on the public (and thus) political agenda. In a democracy—even an imperfect one, as every democracy is—such a change in discourse (sometimes known as "consciousness raising") is probably necessary although not sufficient for genuine change to take place. As the Occupy Movement enters what might be called a demobilization phase, it remains to be seen whether it will have a lasting impact with respect to public attitudes toward economic inequality as well as whether it will foster specific political efforts to reduce the corporate domination of U.S. politics.

# Democracies and Wars

Insofar as there may be a global preference for democracy of one sort or another, reflected in various "democracy movements" worldwide, it is worth asking what implications, if any, such a prodemocracy tendency might have for basic questions of war and peace. It seems a reasonable assumption that if people genuinely seek democracy, then success in this regard constitutes movement toward positive peace, especially as a component of human rights—in this case, the right to democratic self-governance.

A second and less clear-cut question also arises: What, if anything, is the connection between democracy and "negative peace," the prevention of war? At least partly because the Western states generally pride themselves in being democracies, and because it is widely believed that democratic governments are more peaceful than nondemocratic states, it is worth examining the comparative war-proneness of democratic and more authoritarian nations.

The results are a bit disconcerting, at least for people reflexively believing that political democracies are peace-loving nations. Statistically, at least until the second half of the 20th century, no significant difference was demonstrated between the war proneness of democracies and despotisms. Authoritarian Sparta was no more aggressive or expansionist than democratic Athens; similarly, Franco's Spain, Somoza's Nicaragua, and Marcos's Philippines, although dictatorships, were not expansionist. By contrast, during the 19th century in particular, Britain and the United States engaged in numerous expansionist wars. For the United States, these included successful wars against indigenous Native Americans, Mexico, and Spain, as well as the failed War of 1812 against Great Britain (which was undertaken in large part in hopes of annexing what at the time was the British colony of Canada). For its part, Britain completed its acquisition of an immense global empire, it has been said, "in a fit of absent-mindedness" but if so, British imperial expansion involved substantial military adventurism on the part of a democratic country.

## Popular Commitment

A mutually supportive connection between democracy and war, although counterintuitive, should not be all that surprising. In feudal Europe and Japan, the aristocracy had a monopoly on war. This changed substantially with the spread of firearms, which made a commoner capable of stopping a charging horse and penetrating a nobleman's armor. Moreover, the right to keep and bear arms (the Second Amendment to the U.S. Constitution) has been seen by many Americans as fundamental to democracy.

One's perception of the peaceableness of democracies may be strongly colored by the 20th century, in which most democracies became "status quo" powers, unlikely to engage in wars of aggression. However, by the end of that century the United States, in particular, took on the role of world policeman, thereby becoming embroiled, directly or indirectly, in armed conflicts on every continent but Australia and Antarctica. In addition, democracies have proven to be no less likely than more authoritarian states to fight when provoked—and they may be even more fierce in prosecuting such wars. "A democracy is peaceloving," claimed noted diplomat-historian George Kennan (often deemed the intellectual father of "containment" of the former Soviet Union):

It does not like to go to war. It is slow to rise to provocation. When it has once been provoked to the point where it must grasp the sword, it does not easily forgive its adversary for having produced this situation. . . . Democracy fights in anger—it fights for the very reason that it was forced to go to war. It fights to punish the power that was rash enough and hostile enough to provoke it—to teach that power a lesson it will not forget, to prevent the thing from happening again. Such a war must be carried to the bitter end.[5]

Conservative politicians in particular (perhaps surprisingly) have distrusted democracy because of what they saw as its inclination *toward* war. Thus, England's 19th-century prime minister Disraeli maintained that if the British electorate were enlarged, "You will in due season have wars entered into from passion and not from reason." And young Winston Churchill pointed out (correctly) in 1901 that "democracy is more vindictive than Cabinets. The wars of peoples will be more terrible than the wars of kings."

In the late 1930s, Britain and France made concessions to and claimed friendship with Hitler, yet once war was finally declared—and even while Neville Chamberlain was still prime minister—nothing less than the elimination of the Nazi regime was deemed acceptable. The fearsome energy of popular total war, once unleashed, makes it very difficult for accommodations to be made. This is at least partly because as losses accumulate, it becomes all the more important to demonstrate that lives and property have not been expended in vain. Whereas during the numerous 17th and 18th century European "monarchs' wars" (including such historical curiosities as the War of the Spanish Succession, and so forth), rulers were free to end, at their choosing, wars they had often initiated in response to their personal whims or goals, once popular passions are ignited—as is necessarily the case when democracies go to war—it is far more difficult to douse the flames.

Thus, for democracies, political necessity often demands a commitment to total victory. During World War I, France sacrificed hundreds of thousands of young men without ever seriously considering a compromise that might have allowed for Germany to retain Alsace (mostly German speaking) and France to take back Lorraine, whose inhabitants largely identified themselves as French.

A major factor prolonging the Vietnam, Iraq, and Afghanistan Wars was the feeling that, having suffered so many casualties and expended so much national treasure, the United States "must not pull out now." National honor was at stake, as well as the very human reluctance to admit a mistake. For a similar logical fallacy, consider this example: The British and French governments continued to spend money on developing the Concorde supersonic transport plane, even after it was demonstrated to be economically unviable, so that the money already spent would not be seen as wasted. The principle seems to be a general one, even though it is based on faulty logic: Having suffered losses and incurred costs, whether in a war, a financial investment, or even a gambling episode, it is very difficult to back away. Stuck in a hole of their own making, democratic governments are liable to dig themselves deeper, rather than climb out and admit error or defeat.

Despite the above considerations, there is also a potentially important, optimistic, propeace aspect of democracy. Simply stated, it is this: Although democracies are not at all averse to war, it is exceedingly rare for democracies to go to war against each other. The only clear historical case was the War of 1812, between the United States and the United Kingdom, a war that was relatively insignificant and has largely been forgotten. It isn't clear why this is true, but several possibilities exist:

1. Dictatorships are readily personified by the dictator in charge, a situation that quickly lends itself to a commitment to fighting evil as personified by the other side's noxious leader. By contrast, democracies by definition are supposed to reflect the will of the people, so that members of a democratic country seeking to go to war against another democratic country are forced to confront that fact that they are endeavoring to kill people like themselves.

2.  Wars often involve the comforting mythology that the enemy isn't the other side's population but rather, their evil and dangerous leaders. This is more difficult to maintain when the people, rather than a leader per se, are seen as the responsible actors.

3.  Even though, democracies once aroused are liable to pursue their wrath more vigorously than dictatorships, especially the United Kingdom and the United States, it may well be true that most people—as the ones most likely to suffer in the event of war—are typically reluctant to go to war in the first place. If so, than it would seem even less likely that prowar motivation would be generated simultaneously within two separate democratic constituencies.

Whatever the reason(s), it remains possible—perhaps even likely—that a world moving toward democracy may, as a result, also be moving toward greater peace, as such liberal peace theorists as Kant and Oliver Richmond have claimed. Indeed, beyond whatever domestic benefits democracy may convey, the reluctance of democracies to make war on each other may in itself be a powerful reason to encourage—and rejoice in—the spread of democratic government.

# Democracies in Peace Versus War

Peace is not a prerequisite for democracy, but it seems clear that democracies do better in times of peace than in times of war. In fact, whereas democracies do not necessarily lead to peace, the tendency may work in reverse: Peace may predispose governments toward democracy.[6] Certainly, the converse holds: Wars often involve abridgment of rights of dissent and due process, even within democracies. War requires increased discipline, secrecy, unswerving and unquestioning devotion to the state, and obedience to its authority. All of these are easier to achieve with military governments. In fact, the nurturing of democracy in the United Kingdom and the United States may have been facilitated by the fact that in their early history, neither of these nation-states has faced constant military threats; most of their wars were "of choice" rather than of necessity.

During World War II, by contrast, Churchill and his cabinet held almost dictatorial power in otherwise democratic Great Britain; indeed, that war produced a remarkable convergence in the political systems of all participants. There was also widespread suppression of dissent within the United States during World War I, the forced dislocation and involuntary internment of thousands of Japanese Americans in "relocation centers" (milder versions of concentration camps) during World War II, and attempts by some American political and police officials to suppress protest movements as demonstrations against the Vietnam War increased and its popularity sagged. Since 9/11, comparably repressive measures were adopted by the U.S. government and some of its allies in their global war on terrorism.

Some democracies nonetheless retain an abiding sense that the military is subordinate to the civilian sector. In the middle of the Korean War, for example, President Truman was able to fire General MacArthur, the most popular and successful military figure in the country, then at the peak of his powers. Similarly, in 2010, President Barack Obama successfully fired General Stanley McChrystal, top U.S. military commander in Afghanistan, when the latter made apparently disparaging comments about the U.S. civilian political leadership.

Military leaders are specialists in "legitimate" violence; moreover, career advancement within the military typically is enhanced by successful service during real "shooting wars." It follows that they should be more willing, even eager, to enter wars, and moreover, they should be able to do so without the prolonged and divisive procedures found in most democracies. In the nuclear age, which has mandated the need to respond quickly—almost instantly—in order to maintain deterrence, the legal requirement of a formal declaration of war has pretty much been abridged. And whereas the War Powers Act, passed in the aftermath of the Vietnam War, requires that the U.S. Congress approve any executive decision to commit combat forces for longer than 60 days, the reality is that U.S. military forces have been committed by unilateral decision of the president and without any formal authorization from Congress or declaration of war, in Serbia, Kosovo, and Somalia (under President Clinton), in Iraq and Afghanistan (under President George W. Bush), and in Libya (under President Obama), along with the use of remote controlled "killer drones" in Pakistan, Yemen, and elsewhere.

More generally, it can be argued that when it comes to the decision to go to war, democracies are not really democratic at all. The following selection—written by Randolph Bourne in the early days of World War I— conveys a strong sense of despair and disillusionment with governmental activities, even in a democracy:

The Government, with no mandate from the people, without consultation of the people . . . slowly bring[s] it into collision with some other Government, and gently and irresistibly slides the country into war. For the benefit of proud and haughty citizens, it is fortified with a list of the intolerable insults which have been hurled toward us by the other nations; for the benefit of the liberal and beneficent, it has a convincing set of moral purposes which our going to war will achieve; for the ambitious and aggressive classes, it can gently whisper of a bigger role in the destiny of the world. The result is that, even in those countries where the business of declaring war is theoretically in the hands of representatives of the people, no legislature has ever been known to decline the request of an Executive, which has conducted all foreign affairs in utter privacy and irresponsibility, that it order the nation into battle . . .

The moment war is declared, however, the mass of the people, through some spiritual alchemy, become convinced that they have willed and executed the deed themselves. They then with the exception of a few malcontents, proceed to allow themselves to be regimented, coerced, deranged in all the environments of their lives, and turned into a solid manufactory of destruction toward whatever other people may have . . . come within the range of the Government's disapprobation. The citizen throws off his contempt and indifference to Government, identifies himself with its purposes, revives all his military memories and symbols, and the State once more walks . . . through the imaginations of men.[7]

On the other hand, Walter Lippmann, an influential commentator on foreign affairs, maintained that democracies are peaceful because of a certain public inertia:

[A]t the critical junctures, when the stakes are high, the prevailing mass opinion will impose what amounts to a veto upon changing the course on which the government is at the time proceeding.[8]

This perspective suggests that when democracies are at peace, they tend to remain at peace, just as they experience a kind of popular momentum once committed to war.

There is a paradoxical relationship between democracy and war: Once provoked, democratically elected governments fight fiercely, perhaps even more willingly and with greater enthusiasm than their less democratic counterparts, but most democracies tend to remain peaceful, at least when it comes to fighting other democracies. The American experience during the latter part of the 20th century, however, suggests a troubling variation on this theme, namely, a penchant by the United States for brief wars of intervention in the affairs of less powerful nations. The 1983 invasion of Grenada, the 1989 invasion of Panama, the 2001 invasion of Afghanistan, and the 2003 invasion of Iraq by the United States were illegal by most standards of international law, as was the American government's support for the contras in Nicaragua during the 1980s. (By contrast, NATO's military engagement in Bosnia, Kosovo, and Libya were more in accord with international legal obligations, in that they were undertaken as part of a multilateral international commitment.)

Regardless of their blatant illegality, most of these military adventures (excepting the invasions and occupations of Iraq and Afghanistan) were quite successful domestically, temporarily boosting the popularity of President Reagan and both Presidents Bush. These belligerent activities were motivated, at least in part, by the perception (accurate, as it turned out) that the presidents in question would benefit politically . . . at least in the short term, especially as a response to the United States having been attacked. This raises the "wag the dog" specter[9] that presidents and other decision makers may seek to offset their domestic political difficulties by engaging in a quick war or "surgical strike" (as President Clinton did in Afghanistan and Sudan in the 1990s, after al-Qaeda supporters attacked the U.S. embassy in Kenya) that is relatively painless—at least, for the aggressor—and domestically popular. So long as public opinion responds favorably to such wars, especially around election time, democratically elected governments will be tempted to engage in them.

## Can Democracy Be Exported? Should It Be?

It is tempting to assume that a yearning for democracy is universal. Even if this is in fact the case (and there is no clear evidence in this regard), it seems undeniable that there is no "one size fits all" formula for democracy. For example, some long-standing, highly successful democracies—the United Kingdom, Holland, Norway—are also monarchies, whose systems are justified by the claim that hereditary rulers, even when they exercise only symbolic authority, also provide a sense of national unity and continuity. Thus, it is not necessarily isolationist to oppose "nation building," especially given that it is often difficult—perhaps impossible—for politicians and military leaders in one country (e.g., the United States) to prescribe the optimum and most socially acceptable governmental system for another, especially when the recipients of such "assistance" (e.g., Iraq, Afghanistan) have very different historical experience as well as social and religious expectations. What others want for themselves seems destined forever to trump what any country—however well-meaning or imperially strong—wants for them.

It is also widely assumed that democracy and "rule of law" are closely allied, if not synonymous. And yet, many Muslim countries, for example, expect that the religious laws that are to rule (*sharia*, or law in concert with the Koran) must be derived from religious texts (in Egypt, for example, the "rule of law" under the Muslim Brotherhood is supposed to be both secular and sharia), whereas most Western countries assume a much greater degree of separation of church (or synagogue, or mosque) and state.

In addition to the problem of international heterogeneity—the simple yet profound reality that different societies have different traditions and expectations—the export of democracy as an avowed policy goal also runs into the problem that it may serve as a smokescreen for less benevolent intentions, such that the export of democracy could become a *causus bellum* (a reason for war) . . . or at least, what might be called an *excusatum bellum* (an excuse for war)! For example, it was claimed, after the fact, that the Iraq War was actually part of a long-term "Freedom Agenda" designed to "bring democracy to the Middle East."

This claim, too, turns out to have been highly questionable, not only because it manifestly failed, but because as it was being made, the United States maintained close relationships with absolute hereditary monarchies (Saudi Arabia, Bahrain), as well as dictatorships that gave lip service to democracy, but whose actual systems were repressive and highly authoritarian (Egypt, Tunisia, Yemen, Algeria, Jordan). Behind the near-universal diplomatic facade of support for democracy, major countries almost always support governments that they perceive as being useful to them, regardless of their human rights records.

Finally, it must be acknowledged that the enthusiasm that typically surrounds democratic movements worldwide, and that is manifested so dramatically in the immediate aftermath of "success" (namely, the overthrow or forced abdication of a tyrant), often obscures this sobering fact: In many cases, the hardest part of moving toward democracy isn't the liberation of a country but establishing a functioning democratic government . . . however that is defined. It is especially difficult to accomplish this in states that lack a tradition of democratic governance or even of "civil society."[10] For example, shortly after the Arab Spring overthrow of the Mubarak dictatorship in Egypt, huge numbers of citizens of that country were glued to their televisions watching with rapt attention the first genuine presidential debate among independent candidates . . . a first for Egypt, and according to some observers, for the entire Arab world.

On the other hand, historians and political theorists speak of a "Thermidorian Reaction," referring to a time in the French Revolutionary calendar when Robespierre, who had orchestrated much of the terror, was himself overthrown (and beheaded). The reaction itself was a period of relative moderation, a response to the violent excess of the original French Revolution. It isn't uncommon for modern democratic revolutions to have their own Thermidorian Reactions, in which, after having deposed an autocratic government and achieved a degree of democratic governance, countries then slip back into systems not that different from what they had known previously.

## A FINAL NOTE ON MOVEMENTS TOWARD DEMOCRACY

In the concluding paragraphs of Albert Camus' novel, *The Plague*, the residents of Oran (in Algeria) spill into the streets, enthusiastically celebrating the end of a devastating bubonic plague. And yet, the novel's hero, Dr. Rieux, who valiantly fought the plague, observes that such triumphs, although hard won, may only be temporary:

[H]e knew that the tale he had to tell could not be one of a final victory. It could be only the record of what had had to be done, and what assuredly would have to be done again in the never ending fight against terror and its relentless onslaughts, despite their personal afflictions, by all who, while unable to be saints but refusing to bow down to pestilences, strive their utmost to be healers.

And indeed, as he listened to the cries of joy rising from the town, Rieux remembered that such joy is always imperiled. He knew what those jubilant crowds did not know but could have learned from books: that the plague bacillus never dies or disappears for good; that it can lie dormant for years and years . . . and that perhaps the day would come when, for the bane and the enlightening of men, it would rouse up its rats again and send them forth to die in a happy city.

Following the real-life overthrow of Egypt's Hosni Mubarak in 2011, Egyptians similarly flooded into Tahrir Square to celebrate *their* deliverance. A dispassionate observer, however, could not help noting that in many ways the hard work lay ahead, and indeed, subsequent events in post-Mubarak Egypt have shown how difficult it was to persuade the army to relinquish control and to negotiate a democracy that does not devolve into extremism.

At the same time, and despite the difficulties, uncertainties, and downsides of the world's erratic movement toward democracy, it is appropriate to conclude this chapter on a note of admiration and optimism, repeating an earlier observation of Camus's fictional Dr. Rieux, namely "to state quite simply what we learn in a time of pestilence: that there are more things to admire in men than to despise."

## NOTES

1. Named for the artificial grass first employed in the Houston Astrodome, a sports stadium in the United States.

2. Consistent with the maxim that states act more out of their own perceived self-interest than from generalized altruism, it has been claimed that among the reasons the prime ministers of France, the UK and Italy strongly supported NATO intervention in Libya is that they feared that if Gadhafi succeeded in massacring large numbers of his own citizens, this would generate a mass exodus to Europe at a time when their delicate economies would have had an especially difficult time accommodating large numbers of indigent refugees.

3. Rebecca Solnit. "Tomgram: Rebecca Solnit, Hope and Turmoil in 2011." TomDispatch.com. March 20, 2011, http://www.tomdispatch.com/blog/175369/tomgram%3A_rebecca_solnit,_hope_and_turmoil_in_2011/.

4. Hannah Arendt. 1963. *On Revolution*. London: Faber & Faber.

5. George Kennan. 2012 (1951). *American Diplomacy*. Chicago: University of Chicago Press.

6. David Kinsella (2005). "No Rest for the Democratic Peace". *American Political Science Review 99*: 453–457.

7. Randolph Bourne. 1964. *War and the Intellectuals: Collected Essays 1915–1919*. New York: Harper Torchbook.

8. Walter Lippmann. 1989. The Public Philosophy. New Brunswick, NJ: Transaction Publishers.

9. After a movie of that name, in which a U.S. president initiates a fake war in an effort to distract public attention from his involvement in a sex scandal just weeks before his election.

10. The term "civil society," which originates from 19th-century political theory, currently, refers to the range of unofficial, cross-cutting nongovernmental systems and structures that function within most advanced societies, providing coherence as well as civic participation: such things as professional organizations, trade unions, political parties, even seemingly trivial groupings such as book clubs or sports associations. It is considered a significant measure of functioning democracy.

## QUESTIONS FOR FURTHER REFLECTION

1. Do you believe that democracy is the best possible political system? Why or why not?

2. What are some arguments supporting the idea that democracy should be exported to other countries? That it should not?

3. It is widely acknowledged, that if given the opportunity to choose their own government, by election, the population of certain countries (e.g., Algeria) would likely choose leaders who do not support democracy as it is understood in the West. What implications, if any, should this have for foreign policy?

4. Explore the idea of democracy as something other than a formal electoral system at the national level: that is, the implications of "economic" or "social" democracy.

5. Current data suggest that (a) democracies tend not to fight one another but that (b) democracies are not especially waraverse, and, moreover, that (c) when democracies engage in war, they do so with special intensity. Speculate as to the reasons for these three phenomena.

## SUGGESTIONS FOR FURTHER READING

Council on Foreign Relations/Foreign Affairs. 2011. *The New Arab Revolt: What It Means and What Comes Next*. Council on Foreign Relations: New York.

Hamid Debashi. 2012. *The Arab Spring: The End of Post-Colonialism*. London: Zed Books.

James L. Gelvin. 2012. *The Arab Uprisings: What everyone needs to know*. New York: Oxford University Press.

Samuel P. Huntington. 1993. *The Third Wave: Democratization in the Late 20th Century*. Norman: University of Oklahoma Press.

Juan J. Linz and A. Stepan. 1996. *Problems of Democratic Transition and Consolidation: Southern Europe, South America, and Post-Communist Europe*. Baltimore: Johns Hopkins University Press.

Lincoln A. Mitchell. 2012. *The Color Revolutions*. State College: Pennsylvania State University Press.

Lin Noueihed and Alex Warren. 2012. *The Battle for the Arab Spring: Revolution, Counter-Revolution and the Making of a New Era*. New Haven, CT: Yale University Press.

# CHAPTER 22

# NATIONAL RECONCILIATION

South African archbishop and Nobel Peace Prize winner Desmond Tutu (center) with fellow commissioners listening to testimony before the Truth and Reconciliation Commission in 1996.

*Source:* © 2008 Getty Images.

> *We can indeed transcend the conflicts of the past, we can hold hands as we realize our common humanity.*
>
> – Archbishop Desmond Tutu

Just as every human being has a history, so does every society, nation, and country. And just as each person's past will have an impact on his or her present and future, the same applies to societies, nations, and countries. This has implications for positive peace: We cannot simply direct complex social systems toward a given goal (assuming, of course, that such a goal can even be agreed upon!) and assume that those systems will proceed as desired, independent of their histories. Although social history often includes major benefits, all too often it is also marred by massive pain and suffering, which must somehow be overcome if the society's future is to incorporate positive peace.

In the opening sentence of his great novel, *Anna Karenina*, Tolstoy wrote that "All happy families resemble one another, each unhappy family is unhappy in its own way." Although judgment may be reserved regarding the first part of this famous pronouncement, it seems clear there have been many distinct sources of societal unhappiness. Moreover, it is likely that such discontent—sometimes including anger and even rage—must somehow be acknowledged and confronted. In short, societal structures embodying positive peace must take account of past injustices, violence, and, indeed, any number of regrettable and sometimes even terrible abuses.

There is legitimate worry that once a people or a country has experienced lacerating violence, it is not only difficult but also perhaps impossible for the victims to return to a pattern of peaceful coexistence. (It may be difficult for the perpetrators, too, although concern in this regard has focused overwhelmingly on the victims rather than the victimizers.) Could it be that a particularly destructive history might serve as a kind of poison, polluting the future no less than the past?

Regrettably, there is some evidence supporting this gloomy proposition. It has been suggested, for example, that one reason post–Saddam Hussein Iraq had such difficulty forming a democratic and nonviolent society is the legacy of anger and resentment (especially between Sunnis, Shiites, and Kurds) bequeathed by a violent past, one for which the West, including not just the United States but also a repressive British colonial regime, had substantial responsibility.

At the same time, however, there have been hopeful examples of national reconciliation, in which people have carved out a largely nonviolent social prospect despite horrific past abuses. In this chapter, we examine some of these successes, the difficulties encountered, and the techniques employed.

## Truth and Reconciliation Commissions

The most widely used such technique involves the establishment of so-called truth and reconciliation commissions (TRCs). These commissions generally share certain characteristics. Sometimes they are formed by citizen committees, often locally constituted. More often, however, TRCs are established by a recently empowered national government and are given the job of uncovering past wrongdoing, generally atrocities perpetrated by an earlier government. Usually, the goal is not so much to resolve grievances or right past wrongs as to establish an environment in which the present and future will no longer be compromised by bitterness and resentment generated by the actions of an earlier regime. The hope is simple, but nonetheless profound: to facilitate national healing.

With this in mind, such commissions (under various names) have been planned or established in Argentina, Chile, El Salvador, Fiji, Ghana, Guatemala, Liberia, Morocco, Panama, Peru, Sierra Leone, South Africa, South Korea, East Timor, and the United States. Others can be anticipated. Typically, these efforts take place after a country emerges from difficult periods of civil war, unrest, or dictatorship.

These commissions are intended to provide for the victims of government atrocities the partial satisfaction of learning the truth about the past, when possible including clear documentation of abuses: numbers killed, tortured, forcibly exiled, property confiscated, and so forth. "Failure to remember, collectively, triumphs and accomplishments diminishes us," writes an expert on the process. "But failure to remember, collectively, injustice and cruelty is an ethical breach. It implies no responsibility and no commitment to prevent inhumanity in the future. Even worse, failures of collective memory stoke fires of resentment and revenge."[1] In short, the truth often hurts, but failure to acknowledge the truth can hurt even more.

A further benefit of the truth-and-reconciliation process is that it may prevent later historical revisionism (the erasure or whitewashing of the past). In the absence of honest investigation of past abuses, wrongdoers can claim that such events never occurred (for example, Holocaust deniers) or that they were simply the actions of "a few bad apples" (e.g., the official U.S. government explanation of torture at the Abu Ghraib prison camp in post–Saddam Hussein Iraq). Yet another hoped-for payoff of the truth-and-reconciliation process is that it helps victims and their families achieve a kind of emotional closure. Often, however, success requires expressed apology by the perpetrators, which is often difficult to obtain, especially when this is akin to acknowledging guilt, which might expose the confessors to possible prosecution. In hope of circumventing this problem, the various TRCs—most notably in the case of South Africa—have been empowered to grant clemency to perpetrators who "come clean" as to their past misdeeds.

## The Case of South Africa

The standard TRC model is widely acknowledged to be South Africa's Truth and Reconciliation Commission, established by President Nelson Mandela after the fall of that country's apartheid regime. In the South African version, the perpetrators are expected to acknowledge their misdeeds and express contrition, and then, in the ideal case, the victims are expected to offer forgiveness.

To some extent, this commission is credited with having contributed to the relatively nonviolent transition from white minority to black majority rule, all the more remarkable given the viciousness of the white regime under apartheid. South Africa's TRC was created by the "National Unity and Reconciliation Act" in 1995. Here is part of the preamble to that legislation, which provides a good description of the goals of TRCs more generally:

> SINCE the Constitution of the Republic of South Africa . . . provides a historic bridge between the past of a deeply divided society characterized by strife, conflict, untold suffering and injustice, and a future founded on the recognition of human rights, democracy and peaceful co-existence for all South Africans, irrespective of color, race, class, belief or sex; AND SINCE it is deemed necessary to establish the truth in relation to past events as well as the motives for and circumstances in which gross violations of human fights have occurred, and to make the findings known in order to prevent a repetition of such acts in future; AND SINCE the Constitution states that the pursuit of national unity, the well-being of all South African citizens and peace require reconciliation between the people of South Africa and the reconstruction of society; AND SINCE the Constitution states that there is a need for understanding but not for vengeance, a need for reparation but not for retaliation . . .

The commission's motto was "Without truth, no healing; without forgiveness, no future." Headed by Bishop Desmond Tutu (a Nobel Peace Prize winner for his earlier efforts on behalf of ending apartheid), the commission not only took testimony from victims but also was empowered to grant pardons to perpetrators who acknowledged their actions and sought forgiveness. Three years later, in 1998, the commission's final report was delivered to President

Mandela. Former president F. W. de Klerk, as well as the African National Congress (ANC, South Africa's post-apartheid governing party), attempted to block publication, because de Klerk, personally, and the ANC, organizationally, were implicated in gross human rights violations. To many observers, the fact that both current and former rulers of South Africa found the TRC's work objectionable may constitute evidence that the process was fair and impartial. Such efforts are difficult and liable to be fraught with controversy.

When it comes to institutionalizing justice and promoting reconciliation in the aftermath of human rights abuses, some people advocate stern prosecution, while others favor amnesty and impunity for perpetrators. South Africa's TRC is widely seen as representing a third way, steering between these two extremes. It is representative of the dilemma facing many new democracies just emerging from past violations of human rights and whose stability requires a response to this past but whose societies and governments may be so fragile as to be threatened by draconian measures.

The South African TRC had the authority to grant amnesty. As Bishop Tutu put it, "Freedom was exchanged for truth," emphasizing that this referred not only to freedom from apartheid but also to freedom from the tyranny of past abuses. This was controversial, since, in the minds of many people, it resulted in freedom for malefactors to avoid punishment. Tutu emphasized, however, that restorative justice (attempting to make amends to victims) is preferable to retributive justice (punishing the perpetrators), and that the former is consistent with the African cultural tradition of *ubuntu,* which values healing and the encouragement of social relationships over the satisfactions of punishment. Proceedings of the South African TRC were nationally televised, widely watched, and generally credited with helping establish a shared national conscience.

## The German Postwar Experience

One consequence of South Africa's experience with apartheid is that with the end of the white supremacist regime and establishment of a democratically elected government, initially headed by Nelson Mandela, large numbers of victims—mostly, but not entirely, black Africans—found themselves living in close proximity to their victimizers—largely, but not entirely, white members of the South African security service. Each country's experience, however, is different.

The abuses perpetrated by Nazi Germany during World War II, for example, were especially horrific and genocidal. Among the innumerable victims of the Holocaust were approximately 6 million Jews, who were killed. Other victims included Roma ("gypsies"), gays, the mentally ill, political dissidents, and millions of Slavs. Many others were forcibly deported or emigrated, leaving a population consisting largely of perpetrators or those who were (or claimed to be) unknowing bystanders. Post–World War II Germany was therefore less in need of reconciliation between victims and perpetrators than of society-wide reconciliation with its own past.

*Vergangenheitsbewältigung* is a composite German word that speaks to the process of dealing with the past (*Vergangenheit* = past; *Bewältigung* = coming to terms with or mastery of), having the added implication that doing so is a struggle. The philosopher George Santayana famously observed that "those who forget the past are condemned to repeat it."

*Vergangenheitsbewältigung* describes the effort to respond to Santayana's warning, especially with respect to the Holocaust and other atrocities committed by the Third Reich, as well as the complicity of many German civilians. The postwar Federal Republic of Germany ("West Germany" until the postcommunist reunification with its eastern counterpart) assumed the legal obligations of Adolf Hitler's government, including payment of reparations to Israel, yet the German public's acceptance of its moral responsibilities lagged behind.

*Vergangenheitsbewältigung* became a goal of many liberal Germans, beginning around the late 1950s, after the most urgent needs of postwar reconstruction were met. German churches—Lutheran as well as Catholic—have played a significant role in the effort to induce Germans to acknowledge their guilt and to encourage a theology of repentance. German schools constitute another major focus. Curriculum guides typically provide materials and experiences that expose students to the abuses of the Nazi era, including field trips to concentration camps and lectures from Holocaust survivors.

Much of postwar German literature—including, but not limited to, the work of Nobel Prize–winning novelist Günter Grass—has been similarly concerned with coming to terms with that country's past misdeeds. Similarly in the cultural sphere, many sites of atrocities are now commemorated with plaques, and public monuments to Holocaust victims have been widely erected, just as such extermination camps as Dachau, Buchenwald, and Bergen-Belsen are open for visitors. Several years after German reunification in 1999, a Holocaust Memorial was inaugurated in Berlin, to which the German capital had been moved. It is informally known as the "Holocaust-Mahnmal," which is noteworthy since *Mahnmal* carries with it an implication that goes beyond "memorial" or "remembrance" to include "warning" or "admonition."

On the other hand, such efforts do not usually include acknowledgments of personal blame on the part of perpetrators. Indeed, denial, convenient amnesia, and sometimes lying are more common. Notable examples include the case of Kurt Waldheim, once secretary-general of the United Nations and president of Austria, who hid his earlier involvement in a Nazi extermination unit in Greece, and even novelist Günter Grass, who—after routinely excoriating Germans for their widespread complicity in World War II atrocities—only belatedly acknowledged his own enrollment (as a 17-year-old) in the Waffen-SS, a Gestapo-connected military unit.

The German postwar experience of coming to terms—albeit sometimes haltingly—with a regrettable past was revived to some extent after the fall of the Iron Curtain and the reunification of East and West Germany. Thus, the often-brutal actions by employees of the communist state (notably the East German *Stasi,* or secret police) have been widely subjected to efforts at *Vergangenheitsbewältigung.*

## The Postwar Japanese Experience

Although this process in Germany has not been an unmitigated success, it has constituted an admirable effort. By contrast, the people and government of postwar Japan have by and large been resistant to accepting blame and responsibility for their World War II outrages, including the "rape of Nanking," mistreatment of Allied prisoners of war, and the forced enrollment of many women (especially Koreans) as sex slaves. The issue remains a sore point in contemporary Japan, with the widespread claim that (1) no immoral or illegal acts actually occurred, (2) whatever actually happened was in the context of legitimate military actions of self-defense, and/or (3) far from encouraging national reconciliation, acknowledgment of wrongdoing would set right-wing nationalists against left-wing antimilitarists and thus "tear the country apart."

At the same time, Japan's refusal to engage in a process equivalent to Germany's *Vergangenheitsbewältigung* has emerged as a major stumbling block to political harmony between modern Japan and its neighbors—many of them, victims—on the East Asian mainland, notably China and Korea, as well as the Philippines. In this case, national reconciliation has not been a primary driving force, because Japanese society is mostly homogeneous and does not include large numbers of victims living in immediate proximity to their previous tormentors; as a result, international reconciliation has also been inhibited.

## Other Cases

Japan is not unique in this regard. Russia refuses to apologize for the "Katyn Forest" massacre of Polish officers early in World War II; Turkey denies that it perpetrated genocide against Armenians early in the 20th century and indeed, it is literally illegal within Turkey to refer to the Armenian genocide; Chinese government officials remain largely unrepentant for the millions killed under Mao Tse-tung or for the (perhaps) thousands of democracy protesters slaughtered in Tiananmen Square in 1989; and the United States government has not acknowledged any formal guilt for its pre–Civil War history of slavery, its massacres of Native Americans, or the atomic bombing of Hiroshima and Nagasaki. Sadly, this list does not come close to exhausting the roster of abuses that call for reconciliation.

## Latin America and Elsewhere

In Argentina, the report of the "National Commission on the Disappeared" became a best-seller and helped generate widespread awareness about the abuses of that country's "dirty war" (1976–1983). Such publications often include a sense of moral urgency; for example, the Argentina document was titled *Nunca Mas* ("never again"). Democracy now appears well established in that country, and most observers agree that even if they were to slip back into dictatorship, a return to comparable abuses is, as a result of the earlier truth telling, especially unlikely. Similarly, the Guatemalan "Commission of Historical Clarification" not only examined discrimination and marginalization of that country's indigenous population but also indicted military authorities for genocide against contemporary Mayans. Although not yet accepted by the Guatemalan elite, the commission's report has expanded the national dialogue to include what had previously been unmentionable.

Not surprisingly, it is often easier to come to terms with misdeeds when the perpetrators—not to mention the victims—are elderly or deceased. However, there has been a recent trend toward responding more contemporaneously, especially after a transition from dictatorship to democratic rule. During the 1970s and 1980s, for example, many repressive Latin American regimes and other U.S. allies sought to avoid obvious forms of violent repression in order to retain financial and diplomatic support. The result was widespread reliance on clandestine death squads and unacknowledged "disappearances" of political opponents. After the fall of these governments, identification of state-sponsored abuses became widespread, although in certain countries—such as Zimbabwe and the Philippines—TRCs have been authorized, but their reports have either never been completed or not released.

In some countries, dictators have successfully insisted that as part of their willingness to relinquish power, they and their henchmen be guaranteed immunity from prosecution and even from having their misdeeds made public. For example, in Argentina, the National Commission for Forced Disappearances investigated human rights violations, including an estimated 30,000 "disappearances" committed during the so-called dirty war. In nearly every case, however, the commission was empowered only to report on the status of those disappeared and was expressly prohibited from identifying the perpetrators. Next door, in Brazil, a "National Committee on Truth" has been established and charged with examining abuses (torture and assassinations) committed by the military dictators who ruled that country from 1965 to 1985. An interesting outcome of that committee's work is that in the Rio de Janeiro, state government officials announced in 2012 that it would apologize to President Dilma Rousseff for the torture she suffered following her imprisonment during the 1980s for antigovernment activities.

## The Case of the United States

Nor is the United States exempt . . . from abuses or from attempts to respond to them. In 1979, five African Americans were shot to death and 10 wounded in Greensboro, North Carolina, after which the white defendants were acquitted, even though the shootings had been videotaped. More than two decades later, the Greensboro Truth and Reconciliation Commission—the first such formal body ever established in the United States—was established. Its report, presented in 2005, concluded,

> "The passage of time alone cannot bring closure, nor resolve feelings of guilt and lingering trauma, for those impacted by the events of November 3, 1979. Nor can there be any genuine healing for the city of Greensboro unless the truth surrounding these events is honestly confronted, the suffering fully acknowledged, accountability established, and forgiveness and reconciliation facilitated."

Another commission, this one federally appointed, investigated the internment of Japanese Americans during World War II, eventually resulting in the payment of reparations. Also, President Clinton formally apologized for the infamous Tuskegee syphilis experiments, in which African Americans were intentionally left untreated to observe the course of the disease; once again, financial reparations were paid. It remains unclear to what extent such actions constitute mere window dressing or genuine contrition, just as it remains to be seen whether they lead to ultimate reconciliation. Acknowledgment of past abuses may make their repetition less likely in the future. Toward that end, for example, the Australian government organized a commission to report on that country's mid-20th century policy of taking aboriginal children from their homes and indoctrinating them into Anglo culture. One result has been a "National Sorry Day" and recognition that such acts were grievous misdeeds. Similarly, in 2011, an "Indian Residential Schools Truth and Reconciliation Commission" was established in Canada to explore human rights abuses committed by the Canadian Indian residential school system.

# In the Absence of Truthful Reconciliation . . .

Regrettably, instead of truth and reconciliation, some brutal governments are inclined to foster "exaggeration and aggravation," seeking to enhance their public support by playing upon the fears and resentments of their own population. Public celebrations, for example, are often used as opportunities to stick a collective finger in another's eye, or alternatively, to remind a populace of their shared outrage vis-à-vis other groups.

Since the 19th century, for example, Northern Irish Protestants ("Orangemen") have paraded to Drumcree each year on the Sunday preceding the 12th of July. Until the recent Good Friday Accords and its attendant reconciliation between Irish Catholics and Protestants, this parade, along with others during the "marching season," generated predictable violence and considerable anxiety, based upon unreconciled injuries long ago. In 1610, England enacted the "Articles of Plantation," by which the best land was confiscated from the native Irish and given to Crown loyalists, nearly all of them Protestant Scottish and English. In 1641, the displaced Irish rebelled and slaughtered thousands of loyalists, after which in 1649 the English, led by Oliver Cromwell, massacred thousands of Irish. Further Irish rebellion ensued, until eventually the English king, William of Orange, defeated the Irish resistance movement at the Battle of the Boyne in 1690. It is this victory, four centuries ago, that loyalists persisted in celebrating by their annual marches. Moreover, for decades they went out of their way—literally—to route the victory parades through Catholic communities.

Following France's ignominious defeat in the Franco-Prussian War (1871), the newly unified German state annexed the previously French province of Alsace and most of Lorraine. For decades thereafter, the return of these two regions became a French national obsession, with schoolchildren beginning their day by regularly reciting pledges to achieve this goal. Eventually they did, with the "help" of World War I. It was the French yearning for getting even with the Germans that contributed to the pre-World War I Franco-Russian alliance in support of Serbia, against Germany, after the assassination of the Austrian archduke in 1914.

The most troublesome national struggles are those that have been going on for a long time, typically fueled by widespread resentment and unreconciled national anger over past abuses, often reciprocal, even though they may also be asymmetric. Israelis mourn the Holocaust, in which more than 6 million European Jews were murdered—vowing "never again"—while Palestinians regularly and painfully remind themselves about *Al-Naqba* ("The Catastrophe") of Israel's founding and the subsequent expulsion of 750,000 Palestinians from their homes in 1948. In the absence of national reconciliation, historical experience matters, not simply as facts from the past but also because such experience, especially when painful, generates passions and animosity as well as a felt need for revenge and restitution in the present. As a pair of observers, one Israeli and one Palestinian, put it:

> For Israel's Jewish population, this includes displacement, persecution, the life of the ghetto, and the horrors of the Holocaust; and the long, frustrated quest for a normal, recognized and accepted homeland. There is a craving for a future that will not echo the past and for the kind of ordinary security—the unquestioned acceptance of a Jewish presence in the region—that even overwhelming military superiority cannot guarantee. . . . For Palestinians, the most primal demands relate to addressing and redressing a historical experience of dispossession, expulsion, dispersal, massacres, occupation, discrimination, denial of dignity, persistent killing off of their leaders, and the relentless fracturing of their national polity.[2]

Groups and nations often ruminate over past wrongs, reminding themselves of their need to right past wrongs someday. And leaders are often eager to manipulate this inclination for their own ends. For example, consider the history of Serbian aggrievement against Turkish Muslims. In 1989, Slobodan Milošević, then leader of Yugoslavia, announced to an increasingly agitated gathering of Serbs, "No one will ever dare beat you again!" It wasn't lost on Milošević's audience that he was speaking on the precise anniversary of the "Battle of the Blackbirds," near Pristina, the present-day capital of Kosovo. The year was 1389, when invading armies of Ottoman Turks defeated Serb forces. Six hundred years later, Milošević, standing on the same battlefield, setting in motion violent oppression of Kosovars was not simply a case of Milošević reminding his listeners of the unreconciled memory of past pain but of literally reviving it within them, whereupon it fueled fresh outbreaks of murderous violence.

# TRC Downsides and Caveats

At one point in Dante's *The Inferno* (canto XXXIII), Count Ugolino is asked about the abuse he has suffered: "You ask me to renew a grief so desperate," he responds, "that the very thought of speaking it tears my heart in two." He goes on: "But if my words may be a seed that bears the fruit of infamy for him I gnaw, I shall weep, but tell my story through my tears." (In Dante's vision, Ugolino is condemned to spend eternity gnawing on the head of his—equally guilty—opponent; thus both men are punished.) Two disadvantages of TRCs are here revealed: The process itself can be painful, and, to some extent at least, there is powerful motivation to "gnaw" the victimizer(s) and encourage "the fruit of infamy"—that is, revenge—rather than healing. Yet healing may require precisely such a process.

Another possibly unintended consequence of officially sponsored reconciliation is that insofar as it can help victimizers avoid punishment, it may reduce the deterrent effect that might result from meting out legitimate justice. In certain cases, TRCs encourage or require some forms of reparations rather than criminal punishment, a policy that seems more likely to lead to healing. The German government, for example, has paid significant sums to Israel, as partial reparations for the murder of Jews during the Holocaust, and the U.S. government has paid reparations to Japanese American victims of forced resettlement during World War II. Financial compensation seems better than its absence, but it also risks trivializing horrendous abuses by suggesting that money can make up for atrocity. The idea of reparations for slavery in the United States has been floated but rejected, although apologies have been offered. Reconciliation seems unlikely without a context of social justice. As Desmond Tutu notably put it: "How can I reconcile with you when your foot is on my neck?"

It is also important to take account of local cultural traditions, which in some cases demand that bad things must be ignored—rather than confronted—in order to be overcome. After the death of dictator Francisco Franco, for example, Spanish authorities—strongly supported by public opinion—consciously decided not to review the many murders and crimes associated with the Spanish Civil War and the years of fascist tyranny that followed.

Similarly, cultural tradition in Mozambique discourages talking about traumatic experiences. Even though more than 1 million civilians were maimed, tortured, or murdered during the Portuguese occupation of that country and the anticolonial revolution that followed, no public discussion or denunciation of these events has occurred; yet, for the most part, the conflicting parties appear reconciled. Similar postgenocide silence has characterized Cambodia, in this case partly because some prominent officials who were involved in that country's notorious "killing fields" under the Khmer Rouge are still in power and also because the Cambodian style of Buddhism emphasizes that reconciliation can only be hindered by a focus on "justice" or "retribution." One lesson thus appears to be that although much can be learned from the experiences of other cultures, there is no "one size fits all" prescription for national reconciliation.

For example, most of the successful work of TRCs has been in countries that self-identify with a Christian tradition, and reconciliation and forgiveness are explicitly proclaimed to be Christian values (although such values are not universally practiced). It remains unclear whether similar procedures can succeed in cultures with other expressed values, as well as between different religious and cultural traditions.

Moreover, it is reasonable to ask whether a TRC-type process is even necessary for a country to transition from a violent past to a future society operating under the rule of law. Would TRC-sponsored confrontations inhibit such a transition, for example, by generating a culture of lawless impunity or because the perpetrators (as in the case of post-Pinochet Chile) remain so influential that moving against them may endanger a fragile successor democracy? On the other hand, are punishments necessary in order to obtain "closure"? Another problem concerns the selective use of TRCs to further a political agenda. Thus a "Philippine Truth Commission," formed in 2010, was severely criticized by the Philippine Supreme Court as a political witch hunt undertaken by the current government as a way of discrediting its predecessors. And in Sri Lanka, a "Lessons Learnt and Reconciliation Commission" was established in 2010, to investigate various claims of human rights abuse during the Tamil-Sinhalese civil war; although its report was quite extensive, it was also roundly criticized by major human rights organizations such as Human Rights Watch, Amnesty International, and the United Nations as representing an effort by the victorious Sinhalese government to prevent independent organizations from investigating abuses it perpetrated.

## Some Conceptual Debates

One argument holds that the only acceptable response to gross violations of human rights (genocide, ethnic cleansing, etc.) is criminal prosecution and punishment—that is, retributive justice. In addition to satisfying a widespread human desire, retributive justice, it is claimed, helps deter comparable abuses in the future. By their nature, however, TRCs don't do this; instead, they focus on restorative justice, including, but not limited to, the payment of reparations, as well as accepting blame by the perpetrators and encouraging forgiveness by the victims. Two relevant poles of human inclination—vengeance on the one hand and forgiveness on the other—are deep-seated in the human psyche and culturally elaborated in social institutions.

"'The past is never dead," wrote Nobel Prize–winning novelist William Faulkner. "It's not even past." If so, it can only be ignored, not avoided, and not only is there a persistent "duty to remember," but society's encounter with its past is an unavoidable part of its present. But how much farther does this duty go? Is there a duty to achieve justice? And, if so, does this involve only punishment? Reconciliation? Forgiveness?

Even "truth" can be problematic. When it comes to "dirty wars," every side has its preferred version of what really happened, somewhat like the famous Japanese movie, *Rashômon,* which depicts a murder from numerous perspectives, each with its own version of what "really" happened.

Martha Minnow has argued that there may actually be kinds of truth, especially when dealing with complex social phenomena. For example, "empirical truth" refers to whether something happened, and, if so, what were, for example, the actual numbers of rapes, mutilations, murders, and so forth. This is different from "personal truth," the experiences of victims themselves. Then there is "legal" truth, which refers to the forensic requirements that are required to lead to conviction and punishment of perpetrators and which necessarily varies depending on the evidentiary rules of each country (is it, for example, a matter of "beyond reasonable doubt," "the preponderance of the evidence," or "realistic certainty"?). Finally, there is "meaningful truth," which speaks—in predictably contradictory ways—to what the events in question actually mean: The South African security forces, for example, typically maintain that their actions were conducted in defense of the country, just as Latin American military dictators argue that they were protecting their homelands from "communist subversion," either indigenous (as in Chile) or "imported" from such venues as Nicaragua or Cuba.

## Alternatives to Reconciliation

For some, the prospect of effective reconciliation seems to be unrealistically optimistic; for others, the downside to such a process is so great that it simply isn't worth it. But what are the alternatives? One is to ignore the past and attempt to move on. Another is to acknowledge the past, but lightly, and attempt to move on. Yet another—and one that is all too common—is to engage the past but to do so aggressively as a cause of present, future, and escalating cycles of violence—generating a continuing culture of revenge, feuding, and retaliation.

Early in the 20th century, the social scientist R. F. Barton studied a Filipino tribe, the Ifugao, looking at their social rules and how they settled disputes. His findings have become a classic of legal anthropology. "The Ifugao," wrote Barton, "has one general law, which with a few notable exceptions he applies to killings, be they killings in war, murders, or executions . . That law is: A life must be paid with a life."

And here is the testimony of Milovan Djilas, who was born into a perpetually feuding Montenegrin clan and eventually rose to become vice president of the former Yugoslavia. Djilas spanned the interval between ethnic feuding and modernity in his nation, and his insights into vengeance—written nearly 40 years ago—foretell the stubborn enmity that devoured his unhappy land:

> Vengeance—this is a breath of life one shares from the cradle with one's fellow clansmen, in both good fortune and bad, vengeance from eternity. Vengeance was the debt we paid for the love and sacrifice our forebears and fellow clansmen bore for us. It was the defense of our honor and good name, and the guarantee of our maidens. It was our pride before others; our blood was not water that anyone could spill. It was, moreover, our pastures and springs—more beautiful than anyone else's—our family feasts and births. It was the glow in our eyes, the flame in our cheeks, the pounding in our temples, the word that turned to stone in our throats on our hearing that our blood had been shed. It was the sacred task transmitted in the hour of death to those who had just been conceived in our blood. It was centuries of manly pride and heroism, survival, a mother's milk and a sister's vow, bereaved parents and children in black, joy and songs turned into silence and wailing.

Because of the power of such feuding and the vivid historical memory of its participants, in the absence of reconciliation, individuals have often been forced to bear the weight of grudges accumulated by earlier generations. Russian anthropologist Sergei Arutiunov described the situation of many Georgians, Abkhasians, Armenians, and Azeris:

> Among the Caucasus highlanders, a man must know the names and some details of the lives and the locations of the tombstones of seven ancestors of his main line. People fight not only for arable land; they fight for the land where the tombstones of their ancestors are located. Revenge is not only for events today, but also for the atrocities from wars eight generations ago.

It is precisely to interrupt such cycles of violence and in the hope of generating a more peaceful future that scholars, as well as pragmatic politicians, have devoted increasing attention to the process of reconciliation.

## A FINAL NOTE ON NATIONAL RECONCILIATION

It is shockingly easy to destroy a complex structure, compared with building it in the first place or reconstructing it after it has been knocked down. By the same token, it is, unfortunately, much easier to disrupt society than to repair it after serious damage has been done. Conflict—and particularly, violence—often does considerable damage to the social fabric, leaving societies in substantial need of repair, even after the perpetrators may no longer be in power. There is no "one-size-fits-all" solution to the problem of achieving reconciliation after national trauma. However, it is increasingly clear that such reconciliation is not only necessary but also possible and that a truthful, honest recounting of the past can contribute greatly toward achieving a more peaceful future. In this regard, the newly emerging phenomenon of National Reconciliation Commissions recommends itself for serious consideration.

## NOTES

1. Martha Minnow. 2003. *"Memory and Hate." In Breaking the Cycles of Hatred: Memory, Law, and Repair.* Princeton, NJ: Princeton University Press.

2. H. Agha and R. Malley. 2009. "Obama and the Middle East." *The New York Review of Books,* LVI, (10): 67–69.

## QUESTIONS FOR FURTHER REFLECTION

1. Discuss ways of approaching matters of national reconciliation other than through the use of truth and reconciliation commissions.

2. Is it possible to achieve reconciliation without focusing on potentially painful truths?

3. Describe some benefits and problems likely to be encountered in attempting to apply the truth-and-reconciliation model to matters of international tensions instead of—as has largely been the case thus far—restricting it to within-country issues.

4. Make a case (perhaps difficult for most students of peace and conflict studies!) in *favor* of revenge and retaliation.

5. Similarly, make a case for truth and reconciliation with respect to socioeconomic and/or environmental injuries and disputes?

## SUGGESTIONS FOR FURTHER READING

Annelies Verdoolaege. 2008. *Reconciliation Discourse.* Philadelphia: John Benjamins.

Desmond Tutu. 2000. *No Future Without Forgiveness.* New York: Doubleday (Image).

Margaret Soenser Breen. 2005. *Minding Evil: Explorations of Human Iniquity.* Amsterdam: Editions Rodopi BV.

Marie Breen Smyth. 2007. *Truth Recovery and Justice After Conflict: Managing Violent Pasts.* London: Routledge (Taylor & Francis).

Samantha Power. 2007. *A Problem From Hell: America and the Age of Genocide.* New York: Harper Perennial.

# CHAPTER 23

# NONVIOLENCE

Indian leader Mohandas Gandhi, stick in hand, walking with followers during the famous "salt satyagraha" in 1930.

*Source:* © 2008 Getty Images.

*Violence does not mean emancipation from fear but discovering the means of combating the cause of fear. Nonviolence, on the other hand, has no cause for fear . . . . It is nonviolence only when we love those who hate us. I know how difficult it is to follow this grand law of love. But are not all great and good things difficult to do? . . . No man can be actively nonviolent and not rise against social injustice no matter where it occurred.*

M. K. Gandhi

> *"Violence is a method by which the ruthless few can subdue the passive many.*
> *Nonviolence is a means by which the active many can overcome the ruthless few."*
>
> Jonathan Schell, paraphrasing Gandhi

Once the object of skepticism, even scorn, by security specialists and revolutionaries alike, nonviolence has enjoyed increasing professional and political acclaim since Gandhi's experiments with nonviolent civil resistance in the first half of the 20th century. As a principled and strategic global "force more powerful" than violence, nonviolence is gradually winning over the doubters, in large part due to the recent successes of mass nonviolent movements. In this chapter, we focus on its theoretical and practical dimensions, as well as on some towering figures the modern history of nonviolence.

## What Is Nonviolence?

Nonviolence is a word found in many contexts. In English, it consists of two words most people regard as negative: no(n) and violence. The first known use of "nonviolence" in English was in 1920. Nonviolence has two related and sometimes reinforcing meanings:

1.  It can refer, first, to a general philosophy of abstention from violence because of ethical or religious principles (e.g., "She believes in nonviolence."). This is called *principled nonviolence*.

2.  It can also refer to the behavior of people using nonviolent action (e.g., "The demonstrators maintained their nonviolence."). This is called *strategic nonviolence*.

Virtually all the relevant literature on violence and nonviolence assumes that the two are mutually exclusive: either violence or nonviolence. But in real life, the distinction is often less clear-cut. This is relevant for all investigations of specific historical and contemporary conflicts where a range of violent and nonviolent strategies and tactics were adopted. It is also an issue for everyday life situations where *both* physical force and negotiation may be employed to deal with conflicts at the interpersonal and group levels. Accordingly, violence and nonviolence are not absolutes—they lie on a continuum.

The history of nonviolence has two pacifistic traditions, absolute and pragmatic, with some aspects in common. For absolute pacifists, no goal justifies killing other human beings. They are against all forms of harming humans and other living beings. In the pragmatic tradition, nonviolent actions are evaluated mainly according to their importance and efficacy as political tools, as a collection of techniques, means for communication, a vehicle for revolutions and social movements, or as a system of defense. Many within the pacifist tradition actively use pragmatic methods, but many of those using these nonviolent skills do not hold (absolute) pacifist views.[1]

## Violence

Violence may be the worst injury, the most traumatic act, human beings inflict on each other. If a peaceful alien species were to observe human behavior, perhaps the conduct that would most perplex them would be the deliberate infliction of pain, suffering, and death by members of the same species against others of their species, especially when survival is not at stake. (Conversely, of course, belligerent aliens might feel right at home on the Earth of the warlike present!) Identifying violence appears simple—we know it when we see or feel it. But defining violence is tricky.

The noted political philosopher C. A. J. (Tony) Coady, appropriating the *Oxford English Dictionary*, offers a restricted definition of violence in purely physical terms: "The exercise of physical force so as to inflict injury on or damage to persons or property; action or conduct characterised by this."[2] Johan Galtung, on the other hand, has a wider definition: one that includes "direct," "structural," and "cultural" violence, in addition to physical and psychological violence.

The World Health Organization (WHO), in its *World Report on Violence and Health* (2002), has also adopted an expansive definition of violence as: "The intentional use of physical force, threatened or actual, against oneself, another person, or against a group or community, that either results in or has a high likelihood of resulting in injury, death, psychological harm, maldevelopment or deprivation."[3] The four different aspects of violence can be identified: 1. physical, 2. sexual, 3. psychological, and 4. deprivation. The WHO further subdivides each of these into self-directed violence, interpersonal violence, and collective violence.

The Geneva Declaration on Armed Violence and Development (GD) addresses the interrelations between armed violence and development. Although the incidence of armed conflict has declined in recent years, the number of people killed by armed violence has not. More than 740,000 men, women, and children die each year as a result of armed violence. The majority of these deaths—490,000—occur in countries that are not affected by armed conflicts: The GD is designed to support states and civil society actors to achieve measurable reductions in the global burden of armed violence in conflict and nonconflict settings by 2015 (and beyond). It was first adopted in 2006 by 42 nations during a Ministerial Summit in Geneva. The GD is now endorsed by over 100 nations and is the strongest political statement to date that addresses the impact of armed violence within a development context.

In its report, *The Global Burden of Armed Violence* (2008), the GD examined the tremendous burden armed violence—defined as "the intentional use of illegitimate force . . . with arms or explosives, against a person, group, community, or state, that undermines people-centred security and/or sustainable development"—imposes on individuals, families, and communities victimized by lethal armed conflicts and criminality. It finds that the death and destruction of war reduces Gross Domestic Product (GDP) growth by more than 2% annually, and the economic cost of nonconflict armed violence could reach up to $163 billion annually worldwide. The global cost of the insecurity generated by all armed violence is estimated at approximately $400 billion annually. According to the GD, most violent deaths occur in nonwar situations, due to small- or large-scale criminally or politically motivated violence. And weapons matter, with approximately 60% of all homicides committed with firearms.

## Preventing Violence

According to the GD, the consequences of armed violence are felt hardest by the poor and most vulnerable people, particularly in Latin America, Asia, Africa, and the Middle East. But armed violence is preventable, and the GD emphasizes the role of early intervention in saving lives. The WHO concurs, and in "Violence Prevention: The Evidence," lists specific violence-prevention strategies, such as

- developing safe, stable, and nurturing relationships between children and their parents and caregivers;
- reducing access to guns, knives and pesticides;

- changing cultural and social norms that support violence; and
- creating victim identification, care, and support programs.

## Arendt on Violence

One of the 20th century's most eminent political thinkers, Hannah Arendt, offered her own reflections on violence, titled—appropriately—*On Violence*. Arendt wrote against the background of a century (the 20th), which was, according to Arendt, "a century of wars and revolutions . . . a century of that violence which is believed to be their common denominator."

Arendt claims that "warfare has lost much of its effectiveness and nearly all its glamour" because of the "technical development of the instruments of violence," especially nuclear and biological weapons. And she argues that "the chief reason warfare is with us . . . [is] the simple fact that no substitute for this final arbiter in international affairs has yet appeared on the political scene." Although some violence, such as rage, may have "beastly" and or "irrational" sources, according to Arendt, political violence in general and revolutionary violence in particular may sometimes be "deliberate" and even "rational," because it "is the only way to set the scales of justice right again." Arendt's position with regard to violence is nuanced, since she argues that violence may be "effective," and "life itself, the immortal life of the species, nourished . . . by the . . . dying of its individual members . . . is actualised in the practice of violence."[4]

# Nonviolent Peace Theorists and Theories

Having considered some leading views of violence, its nature, varieties, causes, and prevention, we will now examine some leading theorists and practitioners of nonviolence and will then look at the varieties of nonviolent movements, strategies, and tactics.

## Leo Tolstoy

Lev Nikolayevich Tolstoy, known in the West as Leo Tolstoy (1828–1910), was a Russian writer, primarily of world-acclaimed novels (*War and Peace, Anna Karenina,* etc.) and short stories. Later in life, he also wrote political, social, and religious essays. Tolstoy also became noted as a moral thinker and social reformer.

Tolstoy's literal interpretation of the ethical teachings of Jesus, centering on the Sermon on the Mount, caused him in later life to become a fervent Christian anarcho-pacifist. Tolstoy believed being a Christian required him to be a pacifist; this, combined with the persistent waging of war by government, made him a philosophical anarchist as well. His ideas on nonviolent resistance, expressed in such works as *The Kingdom of God Is Within You* and his *Address to the Swedish Peace Congress* (1909), later had a profound impact on such pivotal 20th-century figures as Mohandas Gandhi and Martin Luther King, Jr.

## The Dalai Lama

Tenzin Gyatso, born Lhamo Dondrub in 1935, the 14th and current Dalai Lama, is the leader of Tibetan Buddhism. During the 1959 Tibetan uprising, he fled to India, where he denounced the People's Republic and established a Tibetan government in exile. He has since traveled the world, advocating nonviolent resistance to Chinese rule over Tibet, teaching Tibetan Buddhism, and talking about the importance of compassion as the source of a happy life and for *A Human Approach to World Peace*. In his numerous public appearances, he stresses that during the 20th century, tens of millions of people lost their lives due to violence and the economies of many countries were ruined due to conflicts. The Dalai Lama has proclaimed: "Let the 21st century be a century of tolerance and dialogue."

# Mohandas K. Gandhi

M. K. Gandhi is revered by most Indians as the founder of their nation and also by millions of others as the leading exponent and practitioner of nonviolence and as nearly a modern-day saint. He pioneered the modern use of nonviolent resistance as both a spiritual and philosophical approach to life and an intensely practical technique of achieving political and social change. Gandhi was widely known among Indians as "Mahatma" (Great Soul), for his courage, simplicity, penetrating insight, and the extraordinary impact of his teachings and his life.

Central to Gandhi's worldview was the search for truth, and, indeed, he titled his autobiography *My Experiments With Truth*. Gandhi thought that nonviolent love (*ahimsa*, in Sanskrit) was achievable only through compassion and tolerance for other people; moreover, it required continual testing, experimentation, and constant, unstinting effort. His teachings emphasized not just nonviolence but also courage, directness, civility, and honesty.

## Early Years

Gandhi was born in India, in 1869, to merchant-caste Hindu parents. He remained a devout Hindu throughout his life, although he made room for numerous other religious and ethical traditions and was strongly influenced by pacifist Christianity, as well as the writings of Thoreau and Tolstoy on the rights and duties of individuals to practice civil disobedience when governments intrude on human rights. He married very young (he and his wife were both 13) and studied law in London. After a brief time in India, the young barrister went to South Africa, where he was outraged by that country's system of racial discrimination (there was, and still is, a large Asian—especially Indian—population in South Africa). He remained there for 21 years, leading numerous campaigns for Indian rights, editing a newspaper, and developing his philosophy of nonviolent action as well as specific techniques for implementing it. He was physically abused and arrested many times by British authorities but also served courageously on the British side when he agreed with their positions; for example, Gandhi organized an Indian Ambulance Corps during the Boer War (1899–1902) and the Zulu Rebellion (1906), for which he was decorated by the government.

## Gandhi's Return to India

After achieving some reforms in South Africa, Gandhi returned to India in 1915 and quickly became leader of the Indian nationalist movement, seeking independence from colonial Britain. When the British government made it illegal to organize political opposition, Gandhi led a successful *satyagraha* campaign against these laws.

In 1919, British troops fired into a crowd of unarmed Indian men, women, and children, who had been demonstrating peacefully; nearly 400 were killed in what became known as the Amritsar Massacre. This served to highlight the difference between the steadfast nonviolence of Gandhi's followers and the relative brutality of the colonial government; it also moved Gandhi to refine his techniques of *satyagraha*. In particular, he took the great Sanskrit epic, the *Bhagavad Gita,* to be an allegory not about war but about the human soul and the need for all people to devote themselves, unselfishly, to the attainment of their goals. He urged that for real success, it is necessary to "reduce yourself to zero"—that is, to remove the self-will and striving for personal aggrandizement that so often leads to arrogance or even tyranny.

Gandhi was a small, slight man with indomitable moral certitude and remarkable physical stamina. He frequently underwent fasts to emphasize the importance of personal self-denial and to protest the violence that periodically broke out as less disciplined Indian nationalists rioted against British rule. Following these painful experiences, Gandhi temporarily called off his struggle for Indian independence. During the 1920s, Gandhi continued to fight for the rights of the lowest Hindu caste, the Untouchables—whom he renamed the *Harijan,* children of God—and for miners, factory workers, and poor peasants. He urged Indians to develop cottage industries, notably spinning and weaving, so as to deprive Britain of its major economic advantage in occupying India: markets for English textile products. In addition, hand weaving contributed to the potential of national self-sufficiency (*swaraj*) in India, while also emphasizing the dignity of labor.

In 1930, when the British occupying power introduced the Salt Acts, requiring that all salt in India be purchased from the government, Gandhi led a massive march, 320 kilometers to the sea, where he and his followers made salt from seawater, in defiance of the law. In all, Gandhi spent about 7 years in various jails for his numerous acts of nonviolent resistance, making it respectable—indeed, honorable—for protesters to be imprisoned for their beliefs.

Gandhi was ascetic and intensely frugal, possessing a biting sense of humor: Once, when he visited the British king in London, the half-naked Gandhi was asked whether he felt a bit underdressed for the occasion, to which he replied, "His Majesty wore enough for the two of us." Another time, when asked what he thought of Western civilization, he replied, "I think it would be a good idea."

Gandhi was deeply grieved by the intense periodic violence between Hindus and Muslims, and he opposed the partition of British colonial India into an independent Muslim Pakistan and Hindu India. He was assassinated by a fanatical Hindu, who resented his insistence on religious tolerance, in 1948, a year after India won its independence from Britain. However, Gandhi had accomplished what many thought impossible: gaining independence for a country of 400 million people, without firing a shot. He also showed that a highly spiritual concept—nonviolence—can be an intensely practical tool in the quest for peace, even in the 20th-century world of *Realpolitik,* power, and violence.

## Satyagraha

Perhaps the most important Gandhian concept is *satyagraha,* literally translated as "soul-force" or "soul-truth." Unfortunately, Gandhian *satyagraha* has often been translated into English as "passive resistance," which is like translating *light* as "nondarkness" or defining *good* as "absence of evil." It omits the positive, creative component of its subject. *Satyagraha* is passive only insofar as it espouses self-restraint rather than the active injuring of others. In all other respects, it is active and assertive, requiring great energy and outright courage.

*Satyagraha* requires adherence to love and mutual respect, and demands a willingness to suffer, if need be, to achieve these goals. For Gandhi, satyagraha required strength in practicing nonviolent methods. In his words:

Truth (satya) implies love, and firmness (agraha) engenders and therefore serves as a synonym for force. I thus began to call the Indian movement Satyagraha, that is to say, the Force which is born of Truth and Love or non-violence, and give up the use of the phrase "passive resistance."

As "love-force or soul-force," according to Gandhi:

In the application of satyagraha, I discovered in the earliest stages that pursuit of truth did not admit of violence being inflicted on one's opponent but that he must be weaned from error by patience and compassion. For what appears to be truth to the one may appear to be error to the other. And patience means self-suffering. So the doctrine came to mean vindication of truth, not by infliction of suffering on the opponent, but on oneself.

For Gandhi, the major principles of *satyagraha* are[5]

- nonviolence (*ahimsa*);
- truth—this includes honesty, but goes beyond it to mean living fully in accord with and in devotion to that which is true;
- nonstealing;
- chastity—this includes sexual chastity but also the subordination of other sensual desires to the primary devotion to truth;
- nonpossession—not the same as poverty;
- body-labor or bread-labor;
- control of the palate;
- fearlessness;
- equal respect for all religions;
- economic strategy such as boycotts (*swadeshi*); and
- freedom from untouchability (i.e., elimination of the caste system).

## Gandhi's Rules for Indian *Satyagrahi*

For Gandhi, followers of *satyagraha*

- must have a living faith in God;
- must believe in truth and nonviolence and have faith in the inherent goodness of human nature, which may be evoked by suffering;
- must be leading a chaste life, and be willing to die or lose all one's possessions;
- must be a habitual *Khadi* (homespun cloth textile*)* wearer and spinner;
- must abstain from alcohol and other intoxicants;
- must willingly carry out all the rules of discipline that are issued;
- when imprisoned, must obey all jail rules unless they are specially devised to hurt one's self respect;
- must harbor no anger and to suffer the anger of the opponent;

- must never retaliate to assaults or punishment, but not to submit, out of fear of punishment or assault, to an order given in anger;
- must voluntarily submit to arrest or confiscation of one's own property;
- if one is a trustee of someone else's property, must defend that property (nonviolently) from confiscation with one's life;
- must not curse, swear, or insult the opponent;
- must neither salute nor insult the flag of one's opponent;
- if anyone attempts to insult or assault one's opponent, must defend one's opponent (non-violently) with one's life if need be;
- in prison, must not ask for special favorable treatment; and not to fast in an attempt to gain conveniences;
- must joyfully obey the orders of the leaders of the civil disobedience action;
- must not pick and choose among the orders one obeys; if one finds the action as a whole improper or immoral, to sever one's connection with the action entirely;
- must not make one's participation conditional on one's comrades taking care of one's dependents while one is engaging in the campaign or is in prison;
- must not become a cause of communal quarrels and not to take sides in such quarrels, but must assist only that party demonstrably in the right; in the case of interreligious conflict, one must give one's life to protect (nonviolently) those in danger on either side, and avoid occasions that may give rise to communal quarrels; and
- must not take part in processions that would wound the religious sensibilities of any community.

While Gandhi realized the difficulties encountered by most people who attempted to follow the principles and rules of *satyagraha*, he himself tried, and seems mostly to have succeeded, in doing so.

# Gandhian Nonviolence in Theory and Practice

For some, nonviolence is a way of life, one lived according to one's philosophy and ethical principles. When Gandhi established his first communities, called *ashrams*, in South Africa, and later in India, it was part of his effort to construct a model for how he wanted the whole country to be in the future. His hope was to multiply these "islands" of peaceful, self-sufficient, and disciplined societies, and to create an archipelago of similar villages. For Gandhi, life in the community was an integrated part of his active struggle for a better world, which involved integrating the theory and practice of nonviolence into a coherent whole. He called this strategy the "constructive program." Far from isolating himself and his colleagues in the ashram, Gandhi argued that it was important to make ashram life an enduring action against the malicious aspects of society at large.[6]

## Nonviolent Love and Suffering: *Ahimsa*

A key to understanding Gandhian nonviolence is the concept of nonviolent love, *ahimsa*, the bedrock of *satyagraha*. As Gandhi expressed it, "*ahimsa* is the means; truth is the end." As with the term *passive resistance*, however, defining *ahimsa* as nonviolence does a disservice to the concept, which instead implies active love. It is closer to Albert Schweitzer's principle of "reverence for life," which is not only negative (determination not to destroy living things unnecessarily) but also positive (a commitment in favor of life, especially the life of other human beings).

*Ahimsa* requires deep respect for the other's humanity, an insistence upon sympathy and kindness—but also absolute, unwavering firmness. *Ahimsa* is not meek, mild, or retiring. It implies nothing less than the willingness of each individual to take unto herself or himself the responsibility for reforming the planet and, necessarily, to suffer in the process. Gandhi emphasized that

> ahimsa in its dynamic condition means conscious suffering. It does not mean meek submission to the will of the evil-doer, but it means pitting of one's whole soul against the will of the tyrant. Working under this law of our being, it is possible for a single individual to defy the whole might of an unjust empire to save his honor, his religion, his soul, and lay the foundation for that empire's fall or its regeneration.[7]

And again,

> Suffering is the law of human beings; war is the law of the jungle. But suffering is infinitely more powerful than the law of the jungle for converting the opponent and opening his ears, which are otherwise shut, to the voice of reason. . . . Suffering, not the sword, is the badge of the human race.[8]

The basis for this suffering (which Gandhi termed *tapasya*) is several-fold. For one thing, unless one is prepared to suffer, the depth of one's commitment can be questioned. Moreover, since any serious conflict must lead to suffering, the nonviolent resister's devotion to justice will almost certainly precipitate suffering. *Tapasya* therefore indicates willingness to undergo this suffering oneself and not to shift its burden onto anyone else—including the opponent.

Gandhi's emphasis on suffering is especially difficult for many people to understand or accept. It tends—probably more than any other aspect of his thought and practice—to make Gandhian nonviolence relatively inaccessible to many Westerners. Yet *tapasya* should not be altogether foreign, especially to Christian tradition, given the central importance attributed to Christ's redeeming agony on the cross. In addition, it is not stretching Gandhi's concept too greatly to substitute "courage" for "willingness to suffer." This has the added benefit of helping dispel the frequent misunderstanding that practitioners of nonviolence are cowards, seeking an easy way out of conflict.

## Nonviolence as an Active Force

Gandhi strongly emphasized that *satyagraha* must be distinguished from passive acquiescence or the desire to avoid conflict at any price. The middle class in particular has often been scorned as having an excessive fear of conflict and a corresponding desire to be comfortable at all costs. "The inability of the bourgeois to dream great dreams and ambition noble deeds," according to a biographer of one of Gandhi's most prominent disciples, Martin Luther King, Jr.,

> is revealed in their timidity in the face of violence and conflict. . . . This cowardice also shows itself in what may be called the mercenary impulse, the impulse to hire others to fight one's own battles. This impulse has such concrete manifestations as hiring additional police to

suppress domestic unrest or in spending money for a so-called all volunteer army, rather than personally accepting the obligations of citizenship. . . . [T]hey represent what Gandhi called the nonviolence of the weak. Such nonviolence he took to be counterfeit, a cloak for passivity and cowardice.[9]

Gandhian nonviolence, by contrast, is the nonviolence of the strong, the courageous, and the outraged—not merely passive acquiescence by the weak, the cowardly, or the comfortable. "My creed of nonviolence is an extremely active force," wrote Gandhi. "It has no room for cowardice or even weakness. There is hope for a violent man to be some day nonviolent, but there is none for a coward."[10]

As previously noted, the *satyagrahi* must be prepared to accept beatings, imprisonment, or even absolute truthfulness. It must take the opponent seriously and seek to engage him or her in dialogue and self-examination. It must respect the opponents and permit them to change direction without loss of face.

Traditionally, when conflicts are resolved by violence, they simply involve the triumph of one protagonist over the other. Such a "resolution" may occur via threat or naked force, but the presumption is that one side wins and the other loses: This is what mathematicians call a *zero-sum game* (as in most competitive sports, where for every winner there is a loser, so the sum total of wins and losses equals zero). Even when overtly seeking a compromise—hence, a win-win or positive-sum solution—each side typically attempts to profit at the other's expense and to compromise only when it has no alternative. By contrast, *satyagraha* aims to resolve the source of the conflict rather than to defeat or destroy the opponent. The goal is to persuade the adversary that all parties have more to gain by acting in harmony and love than by persevering in discord and violence. Rather than viewing the other as an enemy to be overcome, the *satyagrahi* considers him or her a participant in a shared search for a just (i.e., "truthful") solution to the problem at hand.

## Ends Versus Means

Not surprisingly, since he attributed so much importance to the process of attaining truth and justice, Gandhi was unalterably opposed to any doctrine in which the ends justify the means. He maintained that there was "the same inviolable connection between the means and the end as there is between the seed and the tree." Of course, a seed can be distinguished from a tree, but, nonetheless, the two are inseparably linked; French philosopher Jacques Maritain wrote that the means of achieving a goal is "in a sense the end in the process of becoming." When the means are pure, the end will be desirable; if the route to political protest is sullied with violence or hatred, the end also will be spoiled. Hannah Arendt concurred, adding that "the practice of violence, like all action, changes the world, but the most probable change is to a more violent world."[11]

For pacifists in the Gandhian mold, violence is reactionary: The more violence, the less revolution. By using violent methods, revolutions and even antiwar movements can build up reservoirs of resentment and hatred, as well as possibly laying the foundations for additional injustice and yet more violence. This stands not only as a warning against violence but also as a caution against letting frustration drive peaceful protest into violent and often self-destructive avenues.

By contrast, violent political activists of the extreme left and right are often prone to make moral compromises, convinced that their vision of the world-as-it-should-be justifies almost any means of attaining it. Lenin, for instance, announced that "to achieve our ends, we will unite even with the Devil." In his poem "To Posterity," Bertolt Brecht, playwright and Marxist, warned about how violence has corrupted and perverted the noblest intentions:

> Even anger against injustice
>
> Makes the voice grow harsh. Alas, we
>
> Who wished to lay the foundations of kindness
>
> Could not ourselves be kind.[12]

Neither the violent left nor the far right has shared Gandhi's acute sensitivity to the relationship between means and ends. And whereas most people would agree that it is desirable to avoid aggression and international intimidation, a Gandhian would also question the legitimacy of employing (i.e., deploying) instruments of violence as means toward those ends.

## Nonviolence in Practice

Cicero, in *The Letters to His Friends,* asks, "What can be done against force, without force?" Students of nonviolence would answer, "Plenty." Moreover, they would question whether anything effective, lasting, or worthwhile can be done against force, *with* force. The Reverend Martin Luther King, Jr., nonviolent leader of the civil rights movement in the United States during the late 1950s and 1960s and a visionary who, like Gandhi, was also intensely practical and result oriented, wrote that "returning violence for violence multiplies violence, adding deeper darkness to a night already devoid of stars. Darkness cannot drive out darkness; only light can do that. Hate cannot drive out hate; only love can do that."[13]

As Gandhi put it, "as evil can only be sustained by violence, withdrawal of support of evil requires complete abstention from violence."[14]

This does not mean, however, that the *satyagrahi* is forbidden anger, even hatred; rather, these feelings are carefully directed toward the various *systems* of evil, rather than toward individuals. Gandhi wrote that

> I can and do hate evil wherever it exists. . . . I hate the ruthless exploitation of India even as I hate from the bottom of my heart the hideous system of untouchability for which millions of Hindus have made themselves responsible. But I do not hate the domineering Englishman as I refuse to hate the domineering Hindus. I seek to reform them in all the loving ways that are open to me. My noncooperation has its roots not in hatred, but in love.[15]

For Gandhi and his followers, it was impossible to elevate oneself by debasing others, just as it debases others by permitting them to dominate one's self.

## Nonviolent Action and Government Reaction

In practice, Gandhi's *satyagraha* took many forms: marches, boycotts, picketing, leafleting, strikes, civil disobedience, the nonviolent occupation of various government facilities, vigils and fasts, mass imprisonments, refusal to pay taxes, and a willingness at all times to be abused by the authorities and yet to respond nonviolently, with politeness, courage, and determination. This, as Gandhi was fond of pointing out, demanded far more strength than is required to pull a trigger, far more courage than is needed to fight or to fight back. Gandhian techniques thus do not offer an alternative to fighting; rather, they provide other, nonviolent ways of doing so. As a result, the nonviolent struggle is, if anything, more intense than its violent counterpart.

The extraordinary courage and humaneness of the Indian *satyagrahis* contrasted dramatically with the ugly violence of the occupying power, thereby helping sway world opinion as well as the British electorate—which became increasingly sympathetic to Gandhi's cause. This is not unusual: Violent governmental overreaction to nonviolent protest historically has had the effect of transforming victims into martyrs, who become symbols of their regime's callous wrongheadedness. For example, in 1819, a nonviolent crowd in Manchester, England, was attacked by soldiers while peacefully listening to speeches calling for the repeal of the Corn Laws. This so-called Peterloo Massacre became a rallying cry for radicals who eventually succeeded in their demands. The slaughter of participants in the Paris Commune of 1871 led to greater solidarity among the French working class. Similarly, violence and brutality directed toward U.S. civil rights workers in the 1960s led to widespread revulsion and moral indignation against the system of racial segregation in the South, just as the Kent State University killings of nonviolent antiwar student protesters in 1970 galvanized sentiment opposed to the Vietnam War.

## Living With and Transforming Violence

For nonviolent campaigns to be successful, the campaigners must have steadfast determination, self-respect, and also (Gandhi would add) respect for the opponent. A favorite expression of 1960s radicals was "power to the people." Followers of nonviolence believe that people are most powerful when they have sufficient moral courage. Courageous nonviolent "warriors" may gradually become immune not only to the threat of violence directed toward them but also to the inclination to employ violence themselves. The latter comes from having sufficient clarity of purpose (Gandhi would call it "selflessness"). As Gandhi saw it, this does not involve a purging of anger but rather a transforming of it: "I have learnt through bitter experience the one supreme lesson to conserve my anger and as heat conserved is transmuted into energy, even so our anger controlled can be transmuted into a power which can move the world."[16]

When a victim responds to violence with yet more violence, he or she is behaving in a manner that is predictable, perhaps even instinctive, which tends to reinforce the aggression of the original attacker and even, in a way, to vindicate the original violence, at least in the attacker's mind: Since the "victim" is so violent, presumably he or she deserved it. Moreover, there is a widespread expectation of countervailing power analogous in the social sphere to Newton's First Law, which states that for every action there is an equal and opposite reaction. Thus, if *A* hits *B* and then *B* hits back, this nearly always encourages *A* to strike yet again. Gandhi was not fond of the Biblical injunction "an eye for an eye, a tooth for a tooth," pointing out that if we all behaved that way, soon the whole world would be blind and toothless! Instead, if *B* responds with nonviolence, this not only breaks the chain of anger and hatred (analogous to the Hindu chain of birth and rebirth); it also puts *A* in an unexpected position. "I seek entirely to blunt the edge of the tyrant's sword," wrote Gandhi, "not by putting up against it a sharper-edged weapon but by disappointing his expectation that I would be offering physical resistance."[17]

Accustomed to counterviolence—and even, perhaps, hoping for it—the violent person who encounters a nonviolent opponent who is courageous and respectful, even loving, toward the aggressor becomes a "victim" of a kind of moral judo in which the attacker's own energy is redirected, placing him or her off balance. "It would at first dazzle him and at last compel recognition from him," wrote Gandhi, "which recognition would not humiliate but would uplift him." And, in fact, many of Gandhi's most bitter opponents were almost inevitably won over. Consider this account of a meeting between the young Gandhi and the legendary General Jan Smuts of South Africa. Gandhi spoke first:

> "I have come to tell you that I am going to fight against your government."

> Smuts must have thought he was hearing things. "You mean you have come here to tell me that?" he laughs. "Is there anything more you want to say?"

> "Yes," says Gandhi. "I am going to win."

> Smuts is astonished. "Well," he says at last, "and how are you going to do that?" Gandhi smiles. "With your help."[18]

Years later, Smuts recounted this meeting, noting—with humor—that Gandhi was correct.

## Nonviolence as a Proactive Force

Nonviolence is often described as nonviolent *resistance,* implying that it is a reaction, a response to some initial force. But, in fact, as practiced by Gandhi and his followers (including Martin Luther King, Jr. in the United States), nonviolence is *pro*active much more than *re*active. These practitioners of politically active nonviolence were masters at taking the initiative and keeping their opponents off balance. Their tactics were unpredictable, spontaneous, radical, and experimental—and, not surprisingly, government authorities found them baffling and exasperating. It is said—of some people and some nations—that "they only understand force," and therefore they cannot be moved by anything other than force or the threat of force. The truth, however, may be precisely the opposite: Those who understand and expect violent force can generally deal effectively with it; after all, it is typically their stock in trade. *Satyagraha*—soul-force rather than physical force—is another matter.

Part of the goal of *satyagraha* is to make the oppressor reflect on his or her psychological unity or similarity with the resister and to change, internally. Consider the analogy of an iceberg, which melts below the water line, invisibly, until suddenly, as the weight shifts, it may flip over. In this way, the consciousness of the oppressor may be changed suddenly and dramatically. "If my soldiers began to think," wrote Frederick the Great, "not one would remain in the ranks." Nonviolence, adroitly and persistently practiced, has the power of inducing soldiers—and government leaders—to think, and, ideally both to learn to love one's opponents and thereby to transform them into one's allies.

# Martin Luther King, Jr. and the U.S. Civil Rights Movement

In the United States, the most influential modern exponent and practitioner of nonviolence was the Reverend Martin Luther King, Jr., who consciously adapted *satyagraha* for use in the American South. King studied Gandhi's philosophy and methods, traveled to India, and emerged as the chief spokesperson, architect, and spiritual leader of the nonviolent civil rights campaign in the United States.

Like Gandhi, King spent time in prison for his nonviolent defiance of unjust laws supporting racial discrimination. His "Letter From Birmingham Jail" is one of the classic statements of the philosophy of nonviolent civil disobedience and the evils of racial intolerance. In it, King also expressed a sense of courage and urgency:

> We know from painful experience that freedom is never voluntarily given by the oppressor; it must be demanded by the oppressed. . . . I guess it is easy for those who have never felt the stinging darts of segregation to say "wait." But when you have seen vicious mobs lynch your mothers and fathers at will . . . then you will understand why we find it difficult to wait.[19]

During the 1950s and 1960s, transportation, restaurants, sports events, restrooms, libraries, and schools were often racially segregated in the American South, with superior facilities reserved for "whites only." Voting rights were often denied or severely restricted by poll taxes, literacy tests, and outright intimidation. Lynching of African Americans was common and racial violence widespread, often led by the Ku Klux Klan, a semisecret band of white supremacists.

Perhaps the seminal event in King's leadership of the civil rights movement was the Montgomery (Alabama) bus boycott, which started in December 1955, when Rosa Parks refused to take a seat in the back of a public bus. After thousands of African Americans walked miles to work rather than use segregated buses, public facilities were eventually integrated. Later, "Freedom Riders," seeking to desegregate interstate bus transportation (in accord with a 1960 Supreme Court decision), endured frequent beatings and mob violence, while state police often failed to provide protection, typically arresting the Riders instead.

Sit-ins began at segregated lunch counters in 1960, in Greensboro, North Carolina, at the soda fountain of a five-and-ten-cent store. With King's encouragement and the guidance and training of local religious and civic leaders, these nonviolent sit-ins, boycotts, and marches quickly spread to more than 100 cities and eventually succeeded in integrating restaurants throughout the South.

These were years when Alabama's governor George Wallace stood in the doorway of the University of Alabama to deny admission to black students and when electric cattle prods, police dogs, and high-pressure water hoses were used against peaceful demonstrators in Birmingham, Alabama. Nonviolent civil rights marchers were herded to jail in Jackson, Mississippi, with the police harassing the marchers and offering them no protection against abusive crowds. Four young black girls were killed by a bomb blast while at Sunday school in Birmingham Baptist Church. Throughout, King maintained a steadfast devotion to nonviolence, based on his perception of Christian principles. "Let no man pull you so low," he was fond of saying, "as to make you hate him."

It is no small task, though, to separate hatred of offenses—or of offending institutions—from hatred of the offenders: to hate murder but love the murderer, to hate oppression but not the oppressor, to hate torture but not the torturer. In this, King once again revealed himself a disciple of Gandhi, showing uncompromising respect, even love, for his opponents, while being equally uncompromising in pursuit of the truth as he saw it. And like Gandhi before him, Martin Luther King, Jr. was assassinated.

But also like Gandhi, King mobilized a nonviolent army of followers, captured the conscience of millions, and achieved monumental legal reforms. He founded the Southern Christian Leadership Conference, which emphasized grassroots, community action in addition to nonviolence, and in 1963, he organized the March on Washington for Jobs and Freedom, also known as the Poor People's March, which brought about 500,000 protestors to the U.S. capital. This effort represented a new dimension of King's nonviolent campaign: extending it from civil rights to a broader concern with social justice for all. His campaign in favor of the Voting Rights Act also helped lead to its passage in 1965. The year before, King was awarded the Nobel Peace Prize.

Shortly before his death, King also started speaking out in opposition to the Vietnam War and the nuclear arms race. "If we assume that humankind has a right to survive," he once wrote, "then we must find an alternative to war and destruction. . . . The choice today is no longer between violence or nonviolence. It is between nonviolence or nonexistence.[20]

# Some Nonviolent Successes

Clearly, there have been many examples of "successful violence," if "success" means conquest of territory, booty, and people; the imposition of a particular social system; or the forcible defeat of would-be aggressors. But it can also be argued that violence, by its nature, inhibits lasting success and sows the seeds of its own instability. When "peace" is imposed by violence or the threat of violence, it is not really peace but rather, violence maintained in a temporary disequilibrium, which is to say, structural violence. The situation in apartheid South Africa was a good example: A kind of "peace" was maintained for decades but only through massive violence, structural as well as direct. It is not surprising that the resulting system was not only destructive of humanistic values but also unstable. (The only surprise, perhaps, is that the demise of South African apartheid was, in the end, relatively nonviolent!) Indeed, the record of much human history can itself be seen as a monument to the *failure* of violence, not to its success.

There have been many cases of successful nonviolent actions, in addition to the well-known examples of Indian independence and the American civil rights movement. Gandhi himself pointed out that nonviolence is far more pervasive in ordinary human life than most of us realize and far more frequent (and successful) than violence:

> The fact that there are so many men still alive in the world shows that it is based not on the force of arms but on the force of truth or love. . . . Thousands, indeed tens of thousands, depend for their existence on a very active working of this force. Little quarrels of millions of families in their daily lives disappear before the exercise of this force.[21]

## The Developing World

One notable example of the recent force of nonviolence was the toppling of Philippine dictator Ferdinand Marcos by the "people power" of Corazón Aquino's followers in 1986. This virtually bloodless coup occurred after Marcos loyalists attempted to rig an election in the dictator's favor. The ensuing protest revolved around persistent nonviolence by Filipino civilians, who at one point interposed themselves between armed forces loyal to Marcos and a small band of dissidents who had declared themselves in support of Aquino and her followers. Newspapers worldwide printed photographs showing Catholic nuns inserting flowers in the barrels of automatic rifles carried by Philippine Army soldiers. Marcos relinquished power and went into exile in the United States when it became evident that his own military would not fire on the unarmed populace (also, after the Reagan administration, which had propped up the Marcos regime, indicated that it was withdrawing support).

A few months later, a similar popular expression of discontent drove Jean-Claude Duvalier, son of longtime Haitian dictator "Papa Doc" Duvalier, from power. Regrettably, the departure of Duvalier did not immediately restore democracy to impoverished Haiti, which still has the highest illiteracy rate and lowest per capita income in the Western Hemisphere, as well as a long tradition of autocratic government. In any event, in Haiti and the Philippines, spontaneous nonviolent movements succeeded in deposing military dictatorships that appeared deeply entrenched, such that traditional violent revolution would probably have led to a large number of casualties.

In 1987, popular discontent in South Korea led to a series of largely nonviolent demonstrations, which in turn caused the military dictatorship to relinquish power and permit the first democratic elections ever held in that country. In Haiti, the Philippines, and South Korea, violent repression of popular resistance—often several or more years earlier—on the part of these dictatorships contributed heavily to the nonviolent popular discontent that ultimately toppled their governments.

## Eastern Europe

In the spring of 1968, under reformist leader Alexander Dubcek, the Czechoslovakian government, under the watchful eye of the Soviet Union, began granting a range of political and economic freedoms, seeking to establish "socialism with a human face." In response, the Soviet Union invaded Czechoslovakia in August, crushing the brief "Prague Spring." Although many Americans think of that Soviet-led invasion as an overwhelming victory for the forces of Soviet repression, in fact the people of Czechoslovakia mounted a remarkable campaign of nonviolent opposition. Although essentially no military resistance was offered to the invading force of nearly 500,000 troops, Czechs and Slovaks for 8 months prevented the installation of a collaborationist government, using general strikes, work slowdowns, clandestine radio broadcasts, and noncooperation by government employees. A compromise (the so-called Moscow Protocols) was reached, which allowed most of the reform leaders to remain in authority; only when riots occurred at Aeroflot offices in Prague—that is, when nonviolent discipline broke down—did Soviet occupying forces remove the reformists and subdue the country.

Twenty-one years later, in the autumn of 1989, after a decade of nonviolent strikes and civil protest in Poland and elsewhere in the former eastern bloc, massive peaceful demonstrations, culminating in "The Velvet Revolution," finally drove the Communist Party from its preeminent place in Czechoslovakia and, ultimately, elsewhere in Central and Eastern Europe. This occurred days after Czech security forces brutally suppressed some prodemocracy demonstrations; outrage at this "police violence" fueled Czech and Slovak determination to replace the discredited government.

In contrast to the Czech experience, the overthrow of Romanian dictator Nicolae Ceauşescu involved violence, mostly directed toward the government leadership. Significantly, moreover, it was public outrage at brutal military response to an earlier nonviolent citizens' protest in the Romanian city of Timisoara that ignited the countrywide revolt.

The Polish trade union movement "Solidarity" followed a strenuously nonviolent path, one that was ultimately successful in changing the Polish government and that served in many ways as a model for the electrifying events throughout Eastern Europe during 1989, whereby an array of unrepresentative, Soviet-backed governments (including Hungary and Bulgaria) was replaced by others, all of them proclaiming democracy—and some of them actually practicing it.

In the words of Polish Solidarity leader Lech Wałęsa, these formidable events, some of the most remarkable in modern times, were accomplished without "so much as breaking a single windowpane."

## Apparent Failures of Nonviolent Resistance

Also in 1989, the world witnessed the spectacle of the People's Republic of China—the world's most populous country and one that has been in the grip of an authoritarian Communist Party–led government since 1949—convulsed by demands for reform and democratization. For several weeks, nonviolent protesters, led by college students but including a wide cross section of the population, occupied Tiananmen Square in the heart of Beijing, with popular demonstrations of more than 1 million people. Prodemocracy protesters also made themselves heard in Shanghai, Nanking, Hunan, and Hong Kong.

Then, the Chinese government cracked down with a brutal military assault; the precise number of casualties is not known but possibly thousands were killed. The government survived these incidents, although it seems likely that the final word on this process has not yet been spoken. Moreover, the bitterness sown by the government's violent repression—which on a larger scale resembles the British Army's Amritsar Massacre in colonial India—may have consequences for the future of China and other governments that practice brutality against nonviolent protesters.

In contrast, the brutal military dictatorship that has oppressed the people of Burma/Myanmar since 1990 has been challenged by nonviolent protests, spearheaded by thousands of Buddhist monks, in solidarity with longtime nonviolent advocate—and Nobel Peace Prize laureate—Daw Aung San Suu Kyi. There now appear to be realistic chances for some form of democracy in Burma. Although the outcome is unpredictable, it is clear that the greater the violence perpetrated, in this case by the Burmese military junta, the less secure the long-term legitimacy of any regime. The same may eventually apply to Chinese occupation and oppression of Tibet.

There is, as Gandhi noted, a special outrage associated with one-sided uses of lethal force. The "Tiananmen Massacre," occurring on a Sunday in June 1989, was not the first "Bloody Sunday" in history: In 1905, a mass of nonviolent Russian peasants in St. Petersburg, led by Father Gapon, attempted to submit a petition to Czar Nicholas. His troops responded by slaughtering hundreds of unarmed people. This led to a general strike, which ushered in some limited democratic reforms on the part of the government but which also signaled the beginning of the end for czarist tyranny, culminating ultimately in the Russian Revolution.

A similar case can be made for the "Kent State Massacre" in the United States, although the numbers involved were far smaller, and the public response was far short of revolution. In this incident, Ohio National Guardsmen killed four students who were part of a crowd peacefully demonstrating in opposition to the U.S. bombing of Cambodia in 1970. It generated widespread outrage in the United States and marked a turning point in citizen respect for the federal government and its prosecution of the Vietnam War.

Nonviolence, especially when contrasted with a brutal government response, has an extraordinary power to influence the human mind. Hence, it may well have a profound role to play in practical politics, even—and perhaps especially—against violent, heavily armed, repressive regimes. In 1989 in China, as in Russia 84 years earlier, the populace, as well as many military leaders themselves, was shocked and infuriated at the heavy-handed use of violence against peaceful demonstrators: "The People's Army," exhorted one communiqué from the Chinese military itself, "absolutely must not attack the people!" When a state does attack its own people, behaving like state terrorists, it is likely that such a regime will quickly lose its legitimacy, its popular support, and, ultimately, its power.

## Interstate Examples

The above examples of nonviolent successes and near-successes refer to conflicts taking place within a given state, rather than between states. Examples of the successful use of nonviolent tactics *between* states are harder to come by, although there are some historical examples.

During the mid-19th century, for example, imperial Austria was seeking to dominate its partner in union, Hungary. The Hungarians were militarily weaker than the Austrians, and they recognized that physical resistance would be useless and probably counterproductive. Instead, Hungarians responded by boycotting Austrian goods, refusing to recognize or cooperate with Austrian authorities, and establishing independent Hungarian industrial, agricultural, and educational systems. Noncompliance proved a powerful tool. For example, Hungarians refused to pay taxes to Austrian collectors. When the resisters' property was seized, no Hungarian auctioneers would sell them, so Austrian auctioneers were imported. But then, no Hungarian would buy the property, so Austrian buyers were imported as well. In the end, the process proved to be a net financial cost to the Austrian authorities. Austria also sought to enforce compulsory military service and the billeting of Austrian soldiers in Hungarian homes, but noncompliance was such that in 1867 the Austrian emperor consented to a constitution giving Hungary full rights within the Austro-Hungarian union.

Many people associate successful independence movements with war and armed rebellion, such as the American Revolution or the independence of Algeria from France. But, in fact, there have been numerous examples of independence achieved by nonviolent means, including the peaceful separations of Canada from Great Britain in the 19th century, of many colonies from Western powers in the decades following World War II, and so on. In 1905, Norway was granted independence from Sweden, with no violence whatever. Shortly before, Norwegian nationalists declared their country to be a free and independent state, almost precipitating a war; in a subsequent plebiscite, all but 184 Norwegians voted for independence, and the Swedish government, acknowledging its "defeat," relented. And Czechs and Slovaks peacefully separated in January 1993.

During World War II, Norway again became an important site of nonviolent resistance to the Nazis. Germany invaded Norway in April 1940, quickly overcoming Norwegian military resistance. Overcoming the people, however, was much more difficult. A pro-Nazi Norwegian, Vidkun Quisling, was made dictator (since then, a *quisling* has entered the lexicon as a local collaborator who helps form a puppet government). Norwegian society spontaneously and persistently undermined the Quisling government, with solidarity on the part of students and the clergy and, especially, by public school teachers, who refused to participate in mandated pro-Nazi indoctrination programs for their students. The Nazis responded by imprisoning and killing many resisters to the regime, but the refusals continued and the country gradually became increasingly ungovernable. As President Franklin Roosevelt put it, Norway became "at once conquered and unconquerable."

During the autumn of 1943, when Denmark was occupied by German armed forces, large numbers of Danes prevented Nazi authorities from seizing 94% of the 8,000 Danish Jews and deporting them to concentration camps. Using improvised methods of communication and transportation, the outnumbered and vastly outgunned Danish citizens succeeded in smuggling most of these would-be victims to safety in Sweden. Another successful resistance tactic was for large numbers of Danes to defy the German authorities by wearing the Star of David, intended to identify Jews. Virtually the entire country—government, religious leadership, trade unions, and professionals—opposed the Nazi efforts at liquidating the Jewish population, and they were largely successful.

Historical evidence suggests that military force has its political and social limits, even when (as in the modern world) such force is technologically almost unlimited. The United States, for example, dropped 8 million tons of bombs on Indochina—the equivalent of about 300 Hiroshima bombs, and 80 times the amount of bombs that Germany dropped on Britain during World War II—but nonetheless lost the Vietnam War. It remains to be seen if a military mailed fist can successfully oppress a resistant population over the long haul. Nonetheless, it is questionable whether governments will move in the near future to de-emphasize the use of violence or the threat of violence in their internal and international affairs.

# Civilian-Based Defense

Advocates of nonviolence are not limited to peace activists and high-minded moralists. More and more hardheaded realists are questioning fundamental assumptions about peace, defense, and security, as the limitations and dangers of traditional military "solutions" become increasingly clear. A classic case, epitomizing what for many is the paradox of reliance on military means of defense, was the Vietnamese village of Ben Tre, which, according to a U.S. major, had to be destroyed "in order for us to save it." In particular, the notion of being defended with nuclear, biological, or chemical weapons leaves many people skeptical.

If nonviolence is to make a real impact on international affairs, however, it needs to be seen as something more than the idiosyncrasy of uniquely empowered saints and martyrs or as an impractical tactic proposed by politically marginal figures. Rather, practitioners of nonviolence must adopt a realistic approach, feasible for a large number of people.

Among the practical suggestions for applying nonviolence to national defense, one of the most organized and realistic involves so-called civilian-based defense, or CBD. (This must be distinguished from "civil defense," or government plans for protecting citizenry in the aftermath of a nuclear war or equivalent catastrophe.) CBD includes a variety of nonviolent techniques intended to make it very difficult if not impossible for a conquering state to govern another and to gain any benefit from its "victory."

The major theorist of CBD, Gene Sharp, has identified about 200 specific techniques of nonviolent action, ranging from general strikes, boycotts, and nonpayment of taxes to removal of street signs and sabotage of electrical services.[22] Civilian defenders will not violently resist the occupation of their country, and substantial hardship, suffering, and even death may well result. But military defenders must also anticipate considerable hardship, suffering, and possibly death, even in a "successful" defensive war. Advocates of CBD emphasize that substantial training would be required, as well as a populace willing to commit itself to the success of its enterprise.

But there is nothing new in this: Military training also requires time, effort, and sacrifice, as well as committed participants. (One important distinction is that CBD demands that the public, not just the military, be the participants.) Moreover, most efforts at nonviolent resistance—for example, Hungary in the mid-19th century, Norway in the early 1940s, Czechoslovakia in 1968, and segments of the "Arab Spring" and "Occupy" Movements of 2011—were spontaneous, unprepared, and largely leaderless. Widespread CBD, well rehearsed and planned in advance, has never really been tried. Given its impressive track record when it was essentially extemporized on the spot, the future of CBD might well be bright indeed if it is ever carried out by a populace that is well trained and prepared. Furthermore, the prospects of having one's soldiers face such a populace, who are committed to denying the invader virtually all fruits of conquest, just might serve to deter invasion no less effectively than the amassing of military forces—and at substantially less cost and risk.

Sharp argues persuasively that under traditional military doctrines, "the capacity to defend in order to deter has been replaced by the capability to destroy massively without the ability to defend." By contrast, CBD would aim to

> deny the attackers their objectives and to make society politically indigestible and ungovernable by the attackers. . . . Potential attackers are deterred when they see that their objectives will be denied them, political consolidation prevented, and that as a consequence of these struggles unacceptable costs will be imposed on them politically, economically, and internationally.[23]

Rather than focusing on moral considerations, Sharp has emphasized the merits of CBD relying on "hardheaded" strategic and cost-effectiveness grounds. He also points out that if nuclear deterrence fails, the results will be utterly catastrophic. By contrast, if deterrence based on CBD fails, the result will be the first opportunity to attempt to implement a truly nonviolent defense.

A national policy of nonviolent CBD would require a state to renounce its interventionist goals in other countries or, at least, to forgo the prospect of direct military intervention in support of economic and political "neo-imperialism." Such states as the United States, Britain, and France have long deployed military forces capable of "projecting power" far from their shores. These forces—including aircraft carriers, long-range fighter-bombers, mobile artillery, and amphibious assault units—are not normally used for defending a state's own borders; rather, their purpose is to intervene (or threaten to intervene) in other nations, generally far from home and most often in the developing world and Middle East. A populace trained and organized for CBD might or might not be able to deter an aggressor. But it could not invade or intimidate a distant country, rendering it similar to—but more assertively nonviolent than—nonprovocative defense. For some people, this is an added advantage of CBD; for others, it is a liability.

There is presently little chance that CBD will soon be adopted as the defense strategy of any major state. However, it need not be initiated all-or-nothing. There is no reason why CBD training could not be gradually integrated into existing military doctrine, after which it would be available to assume a more significant role as part of a transition from offensively oriented forces to those concerned—at first primarily and then exclusively—with defense. Highly respected military and political planners in several European states have been studying the prospects for such a transition. CBD represents a revolution in alternative security thinking, one that is currently bubbling just below the level of official policy but that might well emerge in the 21st century, especially with the end of the Cold War and, with it, many official justifications for the existence of large offensive standing armies.

Counterintuitively, there is some danger that in de-emphasizing the role of traditional military forces and placing the primary burden of defense on the shoulders of the civilian population, CBD could contribute to a kind of militarizing of national cultures, as civilians find themselves forced to confront the essence of national security. The greatest problem, however, is probably a deeply ingrained distrust—on the part of the public as well as the military—of nonviolence as a workable strategy, combined with a widespread fascination with violence and a tendency to rely on it as a last resort, when—in a revealing phrase—"push comes to shove."

# Does Nonviolence "Work"? If So, Why?

When they concern themselves with nonviolence at all, the international media mainly cover such "spectacular events" as masses of protesters occupying central squares in main cities. Nonetheless, contrary to many popular and media-generated perceptions, it is more the rule than the exception that current revolutionary and social justice movements use nonviolent techniques. But on balance, does nonviolence "work"? This question must be placed in an ethical and historical context. What does it mean for something like nonviolence to "work"?

1. To achieve one's short-term political and/or social goals?

Nonviolence does not always succeed, although the historical record suggests that it does so at least as often as violent methods and with far fewer victims.

2. To transform society?

Again, not always, but at least as often as violent methods and once again, with far fewer victims.

3. To improve the human condition and make Earth a more secure place for life?

Too soon to say. But there is not just hope but empirical evidence that nonviolence works, at least in the medium- and long-run.

For example, Maria J. Stephan and Eric Chenoweth have demonstrated that nonviolent struggles against despotism and for self-determination are more likely than violent resistance to achieve their political objectives . . . even in the Middle East:

> "We found that during the period of 1900 to 2006, nonviolent resistance campaigns are about twice as effective as violent ones in achieving their goals. We also found that these trends hold even where most people expect nonviolent resistance to be ineffective—for instance, against dictatorships and highly repressive regimes."[24]

Chenoweth and Stephan researched 323 social-change campaigns from 1900 to 2006. Among their significant findings are that

- campaigns of nonviolent resistance are nearly twice as likely to succeed as violent uprisings;
- far greater numbers of people from more diverse parts of society joined nonviolent campaigns than violent ones. This greater level of participation translates into more people who can demonstrate for change, and withdraw their cooperation from an unjust regime. In short, numbers matter; and
- when nonviolent movements overthrow an unjust regime, the victorious resistance groups are far more likely to establish democracies and protect human rights and far less likely to lapse into civil war than their violent counterparts.

# Prospects for Nonviolence

Despite the appeals of nonviolence, it seems unlikely that states will soon convert their defense to such strategies—whether Gandhian *satyagraha* or CBD. In the long run, however, it can be argued that nonviolence offers hope for the survival of humankind, whereas violence does not.

In fact, nonviolence is not limited to tactics of defending a given people; rather, it is directed toward overthrowing an entire system of relationships based on violence, oppression, and the unjust exploitation of the great majority of humans by privileged elites. Thus, nonviolence is directly relevant not only to the prevention of war but also to the establishment of social justice, environmental protection, and the defense of human rights. It does not aim merely at achieving a more effective national defense but also at a defense of humanity and the planet against destructiveness and violence, by seeking to change the terms by which individuals and groups interact.

The destruction of rain forests, the clear—cutting of temperate zone woodlands, the gouging of the earth in the course of strip-mining, the pollution of water and air, the extinction of plant and animal species, and even the eating of meat and the use of internal combustion engines may all be considered forms of violence, resulting, in a sense, from a lack of *ahimsa*, in Gandhian terms. As former black power leader H. Rap Brown once pointed out, violence is as American as cherry pie.

Sometimes this is presented as reassuring; that is, violence in the United States is nothing new and therefore nothing to get alarmed about. More appropriately, however, it is a warning: Violence is widely considered inimical to humanistic values. Accordingly, it has become commonplace to decry the prevalence of violence in American life, applied not only to international affairs but also to underlying social conditions. Such structural violence includes homicide and abuse of children and spouses, as well as homelessness, drug abuse, environmental destruction, unemployment, poverty, unequal career options, inadequate medical care, and low-quality education.

For some persons deeply committed to nonviolence, the legitimate outrage against violence is sometimes carried to excess; some would claim, for example, that education is violence, child rearing is violence, marriage is violence, and so on. By this point, however, an important distinction has been trivialized, leaving no alternatives but passivity and eventually, death, or else indifference and business as usual. But this is a minority and extreme view; nonviolence is, if nothing else, hardheaded and realistic, demanding that we become immersed, albeit with high ideals, in the actual world.

The leading advocates of nonviolence in the 20th century, Mohandas K. Gandhi and Martin Luther King, Jr., derived the core of their philosophy and the wellsprings of their activism from deeply felt religious faith: Gandhi was a devout Hindu; King was an ordained Southern Baptist minister. Others, by contrast, have emphasized the practical aspects of nonviolence as a tactic for achieving results in the social sphere. For example, Gene Sharp bases his commitment to nonviolent CBD and revolutionary change largely on the utilitarian need for alternatives to violence in meeting social injustice, as well as, forcefully but peacefully, to confront domestic tyranny and international aggression. (Sharp's work, not surprisingly, served as a manifesto for much of the nonviolent Arab Spring movement, especially in Tunisia.)

Advocates of nonviolence have been accused by many conservatives of lacking patriotism, not only because in the past they recommended a less bellicose attitude toward the Soviet Union (among other perceived "threats to American national security") but also because their efforts appear subversive of some mainstream American values. Thus, in an invited memorandum to the Kerner Commission (convened by President Lyndon Johnson to investigate the causes of violence in American life, following the inner-city riots of the mid-1960s), Catholic monk and nonviolence theorist Thomas Merton warned that the sources of violence can be found "not in esoteric groups but in the very culture itself, its mass media, its extreme individualism and competitiveness, its inflated myths of virility and toughness, and its overwhelming preoccupation with various means of destruction."

Nonviolence, Merton emphasized, is likely to be resisted because it will be seen as weakening the position of the world's great powers. There will be other problems. Some government leaders find it much easier, for example, to preside over the rape and pillage of national resources, gaining short-term advantage (including election and reelection) rather than facing the daunting task of working toward a self-sustaining natural ecology. A domestic society purged of structural societal violence might also require a deep rearrangement of current attitudes toward wealth, property, and social privilege. And imagine a state whose military forces are dismantled and which is prepared to defend itself only nonviolently. Wouldn't it be vulnerable to coercion and attack, leading to loss of freedom and very high casualties? On the other hand, Costa Rica abolished its army in 1948 (after the military supported an unpopular dictator who was subsequently overthrown). It has persisted as a model democracy and has never been invaded, even though many of Costa Rica's neighbors have been dictatorships and much of the rest of Central America, especially Honduras, remains quite violent.

Pacifism is tolerated in the United States and many other countries, only as long as it is practiced by small and relatively marginal groups. As Merton has pointed out,

> There is also an implication that any minority stand against war on ground of conscience is ipso facto a kind of deviant and morally eccentric position, to be tolerated only because there are always a few religious half-wits around in any case, and one has to humor them in order to preserve the nation's reputation for respecting individual liberty.[25]

Would it ever be practical to base a state's defense on nonviolent civilian-based tactics and strategies? Some claim that Gandhi succeeded in India and King in the United States only because both Britain and the United States had a long tradition of relatively humane, civilized treatment of others. In fact, the opposite can also be argued: British responses to colonial insurrections (such as the Sepoy Mutiny in India during the mid-19th century) were often extraordinarily brutal, and the U.S. government did not treat its Native Americans with forbearance, at least not at Wounded Knee and other massacres. It is also questionable whether even a Gandhi-led nonviolent resistance movement could have prevailed against a Stalin or a Hitler—but the Danes nonviolently and successfully resisted German occupation, and the Polish and "Velvet" Revolutions in Eastern Europe during the late 1980s were nonviolent waves of secession from the former Soviet Union. In contrast, CBD would likely be helpless against most bombardment attacks, especially those using weapons of mass destruction—but, of course, military defense would be equally helpless. Opponents of nonviolence as a national strategy often point to the slaughter that might take place if a nonviolent country were invaded by a violent opponent. Supporters of nonviolence can point out, however, that in this case the casualties might very well be far lower than if such an invasion were met with countervailing military force.

But the question remains: Beyond nonviolence as a theoretical ideal or as a profound personal witness, will national security policies ever rest on a studied, collective refusal to engage in violence? It is neither psychologically nor politically appealing to contemplate a strategy that allows an aggressor to take over one's country. But neither is it pleasant to contemplate military defense. It may be that military force is merely something with which we are more familiar, not that it is necessarily more effective, especially if the trillions of dollars now expended globally on military and such paramilitary forces as contractors and mercenaries were to be redirected toward nonviolent means of individual and collective self-defense. It may also be that governments would vigorously oppose instituting widespread nonviolent training, not only because it would compete with traditional military efforts but also because such training could empower the population to resist the government, thereby posing a threat to the existing state authorities—even in democracies, which, like most governments, are more comfortable responding in kind to violent provocations and armed resistance than to unarmed, nonviolent protest.

## A FINAL NOTE ON NONVIOLENCE

Efficacious nonviolence, not merely as an ideal but as a practical policy—personal as well as national—seems foreign to most Westerners, including most professed Christians. "Christianity has not been tried and found wanting," noted the English writer G. K. Chesterton, "rather, it has been difficult and left untried." The same can be said, to some extent, about persistent and courageous nonviolence.

What, we may ask, is the future of nonviolence? That is for all of us collectively to determine. Or, alternatively, we might ask: Does the world have a future *without* nonviolence? In his masterpiece, *Leaves of Grass,* the 19th-century American poet Walt Whitman gives this simple answer:

> Were you looking to be held together by lawyers?
>
> Or by an agreement on a paper? Or by arms?
>
> Nay, nor the world, nor any living thing, will so cohere.
>
> Only those who love each other shall become indivisible.[26]

## NOTES

1. Jørgen Johansen. 2009. "Nonviolence: More Than the Absence of Violence." In C. Webel & J. Galtung, eds., *Handbook of Peace and Conflict Studies.* London: Routledge: 143–59.

2. C. A. J. Coady. 1999. "The Idea of Violence." In Manfred B. Steger and *Violence and Its Alternatives,* Nancy S. Lind, eds. New York: St. Martin's Press: 25.

3. WHO. 2012. "An Internationally Accepted Definition of Violence," from "Preventing Violence and Reducing Its Impact: How Development Agencies Can Help." In C. Webel and J. Johansen, eds. *Peace and Conflict Studies: A Reader.* London and New York: Routledge.

4. Hannah Arendt. 1969. *On Violence.* New York: Houghton Mifflin Harcourt: 3–12 and 59–69.

5. These lists are adapted from the Wikepedia article "Satyagraha." http://en.wikipedia.org/wiki/Satyagraha.

6.  M. K. Gandhi. 1955. *Ashram Observances in Action*. Ahmedabad, India: Navajivan Press; and M. Gandhi. 1941. *Constructive Programme, Its Meaning and Place*. Ahmedabad, India: Navajivan Press.

7.  Quoted in E. Easwaran. 1978. *Gandhi the Man*. Petaluma, CA: Nilgiri Press.

8.  Quoted in N. K. Bose, ed. 1957. *Selections From Gandhi*. Ahmedabad, India: Navajivan.

9.  James P. Hanigan. 1984. *Martin Luther King, Jr., and the Foundations of Nonviolence*. New York: University Press of America.

10. Mohandas K. Gandhi. 1940. *An Autobiography: The Story of My Experiments With Truth*. Ahmedabad, India: Navajivan.

11. Arendt. 1969. *On Violence*.

12. Bertolt Brecht. 1976. "To Posterity." In *Poems*. London: Methuen.

13. Martin Luther King, Jr. 1983. "My Pilgrimage to Nonviolence." Reprinted in *The Catholic Worker*, January/February.

14. Mohandas K. Gandhi. 1968. *Selected Works*. S. Narayan, ed. Ahmedabad, India: Navajivan.

15. Gandhi, *An Autobiography*.

16. Quoted in Erik Erikson. 1969. *Gandhi's Truth*. New York: Norton.

17. Quoted in Joan Bondurant. 1971. *Conflict: Violence and Nonviolence*. Chicago: Aldine Atherton.

18. Quoted in Bose, *Selections*.

19. Martin Luther King, Jr. 1964. *Why We Can't Wait*. New York: New American Library.

20. Martin Luther King, Jr. 1983. "My Pilgrimage to Nonviolence." Reprinted in *The Catholic Worker*, January/February.

21. Mohandas K. Gandhi. 1951. *Non-Violent Resistance*. New York: Schocken.

22. Gene Sharp. 2010. *From Dictatorship to Democracy*. 4th U.S. edition. East Boston: The Albert Einstein Institution. Available at http://www.aeinstein.org/organizations/org/FDTD.pdf

23. Gene Sharp. 1985. *Making Europe Unconquerable: The Potential of Civilian-Based Deterrence and Defense*. Cambridge, MA: Ballinger.

24. Terry Messman. 2012. "Discovering the Unexpected Power of Nonviolence: Street Spirit Interview With Erica Chenoweth." http://www.thestreetspirit.org/discovering-the-unexpected-power-of-nonvio-lence-street-spirit-interview-with-erica-chenoweth-4/. Also see Maria J. Stephan, ed. *Civilian Jihad Nonviolent Struggle, Democratization, and Governance in the Middle East*. York: Palgrave Macmillan, 2009; and Erica Chenoweth and Maria J. Stephan. 2011. *Why Civil Resistance Works: The Strategic Logic of Nonviolent Conflict*. New York: Columbia University Press.

25. Thomas Merton. 1980. *The Non-Violent Alternative*. New York: Farrar, Straus & Giroux.

26. Walt Whitman. 1968. *Leaves of Grass*. New York: Norton.

## QUESTIONS FOR FURTHER REFLECTION

1.  What aspects of Gandhian nonviolence are most difficult for Westerners to understand? What aspects are most accessible?

2.  Compare several violent and nonviolent resistance movements. Who are the principal actors, and what are their goals, strategies, and tactics? What are the outcomes for these actors, and what do you conclude about the relative success or failure of violence and nonviolence in these movements?

3. Identify common patterns—and differences—between the Indian campaign for independence from Great Britain and the end of Soviet domination in Eastern Europe. Do the same for the overthrow of apartheid in South Africa, the "orange revolution" in Ukraine, and the democracy movement in China.

4. Suggest nonreligious bases for nonviolence, in the private as well as the public sphere.

5. Evaluate the realistic prospects for civilian-based defense, using actual examples of potential or current international conflict.

## SUGGESTIONS FOR FURTHER READING

Erica Chenoweth and Maria J. Stephan. 2011. *Why Civil Resistance Works: The Strategic Logic of Nonviolent Conflict.* New York: Columbia University Press.

Gene Sharp and Joshua Paulson. 2005. *Waging Nonviolent Struggle: 20th Century Practice and 21st Century Potential.* Manchester, NH: Extending Horizons Books (Porter Sargent).

Gene Sharp. 2010. *From Dictatorship to Democracy,* 4th U.S. edition. East Boston: The Albert Einstein Institution.

Josephy Lelyfeld. 2011. *Great Soul: Mahatma Gandhi and His Struggle With India.* New York: Knopf.

Howard Zinn. 2002. *The Power of Nonviolence: Writings by Advocates of Peace.* Boston: Beacon Press.

James Hanigan. 1984. *Martin Luther King, Jr., and the Foundations of Nonviolence.* New York: University Press of America.

Peter Ackerman and Jack DuVall. 2001. *A Force More Powerful: A Century of Non-Violent Conflict.* New York: Palgrave Macmillan. (Also see the documentary film by this name.)

Richard Gregg. 1959. *The Power of Nonviolence.* New York: Shocken.

# CHAPTER 24

# TOWARD A MORE PEACEFUL FUTURE

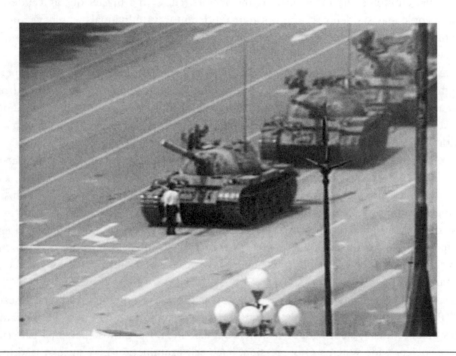

A lone demonstrator—name and fate both unknown—stands down a column of tanks June 5, 1989, at the entrance to Tiananmen Square in Beijing, just after Chinese troops killed many prodemocracy students who had been protesting in the square.

*Source:* © 2008 Getty Images.

> *There are moments when things go well and one feels encouraged. There are difficult moments and one feels overwhelmed. But it's senseless to speak of optimism or pessimism. The only important thing is to know that if one works well in a potato field, the potatoes will grow. If one works well among men, they will grow—that's reality. The rest is smoke. It's important to know that words don't move mountains. Work, exacting work, moves mountains.*
>
> —Danilo Dolci, renowned social activist

Thi**s** will be a brief chapter, not because there isn't much to say but because, fundamentally, personal transformation is, well, personal. Peace may work differently for each of us. Exposure to peace and conflict studies, may, in some cases, not significantly affect the reader's lives. In contrast, PCS may expand some people's consciousness in significant ways, influencing their subsequent behavior and perceptions. We hope that eventually you belong to the latter group!

## Transformations of Self and Society

When exposed to issues that are particularly relevant or arguments that are especially cogent, or simply when emotions and other unconscious factors "click" in a mysterious and little-known manner, people may suddenly see the world in a different way. Individuals who have undergone a religious "conversion experience," for example, often speak of having been "born again," after which everything seems new and different.

Peace and conflict studies does not necessarily aim for a comparable conversion experience, although it sometimes happens. There are many varieties of personal transformation, from the intense and mystical to a practical determination to vote differently, give money to or get directly involved in a particular cause, read another book, take another course, get involved with a social or political movement, or develop a lifelong vocation.

There are many people now working in various ways to help establish a world at peace. Richard Falk calls them "citizen/pilgrims," and they typically focus on specific goals, such as economic conversion; the abolition of nuclear weapons; an end to military interventionism; the abolition of poverty, malnutrition, political oppression, or environmental destruction; the defense of human rights; opposition to a specific war; and a generally more life-affirming rela-tionship between people and their planet, as well as each other. The route of such citizen/ pilgrims, like that of the earlier pilgrims hundreds of years ago, is likely to be long and difficult but not impossible.

It has widely been claimed that peace must start within each individual and then spread out-ward: "Peace begins with me." This implies not only examining one's own life and making changes that seem consistent with one's beliefs but also identifying those personal patterns that reinforce society-wide systems of oppression. Such self-examination may in turn lead to some painful recognitions and decisions: recognizing how one's life may have at times involved the oppression of others and/or questioning what balance is desirable (and feasible) between relative personal privilege and selfless devotion to a cause. For some people, fighting oppression requires breaking out of their own oppression. Minimizing oppressive personal relationships may well be a prerequisite for helping alleviate the oppression of others, and it may work the other way around as well.

To some degree, the world will be a better and less violent place if each individual makes peace in his or her own life. Important as it is, however, the personal transformation involved in making inner peace is only part of the necessary equation; peace must be made not only internally but also externally, out there in the real and sometimes nasty world. No amount of "centeredness," "organic living," "alternative lifestyles," or personal peace will solve the problems of surrogate war in the developing world, of poverty, the denial of human rights, or environmental abuse, to say nothing of the danger of nuclear war. One can think pure thoughts, eat only organic foods, and never think ill of another, but this won't prevent destruction of the rain forests, provide a decent education for a little girl in Mozambique, or prevent the next episode of genocide, terrorism, or "ethnic cleansing." Peace may begin with each of us, but war, at least, is likely to begin elsewhere, and peace must entail significant changes in the world at large. It may be satisfying—and even necessary—to liberate oneself, but it is not sufficient.

In the course of becoming involved in the struggle for peace, an awkward collision may be unavoidable: between a personal ethical commitment to nonviolence and some of the harsh realities of a world in which "freedom," "equality," "justice," and "liberation" may require conflict— preferably nonviolent—with existing authorities if any meaningful change is to occur.

## Stumbling Blocks to Personal Transformation and Empowerment

Sometimes a commitment to peace derives from a kind of transformative experience, perhaps a sudden crash of insight, what has been called a moment of "epiphany," when things are seen with a unique and breathtaking clarity. At other times, it comes slowly and gradually, with the progressive realization that something long suspected is in fact true, as facts, ideas, and personal experiences fit into a coherent whole. Sometimes the appeal is primarily logical; at other times it is emotional and apparently beyond reason. Optimally, both reason and passion are involved. Religious commitment may or may not be involved.

For others, of course, it never comes at all. Nor need everyone be transformed; for most successful social movements, it is only necessary that a critical number—perhaps 10% to 20% of the population, as Chenoweth and Stephan have shown—become sincerely committed to the outcome. Perhaps more are needed for major long-lasting social transformations. In any event, it may well be that the greatest barrier to peace is less the intractability of world problems than the fact that those problems are psychologically and thus politically invisible. Moreover, many of those in the affluent West who perceive these problems tend to respond with either hopelessness or self-defeating violence.

Violence generally evokes its own reaction, comparably violent. As to hopelessness, there are several responses. One is to point out some hopeful possibilities, as we have tried to do in this book. Another is to adopt an existential view that hopelessness is itself fundamental to the human condition, requiring us to struggle—without hope—because that is what it *means* to be human. And yet another is to embrace despair as an indication of our fundamental love for the planet and its living creatures. After all, if we did not care, we would not grieve. And, paradoxically, out of that recognition can come renewed strength.

Hopelessness, in turn, can result from two different sources. On the one hand, there is the literal lack of hope, a denial that solutions even exist or could ever be implemented. On the other hand, there is a frustration that derives from facing life as a small, isolated individual in a very large and complicated world. The issue in this case is not so much an absence of hope as a lack of power or, rather, a perception of one's powerlessness. One purpose of *Peace and Conflict Studies*—the book as well as the discipline—is to provide some empowerment on both levels.

There are also those who refuse to see the world's plight, possibly worrying that the problem of peace is so vast that if they open themselves to its immensity, they would be sucked in, irresistibly, as into a black hole. To these people, we point out that insofar as they see the problem this way, they have already been engulfed, whether they recognize it or not. Admitting their concerns and anxieties and allowing themselves to act on them will be refreshing in the extreme, even exhilarating. And, of course, one needn't devote oneself 100% to planetary betterment, body, mind, and soul. You can support peace, with your votes, volunteer time, occasional financial contributions, and so forth, without disrupting your entire life. To be sure, you can also make a deeper commitment; there is no objective right or wrong in such cases.

Most of us live in a society that in some ways does not really want to confront the world's difficulties and, especially, its own complicity in creating them. In such a society, it is relatively easy to avoid thinking about nuclear weapons, environmental deterioration, and world poverty, not to mention genocide against what are (for affluent Westerners) obscure populations in, say, Sudan or Rwanda. It is easy as well to perceive the world's ills as inevitable—as part of the natural landscape—as many people once imagined slavery to be; similarly, it is easy to practice denial, refusing to recognize what is disconcerting or upsetting, because of an understandable inclination to spare oneself emotional pain. Our current planetary plight—including, but not limited to, global warming—constitutes, paraphrasing former U.S. vice president Al Gore, a huge "inconvenient truth."

But we are rapidly approaching a situation when only an ostrich, head determinedly buried in the sand, will be able to avoid the fundamental issues of avoiding war, confronting violence in all its manifestations (including social and ecological), and establishing a substantive and enduring peace. The Brazilian social activist Paulo Freire coined the term *conscientization* to denote the achievement of first personal and then group awareness. Freire has been primarily concerned with the establishment of social justice, and he calls, accordingly, for "humanization," which is "thwarted by injustice, exploitation, oppression, and the violence of the oppressors; it is affirmed by the yearning of the oppressed for freedom and justice, and by their struggle to recover their lost humanity."

As Freire emphasizes, one of the most important components of personal transformation is empowerment. In some cases, individuals commit themselves to a cause despite a certainty that they will ultimately fail; the most notable example is that of the French existentialist writer Albert Camus, who argued that death makes life absurd and who emphasized that, as a result, it is fundamental to the human condition that we each define ourselves by our struggle against so uncaring a universe—even though, like Sisyphus, we are necessarily doomed to unending struggle and repeated failure. But, for most people, commitment and action are not forthcoming without a sense of efficacy and hope. The image of ultimate failure is not usually considered a reassuring one, likely to recruit many enthusiastic followers. "In order for the oppressed to wage the struggle for their liberation," writes Freire, "they must perceive the reality of oppression not as a closed world from which there is no exit, but as a limiting situation which they can transform."[1]

## Motivating Factors in Personal Transformation

Although oppression is most blatant in the blood-drenched streets of urban conflict zones around the world, in the grinding rural poverty of Sudan and Ethiopia, and in the treatment of political prisoners in Cuba, Israel, and China, it should be clear even to relatively privileged Westerners that we, too, are both contributors to and victims of what has been called "invisible oppression." This includes environmental abuse, economic maldistribution, and the state-sponsored terrorism of nuclear weapons.

Helen Caldicott, Australian physician and influential peace worker, used to recruit antinuclear activists by urging each individual in her audience to "take the world upon your shoulders, like

Atlas." It may be a heavy load, but it is somewhat lighter when shared. And, furthermore, if each of us doesn't do it, who will? Law professor Roger Fisher once made an especially effective plea for personal involvement, when he was speaking at an antiwar symposium. He began by recounting a friend's reaction to the title of his presentation, "Preventing Nuclear War." His friend's response was "Boy, have *you* got a problem!"

In response, Fisher recounted a situation he experienced, when, test-flying a B-17, the pilot had playfully turned off all four engines, demonstrating how the bomber handled with no propulsion. Here are Fisher's own words:

> With all four propellers stationary, we glided, somewhat like a stone, toward the rocks and forests of Newfoundland. After a minute or so the pilot pushed the button to unfeather. Only then did he remember: In order to unfeather the propeller you had to have electric power, and in order to have electric power you had to have at least one engine going. As we were buckling on our parachutes, the copilot burst out laughing. Turning to the pilot he said, "Boy, have *you* got a problem!"

Fisher went on to discuss some of the difficulties as well as the prospects of preventing global war. At the end of his talk, he returned to the hapless B-17, with himself inside, without power and about to crash:

> Well, we didn't crash; we weren't all killed. On that plane we had a buck sergeant who remembered that back behind the bomb bay we had a putt-putt generator for use in case we had to land at some emergency air field that did not have any electric power to start the engines. The sergeant found it. He fiddled with the carburetor; wrapped a rope around the flywheel a few times; pulled it and pulled it; got the generator going and before we were down to 3,000 feet we had electricity. The pilot restarted the engines, and we were all safe. Now saving that plane was not the sergeant's job in the sense that he created the risk. The danger we were in was not his fault or his responsibility. But it was his job in the sense that he had an opportunity to do something about it.[2]

It can be argued that each of us has a duty to contribute to world peace, if only because—like the crew in that stricken B-17—we are all in this world together, and the fate of the Earth is definitely at risk. There aren't even any parachutes. At least as important, however, is the fact that each of us can make a contribution.

Social psychologists have determined that of the various factors likely to motivate people to change their behavior, one of the most powerful is the simple message "You can do it"—that is, evidence that individual behavior will be effective in generating some desirable effect. For example, in one experiment, participants were given three different kinds of information about cigarette smoking, automobile injuries, and sexually transmitted disease. The purpose was to determine which information was most effective in changing the behavior of the participants: (1) details about the noxious consequences of the events (interviews with lung cancer patients, gruesome photos of automobile and sexually transmitted disease victims); (2) statistical data about the probability of experiencing or contracting these outcomes if behavior remains unchanged; and (3) information specifying what preventive measures can be taken and emphasizing their likely effectiveness. The results showed clearly that the third factor, the "efficacy of coping responses," was the most influential in inducing people to change their behavior. Moreover, the first consideration—appeals to fear by emphasizing the noxiousness of the threat—actually served to *reduce* the likelihood that people would engage in adaptive behavior, apparently because such appeals evoked powerful psychological resistance in the participants.[3]

The implications for students, educators, conflict transformers, and practitioners of peace may be important. If significant numbers of people are to change, to break through their crust of denial and indifference, it may be most effective to appeal to their sense of efficacy rather than simply to their rational evaluation of danger or to their raw fear. An additional motivating factor deserves mention: fun. The surprising (and not at all inconvenient) truth is that it can be great fun trying to bring peace to the world. There are few activities that offer more gratification, self-importance, satisfaction of shared struggle on behalf of a greater good, and thus gut-level joy.

## The Social Efficacy of Individual Action

No one can accurately assess the prospects of establishing enduring global peace. Of course, the problems can be identified, and some of the proposed solutions can be discussed. This we have attempted to do. Some of these proposals may be feasible, especially if initiated in combination rather than alone: including switching to nonprovocative defense, de-alerted and gradually eliminated nuclear arsenals, redistribution of global expenditures from the military to social needs, protection of the environment and of human rights, strengthening various world peacekeeping systems in the context of establishing global rather than national security, a widespread shift toward nonviolence, and conscientious collective efforts to address and rectify inequities in wealth.

As to the efficacy of individual action, individuals *can* make a difference—and not only such apparently larger-than-life figures as Mother Teresa, Martin Luther King, Jr., and the Dalai Lama. Moreover, although powerlessness is a self-fulfilling prophecy, so is empowerment. When people are convinced that they are helpless and their behavior is insignificant, they will often behave helplessly and without significance. But the opposite can also be true. "It is within our power," wrote Thomas Paine more than 200 years ago, "to begin the world anew." To some degree, that is what happened when a country was formed based on the principles of democracy and self-government. And the prospect of major transformative change—not only within individuals but in their society as well—is no less true in our time than it was in his. Interestingly, Edmund Burke, writing at about the same time as Paine but espousing a very different view of what the world should be like after the American and French Revolutions, noted that "the only thing necessary for the triumph of evil is for good men to do nothing."

In addition, there is some reason for optimism. The Cold War is over, movements for democracy and social justice are spreading around the world (especially in the Middle East, once thought hostile to such movements), and nuclear weapons are becoming increasingly delegitimized in the minds of some leaders and citizens alike. War itself may be headed in a similar direction. Next might come the elimination of major violent conflicts, the further isolation of terrorism and terrorists, and, eventually, progress toward positive peace. For this process to continue (to some degree it has already begun), at least three things are needed: (1) belief in the possibility of peace, (2) belief in one's personal power and efficacy, and (3) motivation to proceed, whether individually or collectively.

A primary block to the establishment of peace is not so much the actual difficulty of achieving it but rather the *feeling* that it is impossible, the inability or refusal of many people to imagine peace as a realistic prospect. Before anything can be done, it must first be imagined.

Athletics coaches, business leaders, and many actors on the world stage have come to recognize the value of visualization: imagining one's body perfectly coordinated during a gymnastics exercise, envisioning oneself performing Hamlet, and so forth. Subtly, unconsciously, the mind can be essentially "reprogrammed," releasing new potentials and facilitating the accomplishment of things previously thought out of reach. Personal transformation does occur but only after people believe in the possibility of themselves changing, have a positive image of the kind of change they desire, and are positively reinforced by others seeking to accomplish similar goals.

Such an image need not be fine-tuned in every detail. But it must be realistic and feasible. It must not project so far into the future that it seems irrelevant to the present, and it must not make excessive demands on human capacities as we know them. At the same time, it must be idealistic enough to be inspirational, to be worth striving for.

There are many people who believe that the world today stands at the brink of a major transformation. In less than a quarter century, the Internet has changed many personal habits, not to mention world commerce for millions, with effects that are just being glimpsed. National barriers have fallen, not only with the demise of the Soviet Union but also with the growth of continent-wide identity (political, economic, social), especially in Europe. South African apartheid is now a bad memory. And the political and social landscape of the Middle East is being transformed. The very idea that society may change profoundly may itself be the most profound of all social ideas, capable of midwifing remarkable changes.

# Toward the Future

It has been said that the only constant throughout history is change. The future is not optional. This is to say that there will be some sort of future; the question is, *what* sort? In a representative democracy, people who do not vote aren't in the strongest position to complain if they don't get the outcome they want. This is also true for people who don't work for a preferred future.

There is nothing immutable about the world as it exists today. A system based on nation-states could give way to one based on local, semiautonomous communities, just as reliance on nuclear weapons may be replaced by widespread revulsion toward them. Nonviolence could swell and violence could shrink in human affairs. Many aspects of a world at peace could be instituted without disruptive alterations in the basic organization of human society as it now exists. As progress is made and new systems are institutionalized, social change could then be evolutionary rather than revolutionary. It may also be long-lasting.

Among recent exciting developments has been the emergence of connections among social activists who used to work in relative isolation. This is evident in such social and political movements as the "Arab Spring" and the "Occupy Movement." In addition, the worldwide women's and lesbian, gay, bisexual, and transgender (LGBT) movements have gradually emerged from being primarily a concern of middle- and upper-class white people to embrace "sisters" and "brothers" of many different races and economic classes, both straight and gay.

Similarly, environmental concerns are increasingly seen as issues that transcend the interests of people who are economically and socially privileged. There is growing recognition that, if anything, "environmental racism" tends to be particularly a burden for the poor and dispossessed. This recognition of shared interests may augur an exciting future of unforeseen empowerment.

This is a heady time to be alive. Soviet communism and South African apartheid have both collapsed, essentially without a shot being fired. Dictatorships and autocracies around the world are being replaced with nascent democracies. And millions of Westerners have been the streets protesting against the economic tyranny of the superrich. In a world of unprecedented interconnections and increasing democratization, are comparable monumental achievements impossible?

## A FINAL NOTE ON TRANSFORMATION AND THE FUTURE

Achieving sustainable peace is only secondarily a matter of "hardware" involving the manipulation of structures, whether personal, neural, or social. Primarily, the barriers to peace constitute a problem in human "software," in the ways we think and often stubbornly refuse to do so. And herein lies the hope, because there is enormous potential within the human species not only to remove the "bugs" from our own program but also to recreate our lives as we rebuild our world.

Social organizer Saul Alinsky coined a valuable phrase for would-be activists: "Think globally, act locally." There are many avenues for personal involvement, additional training to acquire, and numerous organizations to join, a large number of which are active at the local as well as at the national and global levels. Most people find it difficult to persevere alone, and education is empowering; this is why peace and conflict studies is taught and why various action groups are also so important.

If a little knowledge is a dangerous thing, try getting a lot of knowledge! Remember, as well, that groups have a larger voice than a solitary individual. If you are a "joiner," join. If not, consider acting alone. Either way, when was the last time you stood up for something you believed in and that had such enormous implications for your own future—not to mention the future of the world? And do you *really* have anything more important to do?

## NOTES

1. Paulo Freire. 1970. *Pedagogy of the Oppressed*. New York: Continuum.

2. Roger Fisher. 1981. "Preventing Nuclear War." In R. Adams and S. Cullen, eds., *The Final Epidemic*. Chicago: Educational Foundation for Nuclear Science.

3. R. W. Rodgers and C. R. Mewborn. 1976. "Fear Appeals and Attitude Change: Effects of a Threat's Noxiousness, Probability of Occurrence, and the Efficacy of Coping Responses." *Journal of Personality and Social Psychology* 34: 54–67.

## QUESTIONS FOR FURTHER REFLECTION

1. If you found yourself personally influenced by the material you have encountered in peace and conflict studies, in what way is this influence likely to change you and/or your behavior? If not, why not?

2. What are some major obstacles to personal involvement in peace and social justice movements?

3. Consider the strengths and weaknesses of some contemporary movements for social and political transformation.

4. Discuss the merits of maintaining a high level of hope and even expectation with regard to future successful movements for peace and justice, as opposed to working without explicit hope but with a sense of responsibility and commitment.

5. Discuss the problem of "compassion fatigue" and how it might be overcome.

## SUGGESTIONS FOR FURTHER READING

Alice Walker, Jodie Evans, and Medea Benjamin, eds. 2005. *How to Stop the Next War Now: Effective Responses to Violence and Terrorism*. Novato, CA: New World Library.

Betty Zisk. 1992. *The Politics of Transformation: Local Activism in the Peace and Environmental Movements*. New York: Praeger.

Paulo Freire. 1970. *Pedagogy of the Oppressed*. New York: Continuum.

Randy Shaw. 2001. *The Activist's Handbook: A Primer Updated*. Berkeley: University of California Press.

Jonathan Schell. 2004 *The Unconquerable World: Power, Nonviolence, and the Will of the People*. New York: Henry Holt.

# Author Index

# Subject Index

# About the Authors

**David P. Barash** (PhD, University of Wisconsin) has been with the Department of Psychology at the University of Washington since 1973. His studies span animal behavior and social psychology, with concentrations in sociobiology, psychological aspects of the arms race and nuclear war, peace studies, and animal behavior and evolution. A prolific author, he has written more than 250 technical articles and 31 books ranging from monographs to college textbooks to popular trade titles. His book, *Introduction to Peace Studies* (1991), was the first comprehensive undergraduate textbook in the field of Peace Studies.

**Charles Webel** (PhD, University of California, Berkeley) is professor at the University of New York, Prague. A three-time Fulbright Scholar and graduate of the Psychoanalytic Institute of Northern California, Webel has pursued post-doctoral studies at Harvard University, the Max Planck Institute, and the Universities of Paris, Frankfurt, and Heidelberg. He recently taught in the Peace and Conflict Studies Program at Berkeley and the Honors College of University of South Florida. He is the author or editor of seven books.